EVAGRIUS, *KEPHALAIA GNOSTIKA*

Society of Biblical Literature

Writings from the Greco-Roman World

Number 38

Volume Editor
Sebastian Brock

EVAGRIUS, *KEPHALAIA GNOSTIKA*

A NEW TRANSLATION OF THE UNREFORMED TEXT FROM THE SYRIAC

Translated with an Introduction and Commentary by
Ilaria L. E. Ramelli

SBL Press
Atlanta

Library of Congress Cataloging-in-Publication Data

Evagrius, Ponticus, 345?–399, author.
[Gnostikos. English].
Evagrius's Kephalaia gnostika : a new translation of the unreformed text from the Syriac / translated with an introduction and commentary by Illaria L. E. Ramelli.
p. cm. — (Writings from the Greco-Roman World ; number 38)
ISBN 978-1-62837-039-3 (paper binding : alk. paper) — ISBN 978-1-62837-040-9 (electronic format) — ISBN 978-1-62837-041-6 (hardcover binding : alk. paper)
1. Evagrius, Ponticus, 345?–399. Gnostikos. 2. Theology, Doctrinal—Early works to 1800. 3. Origen. I. Ramelli, Ilaria, 1973– II. Title. III. Title: Kephalaia gnostika. IV. Series: Writings from the Greco-Roman world ; v. 38.
BR65.E923G5613 2015
270.2092—dc23 2015005711

Printed on acid-free paper.

For Angela, Santina, Savina, and Elvira

"There was a time when evilness did not exist, and there will be a time when it will no more exist, whereas there was no time when virtue did not exist, and there will be no time when it will not exist. For the germs of virtue are impossible to destroy."
—Evagrius, *Kephalaia Gnostika* 1.40

Contents

Abbreviations

Aev	Aevum
Aug	Augustinianum
BETL	Bibliotheca ephemeridum theologicarum Lovaniensium
Bijdr	Bijdragen
BLE	Bulletin de littérature ecclésiastique
BWANT	Beiträge zur Wissenschaft vom Alten und Neuen Testament
ByzZ	Byzantinische Zeit*schrift*
Car	*Carthaginensia*
CPG	*Clavis patrum graecorum.* Edited by M. Geerard. 5 vols. Turnhout, 1974–87
EFN	Estudios de filología neotestamentaria
ETL	*Ephemerides theologicae Lovanienses*
FZPhTh	*Freiburger Zeitschrift für Philosophie und Theologie*
GNO	Gregorii Nysseni Opera. Edited by W. Jaeger. Leiden, 1952–
GRBS	*Greek, Roman, and Byzantine Studies*
HTR	*Harvard Theological Review*
IZBG	*Internationale Zeitschriftenschau für Bibelwissenschaft und Grenzgebiete*
JBL	*Journal of Biblical Literature*
JECS	*Journal of Early Christian Studies*
JEH	*Journal of Ecclesiastical History*
JFSR	*Journal of Feminist Studies in Religion*
JHI	*Journal of the History of Ideas*
JTS	*Journal of Theological Studies*
KG	*Kephalaia Gnostika*
KJV	King James Version
Mus	*Le Muséon*
OCP	*Orientalia christiana periodica*
OrChr	*Oriens christianus*
OrChrAn	*Orientalia christiana analecta*

ParOr	*Parole de l'orient*
PG	Patrologia graeca [= Patrologiae cursus completus: Series graeca]. Edited by J.-P. Migne. 162 vols. Paris, 1857–86
PGL	*Patristic Greek Lexicon.* Edited by G. W. H. Lampe. Oxford, 1968
PO	Patrologia orientalis
RHE	*Revue d'histoire ecclésiastique*
RHR	*Revue de l'histoire des religions*
RSPT	*Revue des sciences philosophiques et théologiques*
RSV	Revised Standard Version
SC	Sources chrétiennes. Paris, 1943–
SEAug	Studia ephemeridis Augustinianum
SMSR	*Studi e materiali di storia delle religioni*
SPhilo	*The Studia Philonica Annual*
StPatr	*Studia patristica*
StudMon	*Studia monastica*
SubBi	Subsidia biblica
SVF	*Stoicorum veterum fragmenta.* H. von Arnim. 4 vols. Leipzig, 1903–1924
VC	*Vigiliae christianae*
VSpir	*Vie spirituelle*
WGRW	Writings of the Greco-Roman World
WUNT	Wissenschaftliche Untersuchungen zum Neuen Testament
ZAC	*Zeitschrift für Antikes Christentum*
ZNW	*Zeitschrift für die neutestamentliche Wissenschaft und die Kunde der älteren Kirche*

Introductory Essay
Recovering the True Thought of the Origenian Evagrius: A Needed Reassessment of the Influence of Origen and Gregory of Nyssa on Evagrius

Evagrius Ponticus (345/6–399) was an Origenian, a faithful follower of Origen of Alexandria (d. ca. 255) and of his close disciple Gregory Nyssen, and not—as Guillaumont famously suggested, followed by many—an Origenist of the kind of those who radicalized and distorted Origen's legacy, that is, those known to, and condemned by, Emperor Justinian in 543 and 553. The same reassessment of Origen's true thought—beyond the construals that are a heritage of the Origenistic controversy and partially still hold today—that is needed, and is underway, is also needed for Evagrius's thought. Evagrius's ideas too are indeed undergoing a reassessment, and rightly so. This is necessary, particularly (1) with respect to a unitary vision of his production against a long-standing split between his philosophical and his ascetic works—the former accepted, the latter deemed dangerously "Origenistic"—and (2) with respect to his often misunderstood "Origenism."

Especially in relation to the former issue, Kevin Corrigan's attention to the *Kephalaia Gnostika* (*KG*) and the *Letter to Melania*, or *Great Letter*, and his holistic approach to Evagrius's thought are very helpful. The same holistic approach, without the inveterate fracture between Evagrius's ascetic works and his philosophical works, is also used by Julia Kostantinovsky and Augustine Casiday in their books on Evagrius.[1]

---

1. Kevin Corrigan, *Evagrius and Gregory: Mind, Soul and Body in the Fourth Century* (Burlington, Vt.: Ashgate, 2009). Julia Konstantinovsky, *Evagrius Ponticus: The Making of a Gnostic* (Burlington, Vt.: Ashgate, 2009); Augustine Casiday, *Reconstructing the Theology of Evagrius Ponticus* (Cambridge: Cambridge University Press, 2013).

To address both points, that is, the unitary vision of Evagrius's production and the correction of misunderstandings related to his "Origenism," it is necessary to recover Origen's true thought and thus determine its exact impact on Evagrius's system, as well as to investigate the possible role of the Cappadocians in the transmission of Origen's authentic ideas to Evagrius.[2] Gregory Nyssen in particular is definitely the most insightful and faithful follower of Origen among all patristic thinkers, the one who best understood and developed Origen's genuine ideas. Indeed, a study of Gregory's reception of Origen's philosophy and theology is showing more and more that Gregory is the patristic philosopher-theologian who understood Origen's true thought best of all and misunderstood it least.

Clarifying, to the extent that is possible, which of the Cappadocians transmitted Origen's ideas and their interpretation to Evagrius (who also had direct access to those ideas) is pivotal for the assessment of Evagrius's intellectual heritage. Even some elements of Evagrius's life bear on his ideas and his relationship with those of the Cappadocians, and consequently with those of Origen himself. This reassessment of Origen and Evagrius's thought, and Origen's direct and indirect influence on Evagrius, is one of the most remarkable issues in Greek patristic study.

1. Evagrius's Life Reconsidered in Light of Origen's and Gregory's Influence

The main sources on Evagrius's life are Palladius's *Lausiac History* 38;[3] Socrates's *Church History* 4.23; Sozomen's *Church History* 6.30; and a fifth-century Coptic biography. Other sources are Gregory Nazianzen's will; an anonymous late-fourth-century *Historia Monachorum* (20.15); the anonymous fourth/fifth-century *Apophthegms, Alphabetical Collection* (s.v. "Evagrius"); Gennadius's *Famous People* 6.11 and 6.17; and Jerome's *Letter* 133 and prefaces to *Dialogue against the Pelagians* and to *Commentary on Jeremiah* 4. According to these sources, Evagrius was born in Ibora in

2. See Ilaria L. E. Ramelli, "Evagrius and Gregory: Nazianzen or Nyssen? A Remarkable Issue That Bears on the Cappadocian (and Origenian) Influence on Evagrius," *GRBS* 53 (2013): 117–37.

3. Besides the Greek recensions, there is also a noteworthy Coptic one. See also, e.g., Gabriel Bunge and Adalbert de Vogüé, eds. and trans., *Quatre ermites égyptiens, d'après les fragments coptes de l'Histoire Lausiaque* (Bégrolles-en-Mauges: Bellefontaine, 1994).

Pontus, from a presbyter—ordained in Arkeus by Basil of Caesarea[4]—and "rural bishop" (χωρεπίσκοπος). He received a good education in philosophy, rhetoric, and the liberal arts, thus being "perhaps the best educated in philosophy of all the early monks."[5]

Thanks to Basil and Gregory of Nazianzus, who probably were the compilers of the *Philocalia*, Evagrius became familiar with Origen's ideas. He was ordained a reader by Basil, some time after whose death (which occurred in late 378 or early 379) Evagrius moved to Constantinople to study, according to Socrates and Sozomen, with Gregory Nazianzen.[6] He participated in the 381 Council of Constantinople as a deacon. At this council, during which Nazianzen withdrew from the episcopate of Constantinople, Gregory of Nyssa surely played a core role. Evagrius was ordained deacon by Nazianzen according to Socrates (*Church History* 4.23), and Socrates's affirmation is followed by most scholars, but Palladius indicates Gregory of Nyssa instead. Unlike Socrates and Sozomen, Palladius knew Evagrius personally, as he himself attests in *Lausiac History* 12, 23, 24, 35, 38, and 47, and was a personal disciple of Evagrius, as he claims in *Lausiac History* 23. He devoted to Evagrius a whole chapter of his *Lausiac History*, all of which was composed "in the spirit of Evagrius,"[7] and in chapter 86 he speaks of Evagrius very highly. Palladius was an Origenian monk himself and a friend of the Origenian monks dubbed "Tall Brothers," of Rufinus, and of Melania the Elder. These were in turn close friends of Evagrius.

Palladius is therefore a source worthy of consideration.[8] In *Lausiac History* 86 (PG 34:1188C), Palladius reports that it was Gregory of Nyssa

4. Palladius, *Lausiac History* 38.2.

5. Columba Stewart, "Monastic Attitudes toward Philosophy and Philosophers," *StPatr* 44 (2010): 321–27, esp. 324.

6. "He studied philosophy and sacred Scripture under the direction of Gregory, bishop of Nazianzen" (Sozomen, *Church History* 6.30).

7. See René Draguet, "L'*Histoire Lausiaque*: Une oeuvre écrite dans l'esprit d'Évagre," *RHE* 41 (1946): 321–64; 42 (1947): 5–49.

8. Since Palladius, unlike Socrates, was personally acquainted with Evagrius, he is a firsthand source; while Socrates wrote his information some forty years after Evagrius's death, Evagrius wrote of what happened during his own lifetime. Moreover, Socrates seems to be much better informed on Nazianzen than on Nyssen. This is particularly clear from his *Church History* 4.26, as I have argued in a detailed manner in Ramelli, "Evagrius and Gregory: Nazianzen or Nyssen?" Socrates seems to know nothing of Gregory Nyssen's option for the ascetic life, of his ecclesiastical career, of his anti-Arianism and his theological works. Yet, Nyssen was even more of an Origenian

who ordained Evagrius and was a close friend of his: "After the death of the bishop saint Basil, saint Gregory—the bishop of Nyssa, a brother of the bishop Basil who enjoys the honor of the apostles—saint Gregory, I say, most wise and free from passions to the utmost degree, and illustrious for his wide-ranging learning, became friends with Evagrius and appointed him as a deacon."[9] On this account, it is unequivocally Gregory of Nyssa—the "brother of the bishop Basil" and the "bishop of Nyssa"—who treated Evagrius with friendship and ordained him a deacon. Note Palladius's most praising description of Nyssen in this passage. The reason is easy to guess: Gregory was the closest follower of Origen and the spiritual father of Evagrius, and Palladius profoundly admired both Origen and Evagrius.

The relationship between Nyssen and Evagrius may go back to the former's sojourn in Ibora, between late 379 and 380, when the inhabitants of Ibora asked Gregory to supervise the election of a new bishop. Nyssen and Evagrius were probably together in Ibora at that time. In *Lausiac History* 86 Palladius goes on to say: "When he left, saint Gregory the bishop handed Evagrius to the blessed bishop Nectarius at the great Council of Constantinople. For Evagrius was most skilled in dialectics against all heresies."[10] Gregory is regularly identified by scholars with Nazianzen. However, the Gregory whom Palladius mentions in the immediately preceding sentence, and in exactly the same terms as in the present sentence (ὁ ἅγιος Γρηγόριος ὁ ἐπίσκοπος), is Nyssen. Thus, the Gregory who handed Evagrius to Nectarius may also have been the bishop of Nyssa.

Likewise, the source of Socrates's report in *Church History* 4.23 that Gregory went to Egypt with Evagrius likely referred to Nyssen, since Nazianzen never went to Egypt or Jerusalem after the Council of Constantinople, but Nyssen after Constantinople traveled to Jerusalem late in 381 and in 382, as attested in his *Letter* 3. He may have gone from Jerusalem to Egypt with Evagrius, when Evagrius himself left Jerusalem for Egypt. For

than Nazianzen and Basil were, and this would have been a very interesting aspect to highlight for the strongly philo-Origenian Socrates.

9. Μετὰ δὲ τὴν κοίμησιν τοῦ ἁγίου ἐπισκόπου Βασιλείου προσέχων αὐτοῦ τῇ ἐπιτηδειότητι ὁ σοφώτατος καὶ ἀπαθέστατος καὶ πάσῃ παιδείᾳ λάμπων ὁ ἅγιος Γρηγόριος ὁ Νυσσαεὺς ἐπίσκοπος ἀδελφὸς τοῦ ἐν τιμῇ τῶν ἀποστόλων Βασιλείου τοῦ ἐπισκόπου, προχειρίζεται τοῦτον διάκονον.

10. Ἐκεῖθεν ἐλθὼν ὁ ἅγιος Γρηγόριος ὁ ἐπίσκοπος ἐν τῇ μεγάλῃ συνόδῳ τῇ κατὰ Κωνσταντινούπολιν καταλιμπάνει αὐτὸν Νεκταρίῳ τῷ μακαρίῳ ἐπισκόπῳ, διαλεκτικώτατον ὄντα κατὰ πασῶν τῶν αἱρέσεων.

Evagrius, as all his biographies agree, left Constantinople hurriedly to disembroil himself from an affair with a wife of a high functionary[11] and traveled to Jerusalem (382), where he frequented the Origenians Melania the Elder and Rufinus; the former, as the head of the double monastery where Rufinus too lived, gave Evagrius monastic garb and suggested him to leave for the Egyptian desert. He first headed to Nitria, a cenobitic environment, and then Kellia, where Evagrius practiced a hermitic and extreme form of asceticism and remained until his death in 399.

In Egypt, Evagrius was a disciple of Macarius of Alexandria (d. 394) and especially of Macarius the Egyptian, called the Great, who was converted to asceticism by St. Antony (an Origenian), founded Scetis, and was, like Origen, Antony, and Evagrius himself, a supporter of the doctrine of *apokatastasis*, or universal restoration.[12] Near Alexandria, Evagrius may also have visited Didymus the Blind, the faithful Origenian who was appointed by bishop Athanasius head of the Alexandrian Didaskaleion. Evagrius had disciples himself, among whom were the above-mentioned Palladius, and Cassian,[13] and many pilgrim visitors. He refused the episcopate at Thmuis that Theophilus of Alexandria offered to him. Indeed, Evagrius, like Origen and Gregory Nyssen, tended to emphasize the spiritual authority coming from inspiration, prayer, learning, teaching, and even miracles, rather than that which comes from ecclesiastical hierarchy.[14]

---

11. Sozomen, *Church History* 6.30; Palladius, *Lausiac History* 38.3–7.

12. The former seems to be mentioned by Evagrius in *On Thoughts* (Περὶ λογισμῶν) 33 and 37 and *Talking Back* (*Antirrheticus*) 4.23 and 4.58; 8.26. In *Praktikos* 93–94, instead, the reference seems to be to the latter; Robert E. Sinkewicz (*Evagrius of Pontus: The Greek Ascetic Corpus* [Oxford: Oxford University Press, 2003], xix), however, refers *Praktikos* 94 to Macarius of Alexandria as well. As for St. Antony and Macarius and their adhesion to the doctrine of *apokatastasis*, see Ilaria L. E. Ramelli, *The Christian Doctrine of Apokatastasis: A Critical Assessment from the New Testament to Eriugena* (Supplements to Vigiliae Christianae 120; Leiden: Brill, 2013), the chapter on Antony.

13. For a revisitation of the figure and the works of Cassian, however, with speculative although interesting arguments, see now Panayiotis Tzamalikos, *The Real Cassian Revisited: Monastic Life, Greek Paideia, and Origenism in the Sixth Century* (Leiden: Brill, 2012); idem, *A Newly Discovered Greek Father: Cassian the Sabaite Eclipsed by John Cassian of Marseilles* (Leiden: Brill, 2012).

14. Claudia Rapp, *Holy Bishops in Late Antiquity: The Nature of Christian Leadership in an Age of Transition* (Berkeley: University of California Press, 2005), ch. 3; for the derivation of these ideas from Origen, see Ilaria L. E. Ramelli, "Theosebia: A Presbyter of the Catholic Church," *JFSR* 26.2 (2010): 79–102.

If Gregory Nyssen was with Evagrius in Jerusalem and later in Egypt, or at least was in contact with Melania and Evagrius, this would clarify the reason why Nyssen's dialogue *On the Soul and the Resurrection* was translated into Coptic in Egypt so early, possibly as early as Gregory's very lifetime.[15] This is even more probable in light of the consideration that Nyssen in that dialogue, like Evagrius himself, upholds Origen's theory of *apokatastasis*.[16] Nyssen, in fact, was also in Arabia—close to Palestine and Egypt—shortly after the 381 Council of Constantinople: the council sent Gregory to a church there, for correcting them. While he was in Arabia, Gregory, by request of "those who oversee the holy churches of Jerusalem,"[17] visited Jerusalem, when Evagrius was there at Melania's and Rufinus's double monastery on the Olive Mountain.

In addition to his friendship (and discipleship) with Gregory of Nyssa, Evagrius was Nazianzen's assistant in Constantinople for some time[18] and received instruction from him too, in philosophy and biblical exegesis.[19] Evagrius contrasted "Arians" and Pneumatomachians, like both Nyssen and Nazianzen. Evagrius's *Letter on Faith*, or *Dogmatic Letter*, approximates the Cappadocians' theology so closely that it was attributed to Basil as his *Letter* 8. It supports the Trinitarian formula "one common essence, three individual substances" (μία οὐσία, τρεῖς ὑποστάσεις), which, as I have thoroughly argued elsewhere, derived from Origen.[20]

15. See appendix I in Ilaria L. E. Ramelli, *Gregorio di Nissa: Sull'anima e la resurrezione* (Milan: Bompiani–Catholic University, 2007). The very ancient Coptic translation is also used here in the establishment of a new edition of *De anima et resurrectione*, which is included in the same volume. Now these philological contributions are received in the definitive critical edition *Gregorii Nysseni, De anima et resurrectione* (ed. Andreas Spira and Ekkehardus Mühlenberg; GNO 3.3; Leiden: Brill, 2014), based on all seventy-two available manuscripts.

16. On Evagrius's doctrine of *apokatastasis*, its metaphysical reasons, and its Origenian roots, see Ramelli, *Christian Doctrine of Apokatastasis*, the chapter on Evagrius.

17. Gregory of Nyssa, *Letter* 12.2 (GNO 8.2:17).

18. Gregory mentions Evagrius in his will, written in 381 (PG 37:389–96), as "the deacon Evagrius, who has much worked with me."

19. Sozomen, *Church History* 6.30.

20. For the roots of this formula in Origen, see Ilaria L. E. Ramelli, "Origen's Anti-Subordinationism and Its Heritage in the Nicene and Cappadocian Line," *VC* 65 (2011): 21–49; and idem, "Origen, Greek Philosophy, and the Birth of the Trinitarian Meaning of Hypostasis," *HTR* 105 (2012): 302–50.

Kostantinovsky is right to remark that Evagrius's ideas are not very similar to those of "the Cappadocians,"[21] though in fact they prove to be not very similar to those of Basil (and, to some extent, Nazianzen), but they are quite similar to those of Nyssen (for instance, in metaphysics and eschatology). And Nyssen, in turn, was the most insightful follower of Origen, even more that Basil and Nazianzen were (hence, among much else, his outspoken adhesion to Origen's doctrine of universal restoration, or *apokatastasis*). Consistently, Evagrius, as I mentioned, was close to Origenians such as Rufinus, Melania, the Tall Brothers, John of Jerusalem, and Palladius. To Melania, Rufinus, and John, Evagrius also addressed letters, including the key *Letter to Melania*, or *Great Letter*, to which I will return soon.

Gregory Nyssen was the most faithfully Origenian of Evagrius's friends and probably ordained him a deacon and was with him in Palestine and Egypt. These biographical circumstances help explain Evagrius's acquaintance with Gregory Nyssen's ideas. Remarkable parallels between Evagrius's and Nyssen's ideas, from protology to eschatology, from theology to anthropology, are emerging more and more and in some cases will be highlighted in the present essay and in the commentary below (but an exhaustive analysis is still needed). These parallels can also be explained as common dependences on Origen, but a systematic assessment of the relationship between Evagrius's and Nyssen's ideas is an important desideratum, although Kevin Corrigan has provided some inspiring insights.[22] Gregory's influence on Evagrius also means Origen's influence on Evagrius, and it has to be established which influence was direct and which was mediated by Gregory.

Evagrius's reference to "Gregory the Just" in the epilogue of his *Praktikos*[23] may refer to Nazianzen, as is usually assumed, or to Nyssen: "The high Sun of Justice shines upon us … thanks to the prayers and intercession of Gregory the Just, who planted me, and of the holy fathers who now water me and by the power of Christ Jesus our Lord, who has granted me

21. Konstantinovsky, *Evagrius*, chs. 3–6.

22. Corrigan, *Evagrius*, juxtaposes these two Christian philosophers in respect to some anthropological, ascetic, and mystical issues.

23. Antoine Guillaumont and Claire Guillaumont, eds. and trans., *Évagre le Pontique: Traité pratique, ou Le moine* (2 vols.; SC 170–171; Paris: Cerf, 1971).

growth."[24] Gregory the Just is also cited in *The Gnostic* (*Gnostikos*)[25] 44 concerning the four cardinal virtues first theorized by Plato ("There are four virtues necessary for contemplation, according to the teaching of Gregory the Just: prudence, courage, temperance, and justice"), a topic that Nyssen developed. This fact, together with the metaphors and terminology used by Evagrius in this passage, makes it very likely that the Gregory at hand here was meant to be Gregory of Nyssa, as I will argue more extensively below in the commentary on *KG* 2.25. Likewise, in *Praktikos* 89, as I will contend in the same commentary below, the "wise teacher" of the four cardinal virtues mentioned by Evagrius may easily be Gregory of Nyssa. Therefore, also the "Gregory the Just" mentioned in the epilogue of Evagrius's *Praktikos* is probably Gregory of Nyssa.

The close relationship between Evagrius and Gregory of Nyssa to which Palladius and the source of Socrates point, and the probable connection between Evagrius and the early spread of Nyssen's Origenian work in Egypt, clearly have remarkable implications for Evagrius's ideas and their relationship with those of the Cappadocians and Origen. I indeed suspect that Gregory of Nyssa, the one who best understood and developed Origen's true thought, played an important role in transmitting Origen's authentic ideas to Evagrius. This means not simply Origen's texts, which Evagrius read on his own as well, but also an interpretation of Origen's ideas that was the closest to Origen's genuine philosophy and theology.

Evagrius passed away in 399, just in time to avoid one of the worst bouts of the Origenistic controversy. For he died shortly before Theophilus of Alexandria's Paschal letter against anthropomorphism, which stirred up a revolt among the simpler, anti-Origenian, and anthropomorphite monks, who scared Theophilus and induced his U-turn against Origen and the Origenians. This opportunistic move (for Theophilus was and remained an Origenian, but for a certain period he acted as an anti-Origenian out of fear[26]) brought him to persecute Evagrius's fellow monks in Nitria and Kellia, and especially Evagrius's friends, the above-mentioned Tall Brothers: the monks Ammonius, Euthymius, Eusebius, and Dioscorus. Palladius mentions them together with Evagrius when he speaks of "those belonging

---

24. Translation from Sinkewicz, *Evagrius of Pontus*.

25. Edition: Antoine Guillaumont and Claire Guillaumont, eds. and trans., *Évagre le Pontique: Le gnostique, ou À celui qui est devenu digne de la science* (SC 356; Paris: Cerf, 1989).

26. See Ramelli, *Christian Doctrine of Apokatastasis*, section on Theophilus.

to the circle of saints Ammonius and Evagrius" (*Lausiac History* 24.2). He probably refers to the same people when he mentions "Evagrius's community" (*Lausiac History* 33) and "the circle of saint Evagrius" (35). Evagrius himself attests that he was with Ammonius when they visited John of Lycopolis (*Talking Back* 6.16). Chased by Theophilus from Egypt, the Tall Brothers will be received in Constantinople by Olympia the Deacon—the dedicatee of the Origenian *Homilies on the Song of Songs* by Nyssen, who in the Prologue calls her with deference σεμνοπρεπεστάτη, "most reverend"—and her bishop John Chrysostom. Much of their vicissitudes are known thanks to Palladius, the admirer of Evagrius.

Evagrius's impact was impressive, not only on successive radical Origenists such as Stephen Bar Sudhaili,[27] but also on theologians such as Pseudo-Dionysius, Maximus the Confessor, John Climacus, Isaac of Nineveh, and others.[28] Even much later, Barhebraeus (1226–86), the Syriac bishop and polymath who wrote in Syriac and Arabic on theology, philosophy, history, science, and other topics, and who admired Origen for his *Hexapla* (the first multilingual critical edition of the Bible), described Evagrius as "the greatest of the gnostics."[29] The influence Evagrius exerted is striking, especially on Greek, Syriac, and Latin Christianity. The latter was influenced above all by the Latin writings, or translations, of Cassian and by Rufinus's translations of Evagrius's works. Furthermore, Melania and Rufinus, by means of their scriptorium and their relations, very likely contributed to the spread of Evagrius's Greek works. Others too translated some of Evagrius's oeuvre into Latin, as the existence of two Latin versions of Evagrius's *To a Virgin* (*Ad virginem*) indicate. Jerome too, for a long while, was an admirer of Evagrius, and in *Letter* 4.2 Jerome called Evagrius "reverend presbyter." However, after Jerome's sudden volte-face against Origen,[30] he became hos-

27. See ibid., section on Sudhaili.

28. Columba Stewart, *Cassian the Monk* (Oxford: Oxford University Press, 1998), underlines Evagrius's influence on Cassian; still important is Salvatore Marsili, "Giovanni Cassiano ed Evagrio Pontico, Dottrina sulla Carità e Contemplazione," *Scriptorium* 5 (1951): 195–213. But now Tzamalikos's rereading of the figure of Cassian should at least be taken into account (see above, n. 13). On Isaac of Nineveh's own *Kephalaia Gnostika*, see now Nestor Kavvadas, *Isaak von Ninive und seine Kephalaia Gnostika: Die Pneumatologie und ihr Kontext* (Leiden: Brill, 2015).

29. More generally on Barhebraeus's knowledge and use of the Fathers, see at least David Taylor, "L'importance des Pères de l'Église dans l'oeuvre spéculative de Barhebraeus," *ParOr* 33 (2008): 63–85.

30. See below, in this same chapter.

tile to Evagrius no less than to Origen—a clear indication that he perceived Evagrius as a strict follower of the great Alexandrian.

2. The *Kephalaia Gnostika*, Their Two Versions, and Their Riddles

The *Kephalaia Gnostika* (Γνωστικὰ Κεφάλαια, *Chapters on Knowledge*, or better, *Propositions on Knowledge*, abbreviated *KG*),[31] in six books of ninety propositions (sometimes called "chapters") each, are the third and most advanced piece of a trilogy devoted to monastic life and also composed of the *The Ascetic* (*Praktikos*), sometimes also called the *Kephalaia Praktika* (Κεφάλαια Πρακτικά, *Chapters* or *Propositions on Asceticism*), and *The Gnostic* (*Gnostikos*, Γνωστικός).[32] The *KG* are the masterpiece of Evagrius: he wrote them in Greek, but the whole work is extant only in Oriental versions: in an Armenian adaptation,[33] in Arabic, and above all in Syriac, in two different redactions. The Syriac version discovered by Antoine Guillaumont and called S_2, unlike the other extant Syriac version (S_1) and unlike the other versions in general, is not expurgated; in particular, it is not freed from what was subsequently perceived as dangerously Origenistic. Guillaumont first contended in an article[34] that the original text is S_2, on which I have based my translation and commentary here, which, however, profit from new readings from the manuscript and improvements with respect to Guillaumont's edition. The first critical edition has been Guillaumont's *Les six centuries des "Kephalaia gnostica"* (PO 28.1; Paris: Firmin-Didot, 1958). Guillaumont's hypothesis concerning the priority of S_2 has been followed by virtually all scholars.[35] There are also some Greek fragments of the *KG*, but the Syriac is both complete and much better. The version I have trans-

31. *CPG* 2432. On their literary form, see Endre von Ivánka, "ΚΕΦΑΛΑΙΑ: Eine byzantinische Literaturform und ihre antiken Wurzeln," *ByzZ* 47 (1954): 285–91. For the translation *Propositions on Knowledge*, see below, my first note at the beginning of the commentary.

32. Robin Darling Young, "Evagrius the Iconographer: Monastic Pedagogy in the *Gnostikos*," *JECS* 9 (2001): 53–71.

33. On which see Robin Darling Young, "The Armenian Adaptation of Evagrius' *Kephalaia Gnostika*," in *Origeniana Quinta* (ed. Robert J. Daly; Leuven: Peeters, 1992), 535–41.

34. Antoine Guillaumont, "Le texte véritable des *Gnostica* d'Évagre le Pontique," *RHR* 142 (1952): 156–205.

35. See James W. Watt, "The Syriac Adapter of Evagrius's Centuries," *StPatr* 17.3 (1982): 1388–95; David Bundy, "The Philosophical Structures of Origenism: The Case

lated here is the fuller one, where Evagrius's ideas concerning reality, God, protology, eschatology, anthropology, and allegorical exegesis of Scripture are expressed in a full manner (full but concise and often cryptic, as I will mention).

This does not mean, however, that the *KG*, even in their nonexpurgated version, form a complete work. First of all, this work seems to have been deliberately left incomplete by Evagrius. Babai the Great (569–628), who commented on the *KG*, observes that, instead of the six hundred *kephalaia* promised, Evagrius in fact wrote only 540. According to Babai, the supplement to this incomplete work is to be found in Evagrius's *Skemmata*, or *Reflections* (*CPG* 2433). Babai's version of this work contained only sixty *kephalaia*.[36] On the other hand, Socrates (*Church History* 4.23), when listing Evagrius's works in about 440—only forty years after Evagrius's death—designates this as ἑξακόσια προγνωστικὰ προβλήματα, "six hundred gnostic problems." Either he knew of a complete edition, now lost and unknown to Babai more than one century later, or he ignored that the *KG* were in fact never written in number of six hundred. Second, this incompleteness seems to be structural and to reflect the limits of human theological discourse and what can be expressed of God and of mystical contemplation.[37]

---

of the Expurgated Syriac Version S_1 of the *Kephalaia Gnostika* of Evagrius," in Daly, *Origeniana Quinta*, 577–84.

36. See *Evagrius Ponticus* (ed. W. Frankenberg; Abhandlungen der Königlichen Gesellschaft der Wissenschaften zu Göttingen and Philologisch-Historische Klasse n.s. 13.2; Berlin: Weidmann, 1912), 422–71 = *Pseudo-Supplément des Six Centuries des Képhalaia Gnostica*. The problem is noted by Antoine Guillaumont, *Les "Képhalaia gnostica" d'Évagre le Pontique et l'histoire de l'origénisme chez les grecs et chez les syriens* (Paris: Éditions du Seuil, 1962), 18–22; and Luke Dysinger, *Psalmody and Prayer in the Writings of Evagrius Ponticus* (Oxford: Oxford University Press, 2005), 204.

37. This conclusion has been reached independently by both Monica Tobon and myself. See Monica Tobon, "Reply to Kevin Corrigan," *StPatr* 57 (2013): 27–29, esp. 28: "the 'missing chapters' are in fact 'silent chapters,' corresponding to the passage of the contemplative nous beyond the words of human teachers to the Word himself, beyond image and sign to the unconstrained and uncontainable infinity of God." See now the more articulate treatment by Monica Tobon, "A Word Spoken in Silence: The 'Missing' Chapters of Evagrius' *Kephalaia Gnostika*," in *Studia Patristica LXXII* (ed. Allen Brent, Morwenna Ludlow, and Markus Vinzent; Leuven: Peeters, 2014), 197–210. On mystic apophaticism in Evagrius, see Ilaria L. E. Ramelli, "Mysticism and Mystic Apophaticism in Middle and Neoplatonism across Judaism, 'Paganism' and Christianity," in *Constructions of Mysticism: Inventions and Interactions across the Borders* (ed. Annette Wilke; Wiesbaden: Harrassowitz, 2015).

What makes the *KG* the most difficult text of Evagrius, however, is their concision and lack of explanations. This is because these short sentences were destined to Evagrius's most advanced disciples and presuppose a long path of learning, as well as ascetic training. In order to understand something of these propositions, therefore, it is necessary to be very familiar with the rest of Evagrius's works and his spirituality.

Even if Evagrius's propositions are concise to the point of obscurity, however, the *KG* are very long in comparison with the two other works of Evagrius's monastic trilogy, *Praktikos* and *Gnostikos*. As Monica Tobon remarks, in fact, "the *Kephalaia Gnostika*, the most explicitly contemplative of the three volumes, is four times as long as the other two volumes combined."[38] I use here, and endeavor to improve in some small points, the above-cited edition of Antoine Guillaumont, *Les six centuries des "Kephalaia gnostica."* I will discuss the few textual problems, some new emendations (including those suggested to me by Sebastian Brock), and some more translation problems directly in my commentary.

Guillaumont's French translation is included in his edition, *Les six centuries*, and a new French translation is being prepared by Paul Géhin, as he communicated to me in summer 2012. As of the summer of 2013, there only exist extremely partial English translations, in an article by David Bundy[39] and in a dissertation by Michael O'Laughlin.[40] In respect to these partial translations, the present one is complete, is based on a different edition (with emendations and some different textual choices vis-à-vis those of Guillaumont), and hopefully introduces many improvements in the translation and interpretation of Evagrius's text. What is more, it also provides a full commentary and a substantial critical essay.

The translation provided by Fr. Theophanes (Constantine) in an appendix of his book *The Evagrian Ascetical System* (vol. 2 of *The Psychological Basis of Mental Prayer in the Heart*; Mount Athos: Timios Prodromos, 2006) cannot be considered to be a direct translation of the *KG*, since it is, admittedly, a translation from Guillaumont's French, and not from the Syriac. Indeed, he declares: "We have translated the *Kephalaia Gnos-*

38. Monica Tobon, "Introduction," *StPatr* 57 (2013): 3–7, esp. 4.

39. David Bundy, "The Kephalaia Gnostika," in *Ascetic Behavior in Greco-Roman Antiquity: A Sourcebook* (ed. Vincent L. Wimbush; Minneapolis: Fortress, 1990), 175–86.

40. Michael O'Laughlin, "Origenism in the Desert: Anthropology and Integration in Evagrius Ponticus" (Ph.D. diss., Harvard Divinity School, 1987).

tika of Evagrius Pontikos into English from the French translation of M. Antoine Guillaumont, who translated from the Syriac *version intégrale* (S_2), established by M. Guillaumont, which is, presumably, the authentic Syriac translation of the lost Greek original. The reader should refer to the French, or, better, to the Syriac, in cases of doubt as to the meaning of the text." Something similar would seem to be the case with Luke Dysinger's online version, which is based on the French translation, the Syriac, and assorted Greek fragments (while the Greek retroversion of the Syriac S_1 version, also printed by Dysinger, is unreliable). Some passages from the *KG* are also translated by Julia Konstantinovsky in her aforementioned monograph *Evagrius Ponticus: The Making of a Gnostic*, but they are very far from providing the whole *Kephalaia*.

Antoine Guillaumont deemed the S_2 redaction original, and S_1 expurgated. I tend to agree with this view, which has been received by virtually all scholars, even though I doubt the validity of the related claims by Guillaumont that Philoxenus of Mabbug was the author of the expurgated version (S_1)[41] and, especially, that it is Evagrius's own ideas that were condemned under Justinian. Augustine Casiday is perfectly right, I think, to question this last point, which I also call into doubt, but his argument that S_1 is Evagrius's original redaction and S_2 is a later reworking in a radicalizing Origenistic sense[42] is extremely far from being certain. I shall argue throughout my commentary that S_2 is perfectly in line with Origen's true thought—and not a radicalized version close to the kind of sixth-century Origenism condemned under Justinian—and also with other works by Evagrius himself, including his *Letter on Faith* and *Letter to Melania*. What is there is not what was condemned by Justinian but is Evagrius's original assimilation of Origen's (and Gregory of Nyssa's) ideas, and is very likely to be Evagrius's own product. It is likely that S_1 is an expurgated version, possibly quite old (it is not even to be ruled out that Evagrius himself provided an alternative redaction, even if this is not very probable), but expurgated in an anti-Origenian sense, just as we have expurgated versions of the *Dialogue of Adamantius* or the *History of the Monks in Egypt* (*Historia monachorum in Aegypto*), or even of Eriugena's translations of

41. See John Watt, "Philoxenus and the Old Syriac Version of Evagrius' Centuries," *OrChr* 64 (1980): 65–81; idem, "Syriac Adapter of Evagrius' Centuries"; Ilaria L. E. Ramelli, "Philoxenus and Babai: Authentic and Interpolated Versions of Evagrius's Works?" in idem, *Christian Doctrine of Apokatastasis*.

42. Casiday, *Reconstructing the Theology of Evagrius*, 49, 69–70, and passim.

Gregory of Nyssa's *Creation of the Human Being* (*De hominis opificio*). In all these works, the parts that were dropped in the expurgated redactions were all expressions of Origenian ideas, chiefly those concerning the doctrine of universal restoration.[43]

This is why I chose to translate S_2, moreover exclusively sticking to the Syriac. For "none of the surviving Greek fragments of the *Gnostic Chapters* can be dated before the Second [i.e., Origenistic] Controversy,"[44] and therefore they do not seem to be fully reliable. This text by Evagrius has not yet been translated into English from Syriac and adequately commented on so far, and it is an exceedingly important work by an author who had a great impact on the development of spirituality, of Origenism, and of the spiritual interpretation of the Bible. Evagrius offered the first complete system of Christian spirituality, as noted by Louis Bouyer.[45] As will be clear from the commentary, Evagrius's teaching on prayer emerges more than once in the *KG*, even though Evagrius devoted also a specific treatise to prayer.[46]

3. Evagrius's Works, the Loss of Some in Greek, Their Survival in Translations

Like Origen, Evagrius was made the object of attacks already during his life, and much more so after his death; this explains the loss of a number of his works in Greek and their survival only in ancient translations, mostly into Syriac, but also into Armenian, Latin, and other languages. Many

---

43. See Ramelli, *Christian Doctrine of Apokatastasis*, chapters on the *Dialogue of Adamantius* and Eriugena. On the former, more is in the works.

44. Casiday, *Reconstructing the Theology of Evagrius*, 67.

45. Louis Bouyer, *The Spirituality of the New Testament and the Fathers* (trans. M. P. Ryan; London: Burns & Oates, 1963).

46. See below in the commentary, also with further bibliographical references. Now I limit myself to indicating Irenée Hausherr, "Le traité de l'oraison d'Évagre le Pontique (ps. Nil)," *Revue d'Ascétique et de Mystique* 15 (1934): 34–118; Antoine Guillaumont, "Le problème de la prière continuelle dans le monachisme ancien," in *L'experience de la prière dans les grandes religions* (Louvain-la-Neuve: Presses universitaires, 1980), 285–94; idem, *Études sur la spiritualité de l'Orient chrétien* (Bégrolles en Mauges: Bellefontaine, 1996), 143–50; Gabriel Bunge, "Priez sans cesse: Aux origines de la prière hésychaste," *StudMon* 30 (1988): 7–16. See also Columba Stewart, "Imageless Prayer and the Theological Vision of Evagrius Ponticus," *JECS* 9 (2001): 173–204; Dysinger, *Psalmody and Prayer*.

works by Evagrius (just as some by Gregory Nyssen—for instance, his aforementioned dialogue *On the Soul and the Resurrection*) were translated into Coptic and, probably even before the sixth century, into Syriac. This survival only in translations is especially the case with his most speculative works, and less so with his ascetic works, which were generally judged more innocuous. He was blamed by a monk, Heron, for his teaching during his own lifetime,[47] and it seems that he was criticized because he was too learned and read too much: such a denigration is reflected in the *Apophthegms of the Fathers*.[48]

The main sources of inspiration for his works were Origen's ideas, together with, and partially through, those of the Cappadocians, and particularly of Gregory Nyssen, as I have mentioned, and Neoplatonism. It has been often missed by scholarship[49] that Evagrius was an Origenian, as I said at the beginning of this essay, more than an Origenist: he stuck to Origen's true thought, like Gregory of Nyssa, his other great inspirer. The reading of his thought through the lens of later, radicalized, and distorted Origenism—as though Evagrius's ideas, like Origen's and Didymus's, were those of the Origenists condemned under Justinian—also explains the loss of many of his works in Greek, even though Evagrius, like Origen and Didymus, was perfectly "orthodox" in Trinitarian matters, as is clear from his *Letter on Faith* (as well as in his other works, including the *KG*, as I will

47. Palladius, *Lausiac History* 26.

48. A 233 (Evagrius 7); A 224 (Euprepios 7, but in fact Evagrius); A 43 (Arsenius 5).

49. E.g., Henri Crouzel, "Recherches sur Origène et son influence," *BLE* 62 (1961): 3–15, 105–13; François Refoulé, "La christologie d'Évagre et l'origénisme," *OCP* 27 (1961): 221–66; idem, "Évagre fut-il origéniste?," *RSPT* 47 (1963): 398–402; idem, "La mystique d'Évagre et l'origénisme," *VSpir* suppl. 66 (1963): 453–63; Francis X. Murphy, "Evagrius Ponticus and Origenism," in *Origeniana Tertia* (ed. Robert Hanson and Henri Crouzel; Rome: Augustinianum, 1985), 253–69; Francis Kline, "The Christology of Evagrius and the Parent System of Origen," *Cistercian Studies* 20 (1985): 155–83; Michael O'Laughlin, "Elements of Fourth-Century Origenism," in *Origen of Alexandria* (ed. Charles Kannengiesser; Notre Dame, Ind.: University of Notre Dame Press, 1988), 357–73; idem, "New Questions concerning the Origenism of Evagrius," in Daly, *Origeniana Quinta*, 528–35; Charles Kannengiesser, "Antony, Athanasius, Evagrius: The Egyptian Fate of Origenism," *Coptic Church Review* 16 (1995): 3–8; Lars Thunberg and A. M. Allchin, *Microcosm and Mediator: The Theological Anthropology of Maximus the Confessor* (2d ed.; Chicago: University of Chicago Press, 1995), with reflections on the relationships between Origen, Evagrius, and Maximus; Monika Pesthy, "*Logismoi* origéniens—*logismoi* évagriens," in *Origeniana VIII* (ed. Lorenzo Perrone; Leuven: Peeters, 2003), 1017–22.

point out)—so much so that, as I mentioned earlier, this letter was formerly attributed to Basil the Great. This can help explain the reason why it was tranquilly preserved in Greek.

This letter seems to stem from the years that Evagrius spent with the Cappadocians, but it might also be quite later. Joel Kalvesmaki, building upon Robert Melcher's thesis, suggests that it was written by Evagrius, not from Constantinople around 381 to Christians in Pontus, but to Constantinople from Jerusalem or Egypt in 383 or later.[50] As I mentioned briefly beforehand, this letter follows the Cappadocians' Trinitarian theology with its formula "one common essence, three individual substances," which depends on Origen.[51] Indeed, Evagrius regarded as a heretic anyone who did not believe in the consubstantiality of the persons of the Trinity.[52]

As I will point out in the commentary below, Evagrius's Trinitarian "orthodoxy" is perfectly compatible with the Christology[53] that is found in his *KG* and his *Letter to Melania*. This is not, as is commonly assumed, a subordinationistic Christology, and this comes as no surprise at all in a follower of Origen and Gregory Nyssen, neither of whom was christologically subordinationist.[54] Consistently with what I will argue, Palladius's biography of Evagrius reports an epigram that exalts Evagrius's Trinitarian "orthodoxy," with regard to the Son and the Spirit. As I mentioned earlier in connection with a critical appraisal of Guillaumont's and Casiday's theses concerning Evagrius's "Origenism," Guillaumont's claim that the doctrine condemned at the fifth to eighth ecumenical councils was not that of Origen (as was previously assumed) but that of Evagrius[55] needs to be corrected in turn: the ideas condemned under Justinian and later were largely neither those of Origen nor those of Evagrius but those of later Origenists who radicalized and distorted Evagrius's thinking, and moreover in

50. Joel Kalvesmaki, "The *Epistula fidei* of Evagrius of Pontus: An Answer to Constantinople," *JECS* 20 (2012): 113–39.

51. On Evagrius's *Letter*, see *L'*Epistula fidei *di Evagrio Pontico: Temi, contesti, sviluppi* (ed. Paolo Bettiolo; Rome: Augustinianum, 2000), here especially Paul Géhin, "La place de la *Lettre sur la foi* dans l'oeuvre d'Evagre," 25–58.

52. *Exhortation to the Monks* 45.

53. On which see Konstantinovsky, *Evagrius*, 109–52.

54. See Ramelli, "Origen's Anti-Subordinationism."

55. See Antoine Guillaumont, "Évagre et les anathématismes anti-origénistes de 553," *StPatr* 3 (1961): 219–26; and idem, *Les "Képhalaia gnostica."*

the form these ideas were represented in a dossier prepared by the Sabaite monks hostile to Origenism.[56]

It is obviously because of the hostility and the misunderstandings surrounding his thought that Evagrius's works often survive only in translations.[57] Sometimes, his writings were preserved in anthologies and ascribed to other authors whose orthodoxy was regarded as less suspect, such as Basil and Nilus of Ancyra. "Chapters" (*kephalaia*), or better, "propositions," were compiled by his disciples on the basis of their teacher's ideas.[58] These *Chapters of the Disciples of Evagrius* are over two hundred propositions (κεφάλαια) on asceticism (πρακτική) and knowledge (γνωστική), collected at the beginning of the fifth century. This collection seems to reflect Evagrius's most mature thought and influenced Maximus the Confessor's *Chapters on Love.*

The original Greek of the *Praktikos*, in one hundred "chapters," or propositions, is preserved (it has also been handed down in Syriac, Armenian, Ethiopic, Georgian, and Arabic),[59] just as that of several other ascetic works, mostly collections of sentences, such as those *Sentences to the Monks* (*Sententiae ad monachos*)[60]—in 137 chapters, or propositions, on monastic life, handed down in Greek (in a double recension) and in Latin (also in a double recension), plus Syriac, Coptic, Armenian, Ethiopic, and Geor-

56. István Perczel, "Note sur la pensée systematique d'Évagre le Pontique," in *Origene e l'Alessandrinismo cappadoce* (ed. Mario Girardi and Marcello Marin; Bari: Edipuglia, 2002), 277–97. The comparison between Evagrius's obscure and concise language and the coherent and expanded system of the anti-Origenian sources seems to confirm Perczel's thesis. See Ramelli, *Christian Doctrine of Apokatastasis*, ch. 4, in the section devoted to Justinian and the Origenists.

57. See Antoine Guillaumont, "Le rôle des versions orientales dans la récupération de l'oeuvre d'Évagre," in *Comptes rendus des séances de l'Académie des inscriptions* (Paris: Académie des inscriptions, 1985), 64–74; idem, "Les versions syriaques de l'oeuvre d'Évagre," *OrChrAn* 221 (1983): 35–41; Khalil Samir, "Évagre le Pontique dans la tradition arabo-copte," in *Actes du IVe Congrès Copte* (ed. M. Rassart-Debergh and J. Ries; Louvain-la-Neuve: Université catholique de Louvain, Institut orientaliste, 1992), 2:123–53.

58. Edition by Paul Géhin, ed., *Chapitres des disciples d'Evagre* (SC 514; Paris: Cerf, 2007).

59. Λόγος Πρακτικός (*CPG* 2430).

60. Πρὸς τοὺς ἐν κοινοβίοις ἢ συνοδίαις μοναχούς (*CPG* 2435). See Jeremy Driscoll, *The* Ad monachos *of Evagrius Ponticus* (Rome: Augustinianum, 1991); idem, "Gentleness in the *Ad monachos* of Evagrius," *StudMon* 22 (1990): 295–321; idem, "A Key for Reading the *Ad monachos* of Evagrius," *Aug* 30 (1990): 361–92.

gian—and those *To a Virgin* (*Ad virginem*), fifty-six thoughts handed down in Greek, Latin, Syriac, and Armenian.[61] Susanna Elm considers this text to be a monastic rule rather than a letter to a virgin.[62] Also other sentences (*sententiae*), "chapters"/propositions (*capita*/*kephalaia*), and exegetical works are extant in Greek. Exegetical works that are extant only in Syriac, Coptic, or Arabic are very few; many of them are still available in their Greek original, for instance the *Scholia on Psalms*[63] stemming from catenae or biblical commentaries in which they are attributed to Origen or Athanasius, or from unpublished manuscripts, all deriving from an Evagrian commentary on the Psalms now lost.[64]

On the contrary, only scanty Greek fragments survive from the more speculative *KG*, the object of the present commentary. Likewise another work belonging to the same trilogy as the *KG*, the fifty-chapter *Gnostikos* (Γνωστικός),[65] is preserved in Greek only fragmentarily but survives in full in Syriac, in various recensions, and Armenian. Evagrius's *Talking Back*, or *Antirrheticus*,[66] too is lost in Greek, although it does not contain too bold metaphysical, protological, or eschatological speculations, but it is rather a collection of biblical verses aimed at the destruction of passions. An attempt has been made to reconstruct the original Greek, but the work is preserved only in Syriac, Armenian, and Georgian, in addition to some Sogdian fragments in a double recension.

The same is the case with Evagrius's letters. While the original Greek text is extant even in three recensions—the original, and not later retroversions as in the case of Frankenberg's retroversion of the *KG*—of at least sixty-two epistles of spiritual advice to different addressees, such as Rufinus, Melania the Elder, John of Jerusalem, or Gregory Nazianzen (all Origenians),[67] and the Greek of the *Letter on Faith* is likewise extant along with the Syriac translation, also thanks to the previous attribution of this letter to Basil,[68] the original Greek text is lost in the case of the *Letter to*

61. Παραίνεσις πρὸς παρθένον (*CPG* 2436).

62. Susanna Elm, "The *Sententiae ad virginem* by Evagrius Ponticus and the Problem of Early Monastic Rules," *Aug* 30 (1990): 393–404.

63. Σχόλια εἰς τοὺς Ψαλμούς (*CPG* 2455).

64. See also, e.g., *CPG* 2458.2–5.

65. *CPG* 2431.

66. *CPG* 2434.

67. *CPG* 2437.

68. *CPG* 2439; it was ascribed to Evagrius only in 1923 by Wilhelm Bousset, *Apophthegmata: Studien zur Geschichte des ältesten Mönchtums* (Tübingen: Mohr, 1923),

Melania, where sustained metaphysical, protological, and eschatological speculations are surely put forward. Undoubtedly for this reason, this letter is lost in Greek and is extant only in an Armenian and a double Syriac recension. I shall return very soon to this all-important work, especially on account of its remarkable relevance to the *KG*.

Evagrius's works concern both theology/metaphysics and spiritual ascent and ascetic practice;[69] in this system, asceticism, the *praktikē*, leads to knowledge, *gnōsis*. As I will point out extensively in the commentary, these aspects are closely related in Evagrius and cannot exist independently of one another. As I have mentioned in the initial methodological observations, Evagrius's thought must be approached in its entirety: it cannot be appreciated only for its ascetic insights and advice, while rejected for its metaphysical, protological, and eschatological Origenian implications. It is lamentable that Evagrius's heritage was, so to say, split into two; his ascetic works were deemed good and safe, but his metaphysical, protological, and eschatological speculations—especially those found in his *KG* and *Letter to Melania*—were considered to be bad and dangerous. Evagrius's *Letter to Melania* and *KG*, among much else, clearly teach Origen's doctrine of *apokatastasis*.[70] Here, indeed, Evagrius shows that his conception of the *telos*, the ultimate end of all, just like those of Origen and Gregory Nyssen, is closely related to the rest of his thought, which is entirely oriented toward the *telos* itself. For the *telos* is the perfect realization of God's plan for all rational creatures and for the whole of God's creation.

4. The *Letter to Melania* and Its Relation to the *Kephalaia Gnostika*

The *Letter to Melania*, or *Great Letter*,[71] is the lengthiest of Evagrius's epistles. It focuses on the Trinity, protology, eschatology, restoration (or *apokatastasis*), and spiritual knowledge, issues that also come to the fore in the *KG*. This is why this letter is particularly relevant to, and helpful for, the study of the *KG*. The addressee of the *Letter to Melania* in one of the two Syriac manuscripts in which it is preserved, as in other letters

281–341, and Robert Melcher, *Der 8. Brief des hl. Basilius, ein Werk des Evagrius Pontikus* (Münsterische Beiträge zur Theologie 1; Münster: Aschendorff, 1923).

69. A complete English translation of Evagrius's main ascetic works is found in Sinkewicz, *Evagrius of Pontus*.

70. See Ramelli, *Christian Doctrine of Apokatastasis*, the chapter on Evagrius.

71. *CPG* 2438.

by Evagrius extant in Armenian, is Melania the Elder, who, according to Palladius—as we have seen—definitely converted Evagrius to the ascetic life and gave him his monastic garb. Some scholars do not accept the identification of the recipient with Melania, chiefly because in the Syriac translation Evagrius addresses her thrice as "my lord" (ܡܪܝ). As a consequence, some consider Rufinus—who lived at Melania's monastery and, as I have mentioned earlier, was also a friend of Evagrius's—to be a more probable addressee.[72]

I would not rule out that the recipient was indeed Melania. Palladius in *Lausiac History* 38.8 and 9[73] calls Melania *ἡ μακαρία* Μελάνιον, "the blessed, dear Melanion," using this neutral form as a diminutive and possibly a form of endearment. Evagrius, like his disciple Palladius, may have called Melania Μελάνιον, and Syriac translators may easily have understood Μελάνιον as a masculine, all the more so in that in Syriac there are only masculine or feminine forms, and no neuter. And the neuter in Greek is much closer to masculine than to feminine forms. Also, some scholars think that a masculine address formula for a woman is to be read in a "gnostic" context, as a kind of honorific address: a woman who has transcended the supposed weakness of her gender with her intellectual and spiritual strength and prowess.[74] At any rate, both of the most probable addressees, Melania and Rufinus, deeply admired Origen, as Evagrius also did, and this letter is composed against the backdrop of Origen's theology.

The *Letter to Melania* reveals significant points of contact with the *KG*. Since it is somewhat less concise than the *KG*, it can help a great deal

72. Gabriel Bunge, *Evagrios Pontikos, Briefe aus der Wüste* (Trier: Paulinus, 1986), 194; on 303–28 he also offers a translation of the *Letter to Melania*; Gösta Vitestam, *Seconde partie du traité, qui passe sous le nom de La grande lettre d'Évagre le Pontique à Mélanie l'ancienne, d'après le manuscrit du British Museum Add. 17192* (Lund: Gleerup, 1964), 4–5, also thought that the recipient of the letter was originally a man. Casiday, *Reconstructing the Theology of Evagrius*, 64, is on the same line. Vitestam offers the edition of the Syriac for §§17, 24–25, 33–68. The edition of §§1–32 is provided by Frankenberg, *Evagrius Ponticus*, 610–19.

73. = 86 (PG 34:1193D).

74. Michel Parmentier, "Evagrius of Pontus' Letter to Melania," *Bijdr* 46 (1985): 2–38, esp. 5–6; repr. in *Forms of Devotion, Conversion, Worship, Spirituality, and Asceticism* (ed. Everett Ferguson; New York: Garland, 1999). Parmentier includes an English version of the letter. The title *Letter to Melania* is also kept by Paolo Bettiolo, *Evagrio Pontico: Lo scrigno della sapienza; Lettera a Melania* (Magnano, Biella: Edizioni Qiqajon, 1997).

to understand more of the cryptic *KG*. On the other hand, it must also be taken into account that Evagrius in this letter refrains from committing to paper some of his ideas. To be sure, he is also deploying here a literary *topos*, but it is obvious that he has omitted something—just as in the *KG*. Evagrius himself wants to make this clear by means of repeated allusions. In the opening, in section 1, he states that friends write down in letters thoughts that can be revealed only to those who think alike. A little later, Evagrius insists that in this letter he is writing things that he cannot express fully: "I cannot commit these things to paper and ink, because of those who might intercept this letter; moreover, these important topics are too dangerous to be written down on paper. This is why I cannot say everything" (17). In section 18 he repeats that there are things that ink and paper cannot report. These things should be identified, not with the eventual universal restoration, or *apokatastasis*—of which Evagrius in fact speaks rather overtly, even though it was beginning to be contested in his day, so that Gregory Nyssen felt the need to defend it as "orthodox" Christian doctrine[75]—but probably with the way the Spirit and the Son communicate with the intellect, and with the reasons why the intelligible creation was joined to the sense-perceptible creation. For Evagrius declares that the intelligible creation was joined to the sense-perceptible creation "for reasons that it is impossible to explain here." Moreover, it is of course impossible to speak of the divine mysteries, and in this connection the silence strategy used by Evagrius in this letter seems to parallel that which I have already pointed out—and is finely studied by Monica Tobon—in the *KG*.

Evagrius maintains that, with some rational creatures, the Spirit and the Son communicate directly—although he does not clarify how—but

75. He did so especially in his dialogue *On the Soul and the Resurrection* and in his commentary on 1 Cor 15:28 (*In illud: Tunc et ipse Filius*). See Ramelli, *Gregorio di Nissa: Sull'anima*, for the commentaries on these texts; and idem, *Christian Doctrine of Apokatastasis*, the chapter on Nyssen, for his strategy of defense of this doctrine. I have argued that Gregory supported the *apokatastasis* doctrine in defense of the Nicene Trinitarian orthodoxy (see Ilaria L. E. Ramelli, "Gregory of Nyssa's Trinitarian Theology in *In illud: Tunc et ipse Filius*: His Polemic against 'Arian' Subordinationism and Apokatastasis," in *Gregory of Nyssa: The Minor Treatises on Trinitarian Theology and Apollinarism; Proceedings of the 11th International Colloquium on Gregory of Nyssa (Tübingen, 17–20 September 2008)* [ed.Volker Henning Drecoll and Margitta Berghaus; Leiden: Brill, 2011], 445–78). Evagrius, too, his follower, upheld both the Nicene Trinitarian orthodoxy and the doctrine of universal restoration.

with others, less advanced, they communicate by means of intermediaries, that is, God's sense-perceptible creation, what Evagrius repeatedly calls the "secondary creation" in his *KG*. This is the object of "natural contemplation"[76] (φυσικὴ θεωρία, which will exert a profound influence on Maximus the Confessor[77]). The antecedents to Evagrius's natural contemplation are to be found in Clement of Alexandria (who calls it φυσιολογία) and Origen.[78] This secondary creation, which is the object of natural contemplation, is not evil; on this, Origen had already insisted against "Gnostics" and Marcionites. Far from being evil, the secondary creation is providential and, as Evagrius explains, was wanted by God as mediation, out of love for those who are far from God because "they have placed a separation between themselves and their Creator because of their evil deeds" (*Letter to Melania* 5). God instituted this mediation by means of his Wisdom and Power, that is, the Son and the Spirit. For Evagrius, "the whole ministry of the Son and the Spirit is exercised through creation, *for the sake of those who are far from God*" (ibid.). Something similar was maintained by Gregory of Nyssa, who, in the footsteps of Philo and Origen, claimed that God's operations play a core role in the acquisition of the knowledge of God: humans cannot know God's essence or nature, but they can certainly know God's activities and operations.[79]

In the *Letter to Melania* the Son is called "the hand of God" and the Spirit "the finger of God." Likewise in Evagrius's *Letter on Faith* Christ is called "the right hand of God" and the Spirit "the finger of God."[80] These two peculiar designations are also found in Didymus the Blind's treatise *On the Holy Spirit*[81] and in Ambrose's treatise *On the Holy Spirit* 3.3, where both metaphors occur. Evagrius, Didymus, and Ambrose may have been

76. On natural contemplation in Evagrius, see David Bradford, "Evagrius Ponticus and the Psychology of Natural Contemplation," *Studies in Spirituality* 22 (2012): 109–25.

77. See Joshua Lollar, *To See into the Life of Things: The Contemplation of Nature in Maximus the Confessor and His Predecessors* (Turnhout: Brepols, 2013).

78. See also Paul Blowers, *Drama of the Divine Economy* (Oxford: Oxford University Press, 2012), 316–18.

79. "The Divine as Inaccessible Object of Knowledge in Ancient Platonism: A Common Philosophical Pattern across Religious Traditions," *JHI* 75 (2014): 167–88; and for the reflections of this idea in Evagrius, see Konstantinovsky, *Evagrius*, 47–76.

80. PG 32:265AB.

81. PG 39:1051A, 1076C, and 1077AB, all of these on the Son as "the hand of God," and in 1051BC, on the Spirit as "the finger of God."

inspired by Origen in this respect as in so much else. Evagrius himself does not speak very much of the Spirit in his ascetic works, but this is probably because the Spirit there is often replaced by angels.[82] Evagrius clearly draws on Origen (e.g., *Commentary on Matthew* 13.26)[83] also when he postulates that angels assist humans and are in turn followed by Christ in this assistance. A confirmation for Origen comes from one of the recently discovered homilies on Psalms from Codex Monacensis Graecus 314. In *Homily 2 on Psalm 73,* 1, fol. 129v, Origen remarks that the holy angels cooperated (συνεργοὺς γενομένους) to the salvation and beatitude of Abraham.

Only rational creatures who are particularly close to God do not need the mediation of creation, because they are helped directly by the Son-Logos and the Spirit: "Just as the intellect operates in the body by the mediation of the soul, likewise the Father too, by the mediation of his own soul [i.e., the Son and the Spirit], operates in his own body, which is the human intellect" (*Letter to Melania* 15). Thus, human intellects know thanks to the Logos and the Spirit, who make everything known to them (19); only through the Logos and the Spirit, who are their souls, can they become aware of their own nature (21). In turn, human intellects are the bodies of the Son and the Spirit (ibid.), and the Son and the Spirit are the soul of God. As is clear from Evagrius's argument, the intellect-soul-body tripartition applies both to rational creatures and to the relationship between God and rational creatures, who, as intellects, are the body of God. This is likely to be a development of Origen's notion of the *logika* as the body of Christ-Logos;[84] this concept is also connected with Origen's equation between the body of Christ and the temple, whose stones are rational creatures: this is why in *Commentary on John* 6.1.1–2 the temple is called a "rational building," λογικὴ οἰκοδομή. Also regarding the Son as the soul of God Evagrius was surely inspired by Origen (*Princ.* 2.8.5, where he explicitly describes the Logos as the soul of God). This is a schematic representation of the

82. So Jason Scully, "Angelic Pneumatology in the Egyptian Desert," *JECS* 19 (2011): 287–305, esp. 295.

83. See Joseph W. Trigg, "Christ and the Angelic Hierarchy in Origen's Theology," *JTS* 42 (1991): 35–51.

84. See Ilaria L. E. Ramelli, "Clement's Notion of the Logos 'All Things as One': Its Alexandrian Background in Philo and Its Developments in Origen and Nyssen," in *Alexandrian Personae: Scholarly Culture and Religious Traditions in Ancient Alexandria (1st ct. BCE–4ct. CE)* (ed. Zlatko Plese; Tübingen: Mohr Siebeck, 2016).

relationships that Evagrius posits between the three components of rational creatures and the three persons of the Trinity:

Intellect	>	soul (mediator)	>	body
Father	>	Son and Spirit	>	intellects

Human beings belong to the intelligible creation and are now found joined to the visible creation, with their mortal bodies, "for reasons that it is impossible to explain here" (*Letter to Melania* 13). Evagrius refrains from speaking of the relationship between the fall of the intellects and their acquisition of sense-perceptible bodies, which require the mediation of the soul. He ascribes the role of "soul" to the Logos and the Spirit as well, evidently because of the mediation they perform between the Father and the intellects. Evagrius does not specify whether bodies that are not sense perceptible also require the mediation of the soul. Thus, it is protology—the creation, the fall, and its consequences—that Evagrius omits to explain, by some necessity or convenience, in his *Letter to Melania*, and not so much eschatology.

Indeed, Evagrius does speak of eschatology in terms of universal restoration in this letter, just as he does in a more concise and cryptic way in the *KG*. In sections 22–30 of the letter, in particular, Evagrius expounds some reflections on *apokatastasis*, which he, like Origen, strongly characterizes as a ἕνωσις, a "unification" of the three components of humans (body, soul, and intellect) and of rational creatures with God, in the framework of the elimination of divisions, oppositions, and plurality:

> And there will be a time when the body, the soul, and the intellect will cease to be separate from one another, with their names and their plurality, since the body and the soul will be elevated to the rank of intellects. This conclusion can be drawn from the words "That they may be one in us, just as You and I are One" [John 17:22]. Thus there will be a time when the Father, the Son, and the Spirit, and their rational creation, which constitutes their body, will cease to be separate, with their names and their plurality. And this conclusion can be drawn from the words "God will be all in all" [1 Cor 15:28]. (*Letter to Melania* 22)

As Origen and Gregory Nyssen did, Evagrius also corroborates every argumentative passage of his with a quotation from the Bible. Both scriptural quotations used here by Evagrius were among the favorite quotations of Origen in reference to the ultimate end: John 17:22 for the final unity or ἕνωσις,[85] and 1 Cor 15:28 for both unity and *apokatastasis*.[86] Evagrius teaches that bodies and souls will be elevated to the order of intellects, not only in the *Letter to Melania*, but also in his *KG* (1.65; 2.17; 3.15, 66, 68). I will soon return to these passages both in this essay and below in the commentary: these are among the most prominent passages on *apokatastasis* in the *KG*.

As is evident from the *Letter to Melania* and the *KG*, Evagrius follows both the tripartition of the human being into body, soul, and intellect/spirit and the Platonic tripartition of the soul itself into irascible faculty or part (θυμός, θυμικόν), concupiscible or appetitive faculty or part (ἐπιθυμία, ἐπιθυμητικόν), and intellectual or rational faculty or part (νοῦς, λογικόν), the noblest and most excellent being the last component.[87] This tripartition is evident also in *Praktikos* 89: "The soul of rational beings is tripartite into rational … concupiscible / appetitive … and irascible," and at *Praktikos* 38 and 78. The same tripartition also emerges in a number of passages from Evagrius's *KG* (e.g., 5.27; 4.73; 3.35; 1.84; 3.30; for all of these I refer readers to my translations and commentary below). The excellence of the intellect among the faculties of the soul is proclaimed in *KG* 6.51 ("The intelligent part [i.e., intellect] is the most excellent among all the faculties of the soul") and in 3.6 ("The bare intellect is that which, by means of the contemplation that regards it, is joined to the knowledge of the Trinity") and 3.55 ("In the beginning the intellect had God, who is incorruptible, as teacher of immaterial intellections. Now, however, it has received corruptible sense perception as teacher of material intellections").

---

85. See my volume on John 13–17 (Ilaria L. E. Ramelli, *Gospel according to John III* [Novum Testamentum Patristicum; Göttingen: Vandenhoeck & Ruprecht, forthcoming]). For Evagrius in particular, see Ilaria L. E. Ramelli, "Harmony between *Arkhē* and *Telos* in Patristic Platonism and the Imagery of Astronomical Harmony Applied to the Apokatastasis Theory," *International Journal of the Platonic Tradition* 7 (2013): 1–49.

86. On the use of this verse in support of the doctrine of *apokatastasis* in Evagrius's mentors, Origen and Gregory Nyssen, see Ilaria L. E. Ramelli, "Christian Soteriology and Christian Platonism: Origen, Gregory of Nyssa, and the Biblical and Philosophical Basis of the Doctrine of Apokatastasis," *VC* 61 (2007): 313–56.

87. See Kallistos Ware, "Nous and Noesis in Plato, Aristotle and Evagrius of Pontus," *Diotima* 13 (1985): 158–63; Gabriel Bunge, "'Nach dem Intellekt Leben': Zum sog. 'Intellektualismus' der evagrianischen Spiritualität," in *Simandron, der Wachklopfer: Gedenkenschrift Gamber* (ed. Wilhelm Nyssen; Köln: Luthe, 1989), 95–109; idem, "Origenismus-Gnostizismus: Zum geistesgeschichtlichen Standort des Evagrios Pontikos," *VC* 40 (1986): 24–54; Corrigan, *Evagrius and Gregory*, ch. 5, on the tripartite soul in Evagrius.

Origen famously regarded the soul (ψυχή) as an intellect that has undergone a cooling down (ψῦξις) and due to a lack of ardent love of God and carelessness about its own eternal destiny has fallen down from its original rank, and Evagrius follows him in considering the soul to be a fallen intellect. Thus, in *KG* 3.28, exactly like Origen, Evagrius depicts the soul as an intellect that, because of carelessness, has fallen down from Unity (hence the division between intellect and soul, and further intellect, soul, and body, while initially the intellect was undivided) and, due to its lack of vigilance, has descended to the order of the *praktikē*. In other words, from spiritual contemplation the intellect, now divided into intellect and soul, has descended to practical life, ethics, which in Evagrius coincides with ascesis and the search for virtue and liberation from passions. The same term, πρακτική, with related terms such as πρακτικός, is attested in "pagan" Neoplatonism in the same sense of "ethics."[88] Evagrius himself offers a definition of *praktikē* in *Praktikos* 78: "πρακτική is the spiritual method for purifying the part of the soul subject to passions," its aim being *apatheia*, or impassivity (absence of passions— i.e., of bad emotions).[89] *Praktikē* is deemed by Evagrius the first component of the Christian doctrine: "Christianity is the doctrine of Jesus Christ our Savior, consisting in ethics [πρακτική], philosophy of nature [φυσική], and theology [θεολογική]" (*Praktikos* 1). The intellect, which is distinct from the part of the soul subject to passions, ought to proceed along its own contemplative path toward the angels; if, on the contrary, it proceeds on the path of the soul subject to passions, which should rather be its instrument, it risks ending up among demons (*KG* 2.48).

In this Origenian tenet, and in the Platonic tripartition of the soul, Evagrius's whole ethics and theory of spiritual ascent are grounded. Evagrius's related theory of vices, the "tempting thoughts" (λογισμοί) that lead to the death of the soul, also draws on Origen.[90] The attainment of the perfec-

88. See Olympiodorus, *Prolegomena to Aristotle's Categories* 8.

89. The only monograph devoted to *apatheia* in Evagrius is Monica Tobon, *Apatheia in the Teachings of Evagrius Ponticus: The Health of the Soul* (Burlington, Vt.: Ashgate, forthcoming), esp. ch. 3; see also the essay by Robert Somos, "Origen, Evagrius Ponticus and the Ideal of Impassibility," in *Origeniana Septima: Origenes in den Auseinandersetzungen des 4. Jahrhunderts* (ed. Wolfgang Bienert and Uwe Kühneweg; Leuven: Peeters, 1999), 365–73.

90. See Irénée Hausherr, "L'origine de la théorie orientale des huit péchés capitaux," *Orientalia Christiana* 30 (1933): 164–75, and, below, the commentary.

tion of the *nous*, which consists in knowledge, first requires the perfection of the inferior parts of the soul, those subject to passions—a Neoplatonic idea.[91] Thus, in *On Thoughts* (Περὶ λογισμῶν) 26 Evagrius insists that it is impossible to acquire knowledge without having renounced mundane things, evil, and, after these, ignorance.[92] Clement of Alexandria, who also exerted a certain influence on Evagrius, already posited a similar passage, from the cathartic ("purifying") to the epoptic ("contemplative") mode.[93] The sequence *katharsis*-contemplation (theology) was also clear in Origen, even in one of the newly discovered Homilies on Psalms from Codex Monacensis Graecus 314. In *Homily 1 on Psalm 77*, 5, fol. 223v–224r, Origen observes that in order to practice a correct philosophical-theological-exegetical "zetesis" or investigation one should first purify (καθαρῶς) one's moral behavior (τὰ ἤθη), setting it straight, and only at that point one can aspire to theology (θεολογία) and the investigation into deeper, mystical truths (τὴν ζήτησιν τῶν βαθυτέρων καὶ μυστικωτέρων).

I definitely agree with Augustine Casiday that the *Letter to Melania* cannot be considered to express "isochristic" ideas such as those that were later condemned under Justinian.[94] He rightly observes that when in this letter (at section 22, cited above) Evagrius says that the body and the soul will be raised to the order of the intellect, "there is no compelling reason to think that this elevation destroys rather than, say, consummates or fulfills the body and the soul."[95] I think that indeed a comparison with the *KG* confirms, rather than disproves, this supposition. Casiday opposes the remarks of Antoine Guillaumont: "La christologie d'Évagre est donc absolument identique à celle des moins isochristes et à celle qui forme la partie essentielle de l'origénisme résumé dans les quinze anathématismes de 553. Il y a non seulement identité doctrinale, mais, sur certains points, comme nous l'avons vu, des rencontres littérales."[96] The only point about which I cannot agree with Casiday is that "Origen taught cycles of falling and rec-

91. This has been rightly shown by Blossom Stefaniw, "Exegetical Curricula in Origen, Didymus, and Evagrius: Pedagogical Agenda and the Case for Neoplatonist Influence," *StPatr* 44 (2010): 281–95.

92. See also *KG* 1.78–80 and the relevant commentary below.

93. *Miscellany* (*Stromateis*) 5.70.7–71.2.

94. Augustine Casiday, "Universal Restoration in Evagrius Ponticus' 'Great Letter,'" *StPatr* 47 (2010): 223–28.

95. Ibid., 228.

96. Guillaumont, *Les "Képhalaia gnostica,"* 156.

onciliation, which is precluded by Evagrius's reference to the endless and inseparable unity of God."[97] The reference is to Jerome's *Letter* 124. Jerome, however, ceases to be a reliable source on Origen after his U-turn against him. In fact Origen, exactly like Evagrius, thought that there will be a final unity with God, after which no more falls will be possible. Jerome's letter is much less trustworthy than Origen's own *Commentary on Romans* and many other passages, some of which are preserved in Greek, which I have collected and analyzed elsewhere.[98] Therefore, also in this respect Evagrius did not distance himself from Origen but rather followed in his footsteps.

The passage from the *Letter to Melania* 22 that I have quoted above may also suggest that the three hypostases of the Trinity and the distinction between the Creator and creatures will be obliterated in the very end. This would imply a kind of pantheism such as that which was perceived in the work of Stephen Bar Sudhaili[99] and would indeed place Evagrius within the type of extreme Origenism that was condemned by Justinian, as Guillaumont hypothesized. However, in the immediate continuation of his letter Evagrius openly declares that the three hypostases of the Trinity will continue to subsist in the ultimate end and that the three components of rational creatures will be absorbed in each of the three divine Persons:

> But when it is declared that the names and plurality of rational creatures and their Creator will pass away, it does not at all mean that the hypostases and the names of the Father, the Son, and the Spirit will be obliterated. The nature of the intellect will be joined to the substance of the Father, since it constitutes his body [2 Pet 1:4]. Similarly, the names "soul" and "body" will be subsumed under the hypostases of the Son and the Spirit. And the one and the same nature and three persons of God, and of God's image, will remain eternally, as it was before the inhumanation, and will be after the inhumanation, thanks to the concord of wills. Thus, body, soul, and intellect are (now) separate in number due to the differentiation of wills. But when the names and plurality that have attached to the intellect due to this movement (of will)[100] have passed away, then the multiple

97. Casiday, "Universal Restoration in Evagrius," 224.

98. In Ramelli, *Christian Doctrine of Apokatastasis*, the section on Origen.

99. See ibid., the section on Bar Sudhaili.

100. This meaning of κίνησις is typical of Origen and his tradition, on which Evagrius relies. It is not the case that (as is stated by J. Suzuki, "The Evagrian Concept of *Apatheia* and Its Origenism," in *Origeniana Nona* [ed. G. Heidl and R. Somos; Leuven: Peeters, 2009], 605–11, esp. 608) it is "unique" to Evagrius.

> names by which God is called will pass away as well.... It is not the case that those distinctions [God's names, or *epinoiai*] are inexistent, but those who needed them will no more exist. But the names and hypostases of the Son and the Spirit will never disappear, since they have no beginning and no end. As they have not received them [their names and hypostases] from an unstable cause, they will never disappear, but while their cause continues to exist, they too continue to exist. They are different from rational creatures, whose cause is the Father as well; but these derive from the Father by grace, whereas the Son and the Spirit derive from the nature of the Father's essence. (*Letter to Melania* 23–25)

This passage also makes it clear that the eventual unity cannot be interpreted in a pantheistic sense, as though any distinction between the Creator and creatures should disappear. For Evagrius insists that the unity in the very end will be unanimity of wills and not a merging of substances. Indeed, for Evagrius, just as for Origen, the initial and the final unity are not a confusion of God and creatures but are both a union of wills. The three hypostases of the Trinity have the same will, and all rational creatures shall have the same will, instead of having very different wills, as is now the case, because in the end everyone's will shall be oriented toward God, the highest Good. Moreover, unlike now, when each component in a human being has a different will (so that the intellect wants one thing and the body another), in the end the three components will be reabsorbed into the intellect, so that only the will of the intellect shall remain. Indeed, Evagrius, exactly like Origen, accounts for the present differentiation of rational creatures with the differentiation of their wills, which occurred at the fall. Before the fall, their wills were uniformly oriented toward God, but at a certain point they became fragmented into a multiplicity of acts of volition that had not the highest Good as their object. This is the "movement," as Evagrius, following Origen, calls the movement of will made possible by freedom of will—a gift of God to all rational creatures. Likewise, in *KG* 6.20 Evagrius notes that God created the first creation, of incorporeal realities, and only subsequently the second, that of bodies: the latter came after the *logika*'s "movement," that is, after they dispersed their wills in different directions, instead of toward God alone—this is why Evagrius will soon say in his *Letter to Melania* 26–30 that it was sin to detach the intellects from that unity of will and to diversify intellect, soul, and body. In the very end, at the restoration of all, when God will be "all in all," the differentiation of wills shall cease to exist, since all wills shall finally be directed toward God. "Just as the fire in its power pervades its own body, so will also the *intellect* in its power *pervade the soul*, when the whole of it will be mingled to the light of the Holy Trinity" (*Letter to Melania* 26).

The divine names, or *epinoiai*, too—such as "gate," "shepherd," "rock," and the like—will disappear, since they exist exclusively for the sake of the salvific economy. Evagrius derived this conviction from Origen[101] and also Gregory of Nyssa; the latter, like Evagrius, speaks more of *epinoiai* of God than of *epinoiai* of Christ alone.[102] But while the "economic" *epinoiai* will vanish in the end, the persons of the Father, the Son, and the Spirit will never vanish. The difference between the Son and the Spirit, on the one hand, and the creatures, on the other, is made very clear by Evagrius: the Son and the Spirit stem from the Father *by nature* and share in the Father's very substance, while rational creatures derive from God *by grace* and have a different substance. Indeed, in his *Letter on Faith* Evagrius is adamant that the final deification, or θέωσις, will depend on grace and not on nature: human creatures will be "deities / gods by grace." Again, any similarity with the later "Isochristoi," as well as with a Sudhaili-like pantheism, is to be ruled out.

In his *Letter to Melania* 26, Evagrius draws a parallel between protology and eschatology, as already Origen had done.[103] Evagrius parallels the descent of the intellect to the rank of soul and further of body at the beginning, as a result of the fall and the above-mentioned dispersion of rational creatures' wills, and the eventual elevation of the body to the rank of the soul, and of the soul to the rank of the intellect, when all rational creatures' wills, no more divided into a multiplicity, shall enjoy again perfect unity, once they have returned to be oriented toward God alone:

> There was a time when the intellect, because of its free will, fell from its original rank and was named "soul," and, having plunged further, was named "body." But there will come a time when the body, the soul, and the intellect, thanks to a transformation of their wills, will become one and the same thing. Since there will come a time when the differentiations of the movements of their will shall vanish, it will be elevated to the original state in which it was created. Its nature, hypostasis, and name

101. *On First Principles* 4.4.1.

102. On Gregory's doctrine of divine *epinoiai*, see Tamara Aptsiauri, "Die Allegorese in der Schrift *Leben des Mose* Gregors von Nyssa im Kontext seiner Epinoia-Theorie," in *Gregory of Nyssa Contra Eunomium* (ed. Lenka Karfíková; Leiden: Brill, 2007), 2:495–504.

103. See, e.g., *On First Principles* 2.8.3.

> will be one, known to God. What is elevated in its own nature is alone among all beings, because neither its place nor its name is known, and only the bare mind can say what its nature is.
>
> Please, do not be amazed at my claim regarding the union of rational creatures with God the Father, that these will be one and the same nature in three persons, with no juxtaposition or change.... When the intellects return to God, like rivers to the sea, God entirely transforms them into his own nature, color, and taste. They will be one and the same thing, and not many anymore, in God's infinite and inseparable unity, in that they are united and joined to God.... Before sin operated a separation between intellects and God, just as the earth separated the sea and rivers, they were one with God, without discrepancy, but when their sin was manifested, they were separated from God and alienated from God.... When sin, interposed between intellects and God, has vanished, they will be, not many, but again one and the same.
>
> However, even if I have said that the rivers were eternally in the sea, with this I do not mean that rational creatures were eternally in God in their substance, since, although they were completely united to God in God's Wisdom and creative power, their actual creation did have a beginning; however, one should not think that it will have an end, in that they are united to God, who has no beginning and no end. (*Letter to Melania* 27–30)

It is further clarified here that the final unity (ἕνωσις) will not be a pantheistic confusion but a unity of will—that is, concord. The notion that the "bare intellect" alone can see the nature of God, whose name and place are unknown, is found also in *KG* 2.37 and 3.70 (see the commentary on these *kephalaia* below).

In *Letter to Melania* 30, quoted above, Evagrius draws a fundamental distinction between the eternal existence of the paradigms (*logoi*, or Ideas) of all creatures in God's Wisdom (who is Christ) and their creation as substances only at a certain point, so that they existed not *ab aeterno* in God in their substance but only as paradigms or prefigurations. This important theory too depends on Origen:

> God the Father existed eternally, eternally having his only begotten Son, who at the same time is also called Wisdom.... Now in this Wisdom, which was eternally together with the Father, the whole creation was inscribed from eternity: there was never a time when in Wisdom there was not the prefiguration of the creatures that would come to existence.... Therefore, we do not claim that creatures were never created, or that they

> are coeternal with God, or that God was doing nothing good at first, and then suddenly turned to action.... For, if all beings have been created in Wisdom, since Wisdom has always existed, then from eternity there existed in Wisdom, as paradigmatic prefigurations, those beings that at a certain point have been also created as substances. (Origen, *On First Principles* 1.4.4–5)[104]

Evagrius follows Origen very closely. Origen also thought that, when the *logika* were created as individual substances, they also acquired a fine, immortal body (which may have functioned as *principium individuationis*). Evagrius remarks that, even if rational creatures began to exist as independent substances only at a certain point, they will have no end, because in the *telos* they will enjoy unity with God, who has no end. This remark is probably due to Evagrius's awareness of the "perishability axiom," according to which whatever has a beginning in time will also have an end in time. For Evagrius, rational creatures did have a beginning, but not in the time measured by the stars and the skies of this world, and will have no end.

Moreover, the infinity of God, which Evagrius supports in the last passage quoted from the *Letter to Melania*, was developed especially by Gregory of Nyssa but was found to a certain extent already in Origen, who, for instance, insisted that "the greatness/majesty of God has no limit [πέρας]" and God's providence runs "from the infinite [ἐξ ἀπείρου] to the infinite [ἐπ' ἄπειρον] and even further."[105] In texts that are preserved in Greek and are surely by Origen, God is described as infinite (ἄπειρον) and as being "from infinities to infinity" (ἐξ ἀπείρων ἐπ' ἄπειρον).[106] Origen, Gregory, and Evagrius could find the notion of the infinity of God already in Philo.[107]

---

104. *Deum quidem Patrem semper fuisse, semper habentem unigenitum Filium, qui simul et Sapientia ... appellatur.... In hac igitur Sapientia, quae semper erat cum Patre, descripta semper inerat ac formata conditio et numquam erat quando eorum, quae futura erant, praefiguratio apud Sapientiam non erat.... Ut neque ingenitas neque coaeternas Deo creaturas dicamus, neque rursum, cum nihil boni prius egerit Deus, in id ut ageret esse conversum.... Si utique in Sapientia omnia facta sunt, cum Sapientia semper fuerit, secundum praefigurationem et praeformationem semper erant in Sapientia ea, quae protinus etiam substantialiter facta sunt.*

105. *Selected Passages on Psalms* 144.

106. Respectively in *Against Celsus* 3.77 and *On Prayer* 27.16.

107. See, e.g., Paul Blowers, "Maximus the Confessor, Gregory of Nyssa, and the Concept of Perpetual Progress," *VC* 46 (1992): 151–71; Albert Geljon, "Divine Infinity

In the passage from the *Letter to Melania* I quoted, Evagrius maintains that union with God, who is infinite also in the sense of eternal (a point that was extraordinarily emphasized by Origen, who also used it against a subordinationistic Christology[108]), makes rational creatures eternal. On the infinity of God Gregory Nyssen based his famous doctrine of *epektasis*, the infinite tension of rational creatures toward God and their eternal growth in beatitude.[109] This is why Gregory identified human perfection (τελειότης) with "wishing to attain ever more in the Good."[110] For "no limit could cut short the growth in the ascent to God, since no boundaries can be found to the Good, nor does the progression of desire for the Good end, because it is ever satisfied."[111]

Evagrius criticizes those who assume that habit becomes a second nature (in *Letter to Melania* 32) and claims that a habit can dispel another precedent habit. This replicates Origen's polemic against the "Gnostics," and especially the "Valentinians," and their deterministic division of humanity into different natures. Origen argued practically all of his life against this, demonstrating precisely that a habit can dispel another precedent habit and one's destiny depends on one's moral choices; his doctrine of free will, protology, and eschatology stemmed from his refutation of the "Gnostic" doctrine of different human natures.[112] Evagrius proceeds along the same lines.

Additionally, in *Letter to Melania* 38–39 Evagrius adheres to Origen's differentiation of beings into sense perceptible and intelligible. Remarkably, when he mentions "this perceptible body," composed by God's Wisdom out of the four elements, and subject to God's providence, he points to at least another kind of bodies, which are *not* sense perceptible. This is indeed in

in Gregory of Nyssa and Philo of Alexandria," *VC* 59 (2005): 152–77; Ramelli, *Gregorio di Nissa: Sull'anima*, the second integrative essay on Origen as antecendent; Mark Weedman, "The Polemical Context of Gregory of Nyssa's Doctrine of Divine Infinity," *JECS* 18 (2010): 81–104, on Hilary as antecedent. Now Hilary was influenced by Origen, perhaps also on this score.

108. See Ramelli, "Origen's Anti-Subordinationism," and, for the all-important implications of God's eternity on Origen's philosophy of history and eschatology, idem, *Christian Doctrine of Apokatastasis*, the section on Origen.

109. The model is Moses in *The Life of Moses* 112–113.

110. *The Life of Moses* 4–5.

111. *The Life of Moses* 116.

112. See Ilaria L. E. Ramelli, "Origen, Bardaisan, and the Origin of Universal Salvation," *HTR* 102 (2009): 135–68.

line with Origen and is further confirmed by the Syriac text of the *Kephalaia Gnostika*, in which there is even a specific terminological differentiation between sense-perceptible, heavy, mortal bodies and spiritual, immortal bodies. I will expand on this regularly overlooked differentiation below.

In *Letter to Melania* 46 Evagrius explains that human beings assumed heavy, mortal bodies because of the original fall. On that occasion "they gave up being God's image and wanted to become the image of animals." This description closely resembles Gregory of Nyssa's account of the fall and the equipment of humans with mortal bodies, subject to passions and corruption. Gregory already described this as the abandoning of the image of God and getting closer to animals, especially in his dialogue *On the Soul and the Resurrection*; therefore, at the very end of the dialogue, he posits as the ultimate end (*telos*) the restoration of the image of God.[113] This is also the outcome foreseen by Evagrius, who in the same *Letter to Melania* (53–55) repeats that God created humans in his image, even though he had no need whatsoever of them, and adds that it is impossible that God change his will, and that God wants no one to perish (2 Pet 3:9). This clearly points to the restoration of human beings. Likewise in his treatise *On the Creation of the Human Being* 12 Gregory claims that the human intellect is the image of God and pours God's beautiful image down onto the soul as well, and the latter onto the body, but if the intellect does not orient itself toward God but orients itself toward matter, instead of the beautiful image of God it receives the ugliness of matter. And this is evil, which is the privation of Good and Beauty at the same time. The ontological negativity of evil was shared by Origen, Gregory Nyssen, and Evagrius, as I will point out below and especially in the commentary on *KG* 1.40–41. Consistently with his conviction that with the fall humans gave up the image of God and took up that of animals, in *Letter to Melania* 56–58 Evagrius observes that Christ underwent conception and birth, and curse and death, in order to free humans from all this, which is unnatural to Christ and, in the plan of God, was also unnatural to humans (since these were created to share not in the life of animals but rather in the life of God—what will happen at the final deification, or θέωσις[114]).

113. For the connection between the "theology of the image" and restoration in Gregory, see Ramelli, *Christian Doctrine of Apokatastasis*, the section devoted to him.

114. On θέωσις in patristic thought, see recently Norman Russell, *The Doctrine of Deification in the Greek Patristic Tradition* (Oxford: Oxford University Press, 2004); Ilaria L. E. Ramelli, "Deification (*Theosis*)," in *Encyclopedia of the Bible and Its Recep-*

As is clear from *Letter to Melania* 52, Evagrius also took over Origen's idea of the death of the soul, developed by the Alexandrian in his *Dialogue with Heraclides* and elsewhere; this concept was drawn from Paul and was also present in Philo and in early imperial philosophy.[115] Evagrius in particular remarks that, just as the body dies without food, so does the soul die without its proper nourishment, which is virtue—that is, sticking to the Good. This is entirely in line with Origen's notion of vice or evilness (κακία, the opposite of virtue or goodness) as determining the death of the soul. The effects of evilness on the soul are investigated by Evagrius at length in the *KG*, as we will see.

Evagrius's definition of Christ in *Letter to Melania* 60 is also very interesting to cast light on his intellectual roots and to provide a conceptual background to his cryptic *KG*. He depicts Christ as "the leaven of the divinity who, in its goodness, has hidden itself in the unleavened lump of humanity." This was made in order to "raise the whole lump to all that God is." This description, which seems to allude to Matt 13:33 and Luke 13:21, is surprisingly similar to that given by the Christian Middle Platonist Bardaisan of Edessa shortly before Origen. His words are quoted *ad litteram* by Ephrem in his *Prose Refutations*: "The Logos is the unknown leaven that is hidden in the (human) soul, which is deprived of knowledge and extraneous in respect to both the body and the Logos. If this is the case, the body cannot adhere to the soul, because it is earthly, nor can the soul adhere to the Logos, which is divine."[116] For the Logos is Christ-Logos. Ephrem also attests that Bardaisan, exactly like Origen and Evagrius, assigned to the human being a spirit or intellect in addition to a body and a soul. The soul, according to Bardaisan, possesses no knowledge, which is rather proper to the intellect/*logos*/spirit, that is, the divine part in each human being (as an all-important fragment from Bardaisan preserved by Porphyry

tion (ed. Hans-Joseph Klauck et al.; Berlin: de Gruyter, 2013), 6:468–70. On θέωσις in Evagrius, see Augustine Casiday, "Deification in Origen, Evagrius, and Cassian," in Perrone, *Origeniana VIII*, 2:995–1001.

115. See Ilaria L. E. Ramelli, "1 Tim 5:6 and the Notion and Terminology of Spiritual Death: Hellenistic Moral Philosophy in the Pastoral Epistles," *Aev* 84 (2010): 3–16; and idem, "Spiritual Weakness, Illness, and Death in 1 Cor 11:30," *JBL* 130 (2011): 145–63.

116. C. W. Mitchell, A. A. Bevan, and F. Crawford Burkitt, eds., *S. Ephraim's Prose Refutations of Mani, Marcion, and Bardaisan* (2 vols.; London: Williams & Norgate, 1912–1921), 2:158,20–32.

shows).[117] Evagrius, in his very *Letter to Melania*, similarly declares that in the human intellect the Logos and the Spirit of God operate. I wonder whether Evagrius, who entertained the same concept of the tripartition of the human being, and the same view of *apokatastasis*, knew Bardaisan's thought. Gregory of Nyssa in fact did, like Porphyry and Eusebius (who both had Greek translations of his works available), and Origen too may have known his ideas.[118]

Also, Evagrius's idea—expressed in the passage quoted above from *Letter to Melania* 60—that God, by becoming a human being, allowed all humans to "become God" (in the eventual deification, or θέωσις) is firmly grounded in Origen, from whom it passed on to Athanasius. The latter, at the end of his treatise *On the Incarnation*, famously summed up this train of thought by means of the words "Christ became a human being that we could be deified."

Another pivotal idea of Origen that Evagrius appropriates in his *Letter to Melania* is found in section 62. Here Evagrius makes it clear that to be in the image of God belongs to human nature, but to be in the likeness of God is beyond human nature and depends on one's own efforts. This is exactly what Origen maintained,[119] and in this respect Evagrius seems to stick more to Origen himself than to Gregory of Nyssa, who, even while receiving Origen's "theology of the image," did not insist so much on the distinction between image and likeness. Also in his *Letter to Anatolius* 61 and 18, Evagrius states that the intellectual soul is in the image of God as an initial datum in humans, while likeness must be acquired voluntarily by each one, by means of virtue, just as Origen too thought: "Love manifests the divine image [εἰκών], which is conformed to the Archetype (God), in

117. For these fragments from Ephrem and Porphyry, see Ilaria L. E. Ramelli, "Bardaisan as a Christian Philosopher: A Reassessment of His Christology," in *Religion in the History of European Culture: Proceedings of the 9th EASR Conference and IAHR Special Conference, 14–17 September 2009, Messina* (ed. Giulia Sfameni Gasparro, Augusto Cosentino, and Mariangela Monaca; Palermo: Officina di Studi Medievali, 2013), 873–88.

118. See Ilaria L. E. Ramelli, *Bardaisan of Edessa: A Reassessment of the Evidence and a New Interpretation* (Eastern Christian Studies 22; Piscataway, N.J.: Gorgias, 2009), on the relationship between Origen's and Bardaisan's thought, and here 131–42 on Eusebius's acquaintance with, and Gregory of Nyssa's dependence on, Bardaisan. My conclusions are received by Patricia Crone, "Daysanis," in the *Encyclopedia of Islam* (ed. Kate Fleet et al.; 3d ed.; Leiden: Brill, 2012), 116–18.

119. E.g., in *On First Principles* 3.6.1.

every human.... Your luminous homage to God will be when, by means of the energies of Good that you possess, you will have impressed God's likeness [ὁμοίωσις] in yourself."'

The last sections of the *Letter to Melania* are strategically devoted to the ultimate end (*telos*), the eschatological scenario, when unity (ἕνωσις) and deification (θέωσις) will finally be realized. At section 63 Evagrius describes this not as something natural but as a miracle, a gift from the divine grace. For it is only thanks to God's grace that the nature of rational creatures, which became alienated from God because of the mutability of its free will, should enjoy eternal union with its Creator. Now this too is entirely attuned to Origen's eschatological ideas. For Origen too upheld both the notion of the final *apokatastasis* as unity or unification (ἕνωσις) and its being by grace. Evagrius himself, at section 66, describes "the *telos* of all intellects" as "the union of all these different knowledges in one and the same and unique real knowledge" and as "all becoming this one without end." Also in *Letter* 63, which perfectly corresponds to the final part of the *Letter to Melania*, Evagrius stresses this element of unity, also applying it to the unification of all kinds of knowledge into the "essential knowledge" (of which he speaks a great deal also in the *KG*, as we will see below in the commentary): "all the different and distinct forms of knowledge will fuse together, into *one and the same essential knowledge:* all of those will become *this only knowledge, forever ... the great ark containing all the treasures of wisdom is the heart of Christ*, on which John reclined during the Last Supper." Just because Christ is the ultimate knowledge, being God, who is—as we shall see—"essential knowledge," he is said to be for all rational creatures "the very *telos* and ultimate blessedness."

Evagrius closes his *Letter to Melania* with the metaphor of God as a compassionate farmer, compassion (συμπάθεια) being an important characteristic of the Divinity itself and of the virtuous person.[120] Now, it seems remarkable to me that this is the very same theological metaphor as was used by Gregory of Nyssa in the final section of his dialogue *On the Soul and the Resurrection*. Here God, the good farmer, is said to take care even of the most damaged and worst seeds and to make sure that absolutely all seeds will become fruitful. As Evagrius concludes, "the earth will be blessed, and the farmer, the soil, and those who have been fed will sing glory and praise

120. See Kevin Corrigan and Gregory Yuri Glazov, "Compunction and Compassion: Two Overlooked Virtues in Evagrius of Pontus," *JECS* 22 (2014): 61–77.

to *the First Farmer*, to whom *all the seeds of blessing* belong, *in eternity*." The influence of both Origen and Gregory Nyssen on Evagrius's *Letter to Melania*, as well as on his *KG*—as I will point out below in the present essay and in the commentary—and other works of his, is noteworthy and deserves further investigation.

5. Good and Evil, Gnosis and Ignorance, Virtue and Sin, *Apatheia* and Passions, and Restoration

As I have mentioned, the *Letter to Melania* helps readers understand the *KG*, and this in many respects: for example, metaphysics, ontology, protology, eschatology, and theology. From the metaphysical point of view, in the *KG* too Evagrius highlights the ontological priority of the Good (God) over evil (a lack and negativity). This, according to Evagrius, has momentous eschatological consequences, as Origen and Gregory Nyssen also thought. For the three of them, evil has no ontological consistence: it is not a substance but the result of a bad use of free will. This interpretation, which is the very same as Origen's, is put forward especially in Evagrius's work *On Thoughts* (Περὶ λογισμῶν)[121] 19: the cause of sin is not anything endowed with a substantial existence (ὑφεστὸς κατ' οὐσίαν), but it is a pleasure that is generated by free will, which forces the intellect to make a bad use of God's creatures. Likewise, in one of the thoughts collected by the disciples of Evagrius, evil is presented again as a byproduct of free will, being described as "the movement of free will toward the worse" (*Chapters of the Disciples of Evagrius* 118). The one responsible (αἴτιος) for the appearance of evil, as well as for its disappearance, is the moral subject (ibid. 165).

Thus, at the very beginning of his *KG*, as a founding stone of his metaphysics, Evagrius proclaims: "There is nothing that is opposed to the First

121. See now the edition by Paul Géhin, Antoine Guillaumont, and Claire Guillaumont, *Évagre le Pontique: Sur le pensées* (SC 438; Paris: Cerf, 1998). Very interestingly, the sense in which Evagrius uses λογισμός, as an evil thought inspired by a demon, depends on Origen, as so much else in Evagrius's thinking. See, e.g, *On First Principles* 3.2.4 on *cogitationes* and *Commentary on the Song of Songs* 4.3.4–6, where Origen spoke of thoughts (*logismoi*) inspired by demons and, basically following Stoic ethics, remarked that it is necessary to avert these thoughts from one's mind ("heart") while they are not yet ingrained and it is easier to avoid assenting to them (in reference to the *sygkatathesis* or assent as the turning point that transforms impulses, prepassions and temptations into passions and vices). See also Pesthy, "Logismoi origéniens–logismoi évagriens."

Good, because it is Goodness in its very essence; now, there is nothing that is opposed to the Essence" (*KG* 1.1). Given that the first Good is God, the fact that nothing is opposed to the first Good means that nothing is opposed to God. In fact, evil—the opposite of Good—is nothing. This is why in *KG* 1.89 Evagrius claims, "All rational nature has been naturally made in order to exist and to be capable of knowledge. Now, God is essential knowledge. Rational nature has as its opposite nonexistence, whereas knowledge (has as its opposites) evilness and ignorance. Yet, nothing among these things is opposed to God." Evil, as well as ignorance, cannot be a principle on a par with God and antithetical to God, as it would be in a Manichaean perspective, but it is a lack of the Good that God is, just as ignorance is a lack of the Knowledge ("essential knowledge," as he often calls it) that God is.

Evagrius's idea of knowledge (γνῶσις)[122] is the direct descendant of Clement of Alexandria's crucial notion of γνῶσις, which in its highest degree is inseparable from that of deification (θέωσις). As is clear from *KG* 1.89, the opposite of knowledge for Evagrius is not only ignorance but also evil(ness). This indicates that knowledge in his view goes together with goodness/virtue and cannot be separated from it (I will have many occasions to point this out in the commentary below). Indeed, knowledge, for Evagrius, cannot intrinsically be knowledge for evil but only knowledge for the Good. Evil belongs with ignorance, and not with knowledge. Indeed, in Evagrius's ethical intellectualism—which is parallel to that of Origen and Nyssen—the choice of evil is a result of an obfuscated knowledge.

In one of the most pivotal *kephalaia* in his *KG* (1.41, to which I will devote a very full commentary below, and I refer readers to that), Evagrius hammers home the ontological priority of Good, goodness, and virtue over evil, evilness, and vice. This is not only a moral and chronological priority, but it is also and especially an ontological priority and superiority: "If death comes after life, and illness after health, it is clear that also evil

122. On which see, e.g., Antoine Guillaumont, "La vie gnostique selon Évagre le Pontique," *Annuaire du Collège de France* 80 (1979–80): 467–70; idem, "Le gnostique chez Clément d'Alexandrie et chez Évagre," in *Alexandria: Hellénisme, judaïsme et christianisme à Alexandrie; Mélanges Claude Mondésert* (Paris: Cerf, 1987), 195–201; repr. in *Études sur la spiritualité de l'Orient chrétien* (Begrolles-en-Mauges: Bellefontaine, 1996), 151–60. On Evagrius's theory of a progression from πρακτική to γνωστική and to θεολογική, see idem, "Un philosophe au désert: Évagre le Pontique," *RHR* 181 (1972): 29–56; repr. in *Aux origines du monachisme chrétien* (Begrolles-en-Mauges: Bellefontaine, 1979), 185–212; Kostantinovsky, *Evagrius*, 27–76.

comes after virtue. For it is evil that is the death and the illness of the soul, but *virtue comes even before.*" This is what Origen repeatedly emphasized, for instance in his *Homilies on Jeremiah* 2.1: "In all human beings, what is in the image of God [i.e., virtue] *comes before* the image of evil [i.e., vice]"; it is πρεσβύτερον. So does Evagrius declare that virtue is πρεσβύτερον than vice: it comes before, just as health comes before illness, which is its degeneration. Illness is often meant spiritually by Evagrius, as already by Philo and Origen.[123] On this presupposition, Evagrius follows in Clement's and Origen's footsteps in seeing Christ as the infallible Physician of souls, the only one who will be able to bring all of them back to health.[124] All of these thinkers, like Gregory Nyssen, were indeed consistent in supporting the doctrine of universal restoration and salvation.

In fact, from the ontological (and chronological and moral) priority of Good and virtue over evil and vice, Evagrius, exactly like Origen and Nyssen, infers the eschatological annihilation of all evil in another pivotal *kephalaion* to which I will devote an extensive commentary due to its extraordinary importance in Evagrius's system: "There was a time when evil(ness) did not exist, and there will come a time when *it will no more exist* [ἦν γὰρ ὅτε οὐκ ἦν κακία καὶ ἔσται ὅτε οὐκ ἔσται]. But there was no time when the Good/virtue did not exist, and there will be *no time when it will no more exist.* For the germs of virtue are impossible to destroy." This text of *KG* 1.40, in Syriac, corresponds to that of *On Thoughts* (Περὶ λογισμῶν) 31, preserved in Greek. Evagrius attached so much importance to this pillar of his philosophy that he repeated it not only in these two works, in the very same terms, but even in three more passages: *Letters* 43 and 59, and scholium 62 on Prov 5:14.[125]

In the continuation of *KG* 1.40 and of *On Thoughts* 31 Evagrius adds a biblical reference in which to ground his assertion of the inextinguishability of the germs of virtue: "And what persuades me of this is also the

123. See Ramelli, "Spiritual Weakness, Illness, and Death."

124. See, e.g., *On Thoughts* (Περὶ λογισμῶν) 3 and 10; scholium 2 on Ps 102:3; scholium 9 on Ps 106:20; scholium 6 on Ps 144:15; scholium 2 on Ps 145:7; *Letters* 42; 51; 52; 55; 57; 60. On the spiritual interpretation of illness in Origen, see Ilaria L. E. Ramelli, "Disability in Bardaisan and Origen: Between the Stoic *Adiaphora* and the Lord's Grace," in *Gestörte Lektüre: Disability als hermeneutische Leitkategorie biblischer Exegese* (ed. Wolfgang Grünstäudl and Markus Schiefer Ferrari; Stuttgart: Kohlhammer, 2012), 141–59; in Evagrius, see Monica Tobon, "The Health of the Soul: ἀπάθεια in Evagrius Ponticus," *StPatr* 47 (2010): 187–202.

125. Paul Géhin, ed., *Scholies aux Proverbes* (SC 340; Paris: Cerf, 1987).

rich man who in Sheol was condemned because of his evil and took pity on his siblings. Now, pity is a beautiful germ of virtue."[126] This practice of buttressing every philosophical argument with a scriptural proof was constantly employed by Origen and by Gregory of Nyssa. Evagrius maintains that the germs of virtue—the Good—never die, not even in hell, since they come from God, who is the Good itself. Evil, on the contrary, which was not created by God, will vanish in the end. The eventual disappearance of evil was repeatedly affirmed by both Origen and Gregory Nyssen; the latter even described it in a detailed manner in his short commentary on 1 Cor 15:28 (*In illud: Tunc et ipse Filius*).[127] Moreover, Evagrius was very likely acquainted with the exegesis of the Lukan parable of Dives and Lazarus provided by Gregory Nyssen in his *On the Soul and the Resurrection*, all the more so since Evagrius understands hell exactly as Nyssen presented it there, and as Origen also interpreted it, that is, as "the darkness of the ignorance of those who cannot contemplate God."[128] Evagrius's biblical interpretation, here as elsewhere, is spiritual/allegorical, like Origen's and Gregory Nyssen's. Examples of such an exegesis of Scripture are spread throughout his *KG*, as we shall see below in the commentary.[129] It is remarkable that in *Gnostikos* 21 Evagrius recommends allegorizing only good discourses, and not evil ones, in Scripture.

A similar understanding of hell is found in *Gnostikos* 36, where Evagrius expresses the same concerns as Origen did[130] about divulging

126. See also *Praktikos* 1.65 (PG 40:1240AB).

127. For a full commentary on this short treatise, see Ramelli, *Gregorio di Nissa: Sull'anima*.

128. Giovanni Vannucci, ed., *Philokalia: Testi di ascetica e mistica della Chiesa orientale* (Florence: Libreria editrice fiorentina, 1978), 49.

129. E.g., *KG* 4.46, 53, 56, 79; 5.35, 88; 6.49, 64.

130. Ilaria L. E. Ramelli ("Origen's Exegesis of Jeremiah: Resurrection Announced throughout the Bible and Its Twofold Conception," *Aug* 48 [2008]: 59–78) and Mark S. M. Scott ("Guarding the Mysteries of Salvation: The Pastoral Pedagogy of Origen's Universalism," *JECS* 18 [2010]: 347–68) insist on Origen's prudence in disclosing the *apokatastasis* doctrine to the simple. The latter are the morally immature, those who do good out of fear of punishment and not out of love of the Good, who is God. Origen and Gregory Nyssen seem to me to have used two different strategies, even while sharing the same eschatological doctrine. While Origen used the strategy of not telling immature people about the eventual salvation of all, because he was aware of the moral danger this can entail, Gregory wished to tell everybody (and did so in his *Catechetical Oration*), but through Macrina he also warned people that evil is hard to purify and

his eschatological doctrine to morally immature people: "The highest doctrine concerning the Judgment should remain *unknown to mundane and young people*, in that it can easily produce despise and neglect. For they do not know that the suffering of a rational soul condemned to punishment *consists in ignorance*." Indeed, Evagrius opposes Sheol to paradise, the latter being conceived as a place of knowledge: "Just as paradise is the place of instruction for the righteous, so is hell [or "Sheol"] the torment of the impious" (*KG* 6.8). The implication is again that the torment of the impious will consist in deprivation of knowledge, that is, ignorance. And that torment will come in a variety of degrees, as is clear from *On Thoughts* 18, where Evagrius also insists on the idea of the death of the soul, which, as I have mentioned, was very dear to Origen. Evagrius here even uses Ezek 18:4 and 20 ("the soul that sins will die"), Origen's favorite biblical quotation in this connection.

Beatitude, on the contrary, is identified by Evagrius with the perfect knowledge (γνῶσις) and contemplation (θεωρία) of God—a kind of blessedness that is well suited for rational creatures. Evagrius speaks of contemplation quite frequently in the *KG*—for instance, in 1.27, in which he classifies five forms of contemplation, or θεωρία: the first and highest is the contemplation of God the Trinity, the second is the contemplation of incorporeal realities, the third is the contemplation of bodies, the fourth is the contemplation of the Judgment, and the fifth is that of divine providence. As I will demonstrate below in the commentary, it is probable that these five contemplations are arranged, not in a hierarchical order, but in a "historical" order, starting from God, who is the principle of all, passing on to the creation of intelligent beings, and then of material bodies, until the judgments that close every aeon, the last Judgment, which will conclude all aeons, and God's providence, which accompanies creatures during all aeons and will overcome in the end, at the eventual *apokatastasis* after all aeons and all judgments. In this way, Providence completes Judgment; it does not contradict it. I will return later to the relationship between Judgment and Providence, which also entails the relationship between God's justice and God's mercy.

Evagrius also refers to knowledge, or "gnosis," in *Praktikos* 2–3: "The kingdom of heavens is impassivity (*apatheia*) in the soul, along with the true

---

that the ultramundane sufferings of the wicked will be long and terrible. Evagrius had both strategies before him.

knowledge of beings. The kingdom of God is the knowledge [γνῶσις] of the Holy Trinity, which proceeds along with the intellect's getting closer to it." The process of the intellect's getting closer to God and acquiring ever further knowledge parallels Gregory Nyssen's epecstatic process. The knowledge of the Trinity is the highest of all; the knowledge of created beings is the knowledge of their *logoi*, their paradigmatic reasons and metaphysical forms. Thus, for instance, in *Praktikos* 92 Evagrius cites Antony the Great, who deemed the contemplation of creation aimed at the knowledge "of the nature [φύσις] of creatures." The knowledge of the Trinity is an end (*telos*) in itself, unlike the knowledge of creatures, which is aimed at the superior knowledge of God the Creator; this is why Evagrius stresses: "Let us do everything for the sake of the knowledge of God" (*Praktikos* 32).

The ultimate end (*telos*) of human life—that is, blessedness—is knowledge. This is also based on 1 Tim 2:4–6, a passage dear to Evagrius, where knowledge of the truth is equated with salvation ("God our Savior wants all humans to be saved and to reach the knowledge of the truth"), which is reiterated by Evagrius in *Letter* 56, with a reference to the beatitude in Matt 5:8: "Blessed are the pure of heart, because they will see God." On this basis Evagrius can claim that seeing God—that is, knowing God—is blessedness: Jesus "proclaims them blessed not because of their purity but because of their seeing God; for purity is the impassivity [ἀπάθεια] of the rational soul, whereas seeing God is the true knowledge [γνῶσις] of the Holy Trinity, who must be adored." All rational creatures, according to Evagrius, will reach the knowledge of God and the ultimate blessedness. This is the core of Evagrius's doctrine of universal restoration, or *apokatastasis*, which was already theorized by Origen and Gregory Nyssen, his main inspirers.

Evagrius, like Origen and Gregory, maintained that all rational creatures belong to the same nature and were created equal by God but at some point have become angels, humans, or demons due to the different choices of their free will (the same as Origen and Nyssen maintained). During the aeons human beings, by virtue of their free will, can become good like angels—which is an example of what Evagrius calls "the better transformation"—or evil like demons; this is why he says that they are intermediate between angels and demons (*KG* 4.13). Indeed, rational creatures, for Evagrius just as for Origen, can switch from one order to another between angels, humans, and demons, according to their spiritual progress or regression (*KG* 5.9–11). Spiritual death reigns over demons, because of their choice for evil, whereas spiritual life reigns over angels; humans, being in the aforementioned intermediate state, are ruled by both life and death, again understood in the spiritual sense (*KG* 4.65).

But even if some of the rational creatures (notably, humans and demons) adhered to evil to some extent, this belongs to the moral and not to the ontological sphere: none of the *logika*, according to Evagrius just as according to Origen and Nyssen, is evil by nature, not even demons (*KG* 4.59; see the commentary below). For this would mean making God accountable for evil, something that Origen's, Gregory's, and Evagrius's theodicy could never accept. In *KG* 3.4 the three main categories of rational creatures are characterized by three different kinds of relation to the contemplation of beings, or θεωρία: angels are nourished by it always, humans not always, and demons never. But still, after the vanishing of all evil, the eventual *apokatastasis* will involve all rational creatures, and all will enjoy contemplation and knowledge, eternally.

In this respect, Evagrius is in line with both Origen and Gregory Nyssen, although it is usually assumed that he insists more on the intellectual aspect of contemplation and knowledge.[131] Evagrius, however, does not regard contemplation (θεωρία) as separate from charity-love (ἀγάπη), which is also a dominant element in *apokatastasis* according to both Origen and Nyssen, Origen especially in his commentaries on Romans and on the Song of Songs, Gregory in *On the Soul and the Resurrection* and in his *Homilies on the Song of Songs*.[132] In *KG* 1.86 Evagrius remarks, "*Charity-love* is the excellent state of the rational soul, a state in which the soul cannot *love* anything that is among corruptible beings more than the *knowledge* of God." Love and knowledge are here inseparable.

Gregory Nyssen is very likely to have inspired Evagrius's conviction of the inseparability of knowledge and love. For Gregory, in his dialogue *On the Soul and the Resurrection* 96C, locates knowledge and love together at the highest level, inside the divine life itself: "The life of the divine nature is charity-love [ἀγάπη], since Beauty/Goodness is absolutely lovable to those who know it. Now the divine knows itself, and this knowledge [γνῶσις] becomes love [ἀγάπη]." Moreover, once again just as for Nyssen, for Evagrius too ἀγάπη is no πάθος but impassivity, as is clear, for instance,

131. See Hans Urs von Balthasar, "Metaphysik und Mystik des Evagrius Pontikus," *Zeitschrift für Askese und Mystik* (1939): 31–47; Brian Daley, *The Hope of the Early Church* (Cambridge: Cambridge University Press, 1991), 91.

132. See Ramelli, *Christian Doctrine of Apokatastasis*, sections on Origen and Nyssen.

from *Eulogius* 22: "Charity-love is the bond of impassivity and the expunging of passions.... Love possesses nothing of its own apart from God, for God is Love itself." The link between impassivity (ἀπάθεια, absence of passions, i.e., of bad emotions) and love (ἀγάπη) is also stressed in *Praktikos* 8: "Charity-love is the progeny of impassivity." Precisely because charity-love is no *pathos*, this is why love will abide in the end, in the perfect state, and this is why love is the very life of God, who is supremely free from passions and is perfect knowledge.

The same close connection between charity-love and knowledge is drawn by Evagrius in *KG* 4.50, where he identifies the good and eternal love with that which true knowledge elects, and he declares this love to be inseparable from the intellect, and in *KG* 3.58, where he declares that spiritual love is necessary for one to *learn* the wisdom of beings. It is therefore clear that love is indispensable for knowledge; Evagrius in 3.58 even details that love plays the same role in knowledge as light does in vision, which is itself a metaphor for knowledge.[133] According to Evagrius, then, there can be no separation whatsoever between love and knowledge. Indeed, I have already pointed out that in his view the opposite of knowledge is not only ignorance but also evilness, which results from a lack of love for the Good. Evagrius describes ignorance as "the shadow of evilness" in *KG* 4.29, thus showing that to his mind ignorance and evil cannot exist independently of one another.

Thus, only after the elimination of evil will ignorance also vanish from among rational creatures (*KG* 4.29). The eradication of evil and ignorance from all rational creatures will take place in the eventual *apokatastasis*. That this will be universal and will involve all *logika* is made clear by Evagrius in many passages—for instance, in *KG* 3.72, where "all" are said to be destined to come to the ultimate end, which is knowledge.[134] Consistently with this, Evagrius, like Origen and Nyssen, interprets 1 Cor 15:24–28, which describes the final submission of all to Christ, as the final salvation of all. This submission-salvation will take place through virtue and knowledge, as Evagrius puts it in his allegoresis of Christ's feet in *KG* 6.15: Christ's two feet are asceticism (the πρακτική: ethical life, the pursuit of virtue) and contemplation (θεωρία); now, if Christ "puts *all* enemies under his feet" (1 Cor 15:25), then "all," Evagrius avers, will come to know

133. On Evagrius's theology of light, see at least Konstantinovsky, *Evagrius*, 77–108.
134. For a full discussion of his complex *kephalaion*, see the commentary below.

asceticism and contemplation. This entails that all rational creatures will reach the ultimate perfection in both virtue and knowledge. The universality of the eventual submission-salvation is stressed by Evagrius also in *KG* 6.27, where he argues that "the whole nature of rational creatures" will submit to the Lord. And the final submission of all to Christ will coincide with the eventual salvation of all. Origen first drew this equation between universal submission and universal salvation, which was later developed by Gregory Nyssen in his commentary on 1 Cor 15:28[135] and was appropriated by Evagrius as well. All will submit to Christ, will place themselves "under his feet" by converting to the Good—that is, God—and rejecting evil, and will thereby be saved.

Indeed, in a scholium on Ps 21:29 Evagrius states that the sentence "for he must reign until he has put all his enemies under his feet" (1 Cor 15:25) means that Christ will have to continue reigning "until all the unrighteous [ἄδικοι] have become righteous [δίκαιοι]." In this condition, all will be immortal and will not risk becoming earthly again. At least two passages, one of probable authenticity and the other certainly authentic, show that Evagrius for his exegesis of 1 Cor 15:25 was relying on Origen closely. If *Selecta in Psalmos* (*Selected Passages on Psalms*) 21, preserved in Greek like Evagrius's scholium, is indeed by Origen, this would mean that Evagrius was repeating Origen's exegesis even *ad litteram* (which would not be surprising): "'He must reign until he has put all enemies under his feet' means 'until all the unrighteous have become righteous.'" That this passage is really by Origen (and was therefore taken up by Evagrius word for word) is made very probable by another, surely authentic, passage whose content is the same, albeit in different words: Origen's *Commentary on Romans* 9.41.8, in which 1 Cor 15:25–28 is interpreted—the same passage interpreted by Evagrius—and is joined to Phil 2:10: "But when Christ has 'handed the kingdom to God the Father'—that is, presented to God as an offer *all, converted and reformed*, and has fully performed the mystery of the reconciliation of the world—then they will be in God's presence, that God's word may be fulfilled: 'Because I live—the Lord says—*every knee* will bend before Me, *every tongue* will glorify God.'" Glorification is a sign of voluntary adhesion. This voluntary character of the final submission explains why universal submission for Origen, Eusebius, Nyssen, and Evagrius will coincide with universal

135. See Ramelli, "Christian Soteriology and Christian Platonism"; and idem, "Gregory of Nyssa's Trinitarian Theology."

salvation. The idea that Christ's reign, during which he will submit all, will achieve the conversion and salvation of all, which was typical of Origen, was indeed taken over by Eusebius as well, when he spoke of the θεραπευτική and διορθωτική βασιλεία of Christ, the reign of Christ, during which Christ will heal all those who will still be spiritually ill and he will set right all those who will still be unrighteous.[136] Thus, given the clear antecedents in Origen and Eusebius, besides Nyssen himself, we cannot really say that Evagrius—as Julia Konstantinovsky has suggested[137]—is original on this score.

Origen even maintained that, as long as one single rational creature remains unconverted to the Good, Christ cannot yet submit to the Father (that is, subject his body—i.e., all of humanity and all rational creatures—to the Father), but he has to go on to reign, precisely because during his reign he will convert everyone to the Good, by healing them and setting them right, that is, turning them from unrighteous into righteous. Evagrius in his *Scholia on Proverbs* 355 details that Christ destroys the unrighteous by transforming them into righteous: "Once the impious have ceased to be such, they will become righteous [δίκαιοι]. Indeed, in this passage [concerning the destruction of the impious in Ps 28:28] 'destruction' [ἀπώλεια] means the vanishing of the impiety of that man. Precisely in this way, the Lord brought about the destruction of the publican Matthew, by giving him the grace of righteousness." Evagrius defines righteousness (δικαιοσύνη) in *Praktikos* 89: its task "is to generate the symphony and harmony of all parts of the soul." This definition derives from Plato's definition of justice (δικαιοσύνη). But the very notion that the destruction of the unrighteous performed by Christ is their transformation into righteous, which Evagrius has expounded in his scholium, comes straight from Origen. Even the examples that Evagrius adduces of this destruction-transformation are the same that Origen already adduced: that of Matthew the publican transformed by the Lord into a righteous man, which is adduced in the scholium quoted above, and that of Paul "the persecutor," transformed by the Lord into an apostle of Christ. The

136. See Ilaria L. E. Ramelli, "Origen, Eusebius, and the Doctrine of Apokatastasis," in *Eusebius of Caesarea: Traditions and Innovations* (ed. Aaron Johnson and Jeremy Schott; Hellenic Studies 60; Cambridge: Harvard University Press, 2013), 307–23.

137. "'He must reign till he has put all enemies under his feet.' How this is to happen, however, *constitutes Evagrius' originality*. The defeat of Christ's enemies will come about when all the wicked, including evil men, demons, and the devil himself, become righteous" (Konstantinovsky, *Evagrius*, 157, emphasis mine). Her book as a whole is very good, though.

latter is adduced by Evagrius in a scholium on Ps 17:8–9. Evagrius is here commenting on the fire that is said in Ps 17:8–9 to come from the face of the Lord and identifies it with God's action of "destroying evil habits," so as to transform people into better persons. Evagrius adds two examples: that of Matthew, who was a publican, and that of Paul, who was "a persecutor and a violent man" but became an apostle of Jesus Christ and a righteous man. Likewise Origen, in his *Homilies on Jeremiah* 1.15–16, says: "Who is the person whom 'I (the Lord) shall kill?' It is Paul the traitor, Paul the persecutor; and 'I shall make him live,' so that he may become Paul the apostle of Jesus Christ." As is evident, both the concepts and the very examples, Paul and Matthew, are identical in Origen and Evagrius.

In addition, Evagrius's interpretation of God's fire as God's action of burning away evil from sinners—which Evagrius puts forward again in the scholium on Ps 17:8–9 and elsewhere—is the same as Origen had proposed in many passages—for instance, in *Against Celsus* 6.70: "God is the fire that consumes … every kind of sin"—or in *Homilies on Jeremiah* 1.15–16, where the burning of chaff is interpreted as the purification of sinners from evil. Moreover, the image of God's destroying evil and planting a new garden in its place, employed by Evagrius in a scholium on Ps 43:3 ("God eradicates evilness and ignorance and instead plants virtue and knowledge"), is identical to that used by Origen in the same passage quoted above, *Homilies on Jeremiah* 1.16. Here Origen assures that sin and vice, in all varieties, will be eradicated, so that upon the ruins of evil God may plant the garden of the Good, the new paradise.

Even the main scriptural proofs that Evagrius adduces in support of the doctrine of universal restoration, or *apokatastasis* (1 Cor 15:24–28 and John 17:21–22), are the same with which Origen primarily buttressed it: the submission of all enemies and the annihilation of evil and death during Christ's reign, the handing over of the kingdom to the Father, and the final unity, when God will be "all in all." This is also the basis of Origen's and Evagrius's distinction between the kingdom of Christ and the kingdom of God, the latter being the ultimate reality: "They say the kingdom of Christ is every material knowledge, while that of God the Father is immaterial knowledge."[138] Origen clearly inspired Evagrius also in this case: he identified the kingdom of Christ with the contemplation of the *logoi* of salvation and the accomplishment of the works of justice and the

138. Evagrius, *Letter* 63.

other virtues, and the kingdom of God with the blessed, perfect condition of the intellect.[139] However, the kingdom of Christ is not opposed to that of God but is absorbed into it.

6. The Aeons and the *Telos*

According to Evagrius, the submission of all to Christ, who will hand them to God (on the Origenian exegesis of 1 Cor 15:28), will take place at the conclusion of all aeons, in the very end (*telos*), when all will be brought to unity. As he makes clear in *KG* 6.33, once Christ will no longer be impressed in various aeons and names, then he too will submit to the Father and will delight in the knowledge of God alone. This knowledge is not divided into aeons and increments of rational creatures, but it comes after the end of all aeons, when rational creatures will have stopped increasing. For Evagrius's conception of aeons (αἰῶνες) is the same as Origen's: there are several aeons before the final *apokatastasis*, which will put an end to all aeons.[140] During the aeons, rational creatures increase in virtue and knowledge and get purified; after all this has been accomplished, the series of aeons will cease, and the fullness of God's absolute eternity (ἀϊδιότης) will remain. During the aeons, Evagrius avers, rational creatures will acquire more and more knowledge, with a view to the knowledge of the Trinity (*KG* 6.67), and at the end, after the aeons, God will have rational creatures acquire the essential knowledge of God the Father (*KG* 6.34).

Origen's notion of aeons was misrepresented by Augustine and others during the Origenistic controversy; these people claimed that Origen taught an infinite succession of aeons, without end.[141] This is not the case, and Evagrius knew that Origen in fact taught a finite sequence of aeons, followed by a definitive and eternal *apokatastasis*. Indeed, he closely adheres to Origen when he maintains that the succession of aeons is not infinite, but it had a beginning and will consequently have an end. For instance, in *KG* 5.89 he remarks that the creation of the first aeon was not preceded by a destruction, but it was the beginning of all aeons, and so also the destruction of the last aeon will not be followed by a new aeon,

---

139. Origen, *On Prayer* 25.

140. See Ilaria L. E. Ramelli, "Αἰώνιος and Αἰών in Origen and Gregory of Nyssa," *StPatr* 47 (2010): 57–62; idem, *Christian Doctrine of Apokatastasis*, the chapter on Origen.

141. See Ilaria L. E. Ramelli, "Origen in Augustine: A Paradoxical Reception," *Numen* 60 (2013): 280–307.

but the succession of aeons will cease at that point. Aeons are necessary to rational creatures' spiritual and intellectual development. If aeons should end now, most rational creatures would still be helplessly behind in such a development. Only once they are perfect will God bestow his goods on them, since before that rational creatures would be unable to receive God's richness (*KG* 4.38).

Each aeon is aimed at the knowledge of God on the part of rational creatures: "A world/aeon is a natural system that includes the various and different bodies of rational creatures, because of the knowledge of God" (*KG* 3.36). The very definition of an *αἰών* as a "natural system" is entirely dependent on Origen.[142] According to Evagrius, just as to Origen, each aeon begins with the end of the preceding one, when a judgment takes place about the moral choices made by rational creatures during the preceding aeon. In this judgment, Christ establishes the role and the kind of body that each rational creature will have in the following aeon, on the basis of the moral and spiritual development of each one (*KG* 3.38; cf. 3.47). Thus, the number of judgments corresponds to the number of aeons (*KG* 2.75). Not only in the *KG* but also in his *Scholia* does Evagrius insist on this conception—for instance, in scholium 275 on Prov 24:22: "A judgment is the creation of an aeon that allots bodies to every intellectual creature according to" its moral and spiritual development. In scholium 2 on Ps 134:6 Evagrius further explains that the division of rational creatures into angels, humans, and demons, and their allotment to different places or states, is the result of every judgment. This is why "the exact knowledge of these realms/states and the different bodies [i.e., allotted to angels, humans, and demons] consists in the *logoi* ["criteria, reasons"] regarding the Judgment." A similar principle is expounded in scholium 8 on Eccl 2:10: "we receive knowledge according to our state," or *κατάστασις* (*ἀπο-κατάστασις* is a related term and means the return to the original state without sin).

A systematic investigation into the lexicon of aeons and eternity both in the works of Evagrius extant in Greek, which I have undertaken elsewhere,[143] and in the Syriac translation of his *KG* (I will indicate in the

142. On this notion in Origen, see Panayiotis Tzamalikos, *Origen: Cosmology and Ontology of Time* (Leiden: Brill, 2006), with my review in *Rivista di Filosofia Neoscolastica* 99 (2007): 177–81; and idem, *Origen: Philosophy of History and Eschatology* (Leiden: Brill, 2007), with my review in *Rivista di Filosofia Neoscolastica* 100 (2008): 453–58.

143. In Ilaria Ramelli and David Konstan, *Terms for Eternity: Aiônios and Aïdios*

commentary when the Syriac is an obvious translation of αἰών) definitely confirms that he conceived of a series of aeons preceded by the eternity of God and followed by the eternity of *apokatastasis* in God. Evagrius, also due to the influence of biblical quotations, uses the adjective αἰώνιος more frequently than ἀΐδιος, which refers to intelligible and spiritual things and indicates absolute eternity. This is the eternity of *apokatastasis* itself and of God; in the *telos* all rational creatures will participate in the life of God, and this life is absolutely eternal. Evagrius applies αἰώνιος to God only in scriptural quotations and echoes, and only in reference to God can this adjective bear the connotation of "eternal." In other cases it may mean "remote in time, ancient";[144] it also refers to life in the world (αἰών) to come and the judgment in the next world, which will determine the condition of each one in the αἰών, as long as the αἰών will last. Αἰώνιος is used by Evagrius of punishment in the future αἰών as well, also in the form of a threat.[145] It is also used of fire in the aeon to come,[146] sometimes in connection with the explicit expression αἰὼν μέλλων, "future aeon."[147]

The future aeon, or aeons, will last until *apokatastasis*, when there will come an end to all aeons and there will be no longer either sinners or evil, which did not exist in the beginning and will not endure in the end: "Virtue, the Good, will *consume evil*, and this will come to pass in the future aeon, until *evilness will be eliminated* [τοῦτο δὲ γενήσεται ἐν τῷ αἰῶνι τῷ μέλλοντι, ἕως ἂν ἐκλείπῃ ἡ κακία]."[148] This indicates that the future aeon will last until all evil is eliminated, only after which can the eventual universal restoration finally take place. The eschatological triumphal march of the Good, which progressively conquers evil and consumes it, as Evagrius foresees, was already described by his inspirer, Gregory of Nyssa, in his commentary on 1 Cor 15:28 (*In illud: Tunc et ipse Filius*).

Evagrius calls αἰώνιος the Judgment in the next world, too. In his work *On Thoughts* (Περὶ λογισμῶν), destined to those who have reached impas-

---

in Classical and Christian Authors (2d ed.; Piscataway, N.J.: Gorgias, 2011; Logos Bible Software, 2013), 199–203.

144. See ibid., 47–80.

145. E.g., in *Teacher* 25–26: τῇ ἀπειλῇ τῆς αἰωνίου κολάσεως.

146. E.g., in *On Prayer* (PG 79:1197): punishment ἐν πυρὶ αἰωνίῳ; *99 Sentences Averting from Things Corruptible*, ascribed to Nilus (PG 79:1240).

147. "In the aeon to come," ἐν τῷ αἰῶνι τῷ μέλλοντι, *On Proverbs* p. 101,16 Tischendorf; see also ibid. 104,25, 119,15.

148. *On Proverbs* p. 108,9 Tischendorf.

sivity (*apatheia*) through ascetic life (the *praktikē*) and have become "gnostics" by means of the achievement of knowledge, both punishment and the judgment in the next world are called αἰώνιοι. He speaks of κολάσεως δὲ καὶ κρίσεως αἰωνίου, "punishment and judgment in the next aeon."[149] Evagrius here is referring not to an "eternal judgment" but to a judgment in the other world; indeed, Evagrius, like Origen, as I have mentioned, posited a judgment after each aeon, which determines one's blessedness or purification in the following aeon. Therefore, what will be established in the judgment in the future world will remain until the aeon after that, or until *apokatastasis*. Evagrius invites readers to consider torments in the next world as follows: "think of what awaits sinners: the shame before God and Christ himself … and all the places of punishment: the fire in the next world [πῦρ αἰώνιον], the worm that does not die [ἀτελεύτητος]."[150] Evagrius did not consider either the fire or the worm eternal, but he had no problem using αἰώνιον and ἀτελεύτητος. The same is true of Gregory Nazianzen, Gregory of Nyssa, Origen, and other supporters of the doctrine of *apokatastasis*.[151] Indeed, a passage by Evagrius containing that kind of expressions shows strong affinities with a passage of Nazianzen;[152] here Evagrius uses phrases that could suggest eternity but in fact refer only to the future aeon and not to *apokatastasis*: "Every sinner will be consumed by the otherworldly fire without being able to die; for he will undergo immortal torments," καταναλωθήσεται πᾶς ἁμαρτωλὸς ὑπὸ τοῦ αἰωνίου πυρὸς καὶ οὐ δύναται τελευτῆσαι, ἀθάνατα γὰρ βασανισθήσεται.[153] Like Origen, in fact, Evagrius held that the fire will burn evil in sinners in order to purify them. The Gospel expression πῦρ ἄσβεστον, "inextinguishable fire," is understood not as eternal but as a fire that is not physical and terrestrial but rather precisely αἰώνιον, otherworldly, belonging to not the sense-perceptible realm but the intelligible things of the other world or the aeon to come. This is also the meaning in which Evagrius, like Nazianzen and other patristic authors, uses ἀθάνατον, "immortal, deathless": they call this fire πῦρ ἄσβεστον, ἀθάνατον, and αἰώνιον, not to declare it eternal, but to indicate that it is impossible to extinguish it, unlike the fire of this world, and that it pertains to the other world. All this confirms that Evagrius considered

149. PG 79:1213.
150. *Principles of the Monastic Life* (PG 40:1261).
151. Demonstration in Ramelli, *Christian Doctrine of Apokatastasis*.
152. I point out the close parallel and analyze it in ibid., 444.
153. *Exhortation to the Monks* (PG 79:1237).

the future aeon(s) to precede the eventual and eternal *apokatastasis*. Then there will be no evil left, since all will have been purified in fire, and all will be in God, who will finally be "all in all" (1 Cor 15:28).

Evagrius thinks that during the aeons angels help rational creatures to attain salvation—something also maintained by Origen and Gregory Nyssen—by means of instruction, exhortation, and the liberation from passions, evil, and ignorance (*KG* 6.35). This action takes place thanks to the intellects of the heavenly powers, which are "pure and full of knowledge" (*KG* 3.5) and have learned "the intellections that concern Providence, by means of which (intellections) they urge on those who are inferior to them quickly toward virtue and toward the knowledge of God" (*KG* 6.76). The cooperation of angels to the salvation of rational creatures is repeatedly highlighted by Evagrius, who illustrates the different strategies used by them in *KG* 6.86. According to Evagrius, not only do angels cooperate with Providence, recalling rational souls from evilness to virtue and from ignorance to knowledge, but even celestial bodies—which Evagrius, like Origen and most ancient authors, regarded as animated—and whatever creatures are endowed with spiritual knowledge (*KG* 6.88, 90).

According to Evagrius, just as according to Origen and Nyssen, and partially also to Clement—another Christian thinker, close to Middle Platonism, who exerted a significant influence on Evagrius—suffering is part and parcel of the process of improvement and purification that takes place before the eventual *apokatastasis*. This punishment through fire *purifies* the part of the soul that is liable to passions (*KG* 3.18). Suffering decreed by God is purifying: this is the principle—anticipated by Clement of Alexandria—to which Origen and Gregory of Nyssa also stuck. Evagrius, consistently with his notion of purifying fire, interprets Matt 3:12, on the distinction of chaff and wheat, in the same way as Origen did; he understands that what the divine fire will burn like chaff and destroy are not sinners themselves but their sins and evilness. The wheat in the parable symbolizes virtue, the chaff evilness or vice, and the aeon to come a purifying instrument that will attract the chaff to itself, thus cleaning sinners from vice (*KG* 2.26).

Of the succession of aeons prior to *apokatastasis* Evagrius speaks also in *KG* 2.25, where he uses an agricultural metaphor already employed by Paul in 1 Cor 15: "Just as this body is called the seed of the future ear, so will also this aeon be called seed of the one that will come after it." This metaphor, which also appears in *KG* 1.24, refers to the resurrection, but for Evagrius, just as for Origen and Gregory Nyssen, "resurrection" is not only the resurrection of the body. Indeed, Evagrius distinguishes *three* kinds of resurrection, each of which is a kind of restoration to the original and perfect state: (1) the resurrection of the body, which is the passage from a corruptible to an incorruptible body; (2) the resurrection of the soul, which is the passage from a passible to an impassible soul; and (3) the resurrection of the spirit or intellect, which is the passage from ignorance to true knowledge.[154]

Evagrius refers to the restoration of the intellect also in *KG* 2.15 in terms of its restoration to health, which happens when it receives the contemplation (*theōria*). Evagrius, like Origen and Gregory Nyssen, entertains a *holistic* idea of the resurrection, which will involve, not only the body, but the whole of the human being, including its soul and its intellect. This means that the soul will be freed from passions and will attain impassivity (ἀπάθεια), and the intellect will be illuminated and vivified by knowledge, since the life of the intellect is knowledge. The eventual resurrection-restoration is in fact a total vivification of the dead (*KG* 5.20), not only their physical resurrection, but also the spiritual resurrection of those who have died because of sin and ignorance.

7. Christ, the Attainment of Unity, and Creation

The resurrection-restoration is made possible by Christ. This is a characteristic that I have pointed out in the case of the main patristic supporters of the doctrine of *apokatastasis*, in a systematic study of this doctrine from the New Testament to John Eriugena[155]—and this proves true of Evagrius as well. If we take away Christ, there is no possibility of restoration, and Evagrius stresses in many passages how crucial a role Christ plays in the process that leads to the final restoration of all rational creatures. Now, the extraordinary import of the work of Christ in restoration—with his inhumanation, teaching, death, and resurrection, and Christ's activity as Logos, Wisdom, Teacher and Physician—depends on the fullness of humanity and divinity in Christ. This is a tenet of Origen's, Nyssen's, and Nazianzen's theology (all of them supporters of the doctrine of *apokatastasis*). If Christ were not fully human but only divine, his inhumanation, death, and resurrection would not touch us and the other rational creatures. On the other hand, if Christ were not entirely divine, his inhumana-

154. *KG* 5.19, 22, 25.

155. Ramelli, *Christian Doctrine of Apokatastasis*. See especially the conclusions, and passim.

tion, death, and resurrection would not be salvific and could not affect the restoration of all humanity and all rational creatures. Christ, in Evagrius's view, is together fully God, fully *logikon*, and fully human being.

It is often assumed that Evagrius regarded Christ as not fully divine and had a subordinationistic view of Christ, who, on this interpretation, would not be consubstantial with the Trinity.[156] However, this interpretation is far from being accurate and is mainly based on a faulty reading of *KG* 6.14, which, if interpreted correctly, yields a completely opposite meaning: "'Christ is NOT *homoousios* [consubstantial] with the Trinity; indeed, he is not substantial knowledge as well.' *But* Christ is the only one who always and inseparably possesses substantial knowledge in himself. What I claim is that Christ is the one who went together with God the Logos; in spirit, Christ IS the Lord [i.e., God]. He is inseparable from his body and in unity IS *homoousios* [consubstantial] with the Father." Here the "but" I have highlighted signals that what comes before is not Evagrius's own doctrine but the opinion of an adversary, which Evagrius counters. Evagrius's own idea is introduced by "What I claim is…" For this reason I put the first sentence in quotation marks in my edition. The last sentence, which expresses Evagrius's own position, squarely contradicts the initial one: Christ "IS *homoousios* with the Father" and "IS the Lord" God. This evidently overturns the initial statement by an adversary, that "Christ is NOT *homoousios* with the Trinity." In addition, the adverb "inseparably," in reference to Christ, who possesses "inseparably" the substantial knowledge that is God (according to the definition of God as "substantial/essential knowledge" in *KG* 1.89), is the same as the adverbs that at Chalcedon will describe the inseparability of the two natures of Christ, human and divine (ἀχωρίστως and ἀδιαιρέτως, together with ἀσυγχύτως and ἀτρέπτως, "unconfusedly and unchangeably"). It is not accidental that the adjective "inseparable" is used here by Evagrius exactly to describe the union of the divine and human natures in Christ. Christ is both fully God and fully human; the fact that he is a rational creature, and in particular a human being, does not mean that he is not divine or that he is God only incompletely.

156. E.g., Antoine Guillaumont, *Un philosophe au désert: Évagre le Pontique* (Paris: Vrin, 2004), 375; Claudio Moreschini, *I Padri Cappadoci: Storia, letteratura, teologia* (Rome: Città Nuova, 2008), 307, who ascribes to Evagrius "un subordinazionismo alla maniera origeniana" ("an Origen-like subordinationism"), while neither Origen nor Evagrius were subordinationists; and Konstantinovsky, *Evagrius*, 144.

Thus, the present *kephalaion* does not prove that—as is often repeated[157]—Evagrius considered Christ to be not consubstantial with the other persons of the Trinity, but it rather demonstrates that Evagrius countered such a view and regarded Christ, in his divine nature, as God and as consubstantial with the Father. This was already Origen's and Gregory Nyssen's view, accepted by Eusebius as well, who may even have conveyed Origen's teaching on the *homoousia* of the Father and the Son (i.e., Christ in his divine nature) to Nicea through Constantine,[158] while Nyssen introduced Origen's teaching on "one essence, three individual substances" to Constantinople.[159]

Evagrius is perfectly consistent with this line when in his *Letter on Faith* 3 he declares that the Father and the Son have the same essence or substance (*ousia*). Now, Christ in his divine nature is the Son, while in his human nature he is a human being. This is why Evagrius states that Christ has God the Logos in himself (ibid. 4). This clearly points to the divine nature of Christ. In the very first of his *Reflections* (*Skemmata*), likewise, Evagrius states that Christ qua Christ—that is, qua compound of human and divine nature—possesses the essential knowledge, that is, possesses God, his own divine nature. Consistently with this, even in his biography in Palladius Evagrius is represented as supporting, against "heretics" such as "Arians" and Eunomians, the full divinity of Christ-Logos, the Son of God, who also assumed a human body, soul, and intellect. That Christ in his divine nature is the Son is manifest in *KG* 3.1: "The Father, and only he, knows Christ, and the Son, and only he, the Father," where Christ and the Son meaningfully occupy the same position in the equation.

Christ, who is God in his divine nature, is Life, the Logos of God, and the Wisdom of God. And the *telos*, or ultimate end, of all rational creatures is the divinity, who created them for itself, as Evagrius observes in *KG* 4.1. He also adds there that Christ, the Wisdom of God, grows in the rational creatures of God. Precisely in order to allow all rational creatures to return to God, for whom they were created, as Evagrius explains in *KG* 4.26, Christ assumed humanity, died, and was resurrected, calling all to life in the world to come. This is why he is named the Savior. In *KG* 1.90 Evagrius presents the resurrection of Christ as containing also the resurrection and restoration of all rational creatures, who are now dead because

157. E.g., Konstantinovsky, *Evagrius*, 144–45.

158. Argument in Ramelli, "Origen's Anti-Subordinationism."

159. Demonstration in Ramelli, "Origen, Greek Philosophy."

they are unrighteous: in them the justice of God is dead, as Evagrius puts it. But they will be resurrected, will receive a spiritual body, and will be made righteous. Evagrius is following here in the footsteps of Origen, who read the resurrection of Christ as including (in anticipation) the resurrection and restoration of all rational creatures, who are "the body of Christ."[160]

Christ is the one who "makes" justice, both because he is the judge in the judgments that follow each aeon and in the last Judgment and because he is the agent of the justification of rational creatures by means of his sacrifice and of his eschatological reign of instruction and purification (I have already pointed out how Evagrius thought that during the reign of Christ those who are not yet righteous will be set right). Christ's justice is evident in the partial judgments that take place after each aeon, and in which each rational creature is assigned a given body and place in the world according to its spiritual progress, but Christ's mercy is evident from the fact that he extends divine providence to all, including those who would not deserve it (*KG* 2.59). As I have mentioned, indeed, the *logoi* of judgment for Evagrius are always followed by the *logoi* of Providence. In *KG* 1.72 Evagrius emphasizes again Christ's mercy, which is made clear by the fact that Christ orients even fools away from evilness and toward virtue. Spiritual knowledge itself and contemplation are a gift of divine mercy; Evagrius identifies knowledge with life, since human life was intended for knowledge (*KG* 1.73).

In *KG* 3.57, consistently, Christ's role in the process of restoration is presented as that of a teacher of wisdom to rational creatures. It is remarkable that in his task Christ, according to Evagrius, uses mortal bodies: as I have anticipated while treating the *Letter to Melania*, and as I will show further below, bodies, far from being evil, are a valuable instrument in the process of the instruction of intellects that will lead to *apokatastasis*. Christ providentially leads all *logika* through the aeons in their process of purification and perfecting whose *telos* is *apokatastasis*, characterized by perfect unity, both for Evagrius and for Origen. Indeed, the *logoi* of Providence, as Evagrius explains, have to do with "how Christ leads the rational nature through various aeons, toward union in the holy Unity" (*KG* 4.89).

Christ plays a pivotal role also in the purification of rational creatures in the world to come, with a view to their restoration; this is adumbrated

160. See Ilaria L. E. Ramelli, "Cristo-Logos in Origene: Ascendenze filoniane, passaggi in Bardesane e Clemente, e negazione del subordinazionismo," in *Dal Logos dei Greci e dei Romani al Logos di Dio: Ricordando Marta Sordi* (ed. Alfredo Valvo and Roberto Radice; Milan: Vita e Pensiero, 2011), 295–317.

by the words "the houses of the impious will receive purification" (*KG* 3.9). Only thanks to Christ's work can Evagrius speak of both paradise and hell as overcome in the eventual *apokatastasis*, in the *telos*, which will be participation in the life of the Trinity, "the restoration/completion [*apokatastasis*] of the orbit of all" (*KG* 3.60). As I will argue extensively in the commentary on this *kephalaion*, what escaped Guillaumont and the other commentators is that Evagrius here is playing on the astronomical meaning of ἀποκατάστασις as a return of all stars to their original position after the end of a cosmic cycle, a meaning that Evagrius symbolically applies to the eventual restoration of all rational creatures, both those who are in heaven and those who are in hell. All will experience deification (a leap into the life of the Trinity). Reaching the final unity and delighting in contemplation together with Christ will correspond to participating in divine life, or θέωσις (*KG* 4.8).

The ultimate end is described as the knowledge of Unity in *KG* 3.72 and 4.18. Evagrius, like Origen and Gregory Nyssen, within the framework of Platonism, posits the absolute metaphysical and gnoseological preeminence of the Unity,[161] which characterizes both the beginning and the end. This preeminence is evident, for instance, in *KG* 1.19, where the divinity itself is described as "the One," and the one "who only is." In *KG* 3.1–2 and 3.11 Evagrius describes the Father as "unique in Unity," and the Son as "Monad" and "Unity/Henad." Christ is the only one who has the Unity/Henad in himself, in his divine nature; the incorporeal nature both shows the Wisdom of the Unity (this Wisdom being Christ) and is susceptible of the Unity (to the highest degree in the final deification). Similarly, in *KG* 4.21 Christ only is said to sit to his Father's right, which indicates "the Monad and the Unity/Henad." It seems clear to me that Evagrius was once again inspired by Origen and his fundamental metaphysical principle, that God is Monad and Henad (spelled out in *On First Principles* 1.1.6; see more in the commentary below). Evagrius himself in his *Letter on Faith* explains that "the Monad and Henad/Unity indicates the simple and incomprehensible substance" of God (2.41–42).

161. *KG* 3.33. Cf. Gabriel Bunge, "Hénade ou Monade? Au sujet de deux notions centrales de la terminologie évagrienne," *Mus* 102 (1989): 69–91; idem, "*Mysterium Unitatis*: Der Gedanke der Einheit von Schöpfer und Geschöpf in der evagrianischen Mystik," *FZPhTh* 36 (1989): 449–69; idem, "Encore une fois: Hénade ou Monade?" *Adamantius* 15 (2009): 9–42; Ramelli, "Harmony between *Arkhē* and *Telos*."

Perfect unity will be the outcome of *apokatastasis*. Then, distinctions of merits, which pertain to the stage of judgments in aeons, will be overcome, since all rational creatures will have abandoned passions and evilness by then. Only at that point will the consummate unity of all rational creatures be possible, when all will participate in divine life: "in the Unity there will be no leaders, nor (others) submitted to leaders, but all of them will be gods" (*KG* 4.51); "There will be only bare/naked [or "pure"] intellects who continually satiate themselves from its impossibility to satiate" (*KG* 1.65). The eventual Unity, as is clear from this passage, will be deification: all rational creatures will be gods. They will be pure intellects longing for God and never entirely satiated in their longing, because of the infinity of God. This reflects Origen's notion of an absence of satiety, or *κόρος*, from the final *apokatastasis* (thanks to the presence of perfect love after its manifestation in Christ—what was lacking in the beginning, when rational creatures fell) and Nyssen's epecstatic progress, which is also based on that concept of absence of satiety, with an emphasis on the infinity of God.

The unity that will reign in the end also reigned in the beginning, with the difference that the initial unity was unstable, and many *logika* fell from it, while the final unity will be stable and eternal. Indeed, eschatology is closely connected with protology in Evagrius's thought, just as it is the case with Origen's and Nyssen's thought. This is clear, as I have already showed, in his *Letter to Melania*, but it is clear also in his *KG*, as will become evident. From the *KG* it emerges that God's first creation was the creation of "primary beings"—that is, intelligent creatures—who originally dwelled in a unity of concord that is now lost and will be recovered only in the end, at the restoration of all. That unity, which is also described as essential knowledge (identical with the definition of God the Trinity), was broken because of a differentiation of the intellects' acts of will, as a consequence of which the intellects became souls. I have already discussed above *KG* 3.28, as a parallel to the protology of the *Letter to Melania*, and I have already highlighted that Evagrius, when speaking of sin and vice as "carelessness," is adopting a typically Origenian turn. After the fall of many intellects and their total or partial transformation into souls, God equipped these souls with heavy and mortal bodies subject to passions (in the case of human beings) or dark, immortal bodies subject to passions (in the case of demons). This was the second creation, that of "secondary realities," which resulted from the "first judgment." This judgment, operated by Christ, was the first of a series of judgments, each of which will follow an aeon. In the first judgment, Christ divided rational creatures into angels, humans, and demons, in accord with the gravity of their falls, and transformed their bodies accordingly as well.

8. The Positive Role of Matter and a Crucial but Overlooked Distinction: Different Kinds of Bodies

This second creation, for Evagrius just as for Origen,[162] is neither evil nor a punishment. So, in *KG* 3.53 Evagrius states that "none of the mortal bodies should be declared to be evil." Evil depends on wrong moral choices: it does not lie in the product of any divine act of creation. The secondary creation is rather a providential strategy excogitated by God in order to help the development and restoration of souls to intellects. In the secondary creation there are bodies of different kinds. In this connection it is very important to note a regularly overlooked[163] terminological distinction in the Syriac version of the *KG*, which heavily bears on the exact interpretation of Evagrius's notion of corporeality. There are two different words for "body," one referring to heavy, thick, fleshly, and mortal bodies (*pgr'*, which in Syriac also means "corpse"), and the other also including finer, incorruptible, and immortal bodies (*gwšm'*). Unlike earlier translators, who translated both words as "body," or in French, "corps," in my translation of the *KG* and in my commentary I will methodically take into consideration the important distinction between the two different terms. This has a remarkable impact on the interpretation of Evagrius's thought. I doubt that the Greek corresponding distinction was between σῶμα and σάρξ, since the Syriac translates σάρξ with a third term; so this remains possible but not so probable. It may be more probable that Evagrius, like Origen and the Neoplatonists,[164] added adjectives to σῶμα to specify which kind of body he was speaking of.

Many more hints can be found that indicate that Evagrius, like Origen, Gregory Nyssen, and most Neoplatonists, had in mind different kinds of

162. For Origen, see Ilaria L. E. Ramelli, "'Preexistence of Souls'? The ἀρχή and τέλος of Rational Creatures in Origen and Some Origenians," *StPatr* 56 (2013): 167–226.

163. Even in such insightful papers as Julia Konstantinovsky, "Soul and Body in Early Christian Thought: A Unified Duality?" *StPatr* 44 (2010): 349–55.

164. See Ilaria L. E. Ramelli, "Iamblichus, *De anima* 38 (66,12–15 Finamore/Dillon): A Resolving Conjecture?," *Rheinisches Museum für Philologie* 157 (2014): 106–8.

bodies. For example, in his *Letter to Melania* 38–39, as we have seen, he speaks of "this sense-perceptible body," assembled by God's Wisdom out of the four elements and subject to God's providence. This suggests that there is another kind of bodies that are not sense perceptible. This is perfectly in line with Origen's views and is confirmed by the Greek text of *Praktikos* 49: the intellect "is naturally constituted for prayer even without *this body*," which points to *another* body, different from the mortal. Likewise, when in *KG* 5.19 Evagrius describes the resurrection of the body as a passage from a bad to a good quality—that is, from corruptible and mortal to incorruptible and immortal—this obviously indicates that at least the bodies of the resurrection will be immortal and incorruptible and different from the mortal bodies. What is more, since the resurrection is for Evagrius a restoration to the original state (so that the resurrection of the soul is its restoration from passible to impassible, and that of the intellect is its restoration from ignorance to true knowledge, *KG* 5.22, 25), the restoration of the body to the "better quality" suggests the original existence of an incorruptible body. Also, in *KG* 3.36 Evagrius clearly speaks of "the *various* and *different* bodies of rational creatures," which entails the existence of other bodies than mortal, heavy, and fleshly bodies. There are many other examples in Evagrius's works, including reflections on the bodies of angels and those of demons. I will analyze them in the commentary.

According to Evagrius in his *Letter to Melania*, as I have pointed out earlier, the secondary creation—that is, bodies—is providential and came into being for the sake of those who are far from God. Evagrius also states that the intelligible creation at a certain point was joined to the sense-perceptible creation "for reasons that it is impossible to explain here" (*Letter to Melania* 13). This seems to refer to the union of souls with mortal bodies. Sense-perceptible creation belongs to the "secondary creation," as it is often called in the *KG*, and makes the object of natural contemplation. It is helpful in that, while with some advanced intellects the Spirit and the Son communicate directly, with others they must do so by means of this secondary creation. The latter is not evil, as Origen too clarified in his anti-"Gnostic" and anti-Marcionite polemic. It is neither evil nor a punishment (*KG* 3.53), but it is God's providential strategy for the restoration of souls to intellects.[165] The secondary creation is in fact providential, qua mediation,

165. This has been rightly stressed by Konstantinovsky, *Evagrius*, 27–46, who emphasizes that, according to Evagrius, the body and sense perception are part of the ascent to perfection.

for those who are far from God due to "their evil deeds." This mediation was created by God's Wisdom and Power, the Son and the Spirit, who are absolutely incorporeal, as all the Trinity is (a tenet of Origen's metaphysics as well).[166] But the most advanced rational creatures do without the mediation of the secondary creation.

Indeed, when God's first creation of "primary beings"—rational creatures, or *logika*, who originally dwelled in a unity of concord—experienced a dispersion of the intellects' acts of will, the intellects descended to the rank of souls. Heavy, mortal bodies were thus provided by God for these. This was the creation of "secondary beings," which came after the "first judgment," operated by Christ, who divided rational creatures into angels, humans, and demons according to the gravity of their falls. Christ himself even assumed a heavy, mortal body, and after his resurrection he had a body that revealed how human risen bodies will be (*KG* 4.41). The fact that mortal bodies will vanish at the end of all aeons (*KG* 2.17) does not imply that mortal bodies are not good: they serve their purpose during the aeons. Only, they will have to disappear when all inherit immortality, not because they are evil, but because they are mortal (*KG* 1.58). If the human mortal body is a part of this world, and if "the form of this world will pass," then the form of the mortal body will also pass (*KG* 1.26), simply because it is tied to the present state of things, and not because it is evil. Since Evagrius regards mortal bodies as a positive means for intellects to return to God, as Origen also did, in *KG* 4.60 he warns that those who hate the mortal body hate the Creator as well.[167]

In the eventual *apokatastasis* mortal bodies ("thick bodies") will vanish, when evil will disappear as well, and all secondary beings, to which bodies belong, will cease to exist as such when ignorance will be removed (*KG* 3.68; see the commentary below). The first bodies to disappear will be mortal bodies, which will vanish at the resurrection when they are turned into immortal. At that point evil will also disappear, and no one will sin anymore. Then all bodies will cease to exist as secondary beings, when the body will be elevated to the rank of soul, and the soul to the rank of intellect. In this way, only primary beings (intellects) will remain, because bodies and souls will have been subsumed into intellects. And they will enjoy knowledge; for at that stage ignorance will be definitely removed. But

---

166. E.g., Evagrius, *On Thoughts* (Περὶ λογισμῶν) 41.48–49; *Letter* 39.134–135 Géhin; scholium 1 on Ps 140:2.

167. *KG* 4.62 also blames those who "disparage our body."

while ignorance is closely associated to evil by Evagrius, as I have pointed out beforehand, bodies, and even thick bodies, are not in the least related to evil. Thick bodies will cease to exist when evil too will, but they are neither evil themselves nor the cause of evil. The destruction of evil and ignorance, which will be contemporary with the disappearance of mortal bodies and all secondary beings respectively, is declared by Evagrius, once again, to be a work of Christ, who in Origen, Nyssen, and Evagrius himself is the main agent of *apokatastasis*, as I have already pointed out. In particular, Evagrius maintains that Christ, in his capacity as high priest, intercedes for all rational beings and leads them all to salvation by purifying them from evilness and ignorance (*KG* 5.46). The intercession of Christ as a high priest with a view to universal restoration was greatly emphasized by Origen, who much insisted on the universal and eternal validity of Christ's high-priestly sacrifice.[168]

Kephalaion 3.68, referred to above, mentions two rests of God as the times when the destruction of evil and ignorance respectively will take place. This is related in turn to the "eighth day," the great Sunday. Like Origen, Didymus, Gregory of Nyssa, and Maximus the Confessor, Evagrius identifies the eighth day with the ultimate end and *apokatastasis*. It will be preceded by the Sabbath of rest. In *KG* 4.44 Evagrius identifies the Sabbath as the rest of the rational soul, in which it is naturally made not to trespass the boundaries of its nature. But the rational soul will indeed trespass the boundaries of its creaturely nature—by grace—on the Sunday of the eventual deification (θέωσις). The seventh day will see the healing and corrective reign of Christ on all rational creatures, and on the eighth day, the glorious Sunday, all will return to Unity.[169] Bodies and souls will be subsumed into intellects; what is inferior will be subsumed into what is superior—an eschatological principle that was later developed especially by John the Scot Eriugena.[170]

Once the body has been elevated to the rank of the soul, then the whole of the soul will return to the rank of intellect: the intellect in its power will pervade the soul, when the whole of it will be mingled with the light of the

168. See Ilaria L. E. Ramelli, "The Universal and Eternal Validity of Jesus's High-Priestly Sacrifice: The Epistle to the Hebrews in Support of Origen's Theory of Apokatastasis," in *A Cloud of Witnesses: The Theology of Hebrews in Its Ancient Contexts* (ed. Richard J. Bauckham et al.; London: T&T Clark, 2008), 210–21.

169. Cf. *KG* 4.26; 5.8.

170. See Ramelli, *Christian Doctrine of Apokatastasis*, the section devoted to him.

Trinity (*KG* 2.29). This will happen at the eventual restoration and deification. When the intellects receive contemplation, then the whole nature of the bodies will be eliminated, not because they will be destroyed, but because they will be transformed into souls and souls into intellects, so that the contemplation, or θεωρία, concerning them will become immaterial, since bodies themselves will have become immaterial (*KG* 2.62). In *KG* 3.66 Evagrius observes that the first trumpet at the beginning revealed the coming into being of bodies, and likewise the last trumpet at the end of history will reveal the vanishing of bodies, in that these will be subsumed into souls, and souls into intellects, the superior parts or faculties of souls.

Therefore, any plurality, number, and name will disappear along with all aeons (*KG* 1.7–8) and all bodies, which were useful for life in the aeons. After all aeons have passed away, only the absolute eternity, or ἀϊδιότης, of life in God will remain (*KG* 2.17). Quantity, plurality, and number are attached to secondary beings, what Nyssen would call diastematic or measurable realities that are stretched out in intervals or extensions of space or time.[171] "One" is a number of quantity; quantity is linked with mortal corporeal nature; therefore, number is proper to secondary natural contemplation (*KG* 4.19). This contemplation pertains to secondary beings, those of the second creation, but this creation, as I have already illustrated, will be subsumed into the first. As a consequence, quantity and number will disappear along with the subsumption of secondary realities into primary realities. This description parallels that of the cessation of plurality and names, and even of all divine *epinoiai*, described by Evagrius in his *Letter to Melania*, which I have analyzed earlier. Plurality must cease in the ultimate end, which will be in fact characterized by unity. This does not mean that confusion will arise at that point. Evagrius himself in his *Letter to Melania* is clear that the persons of the Trinity will not be confused, nor will any distinction between the Creator and the creatures disappear. Rather, the unity of which Evagrius speaks will be a unity of concord, as it was also conceived by Origen.

Like Origen, but also like all Platonists, and like most educated people in the imperial age, Evagrius maintains a dualism between the intelligible and the sense-perceptible worlds.[172] However, like Origen and against "Gnostic" and Manichaean perspectives, he is far from seeing matter and

171. On which, see Ramelli, *Gregorio di Nissa: Sull'anima*; and Hans Boersma, *Embodiment and Virtue in Gregory of Nyssa* (Oxford: Oxford University Press, 2013).

172. E.g., *KG* 1.33; 2.35; 4.12; 5.2; 6.2–3, 38–40.

the sense-perceptible realm as evil. Rather, as I have showed, he considers it to be providential, as an instrument of instruction, elevation, and salvation. In *KG* 6.17 too, Evagrius distinguishes the incorporeal nature from the corporeal one, and according to the Syriac translation and its aforementioned terminology of bodies, this distinction seems to be absolute: there are beings that are corporeal—that is, endowed with any kind of body, thicker or finer, mortal or immortal—and there are realities that are absolutely incorporeal—that is, without any kind of body, either fine or thick. God the Trinity, according to both Evagrius and Origen, is absolutely incorporeal. In *KG* 6.20 God is said to have created first the first creation, that of incorporeal realities, including rational creatures, of whom God is the Father, and then the second, that of bodies, which came after the "movement" of rational creatures—that is, after they began to direct their wills in different directions—instead of orienting them only toward the Good, that is, God. The *epinoiai* of God also changed: before the movement, God was good, powerful, wise, and omnipotent; after the movement, God has become Judge, Ruler, Physician, Shepherd, Doctor, merciful and patient, and moreover, Door, Way, Lamb, High Priest, and the like. God's *epinoia* of physician of souls is particularly emphasized by Evagrius,[173] just as by Origen, due to its role in the process of *apokatastasis*. In *On Thoughts* 10 Evagrius notes that the divine Physician applies even drastic remedies, if necessary, for the salvation of the soul, something that was already stressed by Origen. He insisted that Christ, the divine Logos, is such a powerful Physician that there is no spiritual illness that he cannot heal (*Against Celsus* 8.72). As I have remarked earlier on the basis of the *Letter to Melania*, divine *epinoiai*,[174] just as the corporeal creation, for Evagrius are useful for the sake of the salvific economy but will not need to subsist in the end. Similarly, neither will the secondary creation need to subsist in the end.

The first creation, that of incorporeal realities, including rational creatures, is kept distinct from the second also in *KG* 4.58: God (presumably the Father), while creating rational creatures, was in nobody and nothing, whereas while creating the corporeal nature and the aeons he was in his Christ, the creative Logos. Thus, when Christ created the aeons and

173. E.g., in *Letter* 42; 51; 52; 55; 57; 63; *On Thoughts* 3. See Konstantinovsky, *Evagrius*, 112–13.

174. Note again that Evagrius, exactly like Nyssen, regards these *epinoiai* as belonging to God the Trinity and not only to Christ.

the bodies, he had God in himself, so that, on account of Christ's divine nature, we cannot speak of an inferior creative agent, different from God, for bodies. In *KG* 3.19 the ontological distinction between incorporeal and corporeal realities brings about a parallel gnoseological distinction between the primary and the secondary contemplation, the former immaterial, the latter being in matter. The same distinction between two kinds of knowledge and two kinds of creation is kept in *KG* 3.24 and 3.26: the knowledge of the primary nature is the spiritual contemplation that the Creator used in creating the intellects (the primary creation), which alone are susceptible of the divine nature. And the knowledge concerning the secondary nature is a spiritual contemplation that Christ used in creating the nature of bodies and aeons. The succession of aeons, just as bodies, belongs to the second creation and will vanish in the absolute eternity of *apokatastasis* (which is not αἰώνιος or belonging to any aeon, but ἀΐδιος). God's science or knowledge produced primary beings, that is, intellectual realities; secondary beings, bodies, only came after the aforementioned "movement" of rational creatures' free wills (*KG* 1.50). Moses's account of creation in Genesis, according to Evagrius, refers to secondary creation, which took place after the first judgment of fallen rational creatures, whereas there exists no account of God's primary creation, which came to existence before the judgment (*KG* 2.64).

The secondary creation, like all that which was not from the beginning, will disappear in the end, at the universal restoration, not because it will be utterly destroyed, as evil and ignorance will, but because it will be subsumed into what is superior and best; I have already expounded the elevation of bodies to the level of souls and of souls to the level of intellects. *Apokatastasis* thus appears to be the restoration of creatures to the best, that is, the perfection of the intellect, which consists in immaterial knowledge. Now immaterial knowledge is only the Trinity; therefore the intellect will become a seer of the Trinity (*KG* 3.15). The contemplation of the Trinity produces in turn the deification of the creatural intellect, and deification will be the culmination of *apokatastasis.*

Evagrius, just as Origen and especially Gregory of Nyssa, regarded the final *apokatastasis* as the restoration of the divine image in the human being, which was created by God in the beginning but became blurred because of sin. The authentic image of God in the human being is not in the body nor in the inferior faculties of the soul subject to passions—as Philo, Origen, and Gregory Nyssen all agreed (since God is both incorporeal and free from passions)—but in the intellect, the only human faculty that is susceptible of the knowledge of God. *Kephalaion* 6.73 makes it clear that the image of God is the intellect, due to its receptivity of God through knowledge, which is also tantamount to its incorporeality. In this *kephalaion* Evagrius interestingly uses the same "zetetic" method as Origen deployed: first Evagrius presents an explanation for the intellect's characterization as "image of God"—that is, because the intellect is susceptible of God through knowledge; then he presents another explanation, which apparently excludes the former—that is, because the intellect is incorporeal—but finally he shows that both in fact are compatible and even are the same thing. This dialectic structure is similar to that which I have already postulated for *KG* 6.14.

A further clarification comes from *KG* 3.32, where Evagrius explains that the image of God is not what is susceptible of God's Wisdom, since in this way the mortal corporeal nature too would be the image of God. The image of God is rather what is susceptible of the Unity. The mortal corporeal nature can come to know the Wisdom of God as expressed in creation, but only the intellect can know God the Unity/Henad; hence, only in the intellect is the image of God. Thus, in *The Gnostic* (*Gnostikos*) 50 Evagrius urges his reader to endeavor to depict the images (εἰκόνας) by looking at the Archetype, God, without omitting any of the factors that contribute to the reconstitution of the fallen image. This reconstitution is the restoration, or *apokatastasis*, when the image of God will be restored to its original splendor in each intellect. In *Sentence* 58 Evagrius, deeply reminiscent of Origen and in full accord with Nyssen as well, identifies the essence, the true identity of the human being, or better of each rational creature, with what it was at the beginning (the ἀρχή), in God's own plan, before its fall: "If you want to know yourself, who you are, consider not who you have been but *who you were at the beginning*." What rational creatures were in the ἀρχή, before their fall, will be restored in the end, in the eventual *apokatastasis*, when their soul has become entirely pure from passions. Their souls will then become intellects, and intellects will become fully pure in turn and will be immersed in divine life and knowledge.

9. *Apatheia*, *Pathē*, and Charity-Love, Which Is No *Pathos*

The *praktikē*, basically asceticism, aims at virtue and the eradication of passions (*apatheia*), and not simply at their moderation (*metriopatheia*). Evagrius shares the ideal of *apatheia*[175] with Clement of Alex-

175. See Jeremy Driscoll, "*Apatheia* and Purity of Heart in Evagrius," in *Purity*

andria, Origen, Gregory Nyssen, and most Neoplatonists, as well as with the ancient Stoics. He insists on this point, because it is closely related to knowledge and intellectual activity in his view. I have already demonstrated how for Evagrius virtue and knowledge are closely interrelated and interdependent. *Apatheia* and knowledge are as well, given that for Evagrius virtue is essentially absence of passions. The close connection between *apatheia* and knowledge is clear, for instance, in *Praktikos*: "We will say that the absence of passions is the health of the soul, and that its nourishment is knowledge" (56); "Impassivity is possessed by the soul that not only does not suffer for the things that happen but remains imperturbable even at their memory" (67). *Apatheia* is the perfection of the soul that is liable to passions, while knowledge is the perfection of the intellect (*KG* 6.55). The relation between *apatheia* and knowledge is made clear especially by Evagrius's somewhat empirical reflection in *KG* 4.70 that freedom from passions allows for contemplation, for the intellectual activity.

Indeed, the intellect approaches the intelligible realities when it does not unite itself any longer to tempting thoughts (*logismoi*) that come from the part of the soul that is subject to passions (*KG* 1.81). Evagrius even declares that the intellect possesses a creative power when it is free from passions; in this way, intellectual knowledge becomes completely independent of sense perception: "The intellect that has been stripped of its passional thought and sees the intellections of beings does not truly receive anymore the representations that (are formed) by means of sense perceptions, but it is as though another world were created by its knowledge, and it has attracted its thought to itself and rejected the sense-perceptible world far from itself" (*KG* 5.12). A similar idea will return in John the Scot Eriugena.[176] And I have already pointed out this conception in Evagrius's *Letter to Melania* as well. That virtues and *apatheia*—the domain of the *praktikē*—are the prerequisite of knowledge is pithily confirmed by Evagrius in *Scho-*

---

of Heart in Early Ascetic and Monastic Literature (ed. Harriet A. Luckman and Linda Kulzer; Collegeville, Minn.: Liturgical Press, 1999), 141–59; Somos, "Origen, Evagrius Ponticus and the Ideal of Impassibility"; Corrigan, *Evagrius and Gregory*, ch. 4; Tobon, "Health of the Soul"; Suzuki, "Evagrian Concept of *Apatheia*"; Tobon, *Apatheia in the Teachings of Evagrius.*

176. See Ilaria L. E. Ramelli, "Eriugena's Commentary on Martianus in the Framework of His Thought and the Philosophical Debate of His Time," in *Carolingian Scholarship and Martianus Capella* (ed. Sinead O'Sullivan and Mariken Teeuwen; Cultural Encounters in Late Antiquity and the Middle Ages 12; Turnhout: Brepols, 2012), 245–72.

lia on Proverbs 258: the soul, in the sense of the soul subject to passions, is "the mother of the intellect" because "by means of virtues it brings the intellect to light." Of course this is just from the point of view of the present life, since from the protological and ontological point of view the intellect was before the soul, and from the eschatological point of view the soul will be elevated to the rank of intellect.

To Evagrius's mind, just as to Gregory Nyssen's,[177] the ideal of *apatheia* is closely related to the conception of passions as adventitious in rational creatures, secondary, and against nature. Evagrius argues that, since all the faculties that human beings have in common with animals belong to the corporeal nature, then clearly the irascible and the concupiscible/appetitive faculties (in Plato's terminology) were not created together with the rational nature before the movement of will that determined the fall (*KG* 6.85). That is to say, they are adventitious; they do not belong to the authentic human nature, which is the prelapsarian nature of rational creatures, or *logika*. Evagrius in *KG* 6.83 squarely declares the irascible and the concupiscible/appetitive parts of the soul to be "against nature." Their major fault is that they produce tempting thoughts, or *logismoi*, that prevent the intellect from knowing God. Intellects were created by God in order that they might know God; this is their nature. The faculties of the inferior soul that obstacle this knowledge are therefore against nature. This is why, since passions were not at the beginning—being not included in God's plan for rational creatures—they will not endure in the end. However, in *KG* 3.59 Evagrius warns that what is really against nature are not the inferior faculties of the soul per se but their bad use, that is, again, their use against nature, since it is from this that evilness or vice (κακία) derives: "If all evilness is generated by the intelligence, by *thymos* [the irascible faculty], and by *epithymia* [the appetitive one], and of these faculties it is possible to make use in a good and in an evil way, then it is clear that it is by the use of these parts against nature that evils occur to us. And if this is so, there is nothing that has been created by God and is evil." It is clear that Evagrius's main concern in this declaration is theodicy, the same that constantly guided Origen in his own theology. God is not responsible for evil (θεὸς ἀναίτιος: this was already Plato's principle, which later Clement of Alexandria, Origen, Gregory Nyssen, and others repeated many times).[178]

177. See Ramelli, *Gregorio di Nissa: Sull'anima*.
178. See the commentary below.

If passions are against nature, being the result of a use of the soul's faculties against nature, and must therefore be eradicated, what about love (ἀγάπη, charity-love)?[179] Will it have to disappear as well? But I have already pointed out the vital role that love plays in the final restoration in Evagrius's, Origen's, and Nyssen's perspective. They are all adamant that love will never fade away; indeed, it will endure eternally, as Paul already taught. Origen even adduced Paul's argument that "love [ἀγάπη, *caritas*] never falls." This assumption is compatible with the disappearance of all passions in the end simply because Evagrius, like Origen and Nyssen, thinks that ἀγάπη is not a passion (πάθος). Charity-love is indeed so far from being a passion that it derives from impassivity, as is clear from *Praktikos* 81: "ἀγάπη is the product of impassivity." Since in turn impassivity is the goal of asceticism, or *praktikē*, charity-love can be seen as the result of asceticism: "The end of asceticism [πρακτική] is charity-love; that of knowledge is the doctrine concerning God, and the principles of both are faith and natural contemplation" (*Praktikos* 84). Not only does love come from asceticism and impassivity, but, reciprocally, charity-love is also said to overcome the passions of the soul in *Praktikos* 35: "bodily passions are overcome by continence; those of the soul are overcome by spiritual love [ἀγάπη πνευματική]." The interdependence between love and impassivity is made clear in a passage I have already quoted above, *Eulogius* 22: "Charity-love is the bond of impassivity and the expunging of passions.... Love possesses nothing of its own apart from God, for God is Love itself."

Precisely because charity-love is no *pathos* but is rather the progeny and the source of *apatheia* at the same time, and because the Godhead itself is charity-love, this is why love will abide in the end, in the perfect state, and will endure forever. Thus, in *KG* 4.50 Evagrius remarks, "There is one good kind of love, which is forever: that which true knowledge chooses, and it is said to be inseparable from the intellect." Love is inseparable from knowledge and from the intellect; since in the end only intellects will remain (because bodies will be lifted up to the rank of souls, and souls will be elevated to the rank of intellects), it is clear that, if love is inseparable from the intellect, love will exist forever. Indeed, love "is the excellent state of the rational soul, a state in which the soul cannot love anything that is among corruptible beings more than the knowledge of God" (*KG* 1.86). If love is

179. See Ilaria L. E. Ramelli, "Love," in *Encyclopedia of Ancient Christianity* (ed. Angelo Di Berardino; Downers Grove, Ill.: InterVarsity Press, 2014), 2:611–26.

the perfect state of the rational soul, then it is clear that, when all rational creatures have reached perfection, love will always remain. Love, which is related to knowledge, leads to wisdom: whoever has to *learn* the wisdom of the beings needs spiritual *love* (*KG* 3.58). Love, the offspring of *apatheia*, leads straight to knowledge, and with knowledge belongs in the very *telos* of rational creatures.

A strong form of love, which Evagrius, like Origen, Gregory of Nyssa, and later Pseudo-Dionysius, calls desire[180] is even posited by him as the main factor in the continual growth of the intellect in knowledge and in the approximation to God (close to Nyssen's epecstatic, infinite movement of progress and development of rational creatures): "the intellect, when it comes close to the intellections of beings, [will] be filled with desire of the spirit and not abandon admiration" (*KG* 5.29). Love, which is the propulsor of this spiritual development, is the only movement that will remain in the end, in the infinite *epektasis*. The love of intellectual creatures will always strive for the Love that God is.

10. Judgment and Providence, Justice and Mercy

I have analyzed beforehand *KG* 1.27, where I have proposed to read the five contemplations enumerated by Evagrius in chronological order: first the contemplation of God, then the contemplation of incorporeal realities, then that of bodies, then the contemplation of the Judgment, and finally that of divine providence. God existed before anything else; then God created the incorporeal realities (the primary creation), then bodies and aeons (the secondary creation). After each aeon there is a judgment, and after the last aeon there will come the last Judgment. But judgments are accompanied by divine providence, and after the last Judgment, the eventual *apokatastasis* will be the manifestation of divine providence. Judgments and Providence do not contradict one another but reflect, respectively, God's justice and God's mercy. Both are attributes of God; divine justice is made manifest in the judgments after each aeon, when each rational creature will be allotted what it has deserved in the previous aeon, and divine mercy is manifested by the omnipresent action of Providence during all the aeons, even in purifying punishments (in that they are

180. See Ramelli, *Christian Doctrine of Apokatastasis*, the section on Pseudo-Dionysius.

purifying and not retributive), and especially in the final restoration after all purifications have been completed.

This synergy of Judgment and Providence, of divine justice and divine mercy, was stressed above all by Origen, who had to polemicize against the separation of divine justice and divine mercy hypothesized by "Gnostics" and Marcionites.[181] For Origen too, the triumph of divine justice is in the judgments after the aeons, and the triumph of divine mercy and providence will be the eventual *apokatastasis*. Not accidentally, in *Gnostikos* 48 Evagrius quotes with deep veneration and admiration a saying by a faithful follower of Origen, Didymus the Blind, concerning the necessity of meditating on both God's judgment and God's providence: "Always exercise yourself in the meditation of the doctrines concerning Providence and Judgment—said Didymus, the great 'gnostic' teacher [ὁ μέγας καὶ γνωστικὸς διδάσκαλος Δίδυμος]—and endeavor to remember their materials, since almost all people err in these topics. As for the rationale of Judgment, you will find that this lies in the variety of bodies and worlds; that concerning Providence, instead, lies in the turns that from evilness and ignorance bring us back to virtue or knowledge [ἐν τοῖς τρόποις τοῖς ἀπὸ κακίας καὶ ἀγνωσίας ἐπὶ τὴν ἀρετὴν ἢ ἐπὶ τὴν γνῶσιν]."

Providence restores rational creatures to virtue and knowledge; its work will be concluded when this restoration will be universal. Evagrius never separates the idea of the Judgment, with the retribution of rational creatures' deeds and passions or virtues,[182] from that of God's providence, which is prior to that of the Judgment, because it was anterior to the fall, which brought about the necessity of the Judgment: "The *logoi* concerning the Judgment are secondary, as has been said, vis-à-vis the *logoi* concerning movement and concerning Providence" (*KG* 5.24). The rationale concerning the movement is rational creatures' free will, which is a gift of God; this is more important than the Judgment and is prior to the fall, even if it did cause the fall (but not by necessity; indeed, in the end free will shall abide, but it will cause no fall anymore).

That for Evagrius God's judgment is inseparable from God's providence is clear from scholium 8 on Ps 138:16 as well, where also the *logoi* of Providence and Judgment are joined. Providence cares for the spiritual healing of rational creatures and operates on their intellects, which take

181. See ibid., the section on Origen.

182. See, e.g., *KG* 4.33, 38; 6.57.

care of their own souls (*Praktikos* 82). This healing is salvific, because it destroys sins (*KG* 1.28). Evagrius is exactly on Origen's line in thinking that divine providence, which is universally salvific, is not in the least at odds with individual free will, but divine justice rewards each one according to his or her deeds, and divine providence operates at the same time, always allowing each one's will to be free: "God's providence accompanies the freedom of will, whereas God's judgment takes into account the order of rational creatures" (*KG* 6.43). I will highlight below in the commentary the close affinity with Origen's thinking in this respect, to the point of verbal resonance.

Divine providence operates in two ways: (1) it keeps God's creatures, both incorporeal and corporeal realities, in existence; for, without divine grace, no creature could either exist or continue to exist; (2) it converts rational creatures from evilness and ignorance to virtue and knowledge. The first knowledge that was found in rational creatures is that of the Trinity; then, there occurred the movement of free will, Providence, which rescues and never abandons anyone, and then the judgment, and again the movement of free will, Providence, the judgment, and so on with all this, up to the union with the Trinity. Thus, every judgment comes between the movement of free will and divine providence (*KG* 6.59, 75). Aeons, which are the result of each single judgment, come after the first movement of rational creatures' free will and their fall, but before the final and most perfect manifestation of God's providence, which will be *apokatastasis*, after the end of all aeons. Then, not only for Origen, but for Evagrius as well, no one will be in any aeon anymore, but God will be "all in all." Indeed, Evagrius thinks of *apokatastasis* as entailing deification (θέωσις) to the point of downright calling it "the Holy Trinity" in *KG* 6.75.

It is worth noting that Evagrius uses the same biblical passage (the parable in Matt 18:23–25 and Luke 7:41) as Nyssen did to establish that otherworldly punishments will come to an end after "the full payment of one's debt." In Gregory's *On the Soul and the Resurrection* 101–104, Macrina understands Jesus's statement that each one will have to pay off one's debt "up to the last coin" as implying that, once the *last* coin has been paid, the relevant punishment and imprisonment will cease:

> God's right Judgment is applied to all and extends the time of restitution of the debt according to its amount.… The complete repayment of debts does not take place through a money payment, but the debtor is handed to the torturers, until he has paid his whole debt.… Through the

> necessary suffering, he will eliminate the debt, accumulated by means of participation in miserable things, which he had taken upon himself during his earthly life.... After taking off all that which is alien to himself, that is, sin, and getting rid of the shame deriving from debts, he can achieve a condition of freedom and confidence. Now, freedom is assimilation to what has no master and is endowed with absolute power, and at the beginning it was given us by God, but then it was covered and hidden by the shame of debts. Thus, as a consequence, everything that is free will adapt to what is similar to it; but virtue admits of no masters:[183] therefore, everything that is free will turn out to be in virtue, since what is free has no master. Now, God's nature is the source of all virtue; so, in it there will be those who have attained freedom from evil, that, as the apostle says, "God may be all in all" [1 Cor 15:28].[184]

Now, Evagrius refers to the very same parable in *KG* 4.34 and provides of it the same eschatological exegesis as Gregory did: "In the future world/aeon no one will escape from the house of torment into which he will fall. For it is said, 'You will not go out from there until you have given back the very last coin,' that is, up to the smallest amount of suffering." This also means that, after giving back the very last coin, that is, the last amount of deserved suffering, all will at long last be allowed to abandon the house of torment. This parable, indeed, constitutes one of the strongest biblical proofs of *apokatastasis* for both Gregory and Evagrius, as well as for their contemporaries Diodore of Tarsus and Theodore of Mopsuestia, two other significant supporters of the doctrine of *apokatastasis*.[185]

Another major biblical passage with which Evagrius buttressed his *apokatastasis* theory is 1 Tim 2:4–6, which he cites in *Gnostikos* 22: "The 'gnostic' must be neither sad nor hostile: for the former attitude is proper to those who do not know what Scriptures say concerning that which is to happen; the latter, of those who do not want all humans to be saved and reach the knowledge of the truth." One must want all humans to be saved and to attain the knowledge of the truth, which is what God wants. Evagrius maintains here that the awareness of what Scripture reveals concerning the ultimate end necessarily brings joy, and this evidently because the Bible, according to him, announces the eventual restoration and salva-

183. Plato, *Republic* 617E.

184. See Ramelli, "Christian Soteriology and Christian Platonism."

185. See Ramelli, *Christian Doctrine of Apokatastasis*, the section on Diodore and Theodore.

tion of all (*apokatastasis*), which in 1 Tim 2:4–6 is moreover presented as "what God wants." This persuasion, that universal restoration is revealed by Scripture and wanted by God, was shared by all of the supporters of this doctrine in the patristic age, from Origen to Gregory of Nyssa, from Evagrius to Eriugena. These theologians would not have espoused this theory if they had not considered it to be firmly based on the Bible. Hence also their profound conviction, which I have already pointed out, that the final *apokatastasis* depends above all on Christ. Thus, it is ultimately because of his radical metaphysical and eschatological optimism that Evagrius exhorts his disciples to hope, joy, and confidence, for instance, in *Praktikos* 12. In *Praktikos* 20 and 25–26, consistently, Evagrius warns against wrath, hatred, affliction, and memory of suffered injuries. Likewise, in *Praktikos* 27–28 he warns against sadness and lack of confidence and hope in God. Evagrius, who upheld a strong metaphysical, theological, and eschatological optimism, denounces that lacking hope in God's providence is a serious sin, a yielding to the devil (ibid., 46–47). This position, as I have demonstrated elsewhere,[186] was shared by Diodore of Tarsus, another supporter of the *apokatastasis* theory: he criticized those Christians who believed in God but not in divine providence, and for him, not believing in the eventual universal restoration is tantamount to not believing in divine providence, which aims precisely at this restoration.

Once again like Origen, Evagrius reveals a deeply rooted "pastoral" concern in respect to the divulgation of the doctrine of universal restoration, especially among spiritually immature people, those who do good out of fear and not for love. It is better for such people to believe threats of eternal punishment, and thereby keep their fear, since this is what prevents them from sinning (only in the eventual *apokatastasis* will love prevent everyone from sinning). This is why in *Gnostikos* 36 Evagrius warns: "The loftier doctrine [ὁ ὑψηλότερος λόγος] concerning the Judgment should be kept undisclosed to secular people and young people." Secular and young people are the most spiritually immature, who need to believe in a material punishment, and that eternal, whereas the torment of the rational soul will consist in ignorance (ibid.), and this will not be eternal, since ignorance, according to Evagrius, will ultimately vanish, as well as evil will.

Indeed, for Evagrius, just as for Origen, fear of punishments as a deterrent from doing evil is typical of hardly mature people: "Those who have

186. In ibid., section on Diodore of Tarsus.

established virtues in themselves and have entirely mixed to them can no longer remember laws, commandments, or punishment [κολάσεως] but say and do all that which the best disposition advises" (*Praktikos* 70). Love and virtue, and not fear, should urge people to do good—and virtue is primarily love and mercy, which are also the main features of God, the model of all virtues (ibid. 75).

11. Conclusions: Contribution to Research

All of Evagrius's works, both those on theology and metaphysics and those on spiritual ascent and asceticism, help reconstruct his doctrine of intellects and souls, their origin, their relation to the body, the different kinds of bodies, and rational creatures' eschatological destiny. Those two groups of works unfortunately have been kept apart, as I have mentioned at the opening, and have received different treatments: Evagrius's ascetic works were treasured virtually everywhere, but his metaphysical and eschatological speculations, especially in the *KG* and *Letter to Melania*, were condemned. The close connection between Evagrius's doctrine of intellects, souls, and bodies, and that of universal restoration, or *apokatastasis*, is particularly evident in the latter group, the *KG* and *Letter to Melania*. In the *KG* and *Letter to Melania*, Evagrius's reflection on eschatology is clearly related to the rest of his thought, which is oriented toward the *telos*, the ultimate end. This is also the case with Origen and Gregory of Nyssa. For the end is the accomplishment of God's plan for rational creatures; this is why it reflects the beginning, the prelapsarian state.

Evagrius's protological and eschatological ideas reveal remarkable points of contact with those of Origen and Gregory of Nyssa. And such parallels are obvious not only in this respect but also in many others. This is not surprising, since Evagrius absorbed Origen's and the Cappadocians' theology, as well as that of Didymus, another close follower of Origen, whom Evagrius may have frequented personally. In addition, I suspect that Evagrius's biographical and intellectual closeness to Gregory Nyssen is more substantial than is commonly thought. I have provided some evidence that appears significant, but a methodical investigation in this respect seems to be still an important desideratum. Moreover, the close intellectual relationship between Evagrius and Origen and Nyssen is far from being limited to protology and eschatology but invests most aspects of their theology and philosophy.

12. The Present Commentary and Acknowledgments

In the commentary below I shall be focusing on the relation of Evagrius's thought to Origen's and Gregory Nyssen's, and I will point out many more derivations than those already highlighted in the introductory essay. I shall also endeavor to explain every *kephalaion* in the context of Evagrius's thought. I will indicate many internal links within the *KG*, while the parallels with other works of Evagrius will be highlighted, but not in an exhaustive way. Likewise I will not systematically point out all the differences between S_1 and S_2, and the conversation with contemporary scholarship on Evagrius will be well present, as in the introductory essay, though selective.

I am most grateful to Sebastian Brock, the volume editor, whose acute observations have improved my translation, also thanks to new readings of the manuscript that correct Guillaumont's edition, and at points also my commentary. Conversations with many colleagues and friends, especially Kevin Corrigan, Monica Tobon, Mark Edwards, John McGuckin, Robin Darling Young, Charles Stang, and Julia Konstantinovsky, have definitely contributed to my thinking and rethinking about Evagrius's philosophical-theological system. I am most grateful to all of them, as well as to those who attended the many lectures I have given on Evagrius and a reassessment of his thought in Oxford, Cardiff, Bergen, New York, Aarhus, Boston, Durham, Harvard, Emory, Notre Dame, Brown, Rome, Bologna, Munich, Erlangen, Erfurt, Potsdam, Münster, Berlin, Lisbon, London, Leeds, Durham, Chicago, Detroit, Providence, and Malta and at other universities in Europe and the United States during the last decade. I am also deeply grateful to the participants in a workshop I organized at the Oxford Patristics Conference in 2011, where I first had a chance to expound my findings on Evagrius's anthropology: Mark Edwards, Panayiotis Tzamalikos, Christopher Beeley, and all those in attendance. I subsequently co-organized a workshop on theology in Evagrius, the Cappadocians, and Neoplatonism at the Oxford Patristics Conference in 2015 and wish to thank the speakers (Kevin Corrigan, Mark Edwards, Theo Kobusch, and Monica Tobon, besides myself), the respondent, Charles Stang, and the public.

Special thanks to Durham University, where as Senior Research Fellow in 2013 I continued my research into Evagrius in the context of late antique Neoplatonism, and to Jörg Rüpke and Erfurt University for hosting me as a Senior Research Fellow–Gastprofessorin at the Max Weber Centre in the years 2014 and 2015 and offering me a splendid opportunity to work intensely on Evagrius's asceticism in the context of late antique ascetic trends and their social impact. I am also indebted to the Alexander Onassis Foundation for sponsoring my Senior Visiting Professorship in Greek Thought at Harvard Divinity School, Boston University, and other US universities (2014/2015–), where I had, and am having, the opportunity to discuss fruitfully my research into Evagrius. Last but not least, I express my warm gratitude to the WGRW editors and SBL Press, as well as the copyeditor, for receiving the fruit of my long labor in their series and for the preparation of the indexes.

Evagrius Ponticus
[*Propositions on Knowledge*]*

Syriac Nonexpurgated Text (S_2)
English Translation and Commentary

* I place this title in brackets because in MS A, which contains the Syriac version S_2, the title is missing. I have chosen to translate this version because it is the fuller and original version of this work. The title is given, with slight variant readings, in MSS D, E, R, and B, which represent the Syriac version S_1, the expurgated version. The corresponding Greek title that has been handed down is Κεφάλαια Γνωστικά. The word I translate "Discourse," at the beginning of each series of ninety *kephalaia*, and Guillaumont renders "Centurie," is ܡܐܡܪܐ, which corresponds to Greek λόγος. I translate "Discourse" ("First Discourse," "Second Discourse," and so on until the sixth), but it could even be rendered "book," as is customary in ancient Greek literary works: λόγος α′ = book 1, etc. As for κεφάλαια, I prefer to translate it "propositions," at least in the title, rather than "chapters" (the traditional translation), because "propositions" is one of the attested meanings of the term (see *PGL* 748) and corresponds much better than "chapters" to Evagrius's short statements. "Chapters" makes one think of extended chapters of a book, which is not the case with Evagrius's concise and apodictic sentences. The *kephalaia* soon became a classical literary genre in monastic literature, featuring authors such as Maximus the Confessor, Simon the Neotheologian, and Gregory Palamas.

First Discourse

1.1. There is nothing that is opposed to the First Good, because it is Goodness in its very essence; now, there is nothing that is opposed to the Essence.

Evagrius's straightforward introduction, which begins here, is constructed as a sort of theorem. It is different from Origen's discursive and heuristic style in his Περὶ Ἀρχῶν, or *On First Principles*, and of course different too from his exegetical works, although the *KG* heavily relies on Scripture and is grounded in biblical exegesis, no less than Origen's *On First Principles*. The exposition, however, is dry, frequently pithy, and plain, and the chapters are often logically connected to one another with a view to producing a cogent demonstration.

Like Origen, in his first proposition ("chapter") Evagrius maintains that God is essential Good (see, e.g., Origen's *Commentary on Romans* 8.4.125–127: "The only true Good is God, and the image of God's Goodness is the Son, and his Spirit, who is called Good," *unum et uerum Bonum est Deus, cuius imago bonitatis est Filius et Spiritus eius qui dicitur bonus*); evil has no essence, no ontological subsistence, and is doomed to disappear completely in the end. Thus, in the very first chapter we immediately find an assumption that is crucial for the doctrine of *apokatastasis*, which Evagrius shares with Origen, that is, the doctrine of the final restoration of all creatures to the Good, after their purification from evil and the disappearance of evil itself in the end (see on this Ilaria L. E. Ramelli, *The Christian Doctrine of Apokatastasis: A Critical Assessment from the New Testament to Eriugena* [Leiden: Brill, 2013]).

Evagrius derives from Origen also the idea that only God is goodness in essence, while all creatures—that is, all other beings outside of God—are only good by virtue of participation in God, the Good; consequently, they may detach themselves from Good and fall into evil, that is, into nonbeing (e.g., Origen in *Commentary on Romans* 4.5.174–179: “The person who is far from God and does not participate in God is said not to exist either. This was the condition of us Gentiles before we came to recognize the divine truth, and this is why God is said to call those beings that do not exist as those that exist.… ‘Those who exist’ or ‘are’ means those who participate in the One who is,” *qui uero longe est ab eo* [*Deo*], *nec participium eius sumit, ne esse quidem dicitur, sicut eramus nos gentes priusquam ad agnitionem ueritatis diuinae ueniremus, et ideo dicitur Deus uocare ea quae non sunt tamquam quae sunt … qui sunt id est qui participationem habent eius qui est*). Of course, the idea of God as equivalent to the Good itself has its roots in Platonism, and indeed both Origen and Evagrius are Christian Platonists.

A corollary of this strong emphasis on only God being essential Good, and essential Being, seems to be, for both Origen and Evagrius, the doctrine of the *creatio ex nihilo*: it is no accident that Origen, just after claiming that those who do not participate in God and are evil do not even exist, proclaims that God created everything from nothing: God “caused all things to exist out of nothing and by virtue of his power called the things that did not exist that they might be and exist. Nothing was difficult for God in creation, to the point that, when nothing existed, all things suddenly began to exist after being called, just as though they had always been there,” *ex nihilo esse fecit uniuersa et ea quae non erant uirtute potentiae suae tamquam quae essent et subsisterent euocauit, et ita ei in creando nihil fuisse difficile ut cum nihil exsisteret omnia subito uocata ita affuisse, tamquam quae semper extiterint* (*Commentary on Romans* 4.5.185–189; see also *On First Principles* 1.3.3; 2.1.5; *Commentary on John* 1.17). On Origen’s doctrine of *creatio ex nihilo* and his arguments in support of it, see Ilaria L. E. Ramelli, “The *Dialogue of Adamantius*: A Document of Origen’s Thought? (Part One),” *StPatr* 52 (2012): 71–98; idem, “The *Dialogue of Adamantius*: A Document of Origen’s Thought? (Part Two),” *StPatr* 56 (2013): 227–73.

This *kephalaion*, in which the Godhead is declared to have nothing opposed to itself, seems to me to echo Origen’s best follower, Gregory of Nyssa, who inspired Evagrius more than is usually admitted (see the introductory essay) and in *The Life of Moses* 4 stated this very principle: “The Divine admits of nothing opposed to itself.” This principle is for Gregory the point of departure to deduce the infinity of God, which he also found in Plotinus, and which provides the main grounds for his apophatic theology and his *epektasis* doctrine: since the divinity has nothing opposed to itself, “the divine nature is unlimited and infinite.” The very same principle is notably spelled out by Augustine in a work in which Origen’s influence is very strong, *De moribus Ecclesiae Catholicae et de moribus Manichaeorum* (*On the Customs of the Catholic Church and Those of the Manichaeans*) 1.1: "If you search for God's opposite, to be precise, this is absolutely nothing. For the Being has no opposite but nonbeing. Therefore, there is no nature that is opposite to God," *Cui si contrarium recte quaeras, nihil omnino est. Esse enim contrarium non habet nisi non esse. Nulla est ergo Deo natura contraria*. Augustine too upheld the identification of God with the supreme Good: "what is supremely Good and Good per se, not by participation in some good, but by its own nature and essence; other things are good by participation only.… Evil turns out to be not according to the essence but according to privation," *Quod summe ac per se bonum est, non participatione alicuius boni, sed propria natura et essentia; aliud quod participando bonum est.… Malum ostenditur non secundum essentiam, sed secundum privationem* (ibid. 4.6). On Origen's impact on Augustine's anti-Manichaean phase and in particular in his *De moribus*—to the point that Augustine here adhered to Origen's doctrine of *apokatastasis*—see Ilaria L. E. Ramelli, "Origen and Augustine: A Paradoxical Reception," *Numen* 60 (2013): 280–307.

1.2. Opposition exists [i.e., is inherent] in mixtures; now, mixtures exist in bodies: therefore, opposition exists in creatures.

Opposition is not at the level of God but in creation. Evagrius constructs a perfect syllogism: the major premise is that opposition lies in mixtures or arrangements or textures of elements, giving rise to different qualities; the minor premise is that these mixtures lie in bodies; the conclusion one would expect is that opposition is found in bodies. But Evagrius goes one step further and concludes that opposition lies in creatures. This clearly means that "creatures" in his view are coextensive with "bodies." It is notable that Evagrius, thus, seems here to equate creatures with corporeality, which is exactly what Origen had done when he claimed that only the Holy Trinity can live without a body, whereas all creatures are found in a body—of course, different kinds of bodies: from spiritual bodies (those of the *noes* prior to their fall and after their resurrection) to the mortal and corruptible bodies of human beings in their present condition to the bodies of Satan and the demons, which Origen described as a motive of derision on the part of the angels. Evagrius is thus perfectly in line with Origen here, as is often the case—I mean with Origen's *true* thought. For it is not the case that Origen maintained that some creatures, such as the *logika* or *logikoi*—that is, rational creatures—can live without bodies at all, which is usually an assumption underlying the expression "preexistence of souls" in reference to Origen's doctrine of the condition of the *logika* before the fall. For Origen, they were not without any body, like "bare souls," but were endowed with a spiritual body that became thicker, corruptible, and mortal after the fall. See Ilaria L. E. Ramelli, "'Preexistence of Souls'? The ἀρχή and τέλος of Rational Creatures in Origen and Some Origenians," *StPatr* 56 (2013): 167–226. Further investigation into this issue in both Origen and Gregory Nyssen is underway and forthcoming.

That Evagrius, like Origen, equates creatures with corporeal beings does not mean that he, like Origen, did not postulate different levels and degrees of corporeality, from thicker and mortal to finer and immortal. As I shall show, the Syriac text even uses different words in reference to different kinds of bodies.

1.3. Every rational nature is an intelligent substance or essence. Now, our God is intelligible. It is in an indivisible way that he dwells in those in whom he dwells, like the earthly art; however, it is superior to the latter, in that God exists as a personal substance.

Evagrius is referring here to Origen's *logikoi* or *logika* or *noes*, the rational-intellectual creatures that, according to the degree of their love for God or detachment from the Good (that is, God), differentiated themselves into angels, human beings, and demons. He draws a correspondence between the intelligent nature of these creatures and the intelligible nature of God ("our" God, probably as opposed to the views of some "heretics," such as some "Gnostics," who considered God to be unintelligible, or else against some philosophers, such as the Stoics and the Epicureans, who posited material and immanent deities): these rational creatures, therefore, can understand and know God. Here no inkling is given as to whether rational creatures can understand God's essence, that is, God's very nature, or God's activities, or other aspects concerning God. "Intelligible," though, can mean two things, as Porphyry explained well in his *Commentary on Ptolemy's Harmony* 17.13–17: "'Intelligible' [*νοητόν*] means in the proper sense [*ἰδίως*] what differs in essence from sense-perceptible beings; in this sense, only incorporeal beings are intelligible [*μόνα τὰ ἀσώματα νοητά*], and in sum all things that are not bodies. Such was the definition of 'intelligible' among the ancients. In another sense [*ἑτέρως*], 'intelligible' means what can be cognized and apprehended by the intellect [*ἐφ' ὃ δύναται ἐπίστασις γενέσθαι νοῦ καὶ ἀντίληψις*]. In this sense, what is sense perceptible too will be intelligible." Therefore, when Evagrius in the present *kephalaion* claims that God in intelligible, he may mean either that God is incorporeal and immaterial, or that God is apprehensible by the intellect, or both.

A rational creature's intellection of God—on the hypothesis that "intelligible" is taken in the sense of "apprehensible by the intellect"—is described by Evagrius as God's dwelling in that creature. Only God, indeed, exists in a substantial way—that is, as already Origen maintained and as Evagrius has set out already in his first *kephalaion*, only God is the Being and the Good per se. All creatures participate in being and goodness, and thus they exist and are good, in that they participate in God. Thus, rational creatures can understand and know God in that the divinity itself dwells in them, and it does so in an indivisible way. Like the art in the artist or craftsman, so does God dwell in each of the *logika*, with the difference that God exists in a substantial or essential way, whereas the art does not. The art may rather be assimilated to the Ideas that subsist in God's Logos, that is, Christ. Unlike God (and, at an inferior level, the creatures), it is not an existing substance (*qnwm'*, a term often used in Syriac to designate the persons of the Trinity or a hypostasis as an existing substance—on the Origenian background to this notion, see Ilaria L. E. Ramelli, "Origen, Greek Philosophy, and the Birth of the Trinitarian Meaning of Hypostasis," *HTR* 105 [2012]: 302–50).

1.4. Everything that has come to existence either is susceptible of opposition or has been brought to existence from an opposition. On the other hand, not all that is susceptible of opposition is joined with those things that have been brought to existence from an opposition.

This *kephalaion* has to do with creatures and their classification, whereas God has never come to existence and is not susceptible of any opposition, as it has been already stated in 1.1.

1.5. The principles do not generate and are not generated; what is in the middle, on the contrary, does generate and is generated.

A hierarchy is shortly referred to here: what does not generate and is not generated, which is the principle, the transcendent God (the ἀρχή that is plural due to the Trinity: three ἀρχαί, as in Origen); what generates and is generated, that is, the middle causes; and what is generated without being able to generate, that is, material reality. The same definition of the first principle, God, will interestingly be given by a philosopher-theologian who was very well steeped in Christian Platonism: John the Scot Eriugena (ninth century), who knew Origen, Gregory Nyssen, Gregory Nazianzen, Pseudo-Dionysius, and Maximus the Confessor well. He describes God (qua final cause) as "the Nature that is not created and does not create," exactly as Evagrius does here. Eriugena in his *Periphyseon*, or *On Natures*, indeed lists four natures, of which the first and the last are God, first conceived as a causal principle, qua Creator of all, and finally as final cause, at the end of time:

(1) *natura creans et non creata*, "the nature that creates and is not created," that is, God as Creator;
(2) *natura creans et creata*, "the nature that creates and is created," that is, the primordial causes, parallel to the "middle" causes in Evagrius;
(3) *natura non creans et creata*, "the nature that does not create and is created," that is, material, diastematic reality;
(4) *natura non creans et non creata*, "the nature that does not create and is not created," that is, God as final cause, parallel to the principles (of the Trinity) in Evagrius.

1.6. In a comparison, we are something determinate, and one thing is what is in us, and another thing is that in which we are. But that in which we are and that in which is that in which we are, are together.

The determination of a created, diastematic being, as distinct from what surrounds it, emerges by comparison with other created beings. What surrounds us, Evagrius notes, is in turn surrounded by a superior order. In the light of the immediately following two *kephalaia* it is probable that what surrounds us, or "that in which we are," is the aeon—the temporal system of human history—which is in turn included in the eternity (ἀϊδιότης) of God: "that in which is that in which we are." This passage deals again with the classification and hierarchy of beings, at the top of which is God, who also includes everything else. This division is in fact subsumed in a superior unity, as the following *kephalaion* further clarifies.

1.7. When those who are together will be removed, the number [or "the aeon"] also will be removed. And when the latter is removed, what is

in us and that in which we must be (in the future) will be one and the same thing.

Evagrius seems here to be describing the *telos*, in which the number, that is to say, numerical differences, related to the classification and distinction of beings indicated in *KG* 1.6 will disappear. While in 1.6 Evagrius remarked upon the distinction between what is in us and what surrounds us as the determination of each created being, here he refers to the merging of what is in us and what surrounds us. His description seems to point to a deep unity in the *telos*, which was emphasized by Origen as well. One big issue is to understand what exactly this unity means. Should the disappearance of number mean the loss of individual identity? As I have pointed out in the introductory essay, it is probable that both Origen's and Evagrius's true thought meant that the final unity will be a unity of will.

This becomes still more probable if we interpret *mnyn'* as "aeon," which is another possible meaning of this noun besides "number" and "sum" ("nombre" is the rendering of Guillaumont [p. 19]; Fr. Theophanes, who translates from the French, likewise has "number"). The removal of any number is also plausible, given that it is also found in the *Letter to Melania* (provided that there too one must interpret "number"). Here, Evagrius insists on the disappearance of number and plurality in the *telos*. This is what he says in *Letter to Melania* 22–26:

> And there will be a time when the body, the soul, and the intellect will cease to be *separate* from one another, with their names and their *plurality*, since the body and the soul will be elevated to the rank of intellects; this conclusion can be drawn from the following words: "That they may be *one* in us, just as you and I are one" [John 17:22]. And thus there will be a time when *the Father, the Son, and the Spirit, and their rational creation,* which constitutes their body, *will cease to be separate, with their names and their plurality*. And this conclusion can be drawn from the words "God will be all in all" [1 Cor 15:28]. But when it is declared that the *names* and the *plurality* of rational creatures and their Creator will pass away, it does not at all mean that the hypostases and the names of the Father, the Son, and the Spirit will be obliterated. The nature of the intellect will be joined to the substance of the Father, since it constitutes his body [2 Pet 1:4]. Similarly, the names "soul" and "body" will be subsumed under the hypostases of the Son and of the Spirit. And the one and the same nature and the three persons of God, and of God's image, will remain eternally, as it was before the inhumanation, and will be after the

inhumanation, thanks to the *concord of wills* [ܝ ܨܒܝܢܐ]. Thus, body, soul, and mind are (now) *separate* in *number* due to the *differentiation of wills* [ܐܝ ܨܒܝܢܐ]. But when the names and the plurality that have attached to the intellect due to this movement [i.e., of will] have passed away, then the multiple names by which God is called will pass away as well.... It is not the case that those distinctions [i.e., God's *epinoiai*] are inexistent, but those who needed them will no more exist. But *the names and hypostases of the Son and the Spirit will never disappear*, since they have no beginning and no end.

In case one should interpret "aeon" in the present *kephalaion* rather than "number," it is illuminating to bear in mind that the disappearance of every aeon (αἰών) in the *telos* together with the attainment of perfect unity was already foreseen by Origen. In *On First Principles* 3.3.5 the latter states that there will come an end of all aeons, which will coincide with the eventual *apokatastasis*, "when all will be no more in an aeon, but God will be 'all in all'":

> If there is anything superior to the aeons ... one should think of what there will be in the final restoration or *apokatastasis*.... We shall probably understand what there will be at the end of all as superior to any aeon. I am induced to think so by the authority of Scripture, which says: "in the aeon and further" [Micah 4:5]. The fact that it says "further" lets us understand that it means something more than an aeon. And, please, consider whether the Savior's words, "I want them to be with me where I am," and "As you and I are one and the same thing, so they too may be one in us" [John 17:24, 21], may indicate something superior to the aeon and the aeons, and perhaps even to the "aeons of aeons," that is, when no longer all will be in the aeon but "God will be all in all" [1 Cor 15:28].

In the end creatures will no longer be in an aeon, and therefore in history, but will be permeated by God and participate in divine life. This will be the eventual deification (θέωσις, on which see Ramelli, *Christian Doctrine of Apokatastasis*, the chapters on Origen and Evagrius; and Augustine Casiday, "Deification in Origen, Evagrius, and Cassian," in *Origeniana VIII* [ed. Lorenzo Perrone; Leuven: Peeters, 2003], 2:995–1001). In *On First Principles* 2.3.1 too, Origen posits "a stage in which there will be no aeon anymore." In *Commentary on John* 13.3 Origen explains that "αἰώνιος life" will be life in the next aeon, in Christ, but after "αἰώνιος life" there will come the eventual *apokatastasis*, in which all will be not only in the Son but in the Father and the Holy Trinity, and God will be "all in all:" "After *αἰώνιος* life a leap will take place and all will pass from the aeons to the Father, who is *beyond αἰώνιος life*. For Christ is Life, but the Father, who is 'greater than Christ' [John 14:28], is greater than life." *Selected Passages on Psalms* 60 expresses the same idea: "When one is perfected, one sojourns through the aeons in that tabernacle [i.e., Christ, qua αἰώνιος life].... For this tabernacle is αἰώνιος. This tabernacle, to be sure, is a state of perfection, which makes it the Holy of Holies; however, there is a stage that is beyond this and superior to rational creatures. In that state, rational creatures will be in the Father and the Son, or rather in the Trinity. This is why it is said, 'to sojourn in the aeons,' and not 'to dwell stably in the tabernacle.'" That is to say, it is impossible to remain eternally in the aeons—Origen was well aware that αἰώνιος does not mean "eternal" (see Ilaria Ramelli and David Konstan, *Terms for Eternity: Aiônios and Aïdios in Classical and Christian Authors* [2nd ed.; Piscataway, N.J.: Gorgias, 2011; Logos Bible Software, 2013])—because the succession of aeons will come to an end with the eventual *apokatastasis*.

In *Homilies on Exodus* 6.13 as well Origen foresees the end of all aeons: "Whenever Scripture says, 'from aeon to aeon,' the reference is to an interval of time, and it is clear that it will have an end. And if Scripture says, 'in another aeon,' what is indicated is clearly a longer time, and yet an end is still fixed. And when the 'aeons of the aeons' are mentioned, a certain limit is again posited, perhaps unknown to us but surely established by God." When Scripture speaks of aeons, these expressions cannot refer to absolute eternity, which belongs only to God; this also entails clearly that all biblical expressions such as "αἰώνιον fire," "αἰώνιος death," or "αἰώνιος punishment" cannot be interpreted as meaning "eternal" fire, death, or punishment, because there will come an end of all αἰῶνες, when there will be the "leap" from the aeons to God. The perfection that is reached at the end of all aeons, in the eventual *apokatastasis*, is a "coming to be in God." This corresponds to Evagrius's assertion that in the *telos* what is in us and that in which we must be in the future will be one and the same thing.

Both the rendering of *mnyn'* with "number" and its rendering with "aeon" are possible. The following *kephalaion* seems to confirm that the latter translation is indeed possible, and perhaps even probable.

1.8. When that in which we must be in the future was separated, it generated that in which we are. But when that which is in us will be mixed, it will remove that which will be removed with the aeon [or "number"].

Evagrius says here that the initial unity with God, to which we must return in the end, was broken at a certain point in the past and was followed by the present aeon, that is, "that in which we are." But, as already Origen maintained, the αἰών will pass in the *telos*, at the *apokatastasis*, when no one will be found in an αἰών anymore, but God will be all in all (see the commentary on the preceding *kephalaion*). I find it possible that here *mnyn'* means "aeon" besides "number." The αἰών is the sum of all that is included in it, and it will pass away when all that is in it will be finally found rather in God, who will be "all in all" (1 Cor 15:28). At the same time, however, the aeon is also the seat of numbers, which will vanish in the unity of the *telos*. The final unity of the *telos* corresponds to the unity that there was at the beginning, as Origen also maintained (see full documentation in Ilaria L. E. Ramelli, "Origen's Doctrine of the Apokatastasis: A Reassessment," in *Origeniana Decima* [ed. H. Pietras and S. Kaczmarek; BETL 244; Leuven: Peeters, 2011], 649–70).

A corollary emerges here. For Evagrius, just as for Origen and for Gregory of Nyssa, what is normative must be discovered by considering, not the present condition, but the beginning (ἀρχή) and the end (τέλος). One of his aphorisms (PG 40:1269), number 10, precisely expresses this notion: "When you want to understand who you are, look not at what you were but at what you were made from the beginning."

1.9. When we are in that which is, we shall see that which is. When, on the other hand, (we are) in that which is not, we generate what is not. But when those in which we are will be removed, that which is not will no more exist.

God is "that which is" in the proper sense; evil is that which is not. Being in God fully is a condition appropriate to the *telos*, and it will be achieved when all are in God—the Good. As John says, "When God appears, we shall be like God, for we shall see God as God is" (1 John 3:2, which Evagrius is probably echoing here; cf. 1 Cor 13:12). Since God is the Good, to be in evil means to be in what is not, according to the ontological nonsubsistence of evil. Those who are in evil generate evil, which is not (since the condition of being in evil is typical of the present state, and not of the *telos*, I translate the relevant Syriac verbs as presents, which is perfectly possible from the grammatical point of view, rather than as futures, as is done by Guillaumont [p. 21]: "quand nous aurons été … nous engendrerons ce qui n'est pas").

In the *apokatastasis*, when the series of aeons, in which we are currently found, will be over, evil, which does not properly exist, will completely vanish. This notion, which Evagrius expresses in the last sentence of this *kephalaion*, perfectly corresponds to Origen's idea of the *apokatastasis* as the end of all aeons (see above, commentary on *KG* 1.7; see also Ilaria L. E. Ramelli, "Αἰώνιος and Αἰών in Origen and Gregory of Nyssa," *StPatr* 47 [2010]: 57–62) and the final eviction of evil, which becomes its ontological nonsubsistence (see Ilaria L. E. Ramelli, "Christian Soteriology and Christian Platonism: Origen, Gregory of Nyssa, and the Biblical and Philosophical Basis of the Doctrine of Apokatastasis," *VC* 61 [2007]: 313–56).

1.10. Among demons, there are some who oppose the fulfillment of the commandments, and others among them who oppose the acts of understanding nature, and others among them who oppose the talk/discussions about the divinity. For also the knowledge leading to our salvation is constituted by these three (aspects).

Demons oppose the three branches of knowledge: ethics ("fulfillment of the commandments"), physics ("understanding nature"), and metaphysics-theology ("discussions about the divinity"). On this tripartition, see the full treatment below, in the commentary on *KG* 1.13. I have rendered with "talk/discussions" what in Syriac (*mlt'*) corresponds to the Greek λόγοι. It might also be rendered "theories."

Since knowledge favors the salvation of rational creatures, demons try to prevent it. It is indeed typical of Evagrius, as we shall see, to join knowledge to the adhesion to the Good and therefore to virtue: if one adheres to evil and is vicious, one cannot possibly attain knowledge, and vice versa. Knowledge helps virtue, and virtue helps knowledge. This is why Evagrius states that knowledge leads to salvation, and this is also why demons want to hinder this process.

1.11. All those who now have spiritual bodies exercise their royal rule over the worlds / aeons that have come into existence, whereas those who are joined to fleshly bodies that practice the commandments or are opposed will exercise their royal rule over the worlds / aeons to come.

Angels (and probably celestial bodies) have spiritual bodies; fleshly bodies are typical of human beings and have a specific denomination, *pgr'*, different from that of spiritual bodies. From the practical, ethical point of view, these can either fulfill the commandments or the opposite (by translating "that practice the commandments," I follow the marginal addition ܕܦܘ̈ܩܕܢܐ, without which the translation would be "fleshly *praktika* bodies"; but in this case the meaning of the subsequent "are opposed" would lie in darkness). The spiritual developments of human beings may lead them to assume spiritual bodies, like those of angels, in the aeons to come. If they practice the commandments in this aeon, through the *praktikē*, they will exercise rule in the aeons to come, probably after receiving spiritual bodies. For royal rule seems to be attached only to those creatures who have a spiritual body, not to those who have a fleshly body. The relation between bodies and aeons is interestingly drawn by Evagrius in *Skemmata* 35: "An intellect in a body [νοῦς ἐνσώματος] is the spectator of all aeons [πάντων τῶν αἰώνων]." The adjective ἐνσώματος does not detail what kind of body the intellect is in: it may be either a spiritual body or a fleshly, mortal body. The distinction (also terminological in the Syriac of the *KG*) of different kinds of bodies is very important to correctly understand Evagrius's anthropology, protology, and eschatology. See Ramelli, "Preexistence of Souls." The only other scholar who has rightly insisted upon this distinction in Evagrius (albeit very shortly and without noting the Syriac terminological differentiation) is, to my knowledge, Monica Tobon, "Raising Body and Soul to the Order of the *Nous*: Anthropology and Contemplation in Evagrius," *StPatr* 57 (2013): 51–74, esp. 73:

> The perceptible and intelligible bodies are two terms of a triad, of which the spiritual body is the third. The intelligible body is the composite of perceptible body and tripartite soul and equates with the animal body, while the spiritual body is the pure *nous*: source, form and eschatological destiny of the intelligible body. The spiritual body both encompasses and transcends the intelligible body, which in turn encompasses and transcends the perceptible body. Relating this to the three resurrections, that of the body concerns only the perceptible body; that of the soul encompasses both the perceptible and intelligible bodies, while that of the *nous* is the genesis of the spiritual body.

According to her, the spiritual body (*σῶμα πνευματικόν*) is the body reabsorbed in the soul, when the soul is reabsorbed by the intellect, νοῦς. This would presuppose an identification of νοῦς and πνεῦμα.

1.12. That which is without mediation is One. And yet this One for the intermediaries is in all.

The one who is without mediation is God (the Father), who is One in the proper sense, in that the divinity is perfect unity and has no multiplicity in it. Just for this reason it is present in its wholeness in everything for the creatures who live in mediation, so that Evagrius can say that God is "in all," an idea that Gregory of Nyssa developed, by insisting that the divinity, in its power and Providence, διὰ πάντων διήκει, "extends through all." This presence of the divinity in all, which will be perfectly fulfilled in the eventual *apokatastasis* and *theōsis*, when God will be "all in all," for Clement of Alexandria and for Origen is made possible by Christ-Logos, who is, not "simply one" (ἁπλῶς ἕν, like God the Father), but ὡς πάντα ἕν, "all things as One," in that, as Logos, it contains the *logoi* of all things and subsumes this multiplicity into a superior unity. Full documentation on this in Ilaria L. E. Ramelli, "Clement's Notion of the Logos 'All Things As One': Its Alexandrian Background in Philo and Its Developments in Origen and Nyssen," in *Alexandrian Personae: Scholarly Culture and Religious Traditions in Ancient Alexandria (1st ct. BCE–4ct. CE)* (ed. Zlatko Plese; Tübingen: Mohr Siebeck, 2016). Interestingly, from another point of view, Plotinus observed that "the intelligible is everywhere as a whole" and "the many are one [τὰ πολλὰ ἕν], because the *logos* is one and many at the same time [λόγος γὰρ εἷς καὶ πολύς], and all that is, is one [πᾶν τὸ ὂν ἕν]" (*Enneads* 6.4.11.15–16).

1.13. Among the *logika* some have the spiritual contemplation and *praktikē*; others among them, on the other hand, have the *praktikē* and the contemplation; and others among them have hindrance and discernment.

The terminology is Origenian: the *logika* are rational creatures; the Syriac clearly translates Greek λογικοί. It is possible that what I have translated "hindrance" (and what Guillaumont [23] renders "entrave") may also mean "circumspection." What I have rendered "discernment" may also mean "judgment" and even "justice." Evagrius is commenting on the different spiritual endowments of rational creatures. *Praktikē* and contemplation (θεωρία) are parts of the basically threefold division of the Evagrian system, which cannot be separated from one another. In an ascending order, these are: ascetic practice, or πρακτική (broadly corresponding to ethics); natural contemplation, or φυσική (broadly corresponding to physics); and theology, or θεολογία/θεολογική. This division is put forward in *Praktikos* 1 and corresponds to Origen's division of all of philosophy in the preface to his *Commentary on the Song of Songs* 3.2–4: ethics (*ethica*), physics (*physica*), theology (*epoptica*, which deals with "the divine and heavenly things," *de divinis et caelestibus*), and logic (*logica*). Origen posits *epoptica* as the crowning of philosophy, thus regarding theology as part and parcel of philosophy and making clear that theology cannot be studied alone, without philosophical bases (see Ramelli, *Christian Doctrine of Apokatastasis*, 214). Ascetic practice, Evagrius's πρακτική, is broadly what Origen and the Cappadocians meant with "philosophical life."

Evagrius explains the goals of each part of philosophy in *Gnostikos* 49: "The object of πρακτική is to purify the intellect and render it unable to receive passions [ἀπάθεια]. The object of the knowledge of natures [i.e., φυσική] is to make known the answers that are concealed in things. But to separate human intellect from all earthly things and turn it back to the First Cause of all [i.e., God], this is the grace of θεολογία." And in *Praktikos* 84: "The end of ascetic life [i.e., πρακτική] is charity; that of knowledge [γνῶσις] is theology. The beginning in each case is faith and natural contemplation [i.e., φυσική]. The demons that fasten onto the passionate part of the soul are said to oppose ascetic life, those that disturb reason are called enemies of all truth and opponents of contemplation." The stages of *praktikē* and gnosis correspond to the person who practices ascetic virtue (*praktikos*) and that one who has gnosis (the gnostic): "The ascetic [πρακτικός] is one who is concerned solely with the achievement of impassivity (*apatheia*) in the portion of the soul that is liable to passions. The gnostic has the function of salt for the impure and light for the pure" (*Gnostikos* 2–3). Evagrius calls the perfect Christian "gnostic" just as Clement of Alexandria had done.

1.14. Each one of the arts, you see it in the person who is competent in it, whereas you find in all these things the knowledge of the One who is, since our Lord "made everything in Wisdom."

The One who is, is God, who "made everything in Wisdom" according to Ps 103:24. Since God "made everything in Wisdom," the knowledge of God is present in all things through Christ-Logos-Wisdom. This is not the case with the knowledge of a specific art, which is only present in those people who have learned that art.

Here Ps 103:24 is quoted after the LXX, whereas, interestingly, in the corresponding Syriac expurgated version (S_1) it is quoted according to the Peshitta. This ancient Syriac version, as far as the New Testament is concerned, began as a revision of the Old Syriac version (Vetus Syra, second–third century, which contained only the Gospels, and not the Old Testament) and was completed in the fifth century; the earliest of its many manuscripts stem from the fifth and sixth centuries. It soon became the official biblical translation of all the Syriac churches. It was probably propagated from Edessa, and many early manuscripts of it are equipped with the so-called Eusebian Canons. Recent scholarship on the Peshitta is very rich and continually growing. I just refer to Sebastian Brock, *The Bible in the Syriac Tradition* (Piscataway, N.J.: Gorgias, 2006), 17–18, 34–35.

Origen drew upon this verse, Ps 103:24, in order to explain the role of Christ-Logos-Wisdom in creation in *On First Principles* 1.4.5: "We claim neither that creatures are uncreated and coeternal with God, nor that God at first did not do anything good and turned to activity only later, because that famous sentence in Scripture is true: 'You have made all things in Wisdom' [Ps 103:24]. And if indeed all things have been made in Wisdom, since Wisdom has always existed, then in Wisdom there have always been—in the form of a prefiguration and preformation—those things that later on have been also created as substances," *Neque ingenitas et coaeternas Deo creaturas dicamus, neque rursus, cum nihil boni prius egerit Deus, in id ut ageret esse conversum, cum verus sit ille sermo qui scriptus est quia "Omnia in sapientia fecisti." Et si utique in Sapientia omnia facta sunt, cum Sapientia semper fuerit, secundum praefigurationem et praeformationem semper erant in Sapientia ea, quae protinus etiam substantialiter facta sunt.*

In *Commentary on John* 1.19.114–115 Origen uses the same metaphor of the project in the mind of the architect that was already used by Philo to explain the relation between the Logos and the paradigm of the world:

> A house or a ship are built according to architectonic models, so that one can say that the principle of the house or of the ship consists in the paradigms and *logoi* that are found in the craftsman. In the same way, I think, all the things were made according to the *logoi* of the future realities that God had already manifested beforehand in Wisdom. It is necessary to maintain that God founded, so to say, a living Wisdom [i.e., Christ-Logos-Wisdom] and handed it the task of transmitting the structure and forms, and, to my mind, also the substances, from the archetypes contained in it to beings and matter.

The living Wisdom of God, in which everything has been created, is Christ-Logos, who contains all the archetypal *logoi* that are the paradigms of all creation. Likewise, Origen claims in *On First Principles* 1.2.2 that the Son/Logos/Wisdom contained in itself from eternity the "principles," "reasons," and "(metaphysical) forms" of the whole creation (*initia*, *rationes*, and *species* in Rufinus's version, corresponding to ἀρχαί, λόγοι, and εἴδη). These are the Ideas in which every existing being participates. Take, for example, the Idea of Justice: Christ-Logos can be said to be Justice itself, and every being that is just is such insofar as it participates in the Idea of Justice, that is, in Christ: "Our Savior does not participate in Justice but rather is Justice itself, and all the just participate in Christ" (Origen, *Against Celsus* 6.64). This, of course, depends on the Son's own existing from eternity as well as the Father, a point that Origen strongly defended against "pre-Arian" tendencies, according to which "there was a time when (the Son) did not exist." I demonstrated elsewhere that Origen, far from being the inspirer of the "Arians," was the inspirer of the Cappadocians' Trinitarian theology and their anti-Arianism (see Ilaria L. E. Ramelli, "Gregory of Nyssa's Trinitarian Theology in *In illud: Tunc et ipse Filius*: His Polemic against 'Arian' Subordinationism and Apokatastasis," in *Gregory of Nyssa: The Minor Treatises on Trinitarian Theology and Apollinarism; Proceedings of the 11th International Colloquium on Gregory of Nyssa (Tübingen, 17–20 September 2008)* [ed. Volker Henning Drecoll and Margitta Berghaus; Leiden: Brill, 2011], 445–78). Evagrius has followed in his footsteps.

1.15. When the four are eliminated, the five too will be. But when the five are eliminated, the four will not be eliminated together with them.

A possible reference is to the four elements and the five planets, or the five senses. Their elimination refers to the end of this world. When the four elements are eliminated, and therefore matter is eliminated, then also the five senses—that is, sense perception, which is oriented toward matter—or else the five planets, will disappear. However, when sense perception is eliminated, or when the planets are eliminated, this does not mean that matter will disappear altogether. The elimination of sense perception may indeed refer to a person's physical death.

1.16. What has been separated from the five is not separated from the four, whereas what has been separated from the four is also liberated from the five.

If the identification of the four and the five that I have proposed is correct, Evagrius is saying that what has been separated from the influence of the planets is not necessarily separated from the elements constituting matter, but what has been separated from the elements, that is, from matter, is also liberated from the influence of the planets. This may refer to the end of life in this world. The alternative identification of the five with the senses, which I have also put forward, yields the following interpretation: those who have been separated from sense perception, and therefore have no longer fleshly bodies, are not separated from matter altogether, since they can have their bodies transformed into spiritual bodies (we shall soon see that this is the case for Evagrius). But what is separated from matter altogether is also necessarily separated from sense perception.

1.17. When what is in us has changed, those in which we are will also change, and this for many times, until what exists will no longer be denominated by means of modes or ways.

"Those in which we are" are very probably the aeons, denoting the historical conditions of rational creatures (see above, *KG* 1.6–8). These aeons and conditions will change, depending on the movements of the rational creatures' free will and their spiritual development, which is followed by a corporeal change as well (the change of what "is in us"), until the extinction of all aeons in the eventual *apokatastasis*, when all will be in God, and no more in a world or an aeon, and God will be all in all. (Since all in all will be God, it is clear that "means/modalities" or "ways"—two meanings of *pwrs'*, both possible in my view—will subsist no more at that stage; the meaning "limit" is also possible for *pwrs'* according to Michael Sokoloff, ed., *A Syriac Lexicon* [Winona Lake, Ind.: Eisenbrauns, 2009], 1171, meaning 7: "limit, bound." In this case it would mean that there will be no limit anymore when God is all in all, and this would be consistent with the vanishing of pluralities and numbers postulated by Evagrius in his *Letter to Melania* for the *telos*, when God is all in all.) All of this conception is entirely Origenian. See the chapter on Origen in Ramelli, *Christian Doctrine of Apokatastasis.*

1.18. The *telos* of the *praktikē* and of the torment is the heritage of the saints. Now, what is opposed to the first is the cause of the second. And the *telos* of this is the heritage of those who are opposed.

The *praktikē*, as I have mentioned, indicates moral life and development, aimed at the attainment of *apatheia* through ascetic discipline and the obedience to commandments; the torment is purifying suffering. Both ascetic discipline and torments are intended for purification, according to Evagrius just as according to Origen and Gregory of Nyssa. The *telos* will coincide with full spiritual development and, as a consequence, the end of all torments, since purification will have come to an end. What is opposed to moral and spiritual development is clearly the cause of purifying sufferings, which will end in the *telos*. All of this conception is in line with Origen's ideas.

1.19. The knowledge that is in the four is the knowledge of the intellections of creatures, but the knowledge of the One is the knowledge of that one who only is.

God is the only one who IS in the proper sense. The knowledge of God is here differentiated from that of creatures. God is characterized by unity and is for Evagrius, just as for Origen, the only completely nonmaterial being; creatures are characterized by multiplicity and matter (the four elements). The knowledge of material entities is the knowledge of the intellections, or *νοήματα*, of creatures, which are material, whereas the knowledge of God, the One, who is entirely immaterial, is the knowledge of the Being—strictly speaking, the only true Being. Intellections—in Greek, *νοήσεις*—are acts of knowledge by intuition of the intellect; intellections as the content of these intuitions are, in Greek, *νοήματα*. In Gregory of Nyssa, who is more and more emerging as an important inspirer of Evagrius, there are intellections located in Christ-Logos, which also functioned as the intelligible paradigms of the world in the creation. Gregory in *On Perfection* 260B describes Christ-Logos-Wisdom as the seat of all *νοήματα*, intellections, of realities before the creation of the world, in a fashion that closely reminds one of Origen. Through God's *dynamis*—who is again Christ-Logos, as *dynamis* was one of the *epinoiai* of Christ already in Origen—these intellections became creatures, works of God: *ἔργα τὰ νοήματα γίνεται*. Origen had said that they became substances, *οὐσίαι*, in his *Commentary on John* 1.19.114–115. The causes of all things are their *logoi* in the mind of God, or their intellections. Like Evagrius, Origen was clear that an important part of beatitude itself will be the knowledge of these causes. In the next life, Origen maintains, rational creatures will grow intellectually, "because the mind, empowered in its intellect and sensibility, and having achieved perfection, reaches perfect knowledge, without being prevented anymore by the senses of the flesh, but boosted by the senses of the intellect: it discerns clearly and, so to say, face to face the causes/principles of all things.... Its food is knowledge and the understanding of all things and their causes. ... We believe that this food is the contemplation and knowledge of God" (*On First Principles* 1.1.7). Origen telescopes the knowledge of the causes or principles of all things and the knowledge of God because the causes, or *logoi*, of all things are and were in the mind of God.

According to Evagrius, there can be intellections of both sense-perceptible and intellectual realities. In *Chapters of the Disciples of Evagrius* 77 the kind of transforming action of νοήματα on the intellect is made clear: "The intellect can receive only νοήματα, and it assumes the form of each νόημα, as the eye does when it sees itself in mirrors." In prayer, however, all intellections must be put aside, according to Evagrius. His very definition of prayer as "the setting aside of intellections" (ἀπόθεσις νοημάτων; *On Prayer* 71) makes this clear.

This νόησις, or intellectual intuition, is the highest form of knowledge in the progression of kinds of knowledge postulated by Plato (*Republic* 509E–511E):

1. εἰκασία	2. πίστις	3. διάνοια	4. νόησις
imagination	belief	discursive reason	intellectual intuition
1–2. δόξα		3–4. ἐπιστήμη, γνῶσις	
opinion		science, knowledge	

1.20. When only the intellections of all those things that have come to existence by accident will remain in us, then only the One who is known will be known, only he, by the subject who knows.

Evagrius is referring again to the final state of perfection: when all that has come into existence by accident—such as human mortality and all that it entails—has disappeared, only the relevant intellections will remain in us. God, to the contrary, will not disappear but only *is* in the proper sense, and is *known*. God, and the knowledge of God, will never pass away and will exist in the *telos*. In the *telos*, rational creatures will know only God primarily and will know everything in God. This is Evagrius's gnoseological interpretation of 1 Cor 15:28, "God will be all in all," a passage largely deployed by Origen too, in reference to the *apokatastasis*. Just as God will be all goods for each rational creature (according to Origen's and Gregory of Nyssa's interpretation of this passage; see Ramelli, "Christian Soteriology and Christian Platonism"), so will God be the one object of knowledge of all rational creatures, and this one object will subsume in itself all possible objects of knowledge, just as God, the Good itself, subsumes all possible goods. See Ramelli, "Clement's Notion of the Logos," where I extensively argue that this notion in Origen and Nyssen derives from the idea of Christ-Logos *ὡς πάντα ἕν*, already deployed by Clement of Alexandria.

1.21. Goods and evil, those which are considered to be without necessity, some of them are found inside the soul, and others among them outside it. But those which are said to be evils by nature, it is impossible that they come into existence outside it.

Evil by nature, in its proper sense, is sin, which can originate and be found only in a soul, since it is the product of one's wrong will. In its proper sense, evil does not even exist outside the soul's wrong choices, and therefore it is considered by Origen and Evagrius to have no ontological subsistence. See Georgios Lekkas, *Liberté et progrès chez Origène* (Turnhout: Brepols, 2001); Henryk Pietras, "L'apocrifo giudaico *Preghiera di Giuseppe* nell'interpretazione origeniana," in Pietras and Kaczmarek, *Origeniana Decima*, 545–60; and the chapter on Origen in Ramelli, *Christian Doctrine of Apokatastasis.*

1.22. Demons' bodies do have a color and a shape, but they escape our sense perception, in that their admixture (arrangement) is not similar to the admixture (arrangement) of the bodies that fall under our senses. Indeed, whenever they want to appear to human beings, they turn themselves into a complete resemblance of our body, without showing us their own bodies.

Demons are not incorporeal in an absolute sense, but, like angels, they possess bodies; these, however, cannot be perceived by human beings. To indicate the body of a demon, the Syriac here has *gwšm'*, which is different from *pgr'*, the technical word that designates the fleshly body of a human being in the present condition, after the fall. *Pgr'* is the word that here indicates, not demons' bodies, but the bodies that fall under human sense perception. Demonic bodies are not fleshly; they have a texture, an admixture, or an arrangement of elements that is different from that of sense-perceptible bodies, but, according to Origen, they are also very different from angels' spiritual and luminous bodies: they are such as to arouse the laughter of the angels. See Henryk Pietras, "L'inizio del mondo materiale e l'elezione divina in Origene," in *Origeniana Nona* (ed. G. Heidl and R. Somos; Leuven: Peeters, 2009), 653–68. In Evagrius's view, the bodies of angels are fiery, those of humans are earthy, and those of demons are made of pneuma. See Columba Stewart, "Imageless Prayer and the Theological Vision of Evagrius Ponticus," *JECS* 9 (2001): 173–204, esp. 176. Basil in his *Commentary on Isaiah* (which is likely to be authentic) 2.20 admits that demons are incorporeal (ἀσώματοι), but due to a lack of ardent love of God (θείῳ πόθῳ)—the same cause as Origen indicated for the fall—they have in a way become incarnated or fleshly: οἱονεὶ ἀπεσαρκώθησαν, because "they have corrupted themselves with the desire of material things." On demons and their bodies in Origen and the Cappadocians, see also Gregory Smith, "How Thin Is a Demon?" *JECS* 16 (2008): 479–512; Morwenna Ludlow, "Demons, Evil and Liminality in Cappadocian Theology," *JECS* 20 (2012): 179–211; Travis Proctor, "Daemonic Trickery, Platonic Mimicry," *VC* 68 (2014): 416–49.

1.23. The intellections of those realities that are on earth are "the goods of the earth." Now, if the holy angels know them, according to the word of the woman of Tekoa, the angels of God eat the goods of the earth. On the other hand, it is said that "the human being ate the bread of the angels." Therefore, it is clear that some among human beings too know the Ideas of what is on earth.

The intellections are the acts of intellectual knowledge; their objects are the Ideas of the relevant realities (sometimes, like here, the same word in Syriac translates both "intellection" and "Idea"; I capitalize "Idea" because it is taken in a Platonic sense, of course also in the light of the developments of Middle Platonism and Neoplatonism). Evagrius interprets the goods of the earth as the knowledge of the realities that are on earth, and he draws a parallel between "eating" those goods and "knowing" them. This knowledge belongs to angels and some human beings.

The biblical references are respectively to 2 Kgs 14:20 (cf. 14:1–3) and Ps 77:25. Here, as in many other passages both in the *KG* and elsewhere, it is clear that Evagrius, like Origen, applied an allegorical exegesis to Scripture. Indeed, in scholium 15 on Ps 76:21 Evagrius claims that Scripture, besides a literal-historical meaning, also has an ethical meaning, a physical meaning (that is, related to the contemplation of nature), and a theological meaning. Evagrius, like Origen, is convinced that the spiritual meanings of Scripture are concealed to those who are not purified and advanced. Even demons can read Scripture, but without understanding it (*KG* 6.37). In *Gnostikos* 34 Evagrius warns: "You must not interpret spiritually everything that lends itself to allegory, but rather only that which is fitting to the subject; because if you do not act thus, you pass much time on Jonas' boat, explaining every part of its equipment. And you will be humorous to your listeners, rather than useful to them: all of these sitting around you will remind you of this or that equipment, and by laughing [they] will remind you of what you have forgotten" (trans. Dysinger).

The bread of the angels, thus, in the present *kephalaion* is considered to refer not only to manna but also to the knowledge of realities on earth, the "goods of the earth." Indeed, also from his numerous scholia from many passages of Scripture it is clear that Evagrius privileged allegorical and spiritual exegesis, and generally a Christocentric exegesis. Moreover, like Origen, Evagrius, especially in his scholia on Job, demonstrates an attention for the philological establishment of the text, to be sought also through a comparison between the Septuagint and other versions.

1.24. If the wheat ear is in the seed in potency, perfection too is found, in potency, in the person who is susceptible of it. Now, if this is the case, the wheat seed and what is in it are not the same thing, nor the wheat ear and what is in the seed; but the seed of what is included by the ear and the ear of this seed are indeed the same thing. And, indeed, even though the seed becomes an ear, the seed of what is in the ear has not yet received the ear. But when it is liberated from the ear and from the seed, it will have the ear of that first seed.

Of course, Evagrius is here drawing on Paul's assimilation of the bodies of human beings to seeds and crops in 1 Cor 15, a passage on which Gregory of Nyssa also heavily drew in his dialogue *On the Soul and the Resurrection* (*De Anima et Resurrectione*). The seed is the human mortal body, which returns to the earth and dies; the ear is the resurrected body, which comes from the seed, that is, from the death of the mortal body. The risen body is still liable to purifying punishment in the other world if this is needed (Gregory in the aforementioned dialogue even allegorized this purification by means of the imagery of God as the farmer who takes care of the wheat plants in the ways they need, including the most drastic ways—and I have shown in the introduction that this metaphor used by Gregory at the end of his dialogue *On the Soul and the Resurrection* was taken over by Evagrius at the end of his *Letter to Melania*, in a similar eschatological context). Once this purification has taken place, every rational creature will have back its initial ear, planned by God. This represents the incorruptible, glorious, and luminous spiritual body that characterized the *logika* before the fall and will characterize them in the eventual *apokatastasis*.

1.25. Those who want to "sift" us with temptations either examine the intellectual faculty of the soul or endeavor to seize the part that is liable to passions in it, or the (fleshly) body, or what surrounds the body.

The action described here refers to evil angels, that is, demons, who tempt human beings (with a very probable reference to sifting in Luke 22:31, in which the subject of this action is Satan, who wants to tempt Simon Peter—and indeed he did so, when Peter betrayed Jesus thrice; this is Jesus's prediction in Luke 22:31–32: "Simon, Simon, behold, Satan demanded to have you, that he might sift you like wheat, but I have prayed for you that your faith may not fail; and when you have turned again, strengthen your brethren"). Manuscript E, one of the testimonies of the expurgated version (S_1), which for *KG* 1.25 is practically identical to the nonexpurgated version (S_2), in a marginal gloss reads indeed ܡܠܐܟܐ, "angels," meaning evil angels. According to Origen, evil angels can tempt human beings but cannot determine their will, which remains free in any case. See full analysis in Ilaria L. E. Ramelli, "La coerenza della soteriologia origeniana: Dalla polemica contro il determinismo gnostico all'universale restaurazione escatologica," in *Pagani e cristiani alla ricerca della salvezza: Atti del XXXIV Incontro di Studiosi dell'Antichità Cristiana, Roma, Istituto Patristico Augustinianum, 5–7 maggio 2005* (SEAug 96; Rome: Augustinianum, 2006), 661–88. Likewise Evagrius thought that a human being's free will can resist demons, especially by means of virtues, which are acquired through *praktikē*: "Virtues do not prevent demons' assaults, but they keep us safe and unharmed" from those assaults (Αἱ ἀρεταὶ οὐ τὰς τῶν δαιμόνων ὁρμὰς ἀνακόπτουσιν, ἀλλ' ἡμᾶς ἀθῴους διαφυλάττουσιν; *Praktikos* 77). The tempting action of demons on human beings is illustrated by Evagrius also in the prologue to his *Antirrheticus* (*On Talking Back*) 1: "From the rational nature that is under heaven, part of it fights; part assists the one who fights; and part contends with the one who fights, strenuously rising up and making war against him. The fighters are human beings; those assisting them are God's angels; and their opponents are evil demons" (trans. Brakke, slightly modified).

The intellectual soul is opposed both to the inferior faculties of the soul, which are liable to passions, and to the body. These are the three components of the human being: body, inferior soul, and intellectual soul, or intellect. The latter is the main and noblest faculty of the soul. This is the case in most of the Platonic tradition—for example, in Numenius, Plotinus, and Porphyry. Porphyry maintained that the soul is essentially an intellect (*Against Boethus* 243 F.13; 245 F.16) and throughout his *Against Boethus* argued that the *nous* is the core component of the human being, which makes it similar to God. This view was certainly shared by Platonizing thinkers such as Philo and Origen. This is also why Porphyry claimed that the perfection of the human being qua human being consists in voluntary actions, but the perfection of the human being as a divine being and intellect consists in contemplation (Evagrius's θεωρία)—and added that the latter perfection is superior to the former (fr. 165 F [i] Smith). According to Porphyry, only the intellect (νοῦς) and the intellectual reason (νοερὸς λόγος), or the *logos* with its thoughts or Ideas as thoughts of the intellect, are incorporeal entities that subsist separately from any body (*Sentences Leading to the Intelligible* 42).

1.26. If the human mortal body is a part of this world/aeon, and if, on the other hand, "the form of this world will pass," it is clear that the form of the mortal body also will pass.

Evagrius in this syllogism—including a major and a minor premise and a conclusion—is speaking of the fleshly and mortal body (which the Syriac translator indeed calls *pgr'* and not *gwšm'*) that characterizes human beings in the present world, after the fall. This body will pass when the form or shape (Syriac *'skm'* is a transposition of Greek σχῆμα) of this world, or the series of aeons, will pass (which is a quotation from Paul, 1 Cor 7:31), but this does not mean in the least that Evagrius envisages an eschatological condition in which the *logika* will be without bodies. They will have spiritual, incorruptible, and glorious bodies, as they had before the fall. Bodies will be elevated to the rank of souls, and souls to that of intellects, and thus will become spiritual. It is very probable that Evagrius, like Origen, maintained that all creatures have a body, of course in different degrees of fineness and spirituality; only the Holy Trinity can live in an absolutely immaterial condition (see Ramelli, "Preexistence of Souls"). Indeed, it is not the body itself but the shape of this mortal body that is said to pass.

1.27. The main contemplations are five, under which all contemplation is comprised. And they say that the first is the contemplation of the adorable and holy Trinity, and that the second and the third are the contemplation of the incorporeal and the corporeal realities, and that the fourth and the fifth are the contemplation of the Judgment and of Providence.

Julia Konstantinovsky (*Evagrius Ponticus: The Making of a Gnostic* [Burlington, Vt.: Ashgate, 2009], 48) maintains that these five contemplations are arranged in a hierarchical order, from the highest to the lowest levels. Now, it is certainly the case that the θεωρία of the Trinity is the highest; however, it is not clear that the contemplation of Providence, for instance, is lower that that of the Judgment or that of bodies. What I suspect is that Evagrius is following a "historical" order, starting from God, who is the principle of all, passing on to the creation of intelligent beings, and then of material bodies, until the judgments that close every aeon, the last Judgment, which will conclude all aeons, and God's providence, which accompanies creatures during all aeons and which will overcome in the end, at the eventual *apokatastasis* after all aeons and all judgments.

The Holy Trinity comes before anything else, both from the chronological and from the metaphysical point of view, since the Trinity is prior to all creatures. Then comes the contemplation of all realities, both corporeal (all creatures: for the word is not *pgr'* here but *gwšm'*, which includes the bodies of angels, demons, and resurrected humans as well) and incorporeal (Ideas; souls, which are not complete creatures by themselves—it is to be noted that "incorporeal" is used by Evagrius, just as by Origen, sometimes in an absolute sense, referring to a complete absence of any kind of body; sometimes in a relative sense, in reference to bodies that are much lighter and more rarefied and "spiritual" than human mortal bodies are). That the first contemplation or knowledge is that of the Trinity and the second is that of creatures is a notion that comes directly from Origen, *Commentary on the Song of Songs* 2.5.20: "The first task or degree of knowledge is to know and acknowledge the Trinity; the second is to know its creatures," *principale munus scientiae est agnoscere Trinitatem, secundo vero in loco cognoscere creaturam eius.*

After the first two contemplations, the contemplation of the last Judgment is not the last word: after the Judgment and its consequences, including rewards and purifying sufferings, the final contemplation is that of God's providence, which, in Evagrius, just as in Origen, is directed to the *apokatastasis*. Origen, while speaking of the eventual *apokatastasis*, states: "Providence acts in favor of each one, and at the same time it respects each one's free will" (*On First Principles* 3.5.8). A person's free choices invariably have their consequences, and the Judgment will bear precisely upon these free choices and will bring on the relevant consequences (the retributive nature of Judgment is stated by Evagrius also in *KG* 6.57). But this is only one side of the story; for Providence never abandons anyone, and, after due retribution, it will lead all to the *telos*, the end and perfect accomplishment wanted and prepared by God. The respective effects of divine judgment and divine providence are explained in *Gnostikos* 48 by Evagrius, who traces this doctrine back to Didymus of Alexandria (so that its genealogy is clearly Origenian): "Exercise yourself continuously in the *logoi* of Providence and judgment—said the great Knower and teacher Didymus—and strive to bear in your memory their material [expressions]: for nearly all are brought to stumbling through this. And you will discover the *logoi* of judgment in the diversity of bodies and worlds, and those of Providence in the means by which we return from vice and ignorance to virtue or to knowledge" (trans. Dysinger). On these *logoi* of Providence and Judgment, see Luke Dysinger, *Psalmody and Prayer in the Writings of Evagrius Ponticus* (Oxford: Oxford University Press, 2005), 171–95. Before Origen, an important treatment of divine providence, probably known to Evagrius albeit lost to us, was offered by Clement of Alexandria in his *On Providence* (Περὶ προνοίας). The treatise is now extant only in scanty fragments, but Clement's ideas on divine providence can still be gleaned from these and from his *Miscellany.* See Silke-Petra Bergjan, "Clement of Alexandria on God's Providence and the Gnostic's Life Choice: The Concept of *Pronoia* in the *Stromateis*, Book VII," in *The Seventh Book of the Stromateis* (ed. Matyas Havrda, Vit Husek, and Jana Platova; Leiden: Brill, 2012), 63–92.

The double action of Providence for the sake of all rational creatures is explained by Evagrius in *KG* 6.59 (see below).

1.28. Among an abundance of ways, the ways that lead to salvation are three, namely, those that have in common the destruction of sins. Now, two of them have as a property the capacity to deliver from passions, whereas the virtue of the third is that it will also be a cause of glory. Indeed, glory follows the one, and psalmody the other one, and exaltation again the other one.

The elimination of sins brings about salvation. Evagrius here is alluding to three different ways to attain salvation, although he does not explicitly mention them; he presupposes that his readers know them from his teachings. All of these ways to salvation necessarily have in common the destruction of sin, since salvation is incompatible with sin. Delivering from passions is the task of the *praktikē*: moral effort and ascesis. See *KG* 1.10, on the three ways of knowledge leading to salvation; 1.13; 1.18; and 1.25 on the ways in which demons try to hinder human salvation.

1.29. Just as colors, shapes, and numbers pass away together with mortal bodies, likewise matter also is eliminated together with the four elements. For it is with them that matter has the following characteristic: that it did not exist and it came into existence.

Evagrius is speaking not of the elimination of bodies tout court but only of mortal bodies (the specific meaning of Syriac *pgr'*). Matter is made of the four elements (the Syriac is the transliteration of Greek στοιχεῖα; it is the same word that was also used by Bardaisan of Edessa for his "pre-existing beings," which are nevertheless creatures of God; see Ilaria L. E. Ramelli, *Bardaisan of Edessa: A Reassessment of the Evidence and a New Interpretation* [Eastern Christian Studies 22; Piscataway, N.J.: Gorgias, 2009]). Matter, constituted by the four elements (see above, *KG* 1.15, 16, and 19), according to Evagrius was created by God and began to exist at a certain point, just as Origen too maintained, who countered the "pagan" notion of the coeternity of matter with God (see Ramelli, "*Dialogue of Adamantius*" [parts 1 and 2]). Matter did not exist, and then it came into existence, just as all creatures came into existence at a certain moment. And indeed all creatures seem to be considered by Evagrius, as by Origen, to be material, at least to a certain extent; only God is absolutely immaterial and uncreated. Evagrius proclaims the absolute immateriality of God, for example, in *On Prayer* 66–67.

1.30. Only fire is different from among the four elements because of what is alive in it.

According to a philosophical-cosmological tradition that goes back to Stoicism, fire has a special status among the elements. In Stoicism, fire-ether was the only element that was thought to endure at the end of each cosmic cycle; it was the element in which the supreme divinity, Zeus, was considered to contract itself and from which then it expanded again to produce a new cosmos (see Ilaria L. E. Ramelli, *Allegoria, 1: L'età classica* [Milan: Vita e Pensiero, 2004], ch. 2). Evagrius describes the peculiarity of fire as its "being alive." Fire has something living in it. This characteristic can make it somehow closer to God, whom Origen too assimilated to fire (e.g., in *On First Principles* 2.6.6: "That soul which, like iron in fire, always stays in the Logos, always in Wisdom, always in God, well, all that it does, feels, and understands is God. Therefore, we cannot describe as liable to change and alteration the soul that, continuously inflamed by the union with the divine Logos, has come to possess immutability").

1.31. Just as Israel is among the human beings, and the land of Judah among the lands, and Jerusalem among the cities, likewise also the goal of the symbols of the intellections/Ideas is the part of the Lord.

After singling out fire among the elements in *KG* 1.30, here Evagrius singles out a people, a land, and a city as chosen by God. The "part of the Lord" (Deut 32:9) is the portion of something that the divinity has reserved for itself. So is the symbolic-allegorical meaning of the intellections, probably vis-à-vis the literal or more immediate meaning. This is also clarified by the following *kephalaion* (*KG* 1.32), which draws a distinction between the ordinary understanding of things and their spiritual understanding.

1.32. The human beings who have seen something among what is in the natures have only caught the common sight of those natures. For only the just have received the spiritual knowledge of them. He who argues about this resembles one who says: "I was together with Abraham, when he walked on the road with his two wives." The word of this person is true, but he has not perceived the two covenants and has not understood (who are) those who are born from them.

One can know things only by seeing them, or can gain a spiritual knowledge of them, which is the spiritual or symbolic understanding that is referred to in the previous *kephalaion* (1.31). Now Evagrius explains that this spiritual insight is typical of the just only. Here Evagrius's ideal of interpenetration of virtue and knowledge surfaces again: they cannot be disjoined from one another; one cannot be unjust and immoral and nevertheless receive knowledge. This interconnectedness appears everywhere in the *KG* and in other works of Evagrius, for instance, also in his *Scholia on Ecclesiastes*: "It is not things themselves [πράγματα] that are good but the *logoi* of things, by which the rational nature is gladdened naturally and does good; for nothing feeds and waters the intellect like virtue [ἀρετή] and knowledge of God [γνῶσις θεοῦ]" (scholium 15,22–25 on Eccl 3:10–13). Clement of Alexandria and Origen were adamant that virtue and knowledge, especially knowledge of God, go hand in hand and cannot subsist without one another (for this interrelation in Clement, see George Karamanolis, "Clement on Superstition and Religious Belief," in Havrda et al., *Seventh Book of the Stromateis*, 113–30, esp. 117–18). This concept was rooted already in Plato's ethical intellectualism.

The scriptural reference is to Gen 16–17 and Gal 4:22–31. It is Paul who, in the latter passage, discloses the spiritual meaning of Hagar and Sarah, Abraham's two wives. There are some—Evagrius notes—who limit themselves to the literal meaning of this passage, whereas the "just" also grasp its spiritual (allegorical-typological) meaning and see that Hagar and Sarah represent the two covenants.

1.33. Just as each one of the arts needs an acute sense perception appropriate to its own matter, likewise the intellect too needs a spiritual sense, in order to discern spiritual realities.

Evagrius goes on with the discourse that he was developing in the previous *kephalaia*, that is, the differentiation between the immediate sense perception, with the relevant understanding of things, and a deeper perception, which is related to spiritual senses and brings about the spiritual understanding of things. Spiritual senses belong not to the sphere of sense perception but rather to that of the intellect (νοῦς). The theory of spiritual senses, already present in Philo of Alexandria (thanks to his doctrine concerning the "inner human being"), was developed especially by Origen, on whose thought Evagrius heavily, although certainly not slavishly, depends. See Pietro Meloni, *Il profumo dell'immortalità: L'interpretazione patristica di Cantico, 1, 3* (Rome: Edizioni Studium, 1975); and Ilaria L. E. Ramelli, "Philosophical Allegoresis of Scripture in Philo and Its Legacy in Gregory of Nyssa," *SPhilo* 20 (2008): 55–99.

1.34. Sense perception is so constituted as to perceive by itself sense-perceptible realities, whereas the intellect all the time rises up and awaits which spiritual vision will offer itself to it in contemplation.

This is yet another *kephalaion* concerning the difference between physical and spiritual senses, the latter belonging to the intellect (the highest faculty of the soul). Here attention is drawn to the difference between senses and intellect (or physical and spiritual senses) in the process of perception: sense perception perceives material objects by itself, whereas the intellect is declared to perceive spiritual objects as they appear to it in a vision, by offering themselves to it. Spiritual perception, in other words, is contemplation. By implication, it would seem that Evagrius emphasizes here the somewhat passive role of the intellect in contemplation; on the other hand, in *KG* 1.37 Evagrius will explain that this state of the intellect is not passive in the sense that the intellect is invaded by *pathē* or passions but is rather a state of impassivity, or *apatheia.*

1.35. Just as the light, while it allows us to see everything, does not need a light in order to be seen (thanks to it), likewise God, while he makes everything manifest, does not need a light in order to be known in it; for he is Light in his very essence.

Evagrius continues to expound his gnoseological teachings. Here the difference is no more between sense perception and intellectual knowledge but between human sensible vision and knowledge of God. The key element in both cases is light, in the former case physical light, in the latter the spiritual Light that is God. The Godhead needs no illumination in order to know or to be known, because it is Light itself (with a reference to 1 John 1:5: "God is light and in him is no darkness at all," RSV) and rather makes all knowledge possible. The doctrine of knowledge as divine illumination will acquire a prominent status in medieval gnoseology, especially with St. Bonaventura, or Bonaventure. A key text for this so-called theology of light is James 1:17: "Every good endowment and every perfect gift is from above [*sursum*], coming down from the Father of lights [*Pater luminum*] with whom there is no variation or shadow due to change" (RSV). Evagrius also seems to have drawn on the concept of light as a wisdom metaphor in the Old Testament (on which see Horacio Simian-Yofre, "La luce, metafora sapienziale nell'AT," in *Greeks, Jews, and Christians: Historical, Religious, and Philological Studies in Honor of Jesús Peláez del Rosal* [ed. Lautaro Roig Lanzillotta and Israel Muñoz Gallarte; EFN 10; Córdova: Ediciones El Almendro, 2013], 49–66).

1.36. Sense perception and the organ of sense are not the same thing, nor are the subject endowed with sense perception and the sense-per-

ceptible object. Indeed, sense perception is the faculty thanks to which we are in the habit of perceiving material objects; the organ of sense is that in which sense perception dwells; on the other hand, the subject endowed with sense perception is the living being who possesses the senses, whereas the sense-perceptible object is that which falls under the senses. But the intellect is not like this; for it is deprived of one among these four.

The difference between physical and spiritual senses is again at stake here. Evagrius is explaining the reason for this difference and finds it in the fact that one of the four factors that he lists as involved in sense perception is lacking in the case of the intellect. The four factors involved in sense perception are: (1) sense perception itself, that is, the faculty thanks to which humans perceive material objects; (2) the physical organ of sense, such as the eye, the ear, and so forth, in which sense perception dwells; (3) the perceiving subject, endowed with sense perception; (4) the sense-perceptible object, which is perceived by the senses. In the case of intellectual knowledge, one of these factors, probably (2), is lacking, and we have only intellectual intellection, the intelligent subject, and the intelligible object.

1.37. Spiritual sense perception is the impassivity of the rational soul, which is effected by the grace of God.

Evagrius opposes physical sense perception, which is a *pathos* depending on impressions, and intellectual knowledge, which is not a *pathos* but a state of impassivity, or *apatheia*, of the *nous*, or the intellectual or rational faculty in the soul. Evagrius seems to suggest that this state is not natural but is produced by divine grace. *Apatheia* is primarily for Evagrius the goal of *praktikē*, eradicating passions that besiege the inferior faculties of the soul (concupiscible or appetitive, and irascible). The link between asceticism (*praktikē*) and *apatheia*, as well as knowledge, is clear in a number of passages from Evagrius's works, such as *Skemmata* 16: "The ascetic intellect [νοῦς πρακτικός] is the one that always receives the intellections [νοήματα] in a manner free of the passions [ἀπαθῶς] of this world." In *Praktikos* 67 Evagrius explains that the soul possesses *apatheia* not when it is not affected (πάσχουσα) by things but rather when it remains untroubled (ἀτάραχος) by things, and even by their memories. The impassive person is for Evagrius, as for the Stoics, a serene person and not a stone (see Margaret Graver, *Stoicism and Emotion* [Chicago: University of Chicago Press,

2007], who stresses that the Stoic ideal of *apatheia* entailed not the absence of all emotions but only the absence of negative ones, *pathē*, which trouble the soul, whereas *eupatheiai* were not only admitted but also encouraged and regarded positively; cf. Ilaria L. E. Ramelli, *Stoici romani minori* [Milan: Bompiani, 2008]). Indeed Evagrius associates *apatheia* with the inferior faculties of the soul (as in *Gnostikos* 2), with the soul in general (as in *KG* 1.81; see below), with the heart, and with the intellect, or the rational faculty of the soul (as here in *KG* 1.37). Clement of Alexandria, on whose ideas Evagrius relies in several respects—from the definition of prayer as conversation with God to the ideal of the "gnostic"—insisted that *apatheia* is a characteristic of the perfect Christian or "gnostic" (*Miscellany* 7.84.2; cf. 7.13.3). Indeed, like Philo, Clement maintained that a lesser degree of perfection is characterized by *metropatheia*, or moderation of passions, but the highest degree by *apatheia*, or eradication of passions. On Clement's doctrine of *apatheia*, with an overview of previous scholarship, see Judith Kovacs, "Saint Paul as Apostle of *Apatheia*," in Havrda et al., *Seventh Book of the Stromateis*, 199–216.

Apatheia was an ethical ideal for Stoicism and a good part of the Platonic tradition as well. Porphyry, for example, in *Sentences Leading to the Intelligible* 7, states that the soul is joined to the body when it converts to the passions that originate from the body, but *apatheia* frees the soul. Note, however, that in this *kephalaion* Evagrius is speaking of the *apatheia* of the rational soul, the subject of knowledge, and not of the inferior faculties of the soul. The same is to be found in the third of his *Skemmata*: "Impassivity is the tranquil state of the rational soul, which consists in mildness and temperance" (ἀπάθειά ἐστι κατάστασις ἠρεμαῖα ψυχῆς λογικῆς ἐκ πραΰτητος καὶ σωφροσύνης συνισταμένη), where mildness is the impassive state of the irascible faculty, and temperance, the impassive state of the concupiscible/appetitive faculty. Evagrius is also clear that *apatheia* is coextensive with charity-love (*Eulogius* 21.23, where love is described as "the elimination of passions") or is the antechamber of charity-love (ἀγάπη): "These are the words that the fathers always say: 'Faith, O child, is steadied by the fear of God, and this in turn by continence. The latter is made unshakable by patient endurance and hope: from these is born *apatheia*, which brings about charity-love. Now, love is the door to knowledge of nature, which leads to theology and the supreme blessedness" (*Letter to Anatolius* 8). So Evagrius delineates an ascending path from faith to *apatheia* to love to gnosis, the highest peak of which is the knowledge of God. (See Monica Tobon, *Apatheia in the Teachings of Evagrius Ponticus: The Health of the Soul* [Burlington, Vt.: Ashgate, forthcoming]; and Robert Somos, "Origen, Evagrius Ponticus and the Ideal of Impassibility," in *Origeniana Septima: Origenes in den Auseinandersetzungen des 4. Jahrhunderts* [ed. Wolfgang Bienert and Uwe Kühneweg; Leuven: Peeters, 1999], 365–73). The same progression, from faith to charity-love to knowledge, is delineated, more briefly, in *Sententiae ad monachos* (*Sentences to the Monks*) 3: "Faith [πίστις] is the principle/beginning of charity-love [ἀγάπη], and the end/aim of charity-love is the knowledge of God [γνῶσις Θεοῦ]."

1.38. Just as, when we are awake, we say this and that concerning sleep, but then, when we are asleep, we come to know them by experience, likewise of all those things that we hear regarding God when we are apart from God, we shall have the demonstration by experience when we are in God.

Evagrius belongs to a line of Greek theology that was very aware of the limits of human knowledge of God; this line goes back to Origen, who was in turn inspired by Philo (see Ilaria L. E. Ramelli, "The Divine as an Inaccessible Epistemological Object in Ancient Jewish, 'Pagan,' and Christian Platonists: A Common Cognitive Pattern across Different Religion Traditions," *JHI* 75 [2014]: 167–88) and has Gregory of Nyssa as one of its main exponents. Evagrius stresses here that our knowledge of God is very pale in comparison with the knowledge that will be gained by direct experience in the *telos*. At the same time, with the words "when we are in God" he may also be referring to mystical experience as a sort of realized eschatology. What we can know here concerning God is not what God is but are things that are "outside" God or "regarding God" or "external" to God, as Evagrius puts it. This is the same notion that was developed by Origen and Nyssen, when they insisted on the fact that we can know and express only things that are περὶ Θεοῦ, "around God" or "about God," but not God's own nature, so that we do not really know what God *is*, but we can know only what is external to God. It is also notable that in this *kephalaion* the direct knowledge of God by experience is assimilated, not to a state of wakefulness, but to a state of sleep. For human senses and even human intellect are asleep when they experience God. This is a theme that in mystical tradition was present already in Philo and was underscored by Gregory of Nyssa and then Pseudo-Dionysius. In *Gnostikos* 41 Evagrius uses the metaphor, not of sleep, but of silence, with respect to God: "Every proposition has a predicate or a genus, or a distinction, or a species, or a property, or an accident, or that which is composed of these things. But on the subject of the Blessed Trinity, nothing of what has been said [here] is admissible. In silence let the ineffable be adored!" This train of thought too has a long history in ancient apophatic tradition. See Ilaria L. E. Ramelli, "Silenzio apofatico in Gregorio di Nissa: Un confronto con Plotino e un'indagine delle ascendenze origeniane," in *Silenzio e parola nella patristica* (SEAug 127; Rome: Augustinianum, 2012), 367–88.

1.39. When, in the beginning, we came to existence, seeds of virtue were connaturally present in us, but not of evil. For this is not a case of what we are capable of; the potential for it certainly exists in us, for while we are able *not* to become (capable of evil), the power of that which does not exist is not in us, if it is true that the powers are qualities [lit. "mixtures"] and that whatever does not exist is not a quality [lit. "a mixture"].

This fundamental *kephalaion* prepares for the following ones (*KG* 1.40–41), which are among the most important of all of the *Kephalaia Gnostika*. In the beginning, in the ἀρχή (the Syriac uses the words of Gen 1:1 and John 1:1, which in the LXX and the Greek New Testament are ἐν ἀρχῇ), there was no evil in the human being but only seeds of virtue susceptible of development. It is virtue that belongs to the very nature of the human being, not evil. Evil is "that which is not," according to its ontological nonsubsistence (a tenet for Origen and Evagrius, and for Eusebius and Gregory of Nyssa as well). This is also why evil is no power—nor even potency—but a lack of power. This indicates the priority—not only chronological but also and primarily ontological—of Good over evil. And this bears enormous consequences for the whole of Evagrius's thought, just as for Origen's thought.

1.40. There was a time when evil did not exist, and there will be a time when, likewise, it will no more exist, whereas there was no time when virtue did not exist, and there will be no time when it will not exist. For the germs of virtue are impossible to destroy. And what persuades me of this is also the rich man who in Sheol was condemned because of his evil and took pity on his siblings. Now, pity is a beautiful germ of virtue.

1.41. If death comes after life, and illness after health, it is clear that also evil comes after virtue. For it is evil that is the death and the illness of

the soul, but virtue comes even before the intermediate state (between virtue and evil).

I comment on these two core *kephalaia* together, due to their deep contnuity, and I intentionally expand on them, because of their centrality to Evagrius's ontology. Here Evagrius, in accord with what he has claimed in *KG* 1.1 and 1.39, insists on the absolute priority of Good over evil, of virtue over vice, of life over death. In this case, he develops Origen's argument of the derivation of the ultimate end, the τέλος, from the beginning, the ἀρχή: evil did not exist in the beginning (since it was not created by God) and will not exist in the end. Likewise, all negativities, such as death or illness, which Evagrius interprets spiritually, are secondary in respect to the positive entity in relation to which they are defined as "lack" or "privation" (of life, health, etc.). That health comes before illness, as life comes before death and virtue before vice, will be argued also by Proclus, who is likely to have known much of Christian Platonism. He certainly knew Origen and might have known Evagrius as well. In his *Commentary on Plato's Timaeus* 2.63.9–64.9, Proclus claims that health comes before illness; it is primordial and Demiurgic; then comes illness, and then comes Asclepian health, which is a restoration of health after illness. But health in itself comes before illness, and the Demiurge, God the Creator, has in himself the source of health. All this, within a discourse on apokatastasis that Proclus also abundantly developed. See my "Proclus and Christian Neoplatonism: A Case Study," in *The Ways of Byzantine Philosophy* (ed. Mikonja Knežević; Alhambra, CA: Sebastian Press; Kosovska Mitrovica: Faculty of Philosophy, 2015), 43–82; "Proclus of Constantinople and Apokatastasis," forthcoming in the *Proceedings of the Conference Arkhai: Proclus Diadochus of Constantinople and His Abrahamic interpreters, University of Istanbul, 12–16 December 2012*, ed. David Butorac. Evil (1.40) is linked to death (1.41) because the former caused the latter, as Origen and the Bible also claim. Evagrius spells this out in *On Thoughts* (Περὶ λογισμῶν) 38.1: with the fall, "the rational nature was put to death by evil." This death is both physical, in the case of human bodies, which are mortal, and also spiritual, in the case of demons and humans (this is why Evagrius attributes death not only to human beings but to the entire "rational nature"). On the work *On Thoughts*, see Paul Géhin, Antoine Guillaumont, and Claire Guillaumont, eds. and trans., *Évagre le Pontique: Sur les pensées* (SC 438; Paris: Cerf, 1998).

The absolute priority of life over death, both at the beginning and in the end, was steadfastly maintained by Origen, who grounded in this argument his fundamental demonstration that only life will be truly eternal, in his *Commentary on Romans* 5.7.78–88:

> And indeed, if one should posit for death the same eternity as for Life, death will no longer be the contradictory opposite of Life but its equal. For "eternal" will not be the contradictory opposite of "eternal" but the very same thing. Now, however, it is certain that death is the contradictory opposite of Life; therefore, it is certain that, if Life is eternal, death cannot possibly be eternal. This is also why the resurrection of the dead will take place by necessity. For, once the death of the soul, which is the very last enemy, has been destroyed, then also this common death, which we call a shadow, as it were, of that death (of the soul), will necessarily be abolished. And at that point, upon the resurrection of the dead, it will come to pass that the kingdom of death, together with death itself, will be destroyed.
>
> *Et reuera si eadem aeternitas mortis ponatur esse quae uitae est, iam non erit mors uitae contraria, sed aequalis. Aeternum namque aeterno contrarium non erit, sed idem. Nunc autem certum est mortem uitae esse contrariam; certum est ergo quia, si uita aeterna est, mors esse non possit aeterna. Unde et necessarium locum tenet resurrectio mortuorum. Cum enim mors animae, qui est nouissimus inimicus, fuerit destructus, etiam haec communis mors, quam illius uelut umbram esse dicimus, necessario abolebitur. Et tunc consequenter resurrectioni mortuorum dabitur locus ubi regnum mortis pariter cum morte destructum erit.*

This is why in Scripture only life is called ἀΐδιος, "eternal" proper, whereas death is described as αἰώνιος, which means not "eternal" but "belonging to the future aeon." See Ramelli and Konstan, *Terms for Eternity*. Notably, the very same argument of the incompatibility of contradictory opposites (*contraria*) used by Origen to argue that life will exclude death is also employed by him to demonstrate the priority and victory of good over evil: "If you apply the Good, evil is destroyed. For contradictory opposites are annihilated by one another, such as, for instance, fire is extinguished by water and darkness dispelled by light," *Bonum uero si adhibeas exterminatur malum. Contraria namque contrariis perimuntur, sicut per aquam ignis exstinguitur et per lucem tenebrae fugantur* (*Commentary on Romans* 9.24.6–8).

An important point on which Origen insists to support the priority of life over death is that Christ himself is Life, according to John 11:25 and

14:6. Thus, he applies to this equation the above-mentioned argument of the victory of life over death, understood as spiritual death, in his *Commentary on Romans* 5.1.297–303: "This death of sin that has passed on to everyone, when it came to Jesus and attempted to pierce him by means of its sting—for death's sting is sin—was pushed back and destroyed. This is because Jesus was Life, and by necessity death was annihilated by Life," *Ista mors peccati quae in omnes pertransiit, cum uenisset ad Iesum et temptasset eum perforare aculeo suo—aculeus enim mortis peccatum—repulsa est et confracta. Uita enim erat, et mors necessario exterminabatur a uita.*

Evagrius knew these arguments of Origen's perfectly well. The pivotal argument that evil did not exist in the beginning and therefore will not exist in the end was taken up by Gregory of Nyssa too, with whom Evagrius was also well acquainted. In his treatise *On the Titles of the Psalms* (GNO 5:100,21–25), Gregory affirms that evil is not from eternity (*ab aeterno*, ἐξ ἀϊδίου): "The help of the Lord has not permitted that we be residents of hades; this is also because, in proportion to the multitude of pains that derive from sin, we have received the cure from the Physician: and here he makes an even greater philosophical point, asserting as doctrine that *evil is not ab aeterno*." Thus, evil cannot be destined to subsist eternally (see Ramelli, "Christian Soteriology and Christian Platonism"). So, Gregory concludes as follows: "Thus, it has been demonstrated that evil is not *ab aeterno*, nor will it remain forever. For that which has not been forever will not continue to exist forever either" (GNO 5:101,3).

If evil is the death and sickness of the soul, as Evagrius maintains in *KG* 1.41, this death and this sickness cannot prevail, because good and virtue come first, prior to evil and prior even to the neutral state, not only in a chronological sense—insofar as evil entered the world not at the beginning but only at a certain point—but also in an ontological sense. Evagrius's notion derives *verbatim* from Origen: "Virtue is anterior to / more ancient than vice/evilness" (ἡ ἀρετὴ πρεσβυτέρα τῆς κακίας ἐστίν; *Selected Passages on Psalms* [PG 12:1601,3]). Evil is nothing more than a lack of good; good comes first, on the principle of the absolute priority of the positive pole: only Good was in the beginning, and only Good will remain in the end. Origen insisted that evil—that is, sin and spiritual death—was not created by God; thus it cannot have ontological subsistence. For example, in *Commentary on Romans* 6.6.35–37, speaking of the death consisting in the separation of the soul from God that is produced by sin, he states: "God did not create this kind of death [i.e., the death of the soul], nor does God rejoice in the perdition of living beings, but it is due to the devil's envy/hostility if this death entered the world," *Haec mortem Deus non fecit, neque laetatur in perditione uiuorum, sed inuidia diaboli mors haec introiuit in orbem terrarum.* Origen is clearly drawing on Wis 1:13: "The Lord did not create death," *Dominus mortem non fecit*, and 2:24: "It is due to the devil's envy/hostility if this death entered the world," *Invidia diaboli mors introivit in orbem terrarum.* (See Ilaria L. E. Ramelli, "La colpa antecedente come ermeneutica del male in sede storico-religiosa e nei testi biblici," in *Atti del XIV Convegno di Studî vetero-testamentarî dell'Associazione Biblica Italiana: Origine e fenomenologia del male; Le vie della catarsi vetero-testamentaria, Roma-Ciampino, Istituto Il Carmelo, 5–7 settembre 2005* [ed. Ignazio Cardellini; Bologna: Dehoniane, 2007] = *Ricerche Storico-Bibliche* 19 [2007]: 11–64.) Sin and evil derive only from a bad choice; they have no ontological subsistence; they do not even exist: only God/Good exists, and Christ's cross has the power of dispelling all evil: "The power of the cross of Christ is so great that, if one places it before one's eyes, and keeps it steadfastly on one's mind … no concupiscence, no desire, no frenzy, no hostility of sin can overcome, but immediately the whole of that army of sin and flesh that I have listed above is chased away from its presence—indeed, sin itself does not even exist, given that its substance is nowhere but in deeds," *Est enim tanta uis crucis Christi ut si ante oculos ponatur et in mente fideliter retineatur … nulla concupiscentia nulla libido nullus furor nulla peccati superare possit inuidia, sed continuo ab eius praesentia totus ille quem supra enumerauimus peccati et carnis fugatur exercitus—ipsum uero peccatum nec subsistit, quippe cum nec substantia eius usquam sit nisi in opere et gestis* (*Commentary on Romans* 6.1.38–45). Again in 6.7.52–53 Origen insists that death was not made by God: "Passions were fructifying in our limbs, not for God, but for death's sake—that death that God did not create," *Passiones … in membris nostris fructificabant non Deo sed morti, illi morti quam Deus non fecit.*

Even in his *Against Celsus*, a debate with a "pagan" Middle Platonist, Origen insists that evil did not exist at the beginning and therefore will not exist in the end. In one passage he observes that for a philosopher it is very difficult to know the origin of evil, and it is to be hoped that by divine revelation it will be made clear "what evils are, how they *came to existence*, and how *they will be eliminated*" (*Against Celsus* 4.65). For Origen, one can learn from Scripture "how evil first *came to existence* and how it *will be annihilated*" (6.44). Indeed, the death of Christ is the beginning of the destruction of the personification of evil, the devil, "the evil one" (7.17).

Another typical feature that Evagrius derives from Origen is the spiritual interpretation of death and illness, not as affecting the body, but as affecting the soul. Origen has a clear account of this spiritual death in his *Dialogue with Heraclides*, and everywhere in his writings he displays this double interpretation of illness, death, and life. For example, in his *Commentary on Romans* 5.1.249–253 Origen explains that bodily death is only a shadow of the spiritual death brought about by sin and has entered the world as a consequence of spiritual death (which he deems to be the real death): "'And through sin'—Scripture says—'there came about death.' This is undoubtedly the death of which the prophet too is speaking when he states: 'The soul that sins will die' [Ezek 18:4]. Someone rightly called this death of the body a shadow of that death. For wherever the death of the soul goes, the death of the body necessarily follows, just as a shadow follows a body," *Et per peccatum, inquit, mors. Illa sine dubio mors de qua et profeta dicit quia anima quae peccat ipsa morietur, cuius mortis hanc corporalem mortem umbram merito quis dixerit, quocumque enim illa incesserit hanc necesse est subsequi uelut umbram corpus.* Thus, in 4.5.138ff. Origen interprets "the dead" in Rom 4:17 in the sense of those who are dead in their souls due to sin: "'God, who vivifies the dead and calls the beings that are not just as those that are.' As for 'the dead,' we must understand here those who are dead on account of the sin of their soul, because, as Scripture says, 'The soul that sins will die' [Ezek 18:4].... A man who has lost his spiritual senses in his soul, so that he cannot see God, nor hear the words of God, nor perceive Christ's sweet perfume, nor taste the sweet Logos of God, nor do his hands touch the Logos of life, well, this kind of people are called dead, and rightly so," *Qui uiuificat mortuos et uocat ea quae non sunt tamquam quae sunt. Mortuos hic secundum animae peccatum intellegimus, quoniam anima inquit, quae peccat ipsa morietur ... qui spiritales sensus in anima perdiderit ut non uideat Deum neque audiat uerba Dei neque suauem odorem capiat Christi neque gustet bonum Dei uerbum neque manus eius pertractent de uerbo uitae, huiusmodi homines merito mortui appellantur.* A complete prospect of all the possible meanings of "death" in Scripture is provided by Origen both in his *Dialogue of Heraclides*—where Origen lists the death of the body, the death of the soul, which is a big evil, and the death to sin, which is always very good—and, in a still completer form, in his *Commentary on Romans* 6.6.29–43:

> "Death" in Scriptures is one single name but has many meanings. Indeed, the separation of the body from the soul is called "death," but this cannot be said to be either evil or good, since it is in the middle, what is called "indifferent." Again, the separation of a soul from God is named "death,"

> which comes about through sin. This death, which is also called "the wages of sin," is clearly evil.… And again, the author himself of this death, the devil, is called "death," and he is the one who is said to be the very last enemy of Christ, bound to be destroyed [1 Cor 15:26]. But hell, in which souls were imprisoned by death, this too is called "death." And in yet another sense, that death is called praiseworthy by which a person dies to sin and is buried together with Christ; thanks to this a soul is improved and acquires eternal life.

> *Mors in Scripturis unum quidem nomen est, sed multa significat. Etenim separatio corporis ab anima mors nominatur. Sed haec neque mala neque bona dici potest; est enim media, quae dicitur indifferens. Et rursus separatio animae a Deo mors appellatur quae per peccatum uenit. Haec aperte mala est, quae et peccati stipendium nominatur.… Et iterum ipse auctor mortis huius diabolus mors appellatur et ipse est qui dicitur inimicus Christi nouissimus destruendus. Sed et inferni locus in quo animae detinebantur a morte etiam ipse mors appellatur. Dicitur uero illa mors laudabilis qua peccato quis moritur et Christo consepelitur, per quam emendatio fit animae et uita aeterna conquiritur.*

Three of these meanings (bodily death, as an indifferent thing in the sense of the Stoic ἀδιάφορα, spiritual death, and death to sin) are the same as those that are classified by Origen in his *Dialogue* and again in *Commentary on Romans* 6.5.35–41: "this common death" (*mors ista communis*), that is, bodily death; "the death caused by sin, since 'the soul that sins will die' [Ezek 18:4]" (*peccati mors, quoniam anima quae peccat ipsa morietur*); and "the death by which we die to sin together with Christ (*istam mortem qua cum Christo peccato morimur*). Evagrius too uses "death" to indicate physical death, spiritual death, or death to sin. The last kind of death is reflected in *Sentences to the Monks* 21, where death to sin is identified with dying the death of Christ, and in *Chapters of the Disciples of Evagrius* 58, the intellect, that is, the "interior human being" (ὁ ἔσω ἄνθρωπος), dies to sin when it separates itself from "intellections of passions" (ἐμπαθῆ νοήματα).

Evagrius draws on Origen, Clement, Gregory of Nyssa, and even Philo when he speaks of the illness and death of the soul, as well as on the New Testament (see Ilaria L. E. Ramelli, "ΚΟΙΜΩΜΕΝΟΥΣ ΑΠΟ ΤΗΣ ΛΥΠΗΣ (Luke 22,45): A Deliberate Change," *ZNW* 102 [2011]: 59–76). Origen, like already Clement, insisted on the therapy for the ill soul that Christ, in his capacity as physician, provides. This medical, pedagogical, and cathartic view of punishments is so deeply rooted in Origen's mind that he considers even the death inflicted by God after the fall to be a healing and salutary punishment (e.g., *Commentary on Matthew* 15.15; *Homilies on Leviticus* 14.4; *On the Resurrection*, *apud* Methodius, *On the Resurrection*, *apud* Photius, *Library* codex 234: "God enveloped the human being in mortality, so that, through the decomposition of the body, all the evil that was produced in it might die out," νεκρότητι περιβαλὼν αὐτὸν ὅπως διὰ τῆς λύσεως τοῦ σώματος πᾶν τὸ ἐν αὐτῷ γεννηθὲν κακὸν ἀποθάνῃ). Origen indeed describes Christ as a physician of souls whose aim is "to heal *all rational souls* with the therapy that comes from the Logos, to make them friends of God" (*Against Celsus* 3.54). Christ-Logos-Physician can use even drastic remedies (*poenalibus curis*), such as cauterization with fire (*ignis supplicium*), but succeeds in healing the sinner (*On First Principles* 2.10.6; cf. 2.7.3; 3.1.15). Therefore, in *On First Principles* 2.10.6–7 Origen interprets a number of Old Testament passages to show that "God deals with sinners in the same way as physicians do with the sick to restore them to health." And in *On First Principles* 3.6.5 Origen even corrects Plato—who maintained that some people have committed such grave injustices as to become "incurable," ἀνίατοι—by remarking that "nothing is impossible for the Omnipotent; no being is incurable [*insanabile*, ἀνίατον] for the One who created it" (see Ramelli, *Christian Doctrine of Apokatastasis*). For the healing power of the Logos is far superior to the power of sin: "In souls, there is no illness caused by evilness [ἀπὸ κακίας] that is impossible to cure [ἀδύνατον θεραπευθῆναι] for God the Logos, who is superior to all" (*Against Celsus* 8.72).

Like Origen again, Evagrius invokes scriptural evidence to support his thinking: here he refers to the parable of Dives and Lazarus (Luke 16:19–31), which was adduced by Gregory of Nyssa too, in his *On the Soul and the Resurrection*. Even in hell people maintain germs of virtue, because virtue, unlike evil, which is only lack of good, is indestructible. It is the same argument as that maintained by Origen, and then by Gregory of Nyssa, of the indestructibility of the image of God in us: it may be blurred by all sorts of dirt, that is, evil, but it will never disappear, and it will shine forth again in the end.

For the "germs of virtue," Evagrius's original Greek must have been σπέρματα ἀρετῆς. Now the same expression, σπέρμα ἀρετῆς, and the same idea that germs of virtue are naturally present in human souls, was found already in the Roman Stoic Musonius Rufus, *Diatribe* 2, whereas in the ancient Stoa it is unattested. Musonius exerted a heavy influence on Clement and Origen, and indeed Origen repeatedly used σπέρματα ἀρετῆς, so Musonius may have reached Evagrius through Origen. In *Fragments on Psalm* 36:25 Origen argues that "the germs of virtues" (σπέρματα τῶν ἀρετῶν) are themselves virtues. In *Selected Passages on Psalms* (PG 12:1657,49) he remarks, like Musonius and Evagrius, that "the germs of virtues" (τῆς ἀρετῆς … σπερμάτων) are present as a foundation in the soul. *Exegesis of Proverbs* (PG 17:173,34) even has the same text as Evagrius, only shorter—which may point either to a misattribution or to Origen's impact on Evagrius, who in this case would have simply inserted some expansions and dropped tiny points: "There was a time when evil did not exist, and there will be a time when it will no more exist; for the germs of virtue are impossible to destroy/indelible [Ἦν ὅτε οὐκ ἦν κακὸν καὶ ἔσται ὅτε οὐκ ἔσται· ἀνεξάλειπτα γὰρ τὰ σπέρματα τῆς ἀρετῆς]. And what persuades me of this is also the rich man who in Sheol was condemned because of his evil, and yet was not completely immersed in every evil, and took pity on his siblings. Now, pity is the most beautiful germ of virtue [τὸ δὲ ἐλεεῖν, σπέρμα τυγχάνει τὸ κάλλιστον τῆς ἀρετῆς]." The germs of virtue, unlike those of vice, are indestructible, Evagrius claims, because they were planted by God in us, whereas God has never planted the germs of vice, which do not really belong to our nature: they were not part of God's original plan for humanity, and this is why they will not possibly endure in the end. This argument too is patently drawn from Origen (*Commentary on Romans* 6.5.78–102):

> We have said that the apostle drew a comparison between good fruits and bad fruits. For, where he was speaking of bad fruits, he did not say, "You had your fruit, of which you are ashamed," but he rather said: "What fruit did you have?" But where he is speaking of good fruits, he adds, "your." This is, indeed, how he writes: "You have your fruit for your sanctification." By means of this he seems to me to indicate that the bad fruit, the fruit of which one must be ashamed and repent, is not our fruit. Indeed, God did not plant in us the bad plant, which is able to bring about but bad fruits.… Therefore, even if we bring about bad fruits, these are not ours but alien—that is, they belong to sin. But if we bring good fruits in sanctification, these are our own fruits, because human nature received from its Creator the capacity for bringing these good fruits. Those others, the alien ones, indeed, have not been sown in us by God.
>
> *Conlationem diximus fructuum malorum et fructuum bonorum fecisse apostolum, quod ibi quidem ubi de malis fructibus dicebat non dixit "fructum uestrum habuistis in quo erubescitis," sed dixit: "quem ergo fructum habuistis?" Ubi uero de bonis fructibus dicit addit uestrum. Sic enim*

> *scribit: "habetis fructum uestrum in sanctificationem." Per quod indicare mihi uidetur quod fructus malus, fructus erubescendus et paenitendus, non est noster fructus. Non enim malam in nobis arborem Deus plantauit quae fructus malos proferret.... Fructus ergo malos etiamsi afferamus non sunt nostri sed alieni, id est peccati. Fructus uero bonos si afferimus in sanctificatione nostri sunt fructus. Istos enim fructus ut afferret humana natura a conditore suscepit. Nam illi alieni non sunt in nobis seminati a Deo.*

The very metaphor of God as farmer—echoed by Evagrius too in the *kephalaia* at stake with the idea of the germs of virtue planted by God in human souls—in connection with both protology and eschatology was dear to Origen and also to Gregory of Nyssa, who uses it at the end of his dialogue *On the Soul and the Resurrection* to illustrate how God will purify his plants, that is, his creatures, in order to put them into the right condition to enjoy the final *apokatastasis*. Origen also spoke of this agricultural purgation carried out by God with a view to the eternal life for his creatures: "Indeed, every plant, after its winter death, awaits its spring resurrection. Therefore, if we too have been planted together with Christ in his death, it is necessary that the Father, as a farmer, purifies us like branches of the true/genuine vine, that we may bring very much fruit, as Christ himself says in the Gospels: 'I am the true vine, you are the branches, and my Father is the Farmer,'" *Omnis etenim planta post hiemis mortem resurrectionem ueris expectat. Si ergo et nos in Christi morte complantati sumus ei, necesse est ut Pater agricola purget nos tamquam palmites uitis uerae ut fructum plurimum afferamus, sicut et ipse in euangeliis dicit: ego sum uitis uera, uos palmites, pater meus agricola* (*Commentary on Romans* 5.9.65–72; see also 1.15.54–66).

Origen clearly connects the same image to the *apokatastasis* when he comments on Paul's passage in Rom 11 concerning the olive tree composed by Israel and the nations, whose conclusion is the salvation of all Israel and all nations. Origen comments on Rom 11:26 at length, where Paul announces the salvation of "the totality of the nations" (τὸ πλήρωμα τῶν ἐθνῶν: the meaning of πλήρωμα, as is clear from its usage in the LXX, is "totality" and not simply "fullness") and of "all Israel" (πᾶς Ἰσραήλ). In 4.2.88ff. he sees this universal salvation as the eventual realization of the promise made to Abraham, that he would inherit all the peoples of the earth:

> By this symbolic seal, as the apostle (Paul) explains, the justice/justification of faith is indicated, which Abraham deserved to receive before his circumcision, as well as he deserved to become the father of many

> peoples. Now we believe that this symbolic seal will be unsealed when the totality of the nations will have entered, and all of Israel will be saved.... That symbolic seal will be certainly revealed in that time in which, in the very last days, once the totality of the nations has entered, as I have said, all of Israel will be saved.... Thus, what Scripture says, "In you [i.e., Abraham] all the families of the earth will be blessed," means that Abraham was constituted heir of the whole world.
>
> *Per istud ergo signaculum, ut exponit apostolus, iustitia fidei, quam in praeputio positus Abraham accipere meruit, indicatur, et pater esse multarum gentium, quod tunc credimus resignandum cum plenitudo gentium introierit et omnis Israhel saluabitur ... quod signaculum illo utique in tempore dissignabitur cum in nouissimis diebus, postquam plenitudo ut diximus gentium introierit, omnis Israhel saluus fiet.... Quod ergo dicit, "Benedicentur in te omnes tribus terrae," hoc est heredem factum esse totius mundi.*

Origen returns to Israel's salvation in the *telos* several times again, especially in *Commentary on Romans* 8.1.85: "in the eschatological times, when all of Israel will be saved," *in nouissimis, cum omnis Israhel saluus fiet*; and 8.9.107–116:

> So great was God's grace toward this people [i.e., Israel] that, when it was taken away from them, it was powerful enough as to reconcile the entire world with God. What do you think the world will then receive, when this people too will have deserved to be reconciled with God? And what is that which the world will gain from the reconciliation of Israel with God? Paul has briefly indicated this by saying: "Life after death." For Israel will be received when the dead too will by then receive life back, and the world, from corruptible as it is, will become incorruptible, and mortals will be given immortality. For it would seem absurd if, while Israel's offense has donated the world reconciliation with God, their being received should not bestow upon the world something even greater and better.
>
> *Tanta fuit erga gentem istam gratia quae sublata ab ea uniuersum mundum Deo reconciliare sufficeret. Quantum putas tunc merebitur mundus, cum etiam gens ista reconciliari meruerit Deo? Et quid illud sit quod ex reconciliatione Israhel mundus acquirat breuiter ostendit dicens: "uita ex mortuis." Tunc enim erit assumptio Israhel quando iam et mortui uitam recipient et mundus ex corruptibili incorruptibilis fiet et mortales inmortalitate donantur. Absurdum namque uideretur si, cum offensio eorum reconciliationem mundo donauerit, assumptio ipsorum non maius aliquid mundo et praestantius largiretur.*

Origen also adduces scriptural proofs of the final salvation of all Israel: "I shall not condemn the people of Israel for all the misdeeds they have done [Jer 31:37].... There will come from Zion one who will liberate them and will remove his impieties from Jacob, and this I promise them: I shall remove their sins [cf. Isa 59:20–21]," *Ego non reprobabo genus Israhel pro omnibus quae fecerunt … ueniet ex Sion qui liberet et auertet impietates ab Iacob, et hoc illis a me testamentum cum abstulero peccata eorum* (*Commentary on Romans* 8.11.45ff.). As for the salvation of the nations, Origen points out the presence of Christ-Logos even among "pagans" (8.2.100–101): Christ as Logos "is present everywhere and is even among those who do not know him or confess him," *adest ubique et medius est etiam eorum qui ignorant eum et non confitentur*.

When he claims that there was a time or state in which evil did not exist, and therefore there will come a time or state in which evil will no longer exist, Evagrius in *KG* 1.40 is applying the so-called perishability axiom, well known to "pagan" and Christian Platonists alike, and, what is more, he is adapting the anti-"Arian" formula that was used already by Origen (who in fact imported it for the first time from the philosophical cosmological debate into Christian theology): it is not the case that there was a time when *the Son* did not exist, but it is certainly the case that there was a time when *evil* did not exist. This is also why there will surely come a time when it will no more exist. I have demonstrated all this in detail elsewhere (Ilaria L. E. Ramelli, "Alexander of Aphrodisias: A Source of Origen's Philosophy?," *Philosophie Antique* 14 [2014]: 151–205). I have showed that this formula ("there was a time when *x* did not exist"/"there was no time when *x* did not exist," ἦν ποτε ὅτε οὐκ ἦν / οὐκ ἦν ποτε ὅτε οὐκ ἦν) in fact arose in a philosophical milieu, in Alexander of Aphrodisias in connection with the reflection on eternity, but then Origen used it in a theological sense, and so did Eusebius after him, Athanasius, and several other Fathers. This formula, which Evagrius applied to evil, means that evil is not eternal (whereas the Son is absolutely eternal) and thus, as it once did not exist, so it will have to disappear, whereas God is eternal and God is the Good. There was never a time when God-Trinity and the Good did not exist, and there will never be. If Origen's fragments are reliable, Evagrius took his pithy *kephalaion* directly from Origen: "There was a state in which evil did not exist, and there will be one in which evil will not exist anymore" (*Explanation of Proverbs* 5; *Fragments on Proverbs* 5).

Evagrius's very statement that virtue exists forever, and there was no time when it did not exist, and thus there will be no time when it will not exist, directly derives from Origen as well: "Virtue exists always and endures eternally," *Virtutem semper esse et in aeternum manere* (Origen, *On First Principles* 1.3.8).

1.42. God is said to be there where he operates, and where he operates the more, there he is the more present. Now, he operates to the utmost degree in rational and holy natures. Therefore, he is present to the utmost degree in celestial powers.

Angels are, among creatures, the closest to God. God is said by Evagrius to operate and be present in them more than in any other creatures because angels are those who adhere to the Good most closely. According to Origen, whom Evagrius follows, rational creatures differentiated themselves into angels, human, and demons depending on the degree of their detachment from the Good, that is, God, in their turning to minor or apparent goods or to evil. Evagrius too, in the *KG* and elsewhere (e.g., in scholium 33 on Prov 3:19–20) is clear that fallen rational creatures receive bodies and arrangements in aeons that depend on their spiritual and moral condition (κατάστασις), that is, their advancement in the Good or distance from it. Angels are those who have detached themselves from the Good to the least degree or perhaps not at all. This is why God operates in them to the utmost degree. Evagrius's view concerning angels is analyzed by Ellen Muehlberger, *Angels in Late Ancient Christianity* (Oxford: Oxford University Press, 2013), ch. 1.

1.43. The Godhead is in every place, and yet it is not in some specific place. It is everywhere insofar as it is in everything that has come into existence by means of its Wisdom full of modalities. However, it is not in a specific place, because it is not one among those that have come into being.

The preceding *kephalaion* might have given the impression that God is physically or substantially present in a part of the creation rather than in another. The presence of which Evagrius was speaking, however, was a presence of *operation* rather than of substance, in that God operates most of all in angels. But from the physical point of view, the Godhead is nowhere in creation, since it transcends creation; it is not found in any part of creation as an immanent substance (like the deity of the Stoics, for instance), but its trace is present everywhere in creation, since it is the Creator. The Creator's "Wisdom full of modalities," or "variegated," or "endowed with many decorations" (πολυποίκιλος σοφία; Eph 3:10), has created everything that exists, and creation bears the trace of its Creator. The Godhead is present in creation through its Wisdom-Logos, who is Christ. This is a typical Origenian notion (see Ramelli, "Clement's Notion of the Logos"). The divinity cannot be in one specific place, because it is not one among the beings: it transcends all beings since it is the Being itself, and all beings exist in that they participate in God.

1.44. If the kingdom of heavens is known in that which is contained and in that which contains, torment also will be known in that which is opposite to these.

The kingdom of heavens and the torment, a state of suffering, designate two opposite eschatological conditions, which are the result of the Judgment. But in *KG* 1.27 Evagrius has clearly stated that the Judgment and its consequences are not the very ultimate reality to be contemplated. They constitute the fourth contemplation, but they are followed by the fifth, that is, the contemplation of divine providence. At that stage, which corresponds to *apokatastasis*, every opposition will vanish. Thus, suffering, which is opposed to the kingdom of heavens, will also disappear. See also *KG* 1.6–8 and 1.17 for Evagrius's notion of "that in which we are" contained.

1.45. There is nothing among incorporeal realities that is in power/potency in bodies; for our soul is incorporeal.

Here the word for "bodies" is not *pgr'*, designating human mortal bodies, but the more general *gwšm'*, which comprises the bodies of angels and all spiritual bodies, including those of the resurrection. Thus, what is incorporeal and is neither a mortal body nor even a spiritual body must be identified, apart from God, with souls or Ideas. Neither of these are creatures proper: the soul is a part of a creature; Ideas are ideas of creatures. Souls, which are incorporeal, and especially intellectual souls, are not in power in bodies; that seems to mean that when a soul is in a body it is not in its full power. This is an idea that Macrina stressed in Gregory of Nyssa's dialogue *On the Soul and the Resurrection*, which is a Christian remake of Plato's *Phaedo*, and indeed this idea comes straight from that dialogue of Plato's (see my full commentary on this in Ilaria L. E. Ramelli, *Gregorio di Nissa: Sull'anima e la resurrezione* [Milan: Bompiani–Catholic University, 2007]). An alternative explanation, which is supported by the following *kephalaion* (*KG* 1.46), is that an intellectual soul is not in potency or potentiality in a body, where "in potency" is opposite to "in actuality" in the sense of the Aristotelian dialectic between potency or potentiality and act or actuality (δύναμις, ἐνέργεια, ἐντελέχεια). This is indeed the dialectic that underlies the following *kephalaion*, from which it would follow that if souls, qua incorporeal, are not in potency in bodies, then they are not in act therein either. This contradicts Aristotle's definition of a soul as a body's act. This is consistent with Evagrius's stress in *KG* 1.46 on the different nature of intellects and bodies and with Origen's (anti-Aristotelian) refusal to conceive of souls as functions of bodies.

1.46. All that is in power/potency in bodies is naturally found in them also in act. They are of the same nature as those from which they came into existence. But the intellect is free from sight and matter.

Those that are of the same nature as those from which they came into existence are probably bodies. Bodies derive from other bodies and are of the same nature as all bodies; they are material and derive from the four elements. The nature of the intellect, on the other hand, is very different. It has no matter (the Syriac noun *hwl'* is a transposition of ὕλη) and no sight. The word I have translated "sight" has exactly this meaning in Syriac, and in this case it may point to the lack of sense perception in reference to the intellect; however, Guillaumont (p. 39) may be right to suppose that this word perhaps translated εἶδος and that with the latter Evagrius meant "form." In this case, however, "form" should be understood to mean not "metaphysical form"—which the intellect does have—but rather "shape," since the intellect has no physical shape. As a consequence, it would be more probable that, if Evagrius meant "form" in the sense of "shape," the Greek was σχῆμα rather than εἶδος. At any rate, a very possible alternative is "sight" as a metonymy for "sense perception," or in the sense that the intellect cannot be seen.

1.47. There is nothing that is, in potency, in the soul and that can go out of it in act and subsist in its own right; for this [i.e., the soul] is naturally made to be in the body.

This *kephalaion* further confirms that Evagrius agreed with Origen that there cannot exist bare souls, subsisting separately without a body, a soul that "subsists in its own right" (see on this full demonstration in Ramelli, "Pre-existence of Souls"). All creatures have a body, including angels, although there are different degrees of fineness and spirituality in bodies. All souls are naturally made and meant by God to exist in bodies. Only the Holy Trinity can subsist without a body. This, however, does not mean that souls are functions of bodies and are mortal like bodies, as Aristotle maintained.

1.48. All that which is attached to bodies also follows those from which they are born, whereas nothing of these things is attached to the soul.

Bodies produce bodies and all the relevant corporeal properties. These properties are completely extraneous to the soul, which is incorporeal, even though it cannot subsist independently, without a body (see *KG* 1.47). Physical characteristics are passed on from parents to children, but nothing that concerns the soul.

1.49. The Unity (Unification). This, by itself (acting in isolation), is not put into motion, but it is set in motion by the receptivity of the intellect, which, in its carelessness, turns its own face away from it and, due to the privation of it, gives birth to ignorance.

Evagrius traces here a descending hierarchy from the One to the intellect, or *nous*, and explains how intellects fell away from an initial state of unity. This account reflects Origen's thought on the fall of intellectual creatures from the initial unity. It is not the original Unity that is the principle of movement (a term that, in the Origenian language followed by Evagrius, means acts of will, volitions, implying choices between Good and evil), but it is the will of some intellectual creatures who directed themselves elsewhere than the Good constituting the Unity (which was essentially a unity of will rather than a unity of substance: all intellects' wills were directed toward one and the same object, God / the Good). This will, which is an act of movement, is nevertheless described as related to a "reception," "receptivity," or "liability to passions" of the intellect, which is somehow distracted away from the true Good and led astray by lesser or apparent goods, which become the new objects of its deviating will. Evagrius's use of "movement" in the sense of a movement of free will is very frequent, not only in the *KG* but also elsewhere. For instance, in his *Scholia on Ecclesiastes* Evagrius defines προαίρεσις, the fundamental choice by one's free will, as "a certain movement [κίνησις] of the intellect" (scholium 10,1–2 on Eccl 2:11), and in his *Scholia on Proverbs* he defines βουλή, "decision, will, deliberation" as "a certain movement [κίνησις]" (scholium 23,1 on Prov 2:17). The situation described here by Evagrius applies to each single intellect also in the historical time: whenever it turns away from unity, it produces ignorance.

Evagrius describes the defection of intellectual creatures from the blessed Unity as a result of their "carelessness," exactly as Origen had done. According to the latter, indeed, when their ardent love for God, who is Good itself, and their zeal diminishes, rational creatures experience a fall, which Origen described as a ψύξις, a cooling off that transforms intellects into souls (ψυχαί). Note the mention of neglect in connection with the fall and movement in *On First Principles* 2.9.2: "Every intellectual being, neglecting the Good to a greater or lesser extent due to its own movements, was dragged to the opposite of the Good, that is, evil." Origen depicted those rational creatures that do not care for their own spiritual progress and salvation as careless in *On First Principles* 3.5.8: "those who neglect to take care of their own advantage and salvation." In *On First Principles* 2.9.6 neglectfulness is said to be the cause of the fall of those rational creatures; here these are opposed to those who used their free will to progress in their loving imitation of God, instead of detaching themselves from the Good: "Freedom of will either roused each one to progress by means of the imitation of God or dragged each one to deficiency due to neglectfulness," *Libertas unumquemque uoluntatis suae uel ad profectum per imitationem Dei prouocauit uel ad defectum per neglegentiam traxit.* Neglectfulness is so serious a fault that it can make human beings rank among irrational animals (from the moral, and not the ontological, point of view): "Human wisdom, if it turns uncultivated and neglected due to much carelessness in life, becomes like an irrational animal due to incompetence or neglectfulness [*per imperitiam uel per neglegentiam*] even though not by nature" (*apud* Pamphilus, *Apology for Origen* 180). Origen, intellectually minded and hard worker as he is, insists everywhere on the gravity of neglectfulness (ἀμέλεια), disattention (ἀπροσεξία), and laziness (ῥαθυμία, ἀργία). This is no small fault but is the very cause of the fall, qua opposite of the ardent love for God / the Good and attachment to it. Origen's above-mentioned notion of "cooling off" is but another metaphor for the same concept. In the same passage Origen is adamant that "turning away from the better and neglecting it gave rise to the detachment from the Good," *auersio ac neglegentia meliorum initium dedit recedendi a bono*. The same is stressed in *Against Celsus* 6.45: those who adhere to evil are said to do so "due to neglect of the Good," δι' ἀμέλειαν τοῦ καλοῦ.

Against this background it is not surprising that Origen indicates laziness as the factor that opens up the door to the action of demons on one's soul in *On First Principles* 3.3.6. Evagrius himself, in *KG* 3.28 (see below, with the relevant commentary), describes the soul as an intellect that, due to neglectfulness, has fallen down from Unity and, because of it lack of vigilance, has descended to the level of the *praktikē*. Related to neglectfulness is also one of the "evil thoughts," or *logismoi*, that Evagrius systematized (see, e.g., Richard Sorabji, *Emotion and Peace of Mind: From Stoic Agitation to Christian Temptation* [Oxford: Oxford University Press, 2000], and my review in *Aev* 77.1 [2003]: 217–21; see now Kevin Corrigan, *Evagrius and Gregory: Mind, Soul and Body in the 4th Century* [Burlington, Vt.: Ashgate, 2009], ch. 5; Tobon, *Apatheia in the Teachings of Evagrius*, ch. 2). It is the *logismos* of ἀκηδία: "carelessness, indifference, torpor, apathy" (for the exact meaning, see Siegfried Wenzel, "Ακηδια: Additions to Lampe's Patristic Greek Lexicon," *VC* 17 [1963]: 173–76). The gravity of this sin was pointed out to Evagrius by Origen. On ἀκηδία in Evagrius, see Rüdiger Augst, *Lebensverwirklichung und christlicher Glaube, Acedia, religiöse Gleichgültigkeit als Problem der Spiritualität bei Evagrius Ponticus* (Frankfurt: Lang,1990); Christoph Joest, "Die Bedeutung von *Akedia* und *Apatheia* bei Evagrios Pontikos," *StudMon* 35 (1993): 7–53; English translation in *American Benedictine Review* 55 (2004): 121–50, 273–307; Barbara Maier, "*Apatheia* bei den Stoikern und *Akedia* bei Evagrios Pontikos: Ein Ideal und die Kehrseite seiner Realität," *OrChr* 78 (1994): 230–49; R. Pereto Rivas, "Evagrio Póntico y la exclaustración de la acedia," *Car* 28 (2012): 23–35; and Gabriel Bunge, *Despondency: The Spiritual Teaching of Evagrius Ponticus* (trans. Anthony P. Gythiel; Crestwood, N.Y.: St. Vladimir's Seminary Press, 2012); trans. of *Akedia: Die geistliche Lehre des Evagrios Pontikos vom Überdruss* (Köln: Luthe, 1983); for developments, see Siegfried Wenzel, *The Sin of Sloth: Acedia in Medieval Thought and Literature* (Chapel Hill: University of North Carolina Press, 2012). Consistently with this set of ideas, Evagrius, like Origen, places a great emphasis on hard work, effort, and πόνος, which he identifies especially with ascetic labor (see, e.g., *Eulogius* 32.34).

Evagrius agrees with Origen also on the idea—expressed here in *KG* 1.49—that turning away from God, the Good, generates ignorance. Indeed, ignorance is the privation of knowledge and wisdom, and knowledge and Wisdom are primarily Christ-Logos, who is God. Wisdom is the first *epinoia* of Christ, according to Origen. See Ilaria L. E. Ramelli, "Cristo-Logos in Origene: Ascendenze filoniane, passaggi in Bardesane e Clemente, e negazione del subordinazionismo," in *Dal Logos dei Greci e dei Romani al Logos di Dio: Ricordando Marta Sordi* (ed. Alfredo Valvo and Roberto Radice; Milan: Vita e Pensiero, 2011), 295–317.

1.50. All that which has come into existence has come into existence thanks to God's knowledge. But some of these existing beings are primary beings, and some of them are secondary. And (divine) knowledge is more ancient than the primary beings, and movement (is more ancient) than the secondary beings.

God is the creator of all beings, but creatures are divided into primary and secondary beings. The movement of which Evagrius has just spoken in *KG* 1.49 as the beginning of the abandonment of the initial Unity, after what one might call the "fall" of the intellectual creatures, is here declared by him to be anterior to the creation of the "secondary beings." First there was God's knowledge (Christ-Logos-Wisdom, in God); then God's knowledge created the "primary natures," that is, the intelligible beings; these were initially in unity of will with God. When their wills, however, were directed elsewhere and the "movements" began, this "fall" brought about the creation of the present world with its "secondary creatures," among which there surely are mortal bodies, which in the Syriac text are called *pgr'*. Indeed, the identifications I indicate for primary and secondary beings are confirmed by *KG* 1.77 (see below).

1.51. Movement is the cause of evil, whereas virtue is the destructor of evil. Now, virtue is the daughter of names and ways, and the cause of these is, in turn, movement.

Evagrius goes on to speculate on the initial detachment of the intelligences from the Unity with God and among themselves. This detachment, as he has said, was caused by the movements of the intelligent creatures' free wills, which oriented themselves toward lesser or apparent goods instead of adhering to God, the only Good. This detachment from the Good is of course the cause of evil; this is why here Evagrius claims that the "movements" caused evil (or evilness or malice or vice; *byšwt'* in Syriac almost certainly translates Greek κακία, which in Origen too was opposite to virtue and goodness). Germs of virtue were present in the intelligent creatures from the beginning, but they must be developed through a voluntary effort of each one's will (the "movements"). The adhesion to the Good in the end will be better than that obtaining at the beginning, in that it will be the fruit of the moral and spiritual development of rational creatures and will be fully voluntary. This idea, that the *telos* will be even better than the beginning, was typical of Origen as well (see, e.g., Lekkas, *Liberté et progrès*; Panayiotis Tzamalikos, *Origen: Cosmology and Ontology of Time* [Leiden: Brill, 2006], with my review in *Rivista di Filosofia Neoscolastica* 99 [2007]: 177–81; idem, *Origen: Philosophy of History and Eschatology* [Leiden: Brill, 2007], with my review in *Rivista di Filosofia Neoscolastica* 100 [2008]: 453–58; Ramelli, "Origen's Doctrine of the Apokatastasis"), who expressed it in the form of the final achievement of the ὁμοίωσις with God, which depends on personal, voluntary engagement and spiritual development, unlike the condition of being an εἰκών of God, which was an initial datum. So Evagrius here remarks that virtue could not exist without the exercise of free will in the "movement." Thus, the germs of virtue initially implanted by God in rational creatures could not fully develop without the "movement"—and will be perfect in the end, when all evil will be consequently destroyed.

1.52. When the knowledge of those who are the first by virtue of their leading position and who are second because of their coming into being will be in the principalities, then only those who are first in their leading position will receive the knowledge of the Trinity.

This *kephalaion* seems to be speaking of angels, and possibly of the higher ranking among them, who have a leading position and yet came to being as second after the Holy Trinity, which never came into being. The knowledge or science of the Trinity is the highest degree of knowledge, as Evagrius makes repeatedly clear in the *KG*. It should be noted, however, that in Evagrius's view, just as in Origen's and Gregory Nyssen's, human beings too, by means of striving for perfection, can ascend to the rank of angels.

1.53. The devils who fight against the intellect are called "birds"; those who trouble the *thymos*, "animals"; and those who agitate the *epithymia*, "bestial."

Evagrius sticks here to the Platonic tripartition of the soul into *epithymētikon*, or concupiscible faculty; *thymos* or *thymikon*, or irascible faculty; and *logikon*, or *logistikon*, or *nous*, the rational faculty of the soul or the intellect. This tripartition occurs frequently in the *KG*, but also in other works by Evagrius—for instance, in *Praktikos* 86: "The rational soul operates according to nature when its concupiscible/appetitive faculty desires virtue, while its irascible faculty fights for virtue, and the reasoning faculty applies itself to the contemplation of creatures." Demons, and their actions on the various faculties of the soul though passions, are associated with the notion of "ferine." The same was the case in Origen's thought. According to him, sinners are transformed into animals in an allegorical sense, and the transformation of animals into rational beings functions as a symbol of a spiritual evolution. For instance, in a passage preserved both in Greek and in Rufinus's translation of Pamphilus's *Apology for Origen* 180, Origen rejected the transmigration of souls and rather maintained a metaphorical "animalization" of the worst sinners: "Those who are alien to the catholic faith think that souls migrate from human bodies into bodies of animals.... On the contrary, we maintain that human wisdom, if it gets uncultivated and neglected due to much carelessness in life, becomes like an irrational animal [*efficitur uelut irrationabile pecus*] due to incompetence or neglectfulness, but not by nature [*non per naturam*]." Interestingly, the transformation of animals into rational beings as a symbol of moral and spiritual evolution is also reflected in the *Acts of Philip*. See Ilaria L. E. Ramelli, "Mansuetudine, grazia e salvezza negli *Acta Philippi*," *Invigilata Lucernis* 29 (2007): 215–28.

1.54. The plenitude of those who are primary in their principality is without limit, whereas vacuity is contained within a limit. Now, secondary beings are coextensive with vacuity. But they will rest when plenitude will have those who are susceptible of the immaterial science approach it.

The ontological priority of the Good and Origen's and especially Gregory of Nyssa's conception of God as infinite underlie this *kephalaion*. God/Good is the fullness and is infinite; evil is empty and is limited. This argument in Gregory of Nyssa's view also buttresses the doctrine of *apokatastasis* (see Ramelli, *Christian Doctrine of Apokatastasis*, the chapter on Gregory Nyssen). Those who are primary in their principality may be either the highest ranking among the primary beings or even the persons of the Trinity, the only Being without end; all creatures, on the contrary, participate in limitedness. But in the end the *theōsis* will have creatures participate in divine infinitude. Secondary beings according to Evagrius's own definition in *KG* 1.77 (see below, the commentary on this *kephalaion*) are represented by mortal bodies, which are here said to be coextensive with vacuity. Indeed, not bodies tout court but mortal bodies were created only as a consequence of the fall, that is, of rational creatures' detachment from the Good, which led them toward evil and vacuity.

1.55. Only those who are primary in their coming into being will be liberated from the corruption that is in act, whereas there is no one among the beings (that will be delivered) from that which is in potentiality.

Those who are primary, not in their principality but in the order of their coming into being, are creatures, and certainly rational creatures. Secondary beings are mortal bodies (see *KG* 1.77). Rational creatures will be liberated from the corruption that is in actuality, but no creature will be liberated from corruption that is in potentiality.

1.56. The good ones will be the cause of knowledge and of torment, whereas the evil ones only of torments.

It is probable that "the good ones" and "the evil ones" are rational creatures. If so, "the evil ones" are surely demons, while "the good ones" may be angels and possibly good human beings. These expressions might also refer to deeds: bad deeds will have torments as a result; good deeds will result in knowledge as well as possible torment (perhaps due to the persecution that good people may suffer in this world). The hypothesis that "the good ones" and "the evil ones" are rational creatures is also supported by the following *kephalaion*, which focuses on rational creatures.

1.57. Human beings fear Sheol, devils the abyss; but there are some who are more evil than these: the snakes that cannot be charmed.

Sheol is the kingdom of death, without necessarily implying torments or damnation, unlike the abyss. The category of human beings and of devils (or demons), who are rational creatures, seem to be differentiated from that of such irrational creatures as snakes. Snakes "which have no word" is the translation of Guillaumont, but it presupposes correcting *lm'* of the manuscript to *d-ml'*. But according to an autoptic check performed by Sebastian Brock, whom I thank very warmly for sharing this with me, the manuscript actually reads *lm'šp* (ܠܡܐܫܦ), "which one cannot charm." The last two letters, Brock observes, are very faint: this is why Guillaumont missed them. As Brock remarks *per litteras* (personal correspondence), "no doubt Evagrius says this with feeling, having experienced snakes in the Egyptian desert!"

In light of the assimilation of different categories of demons to different categories of animals (in *KG* 1.53), one may easily wonder whether these snakes could also be interpreted allegorically. The loss of rationality, and even of word, may indicate the deepest depravation of rational creatures who have abandoned their prerogatives instead of cultivating them. Of course, the choice of snakes, of all animals (in *KG* 1.53 we had demon-birds, demon-animals, and demon-ferocious-beasts), is not fortuitous: in Gen 3 and Rev 20 Satan is assimilated to a serpent. What is more, in Rev 1:1–3 the serpent, Satan, is thrown into the abyss, to which Evagrius refers here: "Then I saw an angel coming down from heaven, holding in his hand the key of the bottomless abyss and a great chain. And he seized the dragon, that ancient serpent, who is the Devil and Satan, and bound him for a thousand years, and threw him into the abyss, and shut it and sealed it over him" (RSV, slightly modified).

1.58. One of the kinds of death has birth as its primary cause; a second comes from the saints against those who do not live in justice, whereas the mother of the third will be remission. Now, if a mortal is the one that is meant by nature to be released/dissolved from the (mortal) body to which it is joined, something immortal is the one that is not meant by nature to experience this. For all those who have been joined to a (mortal) body will also necessarily be liberated.

In the last sentence, the Syriac word *kul*, "all," may also have the meaning of "all kinds of death." Evagrius describes here three different meanings of "death." The first is the death of the body, physical death, which affects all mortal creatures that have come into being through birth. This is necessary by nature and is a liberation from the mortal body, or *pgr'*. The second is the death of the soul, due to sin, which is the worst kind of death; it is a condemnation, here represented as performed by the saints against sinners. Sin is described as injustice, as opposite to justice, which for Plato was the main virtue of the soul—deriving from its equilibrium—and the first of the cardinal virtues (on justice in Plato, see Jonathan Barnes, "Justice Writ Large," in *Virtue and Happiness: Essays in Honour of Julia Annas* [ed. Rachana Kamtekar; Oxford Studies in Ancient Philosophy Supplements; New York: Oxford University Press, 2012], ch. 2, with a critique of

Socrates's argument about justice in the soul and justice in the state; and especially Paul Woodruff, "Justice as a Virtue of the Soul," in Kamtekar, *Virtue and Happiness*, 89–101). Evagrius himself takes over the definition of justice given by Plato (but attributing it to his own "wise teacher," probably Gregory Nyssen) in *Praktikos* 89.4: "Justice effects a certain symphony and harmony among the [different] parts of the soul."

The third kind of death is death to sin, which is a good. Evagrius makes remission of sins the cause of death to sin. This means liberation from sins. It seems evident that Evagrius is following Origen's classification of the three kinds of death, expressed in his *Dialogue with Heraclides* and elsewhere. See above, commentary on *KG* 1.40–41, and Ilaria L. E. Ramelli, "Origen's Exegesis of Jeremiah: Resurrection Announced throughout the Bible and Its Twofold Conception," *Aug* 48 (2008): 59–78. Death to sin, according to Evagrius, is the life of virtue that is pursued by the *praktikos*: "To separate the body from the soul [i.e., physical death] belongs exclusively to the One who united them [i.e., God], but to separate the soul from the body belongs to anyone who desires virtue. The life of withdrawal has been called by the fathers a preparation for death and flight from the body" (*Praktikos* 52). In the last sentence Evagrius refers to not better specified "fathers," though the concept is clearly Plato's μελέτη θανάτου and flight from the body. Plato's *Phaedo* is the most important text in this respect, and among Christian thinkers it was Gregory of Nyssa who had offered a Christian remake of Plato's *Phaedo* with his dialogue *On the Soul and the Resurrection.* It is therefore probable that Evagrius, when speaking of "fathers," has in mind Gregory Nyssen first of all.

The question of how human beings will be in the resurrection was treated above all by Athenagoras, Origen, Methodius, and Gregory of Nyssa, who devoted specific treatises to this (entitled *On the Resurrection*, or in the case of Gregory, *On the Soul and the Resurrection*). Like Gregory, Origen explicitly denies that any gender differentiation will endure in the resurrection, or any kind of nutrition, which are all traits related to mortality—for example, in *Commentary on Romans* 10.1.24–30: "The kingdom of God, for the sake of which we work hard and run, ought not to be considered to consist in food and drink, but these kinds of things should be regarded as extraneous to the kingdom of God and that future life of ours. For there, just as there will be neither men who take wives nor women who take husbands, but all will be like God's angels, likewise the risen will neither eat nor drink but will be like God's angels," *Regnum Dei, propter quod laboramus et currimus, neque per escam constet neque per potum, sed aliena haec sint a regno Dei et ab illa conuersatione futura. Ibi enim, sicut neque nubunt neque nubuntur, sed sunt sicut angeli Dei, ita neque escam neque potum sumunt, sed sunt sicut angeli Dei.*

1.59. As light and shadow are accidents of air, so virtue and evilness/ vice, and knowledge and ignorance, are joined with the rational soul.

Evagrius speaks very often in these *kephalaia* of virtue and knowledge and their interrelations, as well as of their respective opposites, vice and ignorance. Here he presents all of these as characteristics of rational souls, in the same way as light and shade are accidents of the air. In this way, light is a simile for knowledge and virtue, and shade is a simile for ignorance and vice. Evagrius often speaks of virtue and vice—for example, in *KG* 1.66 and 3.76, where they are seen as necessary choices for an adult person, who must needs adhere either to virtue or to evilness. In *KG* 4.22 virtues are said to be natural for the soul, while vices are against its nature. In *KG* 3.68 Evagrius makes it clear that virtue enables knowledge, and in *KG* 5.66 he remarks that the intellect cannot attain knowledge unless the soul in its passible part has attained virtue. So in *KG* 4.28 Evagrius closely associates "pure virtues" and "true doctrines," and in *KG* 5.37 he maintains that teaching allows the rational soul to rise from evilness to virtue. In *KG* 6.59 Evagrius claims that divine providence pushes rational creatures from evil and ignorance up to virtue and knowledge, both together, inseparably (see also *KG* 6.76 and 6.90). Likewise, in *KG* 5.45 Evagrius states that if one is separated from virtue, one is also separated from science. In *KG* 6.24 Evagrius avers that knowledge leads rational souls both from evilness to virtue and from ignorance to knowledge. And in *KG* 2.7 virtue and evilness or vice in the present life are said to reflect themselves in the future life. Especially *KG* 2.18 is very close to the *kephalaion* under examination here: it states that virtue and knowledge, or evilness and ignorance, are qualities of rational creatures that parallel the qualities of bodies.

The metaphor of the shadow, which is central to the present *kephalaion*, is deployed by Evagrius also elsewhere in the *KG*—for instance, in *KG* 4.29, where he states that "ignorance is the shadow of evilness" or vice, again in the context of a simile: just as the night is the shadow of the earth, so is ignorance the shadow of evilness. Metaphors involving shadows also appear in *KG* 5.14 and 5.17. More generally, metaphors concerning light and shade or darkness are ubiquitous in Evagrius. In *KG* 1.74 knowledge itself is described as light (exactly as in *KG* 1.81), and ignorance as darkness. In *KG* 1.72, light is associated with virtue and knowledge, and darkness with evilness or vice and foolishness or ignorance; at the same time Evagrius remarks that the Lord pushes ignorant people from evilness to virtue. The same passage is indicated as one of the positive transformations in *KG* 2.4. In *KG* 2.26 Evagrius actually claims that in the next world evilness will have to be eliminated. In *KG* 6.15, indeed, Evagrius is adamant that all will reach both practical virtue and contemplation. In *KG* 4.55 virtues are said by Evagrius to be the very "visage" or "face" of a soul, but if a soul does not practice virtue, this visage is rather in a shadow. In *KG* 1.35 the Godhead itself is said to be Light in its very essence, after 1 John 1:5. The intellect will be eschatologically joined to the light of the Trinity (*KG* 2.29; see also 2.90; 5.15, 26). In *KG* 3.58 it is spiritual love that is assimilated to light. The connection between light, knowledge, and love is made clear in *KG* 4.25: light symbolizes spiritual knowledge, and spiritual knowledge in turn, as a lamp, is alimented by the oil of holy love.

1.60. If today they receive the clever steward in their homes, it is evident that yesterday they sat down and modified their bills. Now, it is for this reason that he has been called "clever": the more he has remitted, the more he can receive.

This is an exegetical reflection on the parable of Luke 16:1–8:

> There was a rich man who had a steward, and charges were brought to him that this man was wasting his goods. And he called him and said to him, "What is this that I hear about you? Turn in the account of your stewardship, for you can no longer be steward." And the steward said to himself, "What shall I do, since my master is taking the stewardship away from me? I am not strong enough to dig, and I am ashamed to beg. I have decided what to do, so that people may receive me into their houses when I am put out of the stewardship." So, summoning his master's debtors one by one, he said to the first, "How much do you owe my master?" He said, "A hundred measures of oil." And he said to him, "Take your bill, and sit down quickly and write fifty." Then he said to another, "And how much do you owe?" He said, "A hundred measures of wheat." He said to him, "Take your bill, and write eighty." The master commended the dishonest steward for his shrewdness; for the sons of this world are more shrewd in dealing with their own generation than the sons of light. (RSV)

Those who sit down and modify their bill and then receive the steward, as Evagrius says here, are those who have debts with the master of the steward. The final teaching that Evagrius draws from the parable, "the more he has remitted, the more he can receive," is in line with Jesus's declaration in Matt 7:2; Mark 4:24; and Luke 6:38 that by the measure one measures one will be measured in turn, and with his exhortation in Luke 6:37: "Forgive, and you will be forgiven."

1.61. There exists none among secondary beings that is capable of knowledge, and none among primary beings that originally was in a place.

Primary beings are the intelligible beings, that is, rational souls (and Ideas), according to Evagrius's own definition in *KG* 1.77; secondary beings are mortal bodies (probably including animals, and perhaps also inanimate things). These came into existence after the fall of rational creatures and cannot have any knowledge per se. Primary beings are not mortal bodies and therefore cannot be diastematic, that is, subject to measure, space, and time (διαστήματα, a theme that is particularly developed by Gregory of Nyssa and Origen). This is not to say that souls can exist on their own, without any kind of body. Neither the body per se is a creature, nor the soul per se is, but the human being, or an angel, is a creature and has both a soul and a body (but what kind of body, it depends). Before the creation of the present world, rational creatures were not in a place, but, also according to Origen, they were in Christ-Logos-Wisdom. When they acquired a mortal body, they became diastematic and thus situated in a time and a place.

1.62. Knowledge is said to be in a place when the subject that is capable of it is joined to one of the secondary beings, which is said to be in a place in a real and principal sense.

In light of the immediately preceding passage, it is clear that the subject capable of knowledge is a primary being, a *nous*, an intellectual being, and that this is joined to a secondary being when it acquires a mortal body, which is diastematic—that is, subject to the dimensions of space and time. Thus, it is the mortal body that, properly speaking, is found in a place, not knowledge itself or the intellect/rational soul that knows.

1.63. That rational creatures should come into being in any time or not come into being at all, this depends on the Creator's will; but that they

be immortals or mortals, it depends on their free will, and that they be joined or not to a certain kind or another.

The existence of all rational creatures is decided by God, who creates them, but their existence in mortal bodies or in immortal ones depends on their free will, in that it is a consequence of their free choices. After the fall, some rational creatures acquired a mortal body. It depends on a rational creature's free will that it has one kind of body (mortal) or another (immortal). This corresponds closely to Origen's ideas. This also confirms the terminological distinction between *pgr'* (mortal body) and *gwšm'* (body more generally, including immortal) that I already pointed out in the *KG*.

1.64. The true life of rational creatures is their natural activity, whereas their death is their activity against nature. Now, if the one who is naturally made to cast away the true life is mortal of this kind of death, which of the beings is immortal? This is because every rational nature is liable to opposition.

Evagrius tackles again the motif of the death of the intellectual soul, an Origenian theme (see above, the commentary on *KG* 1.40–41 and 1.58): the soul is mortal of the real death, which comes from the soul's adhesion to sin. Rational creatures should be immortal and were meant to be so—the life of a rational creature is its adhesion to the Good—but they fall into death because of sin. Sin is against the nature of rational creatures, which is good insofar as they were created by God and for virtue. Death is contrary to their very nature. This is the opposition of which Evagrius speaks, which is also related to rational creatures' being constitutively suspended between the choice of the Good and that of evil. I say "constitutively" because free will is a constitutive component of rational creatures according to both Origen and Evagrius. Only God, indeed, is absolutely good in that God is Good itself (*KG* 1.1); creatures are good only insofar as they are created by God and participate in this primal Good. If rational creatures choose not to participate in this Good, they fall into its opposite, evil, which is against their nature. Both Origen and Gregory Nyssen, followed once again by Evagrius, adopted the Stoic theory of *oikeiōsis* to express the idea that the Good is familiar and natural for rational creatures (what the Stoics called πρῶτον οἰκεῖον), while evil is contrary to their nature (see below, *KG* 5.73, and Ilaria L. E. Ramelli, "The Stoic Doctrine of Oikeiosis and Its Transformation by Two Christian Platonists," *Apeiron* 47 [2014]: 116–40).

1.65. In (by) the knowledge of those that are secondary in their coming into being, different worlds/aeons are constituted, and indescribable battles are fought. In the unity, however, none of these things will occur; it will be an indescribable peace. There will be only bare/naked intellects who continually satiate themselves from its impossibility to satiate, if it is true that, according to the word of our Savior, "the Father does not judge anyone but has remitted all the judgment to Christ."

In accord with Origen, Evagrius also foresees the eventual *apokatastasis*, at the end of all aeons, as unity, primarily a unity of will, and peace. It is evident that this passage is also influenced by Gregory of Nyssa's notion of an infinite *epektasis*, in the mention of "bare/naked intellects who continually satiate themselves from its impossibility to satiate." The intellectual creatures will continually tend toward God, who is infinite, achieving a unity among them and with God that is not static but always dynamic. The theme of satiation also is Origenian: God will never fill the intelligences with *koros*, or satiation, in the end.

The right meaning here is "impossibility to satiate" rather than "insatiability," which is the translation of Guillaumont (p. 49: "insatiabilité"), followed by Dysinger, who ascribes this "insatiability" to the intellects ("their insatiability"), even though the possessive suffix in Syriac is singular, *-h*, which refers back to the unity and state of peace mentioned by Evagrius soon beforehand. Fr. Theophanes, although he is translating on the basis of the French rather than of the Syriac, gets closer to the correct meaning and renders "the naked *noes* which always take their fill of its inexhaustibleness," adding in note 5 to this passage: "Correcting the 'insatiabilité' of the text for sense." Indeed, the meaning is that God—and the state of unity with God—will never satiate the intellects: it is the divinity's "impossibility to satiate" ("insatiability" is rather ascribed by Evagrius, after Plato, repeatedly to the concupiscible-appetitive faculty, e.g., in *Eight Evil Thoughts* 1.27). This is essential, because *koros* was the cause of the fall of the intelligent creatures at the beginning, but in the end there will be no new fall, and this thanks to love (*agapē*), which, as Paul avers, "never falls." This is why after all intellectual souls have adhered to God in perfect love, after the manifestation of God's love in Christ, no one will possibly fall again. For this argument, which Origen put forward in his *Commentary on Romans*, see below, the commentary on *KG* 3.46 with the relevant texts. Evagrius in the *KG* makes a great deal of the concept of "bare intellect" or "naked intellect," meaning essentially an absolutely pure intellect. I will return to this later in the commentary.

The reign of the Father will come after that of Christ, who will judge and set right everyone (according to Origen, Nyssen, Eusebius, and Marcellus of Ancyra). The Father will not judge and will not need to: under the Father's reign, when the Son will have handed the kingdom to the Father, after the elimination of all opposite powers and all evil and death, the Father will not need to judge anyone anymore, because all will have been purified at that point, and God will be "all in all" (see Ramelli, "Christian Soteriology and Christian Platonism"). Evagrius's quotation at the end of the *kephalaion*, about the Judgment with which God has entrusted Christ, is from John 5:22.

The initial reference to worlds or aeons may allude either to the sequence of aeons (αἰῶνες) prior to the eventual *apokatastasis*, each aeon being the result of rational creatures' choices and knowledge, or else to the world (κόσμος) given by the knowledge of each rational creature (Evagrius indeed speaks of the κόσμος constituted by a person's διάνοια in *Skemmata* 14 and 38–39)—though Evagrius here speaks of knowledge of secondary creatures, and not of primary creatures, so that the genitive seems objective rather than subjective. Unless Evagrius is here referring again, as in *KG* 1.52, to those "who are second because of their coming into being," who are rational creatures.

1.66. Virtues are said to be before us, on the side on which we have senses, but vices behind us, on the side on which we have no senses. For we are commanded to "flee fornication" and are commanded to "pursue hospitality."

The two scriptural quotations around which this exegetical passage is built are 1 Cor 6:18 and Rom 12:13. The idea that we can see other people's vices but not our own vices was expressed in antiquity by the famous image of Phaedrus (*Fables* 4.10) of the two bags, one of which contains other people's vices and is before us, while the other contains our own vices and is behind us. This image was taken over by Persius in his fourth *Satire* (see Ramelli, *Stoici romani minori*, 1361–515). However, Evagrius does not illustrate exactly the same concept in this *kephalaion* but insists on virtues, which we can see in that they are before us, and vices, which we cannot see because they are behind us. He does not oppose other people's vices to our own but intends to explain the reason why Scripture uses the verb "to flee" in the injunction to avoid vices and "to pursue" in the exhortation to pursue virtues. To flee indicates a detachment from something that we should leave behind; to pursue indicates the action of trying to reach something that is before us. This is why Evagrius adopts the allegory of a spacial location of virtues before us and vices behind us. The very fact that we are built to have senses on the side where virtues are and not on that where vices lie may also refer to the notion that we were naturally made by God for virtue and not for vice (see *KG* 1.40–41 and 1.64, with the relevant commentaries).

1.67. Who knows the constitution of the world and the activity of the elements? And who will understand the composition of this instrument of our soul? Or who will investigate how this is connected with that, which their competences are, and their participation of the one in the other, so that the *praktikē* becomes a chariot for the rational soul that endeavors to reach the knowledge of God?

Here Evagrius is reflecting on the knowledge of the macro- and the microcosm, the material world and the human body, which is the instrument of the soul (σῶμα ὀργανικόν in the Aristotelian tradition, then adopted also in Neoplatonism), and the interrelationship between the body and the soul. The latter was a crucial point of investigation in ancient philosophy, and in Neoplatonism it was widely discussed, both from the "pagan" and from the Christian side. Porphyry in *Life of Plotinus* 13 recounts that for three whole days he asked Plotinus about the way the soul is in the body, and for three whole days Plotinus did not cease to reply. As for the Christian side of Neoplatonism, see Ramelli, "Preexistence of Souls." The rational soul, Evagrius explains, should take as its instrument the *praktikē* itself, the ethical and ascetic discipline, which of course is also meant to discipline the body. The goal of this discipline is, through purification, the attainment of the knowledge of God on the part of the rational soul. Purification is clearly indicated as the goal of *praktikē* in *Praktikos* 78: "*Praktikē* is a spiritual method that purifies the passionate part of the soul" (Πρακτική ἐστι μέθοδος πνευματικὴ τὸ παθετικὸν μέρος τῆς ψυχῆς ἐκκαθαίρουσα). The sequence of purification from passions, attainment of virtue, and knowledge was typical of the Platonic tradition, "pagan" and Christian alike. Porphyry, for instance, in his *Sentences Leading to the Intelligible* 32, likewise placed the cathartic or purificatory virtues before the theoretical and paradigmatic virtues. Evagrius in *Praktikos* 66 also envisages a progression from purifying *praktikē* to gnosis: "An intellect that has, with God's help, successfully accomplished *praktikē* and drawn near to knowledge [νοῦς σὺν

Θεῷ πρακτικὴν κατορθώσας καὶ προσπελάσας τῇ γνώσει], hardly if at all perceives the irrational part of the soul, because knowledge catches it up on high and separates it from perfectible things." In Evagrius it is especially emphasized that virtue and knowledge cannot possibly be disjoined from one another. I shall often have the chance to point this out in the *KG*, but this is not a feature of this work alone. In the eleventh of his *Skemmata*, for instance, Evagrius notes that instruction, that is, the acquisition of knowledge, "is the denial of impiety and worldly desires" (Παιδεία ἐστὶν ἄρνησις ἀσεβείας καὶ κοσμικῶν ἐπιθυμιῶν). Knowledge can be acquired only if one rejects passions and vices.

1.68. A prevalence of intellect and fire is in angels, of *epithymia* and earth in human beings, and of *thymos* and air in demons. And the third ones reach the middle ones through their nostrils, as it is said, and the first ones reach the second ones through the mouth.

Plato's tripartition of the soul is here clearly applied to the threefold classification of the rational creatures: angels, human beings, and demons. Their nature is the same, but they differentiate themselves by means of their choices and the degrees of their elongation from the Good. It is noteworthy that each class of rational creatures is also associated with an element, which suggests that none of them is completely separate from matter and corporeality. This is again in line with Origen's idea that only the Holy Trinity is utterly incorporeal, while all creatures participate in matter to some extent. The very fact that the influence exerted by angels and demons on human beings is described by Evagrius in physical terms ("through the mouth" and "through their nostrils") seems to confirm this. On demonic bodies in the Platonic tradition, see Smith, "How Thin Is a Demon?" In addition to the association with an element, each class of rational creatures is also associated with one of the three parts or faculties of the soul: the intellect (which is prevalent in angels); the concupiscible/appetitive part, or ἐπιθυμία/ἐπιθυμητικόν, in human beings; and the irascible part, or θυμός/θυμικόν, in demons.

1.69. With respect to the one who is the first position in knowledge, there is one who is after him or her, whereas in respect to the one who is in the first position in ignorance, there is no one.

This is because knowledge is positivity, while ignorance is negativity, lack of knowledge. There is no one after the one who is the most ignorant of all, that is, at the peak of negativity, whereas there are others who come after the one who is the most endowed with knowledge; these others are less endowed with knowledge.

1.70. With God, it is said that the first is the one who knows the Holy Trinity, and after this is the one who contemplates the intellections of the intelligible beings; the third, then, is the one who contemplates the incorporeal realities, and the fourth is the one who knows the *theōria* of the worlds/aeons, whereas the one who possesses the impassivity of the soul will be rightly listed as the fifth of these.

After stating in *KG* 1.69 that there are different degrees of knowledge, Evagrius is here describing a hierarchy in knowledge that reflects an ontological hierarchy (described from God's point of view): God (the Holy Trinity); the intellections of intelligible beings or Ideas; the incorporeal realities, which can be souls; and the worlds or aeons, which are the theatre of the transformations of matter. Under these various degrees of contemplation (the Syriac here transliterates Greek θεωρία), the ethical ideal of the impassivity, or *apatheia*, of the soul is placed, which is the domain of the *praktikē*. Therefore, as in *KG* 1.67, Evagrius posits ascesis, purification from passions, and the attainment of virtue as indispensable steps toward the acquisition of knowledge.

1.71. The end of natural knowledge is the holy Unity, whereas the end of ignorance does not exist, as it is said: "for there is no limit/aim to its magnitude."

After explaining in *KG* 1.70 the various levels of knowledge, Evagrius explains the goal of knowledge: the eventual Unity, which is the same as envisaged by Origen. He is here playing on the double meaning of τέλος: both "end," in the sense of goal and perfection, and "limit." While knowledge is oriented to an end of perfection, which is the blessed *telos* of *apokatastasis*, in which Unity will prevail, ignorance has no orientation to an end, because it is not constructive—there is no progress in it. Of course, in the scriptural quotation from Ps 144(145):3 this word, τέλος, bears the second meaning, that is, end as limit (and moreover it refers to God, whose greatness and majesty are said to have no limit, and not to ignorance!). But Evagrius clearly also superimposes the first meaning to it, given that the first meaning is the one that underlies his own initial declaration that the end or goal of natural knowledge is the holy Unity. Unity is the aim and perfection of knowledge. Ignorance, on the contrary, has no goal and no perfection, since it is pure negativity, like all forms of evil.

What is more, the definition of evil—which is the counterpart of ignorance ("ignorance is the shadow of evilness," *KG* 4.29)—as ἄπειρον in the sense of indefinite was well known to Evagrius from Plotinus, who described as ἄπειρον absolute evil (*Enneads* 1.8.9), in turn following Plato. Gregory of Nyssa posited God as ἄπειρον and evil as limited qua opposite of God. It is not to be ruled out that he was consciously "correcting" Plotinus: "Only what is contrary to Beauty and the Good is limited, whereas the Good, whose nature is not susceptible of evil, will progress toward the unlimited and infinite" (*On the Soul and the Resurrection* 97AB). Gregory probably thought that, if evil is ἄπειρον and Good / the Godhead too is ἄπειρον, there is not enough opposition between the two, which therefore risk telescoping into one another. Evagrius, with his inspirer Gregory Nyssen, realized the difficulty and took ἄπειρον in a different sense if it refers to God / the Good, meaning "infinite, unlimited" because there is nothing opposed to the first Good (*KG* 1.1), and if it refers to evil, meaning "indeterminate, indefinite" and "without goal, aimless."

1.72. The Lord has mercy upon the one to whom he gives spiritual knowledge, if it is true that "the just walks in the light, whereas the fool in darkness." ***But*** **the Lord has mercy upon the fool as well, in that he does not punish him at once, or in that he urges/incites him, to bring him from evilness to virtue.**

Evagrius goes on to discuss knowledge in this series of *kephalaia.* "The knowledge of the spirit" (so in Syriac) may mean both "spiritual knowledge" and "knowledge of the spirit" (with objective or subjective genitive); the latter, in turn, may imply both to know the spirit, and what is spiritual, and to know by means of the spirit. The scriptural reference is to Eccl 2:14. Indeed, in *KG* 1.32 Evagrius has already explained that spiritual knowledge is bestowed only on the righteous, and it is characteristic of his thought that virtue and knowledge are impossible to separate but are interdependent.

In the present *kephalaion*, first Evagrius draws a dichotomy between righteous and fools, and it would seem that God has mercy only upon the former, in that he bestows on them spiritual knowledge. But soon he adds that God in fact has mercy also on the latter, and he explains the work of divine providence: to push sinners from evil to the Good. This, of course, entails a very delicate equilibrium between divine providence and human free will. Already Origen was aware of this problem and argued that Providence leads all rational creatures to salvation without compromising their free will (see Ilaria L. E. Ramelli, "Origen, Bardaisan, and the Origin of Universal Salvation," *HTR* 102 [2009]: 135–68, with examples). Cassian, another Origenian belonging to a monastic context, like Evagrius, thought that divine providence will be even very close to *force* one's free will if this is necessary for the salvation of that creature; he would rather sacrifice the pole of human free will than that of God's goodness, omnipotence, and providence. See Ramelli, *Christian Doctrine of Apokatastasis*, the section on Cassian; and, for a new hypothesis on the identity of Cassian, see Panayiotis Tzamalikos, *The Real Cassian Revisited: Monastic Life, Greek Paideia, and Origenism in the Sixth Century* (Leiden: Brill, 2012); and idem, *A Newly Discovered Greek Father: Cassian the Sabaite, Eclipsed by John Cassian of Marseilles* (Leiden: Brill, 2012).

1.73. The life of the human being is the holy knowledge, whereas God's great mercy is the contemplation (*theōria*) of beings. Now, many wise men of this world have promised us knowledge, but "God's mercy is better than life."

Divine mercy (of which Evagrius has just spoken in *KG* 1.72) is, according to the quotation from Ps 63:3, superior to life itself, that is, to knowledge for human beings—since knowledge for rational creatures is their life. Indeed, the initial statement, that the life of human beings is knowledge, may also echo Jesus's words in Matt 4:4: "Man shall not live by bread alone, but by every word that proceeds from the mouth of God" (RSV). Now, God's mercy is the contemplation of beings (one of the contemplations listed in *KG* 1.27); therefore, contemplation is declared to be superior to knowledge. This *kephalaion* is in agreement with Evagrius's teaching that the contemplation of the Judgment is not the last contemplation but is followed by the last contemplation, that of God's providence (*KG* 1.27). God's mercy is closely associated with God's providence, as is also clear from the work of divine mercy as described in *KG* 1.72: to bring rational creatures from evil to the Good.

1.74. The light of the intellect is divided in three parts, that is, in the knowledge of the adorable and holy Trinity, in that of the incorporeal

nature that was created by it, and in the contemplation (*theōria*) of the beings.

Here is yet another *kephalaion* dealing with knowledge (hence the title *Kephalaia Gnostika*, or *Chapters/Propositions on Knowledge*). Intellectual knowledge is classified into three levels, which correspond to three decreasing ontological levels: the highest is that of God the Trinity, then comes that of incorporeal beings, created by God, and finally that of the contemplation of beings, including material beings. All created substances are material to a certain extent. The last element of the triad, the contemplation of beings, has just been identified in 1.73 as "God's mercy." I emend ܘܠܟܝܢܐ into ܘܠܕܟܝܢܐ, for reasons of parallelism: knowledge of the Trinity, knowledge of the incorporeal nature, contemplation of the beings. Without this emendation, the second "knowledge" (that of the incorporeal nature) would be lacking and the parallelism would be lost. This kind of error may have occurred very easily in the manuscript tradition, especially in *ṣertō* script, but also in *esṭrangela*. The incorporeal nature created by the Trinity is both intellectual souls and Ideas, the intelligible realities; not angels, since ܠܐ ܓܘܫܡܢܝܐ means that this nature is not only without a mortal body (*pgr'*) but also without a fine and immortal one (*gwšm'*). This, however, does not mean that Ideas or souls subsist independently; the latter are coupled with a body, whether mortal or not, to form a creature, be it an angel or a human being, or even an animal or a plant.

1.75. If the crown of righteousness is the holy knowledge, and moreover if the gold that includes stones points to the worlds/aeons that have been or that will be, then the contemplation (*theōria*) of the corporeal and the incorporeal nature is the crown that by the just judge is put on the head of the competitors.

Both "gold" and "that includes" are uncertain readings. The initial quotation and the reference to the just judge and to the competitors (the Syriac rendering of Greek ἀγωνισταί) refer to 2 Tim 4:8. Reward for virtue is represented again by Evagrius in terms of knowledge. The knowledge of the aeons is likened to the crown of knowledge that God, the just Judge, bestows on those who have deserved it by means of virtue.

1.76. It is not of the knowledge that is hidden in things that ignorance is made the opposite, but of the knowledge of those who have an under-

standing of things; ignorance, indeed, is not naturally constituted to exist in a corporeal nature.

Evagrius goes on to meditate on knowledge and its opposite, ignorance. Ignorance is in the knowing subject, and not in the objects of knowledge. Ignorance is not naturally constituted to be in a body, which is the object and not the subject of knowledge. Even when this body is not a stone or another inanimate object but is the body of a rational creature, knowledge and ignorance are in the intellect of this creature, and not in its body.

1.77. The secondary nature is the species of the mortal body, while the primary one is that of the soul; the intellect, then, is Christ, the one who is united to the knowledge of the Unity.

An ascending progression is depicted by Evagrius here: mortal body (*pgr'*), soul, intellect-Christ, and unity in the Trinity. The last sentence could also mean: "Christ, who unites (all) knowledge of the (process of) union." I render with "species" the noun ܢܝܫܐ, which Guillaumont rendered "sign" (p. 53). But the secondary nature is not a sign or symbol of the mortal body, but its species, paradigmatic form, and character, even its substance (*nyš'* can mean "paradigm, example, plan" too; see Sokoloff, *Syriac Lexicon*, 916–17, meanings 5, 9, 14), or its manner or mode (for this meaning of *nyš'*, see J. Payne Smith, ed., *A Compendious Syriac Dictionary*, [1903; repr., Winona Lake, Ind.: Eisenbrauns, 1998], 339, meaning *e*); it is the category or genus in which all mortal bodies are included. The assimilation of Christ to the intellect, or *nous*, was already present in Origen. Christ, being the Logos, is intellect. And the intellect in everyone is the image of God, who is Christ. Christ is indeed a synthesis of God and creature.

In his *Letter to Melania* too, Evagrius observes that the Son and the Spirit communicate knowledge directly to the intellect, whereas for some, less advanced, people (those who are "far from God"), they communicate it through the creation: "Just as the intellect operates in the body by means of the mediation of the soul, likewise the Father too, by means of the mediation of his own soul [i.e., the Son and the Spirit], operates in his own body, which is the human intellect" (15). Indeed, human intellects know thanks to the Logos and the Spirit, who make everything known to them (19); they do not become aware of their own nature but through the Logos and the Spirit, who are their souls (21). In turn, human intellects are the bodies of the Son and the Spirit (ibid.). We are the intelligible creation and are now found joined to this visible creation, "for reasons that it is impossible to explain here," Evagrius adds (*Letter to Melania* 13).

As for the psychological content of this passage as well as of *KG* 1.71, which depicts the ascent and progression of the soul, I agree with both Luke Dysinger (*Psalmody and Prayer*, 209) and Julia Konstantinovsky (*Evagrius*, 143) that Evagius offers a symbolic analogy, and not a theological definition such as was anathematized in the 553 Council of Constantinople (anathema 8).

1.78. The first renouncement is the abandonment of worldly things, which takes place thanks to one's will for the knowledge of God.

Evagrius is here meditating on the birth of one's decision to embrace asceticism (the *praktikē*). It is a voluntary decision in which the knowledge of God plays an important role, since it is the ultimate aim of the path of both *praktikē* and, subsequently, *gnōsis*. Once again asceticism and the pursuit of *apatheia* and virtue is not disjoined from the pursuit of knowledge according to Evagrius.

1.79. The second renouncement is the abandonment of evilness, which takes place thanks to God's grace and to the human being's effort.

After the first renouncement, that is, giving up the world (*KG* 1.78), Evagrius introduces the second, that is, giving up vice or evilness or evil (the underlying Greek was very probably κακία). Again, Evagrius lists both human free will and God's grace (or goodness), and the divine factor comes before the human factor in determining the rejection of evil. Once again, he agrees with Origen, who saw the movement toward the *apokatastasis*, and thus the spiritual progression of all rational creatures, as led both by divine providence and by the free will of the *logika*.

Origen rejected Gnostic predestinationism not only in *On First Principles* 3, which is a touchstone of his doctrine of free will and Providence (on which see Ramelli, "La coerenza della soteriologia origeniana"), but again many years later, in his *Commentary on Romans*, where in 7.14.53ff. he puts forward the very same arguments and scriptural examples as in *On First Principles* 3, and indeed he explicitly refers to his own exposition in that book. In this writing he also reflects on the meaning of God's prescience and predestination, especially in 7.6.80–88:

> Those whom God has called—that is, those whom God has called according to the intention of the good person in question—God has also made just. Now, even if this phrase, "according to the intention," is referred to God—that is, these people are said to be called according to the intention of God, who knows that a pious mind and a desire for salvation is in them—not even this will seem to contradict my explanation. For in this way neither does the cause of our salvation or perdition lie in God's foreknowledge, nor will our justification depend on God's call only, nor is the possibility of our being glorified totally taken away from our power.
>
> *Quos ergo uocauit, id est quos secundum propositum boni uocauit, illos et iustificauit. Quod et si secundum propositum ad Deum referatur, hoc est ut secundum propositum Dei, qui sciens in eis religiosam mentem et salutis inesse desiderium, uocati dicantur, non uidebitur his quae exposuimus etiam hoc esse contrarium. Hoc ergo pacto neque in praescientia Dei uel salutis uel perditionis nostrae causa consistit, neque iustificatio ex sola uocatione pendebit, neque glorificari de nostra penitus potestate sublatum est.*

From the beginning, in 1.5.10–13, Origen insists that God's election is never arbitrary or due to a distinction of natures within humanity, as the "Gnostics" maintained: "Paul was not chosen by chance, or because he had a different nature from other people, but he provided the One who knows all things before they happen with reasons for his own election in himself, and it is not due to an iniquitous judgment of God that some sinners are separated (by God) since their gestation," *Neque Paulus fortuitu aut naturali differentia electus est, sed electionis suae causas in semet ipso dedit ei qui scit cuncta antequam fiant, neque peccatores qui separantur a uentre iudicii iniquitate separantur.*

1.80. The third renouncement is separation from ignorance, which is naturally made to be manifested to human beings according to the advancement of their condition.

After speaking of the first and second renouncement in *KG* 1.78–79, that is, giving up worldly things and evil(ness) respectively, Evagrius passes on to the third here. Separation from ignorance parallels separation from evil. Abandoning ignorance clearly means acquiring knowledge, which comes in several degrees, according to the degree of spiritual advancement of each human being. Thus, here we find again the scheme—dear to the

Neoplatonists, as I have mentioned—of *praktikē* first (with the relevant purification) and then knowledge.

1.81. The glory and the light of the intellect is knowledge, whereas the glory and the light of the soul is *apatheia*.

Absence of passions is the goal of ethics (this is a Stoic ideal shared by Origen and Gregory of Nyssa as well), that is, of *praktikē* in Evagrius's terminology; knowledge is the end of intellectual activity. See the commentary on *KG* 1.67, 70, and 80 for the purification–knowledge sequence in Evagrius's thought.

1.82. That which sense-perceptible death customarily performs in us, well, in the same way "the righteous judgment of God" will realize this in the other rational creatures, in the time in which he "is going to judge the living and the dead" and "will reward each one according to his or her deeds."

For Gregory of Nyssa and for Methodius, another follower of Origen, physical death is a positive good, since it puts an end to human sins and prevents them from growing *in infinitum*, and therefore from needing an infinite purification, tantamount to an eternal punishment (see Ramelli, *Christian Doctrine of Apokatastasis*, the chapters on Nyssen and Methodius). The destruction of the mortal body, liable to passions, will provide a point of departure for its rebuilding into a glorious and incorruptible body, free from passions and evil. The other rational creatures who have no mortal body clearly cannot benefit from death in this way, but Evagrius asserts that God will provide them too with something equivalent, and therefore equally salvific, in the eschatological scenario. The contemplation of the Judgment, as I have already pointed out, in Evagrius's thought corresponds to the penultimate stage, the last one being the contemplation of God's providential mercy.

Evagrius's first quotation, on the righteous or impartial judgment of God, is from 2 Thess 1:5; the second, on God's judging the living and the dead, is from 1 Pet 4:5; the third, on the retribution of each one according to one's deeds, is from Rev 22:12.

1.83. If it is true that the Gihon is the Egyptian river that surrounds the whole land of Cush, from which Israel was ordered, by means of one

of the prophets, not to drink, we have also known those three other branches and the river from which the four branches have spread.

This is another piece of allegorical exegesis of the Bible in Evagrius; we shall encounter many in the *KG*. I rendered "branches" what in the Syriac is "heads," which indicated the branches of a river, as is confirmed by the scriptural passages to which Evagrius refers: Gen 2:13, about the four rivers that flowed out of Eden (Pishon, which flows around the land of Havilah, where there is gold; Gihon; Tigris; and Euphrates), and Jer 2:18, which forbids Israel to drink from the rivers of Egypt and Assyria. "The river from which the four branches have spread" is the river that flows in Eden and goes out, dividing into the above-mentioned four branches. Given the prohibition to drink from the Egyptian river, it is clear that Evagrius attaches quite a negative meaning to it, which is reinforced by a negative symbolism of Egypt in *KG* 5.88, where Egypt is labeled "the emblem of every evilness," and *KG* 6.49, where Evagrius hammers home that "Egypt indicates evil," as well as in *KG* 4.64; 5.6, and 21. This association of Egypt with evil and vice was a heritage of Philo of Alexandria and Origen. See below the full commentary on *KG* 6.49.

1.84. Knowledge and ignorance are joined to the intellect, the concupiscible/appetitive part (of the soul) is susceptible of chastity and lust, and the irascible part usually experiences love and hatred. Indeed, the first goes together with the first ones, the second with the second ones.

Evagrius describes how each part of the soul (according to the Platonic tripartition into νοῦς or λογιστικόν, ἐπιθυμητικόν, θυμικόν that is often found in the *KG*) has its own couple of opposites, the first positive and the second negative:

Soul's Faculty or Part	Positive Quality	Negative Quality
Intellect	Knowledge	Ignorance
Epithymētikon	Chastity	Lust
Thymikon	Love	Hatred

It is clear that not only the intellect or rational faculty but also the passionate faculties can have positive aspects. That of the irascible part is love, and even hatred against the right object—that is, evil, the devil, and evil thoughts—can be positive. If it is used against nature, against one's brothers, then it is negative. It all depends on how a person uses her irascible faculty, as Evagrius makes clear in *Eulogius* 11.10:

> The use of the irascible faculty consists in *fighting against the serpent* with hostility, but with gentleness and mildness *exercising patience with charity-love* [ἀγάπη] toward one's brother while battling against the evil thought. The mild person should therefore be a fighter.... But do not turn the use of the irascible faculty to what is contrary to nature, so as to use your irascible faculty against your brother and thus become like the serpent, and friends with the serpent, by consenting to evil thoughts. The mild person, even if she suffers terrible things, does not abandon charity-love [ἀγάπη], since thanks to love she exercises patience and forbearance, kindness and perseverance.

1.85. The intellect wanders when it is affected by passions, and it becomes unrestrainable when it realizes the constitutive matters of its desires. On the other hand, it refrains from going astray once it has become impassive and has got together with those realities that are incorporeal, those that satisfy all its spiritual desires.

The natural objects of the intellect are the intelligible and incorporeal realities; if it is directed to different objects, it deviates and is liable to passions. Passions affect not simply the concupiscible part of the soul, just mentioned in *KG* 1.84, but the intellect, or *nous*, the highest faculty of the soul. Hence the importance of its attaining impassibility. This does not mean that at this point the *nous* has no desires left, but rather it has only spiritual desires, which are classified by Evagrius as good.

1.86. Charity-love is the excellent state of the rational soul, a state in which the soul cannot love anything that is among corruptible beings more than the knowledge of God.

Evagrius too, like Origen and Gregory Nyssen, attaches much importance to charity-love (ἀγάπη). Love will characterize the eventual *apokatastasis* itself and will guarantee that there will be no further falls from that state. Origen developed a long argument to this end in his *Commentary on Romans*, which I have reproduced entirely below, in my commentary on *KG* 5.46 (see there; cf. also commentary on *KG* 1.65). Origen there claimed that love will prevent further falls from the final blessed state on the grounds of Paul's declaration that "love never falls" (*caritas numquam cadit*; ἡ ἀγάπη οὐδέποτε [ἐκ]πίπτει). Evagrius too explains here the reason why love will prevent any further falls: it is because the object of the soul's strongest love is the knowledge of God. This will prevent the soul from choosing any other object of love as preferable to the knowledge of God. Once again Evagrius follows in Origen's footsteps and, identifying charity-love as the perfect state of the rational soul and making the knowledge of God the object of this love, shows that not only knowledge but love too pertains to the ultimate *telos* and perfection of rational creatures. In *KG* 4.50 too, knowledge and love are inseparably joined together (see below, the relevant commentary, as well as *KG* 3.58 and commentary).

As for Gregory of Nyssa, I have already pointed out in the introductory essay that a passage on love and knowledge in his dialogue *On the Soul and the Resurrection* very probably inspired this *kephalaion* of Evagrius.

1.87. All beings have come into existence thanks to God's knowledge. Now, everything that has come into being thanks to something else is inferior to the one thanks to which it has come to existence. This is why God's knowledge is superior to all.

God's knowledge (where, of course, "God's" is a subjective genitive) is the creative agent and as such is superior to all creatures. Now, God's Knowledge, by virtue of its creative function, is very close to God's Wisdom-Logos, that is, Christ, whose role in creation was abundantly underlined by Origen, in the footsteps of Philo of Alexandria and in the light of both John's Prologue (where the creative function of the divine Logos is declared) and Middle-Platonic reinterpretations of the *Timaeus*. See Ramelli, "Clement's Notion of the Logos." If so, Christ-Logos-Wisdom is superior to all creatures.

1.88. Natural knowledge is the true comprehension of those realities that have come into being thanks to the Holy Trinity's knowledge.

God's knowledge, as Evagrius stated in the preceding *kephalaion*, is creative; thus, it works not only on the gnoseological plane but also on the ontological one. Creatures' knowledge works only at the gnoseological level and is applied by them to the beings that were created by God's creative knowledge. Natural knowledge pertains to the realm of physics, the study or contemplation of the natural world.

While the concept of God's knowledge comes close to that of God's Logos-Wisdom, who is Christ (see commentary on *KG* 1.87), here it is also stated, in line more with Gregory of Nyssa than with Origen, that this knowledge is the Trinity's knowledge. In case God's knowledge should be identified with Christ, Christ would be the knowledge of the two other persons of the Trinity.

1.89. All rational nature has been naturally made in order to exist and to be capable of knowledge. Now, God is essential knowledge. Rational nature has as its opposite nonexistence, whereas knowledge (has as its opposites) evilness and ignorance. Yet, nothing among these things is opposed to God.

Not only is God's knowledge the cause of creation, but God is also Knowledge itself, and, with an expression that in Evagrius's work is technical for God, "essential knowledge." All creatures can know insofar as they participate in this Knowledge. At the end of his *Letter to Melania* too, Evagrius describes God as "essential knowledge" and proclaims that in the very end, at the *apokatastasis*, which will imply ἕνωσις (union) and θέωσις (deification), all intellects will share in this knowledge, and all kinds of knowledge will be elevated to the rank of essential knowledge. Evagrius describes here "the *telos* of all intellects" as "the union of all these different knowledges in one and the same and unique real knowledge" and as "all becoming this one without end" (66). Evagrius goes on to say that "all the different and distinct forms of knowledge will fuse together, into one and *the same essential knowledge*: all of those will become this only knowledge, forever.... The great ark containing all the treasures of wisdom is the heart of Christ, on which John reclined during the Last Supper." Just because Christ is the ultimate knowledge, he is said by Evagrius to be "the very *telos* and ultimate blessedness" for all rational creatures (*Letter* 63, which perfectly corresponds to the final part of the *Letter to Melania* I have quoted).

The opening notion of this *kephalaion*, that every rational creature was created by God in order to exist, was prominent already in Origen, who also maintained this as an argument in favor of the salvation of the devil (not qua devil, but qua creature of God): God will never destroy the devil's substance, because God created the devil, and every other rational creature, in order that they could exist. The destruction of even one single rational creature would mean the defeat of God's creative action. See Gabriel Bunge,

"Créé pour être," *BLE* 98 (1997): 21–29; Ramelli, "Christian Soteriology and Christian Platonism"; and my discussion against the assumption that Origen did not believe in the devil's salvation because of his valuing free will (Ramelli, *Christian Doctrine of Apokatastasis*, the chapter on Origen); I argue, on the contrary, that he envisaged that possibility precisely on the basis of the permanence of free will in every creature. Further arguments will appear in a monograph on Origen.

In Evagrius's perspective, the ontological fullness of knowledge is proved by the very fact that its opposite is not only ignorance but also evil. This is because Evagrius has equated God with Knowledge itself, and God is the Good, the opposite of which is evil. In God, as I have already pointed out, knowledge has not only a gnoseological value but also an ontological one (God's knowledge, indeed, is creative). Evagrius's last sentence, that nothing is opposed to God, does not in fact contradict this but takes up *KG* 1.1 and is meant to highlight the absolute positiveness of God, in a radical ontological monism: God is the Being and the Good, and there is no opposite pole that is equal and can stand against it in a metaphysical dualism. Evil is the opposite of Good, but evil is *nonbeing*.

1.90. If today is that which is called Friday, in which our Savior was crucified, indeed, all those who are dead are the parable/image of his sepulcher; those in which the justice of God is dead, which will revive on the third day and will rise, when it will take on a spiritual body, if it is true that "today and tomorrow he works miracles, and on the third day is done."

Evagrius is here drawing on a conception that already Origen maintained: in Jesus's death all humanity has died, and his historical resurrection is the figure of the glorious general resurrection of all humanity, the body of Christ, that will occur in the end. This idea was developed by Gregory of Nyssa as well (see full documentation in Ramelli, "Clement's Notion of the Logos"). Now, it is crucial to remark that for Evagrius, no less than for Origen and Nyssen, this resurrection is not simply the reconstitution of the dead body but a holistic renewal of the whole of the human being, including soul and intellect with their purification and the rejection of evil (death's cause), which is the premise of the *apokatastasis*. This is identified with the third day, that in which everything is accomplished and perfected (the final scriptural quotation is from Luke 13:32).

The Syriac word that I have translated "parable/image" is *pl't'*, which means "simile, riddle, parable." Extensively, it can be taken to mean "image" (better than "symbol" proper). The dead humanity is the image, and the enigmatic expression (like a parable!), of the dead Jesus, who lay in his tomb, and thus the resurrected and restored humanity is represented by the risen Jesus. It is remarkable that the resurrection/restoration is also equated with the restoration of the justice of God, which is said to have died together with Jesus and all humanity. This is the spiritual death of sin, "the real death" according to Origen's definition (see above, the commentaries on *KG* 1.40–41, 58, and 64), from which the resurrection will liberate and save humans. This depends on the fact that Christ is the Justice of God (as Origen insisted, Christ is Justice itself); therefore, when Christ is dead, the Justice of God is dead, and when Christ rises again, the Justice of God is resurrected.

Last, it is to be noticed that the resurrection is indicated as the taking up of a spiritual body, which corresponds to the Pauline *σῶμα πνευματικόν*. Literally, in Syriac it is a "body of spirit," an expression in which of course "body" is not *pgr'*, which designates the mortal, corruptible body, but *gwšm'*, which indicates the bodies that, like the angelic ones, are immortal.

***

In the S_2 manuscript, at this point, the following indication is added: "The first is finished." The corresponding indication in the manuscripts of the S_1 redaction is more elaborated: "The first century is finished, which lacks ten chapters." The idea is that a century should have a hundred chapters (see the introductory essay for the discussion concerning the finished or unfinished nature of the *KG*). The correct rendering of Κεφάλαια Γνωστικά, however, is not "Gnostic Centuries," but "Gnostic Chapters," or better, even "Gnostic Propositions" or "Propositions on Knowledge," as I have suggested.

Second Discourse

2.1. The mirror of God's goodness, and power, and wisdom, is those that in origin were brought into being, something from nonbeing.

Evagrius too, like Origen, supports the notion of *creatio ex nihilo*. Origen in his *Homilies on Genesis* 1.1 remarks that Gen 1:1 ("In the beginning God made heaven and earth," *In principium fecit Deus caelum et terram*) proves that God is "the principle of all," *principium omnium*, so that it is utterly excluded that there is another principle coeternal with God and independent of God. In *On First Principles* 4.4.6 he declares that matter originally lacked in form and order and was not coeternal with God: "'For the earth was invisible and in disorder.' By means of these words Moses seems to have indicated nothing but matter without form.... I deny that matter must be declared to be nongenerated or uncreated, as I have argued above insofar as I could," *Inuisibilem namque et incompositam terram: non aliud eis Moyses quam informem materiam uisus est indicare ... abnuimus ingenitam uel infectam dici debere materiam secundum haec quae in prioribus prout potuimus ostendimus*. In the same work, 1.3.3, Origen rejects the hypothesis of the coeternity of matter with God, precisely within an argument that aims at demonstrating that God created all things: "That all things have been created by God, and that there is no substance that has not received its being by God, is proved by many statements found in all of Scripture. What some people falsely teach about the coeternity of matter with God or the uncreated nature of souls must be rejected," *Quod autem a deo uniuersa creata sint, nec sit ulla substantia quae non ab eo hoc ipsum ut esset acceperit, ex multis totius scripturae adsertionibus conprobatur, repudiatis atque depulsis his, quae a quibusdam falso perhibentur, uel de materia deo coaeterna uel de ingenitis animabus*. Origen brings about another argument as well in order to demonstrate that matter was created by God: "We shall ask them: Was matter created, or is it uncreated, that is, not made? And if they answer that it is uncreated, we shall ask them whether a part of matter is God and a part is the world. If they reply that matter was created, the consequence will undoubtedly be that they will have to acknowledge that the one they call God was created—something that neither their reason nor ours can possibly admit," *Interrogabimus eos: materia facta est aut ingenita, id est infecta? Et si quidem dixerint quia infecta est ... requiremus ab eis si materiae pars quidem aliqua Deus, pars autem mundus est. Si uero responderint de materia quia facta est, sine dubio consequetur ut eum, quem deum dicunt, factum esse fateantur, quod utique nec ipsorum nec nostra ratio admittit* (2.4.3).

That Origen maintained that God created all realities, including matter, is also attested by Rufinus in his *Apology to Anastasius* 6: "God created all things out of nothing.... This is the opinion of Origen and a few other Greeks," *Omnia Deus creauerit ex nihilo.... Hoc sentit et Origenes et nonnulli alii Graecorum.* What is more, Origen's *creatio ex nihilo* theory is clearly proved by a Greek text of Origen himself: *Commentary on John* 1.17.103, where he polemicizes against those who considered matter to be uncreated, or ἀγένητος—"pagan" philosophers but also Christians, mainly "Gnostics" and Marcionites (see Tertullian, *Against Marcion* 1.15); but also Justin, *First Apology* 10.2, refers to a creation out of unformed matter, ἐξ ἀμόρφου ὕλης (see also ibid. 59). Origen contends that God created all beings from nonbeing: ἐξ οὐκ ὄντων τὰ ὄντα ἐποίησεν ὁ Θεός. Likewise, in *On First Principles* 2.1.4 Origen attacks those who assumed the coeternity of matter with God: he admires their mind but rejects their doctrine: "I have no idea why so great and learned men have deemed matter uncreated, that is, not made by God, the creator of all, but have declared its nature and power to be somehow accidental ... since they deem matter to be uncreated and coeternal with the uncreated God," *Nescio quomodo tanti et tales uiri ingenitam [materiam], id est non ab ipso Deo factam conditore omnium putauerunt, sed fortuitam quandam eius naturam uirtutemque dixerunt ... ingenitam dicentes esse materiam deoque ingenito coaeternam.* Origen's refutation is linear: "For how could it not seem impious to declare uncreated that which, if regarded as created by God, turns out to be certainly identical to what is called uncreated?" *Quomodo ergo non uidebitur impium id ingenitum dicere quod, si factum a deo credatur, tale sine dubio inuenitur quale et illud est quod ingenitum dicitur?* Consistently with his refutation, in *On First Principles* 2.1.4 Origen holds that God created both matter and its qualities: "Thus, this matter, which is so much and such as to be enough to constitute all the bodies of the world that God wanted to exist ... receives in itself the qualities that God wanted to assign it," *Hanc ergo materiam, quae tanta et talis est ut et sufficere ad omnia mundi corpora quae esse Deus uoluit queat … recipiens in se qualitates quas ipse uoluisset imponere.* And in 4.4.7 Origen states that no substance can ever exist without qualities ("a substance has never existed without any quality," *numquam substantia sine qualitate subsistit*), which is clearly a claim of basic import for his argument concerning the creation of matter *ex nihilo* against the thesis of its preexistence without qualities. This point will be taken over by Gregory of Nyssa, according to whom matter consists in the union of intelligible qualities, which explains how God created it while being totally immaterial and intelligible, and rules out the preexistence of a material substratum without qualities (see Cinzia Arruzza, "La matière immatérielle chez Grégoire de Nysse," *FZPhTh* 54 [2007]: 215–23; Anna Marmodoro, "Gregory of Nyssa on the Creation of the World," in *Causation and Creation in Late Antiquity* [ed. Anna Marmodoro and Brian Prince; Cambridge: Cambridge University Press, 2015], 94–110; George Karamanolis, *The Philosophy of Early Christianity* [Durham: Acumen, 2013], 101–6). Origen goes on to refute those who think that a preexistent matter was subsequently given qualities (*subiacenti cuidam materiae additas extrinsecus qualitates*). Matter without qualities can only be contemplated by the intellect, "hypothetically and mentally only," *sensu solo ac ratione* (4.4.8). His conclusion makes it clear that Origen engages in the discussion of qualities in relation to matter in order to support the doctrine of *creatio ex nihilo* by denying the preexistence of uncreated matter: "All things have been caused to exist by God, and there is nothing that has not been created but the nature of the Father, of the Son, and of the Holy Spirit," *Omnia quae sunt a Deo facta esse, et nihil esse quod factum non sit praeter naturam Patris et Filii et Spiritus Sancti* (4.4.8).

Evagrius's doctrine of *creatio ex nihilo* situates itself along the lines of Origen's and the Cappadocians' theory. Creation, as Evagrius remarks in the *kephalaion* under examination here, proves God's goodness, because it is completely gratuitous; it proves God's power, because it brought everything into being from nonbeing. It manifests God's Wisdom because it is Christ-Wisdom-Logos who created everything; the following *kephalaion* will be devoted precisely to Christ-Wisdom-Logos as creator.

2.2. In the secondary natural contemplation (*theōria*) we see Christ's Wisdom, full of varieties, that which he used and in which he created the worlds/aeons, whereas in the knowledge that is about rational creatures we have been instructed concerning his substance.

Evagrius goes on to reflect on the creation and its agent, Christ-Wisdom-Logos. Christ's creative Wisdom gave rise to the aeons after rational creatures' fall, and the knowledge of the aeons and all that is in them is identified by Evagrius with the "secondary natural contemplation," that is, the contemplation of the secondary nature, material and postlapsarian. This kind of contemplation reveals Christ's Wisdom qua "full of varieties" (Eph 3:10) precisely in reference to the multiplicity of postlapsarian creation. But the contemplation of the primary nature, prelapsarian rational creatures or *logika*, reveals Christ's substance as divine Logos. The *logika* are related not to the postlapsarian creative work of the Logos but to its substance, in that we are dealing with the Logos, whose substance is the *logos* that is the substance of all the *logika*, or rational creatures. As Origen put it, they were decorations on the Logos's/Wisdom's body before they acquired independent substance as creatures endowed with free will and liable to falling. Origen refers to the very same scriptural passage as Evagrius, Eph 3:10, to support the notion of the Ideas, or *logoi*, of all rational creatures as decorations on Christ's/Wisdom's body (taking πολυποίκιλος in Eph 3:10 to mean "full of various decorations"). The Christian Middle Platonist Bardaisan of Edessa too, very interestingly, shortly before Origen used this peculiar image of decorations to represent the Ideas, or *logoi*, of all beings on the surface of the body of Christ-Logos: in a fragment from his work *On India* reported by Porphyry, these are the figures of all existing beings chiselled on the surface of a statue symbolizing the cosmic Christ. This bears an impressive similarity to Origen's image of the Ideas, or *logoi*, of creatures that were initially found as decorations on the surface of the body of Christ-Logos-Wisdom in *Commentary on John* 19.22.147. These were decorations on the body of Christ-Wisdom as the creator of the world and formed his "intelligible Beauty with many decorations" (πολυποίκιλον νοητὸν κάλλος; ibid. 1.9.55). The notion of Christ-Logos's body covered with decorations representing the Ideas of creatures is identical in Origen and in Bardaisan and is not found in other previous authors (Clement cites Eph 3:10 in his *Miscellany* 1.3.27.1, but joining it to Heb 1:1, and referring it to the variety of God's Wisdom in art, science, faith, and prophecy, and not to the *logoi* of creation on the body of Christ-Logos-Wisdom). Origen might have read Bardaisan's treatise *On India* shortly after its composition in 220–222 C.E., or at least this section. This was interesting to him because of the interpretation of the *Timaeus* and Genesis, and the Christianization of Middle Platonism found in it. If it was known to Porphyry and probably, therefore, in Plotinus's school, it is possible that Origen read it in the same

Greek translation or redaction that was available to Porphyry. Or they may depend on a common, unknown source. See here the commentaries on *KG* 3.22 and 1.43; and Ramelli, *Bardaisan of Edessa*.

In the first of his *Skemmata*, or *Reflections*, which, according to Babai, were meant to complete the incomplete *KG*, Evagrius explains: "Christ, qua Christ, possesses the essential knowledge [i.e., God]; qua creator, possesses the *logoi* of the aeons; and qua incorporeal, possesses the *logoi* of the incorporeal realities." There is no doubt that Christ is creator, for Evagrius, and that Christ is the Logos, who is the creator according to the Johannine prologue. Christ-Logos, for Evagrius just as already for Clement, Origen, and Nyssen, has in himself all the *logoi*, or the Ideas, of all creatures, which he also created as substances eternally. See Ramelli, "Clement's Notion of the Logos." In *Gnostikos* 40 Evagrius makes it clear that Christ, qua creator, holds the *logoi* of all beings, including their first *logos*, which even angels, being creatures, cannot reach: "For each created thing there is not only a single *logos* but a large number, according to the measure of each one. For the holy powers attain to the true *logoi* of the objects, but *not unto the first*, that which is *known by Christ alone*." That Christ is a compound of creature (a rational creature) and God is also clear from the fifth of Evagrius's *Skemmata*: "Christ is the *logikon* who has in himself what is symbolized by the dove descending upon him," that is, God the Spirit. In *Praktikos* 92 the *logoi* of God are consistently said by Evagrius to be found in the nature of all creatures (in a saying attributed to Antony the Great): "One of the sages of that time came to Antony the Just and said: 'Father, how can you endure being deprived of the comfort of books?' And Antony replied: 'My book, O philosopher, is the nature of created beings, and it is there when I want to read the *logoi* of God.'"

In his *Letter to Melania* 30, Evagrius supports the distinction between the eternal existence of the *logoi*, or Ideas, of all creatures in God's Logos—what Origen and Bardaisan represented as decorations on the body of Christ, as I have pointed out—and their creation as substances in time: "*I do not mean that rational creatures were eternally in God in their substance,* since, although they were completely united to God in God's Wisdom and creative power, *their actual creation did have a beginning in time.*" This distinction clearly derives from Origen, *On First Principles* 1.4.4–5:

> God the Father has certainly always existed, always having his only begotten Child, who at the same time is also called Wisdom.... Therefore, in this Wisdom, who had always been with the Father, the creation

> had always been present as an orderly arrangement of chiseled forms, and there was no time when in Wisdom there was no prefiguration of the creatures that would exist.... In this way, we cannot say that creatures are uncreated or coeternal with God, nor, on the other hand, that God suddenly turned to action after a previous period in which he was doing nothing good.... Now, if all creatures have been made in Wisdom, since Wisdom has always existed, then as a prefiguration and preformation there have always existed in Wisdom those creatures that later on have been also created as substances.
>
> *Deum quidem Patrem semper fuisse, semper habentem unigenitum Filium, qui simul et Sapientia ... appellatur.... In hac igitur Sapientia, quae semper erat cum Patre, descripta semper inerat ac formata conditio et numquam erat quando eorum, quae futura erant, praefiguratio apud Sapientiam non erat.... Ut neque ingenitas neque coaeternas Deo creaturas dicamus, neque rursum, cum nihil boni prius egerit Deus, in id ut ageret esse conversum.... Si utique in Sapientia omnia facta sunt, cum Sapientia semper fuerit, secundum praefigurationem et praeformationem semper erant in Sapientia ea, quae protinus etiam substantialiter facta sunt.*

See also above, the commentary on *KG* 1.14.

2.3. The first of all kinds of knowledge is the knowledge of the Monad and of Unity, and spiritual knowledge is more ancient than every natural contemplation. The former, indeed, went forth from the Creator in the beginning and appeared together with the nature that accompanied it.

The priority of the knowledge of intelligible or spiritual realities such as the *logika* over the contemplation of the world has already been emphasized by Evagrius in the preceding *kephalaion*. Now he explains that over the latter, which he calls "natural contemplation" (that is, the contemplation of the natural, material world), and even over the former, which is here called "spiritual knowledge" (that is, the knowledge of spiritual or intellectual things), there is the contemplation of the Unity, which is divine (in the initial Unity all *logika* were included, and they will return to this Unity in God and with God in the ultimate end, with their restoration and deification).

This gnoseological hierarchy clearly reflects an ontological hierarchy: (1) God; (2) intelligible beings; (3) the rest of creation. Evagrius, especially in the last sentence of this *kephalaion*, seems to imply that this ontological and gnoseological hierarchy also has a chronological counterpart: first came God, who is eternal and uncreated; then the intelligible beings, which are nondiastematic, but nevertheless created ("in the beginning"); then the sense-perceptible creation, which was created in the dimension of time. Note that in the last sentence the intellectual creatures are intimated to have appeared together with their bodies, which immediately accompanied them. These were not yet heavy, mortal bodies, but in the prelapsarian state they were light, incorruptible, and immortal, as the risen bodies will be. The last sentence, however, may also mean that "the former," that is, spiritual knowledge, appeared together with the spiritual, intelligible nature that accompanied it.

2.4. While transformations are many, we have received the knowledge of only four (of them): of the first, of the second, of the last, and of the penultimate. And the first is, as has been said, the passage from evilness to virtue, whereas the second is that from impassivity to the secondary natural contemplation (*theōria*), and the third is that from the latter to the knowledge concerning rational creatures, and the fourth is the passage of all to the knowledge of the Holy Trinity.

After delineating the procession from God to intellectual and material creatures in the preceding *kephalaion*, Evagrius here describes the return of the *logika* to God. Indeed, Evagrius here treats the possible and knowable kinds of transformations into a better state, which clearly affect only creatures, not the Creator, who, being perfect in the Good and being Good itself, and being the Trinity itself, the object of the highest contemplation, needs no transformation. Evagrius depicts the ascending hierarchy that passes from purification from evil and passions, and therefore the attainment of *apatheia*, to knowledge, and within the latter from the knowledge of the world to that of the *logika* and finally that of the Trinity.

In the last sentence I propose an emendation, which I have followed in my translation: instead of ܕܡܢ ܟܠܗܘܢ, to read ܕܟܠܗܘܢ (the subsequent insertion of a ܡܢ can easily be explained by a copyist's desire for parallelism). The last sentence would thus mean: "and the fourth is the passage *of all* to the knowledge of the Holy Trinity," instead of "the passage *from all* to the knowledge of the Holy Trinity," which makes very poor sense. It is clear that, in Evagrius's view, just as in Origen's view, all rational creatures will achieve the knowledge of the Trinity in the eventual *apokatastasis*.

2.5. The body of the one who is, is the contemplation (*theōria*) of the beings, whereas the soul of the one who is, is the knowledge of the Unity. And whoever knows the soul is called the soul of the one who is, whereas those who know the body are called body of this soul.

In the first sentence Evagrius is speaking of the body of Christ and the soul of Christ, who, qua God, is called "the one who is," with an obvious reference to Exod 3:14 ("I am who I am" or "I am the One who Is"). It is interesting that in the expression "the body of Christ" the Syriac uses *pgr'*, which indicates a mortal body, not that of angels. Indeed, this is the kind of body that was taken up by Christ during his dwelling on earth. The body of Christ is the contemplation of creatures, while the soul of Christ is the knowledge of God as Unity and the protological and eschatological unity of all *logika* with God.

Origen and Gregory of Nyssa built on the idea of humanity itself as "the body of Christ" and its eschatological consequences (see Ramelli, "Clement's Notion of the Logos"). Evagrius here speaks of the body of Christ in terms of knowledge: those who constitute the body of Christ ("the body of the soul of Christ") are those who know the body of Christ, that is, the contemplation of the beings, and those who constitute the soul of Christ are those who know the soul of Christ, which is the knowledge of the Unity. This knowledge is clearly superior to the contemplation of creatures. Origen also spoke of the "soul of Christ," insisting that Christ-Logos had not only a human body but also a rational soul, a *logikon*. See on this, for example, Christopher Beeley, *The Unity of Christ: Continuity and Conflict in Patristic Tradition* (New Haven: Yale University Press, 2012), the chapter on Origen. See also, in the introductory essay, the treatment of Evagrius's notion of the "body of God" and the "soul of God" in his *Letter to Melania*.

2.6. The ascetic soul that, thanks to God's grace, has won and is detached from the body will find itself in those regions of knowledge where the wings of its *apatheia* will bring it.

Knowledge, of which Evagrius has spoken in the previous *kephalaion*, is here presented as the reward for those souls that have reached *apatheia*, the ethical ideal of Evagrius just as of Clement, Origen, and Gregory of Nyssa. *Apatheia* is the goal of the *praktikē*, which is ascetic life; knowledge follows it and cannot be independent of it, since knowledge—according to Evagrius, just as to most Neoplatonists—cannot dwell in a soul full of passions (see above, *KG* 1.32 and 1.72, and the relevant commentaries). The notion of the soul that has wings when it is free from passions and thus enjoys knowledge is reminiscent, in my view, of Plato's depiction of the winged soul who is immersed in contemplation and knowledge of the Ideas and who loses its wings and falls when it becomes subject to passions.

I also think that Evagrius, in speaking of the reward of the victorious soul, is here echoing Rev 3:12: "The person who wins, I shall make her a pillar in the temple of God, which will never go out." This is the same passage that was commented on by Origen in his *Commentary on John* 10.42.295: everyone who will finally be victorious over sin and evil will become a pillar in the temple of God and will never fall out. This person will never be conquered by evil again. It is also the same passage on which Origen comments in *Scholia on Revelation* 21. It is remarkable that Origen's discourse in the former passage was inserted in his broader argument concerning the eschatological body of Christ constituted by rational creatures and represented by the temple. Origen accepted Revelation, the Apocalypse of John, as belonging to the Scriptures, commented on it, and frequently cited it in his works, moreover making it clear that he identified this John with the author of the Fourth Gospel. But to do so Origen had to interpret this book wholly allegorically. In *On First Principles* 2.11.2–3 he is obviously referring to a literal interpretation of the Apocalypse, too, when he sharply criticizes those exegetes who held that the eschatological beatitude will be made of eating and drinking and other worldly pleasures, and that the heavenly Jerusalem will be an earthly city, made of precious stones, taking literally the description of Rev 21: "But since they have understood the divine Scriptures in a Jewish sense, as it were, on their basis they have envisaged nothing worthy of God's promises," *Iudaico autem quodam sensu scripturas divinas intellegentes, nihil ex his dignum divinis pollicitationibus praesumpserunt.* Rather, he explains, the heavenly Jerusalem of the Apocalypse will be a "city of saints," *civitas sanctorum*, in which each one will be instructed in order to become a living precious stone. After all, that these stones will be human beings was suggested in the Gospel itself, where Jesus not only proclaims that God can turn stones into humans but also identifies Peter with the stone on which the church will be grounded, and Origen was sure that the church eschatologically will coincide with all of humanity, which in turn is tantamount to Christ's mystical body.

Indeed, in his *Commentary on John* 10.35.229 Origen interprets the eschatological temple described in the Apocalypse as the body of Christ, that is, all of humanity renewed. This is why the "living precious stones" of the temple will be rational creatures, after their purification and illumination when necessary. The erection of the temple will be the eschatological resurrection of the "body of Christ," the whole of humanity, which, after the defeat and annihilation of death, will be transformed into the "whole body of Christ constituted by the saints" (10.35.230): "The temple will be raised and the body will be resurrected on the third day.... For the third day will be in the new heaven and new earth, when these bones, the whole house of Israel, will raise, after the victory over death. Thus, the resurrection of Christ from his suffering and death on the cross, which we are still waiting for, embraces the mystery of the resurrection of the whole body of Christ." This eschatological resurrection of the whole body of Christ will be "the blessed and perfect resurrection we hope for" (10.35.232). Again in 10.36.236 Origen describes this eschatological resurrection "of the true and really perfect body of Christ," which is all of humanity or even all rational creatures: "When the resurrection of the true and really perfect body of Christ takes place, then Christ's limbs and bones, which are now dry ... will be put together, bone with bone and joint with joint."

The transformation of the human beings into the precious stones of the divine temple of the Apocalypse is further depicted by Origen in his *Commentary on John* 10.42.295 as the eschatological return of the prisoners—prisoners of sin, thus sinners—who were out of the temple due to their state of captivity, back inside the temple: "This is clearly prophesied regarding the aeon to come to those children of Israel who are in captivity.... Those who were made prisoners at a certain point were once in the temple, and will return there again, when they will be edified again, once they have become the most precious stones." This notion of the eschatological return of all sinners inside the temple—their original dwelling place—after their purification is taken up by Gregory of Nyssa at the end of his dialogue *On the Soul and the Resurrection* (see my full commentary in Ramelli, *Gregorio di Nissa: Sull'anima*, with the reviews by Panayiotis Tzamalikos in *VC* 62 [2008]: 515–23; Mark J. Edwards in *JEH* 60 [2009]: 764–65; M. Herrero de Háuregui in *'Ilu* 13 [2008]: 334–36; Giulio Maspero in *ZAC* 15 [2011]: 592–94; Francesco Corsaro in *Aug* 51 [2011]: 556–59). Here a further quotation from the Apocalypse is fitted in, which parallels the assertion that the precious stones are rational creatures: everyone who will finally be victorious over sin and evil will become a pillar in the temple of God and will never fall out (Rev 3:12):

"For whoever wins, according to John in the Apocalypse, has the promise to become a pillar in the temple of God, and never go out of it." Notably this is, as I have mentioned, the same passage on which Origen comments also in *Scholia on Revelation* 21. The "heavenly Jerusalem," which is "the city of God," with its "gates," is interpreted by Origen in *Against Celsus* 6.23 as the symbol of the entrance of souls into the divine, which is a mystery: "the profoundly mystical contemplation concerning the souls' access to the divine." That this exegesis is allegorical is clearly admitted by Origen (διὰ συμβόλων).

Thanks to Origen's allegorical exegesis, Revelation, which is traditionally regarded as being all about eschatology, turned out to be not at odds with Origen's own eschatological views. Indeed, the Apocalypse of John, per se, does not necessarily oppose Origen's and Evagrius's theory of *apokatastasis*; for, as Origen was well aware, all depends on its interpretation (see Ramelli, *Christian Doctrine of Apokatastasis*, 43–62).

2.7. After death, for the soul these will be inheritances: those that have been for it helps toward virtue or evilness.

The soul will inherit after death, that is, will have as reward, the fruits of its own choices, depending on whether it has chosen virtue or vice. I emend ܝܪ̈ܘܬܐ (the reading of the manuscript) into ܝܪ̈ܬܘܬܐ. The dropping of the first ܬ by haplography is an error that may have occurred extremely easily, all the more in that the meanings of the two words are closely related: the former means "heirs," the latter "inheritances, possessions," that is, those things of which one becomes heir. I prefer "inheritances, possessions" to "heirs" in this *kephalaion* because it is the soul that inherits the consequences of its choices after death, in terms of blessedness or punishment/purification.

2.8. The richness of the soul is knowledge, whereas its poverty is ignorance. Now, if ignorance is privation of knowledge, richness is anterior to poverty, and the soul's health to its illness.

Evagrius returns here to one of the main tenets of his thought, which was already announced in 1.1, his very first statement: the absolute positivity and ontological priority of Good over evil, essentially due to the fact that the Good is God (see also *KG* 1.39–41, with the relevant commentaries). Ignorance is the soul's poverty and its illness, but ignorance, being a lack or negativity, just as all sorts of evil are, is posterior to the positive thing of which it is a lack. The ontological priority of the soul's health and richness, and thus of knowledge, guarantees that the negative pole, which is a mere lack, will not overcome. This ontological theory, which was definitely shared by Origen and Gregory of Nyssa as well, is also one of the main pillars that support their doctrine of *apokatastasis* (in the case of Evagrius this is especially clear from *KG* 1.40; see the relevant commentary above).

2.9. Who knows the operation of the commandments? And who understands the powers of the soul, and how the former heal the latter and lead them toward the contemplation (*theōria*) of the realities that are?

In the previous *kephalaion* Evagrius has touched upon the soul's illness, which is ignorance. Here he explains that the commandments cure the illness of the faculties of the soul, in that they lead it on the right path. The observance of the commandments is identified by Evagrius with the *praktikē*—moral life and ascesis—in *KG* 1.10–11 (see above, the commentary on these *kephalaia*); here the *praktikē* is said to heal the faculties of the soul and lead them toward contemplation. The scheme of ascesis and purification followed by knowledge and contemplation is repeated once again by Evagrius here; the purification-knowledge sequence is typical of his thought and quite frequent in the *KG*.

2.10. Those things that approach us through the senses are desirable; however, their contemplation (*theōria*) is more desirable. But since sense perception does not attain knowledge, because of our weakness, the former is considered to be superior to the latter, which has not yet been achieved.

In this gnoseological statement, which is clearly reminiscent of Plato's theory of knowledge, Evagrius observes that true knowledge does not come through the senses but comes through the intellect, which knows sense-perceptible objects through contemplation and not through the senses. Considering the senses to be superior to the intellect does clearly not reflect the real hierarchy; this only happens because intellectual knowledge (*gnōsis*) has not yet been achieved.

2.11. Concerning whatever has been constituted of the four elements, be this far or close, it is possible for us to receive its resemblance, whereas

only our intellect is for us ungraspable, and God, its author. For we cannot grasp what is a nature susceptible of the Holy Trinity, nor can we grasp the Unity, substantial/essential knowledge.

This is another gnoseological *kephalaion*. Evagrius highlights again the difference between all material realities, which are constituted by the elements and can be perceived through the senses, and the *nous* and God, which are immaterial and intellectual realities. The *nous* is susceptible of the Trinity; indeed, it will receive God in the eventual deification. The definition of God as "substantial knowledge" or "essential knowledge"—implying a knowledge that is creative and immediately results in the constitution of substances or essences (οὐσίαι) and also a knowledge that knows the essence of all beings—will occur again frequently in the *KG*. In this *kephalaion* Evagrius states that we can know material creatures but not our intellect (by which we know and which is susceptible of the Trinity), nor God its Creator, who is Unity and essential knowledge.

2.12. The right (hand) of the Lord is also called "hand," whereas his hand is not called "right," too. And his hand receives increment or diminution; however, this does not happen also to the right hand.

This is an exegetical text, concerning the "right hand" of God, often mentioned in the Bible, and what this expression means, and the "hand" of God, also mentioned in the Bible. The right hand expresses something superior. Its being unsusceptible of increment or diminution makes me think that it is associated with the Son, who is God himself and thus unalterable.

Indeed, in his *Letter to Melania* Evagrius calls the Son "hand of God" and the Holy Spirit "finger of God," and in his *Letter on Faith*, which was preserved as Basil's *Letter* 8, Christ is called "the right hand of God" and the Holy Spirit "the finger of God" (PG 32:265AB; on the *Letter on Faith*, see now Joel Kalvesmaki, "The *Epistula fidei* of Evagrius of Pontus: An Answer to Constantinople," *JECS* 20 [2012]: 113–39). Both images, very interestingly, are also found in the faithful Origenian theologian and exegete Didymus the Blind, *On the Holy Spirit* (PG 39:1051A, 1076C, 1077AB on the Son as hand, and 1051BC on the Spirit as finger), as well as in Ambrose, *On the Holy Spirit* 3.3 (on the Son as hand and the Holy Spirit as finger). Evagrius, Didymus, and Ambrose may have drawn this double image from Origen, with whose writings they were all very well acquainted.

2.13. The primary contemplation of nature was sufficient for the coming into existence of the rational nature, while this too, the second, is sufficient for its return.

The rational nature is very probably to be identified with the *logika*. Their genesis is here said to derive from the primary contemplation of nature, different from the second contemplation, which is the contemplation of the world. The first contemplation is that of God, and from this the rational creatures stemmed. The second contemplation has as its effect the conversion of the *logika*, obviously their return to the Good/God, after their fall. The second or secondary natural contemplation is the contemplation of the material world, and indeed in his *Letter to Melania* too, Evagrius regards this world as a means to achieve the return of rational creatures to God (see Ramelli, *Christian Doctrine of Apokatastasis*, the chapter on Evagrius).

2.14. Those who live in bodies that are alike are not in the same (degree/kind of) knowledge, but in the same world/aeon, whereas those who are in the same (degree/kind of) knowledge are in sameness of bodies and in the same world.

Evagrius says so because the degree of fineness of the bodies of rational creatures (here called *pgr'*, mortal bodies, because he is thinking of the bodies of human beings) depends on their choices and their spiritual advancement. Among those who are in the same world/aeon, some also find themselves in the same degree of knowledge and therefore have the same kind of bodies, mortal bodies in the case of humans, while others do not. Evagrius's conception of the aeons, too, is essentially a moral conception, like that of Origen. Each aeon depends on the judgment that takes place at the end of the preceding aeon and bears on the behavior and moral progress of rational creatures. Each *logikon*'s place in the next aeon depends on its moral development in the previous aeon; thus, each aeon is a moral system, in that it depends on the moral choices of the *logika*. In the end, when all of them will have rejected all evil, no aeon will be needed anymore for their moral improvement, and the series of aeons will come to an end; all *logika* will thus enter the absolute eternity of God, at their *apokatastasis* and deification. See Ramelli, "Αἰώνιος and Αἰών"; idem, "Preexistence of Souls"; Tzamalikos, *Origen: Cosmology.* On the anti-Gnostic notion of aeon in Origen, who refused to describe an aeon as divine or divine life precisely to keep his distance from Gnostic aeons (just as he did with Stoic aeons), see Ramelli, *Christian Doctrine of Apokatastasis*, the chapter on Origen.

2.15. When the rational nature receives the contemplation (*theōria*) that is about it, then also all the faculty/power of the intellect will be healthy.

Evagrius draws again on the idea that the health of the soul is knowledge (evil and ignorance are the illness and death of the soul; see *KG* 1.41 and 2.8, with the relevant commentaries); true knowledge is achieved not through the senses but through the *nous*, or intellect, which is the highest faculty or power of the soul. The intellect will be healthy when it receives the contemplation of rational nature. For the notion of the health or illness and death of the soul, which was deployed in Origen, Philo, and imperial philosophy, see Ilaria L. E. Ramelli, "1 Tim 5:6 and the Notion and Terminology of Spiritual Death: Hellenistic Moral Philosophy in the Pastoral Epistles," *Aev* 84 (2010): 3–16; idem, "Spiritual Weakness, Illness, and Death in 1 Cor 11:30," *JBL* 130 (2011): 145–63.

2.16. Such is the contemplation (*theōria*) of all that has been brought to existence and will be, that the nature that is susceptible of it [i.e., this contemplation] will be able to receive the knowledge of the Trinity as well.

The next and final degree of knowledge, after the contemplation of the whole of creation, is the knowledge of God the Trinity. The *nous*, which is susceptible of the contemplation of all creatures, will also be able to receive the knowledge of God. This is indispensable to the intellect in view of the eventual deification.

2.17. The elimination of the aeons, the abolition of mortal bodies, and the vanishing of names will accompany the knowledge regarding rational creatures, while there will be unanimity of knowledge, in accord with the unanimity of hypostases (individual substances).

Evagrius is here describing the *apokatastasis* after the end of all aeons; the relation of each aeon to the progress of rational creatures is depicted in *KG* 2.14 (see above, the commentary on this *kephalaion*). It is notable that Evagrius speaks of the abolition of *mortal* bodies (*pgr'*) at that stage, but not of all bodies tout court. Indeed, the bodies of the resurrection will be fine, immortal, and spiritual bodies, and there is no mention here of a passing away of these. Names will also disappear as signifiers, in that direct knowledge will render language itself superfluous.

This does not imply that there will be a confusion of substances. Evagrius rather speaks of *unanimity* (ܫܘܝܘܬܐ, "agreement, unanimity," ὁμόνοια) of knowledge, which corresponds to unanimity of substances: for all substances will be unanimous in adhering to the Good and will no longer be burdened by the multiplicity and dispersion of matter, with different kinds of bodies and so on. This, again, does not mean a confusion of substances (unity in the sense of confusion), which is not even implied by the *theōsis* itself, the union of each of the *logika* with the divinity. This is guaranteed by the divinity's transcendence. The canons of the fifth council so-called against Origen, in the fourteenth anathema, reflect what Evagrius says here but entirely misinterpret it (not to mention that these misinterpreted ideas were even ascribed to Origen, whereas they have little to do with Evagrius himself).

Evagrius clarifies enough in his *Letter to Melania* 23–30 that the final ἕνωσις will be not a pantheistic confusion but a unity of will, a concord:

> But when it is declared that the names and plurality of rational creatures and their Creator will pass away, it does *not at all mean that the hypostases and the names of the Father, the Son, and the Spirit will be obliterated.* The nature of the intellect will be joined to the substance of the Father, since it constitutes his body [2 Pet 1:4]. Similarly, the names "soul" and "body" will be subsumed under the hypostases of the Son and the Spirit. And the one and the same nature and three Persons of God, and the same nature and many Persons of God's image, will remain eternally, as it was before the inhumanation, and will be after the inhumanation, thanks to the *concord of wills*. Thus, body, soul, and mind are (now) separate in number due to the *differentiation of wills*. But when the names and plurality that have attached to the intellect due to this movement (of will) have passed away, then the multiple names by which God is called will pass away as well.... It is not the case that those distinctions [i.e., God's *epinoiai*] are inexistent, but those who needed them will no more exist. But *the names and hypostases of the Son and the Spirit will never disappear*, since they have no beginning and no end. As they have not received them [i.e., their names and hypostases] from an unstable cause, they will never disappear, but while their cause continues to exist, they too continue to exist. They are *different from rational creatures*, whose cause is the Father as well; but these derive from him by grace, whereas the Son and the Spirit derive from the nature of his essence.

The intellect, as I have mentioned, is one in nature (οὐσία/φύσις), individual substance (ὑπόστασις), and order (τάξις). However, there was a time when the intellect, because of its free will, fell from its original order and was named "soul," and, having plunged further, was named "body." But there will come a time when *the body, the soul, and the intellect, thanks to a transformation of their wills, will become one* and the same thing. Since there will come a time when *the differentiations of the movements of their will shall vanish*, it will be elevated to the original state in which it was created. Its nature, hypostasis, and name will be one, known to God. What is elevated in its own nature is alone among all beings, because neither its place nor its name is known, and only the bare mind can say what its nature is. Please, do not be amazed at my claim regarding the *union of rational creatures with God the Father*, that these *will be one and the same nature in three Persons*, with no juxtaposition or change.… When *the intellects return to God*, like rivers to the sea, God *entirely transforms them into his own nature*, color, and taste. They will be *one and the same thing*, and not many anymore, in God's infinite and inseparable unity, in that they are *united and joined to God*.… Before sin operated a separation between intellects and God, just as the earth separated the sea and rivers, they were *one with God, without discrepancy*, but *when their sin was manifested, they were separated from God* and alienated from God.… When *sin*, interposed between intellects and God, *has vanished*, they will be, not many, but again *one and the same*. However, even if I have said that the rivers were eternally in the sea, with *this I do not mean that rational creatures were eternally in God in their substance*, since, although they were completely united to God in God's Wisdom and creative power, *their actual creation did have a beginning*; however, one should not think that it will have an end, in that they are *united to God, who has no beginning and no end*.

2.18. Just as the mixtures [or "qualities"] that dwell in them hide the nature of the bodies and uninterruptedly have them pass from one to the other, likewise virtue and knowledge or evilness and ignorance hide the rational nature. Now, if one said that either of the latter came into being naturally together with rational creatures, it would not be right, because it appeared along with the constitution/composition of the nature.

The Syriac text can be translated in two ways: "the mixtures/qualities that dwell in them hide the nature of the bodies" or "the mixtures/qualities that dwell in them are hidden to the nature of the bodies." Likewise, "virtue and knowledge or evilness and ignorance hide the rational nature" or "virtue and knowledge or evilness and ignorance are hidden to the rational nature." I would prefer the first translation in both cases, taking it in the sense that the qualities of bodies and of rational natures cover them, as qualities and accidents intervene upon a substratum, either a body or an intellect. This is also why Evagrius states that ignorance and evilness did not come into being naturally together with rational creatures but arose only afterwards, when the rational nature, after the movement of free will, became composed (in the case of humans, composed of intellect, soul, and mortal body). Evagrius parallels mixtures of elements, giving rise to qualities in bodies (here all kinds of bodies, including the immortal ones, the term being *gwšm'* and not *pgr'*) and virtue and knowledge, or the privation of these, in rational natures. However, he is quick to clarify that only the positive qualities came into being naturally together with rational creatures. In *Letter to Melania* 39–40 Evagrius elucidates the issue of mixtures in bodies: "This sense-perceptible body has been composed from the four sense-perceptible elements by the glorious Wisdom of God; and since it has its composition through them, it also has its life and death, its health and illness through and from them, and none of these is separated from the Providence of its Creator. It is the same case as I said of the movements that conform to the mixtures (qualities) found in it. The mixtures (qualities) are these: heat and coldness, dryness and moisture." Virtue and knowledge, or evilness and ignorance, are the mixtures or qualities of the *logika*. But the two negative qualities, which are a lack of the positive qualities, are not natural qualities of the *logika*, which appeared straight with their coming into being. They appeared afterward. They are not primary, again for the ontological priority of Good over evil, which is an omnipresent tenet of Evagrius's system of thought. What is natural and original to rational creatures are virtue and knowledge (see above, *KG* 1.40–41 and the relevant commentary).

2.19. The knowledge concerning rational creatures is more ancient than duality, and the knowing nature (is more ancient than) all natures.

The knowing nature is the intellectual nature, which comes before all other natures. And the knowing nature is known by the divinity, which is anterior to any duality and is Unity. Evagrius is here overcoming the dual nature of all intellectual knowledge posited by Plotinus, who emphasized it in his discourse on the knowledge of God as necessarily nondual and mystic. Indeed, according to Plotinus, whenever the intellect knows, this immediately produces a duality of knower and known: "For science is reasoning, and reasoning entails multiplicity [λόγος γὰρ ἡ ἐπιστήμη, πολλὰ δὲ ὁ λόγος]. In this way the soul fails to attain the One, because it falls into number and multiplicity [εἰς ἀριθμὸν καὶ πλῆθος πεσοῦσα].... The intellect that knows [τὸ νοοῦν] cannot even remain simple itself [μηδὲ αὐτὸ μένειν ἁπλοῦν] ... since it will make itself double [διχάσει γὰρ αὐτὸ ἑαυτό]" (*Enneads* 6.9.4; 5.3.10.43–44). See Ramelli, "Divine as an Inaccessible Epistemological Object."

2.20. As for the secondary natural contemplation (*theōria*), that which at first was immaterial, in the end the Creator has revealed it by means of matter to the nature of rational creatures.

We have already encountered the second, or secondary, natural contemplation, which is the contemplation of the creation as secondary nature. Here Evagrius explains that at first it was immaterial, because the first creation was intellectual, but then it became material. As Evagrius is clear here, matter is, however, not to be despised, since it is an educative tool for rational creatures after their fall: it is by means of matter that God the Creator reveals the contemplation of beings to rational creatures. The same is stated by Evagrius in his *Letter to Melania*: with some, the Spirit and the Son communicate directly, whereas with others, less advanced, they communicate indirectly, by means of God's creation, meaning the sense-perceptible creation, what Evagrius calls the "secondary creation" often in his *KG* and is the object of "natural contemplation" (φυσικὴ θεωρία). This secondary creation is not evil; on this, Origen had already insisted against "Gnostics" and Marcionites. Far from being evil, it is providential and was wanted by God as a mediation, for the sake of those who are far from God in that, as Evagrius explains in the *Letter to Melania* 5, "they have placed a separation between themselves and their Creator because of their evil deeds." God instituted this mediation by means of his Wisdom and Power, that is to say, the Son and the Spirit. For Evagrius, "the whole ministry of the Son and the Spirit is exercised through creation, *for the sake of those who are far from God*" (ibid.). This is perfectly in line with Gregory of Nyssa's and the Cappadocians' moderate apophaticism and the role that, in their view, God's operations play in the acquisition of the knowledge of God (see Ramelli, "Divine as an Inaccessible Epistemological Object"; and Konstantinovsky, *Evagrius*, 47–76).

2.21. Everything that has come into being declares, "God's Wisdom, full of modalities/varieties." However, among all beings, one that gives information concerning God's nature does not exist.

I have already underlined a reference to Eph 3:10 in Evagrius's *KG* 2.2, and its exegesis by Origen in connection with Christ-Logos-Wisdom (see above, the commentary on *KG* 2.2). This is the second reference, in a gnoseological *kephalaion*. Evagrius, much like Origen and Gregory of Nyssa, explains that it is impossible for us or for any other creature to know, on the basis of any being, the nature or essence or substance of God, but from the creation itself we can come to know the Wisdom of God in its creative activity. This Wisdom is Christ-Logos-Wisdom, the very agent of creation. On the impossibility of knowing God's nature as opposed to God's operations, see Ramelli, "Divine as an Inaccessible Epistemological Object."

2.22. Just as the Logos reveals the nature of the Father, likewise the rational nature reveals that of Christ.

The rational nature of the *logika* makes the nature of Christ known because Christ is the Logos. Christ, in turn, makes the nature of God known because Christ-Logos is God, as is proclaimed at the beginning of the Johannine Prologue: Θεὸς ἦν ὁ Λόγος, "The Logos was (has always been) God."

"Logos" is ܡܠܬܐ here in Syriac, the same word that was already used by Bardaisan of Edessa (d. 222) when he referred to Christ-Logos in his creative function. According to Bardaisan, the Christian philosopher of Edessa who was a contemporary of Clement of Alexandria and was well known to Gregory of Nyssa and probably to Evagrius as well, Christ-Logos, who created this world, is—as he puts it in a fragment preserved by Ephrem—"the power of the primordial Logos." "Power" corresponds to Greek δύναμις. The Logos's being primordial and original is related to its divinity. Precisely because it is God, the Logos was "in the beginning" (John 1:1, echoing Gen 1:1), and the power, or *dynamis*, to which Bardaisan's formula alludes is nothing but an aspect of Christ-Logos. Indeed, in Origen too, *dynamis* is one of the main *epinoiai* of Christ, besides Logos and Sophia/Wisdom, and plays a core role in the doctrine of creation, as Evagrius was well aware.

This conception of Christ as the Power of the primordial Logos was already clear, shortly before Bardaisan, in Justin, one of the first patristic philosophers, influenced by Platonism as well. In his *Dialogue with Trypho*, written when Bardaisan was a child or shortly earlier, Justin calls Christ precisely Dynamis, Logos, and Sophia: "God begot him from himself in the beginning, before all creatures, Power of Logos [δύναμις λογική], … Child, Wisdom, … God, Lord, and Logos" (61.1). Most remarkably, Justin's expression "Power of Logos begotten in the beginning," in reference to Christ, exactly corresponds to Bardaisan's designation of Christ in the aforementioned fragment preserved by Ephrem: "Power of the primordial Logos." I wonder whether this impressive correspondence might indicate that Bardaisan knew Justin's work and thought. It is worthwhile to report Justin's subsequent statement concerning the divinity and eternity of the Logos and its action in creation: "The Logos of Wisdom is itself God, begotten by the Father of the universe, Logos, Wisdom, Power, and glory of the Father"; it is this one who said: "The Lord established me as the principle … before the world; … while God prepared the heavens I was there." Notably, Clement of Alexandria also connected the Logos of God with the δυνάμεις, or Powers, and more precisely with the spiritual powers (see documentation in Ramelli, "Clement's Notion of the Logos"). For Justin, Clement, Bardaisan, and Origen, Christ-Logos is God's Power and Wisdom, by means of which God created the world.

Now, Bardaisan identified this *dynamis* of the Logos with Christ, who is also the Nous of God. This is clear from an impressive passage quoted by Porphyry and concerning a statue that represents the cosmic Christ, Logos containing the *logoi* of all creatures and Nous symbolized by a divine image or *agalma* in a ruling position. It is possible that Bardaisan had also in mind Paul's statement in 1 Cor 2:16, "we have the νοῦς Χριστοῦ," in the sense of "the Nous that is Christ." Christ is the Nous of God. For full documentation, see Ramelli, *Bardaisan of Edessa*, received by Patricia Crone, "Daysanis," in the *Encyclopedia of Islam* (ed. Kate Fleet et al.; 3d ed.; Leiden: Brill, 2012), 116–18.

In John 1:1–2 the Syriac translations of the Greek λόγος are all ܡܠܬܐ, which covers both principal meanings of λόγος, "word, discourse" and "reason/thought," and, as I have mentioned, an author who was contemporary with the earliest Syriac translations and was philosophically minded and well steeped in Middle Platonism and Stoicism, Bardaisan, used exactly the same word when referring to Christ-Logos. He read the biblical account of the creation in the light of Plato's *Timaeus* and, on the basis of the Johannine Prologue, maintained that Christ-Logos was active in the creation itself, in which he operated "according to the mystery of the cross" (full documentation is found again in Ramelli, *Bardaisan of Edessa*).

From the most reliable fragments it results that he used two expressions to indicate Christ-Logos as active in the creation: the aforementioned "power of the primordial Logos [ܡܠܬܐ]" and "Word [ܡܐܡܪܐ] of thought," which is a perfect alternative translation of λόγος, in that it takes into account both its semantic components, the meaning "word" and the meaning "reason." Indeed, the first word of this expression, ܡܐܡܪܐ, means only "word, discourse, treatise, homily" and could not render, by itself, the complexity of the Greek λόγος, and therefore it required the addition of a complement ("thought"). This is all the more interesting if contrasted with some authors who, unlike Bardaisan, were scarcely acquainted with Greek philosophy, such as Aphrahat, who rather uses ܡܐܡܪܐ, "word," in reference to Christ-Logos, and even ܩܠܐ, "voice." For authors such as Aphrahat adhered more to the Genesis literal account than to the Greek conception of λόγος, and they identified Christ-Logos in the Johannine Prologue with the words pronounced by God during the creation, whose effect was the coming into being of things. Given this different understanding of Christ-Logos in John's Prologue and its different denominations, it is meaningful that the Syriac versions of the Bible are unanimous in rendering λόγος in John 1:1–2 with ܡܠܬܐ, "word/reason/thought," not with ܡܐܡܪܐ, simply "word" (or even with ܩܠܐ). See Jesús Luzárraga, *El evangelio de Juán en las versiones siríacas* (SubBi 33; Rome: Pontifical Biblical Institute, 2008).

2.23. The image of God's essence also knows the *theōria* of the realities that exist; however, the one who knows the *theōria* of the beings, it is not the case that this is automatically the image of God's essence.

Those who know the *theōria* of the beings are rational creatures, that is, *logika*; now, the Logos too, in that it is Reason itself, knows that *theōria*, but that does not mean that rational creatures are the Logos. Indeed, Evagrius maintains that they are rational insofar as they *participate in* the Logos. Clearly, the image of God's essence is precisely Christ-Logos. As already Philo and Origen maintained, the human being is in the image of the Logos, who is in the image of God.

2.24. There is only one who has received names that are in common with other beings.

Christ-Logos has acquired a great many appellatives, or *epinoiai*, which are names (mostly occurring in Scriptures) that the Logos shares with many beings and realities, such as "door," "way," "justice," "wisdom," "shepherd," "lamb," and so on. Evagrius inherited from Origen the doctrine of Christ's *epinoiai*. Of course, even if Christ shares these names with creatures and therefore holds them "in common" with them, this does not imply that when these *epinoiai* refer to his divine person they have the same meaning as when they refer to creatures. They have a similar meaning by analogy, but the referee is unique on account of its divinity and transcendence (hence also apophaticism; see, e.g., Ilaria L. E. Ramelli, "Apofatismo cristiano e relativismo pagano: Un confronto tra filosofi platonici," in *Verità e mistero nel pluralismo culturale della tarda antichità* (ed. Angela M. Mazzanti; Bologna: Edizioni Studio Domenicano, 2009), 101–69; and idem, "Silenzio apofatico in Gregorio di Nissa."

2.25. Just as this body is called the seed of the future ear, so will also this aeon be called seed of the one that will come after it.

This *kephalaion* is clearly connected with *KG* 1.24, where Evagrius has explained that the ear is contained in the seed in potency. Evagrius is relying on the Pauline image of 1 Cor 15, on which Gregory of Nyssa likewise commented at the end of his dialogue *On the Soul and the Resurrection*, explaining through this imagery the mystery of the resurrection-restoration. See my full commentary in Ramelli, *Gregorio di Nissa: Sull'anima*. At the same time, in presenting God as the good cultivator who assists the process of development of his plants, liberating them from illnesses and weeds, which represent sins and passions, Gregory was reminiscent of Philo (especially his *De agricultura*, or *On Agriculture*), who was known to Evagrius as well, and of course to Origen, too, who often used agricultural imagery in an allegorical way. For Philo's *De agricultura*, I refer to the English translation and commentary by David Runia and Albert Geljon, *Philo of Alexandria, De Agricultura: Introduction, Translation and Commentary* (Philo of Alexandria Commentary Series 4; Leiden: Brill, 2012).

Evagrius extends the application of the seed/ear metaphor, employed by both Paul and Gregory of Nyssa in reference to the dead and resurrected body respectively, to the present and the future aeon. His point is that both the present body and the present aeon are the germ and seed of the body and the aeon to come. Both a continuity and a transformation are implied. In the case of the aeons, the continuity is a moral one: the consequences of the moral choices of the *logika* in a given aeon will determine the shape and characteristics of the next aeon (see above, the commentary on *KG* 2.14).

In *Gnostikos* 44 too, Evagrius adopts an agricultural metaphor that is again likely to be inspired by Gregory of Nyssa: "There are four virtues necessary for contemplation, according to the teaching of Gregory the Just: prudence, courage, temperance, and justice.… The reception of the first sower's seed and the rejection of what is sown secondarily—this is the proper work of continence, according to Gregory's explanation." Given the above-mentioned allegory of God as the first planter in his *On the Soul and the Resurrection*, and given his description of passions and vice as *epigennēmata* that must be rejected by means of a life of virtue and asceticism, it is probable that Gregory the Just is Gregory of Nyssa (albeit he is generally supposed to be Gregory Nazianzen; see the introductory essay above). Likewise, in *Praktikos* 89, a relatively long chapter, Evagrius expounds the tripartition of the soul according to Plato, with the relevant virtues that are proper to each part of the soul, crowned by justice, which is a virtue of the whole soul. However, interestingly he does not attribute this doctrine—which is again the theory of the four cardinal virtues—to Plato in the least, but rather he attributes it to "our wise teacher" (κατὰ τὸν σοφὸν ἡμῶν διδάσκαλον). It is usually assumed that this unnamed teacher is Gregory of Nazianzus—for instance, by Antoine Guillaumont and Claire Guillaumont (*Évagre le Pontique: Traité pratique, ou Le moine* [Paris: Cerf, 1971], 680–89), followed by Columba Stewart ("Monastic Attitudes toward Philosophy and Philosophers," *StPatr* 44 [2010]: 321–27, esp. 324), who admits, however, that it is unlikely that Gregory Nazianzen transmitted this doctrine to Evagrius but does not propose alternative solutions. I deem it more probable that Evagrius meant Gregory of Nyssa, who used this doctrine extensively in his dialogue *On the Soul and the Resurrection* and elsewhere. And I have suggested in the introductory essay that Gregory's *On the Soul and the Resurrection* was circulated in Egypt and soon translated into Coptic, precisely thanks to the influence of Evagrius there. Evagrius's sympathy for this dialogue was certainly much facilitated by its defense of the doctrine of *apokatastasis*, which Evagrius too upheld. I have suggested in the introductory essay that the "Gregory the Just" mentioned in the epilogue of Evagrius's *Praktikos* too is probably identifiable with Gregory of Nyssa.

2.26. If it is true that the wheat bears the symbol of virtue and the straw the symbol of evilness, the world to come is the symbol of the amber that will attract the straw to it.

Evagrius is here reflecting on another agricultural metaphor: that of the separation of wheat and straw (Matt 3:12), which will take place in the world to come. The Syriac word that I have rendered "amber" is the transposition of the Latin *succinum*, through the corresponding Greek form *σούκινος*. In addition to its decorative function, in the ancient world amber (*ἤλεκτρον*) was known also for its power of attracting things due to its electricity (see Ilaria L. E. Ramelli, "Il *σημεῖον* dell'ambra da Omero a Marziale," *Aevum antiquum* 10 [1997]: 177–90). The attraction of the straw clearly means the liberation of the wheat from it. In this way, Evagrius is clearly referring to the moral function of the aeons, the same as they had in Origen's system: they serve the moral development of rational creatures and their liberation from evil, with a view to their eventual restoration, or *apokatastasis* (see above, the commentaries on *KG* 2.14 and 2.25).

2.27. The intellect, when it looks at intelligible things, sometimes receives their vision separately, and sometimes it also becomes a seer of objects themselves.

The gnoseological difference that Evagrius is here drawing seems to be between a receptive and an active attitude of the intellect (*nous*) in its own knowledge. In receiving visions it is receptive and it does not "become a seer" itself. Evagrius in his *KG* often speaks of the intellect as a seer. In *KG* 2.36 the opposition between receptivity of a revelation and being a seer obtains again ("not to all the seers of intelligible objects the true *logos* concerning them has been immediately entrusted [or "revealed"]"). In *KG* 2.45 the intellect as "seer" is opposed to sense perception, which is never a seer ("The senses and the intellect share sense-perceptible realities, whereas the intellect alone has the intellection of intelligible realities; it becomes a seer of the objects and of the intellections"). In *KG* 3.15 the intellect is said to have to be immaterial in order for it to become a seer of the Trinity, which is absolutely immaterial. In 3.30 the intellect is delineated again as "the seer of the Holy Trinity." In *KG* 3.19 the intellect is described as "a bare seer" (see also 5.84, where the "pure/bare intellect" is presented as "a seer of the holy Unity"). In *KG* 4.7 the question is of how to become a seer of God's Wisdom, who created the world; one cannot do so without the help of Christ-Wisdom. In *KG* 4.90 the knowledge of God is said to be found only in intellectual souls that are seers, because "dialectic is usually found even by souls that are not pure, whereas vision is only in pure souls"; therefore, these alone are seers. In *KG* 5.27 the intellect, as seer, is said to be prevented from seeing by the irascible faculty of the soul as well as by the concupiscible or appetitive (see also *KG* 5.40 for the intellect as seer). On one occasion, in *KG* 3.48, being a seer is associated with the body, but only that of a righteous person. See below, the commentaries on all these *kephalaia*.

2.28. The sensible eye, when it perceives some visible object, does not see its entirety, whereas the intellectual eye, either does not see at all, or, when it does see, surrounds from all parts immediately whatever it sees.

This is yet another gnoseological *kephalaion*, in which Evagrius points out the difference between sense-perceptible and intellectual vision. The latter, when it occurs, is always a global vision, which embraces the totality of its object, whereas the former is necessarily partial. The totality of vision (and of knowledge and thought) was already ascribed to the divinity in Presocratic philosophy: for Xenophanes, the divinity "sees everything as a whole [ὅλον] and hears everything as a whole [ὅλον]." In Plato, the classification of the various kinds of knowledge posits sense perception in the inferior ranks, εἰκασία and πίστις, "imagination" and "belief," both pertaining to the realm of δόξα, or "opinion," whereas knowledge proper, γνῶσις, so celebrated by Evagrius too, is intellectual and is divided into διάνοια, "discursive thinking," and νόησις, "intellectual intuition." The latter is clearly what Evagrius refers to in the present *kephalaion* as the act of the intellectual eye that embraces its object entirely and all at the same time.

2.29. Just as fire in its power pervades its own body, so will also the intellect in its power pervade the soul, when the whole of it will be mingled with the light of the Holy Trinity.

In the eventual *apokatastasis* the soul will be entirely pervaded by its noblest part or faculty, which is the intellect (*nous*). Just as the body will pass on to a better condition, and from mortal it will become immortal and glorious, so will the soul pass on to a better condition and will be all subsumed and absorbed into its best faculty, the *nous*, as opposed to its inferior and worse faculties, which Evagrius identifies with the two inferior faculties of the soul theorized by Plato (irascible, *thymikon*, and concupiscible or appetitive, *epithymētikon*). Here, the strong meaning "in power" seems to be a better rendering than the weak meaning "in potency" or "in potentiality," since the rest of the soul will be subsumed into the intellect when this finally is at the culmination of its power, in the *telos* (and already in this life, as an anticipation, when one is at the top of the spiritual ascent), and not when it exists only "in potency." That the intellect is the best and essential element within the human being, as well as the most prominent faculty of the soul, is a tenet of the Platonic tradition. Porphyry, Plotinus's disciple, who was well acquainted with both his and Origen's writings, and who in turn was known to Evagrius, claimed in his treatise *Against Boethus* that the *nous* is the most essential constituent of the human being, that which makes it similar to God, and that the soul is essentially a *nous*. This was also Plotinus's and Numenius's position. See also George Karamanolis, *Plato and Aristotle in Agreement: Platonists on Aristotle from Antiochus to Porphyry* (Oxford: Oxford University Press, 2006), 293.

As regards fire, in *KG* 1.20 Evagrius has already singled it out from among the other elements on the grounds that it is the only one that is "alive." Then in *KG* 1.60 he has associated fire to the body of angels, the best among rational creatures, explaining that in them there is a prevalence of intellect (in their souls) and fire (in their bodies). The assimilation of the intellectual soul that is entirely pervaded by the light of God to a body that is entirely pervaded by fire here in *KG* 2.29 strongly reminds me of Origen's image of the soul of Christ as entirely immersed in God's Logos so as to become one God with it, just as a body immersed in fire becomes fire. In *On First Principles* 2.6.3 and 6, indeed, Origen discusses the union of divine and human nature in Christ as a union of a soul with the light of the Logos and as a union of iron (representing the soul) and fire (symbolizing the divine Logos), in which divine light prevails over the soul and fire prevails over iron. This image of iron and fire was already adopted by ancient Stoics, especially Chrysippus, to illustrate mixture (μῖξις); it is found in *SVF* 2.471 and 473, preserved respectively by Stobaeus, *Anthology* 1.153, and Alexander of Aphrodisias, *On Mixture* 216. However, according to the Stoics in this case each component in the mixture keeps its own qualities and substance, without a prevalence of one or the other component (fire or iron, in the example given). Origen, on the contrary, indicates that in this union fire informs iron, and light informs the soul:

> The whole soul (of Christ) receives the entire Logos and yields to its light that shines forth.

> The metal that is iron can receive both cold and heat. Now, if a mass of iron is always kept in fire, it receives fire through all of its pores and veins.... Therefore we say that it becomes fire entirely, because nothing can be seen in it but fire; what is more, if one tries to touch and grasp it, one will feel the violence of fire, and not of iron. In the same way also that soul that, like iron in fire, is always in the Logos, always in Wisdom, always in God, well, whatever it does, whatever it thinks, whatever it understands, this is God. Therefore, it cannot be said to be able to turn somewhere else or to be liable to change, since it possesses immutability, being endlessly inflamed by the unity of the Logos with itself.... One must believe that in this soul the very fire of God has taken residence in substance.

> *Tota [anima] totum [Verbum] recipiens atque in eius lucem splendoremque ipsa cedens.* (3)
>
> *Ferri metallum capax est et frigoris et caloris. Si ergo massa aliqua ferri semper in igne sit posita, omnibus suis poris omnibusque venis ignem recipiens ... totam ignem effectam dicimus, quia nec aliud in ea nisi ignis cernitur; sed et si qui contingere atque adtrectare temptaverit, non ferri sed ignis vim sentiet. Hoc ergo modo etiam illa anima, quae quasi ferrum in igne sic semper in Verbo, semper in Sapientia, semper in Deo posita est, omne quod agit, quod sentit, quod intelligit, Deus est. Et ideo nec convertibilis aut mutabilis dici potest, quae inconvertibilitatem ex Verbi ei unitate indesinenter ignita possedit.... In hac autem anima ignis ipse divinus substantialiter requievisse credendus est.* (6)

The very substance of that iron, that is, of that soul, becomes fire; thus, in Origen it is not the case that each component keeps its own substance and qualities, but there is a prevalence of fire over iron, and of the divine light over the soul. This suggests, as in many other cases, an influence from Alexander of Aphrodisias and Aristotle. For Alexander, following Aristotle (*On Generation and Corruption* 1.5.320), in *On Mixture* 9 spoke of a union in which one of the two components overcomes the other but does not eliminate it: it rather informs it, exactly as in Origen's example. Indeed, Alexander in his treatise was precisely criticizing the Stoics. See Ramelli, "Alexander of Aphrodisias." And Evagrius seems to be drawing on Origen's iron/fire metaphor in the present *kephalaion*. He applies this metaphor to the union of the intellect with God and to the transformation of the whole soul into intellect and its deification, since the intellect itself is immersed in God.

2.30. All those of which the holy powers have received the government, they also know their intellections, but it is not necessarily the case that

they are also entrusted with the government of those whose intellections they know.

Evagrius is saying here that the holy powers, probably angels, know the intellections both of those with whose care they have been entrusted and of others with whose care they have not been entrusted. However, of those with whose care they have been entrusted they also certainly know the intellections. For they must necessarily know them very well if they have to take care of them, as instruments of God's providence.

2.31. Human beings live three lives: the first, the second, and the third. And among these lives, the first and the second, it is those who belong to the primary nature who receive them, whereas the third, it is those who participate in the secondary nature who receive it. And the first life is said to come from the One who is, whereas the second and the third from what is not.

Certainly the third life, which pertains to the sense-perceptible world, the "secondary nature," derives from the fall and is the life led in the mortal body, that of human beings; it is said to derive from what is not because it is a consequence of evil. The first, instead, comes from "the One who is," that is, God, according to the definition found in Exod 3:14 ("I am who I am" or "I am the One who Is"), and is the life of angels and of all prelapsarian rational creatures. The second life is probably that of demons, since it is led by intellectual beings but is a result of evil/nonbeing. The tripartition of rational creatures into angels, humans, and demons as a result of their moral choices was a cornerstone of Origen's anti-"Gnostic" system (see Ramelli, "La coerenza della soteriologia origeniana"). These three lives are all attributed to human beings because humans can choose to live the life of angels, if they pursue virtue, or of demons, if they fall into vice. This is an idea already emphasized by Origen and elaborated on by Gregory of Nyssa.

2.32. Just as it is not matters that nourish mortal bodies but their power, so is it not the objects that have the soul grow but their contemplation (*theōria*).

The soul, and especially the intellectual soul, is nourished by knowledge; it grows thanks to the *theōria* of the existing beings—thanks to not the objects themselves, including material objects, but their contemplation, and thereby their intellections.

The dynamic conception of the continuous growth of the soul was especially highlighted by Gregory of Nyssa, who centered his doctrine of *apokatastasis* in it, joining it to the notion of infinite *epektasis* and making life in the beyond strongly dynamic (see Ramelli, *Christian Doctrine of Apokatastasis*, the chapter on Gregory Nyssen; idem, "*Apokatastasis* and *Epektasis* in *Hom. in Cant.*: The Relation between Two Core Doctrines in Gregory and Roots in Origen," forthcoming in the *Proceedings of the XIII International Colloquium on Gregory of Nyssa, Rome, 17–20 September 2014* , ed. Giulio Maspero [Leiden: Brill]). The word I translated "matters" is in Syriac the plural of the transliteration of ὕλη.

2.33. As for the objects of material knowledge, some among them are primary, and some others secondary. And the primary are corruptible in potency, whereas the secondary (are so) in potency and actually.

Evagrius is drawing a distinction among material realities: some, like our mortal bodies, are corruptible both in potency and actually; others, such as perhaps heavenly bodies, are corruptible only in potency. He is obviously drawing on the Aristotelian conception of the potency (potentiality) versus actuality opposition. The corruptibility of matter derives essentially from its multiplicity. This is not a conviction of Evagrius alone but is typical of Plato, who in his protology opposed the One (the Good) to the indefinite Dyad, the principle of opposition and multiplicity, which he associated with matter. He was followed by Plotinus on this score, who was well known to Evagrius, and by Origen, who is the main inspirer of Evagrius. See Ilaria L. E. Ramelli, "Harmony between *Arkhē* and *Telos* in Patristic Platonism and the Imagery of Astronomical Harmony Applied to the Apokatastasis Theory," *International Journal of the Platonic Tradition* 7 (2013): 1–49. Plotinus, however, tended to relate matter to evil, which neither Origen nor Evagrius could accept, essentially because in their view matter was created by God and all that God created is good.

2.34. Just as the lodestone, by its natural power, attracts iron to itself, likewise holy knowledge naturally attracts a pure intellect to itself.

The *nous* is attracted by holy knowledge as by a magnet. Evagrius has already explained that the *nous* can have both an active and a receptive role in intellectual knowledge (*KG* 2.27; see the relevant commentary above). Here the notion of its being attracted by knowledge itself seems to underline the latter. Note the requirement for pureness; Evagrius will often speak of the pure or the bare intellect in the *KG*.

2.35. The intellect (*nous*) too has five spiritual senses, by means of which it perceives the matters that have an affinity to it. Sight reveals its intelligible objects in a bare form; through hearing it receives the *logoi* concerning them; smell delights in the smell that is alien from all deceit, and the mouth receives their tastes; through tact (the intellect) is confirmed, by grasping the exact demonstration of objects.

The doctrine of spiritual senses is fully Origenian and had roots in Philo's conception of the "inner human being" as well. Each kind of sense perception has its corresponding intellectual perception. Of course the objects of spiritual senses are not sensible but intelligible. Evagrius has already introduced the theme of spiritual senses as the intelligible counterpart to sense perception in *KG* 1.33, 34, 36, and 37 (see the relevant commentaries above).

2.36. It is not to all the seers of intelligible objects that the true *logos* concerning them has been immediately entrusted; nor is it those to whom their *logoi* have been entrusted so that they may see them, who also see their objects. There are some people, however, who also get these two distinctions (together), those who are called "firstborn of their brothers."

Evagrius draws here a distinction between seeing intelligible objects, clearly by means of one's spiritual sight, and knowing the true *logos* concerning each of them. Only some persons have both of them together; they are "firstborn" among their siblings (Rom 8:29) because of their privileged status. For the intellect as a "seer," see above, *KG* 2.27 and the relevant commentary. For the "firstborn" and the probable echo of Clement of Alexandria's protoctists here, see below, *KG* 5.10 and the relevant commentary.

2.37. One is, among all beings, without name, and its place is unknown.

The reference seems to be to God. God's true name is unknown, due to the divine ineffability, which depends on divine transcendence and the impossibility for creatures to know God's very essence (a theme that both Origen and Gregory Nyssen developed; see Ramelli, "Divine as an Inaccessible Epistemological Object"), though God has many *epinoiai*. Likewise, God is not diastematic, in that the divinity is not subject to time and space because of its transcendent nature. In his *Letter to Melania* Evagrius also maintains that God has no place because "God has no beginning and no end" (30; cf. 25). The infinity of God, which Evagrius supports, was developed especially by Gregory of Nyssa but was present *in nuce* already in Origen; all of them read it in Philo as well. Ekkehardt Mühlenberg, *Die Unendlichkeit Gottes bei Gregor von Nyssa* (Göttingen: Vandenhoeck & Ruprecht, 1966), has remarked on the absence of authentic theological or philosophical antecedents for Gregory of Nyssa's notion of God's infinity. In Ramelli, *Gregorio di Nissa: Sull'anima*, in the second integrative essay, I indicate antecedents in Origen, and Mark Weedman ("The Polemical Context of Gregory of Nyssa's Doctrine of Divine Infinity," *JECS* 18 [2010]: 81–104) calls attention to another antecedent: Hilary of Poitiers. I observe that Hilary, in turn, was influenced by Origen in several respects and possibly in this as well. Origen was clear that "the greatness [μεγαλωσύνη] of God has no limit [πέρας]" and that God's providence runs "from the infinite [ἐξ ἀπείρου] to the infinite [ἐπ' ἄπειρον] and even further" (*Selected Passages on Psalms* 144). What is more, also because it is attested in texts of sure authenticity and preserved in Greek, God is expressly declared by Origen to be infinite, ἄπειρον (*Against Celsus* 3.77), and to be "from infinities to infinity," ἐξ ἀπείρων ἐπ' ἄπειρον (*On Prayer* 27.16). Gregory of Nyssa grounded in the infinity of God the eternal growth of rational creatures (the model is Moses in *The Life of Moses* 112–113), to the point that he identified human perfection (τελειότης) with "wishing to attain ever more in the Good" (ἀεὶ ἐθέλειν ἐν τῷ καλῷ τὸ πλέον; ibid. 4–5). For "no limit could cut short the growth in the ascent to God, since no boundaries can be found to the Good, nor does the progression of desire for the Good end, because it is ever satisfied" (ibid. 116).

2.38. Whose nature is in the days before the Passion? And whose is the knowledge of the holy Pentecost?

Here is another one in this series of very concise *kephalaia*, this meditating on the mysteries of Christ's inhumanation and Passion, and Pentecost, when the Holy Spirit descended on Jesus's disciples, men and women, to have them proclaim the good news. The nature of Jesus Christ on earth, before the Passion, was human, which also enabled the Passion itself, but this nature was never separate from the divine.

2.39. The five are related to the fifty, and the former are preparers of the knowledge of the latter.

The small group of *kephalaia* that begins with the present one all deals with arithmology, but the "fifty" and, in the next *kephalaion*, the "forty" can refer back to the immediately precedent *kephalaion*, 2.38. In this case the "fifty" would be the fifty days from the resurrection of Jesus to the first Pentecost, and, in liturgy, from Easter to Pentecost, and the "forty" would be the forty days during which Jesus was in the desert, and in liturgy the forty days of Lent. The "five" probably are the five senses, which are presented as a sort of preparation to knowledge of Pentecost and its spiritual meaning. In *KG* 1.15 and 1.16 too Evagrius used "the five" as well as "the four," meaning respectively the five senses (or the five planets) and the four elements that constitute matter (see above, the commentaries on those *kephalaia*).

2.40. The four are related to the forty, and in the former is the contemplation of the forty.

Just after speaking of "the five" in the precedent *kephalaion*, Evagrius speaks now of "the four." He associated the five and the four in *KG* 1.15 and 1.16 too (see above, the commentary on these *kephalaia*). The four probably are the four elements. They constitute matter and are here presented as a basis for *theōria* of the "forty," which, if the interpretation offered above (in the commentary on *KG* 2.39) is correct, would represent Lent and its spiritual meaning, probably related to asceticism (*praktikē*), detachment from matter, and the disciplining of the body made of the four elements.

2.41. There is one who, without the four and the five, knows the forty and the fifty.

The knowledge attained without the four and the five—that is, without the elements constituting matter and the senses—seems to refer to intellectual knowledge (either divine knowledge or the knowledge of rational creatures). This one is said to have the consequences of knowledge without having its material premises. Given that *kephalaia* 2.39, 40, and 41, with their mention of the forty and the fifty, are comprised between 2.38 and 2.42, in which Christ's Passion, Easter, and Pentecost are mentioned, it is possible that "forty" and "fifty" also have a liturgical resonance here too. "Forty" may indeed refer to the forty days between Good Friday and Easter, and "fifty" to the days of Pentecost. Evagrius ascribed allegorical meanings to liturgical details as well. Their spiritual meaning is attainable through intellectual knowledge, separately from sensible knowledge.

2.42. Who will come to the holy Easter, and who will know the holy Pentecost?

This *kephalaion* refers back to *KG* 2.38; both are expressed in an interrogative form, with a binomial question, and both refer to Christ's Passion and resurrection, and to Pentecost. Evagrius focuses on the knowledge of Pentecost and the participation in Easter. The use of the future in this *kephalaion* to express participation in Easter and the knowledge of Pentecost suggests that Evagrius is also thinking of the eschatological Easter, that is, the general resurrection-restoration (in line with Origen's equation between the eschatological resurrection of the body of Christ and the general resurrection and restoration of all humanity; see Ramelli, *Christian Doctrine of Apokatastasis*, the chapter on Origen), and the eschatological Pentecost, the *apokatastasis*. Indeed, this is Easter and Pentecost as a μυστήριον, which will be revealed and find its fullness only in the *telos*. In the Syriac text, both "Easter" and "Pentecost" are transliterations of the relevant Greek liturgical terms: πάσχα and πεντηκοστή.

2.43. There is one who was left in this, and the same will be found again in it.

"This" and "it" are in Syriac feminine pronouns. The "one" seems to be Christ, and Evagrius seems to be referring to his death and resurrection. This is suggested too by the preceding and following *kephalaia*, also dealing with his death and resurrection. In this case, his death and resurrection would have to be understood not only in a historical sense but also in a mystical sense, as embracing the death and resurrection—both physical and spiritual—of all human beings or even—only in the spiritual sense—of all rational creatures.

It is also possible, though uncertain, that Evagrius refers to Christ-Logos, rational nature, as the only *logikon* who never moved away from

God and had no "movement" of will but never ceased to want only the true Good, who is God. This interpretation ought to be read against the backdrop of Origen's claims concerning the *logikon* that was Jesus, the only one who never fell.

An alternative reference might be to the rational nature, the totality of the *logika*, who were left and lost after the initial Unity, with the fall, but will be found again in the eventual restoration, in the final Unity.

2.44. Not all the saints eat (the) bread, but all of them drink the chalice.

The allusions to the death and resurrection of Jesus seem to continue. Of course, the chalice represents the death of Jesus, as is made clear by his very prayer in Gethsemane, in which he calls "chalice," or "cup," his Passion and death (Matt 26:39–42; Mark 14:36; Luke 22:42). In Mark 10:38–39 the possibility is overtly mentioned that Jesus's chalice / cup of death can be drunk by his disciples. Evagrius states that all of the saints drink this cup, thereby participating in Christ's suffering and death. Not all of them, on the contrary, eat the bread; this is restricted to some saints only.

It is uncertain what "eating the bread" represents exactly in this case. In a eucharistic context, the bread of course represents the body of Christ (Matt 26:26, etc.), so that eating the bread represents participation in the body of Christ (1 Cor 11:26–29). It seems odd, however, that not all of the saints should participate in the body of Christ. Likewise, in John 6:32–35, 48–58 Jesus is said to be the true bread from heaven, the bread of life, of which the manna in the desert was a prefiguration. However, again, it would be strange if not all of the saints should enjoy Christ as the bread of life from heaven. Likewise, in Luke 14:15 a man who sat with Jesus at a banquet proclaimed blessed whoever will eat bread in the kingdom of God, but it is difficult to think that not all of the saints will do so. In John 13:18 we even find the opposite of what is stated in this *kephalaion*; for we find one who eats the bread of Jesus and yet is not a saint, Judas: "I am not speaking of you all; I know whom I have chosen; it is that the scripture may be fulfilled, 'He who ate my bread has lifted his heel against me' " (RSV). In Luke 4:4 Jesus declares that a human being lives not by bread alone but by every word of God. If the scriptural reference that Evagrius had in mind is this, the fact that not all of the saints eat bread might allude to their asceticism. One might also think of a reference to John 4:34, where Jesus states: "My food/bread is to do the will of the one who has sent me," but it is difficult to imagine that not all of the saints do the will of God. It may also be that "Not all the saints eat bread" must be taken in a literal sense and the drinking from the chalice in a spiritual sense.

2.45. The senses and the intellect share sense-perceptible realities, whereas the intellect alone has the intellection of intelligible realities; it becomes a seer of the objects and of the intellections.

Sense-perceptible realities are known both by the senses and by the intellect, the former offering of them a sensible knowledge, and the latter an intellectual knowledge. Intelligible realities are instead grasped by intellect alone. On the intellect as a seer, see above (*KG* 2.27 and 2.36 the relevant commentaries). The objects of the intellectual vision are both things themselves and their intellections.

2.46. The craftsman's separable craftsmanship contains its work, and God's Wisdom contains all. And just as the one who, with words, separates the craftsman's craftsmanship from him destroys his work for him, likewise the one who, in his thought, separates God's Wisdom from God destroys all.

Evagrius has already lingered on the creative function of God's Wisdom, who is Christ, in *KG* 1.14; 2.2, and 21 (see the relevant commentaries above). God's Wisdom, in its creative function, is here assimilated to the art of a craftsman, according to a metaphor that was especially deployed by Philo and by Origen in explaining the creative function of the Logos (for Origen, Christ-Logos-Wisdom). See Ramelli, "Clement's Notion of the Logos," and the passages quoted above in the commentary on *KG* 1.14. Evagrius, like Philo and Origen, thinks of the Logos (i.e., Christ) as having in itself all the Ideas of the beings: it is in this form that "God's Wisdom" is said by him to "contain" its works. Since for Evagrius, just as for Origen, God's Wisdom is Christ-Logos, who is God, it is utterly impossible to separate Christ from God, the Son from the Father. This would be tantamount to destroying everything, since all beings subsist in God's Logos.

2.47. The Trinity is not placed together with the contemplation (*theōria*) of the sense-perceptible and the intelligible realities, nor is it counted together with the objects, since that [i.e., the contemplation] is a quality [lit. "a mixture"] and these are creatures, whereas the Holy Trinity is only essential knowledge.

Evagrius proclaims here the absolute excellence of God the Trinity. The Trinity is not an object of knowledge, either sense perceptible or intellectual, nor is it contemplation of these objects of knowledge, but it is essential knowledge itself. An important parallel can be found in Evagrius's *Letter* 28. The definition of God as essential knowledge is repeated in the *KG*, and we have already encountered it in 1.89 (see above, the relevant commentary). The overall message of this *kephalaion* is in line with Philo's, Origen's, and Gregory of Nyssa's conviction that the divinity cannot be known by humans in its essence but can be grasped only by its operations, as reflected in the creation. Evagrius seems also to adhere to Plotinus's view that knowledge implies a duality of subject and object, which is the reason why God, the One, cannot be known as an object of either sense perception or intellection. Indeed, Plotinus posited a kind of mystical union with God, beyond intellectual knowledge, as the only way to experience God's presence. On Evagrius and his sources on this score (Origen, Plotinus, Gregory Nyssen) and their aftermath (Pseudo-Dionysius the Aropagite), see Ilaria L. E. Ramelli, "Mysticism and Mystic Apophaticism in Middle and Neoplatonism across Judaism, 'Paganism' and Christianity," in *Constructions of Mysticism: Inventions and Interactions across the Borders* (ed. Annette Wilke; Wiesbaden: Harrassowitz, 2016).

From the point of view of the Trinity itself, the knowledge that the Trinity has of everything else is neither sense-perceptive, nor even intellectual, but essential: God does not perceive the intellections of all objects but knows their very essence directly. This is because God is the Creator of the essence of each object. Hence also the consequence that God does not know evil, because evil has no essence, no ontological consistence, since it was not created by God but is a lack of Good (see above, *KG* 1.1, 39–41, and the relevant commentaries; see also Ramelli, "Christian Soteriology and Christian Platonism").

2.48. The intellect, if it goes straight along its own path, meets the holy powers, whereas if (it goes along the path) of the instrument of the soul, it will run into the demons.

The instrument of the soul is the body; this is Aristotelian wording, which was taken over in Neoplatonism as well; the Syriac word for "instrument" itself is the transliteration of Greek *ὄργανον* (hence the frequent expression *σῶμα ὀργανικόν*, "organic body," which, depending on the author, means either "body that is the instrument" of the soul or "body endowed with organs/instruments," such as those of sense perception).

According to Plato's conception, expressed by Philo and taken up by Gregory of Nyssa, the intellectual soul, the *nous*, must proceed along its own path, without inclining toward the body and the inferior powers of the soul (*epithymētikon* and *thymikon*, which represent passions; Plato's tripartition of the soul is accepted and often reproduced by Evagrius, including here in the *KG*). The meeting with the holy powers represents the elevation of the intellect to the angelic state, which is also a theme that was dear to Origen and Gregory Nyssen. For both of them a sanctified life—which Origen also interpreted as a true philosophical life—is an angelic life. See, for example, Ilaria L. E. Ramelli, "Theosebia: A Presbyter of the Catholic Church," *JFSR* 26.2 (2010): 79–102. If, on the contrary, the intellect becomes subdued to the body, instead of meeting angels, it will meet demons.

2.49. The one who has been the first to take the ear of the seed is the first of those who have the seed, and the one who has taken the second ear is the first of those who have the first ear; the one who has taken the third ear is the first of those who have the second ear, and likewise concerning the others, until he abandons the last and the first ear, the one who has not the power/potency of the seed in that he is the last.

The ear of the wheat represents the resurrected body, as opposed to the seed, which represents the mortal body, according to Paul's metaphor used in 1 Cor 15. This imagery already has been taken up by Evagrius in *KG* 1.24 and 2.25 (see the commentaries above). Here Evagrius, with this list, seems to refer to a progression in the resurrection. The first who takes the ear of the seed seems to be the first who rose. This seems to be Christ, who is the first of those who have a mortal body; he is also the new Adam, who was the first to take up a mortal human body. The body of Christ was the first to rise but will also be the last, as the general resurrection of all humanity is the eschatological resurrection of the body of Christ, which will be accomplished when the last human being will have risen (for this Origenian conception, see above, the commentaries on *KG* 1.90; 2.6, 42; and Ramelli, "Clement's Notion of the Logos"). When no more mortal bodies are left and all have risen, no more ears (that is, resurrected bodies) will appear. Evagrius may also be referring to the progressive purification and sublimation of bodies, from the mortal body to the risen body and its further refinements (elevation to the rank of soul and, through that, of intellect).

2.50. When those who give birth will have ceased to give birth, then the guardians of the house also will tremble; then also the two heads will gather rose and linen.

The first biblical reference, concerning the guardians of the house, is to Eccl 12:3, in the context of the day of somebody's death; the second, with the mention of rose and linen, might be to Esth 1:6, where the adornments are linked to a feast given by the Persian king. Evagrius is clearly speaking, as in the previous *kephalaion*, of the eschatological times, when no mortal bodies will be generated anymore, but they will rather be resurrected. The guardians of the house in this framework may represent demons, who will tremble because the dead they have in their power may be snatched away from them after the defeat of death and the powers of evil, which produced death. See Ilaria L. E. Ramelli, "1 Cor 15:24–26: Submission of Enemies and Annihilation of Evil and Death; A Case for a New Translation and a History of Interpretation," *SMSR* 74.2 (2008): 241–58.

2.51. The chariot of knowledge is fire and air, whereas the chariot of ignorance is air and water.

The four elements are here divided into two couples, one leading to knowledge and the other to ignorance; however, earth is missing, and it is not to be ruled out that an allegorical meaning is lurking here. Given the association of elements with the bodies of different orders of rational creatures in *KG* 1.68 (where fire is associated with angels, earth with humans, and air with demons), it may be that Evagrius by "chariot" means bodies, all the more so if "chariot" in Syriac translates an underlying Greek ὄχημα, "vehicle." Indeed, the theory of the body—or one kind of body, or more—as a vehicle of the soul, perhaps present already in Aristotle (see Abraham Bos, *The Soul and Its Instrumental Body* [Leiden: Brill, 2003]; idem and Rein Ferwerda, *Aristotle, On the Life-Bearing Spirit* [Leiden: Brill, 2008]), is typical of Neoplatonism, "pagan" and Christian alike, and Evagrius was certainly well acquainted with it. See John Finamore, *Iamblichus and the Theory of the Vehicle of the Soul* (Chico, Cal.: Scholars Press, 1985); and Ilaria L. E. Ramelli, "Iamblichus, *De anima* 38 (66,12–15 Finamore/Dillon): A Resolving Conjecture?," *Rheinisches Museum für Philologie* 157 (2014): 106–8. On this interpretation, the body of angels is fire and air, finer and immortal, and it is a vehicle of knowledge; the human body, mortal and corruptible as it is, is a hindrance to knowledge—as maintained also by

Plato and Gregory of Nyssa in his dialogue *On the Soul and the Resurrection*, which is a Christian remake of Plato's *Phaedo*. Given the association of air with demons, too, the vehicles of ignorance may also be demonic bodies, although water was generally not associated with demons. Demons make the object of the next *kephalaion*, which declares some of them to be endowed with knowledge.

2.52. Some among the demons have called the intelligible things "knowers," whereas some others have also received the knowledge of the intelligible.

For Evagrius, just as for Origen, demons are rational creatures, one of the categories of the intelligences that were initially all alike but got differentiated because of their different choices, originating from the movements of their free will. Some of them became demons, those who most of all separated themselves from the Good. It is left unclarified here whether those demons who have received the knowledge of the intelligible cease to be demons. In Evagrius's perspective, if a *logikon* possesses knowledge, it can hardly stick to evilness/vice, in light of the close interrelation between virtue and knowledge, and ignorance and evilness, according to Evagrius.

2.53. Only One is worthy of worship: the One who uniquely has the Unique.

The only one who is worthy of being worshiped is of course God. As for the Unique whom God only has, this seems to be the only begotten Son. The expression can also refer to God's being essential Unity.

2.54. Knowledge travels/advances not in the regions of ignorance but in the regions of knowledge.

The polarity between knowledge (gnosis) and ignorance (nongnosis) is a constant feature in Evagrius's thought. The present *kephalaion* at first sight seems to be a tautology. In fact, it may focus on the progression of knowledge, which advances among the right conditions. Indeed, it is connected to *KG* 2.51, which speaks of the vehicle of knowledge as opposed to that of ignorance. The imagery always revolves around the progressive movement of knowledge, which is dynamic and increases. This is also a notion that was dear to Origen and Gregory of Nyssa.

2.55. As for ignorance, some have attracted it to themselves out of their own will, and others without their will; and the latter are called "prisoners," whereas the former are named "imprisoners." "The imprisoners," I quote, "have come, and have imprisoned them."

Evagrius goes on to reflect on knowledge and ignorance, here concentrating on ignorance and its genesis. Some have voluntarily chosen ignorance for themselves, and these also seem to take captive others as well. These, that is, the "imprisoners," are probably demons, whereas those who are taken captive by them would seem to be human beings. The final scriptural quotation may come from Job 1:15 (where the subject is the Sabeans), and it is interesting that the corresponding expurgated version rather quotes Eph 4:8, which refers to Christ's ascension to heaven, when he brought the prisoners with him. If the prisoners are those who are prisoners of the demons, that is, of sin, Christ is their liberator from sins.

2.56. The intellect teaches the soul; the soul, in turn, the body. And only a "human being of God" knows the "human being endowed with knowledge."

A human being endowed with true knowledge is recognized as such only by a saint, a "human being of God" (the expression itself is probably an echo of Deut 33:1). This confirms the interconnection between virtue and knowledge I have already pointed out more than once in Evagrius. The first sentence of course reflects the hierarchy body-soul-intellect, which is frequent in Evagrius as well as in Origen, Bardaisan, and Gregory of Nyssa and is also manifested in the gnoseological field: the soul, which is superior to the body, gives it knowledge, and the intellect, which is superior to the rest of the soul, gives knowledge to the rest of the soul.

2.57. We have learned that there are three altars of the heights: the third is simple, whereas the two (others) are composed. And that wisdom which is about the second altar reveals the wisdom of the third, whereas that which is about the first altar comes first vis-à-vis that which is in the second one.

This is another *kephalaion* that focuses on a gnoseological hierarchy, here delineated in three steps. The imagery of the "altars" alludes to various degrees in the progression of the gnosis. However, terminology must be paid attention to: here it is a matter not of "contemplation" (*theōria*) or "knowledge" proper but of "wisdom," ܚܟܡܬܐ, corresponding to Greek σοφία. Evagrius describes wisdom as follows: "wisdom [σοφία] is knowledge [γνῶσις] of corporeal and incorporeal realities and the contemplation in them of judgment and providence" (scholium 3 on Prov 1:2). Wisdom is the main *epinoia* of Christ, together with that of Logos. Knowledge is connected with the Logos-*epinoia* of Christ; Wisdom with his Wisdom-*epinoia*. These are the two main *epinoiai* of Christ; according to Origen, Wisdom is the very first *epinoia* of Christ, even anterior to "Logos," because the Logos itself was from eternity in Wisdom. As Origen remarked in his *Commentary on John*, commenting on John 1:1 ("in the beginning was the Logos," ἐν ἀρχῇ ἦν ὁ λόγος), the Logos "has its hypostasis, or individual substance, in Wisdom, who is the Beginning" (ἐν ἀρχῇ τῇ Σοφίᾳ τὴν ὑπόστασιν ἔχων). See Ramelli, "Origen, Greek Philosophy."

2.58. Those who now live in breadth have been given the three altars, whereas those who live in length and depth will be given them in the world/aeon to come.

Evagrius goes on to speak of the three altars and the wisdom that concerns them, of which he has already spoken in *KG* 2.57. The distinction that he draws in the present *kephalaion* seems to be between rational creatures who live in a diastematic condition, and thus in space and time in this world—that is, human beings during the present life—and rational creatures that are free from διαστήματα—in particular, he seems to be thinking of angels. Humans will attain the three "altars," or the three grades of wisdom, like angels, when they are in the other world. Breadth suggests the stay and wandering in the present aeon, while depth and length suggest a vertical ascent toward God, throughout the aeons. The scriptural reference underlying this *kephalaion* is Eph 3:18–19: "I pray that you may have the power to comprehend, with all the saints, what is the breadth and length and height and depth, and to know the love of Christ that surpasses knowledge." In a scholium on Prov 3:19–20 Evagrius comments precisely on this passage: "That which here [the author of Proverbs] has called 'earth,' Saint Paul denominates 'breadth' [πλάτος], and what are here called 'heavens' Paul in his letter to the Ephesians calls 'height' [ὕψος], and that which he allegorically calls 'abysses' (Paul) denominates 'depth' [βάθος], and the 'clouds dropping water' he calls 'length' [μῆκος]. All these symbolize the rational creatures distributed in orders/arrangements [κόσμοις] and bodies [σώμασιν] according to their state." This confirms the association I proposed of the dimensions mentioned by Evagrius with different orders of rational creatures.

2.59. As for the righteous Judgment of our Christ, the transformation of the bodies, of the lands, and of the aeons indicates it. As for his forbearance of spirit, on the other hand, those who fight against virtue (indicate it). But above all his mercy, it is those who are guided by his Providence without being worthy (that indicate it).

This *kephalaion* connects to *KG* 1.27, in which the contemplation of divine justice, expressed in the Judgment, is followed by that of divine mercy, expressed by Providence. After the resurrection, when bodies will be transformed from mortal to immortal (this is why the Syriac word used here for "bodies" is *gwšm'* rather than *pgr'*), at the end of the aeons, there will come the Judgment, which will be just and will be performed by Christ, but God's mercy will be manifest through the action of divine providence, which leads sinners—who, qua sinners, would not deserve it—to salvation, while respecting their free will. The simultaneous presence of free will and saving divine providence was a deep conviction of both Origen and Gregory of Nyssa. The scriptural reference to the righteous judgment of Christ is to 2 Thess 1:5, which was already quoted in *KG* 1.82.

2.60. The table of Christ is God, whereas the table of those who are exalted is the corporeal and the incorporeal nature.

Evagrius is referring to Luke 22:30, in which Jesus promises his disciples that they will eat and drink at his table in his kingdom, and they will judge the twelve tribes of Israel (perhaps there is also an echo of Jesus's declaration that his own nourishment is performing the will of the Father). Now, Evagrius explains that Christ's table is God, so that to eat the food of that table is to participate in God, that is, in the Good. This is also the line along which Origen and Gregory of Nyssa interpreted 1 Cor 15:28: God will be "all in all," in the sense that God will represent all goods for all, and all will enjoy the summation of the goods in God (see Ramelli, "Christian Soteriology and Christian Platonism"). The corporeal and the incorporeal natures are said to be the table of those who are glorified, probably because they will gain the knowledge of the corporeal and the incorporeal natures, as Christ (by parallelism) knows God. This is also suggested by the immediately following *kephalaion*, which specifically focuses on the contemplation of incorporeal things and of earthly bodies.

2.61. As for the contemplation of incorporeal things, that which originally we have known separately from matter, now we know it while it is entangled in matter. But as for the one that concerns bodies, we have never seen it without matter.

All bodies are corporeal, including the spiritual bodies of angels (this is why the Syriac word for "bodies" here is not *pgr'*, "mortal bodies," but *gwšm'*). On the other hand, intelligible realities like the Ideas are incorporeal, but with the creation of the world these became "entangled in matter." All creatures are endowed with bodies, be these subtle or heavy and corruptible bodies—the same thesis as Origen's (see Ramelli, "Preexistence of Souls"). This is why their *theōria*, or contemplation, is now necessarily linked to matter (in Syriac this noun is the transposition of Greek ὕλη).

2.62. When the intellects have received the contemplation concerning them, then also the whole nature of the bodies will be elevated, and thus contemplation concerning it will become immaterial.

This *kephalaion* is closely connected with the precedent one. There, Evagrius reflected on how a knowledge separate from matter has become a knowledge "entangled in matter." Here the opposite path is delineated, or better, a returning path: the return to immaterial contemplation, in that bodies will be elevated to a level superior to matter. The bodies mentioned here, which will be elevated in the end and whose contemplation will become immaterial ("contemplation concerning it" = contemplation concerning the nature of bodies), are not, or at least not only, the mortal ones (*pgr'*) but the immortal bodies of angels and of resurrected human beings. The nature of all bodies will be raised, elevated, lifted up to a better condition, when the intellects (what Origen called intellects, or *logika*) will have received their own contemplation. Therefore, the contemplation concerning bodies will become immaterial, whereas now it is material. Evagrius in this *kephalaion* is foreseeing a general elevation of each nature to a better state: bodies will be elevated to spiritual bodies, and souls will be elevated to intellects, which is the noblest part of the soul. This elevation of all realities to a better state will be a typical trait of the eschatological thought of John the Scot Eriugena (see Ramelli, *Christian Doctrine of Apokatastasis*, the section on Eriugena). According to Evagrius, as we have already seen, bodies will be upgraded to the rank of souls, and souls to the rank of intellects. This is also why the contemplation concerning bodies will at that point become immaterial.

2.63. Among the kinds of knowledge, one of them will never become material, whereas another will never become immaterial. But that which is material will also be able to become immaterial.

As Evagrius has expounded in the previous two *kephalaia*, the *theōria* of bodies is one of those that will be transformed, from material to immaterial, just as it was initially transformed from immaterial to material. Here, however, he speaks of "knowledge" proper. There is a knowledge of immaterial realities that is expressly said to be unable to become material, probably because there is something immaterial on the ontological plane that cannot possibly become material. This is the case with God. Thus, the knowledge of God will remain immaterial and will not be transformed into material, although the knowledge of God cannot be a direct knowledge of the nature of God, because of divine transcendence. Likewise, there is a knowledge that will always remain material and will never become immaterial, very likely because on the ontological plane there are realities that will remain material without possibly being turned into immaterial. That might refer to mortal bodies (*pgr'*), or more probably to material inanimate entities like minerals. Stones, for instance, are bodies that will never be raised to the rank of souls and, through souls, to intellects. But there is a material knowledge that becomes immaterial, and this refers to the transformations of rational creatures and their reception of different kinds of bodies according to their moral choices. This is the subject of *KG* 2.61–62. The material knowledge of bodies, when these are raised to the rank of souls and, through souls, to that of intellects, will become immaterial.

2.64. Some among the beings came to existence before the judgment, and some after the judgment. And regarding the former, nobody has given an account. Regarding the latter, on the other hand, the one who was on the Horeb offered a description.

Evagrius, drawing on Philo, Origen, and Gregory Nyssen, thinks of an intellectual and a material creation. The account that Moses—the one who was on Mount Horeb—gave in Genesis, according to Evagrius, refers to the second creation; he does not seem to think that the Bible speaks of the first creation. The "judgment," or "act of justice," that separates these two creations is very probably that which followed the fall. Evagrius is indeed clear elsewhere that every aeon is the result of a divine judgment (see, e.g., below, *KG* 2.75 and the relevant commentary), and its arrangement depends on the moral choices of rational creatures in it (see Ramelli, *Christian Doctrine of Apokatastasis*, the chapter on Evagrius). A partial Greek text of this *kephalaion* is provided by Barsanuphius of Gaza (PG 86.1:893A).

2.65. On the basis of those who have reached the perfect fullness of evilness, it is possible to understand the great number of the aeons that have been brought to existence. For it is impossible that in a moment we are perfected in ignorance, because it is also (impossible to be perfected in a moment) in knowledge.

The culmination of evilness and the culmination of ignorance are here identified with one another. Evilness is ignorance; both are defined in a merely negative way, as forms of privation: respectively, privation of Good and of knowledge—and again here the interconnection of virtue and knowledge in Evagrius's thought is clear; I have already pointed it out repeatedly. Moreover, the choice of evil ultimately depends on ignorance, according to an ethical intellectualism that was shared by Origen, Gregory of Nyssa, and Evagrius (see Ramelli, *Christian Doctrine of Apokatastasis*, the chapters on them). Aeons are described by Evagrius, according to the Origenian line, as the theater of the movements of rational creatures and their consequences. Their development toward evil or toward the Good—that is also knowledge, and the choice of the Good depends on knowledge—is very long, and the culmination of both cannot be attained in simply one aeon. Hence the necessity of having many aeons, as the necessary location of the spiritual development of rational creatures. This, in Evagrius's as well as in Origen's opinion, usually takes an enormous amount of time.

2.66. It is not the coming into being of rational creatures that the coming into being of (spiritual) bodies reveals, but it introduced the nature of names, and the composition of the latter shows the difference in order of the former.

Names are related to the genesis of bodies. Before the existence of bodies, names did not exist as well. It is notable that Evagrius is here speaking of *gwšm'*; names, therefore, came into existence together with the production of angelic bodies, not with heavy, postlapsarian bodies. This means that they came into existence when Ideas in God's Logos were transformed into substantial creatures: first of all the rational creatures, the *logika*, each one endowed with a spiritual body. These bodies may have functioned as a *principium individuationis*—hence their relation to names—and a substratum for the substantial individual existence of each *logikon* and for its free will; indeed the body changes as a result of the choices that each *logikon* makes with its own free will. The passage from Ideas in Christ-Logos-Wisdom—like a kind of decorations on its body—to substantial existence was already depicted very well by Origen. See Ramelli, "Clement's Notion of the Logos"; idem, "Preexistence of Souls"; and above, the commentary on *KG* 2.2. Evagrius relates the different orders of names, or bodies, to the different orders of rational creatures; the Syriac word for "order" is based on Greek τάξις.

2.67. The separate ones will become inseparable when they receive the contemplation of the things that had separated them.

Rational creatures, or *logika*, got separated when, from their initial unity of *homonoia* in adhering to the supreme Good, who is God, they began to choose different things, inferior or apparent goods, and some received mortal bodies, the human beings, as opposed to both angels and demons. When they come to know the true nature of the inferior or apparent goods they have chosen and return, all of them, to adhering to the Good, freely, consciously, and voluntarily, they will find themselves in a perfect unity of *homonoia*, inseparable in concord. That the initial and final unity of the *logika* is a unity of will is also clear from the *Letter to Melania*. See above, the commentary on *KG* 2.17; and Ramelli, "Harmony between *Arkhē* and *Telos*."

2.68. Those who possess light bodies are said to be on high, whereas those (who possess) heavy bodies (are said to be) below. And higher than the former are whose who are lighter than they are, whereas below the latter there are those who are heavier than they are.

Evagrius clearly posits a hierarchy of bodies (*gwšm'*, including all kinds of bodies and not only mortal bodies) in different degrees of fineness. In general, the lightness or heaviness of the body is a function of the spiritual development of the *logika*, as is also adumbrated above in *KG* 2.66 (see commentary on that *kephalaion*). The "heavy" bodies are probably the mortal bodies of human beings, and the "light" ones those of angels and/or the resurrected bodies. The bodies that are even heavier than the "heavy" ones may be those of the demons, which are not mortal but which are worse than those of human beings. Origen described them as bodies that constitute an object of derision for the angels (see Pietras, "L'inizio del mondo materiale"). As for those who are lighter than those who have a "light" body, these may be the angels if the "light" ones are the risen bodies, or higher ranks of angels in comparison with lower ranks, such as archangels. Risen human beings and rational creatures who will have attained unity (among themselves, within each of them, and with God) will no longer need heavy and "thick" material bodies, as is also stated in *Chapters of the Disciples of Evagrius* 8: "Just as for a person with an eye illness a collyrium is according to nature more than for someone healthy, likewise for the soul the body [σῶμα] is according to nature. But those souls that are in the healthy monadic state [ἐν τῇ τῆς μονάδος ὑγείᾳ] need no material thickness [τῆς ὑλώδους παχύτητος]." The alternative lies open whether they will have spiritual bodies or no bodies at all in the eventual unity. The same alternative was left open by Origen for the final θέωσις. We have already seen that, rather than speaking of the utter destruction of all kinds of bodies, Evagrius speaks of their elevation to the rank of souls and, through souls, to intellects.

2.69. The Holy Spirit has not revealed to us the first differentiation of rational creatures and the coming into being of spiritual bodies but has manifested to us the present differentiation of rational creatures and the transformation of bodies.

It is notable that Evagrius equates the first distinction of the *logika*, that is, their emerging from Christ-Logos-Wisdom as separate substances, with the coming into being of bodies (*gwšm'*), which are the spiritual bodies that all *logika* had since their beginning as creatures, that is, as individual substances. Only later, after the fall of some *logika*, did mortal bodies appear, as well as the bodies of demons, as distinct from those of angels (see above, *KG* 2.66 and the relevant commentary). In this *kephalaion*,

Evagrius explains that the Holy Spirit has revealed the present differentiation of the *logika* into angels, humans, and demons (different from their first distinction that was their emerging as individual creatures) and the transformation of their bodies, which were differentiated into angelic, human, and demonic, and probably also the distinction between mortal and risen bodies. The Greek text of this *kephalaion* too is preserved by Barsanuphius of Gaza (PG 86.1:893B).

2.70. If it is true that God "made everything in Wisdom," there is nothing that has been created by Him that does not bear—each one of them—a sign of the luminaries.

Creation reveals God in that it was made by God's Wisdom, that is, Christ-Logos, whose creative function is mainly declared in the Johannine Prologue. The *logoi* of Christ-Logos-Wisdom are present and remain in every single creature. These are the signs of the Wisdom of God in every creature, and of course in bodies. The quotation in this *kephalaion* is from Ps 103:24 according to the Septuagint, as it obviously was in the lost Greek original: God "made everything in Wisdom." The Syriac translator in S_2 (the redaction I am translating and commenting on) retained the wording of the Septuagint, whereas in the other redaction, S_1, the wording of the Peshitta for this scriptural verse is adopted. The luminaries are the sun, the moon, and possibly the stars in heaven; at the same time, in Evagrius they also symbolize rational creatures, as will become clear below, and at least the sun can represent Christ, especially with reference to Mal 3:20, where the "Sun of Justice" was interpreted as Christ by many Fathers, and indeed by Evagrius himself in *KG* 3.52 (see commentary below). Also, God as the Good itself was represented as sun (as a Platonic reminiscence). So Evagrius may be meaning, metaphorically, that there is no creature that does not bear the sign of God the Creator and Christ.

2.71. The contemplation of incorporeal realities remains in nonabasement, whereas the one that concerns the bodies, it seems in part liable to abasement and in part nonliable.

The *theōria* of incorporeal realities cannot have any lowering in it, apparently because it is rather bodies that have a hierarchy in fineness and value, and their *theōria* can imply a lowering when it comes to inferior bodies. Of course the hierarchy of bodies depends on the moral and spiritual development of the creatures that have those bodies; therefore the contemplation of the lower bodies also implies the consideration of moral failure.

2.72. If it is true that the knowledge of those things that do not vanish suddenly is primary, it is clear that light bodies are primary and anterior to the heavy ones.

Evagrius has been speaking of a variety of bodies as a function of rational creatures' free will in the past *kephalaia*, and especially in 2.68 and 2.69 (see above, the relevant commentaries). Evagrius's presupposition here is the perfect correspondence between ontology and gnoseology, between the order of being and the order of knowledge. The knowledge of primary realities is primary and anterior to that of secondary realities. Light bodies (*gwšm'*), which are the bodies that all *logika* first assumed at their creation as substances, are anterior to the heavy and mortal bodies that came after the fall of some of these. This posteriority will also have an important eschatological consequence: since all that is not original will not subsist in the *telos*, mortal bodies will not be there. Light bodies, instead, do not vanish suddenly, in a moment. These are the bodies of angels and of resurrected humans; these will be present in the *telos*, although the notion that "they do not vanish suddenly" may suggest that they will actually vanish somehow, but after a long process. Again, this may point to bodies' elevation to the rank of souls and, through souls, to intellects.

2.73. Just as the one who, through his Logos, has revealed to us (the truth) concerning the things of the world to come has not informed us about the coming into being of bodies and incorporeal beings, likewise also the one who has taught us the coming into being of this world has not manifested the passage of bodies and incorporeal beings but explains their differentiation and transformation.

As Evagrius briefly mentioned in *KG* 2.64 (see above, the relevant commentary), the Bible does not offer an account of the creation of incorporeal realities and of spiritual bodies, the bodies that all *logika* had at the beginning, but rather offers an account of their subsequent transformations and of the resurrection and the Judgment in the world to come. Indeed, what is omitted by the Bible, namely, the very creation of the *logika*, was already declared to be an object of rational investigation by

Origen in the preface to his Περὶ Ἀρχῶν, *On First Principles.* There, he said that precisely because this thorny question was not addressed in the divine revelation in Scripture, it was necessary to make it an object of rational investigation. It is remarkable that a couple of centuries later, Gregory of Nazianzus still asserted that this question was open to philosophical inquiry since it was left untouched by Scripture. With this, Nazianzen was clearly defending Origen's philosophical investigation in Περὶ Ἀρχῶν, which by the time of Gregory of Nazianzus had been harshly attacked (see full documentation in Ramelli, *Christian Doctrine of Apokatastasis*, the section on Nazianzen).

2.74. Who has known the primary differentiation, and who has seen the coming into existence of (spiritual) bodies and these various worlds/aeons, these things with which the holy powers have been nourished and have reigned in a blessed sovereignty?

Evagrius has already explained in *KG* 2.64 and 2.73 what scriptural revelation teaches and what it does not. The second category includes the differentiation of rational creatures either from their existence in the Logos as its Ideas to an independent existence as substances or from their concord in adhering to the Good to the differentiation of their free wills. The former is more probable here, because immediately after this Evagrius mentions the coming into being of the spiritual bodies of rational creatures. And rational creatures took up their bodies as soon as they were created as independent substances (see above, *KG* 2.69 with the relevant commentary; see also Ramelli, "Preexistence of Souls").

Now, Evagrius goes on to meditate on the genesis of bodies (*gwšm'*, indicating the spiritual bodies of the rational creatures) and that of aeons, which, according to Evagrius, who is inspired by Origen, depends on the spiritual development of rational creatures—as I have already explained more than once. That of which the holy powers, very probably angels, are nourished is likely to be the knowledge of these aeons and bodies—Evagrius loves the metaphor of nourishment for knowledge—and their sovereignty is likely to be understood as exercised over these aeons. My contention is substantiated by *KG* 2.88, in which it is the contemplation of this world that is said to be a nourishment for humans and other rational creatures. Guillaumont (p. 91) proposes an alternative translation, which is perfectly possible too, from the grammatical point of view: "Ces mondes variés qui ont été nourris par les puissances saintes et ont exercé une royauté bienheureuse." This, however, does not seem to make much sense, especially in that it ascribes sovereignty to the worlds (that is, the aeons). On the nourishment theme in relation to the holy powers and the worlds, see also below, *KG* 2.82 and the relevant commentary.

2.75. As many accountable beings as the Judge has judged, so many aeons he has also made, and the one who knows the number of judgments also knows the number of aeons.

Given that the aeons, for Evagrius just as for Origen, depend on the spiritual development of rational creatures, each of them is the result of God's judgment over that spiritual development, which decides which is the place that each creature must occupy as a result of its moral choices, which is the best suited to the moral progress of each single rational creature, and which is the body that is most suited to the κατάστασις, or state in which each creature is found in that aeon.

It is clear that, just like Origen, and unlike the Stoics, Evagrius too thinks of a limited series of aeons: not an infinite succession but a limited series, however long, after which there will be the restoration, or *apokatastasis*, when all will be no longer in any aeon, but God will be "all in all" (1 Cor 15:28). This is confirmed also by *KG* 6.75, where Evagrius describes the series of aeons, each followed by a judgment, as it is in Origen, and the end of all aeons, which is "the Holy Trinity," of course in reference to θέωσις in the very *telos*. See above, *KG* 1.7, 9; 2.17, and the relevant commentaries; see also Ramelli, *Christian Doctrine of Apokatastasis*, 1–10.

2.76. Just as different orders distinguish rational creatures from one another, so do also the places that are apt to the bodies that are joined to them.

In the last ten *kephalaia* Evagrius has already drawn on the Origenian concept that the *logika* assume different bodies—primarily those of angels, humans, and demons—according to the degree of their spiritual development; here he adds, again like Origen, that each kind of body must also dwell in a place that is appropriate to it. Indeed, depending on their degree of closeness to the Good—that is, God—the *logika*, according to Evagrius just as according to Origen, are divided into different orders: angels, humans, and demons (the Syriac word for "order" is here a transliteration of the Greek τάξις). These different orders have different kinds of bodies, in different degrees of fineness, and mortal or immortal. These different types of bodies (here *gwšm'* is used in a generic sense, embracing both mortal and immortal bodies) in turn require different places in which to live. Human beings, with their mortal bodies, live on earth, in a diastematic reality, but angels and demons live in different dimensions.

2.77. The final Judgment will not show the transformation of bodies, but it will reveal their elimination.

This *kephalaion* refers to the eschatological times. While during the aeons—each marked by a judgment that concludes the precedent aeon—transformations of bodies occur, in the *telos* bodies will all be elevated to a superior state: mortal bodies will no longer exist but will be replaced by immortal and incorruptible bodies; these in turn will tend to be elevated to the soul, and the soul to the *nous*, its most excellent faculty. This scheme of eschatological elevation in the movement of "return" (ἐπιστροφή) will be developed especially by the Christian Neoplatonist John the Scot Eriugena.

In the S_2 redaction, the nonexpurgated one I am following, there is no scriptural quotation here, whereas in the parallel in S_1 by alluding to "the righteous Judge," a reference to 2 Tim 4:8 is introduced ("Henceforth there is laid up for me the crown of righteousness, which the Lord, the righteous judge, will award to me on that Day, and not only to me but also to all who have loved his appearing," RSV).

2.78. Each one of the cohorts of the heavenly powers is constituted either entirely of superior beings, or entirely of inferior ones, or of both superior and inferior ones.

The Syriac noun that I have translated "cohorts" is the transliteration of Greek τάγμα, which has both a military connotation and a connotation of "order." I have endeavored to preserve both in my translation. The idea of order is further emphasized by the hierarchy of superior and inferior heavenly beings. Evagrius seems to be speaking of the various degrees in the hierarchy of angelic creatures (it is unlikely that the inferior heavenly beings should be understood as demons, who are not heavenly, at least after their fall and before their restoration). The original Greek text is preserved in a fragment in the *Scholia in Dionysium*, or *Scholia on Pseudo-Dionysius the Areopagite*, ascribed to Maximus the Confessor (PG 4:173A).

This conception is reflected in the so-called canons of the fifth council against Origen, anathema 5.

2.79. Whoever heads toward knowledge goes toward a positive change of bodies, whereas whoever heads toward ignorance goes toward a negative change.

Evagrius returns to the Origenian notion, developed in the last fifteen *kephalaia*, that the kind of body of every rational creature depends on its moral choices. Those who approach knowledge, and therefore are spiritually advanced, deserve better bodies; those who approach ignorance will also receive an inferior body. For Evagrius, speaking in terms of knowledge and ignorance is tantamount to speaking of good and evil and of virtue and vice. I have already highlighted more than once the interconnection between virtue and knowledge and between vice and ignorance and Evagrius's very definition of ignorance as "the shadow of evilness" (*KG* 4.29; see below, the relevant commentary).

2.80. The contemplation of this instrument of the soul is variegated; that of the instruments of heavenly beings, then, is highly variegated, but the contemplation concerning rational creatures is even more variegated than those, in that those (bodies) are the dwelling places of the knowers, whereas these (rational creatures) are susceptible of the Holy Trinity.

The instrument (in Greek *ὄργανον*) of the soul is the body in a human being, which is now mortal but will be resurrected, and the *theōria* of the bodies is variegated because bodies are very different from one another, and mortal bodies themselves are different from one another, although they share the same nature of mortal bodies (*pgr'*). The instruments of heavenly beings, that is, angels, are their spiritual bodies, and these too are described by Evagrius as different from one another, depending on their hierarchy. Finally, Evagrius concentrates on the *logika* themselves, and not their bodies, which are their dwelling places: the *logika* were created in order to be the recipients of the Trinity, which is essential knowledge and the knowledge of all. The *theōria* of the *logika* too is variegated, even more than that of their bodies, also due to their different acts of will. In the end, however, uniformity and concord will prevail.

2.81. Knowledge has generated knowledge, and always generates the knower.

It is not the rational creature, the "knower," that generates knowledge, but vice versa: it is knowledge itself that produces the knower. This is due to an ontological priority: knowledge is founded in God, who is the ontological absolute *primum*. God is in fact described by Evagrius as "essential knowledge" (see above, *KG* 1.89 and 2.47, and the relevant commentaries, and below, *KG* 4.77 and 5.55, and the relevant commentaries).

2.82. Not the bodies of spiritual powers, but only those of souls, are naturally made to be nourished with the world that is akin to them.

Evagrius has already presented the notion of being nourished by worlds/aeons in *KG* 2.74 (see above, the relevant commentary). The bodies of "spiritual powers" seem to be the spiritual bodies of angels, whereas the bodies of souls seem to be those of human beings, whose intellect has descended to the rank of soul and whose body, now mortal, is an instrument of their soul. As for a world being akin to a certain category of rational beings, I have already pointed out repeatedly that for Evagrius, just as for Origen, worlds/orders/arrangements are established precisely on the basis of rational creatures' moral progress and spiritual conditions. This is also why Evagrius states that every new aeon is constituted on the basis of the judgment that bears upon the previous aeon.

2.83. Just as the senses are changed by the perceptions of different qualities [lit. "mixtures"], likewise the intellect too is changed, when it meditates on contemplations that are different every moment.

In this gnoseological *kephalaion* Evagrius, according to a very old philosophical tradition, describes knowledge as an alteration of the knowing faculty that is produced by the object(s) that it apprehends, in that their qualities change. This is the case both with sense perceptions and with the *nous*'s contemplations, although their respective objects are different.

2.84. There was a time when the Lord was judge only of living beings, whereas there will be no time when he will be judge only of the dead. And there will be again a time when he will be judge only of living beings.

From the formal-rhetorical point of view, this *kephalaion* is structured like *KG* 1.40. From the viewpoint of the contents too, these two *kephalaia* are alike, in that both of them deal with the beginning and the end and highlight a close resemblance between the two: just as at the beginning there was no evil, so will there be no evil in the end (*KG* 1.40), and just as at the beginning there was no death, so will there be no death in the end (*KG* 2.84). This is because death was introduced by evil; therefore, it is obvious that the disappearance of evil will also entail the eventual vanishing of death. This is why at the beginning there were only living beings, before the fall; now after the fall there are both living and dead due to sin; and in the end, after the disappearance of sin, there will likewise be only living beings.

2.85. If it is true that living beings are susceptible of increment and diminution, it is clear that therefore (this is) the opposite of those who are dead, and they receive these things themselves. And if this is in this way, there will be again various bodies, and worlds/aeons will be created that are apt to them.

Evagrius, in the footsteps of Origen, here argues again for the multiplicity of aeons, mainly on the basis of the needs of rational creatures. For each aeon is adapted to the moral development of rational creatures. See above, *KG* 1.7, 9, 11, 17, 65, 70, 75; 2.2, 14, 17, 59, 65, 74, 75, 82, and the relevant commentaries, and below, at least *KG* 6.75 and the relevant commentary.

2.86. The bread of those who are outside is one that is not of the Presence, and their drink is full of flies, whereas the bread of those who are inside is a bread of the Presence, and their drink is harmless.

The metaphor of the Presence or non-Presence bread is parallel to that of a drink full of flies or harmless. The mention of the bread of the Presence is a reference to Exod 25:30 and Heb 9:2.

In *KG* 2.74 and 2.82 Evagrius has already addressed the theme of worlds/aeons as nourishment of rational creatures. And I have already remarked that this nourishment consists in knowledge of these aeons. Being outside and being inside may here refer to the church—the body of Christ—which in the *telos* will coincide with all rational creatures but at the moment includes only some of them.

2.87. The movement of bodies belongs to time, whereas the transformation of incorporeal beings is without time.

Bodies are subject to the laws of space and time (the dimensions, or διαστήματα—hence their being diastematic), but what is incorporeal is not. This distinction between diastematic and nondiastematic was particularly momentous for Origen and Gregory Nyssen (see Hans Boersma, *Embodiment and Virtue in Gregory of Nyssa* [Oxford: Oxford University Press, 2013]; Ramelli, *Gregorio di Nissa: Sull'anima*; and idem, *Christian Doctrine of Apokatastasis*, the sections on Origen and Gregory).

2.88. The contemplation of this sense-perceptible world is given as nourishment not only to human beings but also to other rational natures.

In *KG* 2.74 and 2.82 Evagrius has already addressed the theme of worlds/aeons as nourishment of rational creatures. And I have already remarked that this nourishment consists in knowledge of these worlds (see above, the commentaries on *KG* 2.74 and 2.82). Here he concentrates on this particular world and on its *theōria*.

2.89. The one who, he alone, sits to the right of the Father has, he alone, the knowledge of the right (hand).

The reference is to Mark 16:19. Of course the only one who sits to the right of the Father is Christ. He is said by Evagrius to have "the knowledge of the right," which may symbolize power or justice. Both are connected to Christ, respectively, through the creation of the aeons, which he performed, and the judgments after each aeon and at the end of all aeons, which he also performs.

2.90. Those who have seen the light of the two luminaries, these will see the primary and blessed light, that which we shall see in Christ, when by means of a positive change, we shall rise before him.

The first or primary light is that of Christ, and human beings will see it at the resurrection. The positive change, that is, a change to a better condition, which is mentioned here, is probably to be understood as the change from mortal bodies to immortal ones. But at the same time Evagrius, like Gregory Nyssen and Origen, saw the resurrection, or *anastasis*, as holistic, as a transformation not only of the body but also of the soul (see Ramelli, "Origen's Exegesis of Jeremiah"). And the restoration of the faculties of the soul—the second, spiritual meaning of the "positive change" mentioned here by Evagrius—of course goes together with the *apokatastasis*.

***

At the end of *KG* 2.90, in the manuscript that is the only witness to the S_2 redaction, we find: "The second is finished."

Third Discourse

3.1. The Father, and only he, knows Christ, and the Son, and only he, the Father. The one qua unique in Unity, the other qua Monad and Unity.

This third "century," or discourse, too, like the first and the second, and like Origen's Περὶ 'Αρχῶν, or *On First Principles*, has its beginning in God. The first three *kephalaia* are devoted to God and Christ and are followed by others devoted to the intellectual creatures, who, in the order of beings, come immediately after God. On the structure of Origen's masterpiece, which starts from God and passes on to rational creatures, see Ilaria L. E. Ramelli, "Origen, Patristic Philosophy, and Christian Platonism: Rethinking the Christianisation of Hellenism," *VC* 63 (2009): 217–63. The scriptural reference concerning the Son, who is the only one who knows the Father, is to Matt 11:27.

God, as Evagrius explains here, is unique in Unity; the Son is Monad and Unity—Unity in that the Son is God, and Monad in that the Son is the Logos, the Monad containing the *logoi* of all creatures. This definition comes straight from Clement and Origen, who maintained that God the Father is ἁπλῶς ἕν, absolutely and simply One (= unique in Unity), while the Son, qua Logos-Wisdom, is ὡς τὰ πάντα ἕν, "one as all." See Ramelli, "Clement's Notion of the Logos." Monad and Henad or Unity is the definition of God given by Origen in *On First Principles* 1.1.6: μονάς τε καὶ ἑνάς. If this is the case, it is clear that Evagrius identifies Christ with the Son, given the perfect chiastic structure of this *kephalaion*, in which "Christ" exactly corresponds to "the Son," and depicts Christ-Son as God, as is also clear elsewhere in the *KG* and as I have argued.

3.2. Christ is the only one who has the Unity in himself and has received the judgment of rational creatures.

Christ has been entrusted with the judgment of the *logika* in that he is the Logos. He is said to have the Unity in himself because he is God (the Son). He is at the same time God, the Logos, and a *logikon*, Jesus Christ.

3.3. The Unity is that which now is known by Christ alone, the one whose knowledge is essential.

In *KG* 3.2 Evagrius has just declared that only Christ has Unity in himself; this is why, thanks to this ontological privilege, he is also the only one who knows the Unity. In *KG* 2.89 Evagrius has already stated that Christ, and only Christ, has "the knowledge of the right" hand of God, meaning power and justice. And indeed Christ is the one who is entrusted with the Judgment. Here Christ is said to be the only one who has the knowledge of the Unity, and his knowledge is "essential," or "substantial," in that Christ *is* in the Unity, with God and the Spirit, essentially and not by virtue of participation. The knowledge of Christ is essential in that Christ is God, and the Trinity is described by Evagrius more than once as "essential knowledge." See above, *KG* 1.89; 2.47, 81 and the relevant commentaries, and below, *KG* 4.77 and 5.55, and the relevant commentaries.

It is to be noticed that Evagrius here says that *now* Unity is known only by Christ, which implies that there will come a time in which Christ will no more be alone in this privilege. This will clearly be the *telos*, when the "deification" of rational creatures will have them participate in divine life and "essential knowledge."

3.4. Peculiar to angels is to always be nourished with the contemplation of beings; to human beings is to not always (be nourished with it); and to demons is (to be nourished with it) neither in a time nor without time.

In other *kephalaia* from the Second Part or Discourse, Evagrius has repeatedly spoken of rational creatures as "nourished" with worlds/aeons, or more precisely with the knowledge or the contemplation (*theōria*) of worlds/aeons. Here, he specifically refers to the *theōria* of the existing beings that works as a nourishment for angels and partially for humans—depending on the degree of their moral or intellectual advancement—but never for demons ("never" meaning absolutely never, either in time or outside of the dimension of time). With this, he introduces a fundamental distinction within rational creatures based on knowledge, which in

Evagrius's view goes hand in hand with virtue. As I have already explained several times above, virtue and knowledge are interdependent in Evagrius's thought.

3.5. The intellects of the heavenly powers are pure and full of knowledge, and their bodies are lights that shine over those who get close to them.

In continuity with the last *kephalaion*, Evagrius goes on to speak of the excellence in knowledge proper to angels, which is interconnected with their excellence in virtue. I have repeated several times by now that Evagrius, like Origen, seems to have maintained that all created beings have a body, even angels (and stars), who are not pure spirits but have a luminous, fine, and immortal body (*gwšm'*). Only the Blessed Trinity can live, as an independent substance, without a body. See Ramelli, "Preexistence of Souls."

3.6. The bare intellect is that which, by means of the contemplation that regards it, is joined to the knowledge of the Trinity.

Evagrius speaks often of the bare intellect, for instance in *KG* 3.8 and 3.19 as well (see below, the relevant commentaries). The *nous* is "bare" or "naked" when it is pure to the highest degree; then, its *theōria* and the knowledge of the Trinity, which is the highest degree of knowledge, are united. This kind of intellect is the one to which Evagrius refers in his *Letter to Melania* 15–19, when he claims that those intellects that are close to God do not need the creation as a mediator for their knowledge—a mediation necessary to those who are "far from God"—but directly know through the Son and the Spirit: "Just as the intellect operates in the body by means of the mediation of the soul, likewise the Father too, by means of the mediation of his own soul [i.e., the Son and the Spirit], operates in his own body, which is the human intellect" (15). Indeed, human intellects know thanks to the Logos and the Spirit, who make everything known to them (19). In *KG* 3.19, however, Evagrius does not restrict the bare intellect to the knowledge of the Trinity but associates a bare seer to the primary and secondary contemplation, that is, the immaterial and the material one.

3.7. Each one of the changes is established in order to nourish rational creatures. And those who are (thus) nourished arrive at a better change, whereas those who are not thus nourished (arrive at) a bad change.

The most positive change is probably that which leads a *logikon* from an inferior to a superior order—for instance, from demon to human and from human to angel. The opposite is a change from a superior to an inferior order. Changes in general are established by divine providence ("is established" obviously is a theological passive) for the sake of the spiritual development of the *logika*. If they take advantage of these changes for their own moral progress, they are said to be "nourished" by them. Evagrius uses again the "nourishing" imagery on which he has already relied in several *kephalaia* in reference to the rational creatures, who are "nourished" with contemplation and knowledge.

3.8. The intellect that possesses the last garment is that which knows the contemplation only of all secondary beings.

In *KG* 3.6 Evagrius has explained how a "bare" *nous* is; here he explains how a *nous* that has "the last garment" is. The latter condition is obviously inferior to the former. Indeed, the *theōria* of secondary beings is of course inferior to that of primary beings, that is, intelligible beings. Origen too, and Gregory Nyssen, used the imagery of the garment or tunic of the intellectual soul (χιτών) in connection with the "skin tunics/garments" mentioned by Genesis as the clothes given by God to the protoplasts after their fall. But Porphyry too—who was very well acquainted with Origen's ideas and works, and in turn was known to Evagrius—spoke of the last dress or last tunics of the soul: "In the Father's temple, that is, this world, is it not prudent to keep pure our last garment, the skin tunic, and thus, with this tunic made pure, live in the Father's temple? … We must remove these many garments, both this visible garment of flesh and those inside, which are close to those of skin" (*On Abstinence from Eating Animals* 2.46 and 1.31). See Ramelli, "Preexistence of Souls."

3.9. In the world/aeon to come the bodies of ignorance will be overcome, whereas in that which will be after it the transformation will receive an increment of fire and air, and those who are below will apply themselves to science, if it is true that "the houses of the impious will receive purification" and that Christ "works miracles today and tomorrow, and on the third day is perfected."

The eschatological perspective is composite: the aeon to come will be followed by another one, and the *telos*, symbolized by the third day, will coincide with the perfect accomplishment of the work of Christ. This work, which is represented by his "miracles" (with a quotation from Luke 13:32), is expressly identified by Evagrius with the purification of sinners (with a quotation from Prov 14:9), clearly aimed at their salvation. Luke 13:32 has been already cited by Evagrius in *KG* 1.90, in reference to the resurrection of those in whom God's justice is dead (see above, the relevant commentary). Clearly, this resurrection also implies a purification and a spiritual renewal. Fire and air are the bodies of angels, "chariot/vehicles of knowledge" (see further *KG* 2.51 and the relevant commentary there). Thus, in the future aeons the bodies of ignorance of humans and demons will change into bodies of knowledge, angelic bodies, according to the moral progress of their owners achieved through purification and instruction.

3.10. The intellect that is imperfect is that which still needs the contemplation that is known by means of the mortal corporeal nature.

If the *nous* still needs the secondary *theōria*, which is that of mortal bodies (here the adjective for "corporeal" derives from *pgr'*, designating not the spiritual and immortal body but the mortal body), this is an imperfect *nous*. The perfect *nous* is that which is nourished by the primary *theōria*, and ultimately by the contemplation of God and the reception of essential knowledge (see below, *KG* 3.12).

3.11. The mortal corporeal nature has received Christ's "Wisdom, full of modalities/varieties," whereas it is not susceptible of Christ himself. But the incorporeal nature both shows the Wisdom of the Unity and is susceptible of the Unity.

Evagrius has just spoken of mortal corporeal nature in the previous *kephalaion*, arguing that the *nous* that depends on their *theōria* is still imperfect. Now he goes on to speak of this same nature: the word for "corporeal" is again derived from *pgr'*, which designates mortal corporeality. This can receive Christ's Wisdom, which created it and created all aeons after the fall of the *logika*, but not Christ himself qua Unity, that is, qua God. This can be received only by incorporeal nature. Here the word for "incorporeal" derives from *gwšm'*, also including spiritual bodies; therefore, such an idea of incorporeality, not-*gwšm'*, excludes spiritual as well as mortal bodies. Creatures will receive the Unity in the *telos*. Absolute incorporeality is indeed divine; for creatures this is a limit-hypothesis, which can refer to when bodies will be elevated to the rank of souls and souls to the rank of intellects.

The quotation of Eph 3:10, on Christ as God's Wisdom full of varieties or modalities, is dear to Evagrius, who uses it also in *KG* 1.43; 2.2, and 21. I have already explained Origen's use of this scriptural passage and its striking closeness to Bardaisan in commenting on *KG* 2.2.

3.12. The perfect intellect is that which can easily receive essential knowledge.

Evagrius has spoken in *KG* 3.10 of the imperfect *nous*, which is nourished with the secondary *theōria*. The perfect *nous*, on the contrary, has essential knowledge, which in *KG* 3.3 Evagrius ascribes to Christ; in *KG* 1.89 and 2.47 "essential knowledge" is God the Father and the whole Trinity. See above, the commentaries on these *kephalaia*.

3.13. We have known the Wisdom of the Unity, while joined to the nature that is below it; Unity itself, however, cannot be seen, while joined to some of the beings [or "joined to something deriving from the beings"], and for this reason the incorporeal *nous* sees the Holy Trinity in those beings that are not bodies.

Unity itself can be *received* by the incorporeal nature (as stated by Evagrius in *KG* 3.11), evidently in the *telos*, thanks to the final *theōsis*, but it cannot be seen, as though it were an object of knowledge. It will be an object of mystical experience (and it can already be so, in a mystical experience; see Ramelli, "Divine as an Inaccessible Epistemological Object"). The object of knowledge is rather the Wisdom of the Unity, which is displayed in creation, as is again stated in *KG* 3.11 (see below, the commentary on that *kephalaion*). The Trinity, which is entirely incorporeal, can be seen by the incorporeal *nous* in incorporeal realities, like the intelligible ones.

3.14. A defective soul is that whose faculty that is liable to passions leans toward nothingness.

This *kephalaion* directly depends on Evagrius's strong option for the ontological priority of the Good. The Good is God, and only God is the

Being par excellence (see *KG* 1.1, 39–41, and the relevant commentaries above). Elongation from the Good means inclination toward evil, which is nonbeing. So, the vicious and defective soul, which is enslaved to its own passions, tends to nonbeing.

3.15. If it is true that the perfection of the intellect is immaterial knowledge, as it is said, and immaterial knowledge is only the Trinity, it is clear that in perfection nothing of matter will remain. And if this is so, the intellect, finally bare, will become a seer of the Trinity.

Evagrius has already introduced the equation between immaterial knowledge and God / the Trinity in *KG* 1.89 and 2.47, speaking of "essential knowledge" proper. Essential knowledge is immaterial knowledge. It will be achieved by the *nous* in the *telos*, in perfection, when it will be "bare," a condition that Evagrius presents here as eschatological. In *KG* 3.6 he has already spoken of the "bare intellect," defining it as that which is joined to the knowledge of the Trinity by means of the contemplation concerning it (see also *KG* 3.8 and the commentaries on 3.6 and 3.8). Here again Evagrius describes it as the intellect that will "see" the Trinity and will be bare or naked in that in the *telos* it will be free from what is material and came about as secondary, after the fall. Otherwise it could not see or know the Trinity, which, unlike creatures, is completely immaterial (according also to Origen's conception). At the same time it is to be remarked that in *KG* 3.19 a "bare" seer is also presented as the subject of the primary and secondary contemplations, while in *KG* 3.8 the intellect that knows the secondary contemplation (and not the primary) is said to still have "the last garment" upon it and therefore to be not yet completely "bare" (see above, the commentary on *KG* 3.8).

3.16. The perfect soul is that whose faculty that is liable to passions operates in accord with nature.

This *kephalaion* is closely related to *KG* 3.14. The principle of acting and behaving according to nature is a very old ideal that goes back to Stoic ethics (see, e.g., Ramelli, *Stoici romani minori*). Now, the nature for the rational soul is the *logos*—which for a Christian also means Christ-Logos. The soul that behaves against nature, described in *KG* 3.14, follows passions, which are against the *logos*, and therefore goes toward evil and thus nonbeing. The soul that behaves according to nature, on the contrary, that is, according to the *logos*, is the perfect soul and adheres to Christ-Logos-Virtue. Proclus too, who unlike Evagrius was no Christian but like Evagrius was a Neoplatonist, opposes the passions (τὰ πάθη) that act upon the soul to the intellectual life of the soul, which is the only life in accord with nature for the intellectual soul (τὴν νοερὰν καὶ τὴν κατὰ φύσιν ζωήν), and moreover ascribes this view to Plato (*Commentary on Plato's Timaeus* 3.349.9–12). Likewise, immediately afterward Proclus insists that the soul, if it acts in accordance with its own nature (κατὰ φύσιν), sticks to order, reason, and a reflective and prudent condition (τάξις καὶ λόγος καὶ ἡ λελογισμένη καὶ ἔμφρων κατάστασις). These are characteristics of a mature life, "under the guidance of nature" (τῆς φύσεως ἀγούσης; 3.349.15–21).

3.17. Those who have reached immaterial contemplation, these are also in the same order, whereas it is not the case that those who are in the same order are also in immaterial contemplation since now; for they may still be in the contemplation that concerns intelligible realities, that which, it too, needs a bare intellect, if it is true that it has seen it in a bare manner also at the beginning.

The Syriac word I render "order" is the transliteration of Greek τάξις. Evagrius has already spoken of immaterial knowledge and substantial or essential knowledge; here he speaks of immaterial *theōria*. Those who have this belong to the same order, but it is not guaranteed that those who belong to the same order also immediately have the immaterial *theōria*. Some of these evidently do not have it but only have the *theōria* concerning intelligible things. Since the latter are immediately after God the Trinity in the ontological order, it is clear that for Evagrius the immaterial *theōria*, just as immaterial knowledge and essential knowledge, concerns the divinity itself. The *theōria* concerning intelligible things also requires a "bare" intellect, and Evagrius states that at the beginning as well the intellect saw intelligible things in a bare manner. See also *KG* 3.19 (and the commentary), where a "bare" intellect is presented as involved in both the primary and the secondary contemplation, that is, both the immaterial and the material one.

3.18. Torment is the fiery suffering that purifies the part of the soul that is liable to passions.

The removal of the dirt of evil will be the purification occurring via the πῦρ αἰώνιον, or "otherworldly fire," in the other world; it is the κόλασις αἰώνιος of which the Gospels speak and that means "punishment in the other world" (see Ramelli and Konstan, *Terms for Eternity*, with the reviews by Carl O'Brien in *The Classical Review* 60.2 [2010]: 390–91; and by Danilo Ghira in *Maia* 61 [2009]: 732–34). All passions or affections (πάθη) must disappear from the soul for it to attain purification. Evagrius, like Origen and Gregory of Nyssa, adheres to the ideal of ἀπάθεια, a Stoic and Platonic ethical ideal that had been absorbed already by Philo, Clement of Alexandria, and Origen and will be followed also be Gregory of Nyssa and other Christian Platonists.

Evagrius also sticks to Clement's, Origen's, and Nyssen's conviction that all punishments and sufferings inflicted by God have a therapeutic and purifying aim. Origen steadfastly adhered to this opinion throughout his life and still in his *Commentary on Romans* 8.11.100–111 maintained that purification will be applied through instruction and, in case of necessity, if the instruction will not have produced the desired effect, through fire in the other world, the fire of Gehenna, namely, the πῦρ αἰώνιον, which by no means will be eternal. Its duration will be established for each one by Christ, whose love for humanity is mentioned straightforward:

> But in case one should despise the purification provided by the Word of God and the teaching of the Gospels, one reserves himself for harsh purifications of punishment, that the fire of Gehenna with its torments may purity the man whom neither the teaching of the apostles nor the words of the Gospels have purified, according to Scripture: "And I will purify you with fire until you are clean" [Isa 1:25]. Then, this very purification that is applied by means of the punishment of fire, for how long a time, for how many centuries will require the torment of sinners, well, this can be known only to the One to whom the Father has handed every judgment. This is the One who has loved his creature so much as to empty himself of the form of God for this same creature and take on the form of a slave, humbling himself to the point of dying, because he wanted all human beings to be saved and to come to the knowledge of the Truth.
>
> *Qui uero uerbi Dei et doctrinae euangelicae purificationem spreuerit, tristibus et poenalibus purificationibus semet ipsum reseruat, ut ignis gehennae in cruciatibus purget quem nec apostolica doctrina nec euangelicus sermo purgauit, secundum illud quod scriptum est, "et purificabo te igni ad purum." Uero haec ipsa purgatio quae per poenam ignis adhibetur quantis temporibus quantisue saeculis de peccatoribus exigat cruciatus solus scire potest Ille cui Pater omne iudicium tradidit, qui ita diligit creaturam suam ut pro illa euacuauerit semet ipsum de Dei forma et serui formam sus-*

> *ceperit, humilians semet ipsum usque ad mortem, uolens omnes homines saluos fieri et in agnitionem ueritatis uenire.*

The last sentence is a quotation from 1 Tim 2:4 and assures that Origen was still sure that purification in the fire of Gehenna will come to an end for every human being, however long this punishment can endure—even lasting for many centuries. In fact, this will be a punishment decreed by God, who is good—thence nothing evil is ever decided by God; not even death, when decided by God, can be an evil, but it will be given for the purpose of emendation:

> If you hear God say, "I shall kill and shall make live," you should understand what kind of death is worthy of God to inflict: undoubtedly, that death which brings about life … for David, too, says what follows about God: "When God killed them, they looked for God." This teaches very clearly that, if God kills someone, he kills him precisely in order that this person may die to sin and look for God.… Thus the apostle too handed the sinner to the destruction of his flesh so to save his spirit, that is, in order for him to die to sin and live for God.… Even if God is said to kill and to hand people to death, the death that is given by God must be such as to bestow life. For nothing evil is ever produced by the One who is good. Even if the punishment is harsh and full of pain, however, it is inflicted with the intention of healing and bringing the punished back to health.

> *Si audias Deum dicentem: "Ego occidam et uiuere faciam," intellegere debes quam sit mors quam decet inferre Deum: illa sine dubio quae conferat uitam … sic enim et Dauid dicit de Deo: "cum occideret eos exquirebant eum," apertissime docens quia quem Deus occidit propterea occidit ut peccato moriatur, et quaerat Deum.… Sic et apostolus peccatorem tradebat in interitum carnis ut spiritum faceret saluum, hoc est ut moreretur peccato et uiueret Deo.… Deus etiamsi occidere dicatur et morti tradere, talis quaedam sit mors quae a Deo datur ut conferat uitam. Nihil enim mali datur a bono, licet triste sit, licet doloris plenum, prospectu tamen medendi et contemplatione sanitatis infertur.* (*Commentary on Romans* 6.6.44–66; cf. 1.1.50–57)

In his *Homilies on Jeremiah*, too, Origen expressed the very same idea; see Ramelli, "Origen's Exegesis of Jeremiah."

If nothing bad can possibly be given by God, who is good, according to Plato's principle that "God is not responsible for evil" (θεὸς ἀναίτιος), punishment for bad deeds not only has a therapeutic aim but comes from one's evil actions, and not from God, as Origen affirms in *Commentary on Romans* 11.5.169–171. Such an argument will be rehearsed by Gregory of Nyssa in his dialogue *On the Soul and the Resurrection*: punishment is not God's own aim; God's only purpose is rather the attraction of the soul to Goodness, while the soul's suffering in this process is a sort of side effect produced by the evil itself in which the soul is imprisoned. Origen insists that it is never God who plunges anyone into perdition, and from perdition itself (ἀπόλλυμι, ἀπώλεια) God rescues the lost, as Origen deduces above all from the parables of mercy in Luke 15, which regularly speak of someone or something (the prodigal son, the sheep, the drachma) that was lost but is found again and restored:

> "The Child of the human being has come to look for and save what was lost." And the Lord also says: "I have been sent just to the lost sheep of the house of Israel." … Moreover, in the Gospel the lost drachma is found again by the woman after the cleaning of the house. And the father rejoices when his youngest son repents and converts, because he was dead and returns to life, he was lost and has been found again.… The Lord himself avers: "I shall go search for what is lost." In all of these passages, nowhere does God say to have pushed anybody into perdition himself, but each one suffers because of himself … and the Child of the human being has come to look for what was lost.
>
> *Uenit filius hominis quaerere et saluare quod perierat, et iterum dicit: non sum missus nisi ad oues quae perierunt domus Israhel … sed et in euangelio mina quae perierat, mundata domo, inuenitur a muliere, et gaudet pater super filio iuniore paenitente qui mortuus fuerat et reuixit, perierat et inuentus est … ipse Dominus dicit: et quod perit ego requiram.… In his omnibus nusquam Deus aliquem dicitur perdidisse, sed unusquisque ex se pati … et uenit filius hominis quaerere quod perierat* (*Commentary on Romans* 2.6.35–59).

Likewise, Origen insists that, whenever God is said to kill or destroy, it is only in order to resuscitate and rebuild in a better state (see Ramelli, "Origen's Exegesis of Jeremiah"). For instance, God destroys "Paul the traitor, Paul the persecutor" in order to have him live again as "Paul the apostle of Jesus Christ." Evagrius thinks along the very same lines: "'In the destruction of the impious the righteous will be multiplied': If the impious cease to be impious, they become just. Here, indeed, the term 'destruction' [ἀπώλεια] means the elimination of impiety. In this way, the Lord destroyed Matthew, the tax collector, by bestowing justice upon him" (scholium 355 on Prov 28:28).

3.19. The primary and the secondary contemplations have in common the fact that they have a bare seer, whereas they have (each one) as a property the fact that the one is immaterial, while the other one is in matter.

In both contemplations, or *theōriai*, primary and secondary, the seer is "bare," a concept that Evagrius has already developed in *KG* 3.6, where he has described the bare intellect as joined to the knowledge of the Trinity (see *KG* 3.8, 15, and 17, and the relevant commentaries above). Thus, the difference between the two is not in the subject (the intellect, here called "the seer") but in the object—for that of the primary *theōria* is immaterial, and that of the secondary, material.

3.20. The change/succession of instruments is the transformation from (certain) bodies into (different) bodies, according to the measure of the orders of those that are joined with them.

Evagrius has already used the word "instrument" (the Syriac transliterates the Greek noun ὄργανον) to designate the body, according to the Aristotelian tradition appropriated by Platonists as well (*KG* 1.67; 2.48, 80; see above, the relevant commentaries). Here he uses it again in this sense and explicitly identifies these "instruments" with bodies. Just as Origen thought, Evagrius also maintains that transformations of bodies depend on the degree of moral and spiritual advancement of rational creatures. This is why bodies are instruments: not simply because they are equipped with sense organs but because they indeed are instrumental to the moral stage reached by the *logika* in different times. These stages are here indicated by the word "order," which in Syriac transliterates the Greek noun τάξις. This conception has nothing to do with metensomatosis, which Origen explicitly rejected and Gregory of Nyssa and Evagrius refused to embrace as well. See Ramelli, "Origen's Doctrine of the Apokatastasis"; and idem, "Preexistence of Souls."

3.21. There is in common that the second and third contemplations are in matter, whereas, each one individually, one has a bare *nous* and is of the same order, whereas the third is together with bodies and in different orders.

Evagrius is proceeding downward in the order of contemplation. The second and the third ones are in matter. I translate "in matter" according to my emendation ܒܗܘܠܐ instead of ܕܗܘܠܐ, the reading of the manuscript, and instead of ܕܒܗܘܠܐ, the emendation proposed by Guillaumont (105), which seems to be redundant. In *KG* 3.19 Evagrius has just stated that the secondary *theōria* is "in matter," while the primary is immaterial, and both require a "bare" seer. Now he explains that the third *theōria* too is "in matter," but the second has as a subject a bare *nous*—in agreement with *KG* 3.19—and concerns all beings of the same order (τάξις, indicating the same degree of spiritual development), whereas the third has as a subject *noes* that are joined to bodies and concerns beings that are of different orders.

3.22. The first movement of rational creatures is the separation of the intellect from the unity that is in it.

Evagrius here speculates on protology, and not only. Just as Origen thought, he too maintains that the *noes* first were in the Unity, in Christ-Logos-Wisdom (I have already explained how Origen used the metaphor of their being decorations on the body of Logos-Wisdom). Their creation coincided with their acquiring a substantial existence of their own, thus becoming "rational creatures," and a spiritual body, but the beginning of their movement (meaning the movements of their free will; see *KG* 6.75 and the analogous moral meaning of κίνησις in Origen) took place when they, or some of them, detached themselves from the initial unity of *homonoia*, or concord, that obtained at the beginning, when all of them were oriented to the Good, that is, God, and wanted nothing else, nothing different from the Good. Then the wills of some of them "moved," changed their direction, and oriented themselves toward lesser or apparent goods, or evil. In this way, the initial unity and concord was broken. See Ramelli, "Harmony between *Arkhē* and *Telos*."

This *kephalaion* seems to suggest that this initial story repeats itself for every single *nous*, and indicates that the initial Unity is also in each *nous*—unless we take the final ܒܗ, "in it," in a nonreflexive way, that is, not in reference to the intellect itself but in reference to another indirect object, which may be Christ-Logos and God. Indeed, Evagrius has identified the Unity with Christ-Logos and God in *KG* 1.77; 2.3, 11; 3.1–3, 11, and 13. However, in this *kephalaion* there is no previous mention of Christ or God. In this *kephalaion* Evagrius intimates that the movement of will not only broke the initial Unity and the concord of all intellects but also, on a minor and individual scale, breaks the internal unity of each *nous*, which becomes divided into intellect, soul, and body. The unity of the *nous*, which reflects the unity that is God, will have to be recovered in a process of restoration.

3.23. There is in common that all the aeons are constituted by the four elements, whereas individually each of them has a different kind of mixture.

Evagrius follows again Origen's conception of a limited sequence of worlds/aeons, each one constituted by the four elements of matter. The difference between one and another of them is a difference not in matter but in the combination or mixture that characterizes matter, and thus a difference in quality. Very interestingly, Bardaisan of Edessa, one of the first supporters of the doctrine of *apokatastasis*, indicated the future aeon that will be a prelude, by means of instruction, to the eventual *apokatastasis*, with the expression "a different mixture" or "a different arrangement of things"—the very same concept that Evagrius is expressing here. See my edition, translation, and commentary in Ilaria Ramelli, ed., *Bardaisan on Free Will, Fate, and Human Nature: The Book of the Laws of Countries* (Tübingen: Mohr Siebeck, 2016). There are many interesting parallels between Bardaisan's and Origen's *apokatastasis* doctrines; see Ramelli, "Origen, Bardaisan, and the Origin of Universal Salvation." On matter and qualities in Origen, see also Ramelli, "*Dialogue of Adamantius*" (parts 1 and 2).

3.24. The knowledge of the primary nature is a spiritual contemplation, that of which the Creator availed himself and created [i.e., while creating] the intellects, which only are susceptible of his nature.

Evagrius has spoken several times both of the primary nature, the intelligible one (*KG* 1.50; 2.31), and of spiritual *theōria* (*KG* 1.13); he has also mentioned "spiritual knowledge" in *KG* 1.32, 72; and 2.3, in which spiritual knowledge is said to be anterior to every natural *theōria* (see above, the commentary on these *kephalaia*). Now, God created the intellects by means of spiritual *theōria*, that is, the knowledge of the primary nature or intellectual nature. God created the intellects by knowing them. Only the intellects, qua intelligible beings, can be the recipients of the nature of God, probably in mystical experience, or in the final *theōsis*. At the same time Evagrius also makes it clear what was the reason for

God to create the first, intellectual creation: to have other beings capable of receiving the divine nature. When God created the intellects, he used spiritual contemplation, which is the knowledge of the intellectual nature. This knowledge was present in God's Logos-Wisdom in the form of the Ideas or Logoi of metaphysical forms of the intellectual beings that were to be created. See Ramelli, "Clement's Notion of the Logos."

3.25. The spiritual body and that which is opposite to it will be made not of our limbs or our parts but of an (immortal) body. For it is not the case that death [or "there"] is a change from (given) limbs into (other) limbs, but that from a good or bad mixture to a good or bad transformation.

Gregory of Nyssa in his dialogue *On the Soul and the Resurrection* maintained that the resurrected body will be the same as the dead body, with the same matter, but completely transformed in its quality and texture, so to result in a fine, incorruptible, glorious body, "more beautiful and worthier of love" (see my commentary in Ramelli, *Gregorio di Nissa: Sull'anima*). Evagrius, who was well acquainted with Gregory's ideas, states that the transformation of the body from death to resurrection is not a passage from the limbs of the mortal body to other limbs of the resurrected body, but it will be a change in mixture or texture of elements. It will depend on the goodness of the subject to acquire a spiritual body or its opposite in the resurrection. Evagrius seems to call "spiritual bodies" (of course the Syriac uses *gwšm'*, which includes immortal bodies, and not *pgr'*, which would indicate mortal bodies) those of the blessed at resurrection, and "their opposites" those of the wicked, who will have to undergo purification and thus will be immortal but not yet glorious. Rather, they will represent the wicked characters of their owners. The difference depends on the rational creature itself: whether it is good or bad. This picture, of course, does not describe the ultimate stage, which will come after the purification of all sinners.

It is finally interesting to note that in the corresponding *kephalaion* in the S_1 redaction a reference to 1 Cor 15:42 ("So also is the resurrection of the dead. It is sown in corruption; it is raised in incorruption," KJV) is inserted that in S_2 is lacking.

3.26. The knowledge concerning the secondary nature is a spiritual contemplation, that of which Christ availed himself and created [i.e., while creating] the nature of bodies and worlds/aeons from it.

Here we find an equation between "knowledge" and *theōria* that was latent in many other *kephalaia*. See above, my comments on *KG* 3.24, which is a manifest parallel to this *kephalaion* (3.24 on the primary nature, 3.26 on the secondary nature) and from which the equation between spiritual *theōria* and spiritual knowledge emerges. Both the knowledge of primary nature and that of secondary nature are forms of spiritual *theōria*. Christ created bodies (here *gwšm'*, indicating immortal bodies) and worlds by means of this *theōria*, which functioned as a paradigmatic cause of the cosmos, in accord with the notion of Christ-Logos as a κόσμος νοητός and Demiurge at the same time, as his role in creation was understood, especially by Clement, Origen, and Bardaisan, according to Middle-Platonic categories. See again Ramelli, "Clement's Notion of the Logos"; and, for Bardaisan, Ramelli, *Bardaisan of Edessa*, 107–24.

3.27. The primary contemplation of nature naturally both separates from the intellect and does not separate (from it). Indeed, the one that can be taught is separable, whereas that which is seen in the intellect that "knows" it appears to be inseparable.

In *KG* 2.27 (cf. 2.34) Evagrius has already presented the gnoseological condition of the *nous* as active and receptive together in different respects (see the relevant commentaries above). The *nous* is the subject of the "primary contemplation of nature," which is an intellectual *theōria*. If the latter is in the intellect itself, it cannot be taught to anyone and is inseparable from the intellect, like a mystical experience, whereas if it can be taught it is not "inside the intellect" and is separable. For the dualism that is implicit in knowledge and its overcoming in a "mystical" experience, see Ramelli, "Divine as an Inaccessible Epistemological Object."

3.28. A soul is an intellect that, in its carelessness, has fallen from Unity and, due to its lack of vigilance, has descended to the order of *praktikē*.

In this all-important *kephalaion* Evagrius is once again following Origen, who even expressed this notion by means of an etymology (see above, my commentary on *KG* 1.49, for all the details): ψυχή derives from ψῦξις, a cooling of the intellect, whose fall away from the Good, and from the unity of all intellects in the Good, is due to carelessness, an Origenian idea that Evagrius has already stressed in *KG* 1.49. He also developed this notion in his *Letter to Melania* 26: "The intellect, as I have mentioned, is one in nature, individual substance, and order. However, there was a time when the *intellect, because of its free will, fell from its original order and was named 'soul,'* and, having plunged further, was named 'body.' *But there will come a time when the body, the soul, and the intellect, thanks to a transformation of their wills, will become one and the same thing.* Since there will come a time when *the differentiations of the movements of their will shall vanish,* it will be elevated to the original state in which it was created." In *Letter on Faith* 7 Evagrius likewise depicts our intellect, in the present fallen condition, as "thickened" (παχυνθείς) and imprisoned in "earth and clay" (χοΐ, πηλῷ), that is, the mortal body. This is also why in this state it cannot enjoy "bare" or "pure" contemplation (ψιλὴ θεωρία). Monica Tobon has suggested that in fact for Evagrius the intellect has not descended entirely: "The *nous* remains a *nous* even as it becomes (additionally) a soul and a body; that is, that a part of it remains undescended in the contemplative union with God that it hitherto enjoyed in toto" (Tobon, "Raising Body and Soul," 53). This would be a Plotinian influence: the doctrine of the undescended soul (which subsequent Neoplatonists, such as Iamblichus and Proclus, would reject). If this is the case, Evagrius makes the undescended intellect a point of departure for *apokatastasis.* For, if the intellect has not descended entirely, this is why it can reascend and be restored to its original rank.

According to Origen too, those who, for their carelessness, have neglected to take care of their own spiritual improvement and salvation will be led by divine providence to take care of it and will finally be brought to salvation. See Ramelli, *Christian Doctrine of Apokatastasis*, the chapter on Origen.

The order or level (transliteration of Greek τάξις) of the *praktikē* (the Syriac in this case is not a transliteration but a semantic correspondent of Greek πρακτική), which is the level of the soul embodied in a mortal body liable to passions, in its battle against passions, is inferior to that of the *nous* and the unity it enjoyed in the initial state of *homonoia* in Christ-Logos.

3.29. The sign of the human order is the human body, while the sign of each one of the orders is greatness, forms, colors, qualities [lit. "mixtures"], natural faculties and weakness, time and places, parents and ancestors, increments, ways, life and death, and those aspects that are attached to these.

Differences in bodies and external circumstances that some (e.g., the adversaries of Bardaisan) ascribed to Fate, and that Bardaisan himself ascribed to a fate that is subordinated to God and is ultimately the expression of God's will (see Ramelli, *Bardaisan of Edessa*, 70–107), constitute differences in orders within the same human order. They all depend on God's decision and on the single *logikon*'s spiritual development, according to Evagrius just as according to Origen. The latter, moreover, added as a factor the generosity of some *logika* who accepted incarnation in a mortal body in order to assist the process of redemption (see Ilaria L. E. Ramelli, "Disability in Bardaisan and Origen: Between the Stoic *Adiaphora* and the Lord's Grace," in *Gestörte Lektüre: Disability als hermeneutische Leitkategorie biblischer Exegese* [ed. Wolfgang Grünstäudl and Markus Schiefer Ferrari; Stuttgart: Kohlhammer, 2012], 141–59). It is to be noticed that in the first sentence "human body" is ܓܘܫܡܐ ܐܢܫܝܐ, not ܦܓܪܐ ܐܢܫܝܐ, which would mean "human *mortal* body." This is probably because for Evagrius the human body is not *only* the mortal one but also the immortal body that everyone will take up at the resurrection.

3.30. The intellect is the seer of the Holy Trinity.

In *KG* 1.27 Evagrius has already said that the first of the five main contemplations, or *theōriai*, is the contemplation of the Trinity. The present *kephalaion* is to be understood in the light of *KG* 1.27, and also of 2.27 and 2.45 (see the relevant commentaries). For in *KG* 2.27 Evagrius has said that the *nous*, in looking at intelligible objects, sometimes becomes a seer of them; here the objects are intelligible realities, and in the *kephalaion* under investigation the object is the Trinity. And in *KG* 2.45 Evagrius has stated that the *nous* alone has the intellection of intelligible realities and "becomes a seer" both of the objects themselves and of their intellections. In the present *kephalaion*, the *nous* is a seer of the Trinity itself. This seems tantamount to the reception of essential knowledge by the perfect intellect, of which Evagrius speaks in *KG* 3.12.

3.31. What is the unity of the *nous*, it is possible to say, but what is its nature, it is impossible to say. For, there is no knowledge of the combination of that which is constituted neither of a visible sight nor of matter.

The *nous* is an intelligible reality; therefore, it has no matter and is not visible in any form. This is why the combination or mixture—and therefore the quality—that constitutes it cannot be known, and thus its nature is ineffable. The case is different with the unity of the *nous*, which seems to refer to Christ-Logos, or else to the harmony and intrinsic unity of the *nous*, its being noncomposite (this interpretation is confirmed by *KG* 3.33; see the relevant commentary below); for it is possible to say what the unity of the *nous* is. This unity reflects the Unity that God is, in whose image the intellect was created (as is mentioned in the immediately following *kephalaion*, *KG* 3.32).

3.32. The image of God is not that which is susceptible of his Wisdom, for in this way the mortal corporeal nature too would be the image of God. But that which is susceptible of the Unity is the image of God.

Like Philo, Origen, and Gregory of Nyssa, Evagrius also is convinced that the εἰκών of God in the human being is the *nous*, which is per se incorporeal and is susceptible of the divine Unity, and not their mortal body (here the adjective that I rendered with "mortal corporeal" derives from *pgr'*). Evagrius maintains that corporeal beings are susceptible of God's Wisdom in that they were all created by Christ-Logos-Wisdom.

3.33. The name of immortality reveals the natural unity of the intellect; the fact that it exists forever reveals its incorruptibility. And the knowledge of the Trinity accompanies the first name, whereas the primary contemplation of nature (accompanies) the second.

The *nous* is immortal because it is not composite—it is one and thus cannot die; death, indeed, is disaggregation; it is the division of what is composite, but what is one cannot die. The immortality of the rational soul is one of the tenets of Platonism, from Plato himself to Middle Platonism to Neoplatonism. Furthermore, the demonstration of its immortality based on its unity and simplicity (noncomposition) goes back to Plato himself. Knowledge of the Trinity is said here by Evagrius to be related to immortality and to Unity, because the Trinity is immortal and is Unity, and the primary *theōria* of nature is said to be related to incorruptibility because the primary nature, being intelligible, is itself incorruptible. The insistence on the names of immortality and incorruptibility probably implies a reference to 1 Cor 15:53–54: "For this perishable nature must put on the imperishable, and this mortal nature must put on immortality. When the perishable puts on the imperishable, and the mortal puts on immortality, then shall come to pass the saying that is written: 'Death is swallowed up in victory'" (RSV).

3.34. A demon is a rational nature, that which, because of an excess of *thymos*, has fallen from the service of God.

Evagrius has already ascribed the θυμός, the irascible principle, to demons in *KG* 1.68, where, taking up the Platonic tripartition of the soul, he observed that angels have a prevalence of intellect, human beings have a prevalence of ἐπιθυμία, and demons one of θυμός. Now he explains that it was precisely an excess of θυμός that determined the fall of demons from the initial unity of all rational creatures with God. That this excess of θυμός implies a lack of ἀγάπη, or donative love, which is the principal factor that keeps Unity according to Origen as well, is clear from the following *kephalaion*, in which Evagrius maintains that the virtue that is opposite to the θυμός is precisely ἀγάπη. For Origen's long argument that love will prevent further falls from the final Unity, see below, the commentary on *KG* 5.46 (see also the commentary on *KG* 1.65).

3.35. Knowledge cures the intellect, whereas charity-love cures the irascible faculty (of the soul), and chastity the concupiscible/appetitive part. Now, the cause of the first is the second, and that of the second, the third.

Evagrius here, as often elsewhere, follows Plato's tripartition of the soul into λογιστικόν, θυμικόν, and ἐπιθυμητικόν. The verb that I have translated "cures," from ܐܣܐ, interestingly can mean "restores" as well, so that a reference to the *apokatastasis* may resonate here. Indeed, one of the meanings of ἀποκαθίστημι was precisely that of restoring to health: "healing," "restoration to health," or "replacement of a limb into its original position." In the first century B.C.E. and in the first C.E. this meaning is attested in Apollonius's commentary on Hippocrates's *De articulis* (*On Joints*) 30.38: "It is necessary to bring about the restoration [ἀποκατάστασις] of the above-mentioned limb in the following way" (cf. 10.37: "the tension in the right direction produces the restoration [ἀποκατάστασις] of the limbs to their original place"). Indeed, since illness is against nature, restoration to health can be said to be the restoration into a state that is according to nature: εἰς τὸ κατὰ φύσιν ἀποκατάστασις ἔσται (8.18, an idea that Evagrius takes up in *KG* 1.41; see the relevant commentary above); and the action of putting a displaced limb back to its own place is said to be its ἀποκατάστασις in 2.12. The therapeutic meaning of ἀποκατάστασις is also attested by Archigenes in his medical fragments: "It is to be hoped that those who have fallen ill will be restored to health [εἰς ἀποκατάστασιν ἀχθήσεσθαι]" (71.22). Origen himself played on the meaning of this verb and represented *apokatastasis* as the restoration to spiritual health (see Ramelli, *Christian Doctrine of Apokatastasis*).

The cause of knowledge is love, and the cause of love is chastity. One must begin to cure, and therefore restore, with chastity the appetitive or concupiscible part of the soul, then with charity-love the irascible part (charity-love, ἀγάπη, is described as "the bridle of θυμός" in Evagrius, *Praktikos* 38), and finally will be able to attain knowledge. Here Evagrius's scheme is evident of the necessity of purification from passions by means of *praktikē* in order to attain knowledge. See above, *KG* 1.67 and the relevant commentary.

3.36. A world/aeon is a natural system that includes the various and different bodies of rational creatures, because of the knowledge of God.

The various conditions of rational creatures in each aeon are established by God in his knowledge on the basis of their merits and the degree of their spiritual development. For God knows which condition is the best for each of them for the sake of their development and salvation. Of course, the bodies of the rational creatures are called *gwšm'* because Evagrius here is thinking not only of human beings with their mortal bodies but also of angels and demons.

It is probable, indeed, that here the ambiguous expression "the knowledge of God" refers to God's knowledge, rather than to the creatures' knowledge of God. If the latter were the case—which cannot be ruled out—the expression "because of" should be understood, not without a forcible interpretation, in a final sense: the whole aim of the succession of the aeons is that rational creatures may acquire the knowledge of God. This may imply a reminiscence of 1 Tim 2:4–6: "God our Savior wants all human beings to be saved and to acquire the knowledge of truth"—truth, of course, being Christ/God.

The definition of an aeon as a natural system comes directly from Origen, who postulated a succession of aeons, each one with a specific arrangement for rational creatures, prior to *apokatastasis* into the divine and eternal life, and who refused to conceive an aeon as divine because of his anti-Gnostic polemic (see Ramelli, *Christian Doctrine of Apokatastasis*, the chapter on Origen).

3.37. Stars are superior to one another on the basis of their glory and not in their bodies. However, their size, and their figures, and their distance from one another, and their orbits, are different. And the fact that some of them are inside the shadow of the earth and others outside it, and yet others just on the boundary that separates (the two areas) gives information on their orders and on the government they have been entrusted with by God.

Stars do not differ from one another for their bodies but for their glory, which is greater for one, smaller for another. Evagrius refers to 1 Cor 15:41, but it is interesting that the redaction that I am following, S_2, cites this text according to the Peshitta, whereas the parallel text in S_1 cites 1 Cor 15:41 according to the Greek original: "There is one glory of the sun, and another glory of the moon, and another glory of the stars; for star differs from star in glory" (RSV).

Evagrius's thought concerning the stars as rational creatures who, however, are at the service of God and cannot determine anything in an autonomous way (as the supporters of Fate thought) is similar to that of Origen and of Bardaisan of Edessa, who both were strenuous opponents of the deterministic theory of Fate. See Ramelli, *Bardaisan of Edessa*; and Ute Possekel, "Bardaisan and Origen on Fate and the Power of the Stars," *JECS* 20 (2012): 515–42.

3.38. A judgment of God is the coming into being of a world/aeon, to which he gives a mortal body, in accord with the degree (of development) of each one of the rational creatures.

This *kephalaion* must be read along with *KG* 2.75, in which Evagrius states that the number of judgments corresponds to the number of aeons (see above, the relevant commentary), and with *KG* 3.36, in which a world/aeon is described as "a natural system that includes the various and different bodies of rational creatures." Each aeon is preceded by God's judgment of the merits and the degrees of spiritual development of all rational creatures, and thus God establishes an aeon that is best suited to favor the moral growth of rational creatures, determining the most appropriate condition for each one.

It is remarkable that Evagrius speaks of *pgr'* in reference to the body of each world/aeon, thus making it clear that it is a *mortal* body—like Origen, who took his distance from the "Gnostic" (Valentinian) idea of aeons as divine beings (see above, the commentary on *KG* 3.36). Indeed, according to Evagrius just as according to Origen, every aeon perishes and yields to the following aeon, until in the end there will be no more aeons in which all *logika* are found, but all will be found in God, who will be "all in all." See Ramelli, *Christian Doctrine of Apokatastasis*, the chapter on Origen.

3.39. A part of the fire is capable of burning, and another is incapable. And capable of burning is that which burns sense-perceptible matter, whereas incapable of burning is that which finishes off the disturbance of those disturbed. And the first does not burn the whole of the sense-perceptible mass, whereas the second is able to burn the whole of the mass of the disturbance.

Evagrius is describing the earthly fire, which burns sense-perceptible matter, and the purifying fire, the *πῦρ αἰώνιον* of the other world, established by God, which purifies those who are tormented. For Evagrius too, just as for Clement, for Origen, and for Gregory of Nyssa, the *πῦρ αἰώνιον*, or otherworldly fire, has a purifying function. Finally, the torment will be found to have been consumed precisely by the purifying fire.

3.40. The "last trumpet" is the order of the Judge, who has joined rational creatures to mortal bodies, good or bad. After this, there will be no more bad bodies.

The last trumpet is a reference to 1 Cor 15:51–52: "we shall all be changed, in a moment, in the twinkling of an eye, at the last trumpet. For the trumpet will sound, and the dead will be raised imperishable, and we shall be changed" (in the parallel version, S_1, the reference is to 1 Tim 4:8). The order is the command of the resurrection given by God, who has assigned mortal bodies (*pgr'*) to certain rational creatures, that is, human beings. These bodies are all mortal, but some are good, others bad. After the resurrection and the eschatological purification there will no longer be bad bodies, since all will be glorious and incorruptible. Indeed, there will be no mortal bodies any longer.

3.41. Concerning the contemplation of beings and concerning the knowledge of the Trinity, we and the demons raise a great fight against one another, while they wish to prevent us from knowing, whereas we endeavor to learn.

Like Origen, Evagrius too meditates on the interfering action of demons on human spiritual life, here especially on human *theōria* and knowledge. This action, however, for Origen cannot determine human free will but only disturb it and tempt it. Free will remains free. See Lekkas, *Liberté et progrès*; and Ramelli, "La coerenza della soteriologia origeniana."

3.42. Contemplation is the spiritual knowledge of those realities that were and will be, which lifts the intellect up toward its original order.

From the methodological point of view this *kephalaion* is important, in that it describes the relationship between *theōria* and knowledge (science), two of the key terms in Evagrius's system, which occur again and again in his *kephalaia*. This intellectual activity, contemplation and knowledge, elevates the intellect back to its original condition and rank (the Syriac word for "order" is the transliteration of the Greek τάξις); Evagrius presumably means the prelapsarian condition of the *logika*, before their fall and the transformation of their spiritual bodies into mortal bodies. Contemplation and knowledge are therefore essential to the process of restoration, or *apokatastasis*, just as they were essential to it according to Origen (see Ramelli, *Christian Doctrine of Apokatastasis*, the section on Origen). This restoration will culminate in the subsumption of bodies into souls and souls into intellects.

3.43. Those who now endeavor to reach knowledge possess in common water and perfumed oil (chrism). As a peculiarity, however, and copiously, human beings possess the oil.

Clearly this is one of the passages in which Evagrius uses allegorical interpretations of Scripture and liturgy; here in particular we have the liturgical symbols of water and of perfumed oil; the latter is a reference to Song 1:3. That humans strive to reach knowledge was already introduced in *KG* 3.41 (against demons) and developed in 3.42, where knowledge becomes an instrument of *apokatastasis*. The special association of humans with the oil/chrism may be due to the christological overtones of the chrism itself; Christ is related to humanity in a special way, having assumed humanity.

3.44. The intelligible sun is the rational nature, that which includes in itself the original and blessed light.

Plato of course used the famous metaphor of the sun as an allegorical expression of the Good. Here, Evagrius applies it to the *logika*, rational creatures, especially before their fall, when they were joined in unity of *homonoia* within themselves and with the Good. Then they had in themselves the original light of beatitude, which reminds readers of Origen's description of the prelapsarian union of the *logika* with God as a union of ardent love, as iron in fire. Indeed, it was the loss of their ardor in love, a ψῦξις, that for Origen determined the fall of (some of) the *logika*. Light is a common theme in the *KG*, where it is generally associated with God and with knowledge. The first *logikon*, the source of the original and blessed light, is Christ-Logos.

3.45. Just as it is impossible to say that there is an intellect that is anterior to another intellect, likewise also spiritual mortal bodies are not anterior to *praktika* mortal bodies, if it is true that the transformation that is cause of these two instruments is one and the same.

Noes are not anterior to one another, because they all belong to the same order; the same holds true for bodies, but the problem here is to determine of which bodies (here again called instruments of the souls, with a transliteration from Greek ὄργανον, "instrument") Evagrius is precisely speaking. Indeed, in the Syriac translation "spiritual mortal bodies" seems a *contradictio in adjecto*, and yet in Syriac ܦܓܪܐ ܪܘܚܢܝܐ has exactly this meaning, the adjective indicating "spiritual" and the noun designating a "mortal body," "flesh," and even "a corpse"; it is also the word that is used to indicate the body of Jesus's incarnation, which indeed was mortal and died. It is difficult to figure out the difference between a spiritual mortal body and a *praktikon* mortal body, ܦܓܪܐ ܦܠܚܢܝܐ. It probably refers to a degree of proficiency: *praktika* mortal bodies belong to those who practice asceticism and pursue *apatheia*; spiritual mortal bodies are those of the people who have attained knowledge already on earth. But these mortal bodies belong to the same order, since, as Evagrius argues, they originated from the same transformation, the fall that made human bodies mortal.

3.46. The judgment of angels is the knowledge concerning the illnesses of the soul, which lifts up to health those who have been wounded.

The metaphor of the health or illness of the soul is very old; it is already present in Greek philosophy (*animi medicina philosophia*) and in the Gospels, in which Jesus is presented as the physician of sinners. In patristic philosophy, it was especially developed by Clement and by Origen, who concentrated on the role of Christ-Logos as Physician, a conception that plays a key role in their soteriology and eschatology. See Ramelli, *Christian Doctrine of Apokatastasis*; and, specifically on Origen, see Samuel Fernández, *Cristo médico, según Orígenes: La actividad médica como metáfora de la acción divina* (Rome: Augustinianum, 1999). Evagrius himself has described evilness and sin as the illness of the soul in *KG* 1.41, at the same time establishing the ontological and even chronological priority of virtue over it (see above, the relevant commentary). The angels' knowledge of the illnesses of souls, that is, of their sins and vices, is both a judgment over these and their healing.

According to Evagrius, the illnesses and wounds of the soul can be healed through the relevant knowledge, which is a kind of medicine of the soul. Now, this science is called by Evagrius "judgment of angels." This is an ambiguous expression, depending on the interpretation of the genitive as subjective or objective: do angels judge or are they judged? The parallel with *KG* 3.38 on the judgment of God, there identified with the creation of the world, would suggest that it is angels who judge. The judgments that conclude each aeon are instead performed by Christ, according to Evagrius.

3.47. One is the transformation that happens "in the blink of an eye," which will take place on the basis of a judgment according to the degree of each one and will decree the body of each one depending on the degree of his or her order, so that someone might say that in the parts there is a transformation that is outside what is common, but this is typical of the one who does not know the intellections of the judgment.

The scriptural reference is to 1 Cor 15:52: "In a moment, in the blink of an eye, at the last trump; for the trumpet will sound, and the dead will be raised incorruptible, and we shall be changed." The transformation of which Evagrius is speaking is therefore that of the resurrection. An echo of 1 Cor 15:22–23 is found as well, I think, in the emphasis on the idea of order in connection with the eschatological resurrection/restoration: "For as in Adam all die, so also in Christ shall all be made alive. But each in his own order." The body that is assigned to each one at the resurrection, on the basis of a judgment concerning the degree of his or her spiritual advancement, is of course an immortal body; indeed, the term used in the Syriac text is *gwšm'*, and not *pgr'*, which denotes a mortal body.

3.48. The transformation of the just (is) from mortal bodies that are *praktika* and seers to mortal bodies that are seers or even seers to a high degree.

For a full discussion of this *kephalaion*, see below, the commentary on *KG* 3.50. A Greek text that bears a resemblance to this *kephalaion* and to *KG* 3.50 is found in *Selected Passages on Psalms* 1:5 (PG 12:1097D). The part that corresponds to *KG* 3.48 reads as follows: "The judgment of the just is the passage from a *praktikon* body to an angelic state," Κρίσις ἐστὶ δικαίων μὲν ἡ ἀπὸ πρακτικοῦ σώματος ἐπὶ ἀγγελικὰ μετάβασις. This makes it clear that the change of which the Syriac text speaks takes place as a result of God's decision on the basis of the level of spiritual development of the human being. Instead of the idea of becoming seers, the Greek, which may well be a simplification of Evagrius's original *kephalaion*, has the concept of a transition to an angelic state; and indeed angels are seers to the highest degree. The passage on which Evagrius focuses here, and which I have already pointed out many times in Evagrius, is from *praktikē* (asceticism and striving for *apatheia*) to gnosis, after the attainment of *apatheia*. A similar progression is clearly delineated by Evagrius also in *Skemmata* 21: "When the intellect is in *praktikē*, it is in the intellections of this world. When it is in gnosis, it passes its time in contemplation. Having come to be in prayer, it is in formlessness, which is called the 'place of God.'" The latter expression is dear to Evagrius, who repeatedly uses it, especially outside the *KG*, for example, in *On Thoughts* 40: the intellect, in pure impassivity, transcending all the intellections of objects, in prayer can see the place of God within itself.

3.49. The intellect will not be crowned with the crown of essential knowledge unless it has rejected away from itself the ignorance of the two struggles/contests.

Essential knowledge, which is here presented as a prize for the intellect that has rejected ignorance, is mentioned by Evagrius on several occasions, especially in *KG* 1.89, in which "essential knowledge" is identified with the Godhead itself; *KG* 2.47, in which it is identified with the Trinity; *KG* 3.12, in which Evagrius states that only the perfect intellect can receive it; and *KG* 6.34, in which the "essential knowledge" of God the Father is identified with the Son's image. *Kephalaion* 3.12 is the *kephalaion* that is closest to the present one, which offers further details on the conditions for the intellect to receive this essential knowledge.

This *kephalaion* entirely revolves around agonistic imagery: the word that I have translated "struggles/contests" in Syriac is the transliteration of Greek ἀγών, and the crown is primarily to be understood as the crown of victory in competitions. See Ilaria L. E. Ramelli, "L'*omen* per Acilio Glabrione e per Traiano: Una corona?," *Rivista di Storia della Chiesa in Italia* 55.2 (2001): 389–94.

3.50. The transformation of sinners is the passage that takes place from mortal bodies that are *praktika* and demonic to those that are heavy and dark to a high degree.

Kephalaion 3.48 is obviously the perfectly parallel counterpart to *KG* 3.50 (see the relevant commentary above): the righteous have bodies that are *praktika* and seers, since they exercise *praktikē* and gnosis. Sinners have bodies that are *praktika* and demonic, and therefore characterized by ignorance instead of the vision of the "seers," and here the passage is toward the worse, into demonic-type bodies, which are extremely heavy and dark. This is because sinners evidently have failed to reach the aim of *praktikē*, that is, *apatheia*, but have abandoned themselves to passions and bad conduct. Darkness is associated with demonic bodies also in scholium 8 on Ps 1:5: "The judgment of the just is a passage from a *praktikon* body to angelic bodies; but the judgment of the impious is a transformation from a *praktikon* body into dark and dim [σκοτεινὰ καὶ ζοφερά] bodies."

Precisely for the sake of parallelism between *KG* 3.48 and 3.50, I emend ܐܘ ("or") into ܘ ("and") here in *KG* 3.50 between the adjectives "*praktika*" and "demonic," since in *KG* 3.48 there is ܘ ("and") between "*praktika*" and "seers." Of course, one might also emend with Guillaumont (117) ܘ ("and") into ܐܘ ("or") in *KG* 3.48, but I think that the reverse is preferable for the meaning. Both the just and sinners have *praktika* mortal bodies (*pgr'*), but this quality in the just is joined with the quality of their body of being a seer, whereas in sinners this quality of their mortal body of being *praktikon* is joined with that of being also demonic. It may not simply be the case that, while of course they are in this world, the just have *either* a *praktikon* mortal body *or* that which is a seer, and that sinners have *either* a *praktikon* mortal body *or* a demonic one. Both the just and sinners have a *praktikon* mortal body, but this is joined with the characteristic of being a seer, in the case of the just, or with that of being demonic, in the case of sinners. It is typical of Evagrius, just as of Origen, to think that bodies receive their qualities on the basis of the moral choices of their owners. With qualities they think not merely in terms of physical beauty of health but in terms of angelic, demonic, or mortal and corruptible.

Now, in *KG* 3.48 Evagrius explains that the bodies of the just undergo a transformation into the better, after which they are still mortal bodies (*pgr'*), but they are no more *praktika* and seers together but are exclusively seers; and in *KG* 3.50 he claims that the bodies of sinners become bodies that are mortal but no longer *praktika* and demonic together but are exclusively very heavy and dark. This seems to imply that, instead of being both *praktika* and demonic, they are now exclusively demonic. This is a perfect parallelism with *KG* 3.48. Now, this transformation would not seem to refer directly to the eschatological transformation after the resurrection, or at least not exclusively, because mortal bodies are not said to be transformed into immortal bodies, of whatever kind, but they are still called "mortal" (*pgr'*). Therefore, this transformation seems to take place during the aeons. If taken metaphorically, it could even take place during the present life. Origen too envisaged a change of bodies, between human, demonic, and angelic, during the aeons, and Gregory Nyssen spoke in terms of an anticipation of angelic life and angelic bodies here on earth for ascetics (see Ramelli, *Christian Doctrine of Apokatastasis*, the chapters on Origen and Gregory).

The aforementioned Greek correspondent—although not totally precise, but seemingly a simplification of Evagrius's original *kephalaion*—of this *kephalaion* in *Selected Passages on Psalms* (PG 12:1097D) has: "(The judgment) of the impious is the passage from a *praktikon* body to a condition of darkness and infernal obscurity," (Κρίσις ἐστὶ) ἀσεβῶν δὲ ἀπὸ πρακτικοῦ σώματος ἐπὶ σκοτεινὰ καὶ ζοφερὰ μετάθεσις. The mention of the judgment, which for Evagrius takes place after the end of each aeon, seems to refer to a transformation that takes place during the aeons, in the passage between one aeon and the following one.

3.51. All the transformations that have occurred before the world / aeon to come, some have been joined to excellent mortal bodies, and others to bad ones, whereas those which will occur after the world / aeon to come will join all of them with gnostic instruments.

Kephalaion 3.51 further makes it clear that the changes of which *KG* 3.48 and 3.50 speak (see the relevant commentaries) are to be understood as occurring not at the final resurrection but during the aeons, and even within the present world/aeon. Indeed, in the case of the transformations that have occurred before the future world/aeon the bodies that are mentioned are exclusively mortal bodies (*pgr'*), like those mentioned in *KG* 3.48 and 3.50. Those of the future world, differently from these, are called "instruments" (the Syriac word being a transliteration of Greek *ὄργανον*), that is, instruments of the soul, and are described as "gnostic," that is, endowed with knowledge or capable of knowledge. Gnosis, which comes after *praktikē*, is perfection for humans and is also the characteristic of angels, who are assimilated to seers. After the world to come there will be an improvement of all rational creatures, in accord with Evagrius's ideal of a general movement toward universal restoration.

3.52. The intelligible moon is the rational nature, which is illuminated by the "Sun of Justice."

This *kephalaion*, like *KG* 3.60 (see the relevant commentary below), displays an astronomical allegory. Christ is called, according to Mal 3:20, "Sun of Justice" (this expression, *Sol Iustitiae*, has a long story in patristic exegesis and was one of Origen's favorite designations for Christ); thus, the moon, in that it reflects the light of the sun, is the symbol of rational creatures, who receive knowledge and illumination from Christ-Logos. This is why this symbolic moon is called "intelligible moon," in Evagrius's allegorical exegesis that looks for meanings on the intelligible plane. Therefore, it is legitimate to call it "noetic exegesis." See Blossom Stefaniw, *Mind, Text, and Commentary: Noetic Exegesis in Origen of Alexandria, Didymus the Blind, and Evagrius Ponticus* (Frankfurt: Lang, 2010); and the discussion in Ramelli, "Harmony between *Arkhē* and *Telos*." Evagrius's strategy of looking for the intelligible or noetic meaning of a scriptural detail was already employed by Origen, such as in his exegesis of the creation narrative: here he spoke of "intelligible/noetic trees" (*Homilies on Genesis* 2.4), "intelligible/noetic rivers," "intelligible/noetic woody valleys" in Paradise (*Selected Passages on Numbers* PG 12:581B), and the etymology of "Eden" as ἤδη, "once upon a time," to signify a primeval state rather than a specific garden (*Fragments in Genesis* 236; D15 Metzler).

3.53. Everyone who has become susceptible of the knowledge of God and yet values ignorance more than this knowledge, they say that this person is evil. Now, there is no mortal corporeal nature that is susceptible of knowledge; therefore, none of the mortal bodies should be declared to be evil.

Evil is only in each one's moral choices, not in matter or corporeality per se. Evagrius, like Origen, rejects "Gnostic" and Manichaean claims on this point. Evagrius, indeed, who focuses here on the choice of ignorance instead of knowledge, with a concept that he also develops in *Letter* 29 (586,26–28 Frankenberg), is again perfectly in line with Origen, who insisted about this in his anti-Gnostic polemic, especially against Valentinian predestinationism and the division of humanity into classes or natures. It is precisely on the basis of this polemic, all grounded in theodicy, that his doctrine of *apokatastasis* took shape (see Ramelli, "La coerenza della soteriologia origeniana"; and idem, "Origen, Bardaisan, and the Origin of Universal Salvation"). That theodicy was Origen's first concern in the elaboration of his doctrine of *apokatastasis* was perspicuously realized by Rufinus, *Apology against Jerome* 2.12. Here he remarks that the theoretical basis, grounded in theodicy, of Origen's doctrine of *apokatastasis* was Origen's defense of human free will against determinism and the conciliation of justice and goodness in God. For Origen's aim was "to defend God's justice and respond to those who claim that everything is moved by fate or chance.... It is because (thinkers such as Origen) want to defend God's justice that they maintain that it becomes the great, good, immutable, and simple nature of the Trinity to restore, in the end of all, all of its creatures into the state in which they were created in the beginning, and after long torments, lasting for whole aeons, to finally put an end to punishments," *Dei iustitiam defendere et respondere contra eos qui vel fato vel casu cuncta moveri dicunt.... Dei iustitiam defendere cupientes ... bonae illi et incommutabili ac simplici naturae Trinitatis convenire ut omnem creaturam suam in fine omnium restituat in hoc quod ex initio creata est et post longa et spatiis saeculorum exaequata supplicia finem statuat aliquando poenarum.* Precisely because evil arises from wrong moral choices and the preference for ignorance over knowledge, and bodies make no moral choices, bodies according to Evagrius should not be deemed evil. It is well possible that Evagrius is here opposing Manichaean conceptions, which were alive and well in his lifetime and were also refuted by his contemporary Diodore of Tarsus.

3.54. In the blink of an eye the cherubim were called "cherubim," Gabriel "Gabriel," and the human being "human being."

In 1 Cor 15:32 (to which Evagrius is referring here, as in *KG* 3.47), the image of the eye blink is connected with the final resurrection, transformation, and judgment. In this *kephalaion*, differently from *KG* 3.47, it seems to refer, not to the last, but to the first transformation and judgment, those which followed the initial fall and determined the differentiation of the *logika* into angels—including categories of angels, such as the cherubim, and single angels and archangels, such as Gabriel—and human beings.

3.55. In the beginning the intellect had God, who is incorruptible, as teacher of immaterial intellections. Now, however, it has received corruptible sense perception as teacher of material intellections.

Evagius is here referring to the initial state in which the *nous* was not joined to a mortal body, endowed with material sense perception. In that state, its intellections were not material but immaterial, and in this it was taught by God, who is incorruptible, unlike mortal bodies. It is remarkable that the expression that I have rendered "in the beginning" reproduces ἐν ἀρχῇ in Gen 1:1 and John 1:1. Evagrius intentionally refers the biblical "beginning" to the initial state prior to the constitution of the present world.

The distinction between learning directly from God and learning from sense perception in the present world is explained better by Evagrius in his *Letter to Melania*. With some, he states there, the Spirit and the Son communicate directly—even if Evagrius does not explain how—whereas with others, less advanced, they communicate indirectly, by means of God's creation, meaning the sense-perceptible creation, what Evagrius calls the "secondary creation" in his *KG* and is the object of "natural contemplation" (φυσικὴ θεωρία). This secondary creation is not evil; on this, Origen had already insisted against "Gnostics" and Marcionites. Far from being evil, it is providential and was wanted by God as a mediation, for the sake of those who are far from God in that "they have placed a separation between themselves and their Creator because of their evil deeds" (*Letter to Melania* 5). God instituted this gnoseological mediation by means of his Wisdom and Power, that is to say, the Son and the Spirit. According to Evagrius, "the whole ministry of the Son and the Spirit is exercised through creation, for the sake of those who are far from God" (ibid.).

3.56. Spiritual knowledge is "the wings of the intellect"; the knower is the intellect of the wings. And if this is in this way, the objects (of knowledge) bear the sign of the trees, those on which the intellect dwells, and it is delighted by their leaves, and tastes their fruits, by continually hastening toward the tree of life.

Here Evagrius is clearly alluding to Plato's famous metaphor of the wings of the soul, which is primarily the intellectual soul, which loses its wings when it decays from the contemplation of eternal realities ("the Ideas"). The same discourse of Plato was well present, in years very close to Evagrius, to Gregory of Nyssa's mind, when he offered his Christian reelaboration of Plato's *Phaedo* in his dialogue *On the Soul and the Resurrection*. See Ramelli, *Gregorio di Nissa: Sull'anima*, with new edition and a complete commentary and essays.

This assimilation of the *nous* to a winged creature in the present *kephalaion* facilitates the imagery of the *nous* dwelling on a tree, like a bird. But the conceptual connection is the most important one, and it revolves around knowledge: the tree of paradise is the tree of knowledge in Gen 2:9 (mentioning the "tree of life" and "tree of knowledge"), which is referred to here, and the *nous* dwells on it in that it knows, and the objects of knowledge are signs of this tree of knowledge. The *nous* clearly hastens toward the tree of life through knowledge, which also shows that intellectual life coincides with knowledge.

3.57. Just as those who transmit [i.e., teach] children the letters write them on tablets, in the same way Christ too, while he teaches his wisdom to rational creatures, has traced it in the nature of the mortal body.

In *KG* 3.55 and in the *Letter to Melania* Evagrius has expounded how the material world, created by Christ, functions as a mediator of knowledge for fallen rational creatures (see above, the commentary on *KG* 3.55). Evagrius has already recalled the metaphor of Christ as healer or physician (*KG* 1.41 and especially 3.46; see the relevant commentaries); now he insists on that of Christ-Logos as a teacher, which was already exploited by Clement and Origen. Christ-Logos illuminates the *logika*. Christ is here described as teaching his wisdom to the *logika*. The Syriac word for "wisdom" is the translation of Greek σοφία, which is one of the main *epinoiai* of Christ, according to Origen the very first *epinoia*, even anterior to Logos. Now, Christ teaches the *logika* this divine Wisdom by "tracing it in the nature of the mortal body [*pgr'*]." This seems to be a reference, either to the incarnation of the *logika* into mortal bodies, thus in the case of human beings, or, even more probably, to the incarnation of Christ-Logos-Wisdom in a mortal human body. The incarnation of divine Wisdom itself becomes a way to teach this Wisdom to rational creatures.

3.58. The one who is going to see written things needs light, and the one who is going to learn the wisdom of beings needs spiritual love.

This is another *kephalaion* bearing on knowledge and on the similitude between spiritual knowledge and writing/reading. The focus is here on the role of light, which allows people to read; its intelligible correspondent is spiritual love, which therefore has an illuminating function. This, indeed, allows intellects to receive "the wisdom of beings." See above, the commentary on *KG* 1.86 concerning the importance of charity-love in the acquisition of knowledge.

The association of love and light in reference to God/Christ of course goes back to the New Testament, with the Johannine definition of God as *ἀγάπη* in 1 John 4:8, and the double definition of God as both *light* and *love* is found in 1 John 1:5 ("God is light") and 4:8 ("God is love"). And the connection with the third element of this *kephalaion*, that is, *knowledge*, is made clear in 1 John 3:2: the culmination of knowledge will take place when "we shall see God as God is." I think Evagrius was ultimately relying on, and inspired by, this cluster of notions from 1 John.

3.59. If all evilness is generated by the intelligence, by *thymos*, and by *epithymia*, and of these faculties it is possible to make use in a good and in an evil way, then it is clear that it is by the use of these parts against nature that evils occur to us. And if this is so, there is nothing that has been created by God and is evil.

This *kephalaion* is closely related to *KG* 3.53, where Evagrius has declared that evil originates not from the body, which per se is good qua creature of God, but from the intellect and its bad choices, thus from human free will. Here Evagrius returns to this point, closely examining the three faculties of the soul, according to the Platonic tripartition that he follows everywhere: the intellect and the two inferior parts, the irascible faculty, or θυμός, and the concupiscible/appetitive faculty, or ἐπιθυμία. It is their use against nature that determines evil, whereas their use according to nature produces good. This is in line with what Evagrius says in *KG* 1.64, where the natural activity of rational creatures is identified with their very life, and their death with their activity against nature, that is, against the Logos (see above, the relevant commentary). In *KG* 3.16, Evagrius defines the perfect soul as that whose faculty that is liable to passions—that is to say, its θυμός and ἐπιθυμία—operates in accord with nature. In the present *kephalaion*, it is the use of the three faculties of the soul against nature or according to nature that determines evilness or goodness. The inferior faculties of the soul, which were added later, are not bad, but their use against nature is. The final statement of Evagrius in the present *kephalaion*, that nothing made by God is evil, takes up the main principle of theodicy that was already defended by Origen against Valentinianism and by Clement, who repeatedly quoted the Platonic motto Θεὸς ἀναίτιος, "God is not responsible for evil" (see Ramelli, *Gregorio di Nissa: Sull'anima*, with wide-ranging documentation). Evagrius also deals with the central problem of this *kephalaion* in his *Letter* 29 (586,22–25 Frankenberg).

3.60. The morning star is the symbol of the saints, whereas the evening star is the symbol of the souls who are in Sheol. But the restoration/completion of the orbit of all is the Holy Trinity.

Here is another *kephalaion* that, like *KG* 3.52 (see the commentary), plays on astronomical terminology. In the Greek original, now lost, the term ἀποκατάστασις, "return," "restoration," "completion" (in reference to an orbit) must have been employed in this passage. This is evident from the allegorical reference to the return of the stars to their original position, which was precisely called ἀποκατάστασις, using an astronomical *terminus technicus* that here is applied to the restoration of all, both the saints and those who will be in Sheol (Evagrius indeed plays on the astronomical meaning of ἀποκατάστασις as well as its medical meaning, for which see above, *KG* 3.35 and the relevant commentary). Also, the Syriac term for "sign" most probably reflects the Greek σημεῖον, which was often used in reference to stars, heavenly bodies, and constellations; thus, the "sign of the east" and the "sign of the west" are the morning and the evening star, representing the saints and the prisoners in Sheol respectively (in this case the death indicated by Sheol must be understood as spiritual death due to sin, since it is the wicked who are opposed to the saints and not the dead in general).

It seems to me remarkable that Basil, too, the one who made Evagrius a lector and who surely exerted an intellectual influence on him, in his own most Origenian work, his *Commentary on Isaiah*, used the astronomical *apokatastasis* as a metaphor of the *apokatastasis* of human beings to their original condition: "Because 'the stupid changes like the moon,' the text indicates that the compassionate one, who loves his brother, celebrates a feast for his return to the light, which the stupid had left, and his restoration to the original state achieved through repentance—as though he were celebrating as a new moon feast the beginning of his life in light, since his brother left the light by turning toward the worse, but returned again to it by converting/turning back," ἐπειδὴ Ὁ ἄφρων ὡς σελήνη ἀλλοιοῦται, τὴν πρὸς τὸ φῶς ἐπάνοδον, ὅπερ ἐξέλιπεν ὁ ἄφρων, καὶ τὴν διὰ μετανοίας εἰς τὸ ἀρχαῖον ἀποκατάστασιν ἑορτὴν ἡγεῖσθαι τὸν φιλάδελφον καὶ συμπαθῆ, ὁ λόγος βούλεται· οἱονεὶ νουμηνίαν ἄγων τὴν ἀρχὴν τοῦ ἐν φωτὶ βίου· ἐπειδὴ ἐξέλιπε μὲν τὸ φῶς διὰ τὴν εἰς τὸ χεῖρον τροπὴν ἐπαλινδρόμησε δὲ πάλιν πρὸς αὐτὸ διὰ τῆς ἐπιστροφῆς (*Commentary on Isaiah* 1.30). On the authenticity of his *Commentary on Isaiah*, see the documentation in Ramelli, *Christian Doctrine of Apokatastasis*, the section on Basil, and now "Basil and Apokatastasis: New Findings," *Journal of Early Christian History* 4 (2014): 116–36.

The French translation by Guillaumont (p. 123: "le signe de l'orient est le symbole des saints, le signe de l'occident les âmes qui sont dans le Schéol, mais l'accomplissement du retour de la course de tout est la Trinité sainte"), the English versions based on the French, by Dysinger ("The 'sign of the East' is the symbol of the saints, and the 'sign of the West' of the souls which are in Sheol. But the achievement of the return from 'the race' by all is the Blessed Trinity") and by Fr. Theophanes ("The sign of the east is the symbol of the saints, and the sign of the west, the souls which are in Sheol. But the accomplishment of the return of the 'course' of all is the Holy Trinity"), and the later retroversion into Greek (Σύμβολον τῆς ἡμέρας ἀνατολῆς ἐστι τὸ τῶν ἁγίων σύμβολον, τῶν δὲ δυσμῶν αἱ ἐν ᾅδου ψυχαί: τελείωσις δὲ τοῦ τοῦ παντὸς δρόμου ἐστιν ἡ ἁγία Τριάς), all miss this fundamental reference to the astronomical lexicon, and thus also the reference to the *apokatastasis*, which is apparent here.

The reference is first of all to the astronomical sense of the Greek term ἀποκατάστασις, but it immediately acquires also the eschatological meaning. The "course," which I translate as "orbit" and in Greek must have been δρόμος, is usually understood as a reference to 2 Tim 4:7, but it is the course of the stars, and the distance between the morning and the evening stars, east and west, is overcome by the return of all stars to their original position, in the *apokatastasis*, which brings all to their original state, in conformity with God's original plan. It also reveals that the morning star and the evening star are one and the same. The *apokatastasis* was expressly related to the Trinity already by Origen, as the perfect unity of all in the unity of God, after the reign of Christ and the handing over of all by him to the Father, when God will be "all in all" (1 Cor 15:28). See Ramelli, "Harmony between *Arkhē* and *Telos*."

3.61. Virtues show the secondary natural contemplation to the intellect, and this (contemplation) shows it the primary (natural contemplation), and the latter in turn shows it the holy Unity.

As on many other occasions elsewhere in these *Kephalaia*, Evagrius follows the ascending hierarchy of *theōriai*: secondary, primary, and that of Unity. The latter is the Unity of God and in God, in which rational creatures are called to participate through the "deification," or θέωσις (on which see Ilaria L. E. Ramelli, "Deification (Theosis)," in *Encyclopedia of the Bible and Its Reception* [ed. Hans-Joseph Klauck et al.; Berlin: de Gruyter, 2013], 6:468–70). Note that the first step, even before the lower knowledge, is virtue, which one exercises in the *praktikē*. This enables the lower knowledge, the latter in turn enables the higher knowledge, and this finally enables the top: the attainment of Unity. Once again virtue and knowledge go together in Evagrius's system. Virtue enables knowledge, and knowledge enhances virtue.

3.62. Intelligible stars are rational natures who have been entrusted with illuminating those who are in darkness.

Like *KG* 3.52 and *KG* 3.60 (on which see above, the relevant commentaries), so also does *KG* 3.62 revolve around astronomical terminology and imagery. Stars were actually considered to be rational or semi-divine beings in antiquity, but here Evagrius explicitly mentions *intelligible* stars—the noetic counterpart of ordinary stars—thus making it clear that these rational creatures have allegorically the same illuminating function as the stars that are seen in the sky. However, they illuminate not the earth but those intellects that are in darkness. The illumination metaphor has been applied by Evagrius to the gnoseological field in several other *kephalaia*, especially *KG* 1.35, in which it is the Godhead to have an illuminating function, in that it is light in its very essence; *KG* 3.52, in which Christ, qua Sun of Justice, is said to illuminate the rational nature as a sort of moon (here too with an astronomical allegory!); and *KG* 3.58, in which spiritual love is assigned the illuminating role of light in the dispensation of "the wisdom of beings" to rational creatures (see above, the commentaries on these *kephalaia*).

3.63. Of the one whose knowledge is finite, the ignorance is also finite, and of the one whose ignorance is infinite, the knowledge too is infinite.

Who are the beings Evagrius is thinking of here? The first half of the *kephalaion* seems to be easier to interpret: human beings and rational creatures have a limited knowledge, and also a limited ignorance. The genitive depending on "knowledge" and "ignorance," however, can also be an objective genitive, meaning that the knowledge, or the ignorance, that someone can have of creatures is limited, just as they are in their own nature.

The second part of the *kephalaion*, instead, probably alludes to God, who possesses an infinite knowledge (the genitive is subjective here) and at the same time is the object of an infinite ignorance (with objective genitive). Indeed, it is not the case that God infinitely lacks knowledge, but God is rather infinitely unknown. Evagrius is following here the tradition of apophaticism and negative theology that has roots in Philo, Clement, Origen, and Gregory of Nyssa (see Ramelli, "Divine as an Inaccessible Epistemological Object"). He may also echo Gregory Nyssen's notion of God as infinite. Since God is infinite, one could know God only by an infinite knowledge.

3.64. If among the things that are eaten there is none that is sweeter than honey and than honeycomb, and if, on the other hand, the knowledge of God is said to be sweeter than these things, it is clear that there is nothing among all that is on earth that provides delight as the knowledge of God does.

Evagrius, who likes ascending hierarchies, here draws one based on delight, which ascends from sense-perceptible delight—in particular that of taste before especially sweet foods—to spiritual delight, culminating in the knowledge of God, which can be regarded as productive of a mystical delight. Evagrius is very probably alluding to Ps 18(19):10: "More to be desired are they than gold, even much fine gold; sweeter also than honey and drippings of the honeycomb" (RSV); this is also why I rendered "the knowledge of God is said to be *sweeter than*" instead of the more generic "the knowledge of God is said to be *superior to*," which was given by Guillaumont (p. 123: "la science de Dieu soit dite supérieure à ces choses"), followed by Dysinger ("the knowledge of God is said to be superior to these things") and Fr. Theophanes ("the gnosis of God might be said [to be] superior to these things"). From the grammatical and lexical point of view, the Syriac text can be rendered in both ways, "sweeter than" and "superior to," but the quotation from the psalm—which was in fact missed by Guillaumont—makes it clear that ܝܬܝܪ ܡܢ, "more than," refers back to the adjective "sweet" rather than bearing the absolute meaning "superior to."

3.65. Those angels who taught human beings from the earth, in the world to come will constitute them heirs of their direction.

Evagrius takes up the theme of angelic teaching, which was already present both in Origen and in Gregory of Nyssa. Origen thought of an instruction from angels preceding that coming from Christ-Logos (see all documentation in Ramelli, *Christian Doctrine of Apokatastasis*, the chapter on Origen), and Gregory in his short treatise *On Babies Prematurely Snatched from This Life* imagined angels teaching babies who died too early to achieve maturity and knowledge on this side.

Unlike the latter, Evagrius here speaks of an instruction provided by angels already here on earth to human beings, who subsequently, in the other world, will enjoy the fruit of this instruction. Evidently this is because they have already been able to make spiritual progress thanks to this instruction, here called "direction" or "government" in that it is a spiritual direction.

3.66. Just as the first trumpet revealed the coming into being of (spiritual) bodies, so also will the last trumpet reveal the vanishing of (spiritual) bodies.

This is one of the several parallels drawn by Evagrius, just as by Origen, between the ἀρχή and the τέλος. He has already spoken of the "last trumpet" in *KG* 3.40, in which he identified it—in reference to 1 Cor 15:52—with the command of the resurrection given by God, who has assigned mortal bodies (*pgr'*) to human beings. These mortal bodies are, some good, others bad. After the resurrection there will be no longer bad bodies, since all will be glorious and incorruptible.

In the present *kephalaion* Evagrius connects the "last trumpet," which is eschatological, with the "first trumpet," which is protological, and moreover speaks no longer of mortal bodies (*pgr'*) but of spiritual bodies (*gwšm'*). The first trumpet refers here to the coming into being of the *logika* as creatures emerging from Christ-Logos and endowed at that moment with spiritual bodies. What the last trumpet here, which is the pendant to this first trumpet, reveals does not seem to refer to the resurrection, with the passage from mortal to immortal bodies, but to an even more advanced stage, probably that of the θέωσις of rational creatures, with a passage, by grace, from the creaturely to the divine life. The vanishing of bodies as such will not necessarily result from their abolition or destruction but rather from their elevation to the rank of souls and, through souls, to intellects.

3.67. The whole secondary natural contemplation bears the sign of milk, whereas the primary one bears the sign of honey. And this is "the land where milk and honey flow."

The symbol of honey was already used by Evagrius in 3.64, with a quotation from the Psalms, to symbolize the delight brought about by knowledge. Here too, where the quotation is from Exod 33:1–3 ("The Lord said to Moses, 'Depart, go up hence, you and the people whom you have brought up out of the land of Egypt, to the land of which I swore to Abraham, Isaac, and Jacob, saying: To your descendants I will give it.... Go up to a land flowing with milk and honey," RSV), honey, joined with milk, is a symbol of spiritual delight. These symbols describe both natural *theōriai*, primary and secondary—the former concerning the intelligible realm, the latter bodily creatures—depicted by Evagrius in *KG* 3.61 as leading to the final Unity with God and in God, which is the culmination of spiritual life.

3.68. Just as the first rest of God indicates the removal of evil and the vanishing of thick bodies, likewise the second too indicates the vanishing of bodies, secondary beings, and the diminution of ignorance.

This passage offers an elucidation to *KG* 3.40 and 3.66, which respectively speak of the resurrection-restoration and of the restoration-deification. The elimination of heavy, terrestrial bodies will occur in the resurrection, with their transformation into fine bodies—as they were before the fall. At that stage the diminution of evil will also take place (ܡܒܨܪܘܬܐ can also mean "inferiority"; indeed, the inferiority of evil vis-à-vis Good/God will be made manifest, and evil will progressively disappear), which is the fundamental premise of *apokatastasis* for Origen, Gregory, and Evagrius (see Ramelli, "Christian Soteriology and Christian Platonism"). In particular, Origen, followed by Gregory Nyssen, argued from 1 Cor 15:28 that, since God "will be all in all," in the *telos* "we cannot admit of evil, lest God may be found in evil." The final eviction of evil is also a consequence of its ontological negativity, which is a tenet of Origen's and Nyssen's thought, and is precisely the notion that Evagrius posits at the very beginning of the *KG* and constantly repeats all over: the absolute ontological priority of Good—that is, God—over evil (see above, the commentaries on *KG* 1.1 and 1.39–41).

The reference to the rest of God seems to be taken from Gen 2:2, but it is here divided into two and transposed to the eschatological times, according to the conception, then prominent in Maximus the Confessor, that the *telos* will be the eighth day, following the seventh day, of the rest (see Ramelli, *Christian Doctrine of Apokatastasis*, the section on the Confessor). Here Evagrius draws a connection between the first rest of God and the resurrection, with the transformation of mortal into immortal bodies at the resurrection and the complete eviction of evil; then he draws another connection, between the second rest of God and the final θέωσις, when rational creatures will be freed from ignorance, which is the counterpart of evil, and from bodies, which are not at all evil (indeed, they do survive the destruction of evil) but are "secondary entities" vis-à-vis God, and in the eventual deification rational creatures will participate in divine life. Bodies, secondary beings, will be elevated to the rank of souls and, through souls, to intellects, primary beings, which will experience "deification." Again, the words that I have translated "will reveal the diminution of ignorance" might also mean "will reveal the inferiority of ignorance," clearly vis-à-vis knowledge, that is, God, who for Evagrius is "essential knowledge." This is also why the manifestation of this ontological inferiority immediately determines the elimination of ignorance.

3.69. From that contemplation from which the intellect has been constituted it is impossible that anything else be constituted, unless this too is susceptible of the Trinity.

The *nous* was created by a unique *theōria*, which is obviously divine and cannot give rise to anything else but what is, like the *nous*, a receptacle of the Trinity. This also suggests that for Evagrius the first, intelligible creation, that of the *noes*, was totally gratuitous, and the Trinity thus aimed at having receptacles of itself. This *kephalaion* is closely related to *KG* 3.24, which speaks of the divine contemplation that constituted the intellects, and moreover describes the latter as susceptible of God: "The knowledge of the primary nature is a spiritual contemplation, that of which the Creator availed himself and created [i.e., while creating] the intellects, which only are susceptible of his nature" (see above, the relevant commentary). Of course, the eventual, perfect reception of the Trinity on the part of all intellects will occur in the final deification (θέωσις). This, indeed, requires perfect intellects, as is clear from *KG* 3.12: "The perfect intellect is that which can easily receive essential knowledge," which Evagrius repeatedly identifies with God the Trinity. This conception of deification is deeply rooted in Origen and Athanasius. The divinization of the whole of humanity will be fully accomplished in the eventual *apokatastasis*. In *Commentary on Romans* 3.1.133ff., for instance, Origen explains that humanity lost its divine condition with the fall, but it will recover it in the *telos*, marked by God's being "all in all" (1 Cor 15:28):

> All human beings by nature have become "children of wrath," from their initial state of being gods and children of the Most High, and for this reason they have been called humans.... "I have said: You are gods, you are children of the Most High," and God added: "*all of you*." Now this addition has interconnected the whole human race at the same time under this title (of gods and children of the Most High).... Now this is a mystical prediction of what will happen in the future, that we may interpret God's words, "I shall destroy the human being," in the sense of what God says by means of his prophet: "Look, I destroy your iniquities like a cloud." This must be understood in the sense that God will destroy the human being qua human being and after that will make it a god, when God will be "all in all."

> *Omnes enim homines natura filii irae effecti sunt, ex eo quod erant dii et filii Excelsi et per hoc homines appellati sunt.... "Ego dixi: dii estis et filii Excelsi," et addidit: "omnes." Quae adiectio omne simul sub hoc titulo humanum conexuit genus ... sub mysterio de futuris praedictum ut eo modo sentiatur quod dictum est, "deleam hominem," quo et per profetam dicit Deus: "ecce enim deleo sicut nubem iniquitates tuas," ut uideatur delens eum secundum hoc quod homo est, post haec facere eum deum tunc cum erit Deus omnia in omnibus.*

3.70. It is proper to the bare intellect to say what its nature is, and now there exists no clear answer to this question, whereas in the end there will be not even the question.

The theme of the "bare *nous*" has been already introduced and developed by Evagrius in *KG* 3.6, in which the bare *nous* is described as joined to the knowledge of the Trinity by means of the *theōria* that regards it. In *KG* 3.15 Evagrius further explains that this knowledge of the Trinity only is immaterial knowledge and it constitutes the perfection of the *nous*; the latter, "finally bare," will become "a seer of the Trinity." Again, in *KG* 3.17 Evagrius has explained that the *theōria* that concerns intelligible realities requires a bare *nous*, as it was at the beginning, when the *nous* could see the intelligible realities in a pure manner. Finally, in *KG* 3.19, the primary and secondary *theōria* are both characterized by a *nous* that is "a bare seer." See above, the commentaries on these *kephalaia*.

In the present *kephalaion* Evagrius states that only such a *nous* has the ability to know and reveal its own nature. A very close parallel and elucidation comes from Evagrius's *Letter to Melania* 26: "But there will come a time when the body, the soul, and the intellect, thanks to a transformation of their wills, will become one and the same thing. Since there will come a time when the differentiations of the movements of their will shall vanish, it will be elevated to the original state in which it was created. Its nature, hypostasis, and name will be one, known to God. What is elevated in its own nature is alone among all beings, because neither its place nor its name is known, and only the bare intellect can say what its nature is." As long as the *nous* is not yet bare, it is impossible to express the nature of the *nous*. This is why Evagrius affirms that there exists "no clear answer" to the question of the nature or essence of the *nous* (the adjective I have translated "clear" is omitted in Guillaumont's translation [p. 127]: "il n'y a pas de réponse," and in the versions that follow his translation: "now there is no reply" [Dysinger] and "there is not now a response" [Fr. Theophanes]; similarly, the Greek retroversion simply renders ἀπόκρισις without any attributive adjective). In the eschatological condition, when the bare *nous* will know the Trinity in θέωσις, as a recipient of the Trinity, the question itself of the definition and nature of the *nous* will become useless. That Evagrius is here thinking precisely of the eschatological θέωσις seems to be confirmed both by the above-quoted parallel in *Letter to Melania* 26 and by the immediately following *kephalaion*.

3.71. Just as the human being, when it received the insufflation, became a "living soul," likewise the intellect too, when it has received the Holy Trinity, will become a living intellect.

The scriptural reference to the insufflation of the breathing of God into the nostrils of the human being, who thus became a "living soul," is to Gen 2:7, in turn quoted by Paul in 1 Cor 15:45. Paul's passage, which Evagrius surely had in mind, draws a parallel between the first human being, Adam, who became "a living soul," and Christ, the new Adam, "the last human being," who "became a life-giving spirit." Paul is obviously playing on the ψυχή-πνεῦμα opposition. A similar opposition, indeed, is also drawn by Evagrius in the present *kephalaion*, but between two levels pertaining to rational creatures: that of the ψυχή, or soul (which for Origen, as I have already illustrated, derives from a "cooling down" of the *nous* and thus a decadence from the highest intellectual level, due to a loss of ἀγάπη in the adhesion to the Good), and that, superior, of the νοῦς, or intellect. Just as the ψυχή became "living, alive" when it received the insufflation from God, so will the νοῦς become "living, alive" when it receives the Trinity. This will happen in the *telos*, with the θέωσις, when the intellect will be susceptible, and recipient, of God the Trinity.

It is notable that in both cases the life-giving principle, for the soul and for the intellect, is God, in the first case through the insufflation, and in the second through the presence of the Trinity in the intellect itself, which received the Trinity and participates in divine life.

3.72. The heritage of Christ is the knowledge of the Unity. Now, if all will become coheirs of Christ, all will know the holy Unity. However, it is impossible that they become his coheirs unless they first have become his heirs.

Like the two preceding *kephalaia*, this too focuses on the *telos*, which moreover is here described in universalistic terms. Evagrius delineates two stages, the first of which is necessary to attain the second: first to become heirs of Christ, then to become his coheirs, sharing his own heritage, and therefore to become heirs of God (the scriptural reference is to Rom 8:16–17, where both these kinds of heritage are joined: "It is the Spirit himself bearing witness with our spirit that we are children of God, and if children, then heirs, heirs of God and fellow heirs with Christ, provided we suffer with him in order that we may also be glorified with him," RSV). It is manifest that the notion of "inheriting God" alludes again to the final θέωσις. All will achieve the θέωσις and will know the final Unity (in which the "heritage of Christ" consists). Both θέωσις and ἕνωσις were the marks of the *telos* also for Origen. In particular for the "unity," see Ramelli, "Harmony between *Arkhē* and *Telos*"; and my volume on John 13–17 (Ilaria L. E. Ramelli, *Gospel according to John III* [Novum Testamentum Patristicum; Göttingen: Vandenhoeck & Ruprecht, forthcoming]).

3.73. If it is true that the day of the Lord comes like a thief during the night, nobody knows, among all those who are in the house, at what time or on which day he will rob those who are sleeping.

This is a short exegetical passage on 1 Thess 5:2, on the unpredictability of the arrival of the *eschaton*.

3.74. All that which is of the nature of the mortal body and is called "holy," this is sanctified in the Logos of God, and all that which, among rational creatures, is defined "holy," this is sanctified in the knowledge of God. But there are yet some among the latter who are sanctified by the Logos of God, like babies, who are susceptible of knowledge.

The reference is to 1 Tim 4:4–5: "Everything created by God is good.... It is consecrated by the *logos* of God." Evagrius here means that with the incarnation, Christ, who is God's Logos, has sanctified the nature of the mortal body (*pgr'*) by taking it up. The *logika* are sanctified by the knowledge of God, gnosis being the goal and sanctification of the *nous*. Among the *logika*, some are still immature, that is, babies, whose *logos* is not yet developed; thus they are susceptible of knowledge potentially. This particular statement concerning babies who possess the *logos* only in potency should be read along with *KG* 4.76, on the faculties of babies, before and after birth, and adults (see my commentary below). There, the watershed of the *logos* will become prominent, but it will also prove extremely dangerous, in that Evagrius will show that it can have humans lead an angelic life, if they follow virtue, but also a demonic life, if they follow evilness.

3.75. What is unclean becomes so either because of a usage that is against nature or because of evilness. And everything that, against usage, is considered to be contaminated, this is from the mortal corporeal nature, but what is contaminated by evilness, this is said to be from the rational nature.

As Evagrius will explain in the next *kephalaion*, and as he has already explained in *KG* 3.53, evilness is proper not to the body but to the rational faculty (see above, the commentary on *KG* 3.53, and below, that on *KG* 3.76). It is the *logos* that can choose between virtue and evilness. The latter is assimilated to the "dirtiness" of the rational nature. This is its way of being unclean. A similar image was used by Gregory of Nyssa in his dialogue *On the Soul and the Resurrection*: he assimilated the evil committed by each one to a sort of thick, dirty glue that sticks to the sinner's soul. This will be extremely difficult and painful to remove for the sinner to be purified and to return clean in the end, which is the goal that God wants to achieve with this painful purification. See my commentary in Ramelli, *Gregorio di Nissa: Sull'anima*. In the mortal body, it is usage against nature that makes something unclean, but contamination by evilness or vice (κακία) comes from the intellect and the will that proceeds from it.

3.76. While we are formed in the womb, we live a life of vegetables; when we are born, on the other hand, (we live) a life of animals. But after we have become adult, we live either a life of angels or a life of demons. Now, the cause of the first level of life is animated nature, that of the second one is sense perception, but that of the third one is the fact that we are susceptible of virtue or of evilness.

Evagrius is here following a widespread assumption in ancient philosophy (mainly Aristotelian and Stoic) that finds one of its clearest expressions in Hierocles the Stoic. Relying on the basically Aristotelian tripartition of the soul into vegetative (with living functions like nutrition and growth, which humans have in common with plants), animal (with sense perception and local movement, which humans have in common with animals), and rational (with the *logos*, which is a prerogative of humans), Evagrius observes that the first, most elementary level of the soul is that which functions immediately, between conception and birth; the second level, the animal one, begins to operate in the young human being, and finally the *logos* too develops, bringing the human being to maturity. At this point, however, Evagrius warns, everything depends on the choices that one makes by means of his or her own *logos*: if these are for the Good, inspired by virtue, one will transcend even human life and lead the life of angels; if these choices, on the other hand, are for evil, inspired by evilness, one will decay to demonic life.

On Hierocles the Stoic's scheme of the development of the human soul from the womb to adulthood, see Ilaria L. E. Ramelli, *Hierocles the Stoic* (trans. David Konstan; Leiden: Brill, 2009), with wide-ranging commentary on Hierocles's *Elements of Ethics*. That the baby animal or human, in an egg or inside its mother, is a mere φύσις, without an animal soul but more like a small vegetable, is a doctrine that goes back to Chrysippus *SVF* 2.806, who believed that such a little one, between conception and birth, "is naturally nourished like a plant. But when it is born, the *pneuma*, cooled and tempered by the air, changes and becomes an animal: thus it is not inappropriate that it is called soul [ψυχή] in relation to cooling [ψύξις].... (2) He says that the soul is produced when the fetus is born, as the *pneuma* changes because of cooling, as if by tempering.... (3) The Stoics say that *pneuma* in the bodies of fetuses is tempered by cooling and that as it changes from a 'nature' [φύσις] it becomes a soul.... (4) The *pneuma* yields the soul itself ... when, by cooling and, as it were, immersion in the air, it is kindled or tempered." According to *SVF* 2.787, the Stoics held that the *pneuma* of the φύσις was colder and more humid that that of the ψυχή. The point is attested also in *SVF* 2.805, in which the same metaphor of tempering appears ("like incandescent iron immersed in cold water") that is used by Hierocles. The same set of ideas is expressed too in *SVF* 2.756–757: "The Stoics say that it [the embryo] is part of the belly, and not an animal. For just as fruits are parts of the plants and fall off only when they are ripe, so too the embryo does"; "They say that [the embryo] is not an animal but is nourished and grows like trees: they do not have impulses and aversions as animals do." Hierocles goes back to Old Stoicism when he adopts the theory that φύσις in prebirth animals is transformed into ψυχή. For, in Middle Stoicism, Panaetius had abandoned this notion. Aristotle also considered the active life of a baby animal in the womb to be similar to that of a plant. Galen, *The Formation of a Fetus* 6 (4:700 Kühn), indeed assimilates the Stoic φύσις, which is characteristic of prebirth baby animals before they become ψυχαί, to Aristotle's vegetative soul and Plato's appetitive soul, although he is aware that the Stoic φύσις is not soul proper.

Thus, Hierocles at the very beginning of his *Elements of Ethics* describes the evolution from vegetative to animal to rational soul as follows:

> During all this time—I mean that which goes from conception to birth—it remains as a nature [φύσις], that is a *pneuma* (breath), transformed from the status of a seed and proceeding from the beginning to the end in a preestablished order. Now, in the first phases of this period of time the "nature" is a kind of particularly dense *pneuma* and far removed from soul; following this, however, and once it has nearly arrived at birth, it thins out, buffeted as it is by continuous doings, and, in respect to quantity, it is soul. Thus, once it arrives at the exit it is adapted to the environment, so that, toughened, so to speak, by this, it changes into soul.... The nature of the embryo, when it has become mature, is not slow to change to soul, when it comes out into the surrounding environment. For this reason, everything that comes out of the uterus is immediately an animal.... One must therefore understand that, from this moment, an animal differs from a nonanimal in two respects, that is, in sense perception [αἴσθησις] and in impulse [ὁρμή].... The entire class of irrational animals, not just those that are less endowed by nature but also those that exceed us in speed, size, and strength, nevertheless they perceive our [i.e., human beings'] superiority in respect to the *logos*.

Once he has reached the level of the *logos*, Evagrius adds that at this point all depends on the use that each rational creature makes of it, for the Good or for evil. The idea that one can lead an angelic or a demonic life was especially developed by Origen and Gregory Nyssen.

3.77. Of those whose life and death the Holy Spirit has narrated to us, it has also announced to us in advance the resurrection that will take place.

The narration provided by the Holy Spirit seems to be identifiable with that of the Bible, in which indeed the future resurrection is also announced, especially in the Gospels and Paul, but, according to an interpretation, also in Ezekiel, in some Psalms, and elsewhere.

3.78. Angels and demons come close to our world, whereas we do not get close to their worlds. For we cannot have angels get closer to God, nor do we consider making demons more contaminated.

Angels and demons can influence human beings (an idea that was supported by Origen as well, who, however, did not admit of any *determination* of human free will on their part; see Ramelli, "La coerenza della soteriologia origeniana"), in that they respectively endeavor to bring them closer to the Good or farther from it. But human beings, in turn, do not influence angels or demons, bringing angels closer to God—what human cannot do because of their inferiority to angels—or making demons even more perverse—what humans do not care to do. As Evagrius has explained in *KG* 3.76, indeed, it is humans who, thanks to their *logos*, at least when they are adult, find themselves in an intermediate position and can be like angels, if they follow virtue, or else like demons, if they follow evilness.

A Greek parallel to this *kephalaion* is found in Nilus, *De malignis cogitationibus* (*On Evil Thoughts*) 20 (PG 79:1221D–1224A). Similar reflections are also found in Evagrius's *Letter* 56, preserved in Syriac: "Teach your brothers this gentleness, so that they give themselves to anger only with difficulty. For no evil makes the intellect into a demon as much as anger through the troubling of wrath. Thus it is said in the psalm: '[their] anger is like that of the snake' (Ps 57:5). And do not consider a demon to be anything other than a human being aroused by anger and deprived of perception! Although the bodies of the demons have color and form, they elude our perception, because their quality is the quality of bodies beyond our perception Therefore, if they wish to appear to someone, they imitate our bodies in various ways and do not show their own bodies" (*Letter* 56.4, trans. Dysinger with some modifications). The last part of this section parallels *KG* 1.22, in which it is also stated that the bodies of demons have a color and a shape, but they escape human sense-perception. So whenever they want to appear to humans, they imitate a human body, without showing us their own bodies. But the first part of *Letter* 56.4 focuses on the tempting action of demons, or better, on the effects of passions, especially anger, namely, the transformation of a human *nous* into a demon. The very definition of a demon as a human being aroused by anger is in perfect agreement with Origen's conviction that humans, demons, and angels belong to the same nature and are only different due to their moral choices.

3.79. Those who now are in the underworld will draw those beings on earth who have now transgressed toward an evilness without measure, the miserable!

I read *'brw* in the Syriac text, after a suggestion by Sebastian Brock. Those who are in the underworld are not so much the dead but, very probably, demons, all the more so in that Evagrius in *KG* 3.78 has just explained that demons, as well as angels, can exert an influence over humans. This is the same sense of "underworld" as is found in Origen's and Nyssen's interpretation of Phil 2:10–11, on the bending of all knees before Christ, in heaven, on earth, and in the underworld, denoting the voluntary submission of all rational creatures to Christ, angels (in heaven), humans (on earth), and demons (underneath). See especially Gregory of Nyssa, *In illud: Tunc et ipse Filius* (commentary on 1 Cor 15:28) 20; and Origen, *On First Principles* 1.2.10 and 1.6.2, where Phil 2:10–11 is quoted in this connection, and everyone's submission to Christ in heaven, on earth, and in the underworld (angels, humans, and demons) is understood as the salvation of all, in that it is fully voluntary and entails conversion and spontaneous adhesion. In *On First Principles* 1.2.10 the spontaneity of this submission is clear: "If every knee bends before Jesus, without doubt Jesus is the one to whom all beings are subject, and the one who has power over all, and through whom all beings are subjected to God the Father. Indeed, they will be subjected through wisdom, that is, by means of rational discourse, and not by violence and necessity.... All will be subjected with most pure and effulgent glory, with reason and wisdom, and not by violence or necessity," *Si omne genu flectitur Iesu, sine dubio Iesus est cui subiecta sunt omnia, et ipse est qui potentatum agit in omnibus, et per quem subiecta sunt Patri omnia. Per sapientiam namque, id est verbo ac ratione, non vi ac necessitate, subiecta sunt … purissima ac limpidissima gloria cum ratione et sapientia, non vi ac necessitate, cuncta subiecta sunt.* In the second passage, *On First Principles* 1.6.2, the universality of the submission in Phil 2:10 is stressed, and the knees that will bend in heaven are identified with those of angels, and those that will bend in the underworld are interpreted as those of demons: "All those who will have knelt in the name of Jesus and by this sign will have showed their subjection to him will be called back to one and the same end. These are the creatures in heaven, on earth, and in the underworld, that is to say, the whole universe," *In unum finem revocantur omnes hi qui, in nomine Iesu genu flectentes, per hoc ipsum subiectionis suae insignia declararunt, qui sunt caelestium et terrestrium et infernorum, in quibus tribus significationibus omnis universitas indicatur.*

This *kephalaion*, therefore, is closely connected with the preceding one, dealing with the demons' evil influence on humans.

3.80. The corporeal and the incorporeal nature are both knowable, but only the incorporeal nature is knowing. Now, God is both knowing and knowable, but he does not know as the incorporeal nature does, nor is he known as the corporeal and the incorporeal nature are.

The knowledge of God, both active and passive, is totally different from that of creatures. The Godhead knows and can be known, but it does not know in the way in which created intellects do, nor is it known as all creatures are. This is due to God's transcendence (see Ramelli, "Divine as an Inaccessible Epistemological Object"). This is also why the knowledge of the Trinity is reserved to the final θέωσις, according to Evagrius.

It is to be noticed that here the division between corporeal and incorporeal nature refers not to mortal bodies (*pgr'*) but to all bodies, including immortal and spiritual bodies (*gwšm'*). God transcends all, corporeal and incorporeal, qua Creator of all.

3.81. The one who knows God has either the knowledge of his nature or that of his Wisdom, that which he used in creating everything.

This *kephalaion* is closely related to the preceding one and deals with the knowledge of God, in the sense of an objective genitive: how can an intellect know God? Either knowing the divine nature itself with an intrinsic knowledge that Evagrius seems to postpone to the final stage of θέωσις, or knowing God's Wisdom, who is Christ, the agent of the creation (Evagrius has repeatedly mentioned that Christ-Wisdom is the creator of the aeons and bodies, for instance, in *KG* 1.43; 2.2, 21, 70; 3.11, 13, 57; see above, the commentaries on these *kephalaia*). This is the kind of knowledge of God that is available in the present stage: knowing God from divine *energeiai*, or operations. This distinction between the present unknowability of God's nature and the knowability of God's *energeiai* is also typical of Nyssen, who drew it from Origen, and will be taken up again by Maximus the Confessor. See Ramelli, "Apofatismo cristiano."

3.82. Blessed is the one who by means of objects receives the demonstration of God's grace, but blessed also the one who by means of knowledge can perform an investigation concerning them.

The knowledge of God, in the present state, ordinarily comes through creation, as has already been explained in the previous *kephalaion* (see commentary there). Creatures show God the Creator's grace. Knowledge implies an investigation, and active examination. In this, Evagrius takes over Origen's fundamentally investigative conception of knowledge, which was also appreciated by Nyssen and subsequently tended to disappear in patristic philosophy. A research is in progress on this, focusing on Origen's "zetetic" attitude and its aftermath.

3.83. Faith is a voluntary good that leads us toward the beatitude to come.

Faith is not only a good, which is obvious, and leading to blessedness in the world to come, which is again a shared view among Christian authors and deeply rooted in the New Testament, but it is a *voluntary* good (the Syriac adjective lexically corresponds to Greek ἑκούσιος). This point is noteworthy, since there was no agreement about faith being by grace or voluntary on the part of each one, or else voluntary and at the same time helped by God's grace (see Ramelli, *Christian Doctrine of Apokatastasis*, the section on Cassian). It is probable that Evagrius, like Origen, wanted to stress that faith cannot be forced upon anybody—just as the Good must be chosen freely—but has to be freely embraced in order to be salvific. The voluntary nature of faith is stressed by Evagrius also in a scholium on Ps 115:10: "Faith is the rational assent of a soul endowed with free will [ψυχῆς αὐτεξουσίου λογικὴ συγκατάθεσις]." Evagrius here uses philosophical terminology (συγκατάθεσις, αὐτεξούσιον). When a soul embraces faith, it gives an assent that is rational and free, free will being for Evagrius, just as for Origen, constitutive of a rational creature. This is why Origen maintained that rational creatures will never lose their free will (*manere quidem naturae rationabili semper liberum arbitrium non negamus*; *Commentary on Romans* 5.10.187).

As for the role of faith in leading to the future state of beatitude, which is the restoration to the initial blessedness, this point, which is made in the present *kephalaion*, is supported and expanded in *Chapters of the Disciples of Evagrius* 198: "The intellect needs faith to be able to receive the divine law with a good hope, with a view to the perfect purification of its virtuous life, so that it may return to its original state [ἀρχαίαν κατάστασιν] prior to the movement, in which thanks to perfect charity-love [διὰ τῆς τελείας ἀγάπης], it will reach unity with its Archetype in the Holy Spirit. There will be union of hypostases, abolition of numbers, liberation from change, cessation of opposition … fulfillment of the progress of the children (of God), the knowledge of the Holy Trinity in power/potentiality, and the peaceful kingdom of the Holy Unity, without war." Here the very description of *apokatastasis* owes much to Origen's view of the restoration.

3.84. The whole of the secondary natural contemplation bears the symbol of stars. Now, the stars are those who have been entrusted with the task of illuminating those who are in the night.

Evagrius is here offering another of his astronomical metaphors, such as those that I have already highlighted and explained in *KG* 3.52, 60, and 62, the last one especially dealing with the intellectually illuminating function of "stars": "Intelligible stars are rational natures who have been entrusted with illuminating those who are in darkness" (see my commentary above). These are clearly the same metaphorical "stars" that are mentioned in the present *kephalaion* and that cast light on those who are found in the darkness of night. Evagrius meant that these stars are rational creatures who illuminate other rational creatures in their contemplation. This illumination comes from virtues, as is suggested by *KG* 3.61, which seems to offer a valuable clue to the comprehension of the present *kephalaion*, since Evagrius states therein that "virtues show the secondary natural contemplation to the intellect." Virtues therefore might be the stars that illuminate the intellects in its secondary natural *theōria*. But in the light of the identification of stars with rational natures in 3.62, one can surmise that Evagrius by "stars" here means virtuous rational creatures.

The whole imagery of light, darkness, and illumination, which is dear to Evagrius, is perfectly attuned with the theme of knowledge and *theōria*. Here the question is specifically of secondary natural contemplation, that is, the *theōria* of the secondary nature, which is the material world. This contemplation itself can be understood as symbolized by the stars and therefore as illuminating those who are in darkness. Indeed, I have already observed (in the commentary on *KG* 3.55, above) that in his *Letter to Melania* Evagrius taught that the secondary nature, the present world, for the majority of rational creatures is the only means of attaining knowledge, while only some elect can know directly, thanks to an illumination by the Son and the Spirit—hence, for most *logika*, the necessity of using the secondary nature as illuminating them. This is precisely what Evagrius is also stating in the present *kephalaion.*

3.85. All those who are baptized in water receive a delightful perfume, whereas the One who baptizes, it is he who has the perfumed oil.

The One who baptizes is Christ, whose name, ܡܫܝܚܐ (the Syriac equivalent of Greek Χριστός, "the anointed one"), has the same root as ܡܫܚܐ, here employed for "oil" (cf. Greek χρῖσμα). This oil is perfumed, and from its perfume the baptized receive their own perfume. The oil is also referred to in *KG* 3.43. Origen too used the Christ-oil-anoint wordplay to indicate that all Christians are anointed by Christ with his perfumed oil.

3.86. Blessed is the one who has loved nothing from the secondary natural contemplation except the contemplation itself.

One should not love the objects of the secondary natural *theōria*, because they are inferior in the order of being (as Evagrius has already expounded, e.g., in *KG* 1.50, 54, 61, 65, 77; 2.31; see also *KG* 3.68, in which he distinguishes between primary and secondary beings; *KG* 2.33, in which the distinction is between primary and secondary objects of knowledge; *KG* 3.8, 10, 19, 26, 61, 67, on secondary *theōria*). But the *theōria* itself should be loved, since it is indispensable on the path to gnosis. This ascending path has been described by Evagrius in *KG* 3.61: virtues show the secondary natural *theōria* to the intellect, and this *theōria* in turn shows the primary natural *theōria* to the intellect, and the primary natural *theōria* finally shows the intellect the holy Unity. Thus, the secondary natural *theōria* is necessary in this path.

3.87. Blessed is the one who has hated nothing from the primary contemplation of natures, except their evilness.

Nothing must be hated in the primary natural *theōria*, which is the contemplation of the *logika*, because these are all creatures of God and therefore are good. But what is evil in them, which was not created by God and does not belong to their nature, but is a consequence of their wrong choices based on their free will, this must be hated.

I render "of natures" in the plural although the manuscript has no sign of plural in ܕܟܝܢܐ, but Guillaumont (p. 133) rightly supplied it, because the pronoun "their" in "their evilness" (ܒܝܫܘܬܗܘܢ) makes it clear that the noun to which it refers is a plural.

3.88. Blessed is the one who has reached the knowledge that cannot be abolished (beyond what cannot be, it cannot be gone).

The knowledge that cannot be abolished or surpassed or outdone is the supreme knowledge of the Trinity, the end of the path of gnosis. There is no higher knowledge that can replace it, and it goes together with the final θέωσις.

3.89. Just as our mortal body, while it is generated by our parents, cannot possibly generate them in turn, likewise the soul too, which is generated by God, cannot possibly give him back knowledge. Indeed, "what shall I render to the Lord in exchange for all the gifts he has bestowed upon me?"

The generation of the soul on the part of God is conceived by Evagrius in terms of knowledge and of the gift of knowledge. Hence it is also clear that Evagrius is principally thinking of the intellectual soul. It is primarily the *nous* that is in the image of God and, like God, is endowed with knowledge. The latter, thus, is the principal gift of God, which subsumes all of God's gifts, which are mentioned in the scriptural quotation from Ps 115:3. Given the enormity of the gifts of God, it is utterly impossible for a human being to reciprocate them.

3.90. Demons do not cease to calumniate the knower, even when this is not culpable, so to attract his intellect to themselves. For a sort of cloud lies over the mind and pushes the intellect away from contemplation, while it reproaches demons as calumniators.

The knower, or "gnostic" (of course in Evagrius's and Clement's sense rather than in reference to the historical, complex phenomenon of "Gnosticism"), is the object of the tricks of demons. Evagrius returns here to this theme, which he has already developed in several preceding *kephalaia*: demons endeavor to negatively influence the spiritual life of humans, although, according to Origen, they cannot determine human will, which remains free.

***

In the S_2 manuscript, at this point, the following indication is added: "The third discourse/book is finished." As usual, the Syriac word for "discourse/book" corresponds to Greek λόγος.

Fourth Discourse

4.1. God planted rational creatures for himself. His Wisdom, in turn, has grown in them, while she read them writings of all sorts.

This first *kephalaion* of the present series addresses the problem of the end of God in creation, which was an entirely gratuitous action. It displays, as Evagrius has stated in *KG* 2.1, God's goodness, power, and wisdom. Goodness, because it was gratuitous and unselfish, and because it shows that God is the absolute Good (cf. *KG* 1.1 and the relevant commentary); power, because God brought everything into being from nonbeing; wisdom, because it was performed by God's Wisdom itself, Christ-Logos, and because its very order and beauty show the Creator's wisdom. Now, in the present *kephalaion* Evagrius specifically addresses the question of the creation of the *logika* or *noes*: the divinity created them for itself. This notion is related to the idea (which underlies *KG* 2.80 and 3.24 as well; see above, the relevant commentaries) that the Godhead created the *noes* that they might be recipients of it. God's Wisdom, Christ-Logos, who is also their creator, must grow in them through an education that is here expressed by means of the metaphor of "reading," again along the lines of the presentation of Christ as παιδαγωγός, especially dear to Clement and Origen. The instruction provided by Christ-Logos, the Wisdom of God, to the *logika*, in Evagrius's view, passes through the various *theōriai*, and has as its goal the knowledge of the Trinity and the participation in it, which is the θέωσις.

Another metaphor here is interesting: the agricultural metaphor of God as a "planter," who "planted" the *logika* for himself. This kind of imagery applied to God goes back at least to Philo's *On Agriculture* and was developed by Origen and Gregory of Nyssa in respect both to protology and to eschatology (see above, my commentary on *KG* 2.25).

4.2. God's knowability is in those who are primary in their coming into being, whereas his unknowability is in his Christ.

What I have translated "God's knowability" and "unknowability," in order to maintain the Syriac wording, are probably to be understood respectively "what can be known of God" and "what cannot be known." The former Syriac phrase, ܝܕܝܥܘܬܗ ܕܐܠܗܐ, in the Peshitta translates Rom 1:19, τὸ γνωστὸν τοῦ Θεοῦ. Now, what can be known of God, according to Evagrius, is found in primary creatures, that is, the intelligible beings (see *KG* 1.50 and 1.61, with the relevant commentaries). What is unknowable of God, on the other hand, is found in Christ, who is no creature but is the Godhead itself. Once again the principle is asserted that the divinity is known in its creation whereas it is unknowable in its essence, a principle that was developed especially by Origen and Gregory of Nyssa (see above, the commentary on *KG* 3.81; see also Ramelli, "Apofatismo cristiano").

4.3. The knowability of Christ is in those who are secondary in their coming into being, whereas his unknowability is in his Father.

This *kephalaion* is a perfect pendant to the preceding one; there, the question was what is knowable in God; here it is what is knowable in Christ, and again a fundamental role is played by Christ's double nature, human and divine. What is knowable of Christ is found in mortal corporeal beings, which Evagrius calls "secondary beings" (e.g., in *KG* 1.50, 54, 61, 62, 77; 3.8, 68), since Christ both created them and in his human nature did take up human mortality; what is unknowable of Christ is Christ's divine nature, in that Christ is God, and Christ's divinity is in God the Father. Once again, what is knowable of God is his creation, his operations, his *energeiai*, while what is unknowable is the divine nature itself, which Christ shares with the Father.

4.4. The heir of Christ is the one who knows the intellections of all the beings that (came) after the original judgment.

The notion of becoming heirs of Christ has been already introduced by Evagrius in *KG* 3.72, in which he states that first all will have to become heirs of Christ for them to be able to become his coheirs, which will mean to acquire the knowledge of the Unity, in the final θέωσις (see above, the relevant commentary). Here Evagrius further explains what being "heirs of

Christ" consists in: in knowing the intellections (from ܣܘܟܠܐ, meaning "intelligence, understanding, thought, sense, meaning") of all beings as they have been after the first judgment, which surely is the original judgment that followed the fall of the *logika* and determined their differentiation into angels, humans, and demons. Therefore, this stage of knowledge comes first (being "heirs of Christ"), and then comes the knowledge of the Unity in the *telos* (being "coheirs of Christ," i.e., sharing Christ's own inheritance).

4.5. What is knowable is manifested to the knower partially in the knower and partially in the nonknower.

This is a series of gnoseological *kephalaia*, and Evagrius concentrates here on the manifestation of what is knowable to the *nous*, the "knower." Given that the objects of knowledge have been identified by Evagrius more than once with both primary and secondary beings, it is likely that the "knower" and the "nonknower" in which what is knowable is partially manifested are to be identifiable with primary and secondary beings respectively. Primary, intellectual beings, indeed, have the faculty of knowing and thus are "knowers"; secondary, corporeal beings are not receptive of knowledge and therefore are "nonknowers." What is knowable, however, is revealed to the intellect both in primary and in secondary beings, which are all objects of knowledge, even though only the former are subjects of knowledge. Indeed, in *KG* 1.61 Evagrius has explicitly stated that "there exists none among secondary beings that is capable of knowledge" (see the relevant commentary above).

4.6. A part of what is knowable comes into existence in the pure, and a part in those who are not pure. And whatever comes into being in the former is called spiritual knowledge, whereas what happens to the latter is named natural contemplation.

Evagrius in these gnoseological *kephalaia* goes on to reflect on what is knowable and how this is manifested to the intellect. First of all, he draws a distinction between intellects that are pure and those that are not pure. He has already spoken of pure or impure intellects in *KG* 1.65, where he affirms that in the final unity of θέωσις there will be only pure (or "bare") *noes* who will satiate themselves from God's impossibility to satiate; in *KG* 2.34, where Evagrius observes that "holy knowledge" attracts a pure *nous* to itself; and in *KG* 3.5, in which the intellects of the heavenly powers are said to be "pure and full of knowledge" (see the relevant commentaries above). Pure *noes* are thus associated with knowledge, and in particular with "holy" knowledge; in the present *kephalaion*, likewise, they are associated with "spiritual knowledge," which comes into being in them. Impure intellects, on the other hand, are associated with "natural *theōria*," which moreover is said to "happen" to them rather than being formed in them.

Evagrius has already described in several *kephalaia* what natural *theōria* is, and he has also distinguished between primary and secondary natural *theōria*. In *KG* 2.2 the secondary natural *theōria*—that is, the study of the world, in which the Creator's Wisdom appears—is opposed to the higher knowledge concerning rational creatures, the science of the *logika*. In *KG* 2.3 he has depicted "spiritual knowledge" as more ancient than every "natural contemplation." Above both the knowledge of intelligible realities and the contemplation of the world is the contemplation of the Unity. In *KG* 2.4, the secondary natural *theōria* is presented as a step that leads to the superior step of the knowledge concerning rational creatures, which is surpassed only by the knowledge of the Trinity. Secondary natural *theōria* appears again in *KG* 2.20 and 3.67, where it is coupled with the first or primary one, and 3.61, where it is said to be shown by virtue to the intellect, and to show in turn the primary natural *theōria* to the intellect. Finally, in *KG* 3.86–87 Evagrius parallels and opposes the "secondary natural *theōria*" and the "primary *theōria* of natures," which concerns the *logika*, whose evilness alone must be hated. See above, the commentaries on these *kephalaia*.

In the present *kephalaion*, Evagrius associates spiritual knowledge to pure intellects. Now, in *KG* 1.32 and 1.72 he has already explained that only the righteous receive spiritual knowledge, and in *KG* 2.3 he has established the priority of "spiritual knowledge" over "natural *theōria*," both primary and secondary (see above, the relevant commentaries). Therefore, in the present *kephalaion* Evagrius is perfectly coherent when he assigns the former to pure intellects and the latter to impure ones.

4.7. The One who has put "the Wisdom full of varieties/modalities" in beings, this also teaches to those who want it the art of how one easily becomes a seer of it.

Evagrius is quoting Eph 3:10 once again, after referring to it in *KG* 1.43; 2.2, 21; and 3.11 (see above, the relevant commentaries), usually in reference to the manifestation of God's Wisdom, Christ-Logos, in creation. He created all creatures according to the intelligible models that were in him, and this is why Wisdom, who is one, is also multiple and "full of varieties," containing the *logoi* of all things. Now in the present *kephalaion* Evagrius adds that Christ-Logos, the agent of creation qua Wisdom, is at the same time also the διδάσκαλος who bestows the knowledge of this Wisdom and its manifestations in creation upon those who want to learn. Here the element of voluntarism on the part of rational creatures is joined to the passive notion of receiving knowledge. The very expression "to become a seer" conveys an active meaning.

4.8. The coheir of Christ is the one who comes to be in Unity and delights in contemplation together with Christ.

In *KG* 3.72 Evagrius has maintained that one must become a "heir" of Christ in order to become his "coheir" as well, and thus inherit the "knowledge of the Unity"—the supreme kind of knowledge—together with Christ (see above, the relevant commentary). And in *KG* 4.4 he has just explained what it means to become a "heir of Christ": it means to know the intellections of all the beings that came after the original judgment. In the present *kephalaion* he returns to the definition of being "coheirs of Christ." As in *KG* 3.75, where he defined this with inheriting the knowledge of the Unity, here he defines this with getting to the Unity and joining Christ in his contemplation. Evagrius is most probably depicting the *telos* that consists in θέωσις. Indeed, being coheirs of Christ is participation in divine life, since Christ is God.

4.9. If the heir is one thing and the heritage is another, the Logos is not the one that inherits, but it is Christ who inherits the Logos, which is the heritage, because whoever inherits in this way is united to the heritage, whereas God the Logos is free from union.

Evagrius goes on with his considerations on what it means to be a coheir of Christ, and what it is that Christ will inherit in the end, and in which his coheirs will participate. Christ—the union of a human *logikon* and God—will inherit the Logos, who is God, and not vice versa, and all those *logika* who are coheirs of Christ inherit the same heritage as Christ does, that is, the Logos, and are in unity with it. The reference is again to the final *telos* of unity.

The definition of the Logos is here noteworthy: the Syriac text has ܡܠܬܐ ܐܠܗܐ, rather than the more common ܡܠܬܐ ܕܐܠܗܐ, which would mean "the Logos of God." The former expression, on the other hand, unless it should be emended with the addition of the *nota genetivi* ܕ, means "the Logos-God" or "God the Logos," "the Logos that is God." I suspect, however, that it ought not to be emended, because of the very context, and because of two precise parallels: one is *KG* 4.80, in which exactly the same expression is found, without *nota genetivi* (see below, my commentary on *KG* 4.80), and the other one is *KG* 4.18, in which Evagrius draws a distinction between Christ—who is human, *logikon*, and divine—and the Logos qua God (see below, my commentary on *KG* 4.18). Evagrius is speaking ofthe Logos qua God, not as heir—this is the person of Christ—but as heritage. So far, Evagrius has explicitly nominated the Logos only thrice, and never in the form "God the Logos." In *KG* 2.22 the Logos is Christ-Logos, who acts as an intermediary between the *logika* and the Father: the rational, *logikē* nature reveals the nature of Christ (clearly qua Logos) and the Logos in turn reveals the nature of the Father. In *KG* 2.73 the Logos is the Logos of God, who has revealed to us the truth concerning the things of the world to come, without, however, informing us about the coming into being of bodies and incorporeal beings. The very syntagma "the Logos of God" is finally found in *KG* 3.74, where Evagrius says that it has sanctified "the nature of the mortal body" and babies, who are *logika* only potentially and susceptible of knowledge.

Here in *KG* 4.9 the Logos is to be understood "the Logos qua God," which is free from union insofar as it is the heritage itself and not the heir. It is Christ and all the *logika* his coheirs who participate in the heritage and are united, not the heritage itself, God the Logos, which is participated in and maintains its transcendence. With "Christ" Evagrius here designates the union of divine, rational, and human nature in Jesus Christ; with "God the Logos" he designates his divine nature independently of that union. For ܡܠܬܐ ܐܠܗܐ, see also *KG* 5.48; 6.14, and 18.

4.10. Some of the writers of true doctrines have fallen from the primary contemplation of nature, some others from the secondary one, and yet others have even deviated from the Holy Trinity.

Evagrius here lists the three gnostic levels from which it is possible to fall: that of the Trinity is of course the highest, then comes the primary natural contemplation (that of intelligible realities), and then the secondary one (that of corporeal realities). It is from these levels that some of those who wrote true doctrines descended. Plotinus also spoke of primary or secondary contemplation. For Plotinus, primary contemplation is the contemplation of the One, and secondary contemplation is that of the intelligible (δεύτερα θεάματα, *Enneads* 6.9.9.11). On natural contemplation in patristic authors, see also Joshua Lollar, *To See into the Life of Things: The Contemplation of Nature in Maximus the Confessor and His Predecessors* (Turnhout: Brepols, 2015), ch. 13: "The Contemplation of Nature in the Greek Fathers."

4.11. If it is true that God is known by means of the corporeal and the incorporeal natures, and indeed the two contemplations of these (natures) vivify rational creatures, it is well said that God "is known inside the two living beings."

The scriptural quotation is from Hab 3:2. God is known by the *logika* through two kinds of living beings, corporeal and incorporeal, and it is this knowledge that vivifies the *logika*. Evagrius has already remarked that life for intellectual beings is knowledge (*KG* 1.73) and death is ignorance and evil (*KG* 1.41; see the relevant commentaries above).

4.12. The intelligible circumcision is a voluntary distancing from passions, which (takes place) thanks to the knowledge of God.

The allegorical meaning of circumcision, more precisely its intelligible or noetic meaning, is the rejection of πάθη (an interpretation that goes back to Philo and was also maintained by some rabbis; see Anna Tzvetkova-Glaser, *Pentateuchauslegung bei Origenes und den frühen Rabbinen* [Frankfurt: Lang, 2010], 179–80), according to the ideal of ἀπάθεια that Evagrius shared with Origen and Gregory of Nyssa (on this ideal in Nyssen and Origen, see Ilaria L. E. Ramelli, "Tears of Pathos, Repentance and Bliss: Crying and Salvation in Origen and Gregory of Nyssa," in *Tears in the Graeco-Roman World* [ed. Thorsten Fögen; Berlin: de Gruyter, 2009], 367–96; and idem, *Gregorio di Nissa: Sull'anima*). It is notable that this rejection is traced back by him to the knowledge of God, which acquires a priority in this ethical field as well: only those who know God can also renounce passions. The interrelationship between virtue and knowledge is thus once again clear.

4.13. Those who have participated in flesh and blood are babies. Now, whoever is an infant is neither good nor evil. Therefore, it is well said that human beings are intermediaries between angels and demons.

This *kephalaion* is closely connected with *KG* 3.76, in which Evagrius has traced the development of the human soul from a vegetative level in the womb to an animal level in babyhood (which in the present *kephalaion* is represented by Heb 2:14), to the rational level in adulthood. There, he warned that the gift of the *logos* can be used by human beings in two opposite ways, either for the Good, if one follows virtue, or for evil, if one follows evilness. The former conduct elevates the human being to the rank of angels, and the latter degrades it to that of demons, an idea that here is repeated. Here, human beings are assimilated to babies, who are neither good nor evil, in the sense that they are neither completely good, as angels are, nor so evil as demons are. If humans were completely good, they would be angels, and if they were much worse than they are, they would be demons (I do not say, "if they were completely evil," because demons themselves are not completely evil, since they are creatures of God—if they were completely evil, they would cease to exist). At other times, indeed, Evagrius speaks of an assimilation of humans to angels or to demons over the aeons, depending on their moral choices.

4.14. Just as the pledge that is in mortal bodies is a small part of the body, likewise also the pledge that is in the kinds of knowledge is a certain part of the knowledge of beings.

It is not entirely perspicuous what Evagrius here means with pledge or deposit in reference both to mortal bodies and to knowledge. The pledge that is in mortal bodies may be the promise of their future resurrection (with a possible allusion to 2 Cor 5:5); likewise, the pledge that is in the various kinds of knowledge, sciences or gnoses, may be the promise of the full future knowledge. Mortal bodies are just a small part of all bodies, and single kinds of knowledge are just a small part of all knowledge.

4.15. If the whole world/aeon of the human beings is an aeon of babies, there will come a time in which they will reach adulthood, that which is suitable to the just or to the impious.

Evagrius has already spoken twice, in *KG* 3.76 and 4.13, of the development of rational creatures from babyhood to adulthood, a passage in which the watershed is given by the appearance of the *logos*, which can pursue the Good or evil, and thus can assimilate the human being to angels or demons. And in *KG* 4.13 he has assimilated humans to babies, who are neither good nor evil and are therefore in an intermediate state between angels and demons (see above, the relevant commentary). Now the whole *αἰών* of human beings, that is, their arranged totality in the present aeon, is represented as it were at the stage of babyhood, which has no goodness or evilness, because it comes before moral choices; when it reaches adulthood, then there will intervene a division between the just and the impious, based on the moral choices of each one. This will probably entail the transformation of some into angels, and others into demons.

4.16. The only begotten is the one before whom no one else has been generated, and after whom no one.

This reflects on the nature of Christ as only begotten Child of God and sharing in divine nature. Here the divide—exasperated by the "Arian" controversy—between Son of God, consubstantial with God, and creatures of God is manifest.

4.17. "On high" is said to be the place to which knowledge leads those who possess it, "down" the place to which ignorance (leads) those who possess it.

Biblical spatial locutions are interpreted according to the noetic coordinates of knowledge and ignorance, which are fundamental in Evagrius's system and especially in these *Chapters/Propositions on Knowledge.*

4.18. The intelligible anointing is the spiritual knowledge of the holy Unity, and Christ is the one who is united to this knowledge. And if this is so, Christ is not the Logos originally, just as the Anointed One (Messiah) is not God originally, but this is Christ thanks to that one, and he is God thanks to him.

Evagrius goes on with his noetic exegesis, and at the same time with his reflection on the divinity of Christ, which he has begun in *KG* 4.16 (see above, the relevant commentary). The "anointing" immediately establishes an etymological reference to Christ, the Anointed One; the Syriac is related to the Semitic epithet Messiah. The anointing that characterizes Christ is described by Evagrius as the highest form of knowledge, the "spiritual knowledge of the holy Unity," as defined in *KG* 2.3 (see my commentary there). Since Christ is united to this knowledge and is a human-divine compound, Christ is not the Logos originally and immediately, and, qua Anointed One, is not God immediately, but is God and Logos, thanks to God the Logos. In *KG* 4.9 Evagrius has already distinguished Christ from the Logos-God, making of the former the heir, with all his coheirs, and of the latter the inheritance. The last sentence, "this is Christ thanks to that one, and he is God thanks to him," points to the so-called *communicatio idiomatum* between the creaturely nature—human and rational—and the divine nature within the same person of Christ.

The present *kephalaion* seems to be reflected, and misunderstood, in the so-called canons of the fifth council against Origen, anathema 8.

4.19. "One" is a number of quantity. Now, quantity is linked with mortal corporeal nature. Therefore, number is proper to secondary natural contemplation.

This is one of Evagrius's syllogisms, with a major and minor premise, and a conclusion. As he has made clear more than once, secondary natural contemplation refers precisely to the mortal corporeal nature, which explains the cogency of this syllogism. Of course, here "one" is taken in a numeric sense, and not in the protological sense of the principle of unity (see Ramelli, "Harmony between *Arkhē* and *Telos*" on this). The disappearance of all numbers and quantities along with all diastematic nature is announced by Evagrius in his *Letter to Melania*, as well as in his *Letter on Faith*, corresponding to *Letter* 8 ascribed to Basil (PG 32:249A). In *Letter to Melania* 22, in particular, Evagrius announces the eschatological abolition of numbers and divisions:

> And there will be a time when the body, the soul, and the intellect will cease to be separate from one another, with their names and their *plurality*, since the body and the soul will be elevated to the rank of intellects; this conclusion can be drawn from the following words: "That they may be *one* in us, just as you and I are one" [John 17:22]. And thus there will be a time when the Father, the Son, and the Spirit, and their rational creation, which constitutes their body, *will cease to be separate, with their*

names and their plurality. And this conclusion can be drawn from the words "God will be all in all" [1 Cor 15:28].

See above, the commentary on *KG* 1.7. The ultimate end, characterized by deification, will be an undivided state, marked by a condition of unity, as underscored by Maximus the Confessor in very similar terms: deification is "the undivided [ἀδιάστατος] state of the pure union [ἑνότης] of the beginning and the end" (*To Thalassius* 59).

4.20. The first begotten is the one before whom nobody has been generated but after whom others have come into being.

This *kephalaion* is a pendant to *KG* 4.16: there, Evagrius defines the only begotten, in reference to Christ as God and Child of God (see above, the relevant commentary). Here he defines the first begotten, which again may apply to Christ as new Adam and first begotten of all humans (see Rom 8:29–30: "For those whom he foreknew he also predestined to be conformed to the image of his Son, in order that he might be *the firstborn among many siblings*. And those whom he predestined he also called; and those whom he called he also justified; and those whom he justified he also glorified," RSV, slightly modified).

4.21. The anointing either indicates the knowledge of the Unity or denotes the contemplation of beings. Now, if it is true that Christ is anointed more than the others, it is clear that he is anointed in the knowledge of the Unity. This is why he only is said to sit to his Father's right, that which here, according to the norm of the gnostics, indicates the Monad and the Unity.

In *KG* 4.18 Evagrius, in his noetic exegesis, has already stated that Christ's anointing is the supreme knowledge, the spiritual knowledge of the Unity. A second sense of "anointing" (= the *theōria* of beings) is inferior and refers not to Christ, to whom the eminent sense refers, but to other *logika*, who are creatures. That Christ is anointed "more than the others" might be a reference to Ps 44:8. Also, Christ's sitting to the right of the Father is a reminiscence of Mark 16:19; Eph 1:20; Col 3:1; Heb 10:2. Christ's privilege to sit at the right hand of the Father is here allegorized by Evagrius as the Monad and the Unity. Evagrius has already explained, in *KG* 3.1, that the Father is unique in Unity, and the Son is Monad and Unity;

for the derivation of this concept, and the very expression μονάς τε καὶ ἑνάς (in reference to God), from Origen, see above my commentary on 3.1.

4.22. Just as those who offer symbolic sacrifices to God burn the bestial movements of the soul by means of virtues, in the same way those who sacrifice to demons destroy the natural activities of the soul by means of vices.

These symbolic sacrifices offered to God seem to echo Paul's λογικὴ λατρεία (rational or spiritual worship), and the theme of following virtue or following vice and thus associating oneself to demons is parallel to that developed in *KG* 3.76 and 4.13 (see above, the relevant commentary). The natural activities of the soul are oriented to the Good. Evilness is against nature; it was not implanted by God at the beginning in human beings. It is no creature of God, and is not natural for a soul. The same characterization of vices and passions as not belonging to the nature of the soul but as sort of accretions against nature is also found in Gregory of Nyssa's *On the Soul and the Resurrection* (see my commentary in Ramelli, *Gregorio di Nissa: Sull'anima*). Virtues destroy the bestial movements of the soul—which are against the rational nature and are rather proper to irrational creatures—as in a sacrifice.

4.23. The kingdom of God is not Moses and Elijah, if it is true that the former is contemplation, whereas the latter are holy human beings. Therefore, how is it that our Savior, after promising the disciples to show them the kingdom of God, showed them himself, Moses, and Elijah on the mountain, with a spiritual body?

This is a biblical exegetical *kephalaion*, as many others are in the *KG*. Evagrius presents what seems to be a contradiction in Matt 17 and Mark 9 (cf. Luke 9) in the episode of Jesus's transfiguration. The body of the transfiguration is a spiritual body, that which will characterize the kingdom of God.

4.24. The firstborn from among the dead is the one who rose from among the dead and first took up a spiritual body.

This *kephalaion* returns to the theme already addressed in *KG* 4.16 and 4.20, and it refers again to Christ, who is now described as the firstborn from among the dead (see Col 1:18; Rev 1:5). The body of the resurrection is a spiritual body, both that of Christ and that of all human beings, who will be resurrected.

4.25. Just as the light that shines in our holy temples is the symbol of the spiritual knowledge, likewise also that of pagan temples is the sign of false teachings and conceptions. And the former is alimented by the oil of holy love, while the latter by mundane love, which loves the world and the things that are in it.

The opposition is between the temples in which the true God is worshiped and "pagan" temples. These are respectively the symbols of spiritual knowledge, the highest kind of knowledge, and of false knowledge. Now, the difference between these two opposite kinds of knowledge depends on a radical difference of the kind of love that nourishes each of the two: one directed toward God, the true Good and the source and summation of all goods, and the other toward the world, toward disparate and apparent goods. Evagrius inherited Origen's idea of the crucial importance of love: the first fall was caused by a loss of love for God, and the final unity in the *apokatastasis* will be kept forever only thanks to love, for God and reciprocal (see below, *KG* 5.46, with the whole text). Like Origen himself, Evagrius constantly joins philosophical argument with scriptural support; his reference to the love of the world and the realities that are in the world comes from 1 John 2:15: "Do not love the world or the things in the world. If any one loves the world, love for the Father is not in him" (RSV).

4.26. If it is the case that on the third day Christ "is done/perfected" and that, the day before, the one who gathered wood in the desert "was burned," it is clear that today it is the day that is called Friday, at whose eleventh hour the peoples have been called by our Savior to eternal life.

The *apokatastasis* will be on the eighth day, the eternal Sunday, the third day from the death of Christ; Friday is now, which also reproduces the Friday of the Passion that, toward the end of the day (at the "eleventh hour"), performs the salvation of the peoples (this is a reference to Matt 20:6–7). Evagrius has already presented the same quotation from Luke 13:32 in *KG* 1.90, in which he has stated as well that "today is that which is called Friday, in which our Savior was crucified" (see above, the relevant commentary). Luke 13:31–32 is indeed a declaration by Jesus himself directed to Herod about his own miracles and death: "At that very hour some Pharisees came, and said to him, 'Get away from here, for Herod wants to kill you.' And he said to them, 'Go and tell that fox, "Behold, I cast out demons and perform cures today and tomorrow, and the third day I finish my course"'" (RSV). But, like Christ, all will rise on the third day, when Christ will be "done" after working miracles on the first two days, that is, "today and tomorrow." In *KG* 3.9, the same quotation from Luke concerning Christ, who "works miracles today and tomorrow, and on the third day is done" or "is perfected," is in the service of the description of what will happen during the eschatological Friday, Saturday (the reference to the man who gathered wood on this day is to Num 15:32–36, though "burned" is surprising, since the biblical text has "stoned," because he acted thus on the Sabbath), and Sunday: the bodies of ignorance will be overcome, then will be transformed with an increment of fire and air (meaning that they will be transformed into angelic bodies), and those who are below will apply themselves to science, so that "the houses of the impious will receive purification." After this purification, Christ will be "done," which means that he will have accomplished his task, which is the purification of sinners (his "working miracles"). Only then will the final *apokatastasis* take place on the great Sunday. This is the accomplishment of all peoples' call to eternal life on the day of Christ's sacrifice, which is referred to in the present *kephalaion*. Origen even claimed that Christ himself will be unable to accomplish his own eschatological resurrection-restoration until he has completed his task, that is, until the last sinner will have become righteous. Christ will have finished the "work" assigned to him by the Father, to which he refers in John 17:4, after making even the last sinner just. For as long as even one rational creature remains outside the body of Christ and the submission to him, Christ will not be able to submit to God and perform the restoration of his own body. In all humanity—the body of Christ-Logos—made perfect by him, Christ will accomplish his work, as the result of which "God will be all in all" (Origen, *Homilies on Leviticus* 7.2.6; *Commentary on John* 28.21.185).

4.27. The image of the one who had to be baptized that appeared to the Baptist, was it in the primary contemplation, or in the secondary one, or even in the third one? And moreover, if it is possible that the Unity be impressed in a form like that. But there is the risk that we may make this known patently; thus, let this (image) be examined (only) among those who know.

This is an exegetical reflection on how John the Baptist recognized Jesus as the one whom he had to baptize. The questions, in a "zetetic" fashion that resembles Origen's, are two: (1) In which contemplation did the Baptist have this revelation? (2) Is it possible that the Unity was impressed in the "image of the one who had to be baptized"? Since Christ is God, the Godhead is the supreme Unity, which should have been impressed in the "image" received by the Baptist. The problem is mainly gnoseological.

In the last sentence the Syriac text is very faint: the reading of the manuscript, "you will correct [ܬܬܪܨ] this image," is uncertain, as Guillaumont himself (147) warns. However, he follows this reading in his translation and is followed in turn by Dysinger ("you will correct this symbol among the *gnostikoi*") and Fr. Theophanes ("you will correct this symbol among the gnostics"). I hypothesized an emendation into "you will make this image known," or "you will reveal/manifest [ܬܒܪܨ] this image," only to the gnostics, that is, those who have knowledge. From the paleographical point of view, the transformation of ܬܬܪܨ into ܬܒܪܨ is very easy, and the meaning of the sentence after the correction is much more satisfactory. Sebastian Brock, whom once again I thank warmly for sharing his reading with me, feels "pretty confident" that the correct reading of the manuscript at this point is ܬܬܒܨܐ; this lends a sense that is very similar to the preceding one and has the best chances to be correct: "let this (image) be examined (only) among those who know," the gnostics.

The "image" in this sentence is probably again that which is mentioned at the beginning of the *kephalaion* and around which Evagrius's gnoseological questions revolve. This "image," according to the last sentence, should be made known only to, or examined only by, those who have knowledge. Clement and Origen also had this concern to make things progressively known to those who can receive them. See, for example, Ilaria L. E. Ramelli, "The Birth of the Rome–Alexandria Connection," *SPhilo* 23 (2011): 69–95, esp. last section; and idem, "The Mysteries of Scripture: Allegorical Exegesis and the Heritage of Stoicism, Philo, and Pantaenus in Clement," forthcoming in the Proceedings of the Second Internationale Colloquium Clementinum, Prague-Olomouc 29–31 May 2014 (ed. Veronica Cernuskova, Vit Husek, and Jana Platova; Leiden: Brill, 2016).

4.28. The intelligible unleavened breads are the state of the rational soul that is constituted by pure virtues and true doctrines.

Evagrius is interpreting allegorically, in the line of Philo, Origen, and Nyssen, the ritual prescriptions of the Old Testament. Indeed, just as in *KG* 4.12 Evagrius has given the allegorical meaning of circumcision in ethical terms, thereby explaining what the "intelligible circumcision" is (i.e., a distancing from πάθη), so does he explain here what the "intelligible unleavened breads" (in reference to Deut 16:8) are: the state of the rational soul characterized by both pure virtues and true doctrines. This is noetic exegesis, the search for the meaning of a detail in Scripture on the intelligible plane. Note the joining of ethical and gnoseological goods, virtue and truth (ethical and theoretical virtues, according to the Aristotelian scheme—what Dante will still indicate as the goal of human life: "to pursue virtue and knowledge," "seguir virtute e conoscenza"). As I have already pointed out more than once, these two planes are never disjoined for Evagrius: there cannot be virtue without knowledge, or knowledge without virtue. This is an approach that is ultimately indebted to ethical intellectualism, which goes back to Socrates and Plato and has an important part in the thought of Origen and Gregory of Nyssa, as well as of Origen's fellow disciple at Ammonius Saccas's: Plotinus. In *Enneads* 6.8.6.36–38 Plotinus pithily describes will as an intellectual act: "Will is the intellection / the intellectual activity [ἡ δὲ βούλησις ἡ νόησις]. The latter is called will because it conforms to the intellect. For we maintain that the will follows what conforms to the intellect." For Origen, Plotinus, Gregory, and Evagrius, the choices of our free will depend on our knowledge; if our intellect is obnubilated, our free will is much less free. True freedom, for Evagrius just as for Plato, Origen, and Nyssen, is the freedom to choose the Good.

4.29. Just as, if the earth were destroyed, then the night would no more exist on the face of the firmament, likewise, once evilness is removed, then ignorance will no longer exist among rational creatures. For ignorance is the shadow of evilness: those who walk in it, as in the night, are illuminated by the (lamp) oil of Christ and see the stars, in accord with the knowledge that they are worthy of receiving from him. And they too, the stars, will "fall" for them, unless they immediately turn toward the "Sun of Justice."

This is another *kephalaion* in which Evagrius uses astronomical allegory in reference to *apokatastasis*, as in 3.60 (see the relevant commentary above). The union of virtue and knowledge, which Evagrius has stressed in the last *kephalaion*, *KG* 4.28, has its negative counterpart in the union of evilness and ignorance, which is the focus of the present one. Just as the night is the shadow of the earth, as Evagrius explains with a simile, so is ignorance the shadow of evilness. This *kephalaion* in particular concerns the *telos*, which, according to Evagrius, just as to Origen and Gregory of Nyssa, will be characterized by the complete eviction of evil and *apokatastasis* (see Ramelli, "Christian Soteriology and Christian Platonism"). And this will go together with the elimination of ignorance and the shining of knowledge among the *logika*. Of course, a key role in this is played by Christ, the Anointed, whose lamp oil illuminates the *logika*. Christ-Logos, according to Evagrius just as to Origen, has a fundamental gnoseological and illuminative function for the *logika*. The blending of virtue and knowledge—typical of Evagrius, as I have often remarked so far—is evident from the very characterization of Christ as *Sol Iustitiae* (from Mal 3:20), which already appeared in *KG* 3.52: Christ enlightens rational creatures both with knowledge and with virtue.

The fall of the stars is a reference to Rev 6:13 or Judg 5:20. The illuminating function of the stars has been declared, in an allegorical way, by Evagrius in *KG* 3.62 and 3.84, in which he speaks of intellectual stars (see above, the relevant commentaries). Their enlightening task is parallel to that of Christ as *Sol Iustitiae*; this is why they are said to fall for those *logika* who do not turn to the Sun of Justice. These are those who refuse to be illuminated and acquire knowledge, and thus virtue. Ultimately, however, all evil and all ignorance will be obliterated, according to Evagrius.

4.30. If the wealth of God, that which is to come, is the spiritual contemplation of the worlds/aeons that will come into existence, those who reduce the kingdom of heaven to the palate and the belly will be confused.

The identification of the kingdom with the contemplation of the aeons to come is drawn directly from a passage ascribed to Origen, *Selected Passages on Psalms* 144, where the kingdom is identified with the contemplation of both the past aeons and the aeons to come, *τῶν γενησομένων αἰώνων*. The reference to the wealth of God is to Rom 11:33. Origen criticized harshly those who interpreted God's promises, especially in the Apocalypse, in a literal and earthly way, imagining the kingdom as full of enjoyments of the belly. In *On First Principles* 2.11.2–3 he sharply criticizes those exegetes who hold that the eschatological beatitude will be made of eating and drinking and other worldly pleasures and that the heavenly Jerusalem will be an earthly city, made of precious stones, taking literally the description of Rev 21: "Some people, yielding, in a way, to their enjoyment and desire, think that God's promises for the future must be expected to consist in pleasure and bodily indulgence, since they do not follow what the apostle Paul meant about the resurrection of a *spiritual* body. They have rather understood the divine Scriptures, so to say, in a Jewish sense, and therefore they have not presumed out of them anything worthy of the divine promises," *Quidam ergo ... magis delectationi suae quodammodo ac libidini indulgentes ... arbitrantur repromissiones futuras in voluptate et luxuria corporis expectanda ... apostoli Pauli de resurrectione spiritalis corporis sententiam non sequentes. Iudaico autem quodam sensu scripturas divinas intellegentes, nihil ex his dignum divinis pollicitationibus praesumpserunt.* Rather, Origen explains, the heavenly Jerusalem of the Apocalypse, or Revelation, will be a "city of saints," a *civitas sanctorum*, in which each one will be instructed in order to become a living precious stone: "The intellect, fed on the food of Wisdom up to absolute perfection, will be restored into the image and likeness of God, exactly as the human being was created at the beginning, so that, even if one should pass away from this life without having been well instructed, but with laudable deeds, one may be taught in that famous Jerusalem, city of saints, and thus be instructed and formed, and transformed into a living stone, precious and elect," *Sapientiae escis nutrita mens ad integrum et perfectum, sicut ex initio factus est homo, ad imaginem Dei ac similitudinem reparetur: ut etiamsi quis ex hac vita minus eruditus abierit, probabilia tamen opera detulerit, instrui possit in illa Hierusalem civitate sanctorum, id et edoceri et informari et effici lapis vivus, lapis pretiosus et electus.* After all, that these stones will be the human beings was suggested in the Gospel itself, where Jesus identifies Peter with the stone on which the church will be grounded, and Origen was sure that the church eschatologically will coincide with all of humanity, which in turn is tantamount to Christ's mystical body. Evagrius's *kephalaion* is along the same lines: the goods of God's promises are identified by him with spiritual *theōria*, which is the highest kind of *theōria*. That will have as its object the future aeons, precisely those of the kingdom, which is the preparation of the *telos*.

4.31. Just as the star that is hidden by the interposition of another one is higher than the latter, likewise the one who is much humbler than another, in the world to come will be found much higher than the latter.

Again, here is an astronomical simile, like that used in *KG* 4.29 (see the relevant commentary above). The world to come will reveal the true worth of rational creatures. This notion draws upon several Gospel passages, bearing on the future exaltation of those who humble themselves.

4.32. The lobe of the liver is the first (tempting) reasoning, which is constituted by the concupiscible faculty of the soul.

The scriptural reference to the lobe of the liver seems to be to Exod 29:13, which here, once again, is interpreted at the noetic level. I render with "(tempting) reasoning" the Syriac translation of Greek διαλογισμός. The concupiscible part of the soul is the part governed by *epithymia*, according to Plato's tripartition of the soul in *logikon*, *epithymētikon*, and *thymikon*, which Evagrius regularly takes up. Tempting reasonings emerge from the two irrational parts of the soul.

4.33. Those who are without mercy, after their death demons who are without mercy will receive them. As for those who are even more merciless, (demons) worse than these will receive them. And if this is so, it escapes those who make their soul exit their body which kind of demons will receive them after their death. Indeed, there is also the saying that nobody among those who leave according to God's will shall be handed to demons like those.

The demons who will receive the dead will be as merciless as they were on earth. Those who commit suicide are represented here as the most merciless of all; accordingly, they are said to be received by the most merciless demons after death.

4.34. In the future world/aeon no one will escape from the house of torment into which he will fall. For it is said, "You will not go out from there until you have given back the very last coin," that is, up to the smallest amount of suffering.

Evagrius, Origen, Gregory Nyssen, and other Fathers who supported the doctrine of *apokatastasis* nevertheless were adamant that all the evil that each one has committed must necessarily be purified, and this purification cannot be attained but through suffering, although suffering itself is not the primary aim of God in this but rather an inevitable side effect of this purification from evil, which is the *telos* of all (this is particularly clear in Nyssen's dialogue *On the Soul and the Resurrection*; see my commentary in Ramelli, *Gregorio di Nissa: Sull'anima*). Only, these Fathers were all convinced that this purification will finally come to an end. And Evagrius shared this conviction, also because of his fundamental assumption of the ontological priority of the Good and the limitedness and nonsubsistence of evil, and of the limitedness of human earthly life and capability to sin (a motif developed by Origen, Methodius, and Nyssen).

Indeed, here attention is drawn by Evagrius to the κόλασις αἰώνιος, that is, punishment in the next world/aeon (Syriac ܥܠܡܐ renders Greek αἰών). The reference to the parable in Matt 5:26 is the same as that which we find in Gregory of Nyssa's above-mentioned dialogue *On the Soul and the Resurrection*, where Macrina uses it to show that punishment in the next world will be exactly commensurate to one's sins; thus, everyone will certainly pay his or her debt "up to the very last coin," but there will come a "last coin" sooner or later, and so all punishments will eventually come to an end. Macrina stresses that even the smallest sin will have to be repaid through a minimum amount of suffering; there will be a complete and exact retribution, but this very exactitude implies a precise *measure*: if punishment will be exactly commensurate with sins, this means that it will not be infinite and that it will cease for each person at a certain point. This idea of the measure applied to otherworldly sufferings is prominent in Diodore of Tarsus and Theodore of Mopsuestia. See Ramelli, *Christian Doctrine of Apokatastasis*, the section on them.

I think that both Evagrius and Gregory of Nyssa were inspired by Origen in their exegesis of Matt 5:26. In his *Commentary on Romans* 5.2.170–176, Origen states both that purification for one's sins will last until the smallest sin has been abolished—much insisting on this, like Macrina, for a pedagogical purpose—and that there will surely come an end for this purification: "It is promised that at a certain point one will certainly exit that prison; however, it is also indicated that it is impossible to go out unless each one has paid back even the very last coin. Now, if even the punishment corresponding to a coin, that is, the very smallest sin, is not remitted unless it is cleared in prison and through torments, how can one relax in hopes of going unpunished or regard the gift of divine grace as a permission to sin freely?" *Quamuis enim promittatur exeundum esse quandoque de carcere, tamen designatur non inde exiri posse nisi reddat unusquisque etiam nouissimum quadrantem. Quod si etiam quadrantis quod est minimi peccati poena non remittitur nisi in carcere et per supplicia luatur, quomodo quis spe impunitatis resoluitur aut donum gratiae peccandi libertatem putabit?*

From Origen, and perhaps also from Didymus the Blind, Evagrius also inherited the awareness that αἰώνιος in the Bible is far from meaning only "eternal." This is clear not only from Origen's own linguistic use (see wide-ranging analysis in Ramelli and Konstan, *Terms for Eternity*; and for Didymus, see Ramelli, *Christian Doctrine of Apokatastasis*, the chapter on him) but also from his theoretical declaration in *Commentary on Romans* 6.5.112–129:

> In Scriptures eternity must be understood sometimes as without end but sometimes as coming to an end, if not in the present aeon, at least in the future one; and sometimes eternity means a certain amount of time, or the duration of the life of a single human being.... "And he will be your slave for eternity [εἰς αἰῶνα]": here the author with "eternity" undoubtedly meant the duration of the life of a human being.... "But the earth endures eternally": here "eternally" means "for the duration of the present aeon." But when Scripture says, "life eternal," one must look at what the Savior himself said: "This is life eternal: that they may come to know you, the only true God, and the one you sent, Jesus Christ." And again: "I am the Way, Truth, and Life," ... "And thus we shall be always with the Lord." Now, just as being always with the Lord has no end, so also must life eternal be considered to have no end.
>
> *Aeternitas in Scripturis aliquando pro eo ponatur ut finem nesciat, aliquando uero ut in praesenti quidem saeculo finem non habeat, habeat tamen in futuro; aliquando uel temporis alicuius uel etiam uitae unius hominis spatium aeternitas appelletur ... "et erit tibi seruus in aeternum": aeternum hic sine dubio tempus uitae hominis posuit ... "terra autem in aeternum stat": hic aeternum praesentis saeculi tempus ostendit. Ubi uero dicit "uitam aeternam" ad illud aspiciendum est quod ipse saluator dixit: "haec est autem uita aeterna: ut cognoscant te, solum uerum Deum, et quem misisti, Iesum Christum"; et iterum: "ego sum uia et ueritas et uita"; ... "et ita semper cum Domino erimus." Sicut ergo semper esse cum Domino finem non habet, ita et uita aeterna nullum finem habere credenda est.*

Also in *Commentary on Romans* 10.43.76–78 Origen explains that the biblical expression εἰς τοὺς αἰῶνας τῶν αἰώνων in Scripture means a very long stretch of time: "As for the biblical expression 'for ages and ages,' usually the divine Scripture indicates with this a very long and unmeasurable stretch of time" (but still time and not eternity), *in saecula uero saeculo-*

rum quod ait moris est scripturae diuinae immensitatem per hoc temporum designare.

4.35. If it is the case that the gift of languages is a gift of the spirit, and that demons are bereft of this gift, they do not speak in languages. They say, however, that, thanks to learning, they know the languages of human beings. And it is not surprising if they possess this by means of receptivity, in that their constitution is coextensive with the constitution of the world. Now, someone said that their languages too are varied, because of the variety of human beings. There are some who say that among them there are even ancient languages, so that there may be found opposing the Hebrews those who use the Hebrew language, opposing the Greeks those who speak Greek, and so on.

The gift of languages spoken without a previous study refers to the Pentecost episode in Acts 2:4–13., in which this is presented as a gift from the Spirit, probably a reversal of the Babel episode of the initial differentiation of languages. Evagrius also declares that this Pentecost gift comes from the Spirit. Therefore, demons do not absolutely have this gift from the Spirit; however, they do learn languages, being rational creatures, and use them to tempt humans. In the penultimate line of the text there is a misprint in Guillaumont's edition, with respect to the manuscript: ܠܥܘܢ̈ܝܐ should be ܠܝܘܢ̈ܝܐ.

4.36. The intelligible fat is the thickness that, due to evilness, sticks to the intellect.

In several previous *kephalaia* Evagrius has already explained what is the intelligible unleavened bread (*KG* 4.28), the intelligible circumcision (*KG* 4.12), and intelligible stars (*KG* 3.62 and 3.84; see the relevant commentaries above). Here he elucidates the meaning of "intelligible fat." This image (and the one in *KG* 3.75, in which Evagrius has already introduced the notion of dirtiness and contamination of the rational nature) is close to Gregory of Nyssa's notion of the thick and dirty glue, mud, or crusted dirt that sticks to one's intellectual soul whenever one commits evil and that will have to be removed, which will produce acute suffering (in *On the Soul and the Resurrection* 100A; see my commentary in Ramelli, *Gregorio di Nissa: Sull'anima*). The Greek text of this *kephalaion* is to be found in *Selected Passages on Psalms* 16:9–10 (PG 12:1220CD). Evagrius's allegorization here is also close to Origen's metaphor of the "fattening, thickening" of the (intellectual) soul.

4.37. They say that, among animals, some draw their breath from outside, others from the inside, others from what is around them, and yet others from all sides. And those that draw it from outside are said to be the human beings and all those that have lungs, whereas those that draw it from inside are fishes and all those whose muteness is complete [or "whose throat is large"]; again, those that draw it from what is around them are the bees with their wings (literally, "with the spathe of their wings"). Those who draw it from all sides, on the other hand, are the devils (demons) and all those rational creatures who own aerial immortal bodies.

In addition to "and all those whose throat is large," which is the rendering of Guillaumont (153, on the basis of the interpretation of ܚܪܫܐ as a synonym of ܚܪܘܫܬܐ, followed by Dysinger ["all those with large throats"] and Fr. Theophanes ["all those of whom the gullet is large"], and on the basis of a reference to fish breathing in the Syriac translation of Basil's *Hexaemeron*, which uses *ggrt'*), a possible alternative translation may be "and all those whose muteness is complete" (literally, "extended"). Indeed, ܚܪܫܐ, which is unattested elsewhere, may well come from ܚܪܫ, "to be mute, silent," and this meaning would be extremely apt to the relationship drawn here by Evagrius between these animals and fishes, which clearly belong to the category of completely mute animals.

Human beings in this life, having mortal bodies, breathe through their lungs. Other *logika*, on the other hand, have immortal bodies; demons, in particular, have immortal bodies made of air (the Syriac adjective "aerial" comes from Greek ἀήρ) and their breathing does not pass through a specific duct—demons have no nose—but they pull air all over. The bodies of demons, although immortal like those of angels, are imagined by Evagrius as very different from those of the latter. Indeed, Origen thought that the body of Satan and his followers are such as to arouse the laughter of angels. See Pietras, "L'inizio del mondo materiale." In *KG* 2.51 Evagrius has already opposed the bodies of demons to those of angels: the latter are "the chariot of knowledge" and are composed of "fire and air," whereas the former are "the chariot of ignorance" and are composed of "air and water" (see above, the relevant commentary). In *KG* 1.68 Evagrius has also explained that in the bodies of angels fire prevails, in those of human beings earth prevails, and in those of demons air does. This is also why demons reach humans through their nostrils, Evagrius claims (see above, the relevant commentary). Demons have no nostrils but, as is clear from the present *kephalaion*, pull air from all directions, and their very bodies are made of air. Concerning bees, the Syriac text literally speaks of "the spathe of their wings." A spathe is a large sheathing bract enclosing the flower cluster of certain plants, such as palms. Evagrius uses this term metaphorically, probably alluding to the form and the movement of the bees' wings, as though bees breathed through their wings.

4.38. In the aeon to come, the irascible man will not be counted along with angels, nor will he be entrusted with a leading position. For he does not see because of passion, easily gets angry with those who are led by him, falls from vision, and throws those people into risk. Now, these two things are alien to the angelic order.

Evagrius here reflects on the effects of *thymos*, the irascible faculty of the soul, one of the two passional parts of the soul together with *epithymia*, or the concupiscible faculty. These effects are incompatible with the order (the Syriac word is the transliteration of Greek τάξις) of angels, which cultivates the rational soul. In *KG* 1.68 Evagrius has declared that in demons there is a prevalence of *thymos*; one suspects that here he is saying—like Origen—that human beings who have an excess of *thymos* in this aeon and do not correct themselves will become demons in the next aeon. Indeed, in *Letter* 56.4 Evagrius warns that anger can transform a human *nous* into a demon and even describes a demon as a human being aroused by anger.

4.39. If in the aeons to come God will show his richness to rational creatures, it is clear that he will do so in those that will come into being after that which is to come, in that before this rational creatures will be unable to receive his holy richness.

Evagrius follows Origen once again in envisaging a long series of aeons, which are the theater of the spiritual education and development of the *logika*; at the end of these aeons there will come universal *apokatastasis*. See Tzamalikos, *Origen: Philosophy of History*; Ramelli, "Αἰώνιος and Αἰών"; and idem, *Christian Doctrine of Apokatastasis*. Like Nyssen, Evagrius thinks of the progressive and infinite approach of rational creatures to God in terms of being more and more receptive of God, like Gregory of Nyssa (see Ramelli, *Gregorio di Nissa: Sull'anima*). Here Evagrius's reflection is based on Eph 2:7: "in the aeons to come God will show the immeasurable richness of his grace in kindness toward us in Christ Jesus." This is the same passage that Origen used to argue that there will be more aeons before the eventual restoration. Indeed, in his treatise *On Prayer* 27.15 Origen relied on Heb 9:26 ("he has appeared once for all at the end of the aeon to put away sin by the sacrifice of himself") together with Eph 2:7, where he found support for his claim that there will be an end to the aeons and that Christ's sacrifice was made once and for all. These aeons display God's grace because they point to one end, the final restoration of all, attained by all rational creatures' voluntary adhesion to the Good and thanks to God's grace. After it, there will be no more aeons but the absolute eternity (ἀϊδιότης) of *apokatastasis*.

4.40. The key of the kingdom of heaven is a gift of the Spirit, that which little by little reveals the intellections of the *praktikē* and of nature, and of the *logoi* concerning God.

The scriptural reference is to Matt 16:19. In this exegetical passage Evagrius offers an allegorical reading of this "key." A key opens; thus, this key discloses the intellections of ethics, the knowledge of nature, and that of God, of course in a progression toward the summit of knowledge. In *Praktikos* 2 Evagrius likewise describes the kingdom of heaven as a synthesis of *praktikē* and knowledge, distinguishing it from the kingdom of God, which is pure knowledge: "The kingdom of heaven is impassibility of the soul accompanied by the knowledge of beings" (*Praktikos* 2); "The kingdom of God is knowledge of the Holy Trinity coextensive with the substance of the mind and surpassing its incorruptibility" (*Praktikos* 3; trans. Sinkewicz). The kingdom of God, according to 1 Cor 15:28, will result from the kingdom of Christ, once Christ has handed it over to God the Father, that God may be "all in all." This is why in *On Faith* 7 Evagrius speaks first of the kingdom of Christ, allegorizing it with the whole of material knowledge, and then of the kingdom of God the Father, allegorizing it as immaterial contemplation and contemplation of the divinity. But he adds that Christ too is the *telos* no less than the Father is, since—as Origen too maintained—the whole Trinity is the ultimate *telos*. And Christ performs the resurrection from material knowledge to immaterial contemplation.

The notion that the kingdom of God will consist essentially in contemplation is inspired by Origen. In the dubious, but probably authentic,

Selected Passages on Psalms 144 he defined the kingdom of God as a contemplation of the past aeons. Evagrius in the present *kephalaion* highlights the role of the Spirit in the acquisition of knowledge; in his *Letter to Melania* too he speaks of this role, saying that the most perfect of the *logika* receive knowledge directly from the Spirit and the Son, whereas the less perfect need the material world as an intermediary.

4.41. Christ to human beings, before his coming, showed an angelic body; to the last, however, it is not that (spiritual) body that he has now that he has shown, but he has revealed to them that which they will have.

The manifestations of Christ before his incarnation in a mortal human body were in an angelic body (it is noteworthy that here the Syriac has *pgr' ml'ky'*, which seems to be a *contradictio in adiecto*, given that *pgr'* properly indicates a mortal body, which would seem incompatible with an angelic body; an explanation might be that the Old Testament apparitions of Christ, for example to Abraham, Isaac, or Lot, usually speak of a "human being" or "human beings"). Origen, like Evagrius here, interpreted christologically the three figures who appeared to Abraham; on the exegesis of these figures in early Christianity, see Bogdan Bucur, "The Early Christian Reception of Gen 18," *JECS* 23 (2015): 245–72. After his resurrection, Christ showed which bodies human beings will have at their own resurrection. Here, the word that indicates the body that Christ has now and that which humans will have at the resurrection is *gwšm'*, which indicates indeed an immortal body.

4.42. The promise of the "hundredfold gain" is the contemplation of beings, whereas "eternal life" is the knowledge of the Holy Trinity. "This is," I quote, "eternal life: that they may know You, the only true God."

The first scriptural reference, with the promise of the hundredfold gain already in this world and life eternal in the next to those who follow Jesus, is to Matt 19:29; the second, with the definition of eternal life as the knowledge of God, is to John 17:3, in Jesus's great farewell discourse (on the reception of this verse in patristic theologians, see my volume on John 13–17 [Ramelli, *John III*]). The highest form of knowledge, indeed, as Evagrius repeatedly states in these *kephalaia*, is the knowledge of God the Trinity, which is superior to the *theōria* of all beings. Those who follow

Jesus therefore receive the contemplation of beings in the present aeon and the knowledge of God the Trinity in the next.

4.43. Christ, who appeared to Jacob on the ladder, if he represents the natural contemplation, then the metaphor of the ladder gives indications concerning the path of the *praktikē*. But if he symbolizes the knowledge of the Unity, then the ladder is the image of all aeons.

This *kephalaion* connects back to *KG* 4.41, concerning the apparitions of Christ mentioned in the Old Testament. Evagrius interprets the angels in Jacob's vision of the ladder in Gen 28:12–13 as manifestations of Christ as well. As Origen often did, so does Evagrius too propose multiple possible interpretations of the same scriptural passage or detail. Here he offers that Christ in that vision can represent either the "natural *theōria*" or the superior "knowledge of the Unity." In the latter case, the ladder itself would be the symbolic representation of all aeons and all that is included in them, that is, of all that exists and has existed and will ever exist, at the very end of which sits God the Unity. Thus, while in *KG* 4.42 life in the aeons (ζωὴ αἰώνιος) is identified with the knowledge of God the Trinity, here the end of all aeons is identified with the knowledge of God the Unity. As in Origen, the sequence of the aeons becomes in this way a path that leads to God.

4.44. The Sabbath is the rest of the rational soul, in which it is naturally made not to trespass the boundaries of its nature.

In many *kephalaia* Evagrius offers the allegorical interpretation of cultic details in the Old Testament. Here he proposes that of the Sabbath, the seventh day of rest proclaimed by God and even observed by God himself in creation. In the Sabbath, Evagrius observes, the rational soul will not trespass the boundaries of its nature of rational creature. The rational soul will indeed trespass the boundaries of its creaturely nature only on the Sunday of the final θέωσις, and that by grace alone. On the eschatological Sabbath and Sunday, see also *KG* 4.26 above and the relevant commentary; cf. 3.68.

4.45. It is not those who worship (God) but those who offer them sacrifices that the divine powers reject. And this we have clearly learned in the (book of) Judges, with Manoah.

The reference is to Judg 13:15–21, where the angel of the Lord does not accept a sacrifice from Manoah and her husband, the future parents of Samson, for himself but rather exhorts them to burn a sacrifice to God. Angels, here called "the divine powers," do not want to become the object of worship, since they are creatures. The only legitimate object of worship is the Creator, God.

4.46. The "four corners" mean the four elements, and the object that has appeared symbolizes the thick world; and the various animals are the images of the order of the human beings. And this is what appeared to Peter on the roof.

The reference is to Peter's vision in Acts 10:11–16. The elements are those that constitute the material world: fire, water, earth, and air (the Syriac term is the transliteration of Greek στοιχεῖον). Evagrius has just spoken of them as the constituents of matter in *KG* 1.15–16; 2.40–41; and 3.23 (see commentaries above). The allegory of different moral kinds of human beings represented as animals was also dear to Origen. See Ramelli, "Mansuetudine, grazia e salvezza"; and, for the relation to Origen, see idem, *Christian Doctrine of Apokatastasis*, the section on the *Acts of Philip.*

4.47. With those who approach difficult subjects and want to write upon them the demon of anger battles night and day, the one who is accustomed to blinding the thought and depriving it of spiritual contemplation.

The action of demons on humans is a theme that is dear to Evagrius, and we have already encountered it several times. The effects of anger are here described in terms of a loss of spiritual sight. Evagrius here specifically speaks of the demon of anger; to all demons in general he attaches an excess of *thymos* in *KG* 1.68; 3.34; and perhaps 4.38; later he will resume this idea in *KG* 5.11 (see above and below, the relevant commentaries). The blinding effects of anger are denounced by Evagrius also in *Gnostikos* 5: "All virtues clear the road for the gnostic; but superior to all others is absence of anger. Indeed, one who has touched knowledge and is easily moved to anger is like a man who pierces himself in the eyes with a metal stylus" (trans. Dysinger, slightly modified).

4.48. The intelligible "turban" is faith that does not deflect and is not susceptible of fear.

The scriptural reference is to Exod 28:4, where a description of the priestly garments of Aaron is given: "These are the garments that they shall make: a pectoral, an ephod, a mantle, a coat of checker work, a turban, and a belt; they shall make holy garments for Aaron your brother and his sons to serve me as priests." As often, in the footsteps of Origen, Evagrius explains symbols and figures that appear in the Bible, especially the Old Testament, in an allegorical way, in reference to intelligible realities (what we could call noetic exegesis). In other *kephalaia* Evagrius will likewise allegorize other elements of the priestly garments in Exod 28:4—for instance, in *KG* 4.66 the intelligible pectoral of the high priest, in *KG* 4.69 the intelligible mantle, in *KG* 4.75 the intelligible ephod, and in *KG* 4.79 the intelligible belt of the high priest. Evagrius is likely to have had in mind the similar allegorization of the high-priestly garments offered by Gregory of Nyssa in *Life of Moses* 2.190–201. For a commentary on Gregory's passage, see now Ann Conway-Jones, *Gregory of Nyssa's Tabernacle Imagery in Its Jewish and Christian Contexts* (Oxford: Oxford University Press, 2014).

4.49. There is one among all pleasures that is coextensive with the constitution of the intellect: that which follows knowledge; for all of them will pass together with the aeon(s) to come.

All pleasures will pass, like all πάθη, at the end of time; only the intellectual pleasure that accompanies knowledge will remain, because this is not a πάθος. It is, rather, coextensive with the constitution, or σύστασις, of the *nous* in that it follows knowledge, the peculiar activity of the *nous*, or intellectual soul. Knowledge will not pass away with the passing away of the future aeon or aeons, in the eventual *apokatastasis*, and likewise the noetic pleasure that accompanies it will not pass away.

An analogous argument is developed by Gregory of Nyssa in his dialogue *On the Soul and the Resurrection* in reference to ἀγάπη, or charity-love: all πάθη will pass in the *telos*, in that they belong to the inferior faculties of the soul and do not belong to the very nature of the soul, which is the intellectual nature. They are external and posterior accretions, spurious. But ἀγάπη will not pass away in the *telos*, because ἀγάπη is no πάθος. It belongs to the intellectual soul itself. See my commentary in Ramelli, *Gregorio di Nissa: Sull'anima*; and idem, "Tears of Pathos." Proclus will distinguish a mortal soul (θνητή, consisting of the nutritive, perceptive, and appetitive life: φυτική, αἰσθητική, ὀρεκτική ζωή) from the immortal soul (ἀθάνατος). The former is born subsequently, together with the body (ἀπογεννᾶται μετὰ τοῦ σώματος), while the latter exists prior to the body and is bound to the body (ἐνδεῖται) only at a certain point (*Commentary on Plato's Timaeus* 3.321.25–32).

That Evagrius's argument here is exactly parallel to that of Gregory of Nyssa concerning ἀγάπη is confirmed by the immediately following *kephalaion*, in which Evagrius precisely refers to ἀγάπη and to its permanence in the *telos*, exactly on the grounds that this belongs to the intellect proper. It seems to me that this is one of the many instances in which Evagrius is inspired by Gregory Nyssen, who is likely to have had on him much more influence than is normally assumed (see Ilaria Ramelli, "Evagrius and Gregory: Nazianzen or Nyssen? A Remarkable Issue That Bears on the Cappadocian (and Origenian) Influence on Evagrius," *GRBS* 53 [2013]: 117–37; and Corrigan, *Evagrius and Gregory*; but a systematic work on Gregory's influence on Evagrius is still missing).

4.50. There is one good kind of love, which is forever: that which true knowledge chooses, and it is said to be inseparable from the intellect.

This *kephalaion* is parallel to the preceding and finds a very close correspondence in Gregory of Nyssa, who in turn was inspired by Origen on the permanence of charity-love, ἀγάπη, in the eventual *apokatastasis* (see above, the commentary on *KG* 4.49). Just as with the pleasure of which Evagrius has spoken in *KG* 4.49, likewise ἀγάπη here is associated with true knowledge and the *nous* that pursues true knowledge. In *Praktikos* 81 and 84 too, Evagrius talks of love as the offspring of *apatheia* and the end of the *praktikē*, ethical life (see Corrigan, *Evagrius and Gregory*, ch. 9). Love is indeed described by Evagrius as the source of all virtues and of *apatheia*, which is the goal of *praktikē* (*Eulogius* 30.32). Evagrius thus posits a deep interrelation between charity-love and *apatheia*, and thereby between love and *praktikē*. In the present *kephalaion*, however, love is connected not simply to *praktikē* but to knowledge (gnosis), which for Evagrius is one step further and bears on the *telos*, and this is remarkable because this conception goes in the direction of Origen and Gregory of Nyssa, who located love straight in the ultimate *telos*.

Bardaisan of Edessa, whose treatise against Fate was known both to Gregory of Nyssa and to Diodore of Tarsus in the time of Evagrius, and may have been known to Evagrius as well, likewise stated that the good kind of love endures forever and is the love of truth—an idea that is strikingly close to that expressed in the present *kephalaion*: "one thing is concupiscence and another is love, and one thing is friendship and another is conspiracy. And we should easily understand that the ardor of love is called concupiscence; now, even if in it there is the pleasure of a moment, however, it is far different from the love of truth, whose beatitude, forever, is not destroyed and is not annihilated" (my translation from Ramelli, ed., *Bardaisan on Free Will*). Here "love of truth" can either be a Syriac turn of phrase for "true love," conceived in opposition to ephemeral passion or concupiscence, or mean "love for truth, loving truth" such as a philosopher and theologian can have. This would also explain the declared eternity of this love, since for the Christian Bardaisan, Truth itself is Christ (in an important fragment Bardaisan describes Christ's mission as "he taught the truth and was lifted up"; see Ramelli, *Bardaisan of Edessa*, 229–31). This kind of love, eternal and incorruptible, whose fruition is inexhaustible, is the same as Origen saw allegorized in the Song of Songs, which in his commentary is interpreted as the expression of the love between the soul and Christ and between the church and Christ.

The Greek text that corresponds to this Syriac *kephalaion*, incomplete, is preserved by Leontius of Byzantium, *Against the Nestorians and the Eutychians* 1 (PG 86.1:1285AB).

4.51. In the secondary natural contemplation, some are said to be leaders, and some to be subject to leaders, according to necessity. But in the Unity there will be no leaders, nor (others) submitted to leaders, but all of them will be gods.

The final *apokatastasis* will culminate in the glorious θέωσις. When all rational creatures are deified, and unified among them and to God (according to the characterization of the *apokatastasis* as θέωσις and Unity that is already clear in Origen), there will be no room for any hierarchy anymore. The final sentence, that all will be gods, may echo John 10:34–35, interpreted in an eschatological sense: "Jesus answered them, 'Is it not written in your law, "I said, you are gods"? God called them gods to whom the word of God came.'" Jesus in turn refers to Ps 82:6, where God proclaims: "You are gods, you are all children of the Most High."

4.52. The intelligible plate is the knowledge of the Holy Trinity.

The priestly πέταλον, a reference to Exod 28:36, was a plate upon which the name of the Lord was engraved. It was worn by Aaron and the Jewish high priests on their foreheads. Since it represents God, its intellectual meaning is the knowledge of God the Trinity, the highest form of knowledge. This is one of the many *kephalaia* in which Evagrius offers the intellectual meaning of cultic details in the Old Testament, such as circumcision, the high priest's turban (on which the πέταλον itself was fixed), and so on (see above, the commentary on *KG* 4.48).

4.53. Knowledge is diminished and descends among those who build up the tower with evilness and with false doctrines. Ignorance and confusion of ideas occur to them, just as also to those who were building the tower.

Once again, Evagrius insists on the necessity that knowledge and virtue go together, just as knowing the Good and choosing it go together in his ethical intellectualism (see especially my commentary on *KG* 4.28, above); knowledge cannot be joined to vice, or it will ruin, like the tower of Babel in Gen 11:4–9, a passage that was already the object of Philo's allegory in *De confusione linguarum* (*On the Confusion of Languages*). The Babel episode symbolizes the beginning of ignorance and confusion. The gift of speaking in tongues conferred by the Holy Spirit to the first followers of Christ at Pentecost is a kind of reversal of the division of languages and the beginning of incomprehensibility at Babel, and Pentecost is repeatedly mentioned by Evagrius as containing a great mystery (see above, *KG* 2.38–42 and 4.35, and the relevant commentaries).

4.54. Words in all languages make names known, and objects in turn are known. Thus, the words of the apostles, which were pronounced in the Hebrew language, were transformed into the words and names of different languages, and thanks to this all peoples have known what has been revealed.

That Evagrius saw the Pentecost gift of tongues as a reversal of the Babel differentiation of languages is confirmed by the very fact that the present *kephalaion* on the Pentecost gift of languages comes immediately after *KG* 4.53, which refers to the Babel episode (see the relevant commentary above). Evagrius indeed in the present *kephalaion* is referring again to Acts 2:4–12, of which he has already spoken in *KG* 4.35 (see the relevant commentary above):

> And they were all filled with the Holy Spirit and began to speak in other tongues, as the Spirit gave them utterance. Now there were dwelling in Jerusalem Jews, devout men from every nation under heaven. And at this sound the multitude came together, and they were bewildered, because each one heard them speaking in his own language. And they were amazed and wondered, saying, "Are not all these who are speaking Galileans? And how is it that we hear, each of us in his own native language? Parthians and Medes and Elamites and residents of Mesopotamia, Judea and Cappadocia, Pontus and Asia, Phrygia and Pamphylia, Egypt and the parts of Libya belonging to Cyrene, and visitors from Rome, both Jews and proselytes, Cretans and Arabians, we hear them telling in our own tongues the mighty works of God." And all were amazed and perplexed, saying to one another, "What does this mean?" (RSV)

Evagrius reflects here on the passage from language to knowledge.

4.55. The words of virtues are the mirrors of virtues. Now, the one who listens to the words but does not put them into practice, this one sees virtue as in a shadow, virtue, which is the visage of the soul.

I have highlighted several times that for Evagrius the interrelation of knowledge and virtue is fundamental; here he meditates on the correspondence between language, knowledge, and virtue. The definition of virtue as the face of the soul refers to the manifestation of the intellectual soul and its knowledge in the choice of the Good. Knowledge of virtue without the practice of virtue is false knowledge, just an appearance of knowledge.

4.56. The intelligible ephod is the condition of the rational soul in which the human being is accustomed to practice in it his or her virtues.

Here is another of the long series of *kephalaia* in which Evagrius, in the footsteps of Origen, interprets a cultic detail of the Old Testament (here Aaron's ephod in Exod 28:4) on the intelligible plane. The ephod is interpreted allegorically as a sort of *habitus*, that of practicing virtues, the importance of which Evagrius has just highlighted in *KG* 4.55 (see above, the commentary). The same interpretation in terms of *habitus* will appear again in *KG* 4.75 (see the relevant commentary below). Gregory of Nyssa, too, had interpreted the ephod as virtues in *Life of Moses* 2.190, 196. More generally he had interpreted the priestly vestments as "the graces of virtues" in *On the Lord's Prayer* 3.

4.57. Christ was seen as Creator in the multiplication of the bread, in the wine of the wedding, and in the eyes of the blind man by nature.

In the three miracles that are mentioned here (that of the multiplication of the loaves in Matt 14:15–21; 15:32–38 and parallels, in Syriac literally called the miracle of "the bread of quantity"; that of the wedding feast at Cana in John 1:10; and that of the man who was born blind in John 9:1–7) Christ manifests himself as the Creator in that he has created both the bread and the wine and the blind's sight out of nothing. Christ-Logos is indeed creator, according to the Johannine Prologue. In Jesus's miracles Evagrius finds the manifestation of the creative function of the Logos. Origen used precisely the creative function of Christ-Logos to affirm his restorative absolute power: "no being is incurable for the one who created it" (*On First Principles* 3.6.5); if Christ heals the incurable, this means that he is also the Creator—with this Origen was also correcting Plato's assertion that some sinners are "incurable" (see Ramelli, *Christian Doctrine of Apokatastasis*, the chapter on Origen and the conclusions). Especially in the last words about the blind man, Evagrius seems to be drawing on Origen's connection between creation and healing by Christ-Logos-God.

4.58. God, while creating rational creatures, was not even in anything, whereas while creating the corporeal nature and the aeons that derive from it, was in his Christ.

Evagrius goes on to reflect on the creative function of Christ-Logos, which he has underlined in *KG* 4.57 (see above, the relevant commentary) and which he applies here to the creation of the corporeal nature and the relevant aeons. The first creation, that is, the intelligible creation that gave rise to the *logika* as creatures and substances of their own, was not "in Christ." This creation is also ascribed to God, but God was "in nothing" during the creation of the *logika* (an expression that probably aims at stressing the notion of *creatio ex nihilo*), whereas God was in Christ during the creation of the corporeal nature, to which the biblical account of creation refers. Even when God was in nothing, however, Christ as God was in God.

4.59. If it is true that an essence is not said to be superior or inferior to another essence, and, on the other hand, a devil/demon has been called

by our Savior worse than another devil, it is clear that it is not in their essence that devils are evil.

Evagrius picks up a point that was forcefully made by Origen in his polemic against the "Gnostics," especially against Valentinianism: the differentiation of rational creatures into angels, humans, and demons depends on the choices of their free will, and not on their nature, which is the same for all of them. From this argument Origen even developed his whole theodicy and ultimately his eschatology (see, with several arguments, Ramelli, "La coerenza della soteriologia origeniana"; idem, "Origen, Bardaisan, and the Origin of Universal Salvation"; and idem, "Origen, Patristic Philosophy, and Christian Platonism"). Evagrius takes up this point, here arguing very succinctly through a syllogism:

> major premise: no essence or nature is superior or inferior to another;
> minor premise: now, a demon can be worse (or better) than another;
> conclusion: therefore, it is not by their nature that demons are evil.

Indeed, demons are evil on account of their evil moral choices and not of their nature, which was created by God.

The scriptural reference to Jesus calling a demon worse than another is to Luke 11:26.

4.60. To those who blaspheme against the Creator and speak ill of this mortal body of our soul, who will show them the grace that they have received, while they are subject to passions, to have been joined to such an instrument? But to witness in favor of my words are those who in visions of dreams are scared by demons, and when they awake they take refuge as among angels, when the mortal body suddenly awakes.

The mortal body is a gift that God has given to human souls in the present condition; being created by God, it cannot be evil. Here, as elsewhere, Evagrius calls it an "instrument," the transliteration of Greek ὄργανον, of the soul, with an Aristotelian terminology (in *KG* 1.67; 2.48, 80; 3.20, 45, 51; see the relevant commentaries above; see also below, *KG* 6.72 and the commentary on it). According to Evagrius, indeed, who agreed with Origen, Methodius, and Nyssen on this score, its very mortality is providential and is a good, in that it puts a limit to sin and paves the way for restoration (see Ramelli, *Christian Doctrine of Apokatastasis*, the chapters on Origen, Methodius, and Gregory). As is rightly noted by Sebastian Brock (personal correspondence), the penultimate line of the Syriac in Guillaumont's edition has a misprint: it should read ܕܠܘܬ ܡܠܐܟ̈ܐ.

4.61. The elucidation is the explanation of commandments for the comfort of simple people.

I prefer to render "elucidation" rather than "interpretation" (chosen by Guillaumont [p. 163]: "interprétation," followed by Dysinger and Fr. Theophanes, who both render "interpretation"), first of all because it is closer to the meaning of the relevant Syriac word, and because Evagrius is here referring to an explanation that is not an allegorical interpretation. Like Clement and Origen, indeed, he reserves the allegorical, noetic interpretation of Scripture to the advanced, while leaving the literal, historical, or moral elucidation to the "simple" (see Ilaria L. E. Ramelli, "Origen and the Stoic Allegorical Tradition: Continuity and Innovation," *Invigilata Lucernis* 28 [2006]: 195–226).

4.62. It is necessary for the intellect to be instructed either on incorporeal beings or on bodies of any sorts, or else simply to see objects. For these things are its life. But it will not see incorporeal realities when it is contaminated in its free will, nor will it see spiritual bodies when it is deprived of the instrument that shows it sense-perceptible objects. Therefore, (as for) those who despise the Creator and also disparage our body, what will give them to a dead soul for contemplation?

The life of the *nous* is vision and knowledge, but once again Evagrius does not disjoin knowledge from virtue: a lack of virtue determines an impairment of knowledge in the *nous*. Evagrius has already spoken in the *KG* about the life of the intellect: in *KG* 1.64 he has mentioned what is true life for a rational creature; in *KG* 1.73 and 4.42 he has equated life with knowledge; and in *KG* 1.40–41 he has identified the life of the soul with virtue and knowledge—the opposite is the illness and death of the soul. In the present *kephalaion* Evagrius's expression "dead soul" might seem to be a *contradictio in adiecto*, the soul being immortal, but Evagrius is probably referring to the spiritual notion of the death of the soul, which has a rich tradition behind it (see my commentaries on *KG* 1.40–41 and 2.15, above;

and Ramelli, "Spiritual Weakness, Illness, and Death") and was emphasized especially by Origen. In his *Dialogue with Heraclides* he insisted that "the soul is mortal of the real death." Thus, here Evagrius observes that a soul that is dead because its free will is contaminated cannot enjoy contemplation either, which is the life of the intellectual soul. Such a soul is deprived of its proper life and is therefore dead.

4.63. The "mercy seat" is spiritual knowledge, which leads the souls of the *praktikoi*.

This is another of the many *kephalaia* in which Evagrius interprets in an intelligible way the cultic prescriptions of the Old Testament. Here in particular he is referring to the "mercy seat" (ἱλαστήριον, "propitiatory") of Exod 25:17, which is taken to be a representation of the highest kind of knowledge: spiritual knowledge. Both Origen (in *Commentary on Romans* 3.8.3–5 and elsewhere) and Gregory of Nyssa (*Life of Moses* 2.182–183) had interpreted the propitiatory spiritually as Christ. Evagrius allegorizes the propitiatory as spiritual knowledge, but in *KG* 4.18 he closely associates Christ with the spiritual knowledge of the holy Unity (see also 4.21 and the relevant commentaries).

4.64. If it is true that, as for the ancient Israel, many people who were not from Israel accompanied it, perhaps also with the new Israel: many have come out of Egypt, haven't they?

The historical Israel is here assimilated to the new Israel, the elect people. Many people composing the former were not Israelites themselves; likewise, many composing the latter come from "Egypt" (with a reference to Exod 12:38), traditionally interpreted (by Philo and Origen; see Sarah J. K. Pearce, *The Land of the Body: Studies in Philo's Representation of Egypt* [WUNT 208; Tübingen: Mohr Siebeck, 2007]; and Ramelli, "Philosophical Allegoresis of Scripture") as the land of vice and captivity to passion. But they can convert to become the true Israel. Indeed, they will accompany the true Israel. Evagrius seems to be alluding to the inclusion of sinners among the elect, which will take place after the purification of sinners in the eschatological times. In this case, this would be another allusion to the doctrine of *apokatastasis*. The translations of Dysinger and Fr. Theophanes follow the French version of Guillaumont and do not grasp the rhetorical nature of the negation (Guillaumont [p. 165]: "Si l'Israël ancien, beaucoup qui n'étaient pas d'Israël l'ont accompagné, est-ce qu'aussi avec l'Israël nouveau beaucoup d'entre les Égyptiens ne sont pas sortis?"; Dysinger: "If ancient Israel, of whom many were not [part] of Israel, accompanied him, is it also thus with the new Israel—that many among the Egyptians did not go out?"; Fr. Theophanes: "If many who were not of Israel have accompanied the ancient Israel, is it that, with the new Israel also, many from among the Egyptians have not gone out?").

4.65. The whole rational nature is divided into three parts, and life reigns over one, death and life over the other one, and only death over the third.

Here, just as in *KG* 4.62, Evagrius is referring to spiritual life and spiritual death, the latter being the death of the soul determined by evil. It is clear, therefore, that the three groups described in this *kephalaion* are angels, humans, and demons (the three groups of *logika* distinguished by Origen after the fall). Spiritual death takes hold of demons completely and of human beings partially. Angels are immune on account of their goodness.

4.66. The intelligible pectoral/girdle is the hidden knowledge of the mysteries of God.

Here is yet another of the many short *kephalaia* in which Evagrius interprets in an intelligible way the cultic prescriptions of the Old Testament. Here he is referring to the "pectoral" or "breastplate" of Exod 28:4. The "breast" suggests the idea of concealment; this is why Evagrius relates it to the secret knowledge of the mysteries of God. It must be noted that Exod 28:4 (cf. 28:40 for "girdle") in the Septuagint has "pectoral," but the Syriac translation of Evagrius here has "girdle," which is the reading of the Peshitta. It seems probable that Evagrius's original Greek text followed the Septuagint but that the Syriac translator checked the biblical text against the Peshitta and followed the latter. Gregory of Nyssa interpreted the pectoral as representing virtues and steadfastness in the Good but also as a "covering of the heart" that symbolizes contemplation (*Life of Moses* 2.199–200). This may easily have influenced Evagrius's exegesis.

4.67. The objects that, by means of sense perception, fall under the soul's (awareness) move it in order to have it receive their forms, because this is the work of the intellect: to know, in the same way as in the case of ani-

mals that breathe from outside. And it falls into danger unless it works, if it is true that, according to the saying of Solomon the wise, "The light of the Lord is the breathing of human beings."

As Evagrius has already stated in *KG* 4.62, the life of the intellect is knowledge (see the relevant commentary above). This is so vital an activity for the intellectual soul that it is here assimilated to breathing (also through the reference to Prov 20:27). If an intellectual soul renounces this activity, it falls into death. For a classification of creatures on the basis of the ways they breathe, see above, *KG* 4.37 and the relevant commentary.

4.68. This mortal body belonging to the soul is symbolized by a house; sense perceptions are symbolized by the windows, through which the intellect observes and sees sense-perceptible realities.

Evagrius constructs here a gnoseological metaphor: the mortal body is represented by means of the image of a house; the intellect is inside, and the windows represent sense perception, in its various organs, through which external sense-perceptible objects are apprehended by the *nous*. For what knows is the *nous* and not the senses. This is a point on which Gregory of Nyssa, with his sister and teacher Macrina, insisted particularly in the dialogue *On the Soul and the Resurrection*, very well known to Evagrius.

4.69. The intelligible mantle is the spiritual teaching that gathers those in error.

This is another of the many *kephalaia* in which Evagrius interprets the cultic prescriptions of the Old Testament on the intelligible plane, in the footsteps of Origen. Here he is referring to the "mantle" or "coat" of the high priest as described in Exod 28:4 (a passage on which Evagrius comments more than once). Those who are wandering in error are dispersed; only true teaching can put an end to this state.

4.70. It is not for everyone to say, "I will take my soul out of prison," but this belongs to those who, because of the purity of their soul, can, even without this mortal body, get close to the contemplation of beings.

The scriptural reference to the liberation from prison is to Ps 141:8. It is interesting that the mortal body is equated to the "prison" of the psalm, according to imagery that was already present in Plato and was taken up by Gregory of Nyssa in his Christian *Phaedo*, his dialogue *On the Soul and the Resurrection*. Evagrius is on the same line when he presents the soul that, free from the bonds of the body, can more easily attend to *theōria*. See my commentary in Ramelli, *Gregorio di Nissa: Sull'anima*. Evagrius, like Origen and Nyssen, integrates Plato's vision and biblical quotations. The purity of the soul refers to the intellectual soul, when it is not contaminated by passions pertaining to the inferior faculties of the soul. Contemplation (which corresponds to Plato's contemplation of the Ideas) is a state that Evagrius too, like Plato and Nyssen (in *On the Soul and the Resurrection*), presents as a *praeparatio mortis*. See again my commentary in Ramelli, *Gregorio di Nissa: Sull'anima*.

The Greek text of this *kephalaion* is preserved in *Selected Passages on Psalms* 141:8 (PG 12:1668B).

4.71. If one of the senses fails, it strongly saddens those who are deprived of it. Who will be able to bear the privation of all of them, which will happen all of a sudden and will liberate it from the wonder at (all) bodies?

I have rendered "all bodies" for the Syriac plural *gwšm'*, which designates immortal bodies, and occasionally all bodies, mortal and immortal, when taken in an inclusive sense. The privation of all senses together will occur, as it seems, at death. Evagrius, like Origen, Methodius, and Nyssen, highlights the positive aspect of physical death. See above, *KG* 1.82 and 4.60, for the conception of physical death as providential. In the absence of sense perception, we shall cease to admire bodies and conceivably shall reserve our wonder for spiritual realities. An alternative, possible but less probable, translation of the last sentence is: "that (exists) in (spiritual) bodies."

4.72. The intelligible breeches are the mortification of the concupiscible faculty, which takes place thanks to the knowledge of God.

The scriptural reference is to Exod 28:42. This is one of the many short *kephalaia* in which Evagrius, following Origen, offers an allegorical interpretation of cultic prescriptions and objects in the Old Testament, on the intelligible plane. This *kephalaion*, in particular, is close to Evagrius's interpretation of the intelligible circumcision in *KG* 4.12 (see above, the relevant commentary); both the breeches and circumcision symbolize the restraining of passions. Evagrius, as ever, follows Plato's tripartition of the soul. In order to overcome passions, which are related to the two inferior parts of the soul (*epithymētikon*, *thymikon*), Evagrius states that the knowledge of God is necessary. Once again *praktikē*—aiming at *apatheia* and virtue—and gnosis go together; Evagrius constantly warns that they are interdependent.

4.73. The one whose intellect is with the Lord all the time, and whose irascible part is full of humility thanks to its remembering God, and whose concupiscible/appetitive part is entirely oriented toward the Lord, it is for such a person not to fear his or her enemies, those which circulate outside our mortal bodies.

This *kephalaion* confirms the preceding one: it is the knowledge of God and closeness to God that determine the eradication of passions. Evagrius here depicts the ideal situation of a person who is entirely oriented toward God in the three components of her soul: intellect (*nous*), irascible faculty (*thymikon*), and concupiscible faculty (*epithymia* or *epithymētikon*), according to Plato's division of the soul. The enemies that the person who has attained this must not fear are most probably demons, with their tempting activity.

4.74. Those among the saints who now have been released from bodies and have joined the choirs of angels, it is clear that these ones also came to our world/aeon because of the economy.

Origen also thought that some *noes* became incarnated in a mortal body not because of a fault of their own and thus for their need for an education and purification, since they should have remained among the angels, but out of sheer generosity, in order to assist the process of spiritual education and salvation of other rational creatures (e.g., *On First Principles* 2.9.7; *Commentary on John* 2.31.187f.). This idea is found again in the Neoplatonist Iamblichus, who (in *On the Soul* 29 Finamore and Dillon) expounded a doctrine that has no correspondence in Plato and therefore would not seem to come from him: some souls do not descend into the material realm as a consequence of sins they must expiate, but they descend even if they are "immaculate," for the sake of salvation, purification, and perfection of this realm: "The soul that descends for the salvation, purification, and perfection [ἐπὶ σωτηρίᾳ καὶ καθάρσει καὶ τελειότητι] of this realm is immaculate in its descent." Origen displays the very same notion and possibly inspired Iamblichus. This is what Evagrius also states: such rational creatures have come into this world/aeon for the sake of the salvific economy (the Syriac word is the perfect correspondent of Greek οἰκονομία).

4.75. The intelligible ephod is the justice of the soul with which the human person customarily adorns herself with irreproachable works and doctrines.

In *KG* 4.56 Evagrius offered an allegorical interpretation of Aaron's ephod in Exod 28:4 in terms of virtuous *habitus* (see the commentary there). Here one virtue, justice, is especially highlighted and related again to a *habitus*. Justice has both a theoretical and a practical component: right doctrines and right works. This is consistent with Evagrius's idea—which I have highlighted already many times—that knowledge and virtue go together, which is in turn one of the expressions of the ethical intellectualism that he shares with Origen and Gregory of Nyssa. Gregory also singled out justice as the noetic counterpart of the high priest's garments, but more with reference to the shoulder pieces (*Life of Moses* 2.198).

4.76. The one who is liable to passions and prays that his departure may occur soon is similar to a man who is ill and asks the joiner to break up his bed soon.

The present life, which takes place in a mortal body, should be seen as an opportunity for purification and moral improvement, which is connected with the discourse that Evagrius has developed in *KG* 4.74 (see above, the relevant commentary). It is good to exit the mortal body once one is purified from passions, and not while one is still liable to passions—clearly because, if one has not been purified in this life, one will necessarily have to be purified in the other world. The present *kephalaion* of course relies on the notion of illness and death of the soul, which was already present in the New Testament and in Platonism and was especially dear to Clement and Origen, who elaborated the doctrine of Christ-Physician in relation to it. The same notion is at work in *KG* 1.41 (see the relevant commentary).

The Greek of this *kephalaion* is found in Dorotheus, *Didaskaliai* 12 (PG 88:1749D–1752A).

4.77. Objects are outside the intellect, whereas the contemplation concerning them is constituted inside it. This is not the case, however, with the Holy Trinity, for it is only essential knowledge.

In the case of human intellects, there is a dualism between the knower and the known object: objects of intellectual knowledge are outside the *nous*, but their *theōria* is inside the *nous*. In the case of the Trinity, there is no such dualism, since the Trinity itself is substantial or essential knowledge, as Evagrius has also declared in *KG* 1.89 and 2.47 (see above, the relevant commentaries). See Ramelli, "Divine as an Inaccessible Epistemological Object." Of course, in the case of the Trinity the question revolves around the transcendence of God in respect to both the objects of God's knowledge and the subjects of the knowledge of God. The Trinity, being essential knowledge also in the sense that it knows all beings in their essence or substance, is creative knowledge, because by knowing their essence, it immediately constitutes them in their substance. Instead of immediacy, creaturely intellectual knowledge is marked by dualism, as Plotinus also stressed (see my "The Divine as Inaccessible Object").

4.78. Christ is inherited and inherits, whereas the Father is only inherited.

Evagrius already insisted on the notion of the inheritance of Christ and distinguished what Christ inherits and Christ as the inheritance itself, in *KG* 4.18 and elsewhere, especially in 4.9, in which he said that Christ (qua union of human and divine nature and synthesis of all humanity) will inherit God the Logos (divine nature, which is also inherited by all humanity through Christ; see above, the relevant commentaries). The Father, who is transcendent and has no mediation, is the inheritance of Christ and of all those who are coheirs with Christ, whereas Christ, who is God and Logos and a *logikon*, a human being, is both inherited by the *logika* and inherits. At the same time, Christ inherits all the rational creatures who will be submitted to him and will constitute his kingdom, which he will present to the Father (1 Cor 15:28). See Ramelli, "Clement's Notion of the Logos."

4.79. The intelligible belt of the high priest is the humility of the irascible faculty, which strengthens the intellect.

Here is yet another short *kephalaion* dealing with the allegorical interpretation of cultic details of the Old Testament on the intellectual plane.

Here the reference is to Exod 28:4, on which Evagrius has already commented more than once. Evagrius relies here again on the Platonic tripartition of the soul into intellect (or rational soul, *logikon*), irascible faculty (*thymikon*), and concupiscible or appetitive faculty (*epithymētikon*). The second and third part are prone to passions, and the way to overcome the passion of the *thymikon* is here identified with humility, which tames the irascible tendency of this faculty (particularly dangerous according to Evagrius, since it leads the soul to acquire demonic traits). At the same time, this disposition strengthens and fortifies the *nous*, the intellectual part of the soul.

4.80. It is not God the Logos, primarily, who descended to Sheol and ascended to heaven, but Christ, the one who has the Logos in himself. For the mortal, ordinary body is not susceptible of knowledge, whereas God is known.

The distinction between the Logos qua God and Christ has already been introduced by Evagrius in *KG* 4.9, where he also uses the same expression, "God the Logos" or "the Logos-God" (see above, my commentary on *KG* 4.9, where I also argue against an emendation of "God the Logos" into "the Logos of God," with the addition of a *nota genetivi*). Here the distinction is based on Christ's death, *descensus ad inferos*, resurrection, and ascension. It is not God the Logos that has died, has descended to the dead in Sheol, and has risen, but Christ, in that he took up humanity and more specifically a human mortal body. Otherwise he could not even have died. At the same time, in addition to having humanity in himself, Christ has also God the Logos in himself, in his own double nature, human and divine.

4.81. Every contemplation, from the point of view of its intellection, is immaterial and incorporeal. However, that which possesses or does not possess objects that fall under it is said to be material or immaterial.

Every *theōria* is immaterial (without ὕλη, of which the Syriac word is the transliteration) and incorporeal (without any body, including immortal bodies, or *gwšm'*) in its intellectual content, although its objects, which are either material or immaterial, determine its being material or immaterial.

4.82. The "refuge" is the mortal *praktikon* body of the soul that is liable to passions, which liberates it from the demons that surround it.

Evagrius is here referring to Josh 20:2–3, concerning the "cities of refuge" established for sinners, in another of the several *kephalaia* in which he interprets details of the Old Testament in an allegorical way, in reference to the *nous* and human soul in general. The intelligible refuge is a refuge from demons, which torment the soul by means of passions. Note the positive role ascribed here by Evagrius to the mortal body, provided that it is exercised in the *praktikē*. This positivity relates to what Evagrius was saying in *KG* 4.76 about the sojourn in the mortal body as an opportunity for purification and improvement (see the relevant commentary above).

4.83. The one who escapes the mortal body while he is not pure should consider whether the relative of the killed person will stand at the door and will accuse him.

From the exegetical point of view this *kephalaion* is the continuation of the preceding one: that one commented on Josh 20:2–3 on the "cities of refuge"; this one comments on Josh 20:4–6: the unintentional killer "shall flee to one of these cities and shall stand at the entrance of the gate of the city, and explain his case to the elders of that city; then they shall take him into the city, and give him a place, and he shall remain with them. And if the avenger of blood pursues him, they shall not give up the slayer into his hand; because he killed his neighbor unwittingly, having had no enmity against him in times past" (RSV). But this *kephalaion* is also connected to *KG* 4.76, in which Evagrius explains that it is better not to leave the body until the soul is not purified, otherwise one will still need purification after death (see above, the relevant commentary).

4.84. Knowledge is not a quality [lit. "mixture"] of bodies, nor are colors qualities (mixtures) of incorporeal realities, but knowledge (is a quality) of incorporeal realities, whereas color (is a quality) of bodies in an accidental way.

When he says that knowledge is not a quality of bodies, or is not constituted by a mixture of bodies, Evagrius is speaking not only of mortal bodies (*pgr'*) but of bodies in general. Knowledge is in fact a quality of incorporeal realities, such as the *nous*. A color is a combination of bodily components, and this should be kept distinct from the intellectual plane, where knowledge is a combination of incorporeal components.

4.85. Demons overcome the soul when passions multiply, and render the human being insensitive while they quench the faculties of his sense organs, lest, when one of the objects that are close is found, it cause the intellect to come up as from a deep pit.

Following the line of Origen, who thought that demons tempt but cannot determine human free will, Evagrius has already spoken in several *kephalaia* of the tempting action of demons against human souls. Now he observes that passions (πάθη) are the instruments of this temptation; they occlude sense perception, which is the beginning of knowledge. Indeed, passions are opposite to knowledge, which Evagrius has defined as the life of the intellectual soul. Demons, through passions, endeavor to kill the intellectual soul.

4.86. The intellect that possesses a body does not see incorporeal realities, and when it will be without a body, it will not see bodies.

Evagrius resumes the whole discourse of Plato, taken up by Gregory of Nyssa in his dialogue *On the Soul and the Resurrection*, on the soul that contemplates the Ideas all the better the further it is removed from the body and from passions (see Ramelli, *Gregorio di Nissa: Sull'anima*). The Syriac word for "body", here is *gwšm'*, which indicates that Evagrius is meaning not only mortal bodies but also spiritual and immortal bodies. The question at stake here is "vision" proper—of course, noetic vision, since the subject is the intellect. The *nous*, while it is in a body, cannot see incorporeal realities; in the *telos*, it will no longer be in a body, and it will not be able to see bodies anymore.

4.87. Every contemplation is seen in an object that underlies it, apart from the Holy Trinity.

In *KG* 4.81 Evagrius has already drawn a difference between material and immaterial *theōriai*, depending on their objects, after stating that, from the point of view of the intellections themselves, all *theōriai* are immaterial. Now he remarks that the *theōria* of the Trinity is the only one that is not seen in an object underlying it. It is spiritual contemplation and precisely "essential knowledge," which for *logika* is achieved in the Unity of the final θέωσις. There, there will be no duality of subject and object. The Trinity itself knows in an essential way, being the creator of the essence of all beings; this is why it can know all of them not from the outside but in their very essence. On dual and nondual knowledge, the former being of the intellect and the latter of the Trinity, see above, *KG* 4.77 and the relevant commentary.

4.88. Among the three altars of knowledge, there are two that have a circle, whereas one is seen without a circle.

The idea conveyed by this *kephalaion* may be that two kinds of knowledge are circumscribed and limited, whereas the third is unlimited. The two limited kinds of knowledge seem to be the knowledge of corporeal realities and that of incorporeal creatures, those that Evagrius calls secondary and primary; the third kind of knowledge is that of the Trinity, which is unlimited just as the Trinity is, which is "essential knowledge" (see above, *KG* 4.77 and 4.87, with the relevant commentaries). The infinity of God is a trait that characterizes Gregory of Nyssa and goes back to Origen. On the three altars, see *KG* 2.57–58 above and the relevant commentaries.

4.89. Who will expound the grace of God? And who will investigate the *logoi* of Providence, and how Christ leads the rational nature through various aeons, toward union in the holy Unity?

Evagrius completely agrees with Origen that the final *apokatastasis* will be made possible, primarily, by the grace of God and not by just a metaphysical necessity. Origen, in his treatise *On Prayer* and in his *Commentary on Romans* (from the catenae, 22.1), combines different Pauline quotations (Rom 6:23; Eph 2:7; Heb 9:26) when he states: "Eternal life is a free gift [χάρισμα] from God: it does not come from us, but it is God who has bestowed on us this present [Θεοῦ τὸ δῶρον]." Christ is the main agent of God's grace: he accomplishes the action of Providence—that is, he brings all rational creatures through the sequence of aeons to the *telos*—at the end of all aeons. Evagrius evidently adopts Origen's idea of the sequence of aeons followed by the end of all aeons in the absolute eternity (ἀϊδιότης) of *apokatastasis*, which is characterized by a perfect unity (in accord with Jesus's solemn prayer for unity at the Last Supper, as recounted in John and of which the Origenian Fathers made so much; see my volume on John 13–17 [Ramelli, *John III*]). In this passage it is clear that, in Evagrius's view, just as in Origen's, the eventual *apokatastasis* results from the work of Christ-Logos and God's providence and grace and is not analogous to "pagan" doctrines that render the restoration of all things a consequence of necessity (the latter accusation was leveled during the "Origenistic controversy" and is sometimes repeated even in modern debates).

That eternal life that overcomes any death and characterizes universal *apokatastasis* comes from divine grace is made clear by Origen in several passages, in particular in *Commentary on Romans* 5.6.65, where he is commenting on Rom 5:20: Paul "shows that the remedy brought about by Christ's grace is much greater [than Adam's sin].... Christ's grace has overflowed.... This is the grace that will have chased sin out of Christ's kingdom [i.e., during his eschatological reign], and along with sin death too will necessarily have been thrown out, that grace, through justice, may finally regain its full power in us, and in the place of death there may be established life eternal.... Where there were sin and death now there are grace, justice, and eternal life," *Multo maiora ostendit esse quae per gratiam Christi ad remedium conlata sunt.... Superabundauit gratia Christi ... gratia ergo est quae de regno suo peccatum eiecit et expulit, cum quo necessario etiam mors pariter expulsa est, ut ita demum regnum sibi in nobis gratia per iustitiam uindicaret et ubi mors fuerat aeterna uita consisteret ... ubi peccatum fuit et mors ibi nunc est gratia et iustitia et uita aeterna.* Again in 6.6.1–14 Origen observes that death is the price of sin, but life eternal is not a remuneration for anything, but it is rather a grace, since it is incommensurable with any good deed we may have done: "For the wages of sin is death, but life eternal in Christ Jesus is a gratuitous gift of God [Rom 6:23].... It would have been unworthy of God to give his soldiers a stipend as something due, but he rather gives them a gratuitous gift, which is eternal life in Christ," *Stipendia enim peccati mors, gratia autem Dei uita aeterna in Christo Iesu.... Deum uero non erat dignum militibus suis stipendia quasi debitum aliquod dare, sed donum et gratiam, quae est uita aeterna in Christo* (note the use of the argument of what is "worthy of God," which is typical of Origen). In fact, there is no possible comparison even between our present merits and tribulations and the future glory, which, in Paul's world, will be "an eternal weight of glory, in abundance and superabundance" (2 Cor 4:17): on this *supra modum in immensum aeternae gloriae pondus* Origen reflects in *Commentary on Romans* 7.2.33ff.

4.90. The knowledge of God needs, not a dialectic soul, but (the faculty of spiritual) vision. For dialectic is usually found even by souls that are not pure, whereas vision is only in pure souls.

The knowledge of God implies no separation or dualism (see above, *KG* 4.77 and 4.87, with the relevant commentaries), and thus no dialectics, but requires pureness. Only a pure soul can be a seer of God. It is to be noticed that in the Platonic tradition dialectics was the first and highest expression of philosophy (so that the philosopher must be διαλεκτικώτατος). But the knowledge of God transcends philosophical knowledge in that it is a mystic vision that takes place in presence, in the union with God, of which Evagrius has just spoken in *KG* 4.89, and the very θέωσις.

***

After the end of this *kephalaion* the manuscript has: "The fourth discourse/book is concluded."

Fifth Discourse

5.1. Adam is the type of Christ, whereas Eve is that of the rational nature, since because of the latter Christ went out of his paradise.

The Syriac word for "type," ܛܘܦܣܐ, is a transliteration of Greek τύπος. To use relative and discussed categories, the exegesis that Evagrius offers here is both typological and allegorical together. That Adam is the "type" of Christ is an example of what is traditionally called typological exegesis, in which characters and figures in the Old Testament are interpreted as prefigurations of new characters and realities. This particular typology is already found in Rom 5:14, to which Evagrius is referring here. However, the interpretation of Eve as a symbol of the whole rational nature is more allegorical than strictly typological. Such a blending of typology and allegory was already typical of Origen. See Peter Martens, "Revisiting the Allegory/Typology Distinction: The Case of Origen," *JECS* 16 (2008): 283–317; Ilaria L. E. Ramelli, "Typology," in *The Encyclopedia of Ancient History* (ed. Roger S. Bagnall et al.; London: Wiley-Blackwell, 2013), 12:6898–6900; doi:10.1002/9781444338386.wbeah05187; and idem, "Origen and the Stoic Allegorical Tradition." On the necessity of overcoming the typology/allegory divide and terminology, see also Bucur, "The Early Christian Reception."

Evagrius's exegesis relies on the following idea: just as Adam was chased out of paradise because of Eve's transgression, so has Christ left his own paradise—that is, his immanent life in the Father, his being God—because of the transgression of the *logika*; thus he took up humanity and became the Savior.

5.2. The listeners of the sense-perceptible church are separated from one another only by places, whereas those of the intelligible one, which is opposite to the former, (are separated) by places and by (kinds of) bodies.

Like Origen, Evagrius here distinguishes the visible church and the intelligible one, even to the point of stating that they are opposite to each other. Origen regarded the church, ordained ministries, sacraments, and liturgy as both physical-historical and spiritual-symbolic. Thus, baptism can be either visible or invisible, that is, intelligible; each church has a visible bishop and an invisible and intelligible one (*Homilies on Leviticus* 24.1 and 13.5); the Eucharist is not only the sacramental bread consecrated by a presbyter but also the reading, listening to, and meditation on Scripture, "the body of Christ" (*On Passover and Easter* 26.5–8; 33.20–32). The nourishment of the soul is not only the eucharistic sacrament but reading the Bible (*Homilies on Leviticus* 9.7; *Homilies on Jeremiah* 4.6.18; *Homilies on Numbers* 27.1; *Homilies on Genesis* 10.3). The intellectual and spiritual aspect prevails over the liturgical-sacramental. According to Origen, all Christians share the priestly office; a person who is not formally ordained on earth can be worthier of priesthood than one ordained. For only those who have an understanding of God are worthy of being called priests: "Only those who understand God and are capable of knowing God" (*soli sunt qui intelligent Deum et capaces sint scientiae Dei*), and not those who observe a merely physical pureness. The true priest is a person who "knows and understands one's own sins," and a presbyter should be chosen on account of one's eminence in every virtue (*Homilies on Leviticus* 2.1; 6.3). The true priests are those who, independently of ordination, "devote themselves to the divine Word and truly exist for the service of God alone" (*Commentary on John* 1.10–11).

In Origen's view, in sum, ordained ministry is found not only in the earthly church but also and primarily in the heavenly or spiritual church. For instance, some deacons, presbyters, and bishops who belong to the earthly church but are unworthy of their office do not belong to the spiritual church; conversely, some who are not ordained in the earthly church but are worthy of priesthood are in fact presbyters and bishops in the latter (*Commentary on Matthew* 16.20–23; *Series* 12). Origen remarks that an ecclesiastical person can have authority over another who is in fact much better gifted, "just as Jesus was subject to Joseph" (*Homilies on Luke* 20); an autobiographical echo is likely here, since the wonderfully gifted Origen was subject to his much more mediocre bishop, who in fact was jealous of his capacities and success. Origen does not stop warning that true teachers are not necessarily churchmen; some ordained ecclesiastical ministers, on the contrary, are in fact not teachers, because they do not possess Jesus, who is the Logos and Wisdom of God (*Homilies on Luke* 18). One should aspire to be called a presbyter/elder (*presbyteri et seniores*) on account of the spiritual perfection, seriousness, and constancy of his or her "inner human being" (*pro interioris hominis perfecto sensu et gravitate constantiae*) rather than on account of the ordained office of presbyter (*pro officio presbyterii*; *Homily* 4 on Ps 36, section 3). Of course the "inner human being" is neither male nor female. Indeed, relying on Gal 3:28, Origen explicitly remarks that the church, and every soul, like Christ himself, who can be called both Bride and Bridegroom (*Commentary on the Song of Songs* 1.6.14; *Homilies on Genesis* 14.1), is beyond gender: "These realities of which Scripture is speaking here must be understood as superior to the masculine, neuter, or feminine gender, and to whatever is related to this, and not only the Logos of God but also its church and every perfect soul. Indeed, the apostle Paul too says so: 'In Christ there is neither male nor female,'" *Super masculinum tandem et neutrum ac femininum genus et super omne omnino quod ad haec respicit esse cogitanda sunt ista de quibus sermo est, et non solum Verbum Dei, sed et ecclesia eius atque anima perfecta. Sic enim et Apostolus dicit: In Christo enim neque masculus neque femina* (*Commentary on the Song of Songs* 3.9.3–4). In such a perspective it clearly makes no sense to reserve ecclesiastical ministries for just one gender. Origen warns that perfection is not conferred on a person automatically by the ordination to an ecclesiastical ministry (*Homilies on Jeremiah* 11.3). Not only bishops and presbyters but also and especially teachers, theologians, and saints form the apostolic succession: "Whenever the Savior sends someone for the salvation of humans, the messenger is an apostle of Jesus Christ" (*Commentary on John* 32.17.204). Thus, the Samaritan woman and other women are apostles (ibid. 13.28.169). For the church rests not only on the apostle Peter but on a number of Peters/Rocks, who can be women: "All those against whom the gates of hades will not prevail, who have in themselves a work called Peter the Rock, are also Peters/Rocks" (*Commentary on Matthew* 12.10–11; cf. *Series* 139). Therefore, Jesus gives "the keys of the kingdom" and the relevant faculty of "binding and loosing" not only to Peter but also to these other Peters/Rocks, whereas an ordained bishop who judges unrighteously has not "power of the keys" (*Commentary on Matthew* 12.14). Evagrius continues on Origen's lines when he meditates on the visible church and the spiritual church and their distinction and even opposition.

Places are said by Evagrius, in the *kephalaion* under examination here, to separate those who belong to the sense-perceptible church (hearers or listeners are those who are instructed) from one another, and this is perfectly clear in that the church in this world is a diastematic reality, in space and time. As for the intelligible church, Evagrius says that those who belong to it are separate from one another also by means of different kinds of bodies (*gwšm'*). This can be an allusion to the difference between the mortal bodies of Christians on earth and the immortal bodies of the resurrection, but it can also imply a more inclusive range of rational creatures in the "intelligible church," also comprehensive of angels—and, after the resurrection, of risen human beings.

5.3. Just as those who dwell in this aeon have quite a small sight over the world to come, in the same way those who are in the last aeon see some luminous beams of the Holy Trinity.

Evagrius, like Origen, sees the succession of aeons in the history of salvation (of which he has already spoken in *KG* 4.89; see the relevant commentary above) as an uninterrupted spiritual growth. Thus, in each stage something of the future is already seen, but only a very little bit, given that spiritual development is required to access the subsequent stage, and in the last stage before *apokatastasis* and θέωσις (that is, the last aeon, since all aeons will be over in the eventual *apokatastasis*) the Trinity itself will become visible. The vision of the Trinity and participation in divine life will indeed characterize the final θέωσις.

5.4. An archangel is a rational substance who has been entrusted with the *logoi* of Providence, of Judgment, and of the worlds/aeons of angels.

An "archangel" in Syriac is, literally, a "chief of angels." These creatures, perfect *logika*, are endowed with the *logoi* of the Judgment and of Providence, which form the last two contemplations ot *theōriai* in *KG* 1.27 (see the relevant commentary there). Being superior in order to angels, archangels are also entrusted with the *logoi* of the worlds/aeons of angels, thus their arrangement, spiritual growth and adherence to the Good, and their cooperation in the process of *oikonomia*.

5.5. Two of the aeons purify the part of the soul that is liable to passions, one of them by means of the *praktikē*, and the other by means of harsh torment.

Evagrius refers here to the present and the future aeon. The present one is that in which the ascetic training of the soul purifies it from passions.

The future one is that in which torments (the biblical πῦρ αἰώνιον, or "fire of the aeon to come") will purify sinners. It is clear that Evagrius too, like Origen and Gregory of Nyssa, understood expressions like πῦρ αἰώνιον or κόλασις αἰώνιος as "fire/punishment in the world to come, in the aeon to come," and not at all as "eternal fire/punishment." See Ramelli and Konstan, *Terms for Eternity*. Evagrius, like Origen, Clement of Alexandria, and Gregory Nyssen, clearly thinks of punishment as endowed with a purifying function, not in retributive terms. What has not been purified in the present world shall have to be purified in the next in a more drastic way. See Ramelli, *Christian Doctrine of Apokatastasis*, the chapters on Clement, Origen, Gregory of Nyssa, and Evagrius.

5.6. The contemplation of angels is named heavenly Jerusalem and Mount Zion. Now, if those who have believed in Christ have got close to Mount Zion and to the City of the Living God, then those who have believed in Christ have been and will be in the contemplation of angels, that out of which their forefathers came when they descended to Egypt.

Evagrius applies here a transitive principle based on the interpretation of scriptural references. Since the *theōria* of angels is identified with the biblical symbols of the heavenly Jerusalem and Mount Zion, and faith in Christ in turn is related to them, then faith in Christ is identified with the angels' *theōria*. Now faith in Christ, in the form of this *theōria*, is ascribed to the ancient Hebrews before their descent to Egypt. (Paul also suggested this for the Israelites after their exodus from Egypt, when he stated that the Hebrews in the desert drank from a spiritual rock that was Christ himself. It is also what later theology would theorize as faith in the Christ to come.) In turn, Egypt being the symbol of vice, passions, and idolatry, the descent to Egypt and the detachment from the adherence to Christ-Logos can be ascribed to any soul who embraces passions and evilness; adherence to Christ-Logos is tantamount to embracing virtue and the Good. This is faith in Christ, the *theōria* of angels, and approaching the heavenly Jerusalem.

5.7. An angel is a rational substance who has been entrusted with the *logoi* concerning Providence and the Judgment and concerning the worlds/aeons of human beings.

As in *KG* 5.6, Evagrius goes on here to speak of angelic creatures. This *kephalaion* is a perfect parallel to *KG* 5.4, in which Evagrius has explained which are the *logoi* archangels have been entrusted with: the *logoi* of Providence, of Judgment, and of the worlds/aeons of angels (see above, the relevant commentary). Here he explains which are those that have been handed to angels. Two are the same as the archangels' *logoi*: those of the final Judgment and of Providence, which coincide with the last two *theōriai*. The third kind of *logoi* is different, according to the different orders of angels and archangels: the former are entrusted with the *logoi* of human beings in their different stages of development, while the latter are entrusted with the *logoi* of angels themselves.

5.8. Those who have worked their ground for the six years of the *praktikē*, it is not in the eighth year but in the seventh that these will feed orphans and widows; for in the eighth year there are no orphans or widows.

This is another *kephalaion* that, like *KG* 3.68 and *KG* 4.26 (see the relevant commentaries above), applies the notion of "the eighth day" to the final *apokatastasis*. The immediate reference is here to Exod 23:10–11, in which the seventh year is instituted as a Sabbatical year meant for the benefit of the poor ("For six years you shall sow your land and gather in its yield, but the seventh year you shall let it rest and lie fallow, that the poor of your people may eat," RSV). Here the poor are exemplified by widows and orphans. In the *apokatastasis*, the "eighth year," there will be no poor left. The current aeon is assimilated to the six years, and the agricultural work in it is taken by Evagrius to represent the moral work at the level of the *praktikē*, with the spiritual development that it produces. The "seventh (year)" is the aeon, or aeons, to come, when the poor will be fed, virtue will be rewarded, and sins will be purified, and the "eighth year" will be the eventual *apokatastasis*, when there will be no evil left, no suffering, no poor. This scheme of the six days–seventh day–eighth day is also taken up by Maximus the Confessor (see Ramelli, *Christian Doctrine of Apokatastasis*, the chapter devoted to him).

5.9. Some among human beings will feast together with angels, whereas others will mingle with the hosts of demons, and yet others will be tortured along with contaminated human beings.

The common feast of humans and angels is described by Gregory of Nyssa at the end of *On the Soul and the Resurrection* (see full commentary in Ramelli, *Gregorio di Nissa: Sull'anima*). But that refers specifically to the final *apokatastasis*, whereas Evagrius here seems to refer to a stage before *apokatastasis*, in the aeon to come, in which the purification of sinners will also take place. The "contaminated human beings" mentioned here are precisely those who have sullied themselves with sin, which both Evagrius and Nyssen metaphorically represent elsewhere as a kind of dirty glue, mud, or fat that sticks to evildoers (see above, the commentary on *KG* 4.36). Evagrius also alludes to the assimilation of human beings to angels or demons according to their moral choices.

5.10. The firstborn are rational natures who, in each one of the aeons, get close to the positive transformation.

Evagrius here may be alluding to Exod 22:29 ("The first-born of your sons you shall give to me," RSV), but more easily, I suspect, he will have in mind Clement of Alexandria's firstborn or protoctists, the "first founded" or "first created" but also "firstborn," given their partial identification with both Christ-Logos and the Spirit. In Clement's view, indeed, "the protoctists are both 'angelic powers' and 'powers of the Logos' that mark the passing of divine unity into multiplicity, and, conversely, the reassembly of cosmic multiplicity into the unity of the Godhead" (Bogdan Bucur, *Angelomorphic Pneumatology: Clement of Alexandria and Other Early Christian Witnesses* [Leiden: Brill, 2009], 40). "For Clement the Holy Spirit is a plural entity consisting of the seven highest angels, or … the hypostasis of the Spirit is functionally absorbed and replaced by the protoctists, or, as I am inclined to think, … Clement interpret[s] the protoctists as an angelomorphic representation of the Spirit" (ibid., 83). In *Extracts from the Prophets* 56.7 the seven main angels, the archangels, the protoctists, are said to achieve peace and contemplation of God after having served divine providence. On the protoctists in Clement, see also Alain Le Boulluec, *Clément d'Alexandrie: Les Stromates; Stromate V, Tome II; Commentaire, bibliographie et index* (SC 279; Paris: Cerf, 1981), 143–44.

Evagrius has already spoken of the "firstborn" in *KG* 2.36 and 4.24, the former referring to the most advanced among rational creatures and—with a very probable Clementine reminiscence—models of gnosis (those who both see the intelligible objects and know the true *logos* concerning them), like here, and the latter especially referring to Christ ("The firstborn from among the dead is the one who rose from among the dead and first took up a spiritual body"). See the relevant commentaries above. The spiritual advanced state of these *logika* in each aeon, and thus their improved condition in the next one, is here presented as the reason why these *logika* are called "firstborn." Indeed, they are the first to reach a degree of spiritual advancement to which all rational creatures will arrive at long last, in the end, through purification and illumination.

5.11. From the order of angels come the order of archangels and that of the psychic; from that of the psychic, that of demons and that of human beings; from that of human beings, angels and demons will derive in turn, if it is true that a demon is the one who, because of excess of *thymos*, has fallen from the *praktikē* and has been joined with a dark and extended (immortal) body.

As in the immediately preceding *kephalaia*, Evagrius here goes on to speak of angelic creatures. Spiritual progression or regression determine, according to Evagrius, just as according to Origen, a transformation from a kind ("order" is in Syriac the transliteration of Greek τάξις) of *logika* into another, the main being angels, humans, and demons. This does not entail a transformation of nature, which is the same for all the *logika*. These changes can occur throughout the aeons, but not in the *telos*. The body of demons is described by Evagrius in terms that are very similar to those employed by Origen (on which, see Pietras, "L'inizio del mondo materiale"). It is a body that, unlike spiritual bodies, is diastematic, and above all it is dark, unlike human mortal bodies, and unlike the luminous spiritual bodies of the saints and the angels. However, it is not mortal, unlike human earthly bodies.

As for the initial sentence, Guillaumont (p. 181) proposed a textual emendation: the removal of ܘ before ܕܢܦܫܢܐ and its transposition before ܛܟܣܐ ܕܪ̈ܝܫ. This would allow the following translation: "From the order of angels come the order of archangels and that of the psychic." The underlying idea, according to Guillaumont, is that it is not archangels and psychics who derived from angels but the psychic who derived from both angels and archangels. Now, that the psychics are a secondary stage that intervened after the fall of the *noes* is beyond doubt: Evagrius is clearly referring to Origen's idea of the initial transformation of (some) *noes* into souls (ψυχαί) because of a cooling down (ψῦξις) of their ardent attachment to God, the Good. From these came both human beings and demons, who are the coolest of all in their lack of love for God. Human beings can in turn give rise to both angels and demons, according to their spiritual progression toward the good or toward evil. Evagrius mentions archangels only at the beginning of this *kephalaion* and in *KG* 5.4 (see the relevant commentary there). Now, translating according to Guillaumont's emendation (followed by Fr. Theophanes: "From the order of angels and from the order of archangels comes the order of souls") would imply that before the fall and the cooling of the *noes* there were angels and archangels, distinct from one another. But this would introduce a hierarchy among the *logika* at the beginning, whereas Evagrius, following Origen, rather thought that the differentiation of rational creatures into orders came about only as a result of the fall (and will likewise disappear in the ultimate end). The Syriac text seems to make good sense as it is: from a situation of nondifferentiation among all *logika*, who were all "angels," a differentiation appeared at a certain point, depending on the conduct of the various *logika*. Thus, the best became archangels, ruling over inferior angels, and the worst became "psychic," who in turn developed either into human beings or into demons. Demons can also derive from humans out of an excess of anger (on this see also *Letter* 56.4). A further argument in favor of my interpretation is given by the structure of the *kephalaion* itself: the first three sentences are all parallel, "from A come B and C," B and C being two developments, one better and one worse:

(1) from A (angels) come B (archangels, better) and C (the "psychic," worse);
(2) from A (the "psychic") come B (demons, worse) and C (human beings, better);
(3) from A (human beings) come B (angels, better) and C (demons, worse).

The transformation of 1 along the lines suggested by Guillaumont would break the parallel, introducing a different structure, "from A and B comes C," in which moreover there would be not a positive and a negative development but only one negative ("the psychic"), from a double premise (angels *and* archangels).

The Greek parallel of the three initial sentences is preserved in the *Scholia on Pseudo-Dionysius the Areopagite* ascribed to Maximus the Confessor (PG 4:173B). This text seems to be reflected also in the fifth anathema of the canons of the fifth council against Origen (Giovanni Domenico Mansi, *Sacrorum conciliorum, nova et amplissima collectio*, 9:397), combined with 2.78.

5.12. The intellect that has been stripped of its passional thought and sees the intellections of beings does not truly receive anymore the representations that (are formed) by means of sense perceptions, but it is as though another world were created by its knowledge, and it has attracted its thought to itself and rejected the sense-perceptible world far from itself.

This *kephalaion* emphasizes the big difference, in the ontological and the gnoseological order, between the sense-perceptible and the intelligible plane. The *nous* that has attained *apatheia* transcends the sense-perceptible world; therefore, it cannot receive sense-perceptible representations proper, as if it were liable to being transformed by them, but its knowledge *creates* another world, intelligible and transcendent. This is the very same idea of intellectual knowledge that centuries later the Christian Neoplatonist John the Scot Eriugena will express: "when I imprint their phantasms [i.e., impressions of objects of knowledge] in my memory, and when I treat these things within myself, I divide, I compare, and, as it were, I collect them into a certain unity, I perceive a certain *knowledge of the things that are external to me being created within me*" (*Periphyseon, On Natures*, 4,765C, version v).

It is to be noticed that Evagrius introduces a very important condition: that the *nous* be free from passions. Otherwise, the *nous* loses much of its transcendence and declines to the plane of the sense-perceptible world itself. Evagrius, as usual, keeps knowledge and virtue—the intellectual and ethical planes—together. His background is Plato's metaphorical argument on the intellectual soul who puts on or loses its wings: in the former case, the *nous* will maintain its transcendence and will be occupied in the contemplation of the Ideas, intelligible realities; in the latter, when it is overcome by the passional parts of the soul, it will become involved in the lower, sense-perceptible world and will lose its transcendence and its capacity for intellectual knowledge.

An interesting expression of the notion that the most advanced intellectual souls do not need the mediation of sense perception for knowledge is found in Evagrius's *Letter to Melania*. With some, the Spirit and the Son communicate directly—although Evagrius does not explain how—whereas with others, less advanced, they communicate indirectly, by means of God's creation, meaning the sense-perceptible creation, what Evagrius calls the "secondary creation" (this terminology repeatedly appears in *KG*). This secondary creation is not an evil; on this, Origen had already insisted against "Gnostics" and Marcionites. Far from being an evil, it is providential and was wanted by God as a mediation, for the sake of those who are far from God in that "they have placed a separation between themselves and their Creator because of their evil deeds" (*Letter to Melania* 5). God instituted this mediation by means of his Wisdom and his Power, that is to say, the Son and the Spirit. For Evagrius, "the whole ministry of the Son and the Spirit is exercised through creation, *for the sake of those who are far from God*" (ibid.). This is perfectly in line with Gregory of Nyssa's and the Cappadocians' moderate apophaticism and the role that, in their view, God's operations play in the acquisition of the knowledge of God (see Ramelli, "Silenzio apofatico in Gregorio di Nissa"; and Konstantinovsky, *Evagrius*, 47–76). Only those rational creatures who are very close to God are helped directly by the Logos and the Spirit, without the mediation of creation: "Just as the intellect operates in the body by means of the mediation of the soul, likewise the Father too, by means of the mediation of his own soul [i.e., the Son and the Spirit], operates in his own body, which is the human intellect" (*Letter to Melania* 15). Indeed, human intellects know thanks to the Logos and the Spirit, who make everything known to them (19); they do not become aware of their own nature but through the Logos and the Spirit, who are their souls (21). In turn, human intellects are the bodies of the Son and the Spirit (ibid.). We are the intelligible creation and are now found joined to this visible creation, "for reasons that it is impossible to explain here" (*Letter to Melania* 13).

5.13. The intelligible "cloud" is the rational nature who has been entrusted by God with the task of letting those who sleep far away drink from it.

Evagrius may refer here to the "thick cloud" from which the Lord spoke to Moses (Exod 19:9), or to Exod 13:21–22, where the Lord is said to have gone before the Israelites in the desert every day in "a pillar of cloud" to lead them, and 40:38:

> Then the cloud covered the tent of meeting, and the glory of the Lord filled the tabernacle. And Moses was not able to enter the tent of meeting, because the cloud abode upon it, and the glory of the Lord filled the tabernacle. Throughout all their journeys, whenever the cloud was taken up from over the tabernacle, the people of Israel would go onward; but if the cloud was not taken up, then they did not go onward till the day that

> it was taken up. For throughout all their journeys the cloud of the Lord was upon the tabernacle by day, and fire was in it by night, in the sight of all the house of Israel. (RSV)

The same desert episode is recounted in Num 9:17: "And whenever the cloud was taken up from over the tent, after that the people of Israel set out; and in the place where the cloud settled down, there the people of Israel encamped" (RSV). In Deut 31:15 God is said to have appeared near Moses's tent "in a pillar of cloud." The desert episode, with the cloud and the notion of the drink provided by Jesus, is also mentioned by Paul in 1 Cor 10:1–4: "I want you to know, brethren, that our fathers were all *under the cloud*, and all passed through the sea, and all were baptized into Moses *in the cloud* and in the sea, and all ate the same supernatural food and all *drank the same supernatural drink*. For they drank from the supernatural Rock which followed them, and the Rock was Christ" (RSV). In Rev 10:1 a mighty angel is wrapped in a cloud; he holds a scroll and performs a revelatory function. In Rev 14:14 a cloud is presented upon which "one like a child of a human being appears." The reference to both the cloud and the action of drinking from it makes it probable that Evagrius was thinking of Exodus through 1 Cor 10:1–4.

As in many other short exegetical *kephalaia* devoted to a detail of the Old Testament, in the footsteps of Origen, Evagrius offers an allegorical interpretation of this cloud. Evagrius interprets this noetic cloud as the symbol of those more perfect *logika* who help others to acquire the knowledge of God. Elsewhere, in *KG* 3.62, he likewise identifies these angels with stars for their illuminative function (see above, the relevant commentary).

5.14. Just as, when the sun rises, even those things that are only a little bit raised over the earth produce a shadow, in the same way too the objects (of knowledge) appear in an obscure way to the intellect that begins to get close to the intellections of the beings.

This reflection on the gnoseological activity of the *nous* in its progress is closely related to *KG* 5.12 and 5.15 (see the relevant commentaries). The *nous*'s capacity for knowledge depends on its advancement, and its advancement in turn heavily depends on the *nous*'s liberation from passions. Once more, Evagrius insists on the close connection between knowledge and virtue. The intellect's capacity for knowledge is seriously impaired if it lacks virtue. The obscurity in which objects appear is like the shadow that bodies project when the light of the sun strikes them. The shadow is darkness, but at the same time it implies the light of the sun, and it becomes smaller and smaller as the sun progresses in the sky. The ambivalence of the shadow in a metaphorical framework is also alluded to by Evagrius in *KG* 4.29 (see the relevant commentary above). There Evagrius draws another simile: the night is the shadow produced by the earth when the light of the sun strikes it. Without the earth, as well as without the sun, there would be no night. Likewise, ignorance is the shadow of evilness: it could not exist without evilness, or without the light of Christ, the "Sun of Justice."

5.15. The intellect that has been stripped of passions becomes entirely like light, illuminated as it is by the contemplation of beings.

This *kephalaion*, which is closely related to the preceding one, which speaks of knowledge in terms of light (see my commentary on it and on *KG* 1.35), makes it extremely clear how profoundly knowledge depends on virtue: only a *nous* that is free from passions can know. Notably, in the Syriac text the expression "that has been stripped of passions" can also be understood as "that has despoiled itself from passions" or "has taken off passions." The underlying metaphor is obviously that of the "bare/naked *nous*," which Evagrius has already introduced in *KG* 3.6, 15, 17, 19, and 21 (see above, the relevant commentaries). Only a *nous* that has reached a perfect state of "nakedness" can attain the highest degree of knowledge. In the present *kephalaion* Evagrius speaks of the *theōria* of existing beings, which is one degree inferior to that of the Trinity. This is said to illuminate the intellect that is finally *apathēs* and thereby becomes like light. In *KG* 1.35 God is described as Light, which illuminates the intellect, and in the *Chapters of the Disciples of Evagrius* 78 the light of the intellect is said to increase in prayer—therefore in a direct relation to God: "when the intellect is progressing in prayer, it will see its own light become more brilliant and shining." Light and prayer are associated by Evagrius also in *On Talking Back* 6.16, where he reports John of Lycopolis's opinion that the mind can be illuminated during prayer only thanks to the grace of God. That prayer entails a relation between the praying intellect and God is clear from Evagrius's very definition of prayer as "the intellect's conversation [ὁμιλία] with God" in *On Prayer* 3, a definition that is so important as to be repeated in *Skemmata* 28 and 31 and in scholium 1 on Ps 140(141):2, and echoed in *On Prayer* 4, 34, and 55. This definition comes from Clement of Alexandria,

Stromateis (*Miscellaneous Books*) 7.39.6; cf. 7.73.1–3 (on this definition of prayer in Clement, see Henny F. Hägg, "Prayer and Knowledge in Clement of Alexandria," in *The Seventh Book of the Stromateis* [ed. Matyas Havrda, Vit Husek, and Jana Platova; Leiden: Brill, 2012], 131–42, esp. 132–35). According to Stewart, "Imageless Prayer," 191, "Evagrius' use of that definition of prayer inherited from Clement of Alexandria is more than just a bow to tradition. Prayer is an encounter with a personal God, and Evagrius keeps biblical words and imagery in play even in his description of the highest stages of prayer." On Evagrius's teaching on prayer, see Irenée Hausherr, *Les leçons d'un contemplatif: Le Traité de l'oraison d'Evagre le Pontique* (Paris: Beauchesne, 1960); Gabriel Bunge, *Das Geistgebet: Studien zum Traktat* De oratione *des Evagrios Pontikos* (Köln: Luthe, 1987); idem, "Aktive und kontemplative Weise des Betens im Traktat *De oratione* des Evagrios Pontikos," *StudMon* 41 (1999): 211–27; Augustine Casiday, *Reconstructing the Theology of Evagrius Ponticus* (Cambridge: Cambridge University Press, 2013), 136–66. For a defense of Christian prayer by Justin and other patristic theologians against arguments for the uselessness of prayer, see Dylan Burns, "Care or Prayer? Justin Martyr's *Dialogue with Trypho* 1.4 Revisited," *VC* 68 (2014): 178–91.

5.16. The intelligible "darkness" is the spiritual contemplation that contains in itself the *logoi* of Providence and of the Judgment of those who are on earth.

The scriptural reference is to Exod 20:21 and the "darkness" in which God was, a passage that was deployed by Philo, Origen, and Gregory of Nyssa as a hint of God's unknowability (see Ramelli, "Philosophical Allegoresis of Scripture"; and idem, "Divine as an Inaccessible Epistemological Object"). The reference to darkness, indeed, is related to the theological conception of apophaticism. Philo, interpreting Moses's ascent into darkness, in *On the Posterity of Cain* 14, takes darkness as representing spiritual contemplation, "conceptions concerning the Existent Being that belong to the recess [ἄδυτα] where there are no material forms" (with an imagery probably also influenced by the emptiness and darkness of the temple's *adyton* in Philo's day). Here Evagrius does not refer darkness to the inaccessible nature of God but to the contemplation of the *logoi* of Providence and of the Judgment, which seem obscure to those on earth (as is further confirmed by *KG* 5.23). This passage is linked with *KG* 5.13, but also to 5.4 and 5.7, in which the *logoi* of divine providence and of the Judgment are said to have been given to angels and archangels (see above, the relevant commentaries). They are the contents of the spiritual *theōria* that is proper to them.

5.17. Just as the waves, when they rise, produce a shadow, and immediately they appear without a shadow, in the same way, when the intellections of beings will flee away from the pure intellect, they will be immediately known in turn.

This *kephalaion* is connected with *KG* 5.14, with its reflection on how shadow, representing ignorance, is related to knowledge and depends on the degree of purity of the *nous*. See the relevant commentary above. Here the simile concerns a much more mutable kind of shadow, that of waves, which change continuously. The intellections of beings are known by the pure intellect precisely when they flee away from it.

5.18. Demons only resemble colors, shapes, and size, whereas the holy powers also can [lit. "know"] change the nature of the (immortal) body, while they prepare it for the functions that are necessary. And this occurs among composite beings, whereas of the incorporeal nature there are no intellections like these, as has been said.

Guillaumont has proposed here an emendation (185): to read ܠܡܫܬܚܠܦܘ instead of ܠܡܫܚܠܦܘ and to understand, "savent se transformer aussi en la nature," "they also can transform themselves into the nature," which is closer to the nonexpurgated version S_1. Now, I think that Guillaumont's emendation is possible but unnecessary: angels alter and transform their own immortal and spiritual bodies (which indeed here are called *gwšm'*) into the bodies they need to assume, even changing the nature of their bodies, for instance, into diastematic bodies, and not simply transforming their qualities (color, shape, size), as demons do. Both Dysinger and Fr. Theophanes are right not to follow the emendation and to render, respectively: "the holy powers also know how to transform the nature of the body" and "the holy powers know (how) to transform also the nature of the body."

Both demons and angels are composite beings, corporeal in their (immortal) bodies and incorporeal in their *nous*. Incorporeal realities, like *noes* and Ideas, do not admit of intellections concerning bodies and transformations of bodies and of bodily qualities.

5.19. The resurrection of the mortal body is a passage from a bad quality [lit. "mixture"] to an excellent quality [lit. "mixture"].

This is the first of three closely related *kephalaia* in this book that demonstrate that Evagrius, like Origen and Nyssen, had a holistic conception of the resurrection: it is the resurrection not only of the body but of all the components of the human being—the body, the soul in its inferior parts, and the superior faculty of the soul, the *nous*.

Here, in the first of these three *kephalaia*, Evagrius concentrates on the resurrection of the body. The mortal body will pass from a bad quality to a good one, from mortality to immortality, from corruptibility to incorruptibility, from illness to health, from ugliness to beauty, and so on. Evagrius is on the line of Origen and of Adamantius in the *Dialogue of Adamantius* in maintaining that the individual body is the same and not another once resurrected, but its qualities are transformed (see Ramelli, "Preexistence of Souls."). Evagrius identifies the resurrection of the body with the transformation of the same body from one mixture to another, keeping the same elements (the Syriac noun *mwzg'* literally means "mixture"; from different mixtures of elements then come different qualities). As Gregory of Nyssa also suggests, the body remains the same, but its texture is finer. The elements remain the same, but their composition and mixture change. For Origen and Nyssen, see Ramelli, "Origen's Exegesis of Jeremiah"; and idem, *Gregorio di Nissa: Sull'anima*.

On the "triple resurrection" of *KG* 5.19, 22, and 25, see Tobon, "Raising Body and Soul." Her analysis is sound; what I deem very important to add is that this notion of threefold resurrection and its relation to restoration/*apokatastasis* comes from Origen, and partially Gregory of Nyssa. It is also from Origen that Evagrius derived the close correspondence and dependence of the kinds of bodies and souls from the choices of the *nous*.

5.20. Life has vivified at the beginning living beings; subsequently, those who are alive and those who die; in the end, it will vivify also the dead.

This *kephalaion* is related to *KG* 5.19, 22, and 25, in that all of these treat the resurrection (see the relevant commentaries). The final vivification mentioned in this *kephalaion* is indeed the resurrection, which must be understood as indicated by the three other *kephalaia*: that is, a resurrection of the body, of the soul, and of the intellect or spirit. On each of these planes—as was maintained by Origen and Gregory of Nyssa as well—there will be a return from death to life. As for the initial statement that life originally vivified living beings, this seems to be a reference to the ἀρχή, when, before the fall, all existing beings, God and the *logika*, were alive. This, of course, refers not simply to physical life, as there were no mortal bodies then, but to spiritual life: no one of the *logika* had yet received evil in itself, and with it spiritual death. All of them were in the life of God, the Good, and they will return to it in the *telos*, in the final θέωσις, after the purification and disappearance of evil, which is the primary cause of death, spiritual death and physical death. Indeed, the death of the body followed the death of the soul "like a shadow" (*velut umbra*, in Origen's words). This was indeed Origen's idea as well. On evil being the cause of death in Origen, see Ilaria L. E. Ramelli, "Death," in *Encyclopedia of Ancient Christianity* (ed. Angelo Di Berardino; Downers Grove, IL: InterVarsity Press, 2014), 1:673–81.

The sentence concerning "those who are alive and those who die" refers to the present, intermediate state of things, during the aeons, after the fall and before the final *apokatastasis*. Now, some of the *logika* are spiritually alive, in that they adhere to the Good, and some are dying, insofar as they choose evil (note that Evagrius says that they "die" or even "are dying," ܡܝܬܝܢ, whereas in the last sentence he uses "the dead," ܡܝ̈ܬܐ, because during the aeons death is not a definitive condition, since spiritual improvement is always open, and in the end there will be the resurrection of the dead, not only physical, but also spiritual); moreover, in the case of human beings, some are physically dead and some are alive. But in the *telos*, death—both spiritual and physical—will disappear, and all the dead will be vivified, in body, soul, and spirit. Spiritual resurrection will entail the rejection of sin and life in God.

5.21. It is not in all the aeons that you will find Egypt; in the last ones, on the contrary, you will see Jerusalem and Mount Zion.

This is another *kephalaion* devoted to eschatological realities, and in particular to the continuous improvement of the *logika* throughout the aeons, with a view to the eventual restoration. Evagrius has already interpreted the heavenly Jerusalem and the Mount of Zion, as well as Egypt, in *KG* 5.6 (see the relevant commentary, above) and will return to their spiritual interpretation in *KG* 6.49 (see below, the commentary). In *KG* 5.6 he has identified the heavenly Jerusalem and Zion, the heritage of those who have believed in Christ, with the *theōria* of angels. Descending to Egypt, the symbol of evil, is tantamount to coming out of the *theōria* of angels. In *KG* 6.49, Evagrius explicitly describes Egypt as the symbol of evil (see also *KG* 4.64 and the commentary) and the heavenly Jerusalem and Zion as the symbols of the highest *theōria*, that of incorporeal realities, and of the highest reality, the Trinity. In the eschatological scenario, rational creatures will abandon Egypt/evilness and reach the contemplation of incorporeal realities (Jerusalem) and the Trinity itself (Zion) in the θέωσις. I emend ܒܐܚܪ̈ܢܐ ("in the others," i.e., aeons) into ܒܐܚܪ̈ܝܐ ("in the last," i.e., aeons) according to the suggestion of Guillaumont (p. 185), who, however, has not followed it in his own French translation ("dans les autres"). This is much more satisfactory from the point of view of the meaning; moreover, it is very probable that a similar mistake occurred in the scribal tradition: the confusion between *nun* (ܢ) and *yud* (ܝ) is extremely easy from the palaeographical viewpoint.

5.22. The resurrection of the soul is the return from the condition of vulnerability to passions to the condition without any passions.

See above, the commentary on *KG* 5.19, for the relation of this *kephalaion* to *KG* 5.19 and 5.25; these three bits must be read together. After explaining in *KG* 5.19 what the resurrection of the body is, that is, a passage from bad qualities, or a poor arrangement of elements, to good qualities, or a fine arrangement of elements, here Evagrius explains what the resurrection of the soul is: it is likewise a passage, not to a different soul, but from liability to passions to *apatheia*, which is the ethical ideal of Evagrius just as it was of Clement, Origen, and Gregory of Nyssa (see Ramelli, *Gregorio di Nissa: Sull'anima*; and idem, "Tears of Pathos"). This pertains to the *praktikē*, the ethical and ascetic endeavor.

It is to be noticed that Evagrius does not simply speak of a "passage" to *apatheia*, but he mentions a "return" proper. The reference is clearly to the ἀνάστασις understood as ἀποκατάστασις, the restoration to the original state, in which the soul was not liable to passions. This comes through the restoration and renovation of the faculties of the soul, which accompanies the transformation of the body. This is also the way in which Maximus the Confessor maintained that the resurrection should be understood in the writings of Gregory of Nyssa: much more than the mere reconstitution of the body (see Ramelli, *Christian Doctrine of Apokatastasis*, the chapter on Maximus the Confessor). Indeed, the restoration of the soul is its restoration to life after death, and Evagrius is clear in *KG* 1.41 that the death and illness of the soul are posterior to its life and health; its restoration, therefore, will be a return to its primeval condition of life. This is why it is its resurrection from death.

Evagrius is again following the tripartition of the human being into body, soul, and intellect, which is Platonic in its origin (*Timaeus* 30B4–5) but also had resonances in St. Paul (1 Thess 5:23); see Ilaria L. E. Ramelli, "Tricotomia," in *Enciclopedia Filosofica* (ed. V. Melchiorre; Milan: Bompiani, 2006), 11772–76. This is why, after speaking of the resurrection of the body (*KG* 5.19), Evagrius treats here that of the soul (the *praktikē* soul, which strives to liberate itself from the passions that besiege its inferior parts, the *thymikon* and *epithymētikon*) and finally, in *KG* 5.25, that of the intellect, the highest faculty of the soul.

5.23. The various movements and the different passions of rational creatures have compelled by force the intellections concerning Providence to be seen in an obscure way, whereas their different orders have made the intellections concerning the Judgment concealed.

Since the fall, the *logika* have been constantly characterized by the movements of their free will, which are directed toward different objects. The diversity of the movements of their free will (according to a typically Origenian lexicon; see Ramelli, "Origen, Bardaisan, and the Origin of Universal Salvation") is parallel to that of their passions, or πάθη. Passions and the choice of evil obscure the intellectual sight—as Evagrius has already explained several times, clarifying his view of the close interrelationship between virtue and knowledge. Here, in particular, the knowledge that is obscured by passions and evilness, and by the differences that appeared among the *logika* as a result of the fall, is said to be that of divine providence and the Judgment. These are the last and the penultimate *theōriai* according to Evagrius's own classification in *KG* 1.27 (see above, the relevant commentary). The priority of Providence over the Judgment according to Evagrius is already intimated in *KG* 1.27 and is made even clearer in the immediately following *kephalaion* (5.24). On the "darkness" in which the *logoi* of Providence and Judgment are enveloped in this world, see above, *KG* 5.16 and the relevant commentary. Here Evagrius explains the reason for this darkness and obscurity.

5.24. The *logoi* concerning the Judgment are secondary, as has been said, vis-à-vis the *logoi* concerning movement and concerning Providence.

This *kephalaion* is closely related to the preceding one for its focus on divine judgment and providence. Evagrius has already stated in *KG* 1.27 that after the contemplation of the Judgment there will come the contemplation of divine providence. Since the ultimate end specularly reflects the beginning, this means that divine providence is ontologically prior to divine judgment, which is what Evagrius expounds in the present bit. He associates the *logoi* of movement with those of Providence because it was from the first movements (of will) of the rational creatures that divine providence began to operate. The Judgment is a consequence of the movements of the *logika*'s free will as well, but Providence is primary vis-à-vis it.

5.25. The resurrection of the intellect is the passage from ignorance to knowledge of the truth.

Kephalaia 5.22 and 5.25, which treat the resurrection of the soul and the intellect respectively, are closely related to 5.19, which deals with the resurrection of the body (see the commentaries, above). I have already noted that Evagrius follows Origen in his twofold conception of death, both physical and spiritual. The same is the case with his twofold conception of resurrection: physical (the resurrection of the body, with its transition to incorruptibility, the "superior quality") and spiritual—that is, the resurrection of the soul in both its superior and its inferior parts. The superior part is the intellect, the *nous*, whose resurrection is said to be the passage from ignorance to knowledge, since gnosis is the perfection of *nous*. The inferior parts, in accord with Plato's division, adopted also by Gregory of Nyssa in his dialogue *On the Soul and the Resurrection*, are the *epithymētikon*, or concupiscible/appetitive faculty, and the *thymikon*, or irascible faculty (in *KG* 5.27, as well as elsewhere, Evagrius clearly takes over this classification; see below, the relevant commentary). Since these parts are vulnerable to passions, their resurrection consists in their passage to impassivity. But the resurrection of the *nous* is the passage from ignorance—"the shadow of evilness" for Evagrius (*KG* 4.29)—to gnosis. Thus, the concept of resurrection is very rich and complex in Evagrius: it involves the whole of the human being, not merely his or her body. In his *Letter on Faith* Evagrius also reflects on the resurrection of the intellect, taking Jesus's promise of resurrecting his saints as a reference precisely to the resurrection of the intellect: "What does Jesus say in the Gospel? 'And I will resurrect him in the last day,' meaning by 'resurrection' [ἀνάστασις] the transformation from material knowledge to immaterial contemplation, and calling 'the last day' that knowledge [γνῶσις] beyond which there is no other. Our mind has been resurrected and roused to the height of blessedness only when it shall contemplate the Logos as Monad and Henad." The resurrection of the *nous* takes place in the *telos*, when it attains perfect and ultimate knowledge, but has its anticipation here and now. Note also the definition of the Logos as Monad and Henad, which Casiday (*Reconstructing the Theology of Evagrius*, 214) finds "a decidedly odd expression," but is in fact a further proof that Evagrius is following Origen *ad litteram* and that for Evagrius, Christ-Logos is God. Indeed, "Monad and Henad," μονάς τε καὶ ἑνάς, is Origen's definition of God, ὁ θεός, in *On First Principles* 1.1.6: given the technical nature of this expression, Rufinus preserved the original Greek here. That "Monad and Henad" is the definition of God is clear from another passage of Evagrius's *Letter on Faith*: "The Monad and Henad indicates the simple and incomprehensible substance" of God (2.41–42).

This holistic concept of the resurrection, as I have mentioned, has its roots in Origen and appears also in Gregory of Nyssa, who in his dialogue *On the Soul and the Resurrection* defines the resurrection (ἀνάστασις) as "the restoration of our nature, that is, human nature, to its original state" (ἡ εἰς τὸ ἀρχαῖον τῆς φύσεως ἡμῶν ἀποκατάστασις). This entails not only the resurrection of the body but also the purification from sin, impassivity, illumination, and knowledge.

The strong assertion of the eventual resurrection of the entire human being, in all of its faculties and component parts, perfectly corresponds to the conviction—which Evagrius shares, again, with Origen—that death cannot be the ultimate reality, whether it is physical or spiritual death. One of Origen's arguments in this connection was drawn from Rom 8:38: death will not be able to separate anyone from God forever. And this applies not only to physical death but above all to spiritual death, the death of sin that separates the soul from God: "Death, as he says, must be understood as the enemy of Christ that will have to be destroyed as the last, as I have explained above. Now, this enemy is called 'death' because, just as this common death separates the soul from the body, likewise it endeavors to separate the soul from the charity-love of God: and this is precisely the death of the soul," *Mors, quod dicit ille, accipiendus est quem supra exposuimus inimicum Christi destruendum nouissimum dici. Qui utique propterea mors dicitur, quia sicut haec communis mors animam separare a corpore, ita ille contendit animam separare a caritate Dei, et haec utique est animae mors* (Origen, *Commentary on Romans* 7.10.48–53). Now, Paul affirms that not even this death will ever be able to separate us from God's love.

Thus, even after such a death there will be a resurrection, not physical in this case, but spiritual.

It is evident from *KG* 5.19, 22, and 25 that Evagrius also adheres to the threefold conception of the human being, divided into body (σῶμα), soul (ψυχή), and intellect (νοῦς) or spirit (πνεῦμα), that was typical of Origen, St. Paul, and several Middle-Platonists and Roman Stoics, such as Marcus Aurelius (cf. Ramelli, "Tricotomia"). From Origen this conception passed on to Gregory of Nyssa and Evagrius. Among Origen's writings, one of the many passages that display this anthropological trichotomy (which also corresponds to the threefold interpretation of Scripture theorized by him in *On First Principles* 4; see Ilaria L. E. Ramelli, "The Philosophical Stance of Allegory in Stoicism and Its Reception in Platonism, Pagan and Christian: Origen in Dialogue with the Stoics and Plato," *International Journal of the Classical Tradition* 18.3 [2011]: 335–71) is *Commentary on Romans* 1.12.16–21, where Origen grounds this tripartition precisely in Paul (1 Thess 5:23): "That these three components are found in the human being, Paul makes it clear in his letter to the Thessalonians, when he states: 'That your body, soul, and spirit may be preserved intact in the day of our Lord Jesus Christ,'" *Haec enim tria esse in homine designat ad Thessalonicenses scribens cum dicit: "ut integrum corpus uestrum et anima et spiritus in die Domini nostri Iesu Christi seruetur."* And in the same *Commentary on Romans* 1.21.40–47 Origen ascribes this threefold vision of the human being to the whole of Scripture: "We often find in Scripture that the human being is said to be spirit, body, and soul. In fact, when it is said that the flesh has desires that are opposite to the spirit, and the spirit has desires that are opposite to the flesh, the soul without doubt is posited in the middle, so to either yield to the desires of the spirit or incline to the concupiscence of the flesh," *Frequenter in Scripturis inuenimus … quod homo spiritus et corpus et anima esse dicatur. Uero cum dicitur quia caro aduersus spiritum concupiscit, spiritus autem aduersus carnem, media procul dubio ponitur anima, quae uel desideriis spiritus adquiescat uel ad carnis concupiscentiam inclinetur.*

Knowledge of truth is the will of God for all human beings, according to 1 Tim 2:4: "God wants all human beings to be saved and to reach the knowledge of truth." This is the goal of the *logika*'s life. Evagrius explicitly appeals to this scriptural passage in *Gnostikos* 22: "The gnostic must be neither sad nor intimidating. For the former is ignorance of the *logoi* of things that have come into existence; the latter does not want 'all humans to be saved and come to knowledge of the truth' [1 Tim 2:4]."

5.26. Just as it is not the same thing that we see the light and that we speak of the light, in the same way it is not tantamount that we shall see God and that we can grasp something concerning God.

To see God will belong to the final condition of θέωσις; now we can only think and understand something of God. The latter is the goal of theology while we are on earth. The fundamental difference between knowing God (in the divine essence) and knowing something "concerning God," "around God," "about God," περὶ Θεοῦ, was accurately developed by Philo of Alexandria, Origen, and, even more, Gregory of Nyssa. See full treatment in Ramelli, "Divine as an Inaccessible Epistemological Object." Evagrius is well acquainted with this tradition of Christian apophaticism, which has roots also in Clement and, earlier, in Philo. See Ramelli, "Philosophical Allegoresis of Scripture."

5.27. The irascible faculty, when it is troubled, blinds the seer; the concupiscible/appetitive faculty, when bestially moved, hides the visible objects.

The Platonic tripartition of the soul, which Evagrius assumes in many *kephalaia*, underlies the present one as well. The irascible faculty or part of the soul is the θυμός or θυμικόν; the concupiscible appetitive or desiderative faculty, characterized by greed and lust, is the ἐπιθυμητικόν. These are the two main headings under which passions are classified. These are "bestial" in that the irrational movements and faculties of the soul assimilate humans to animals; this notion was dear to Gregory of Nyssa (who develops it in *On the Soul and the Resurrection*) and is taken over by Evagrius also in *KG* 6.85 (see the relevant commentary below) and *Letter to Melania* 46. The effects of πάθη on knowledge, and the interrelationship between knowledge and virtue, is a constant motif in Evagrius's thought and is here expressed clearly. Anger, desire, and related passions obfuscate the rational soul's sight. In this state, knowledge is severely impaired. In this *kephalaion*, in particular, a difference between the specific effects of the irascible and the concupiscible faculties is underlined: the former acts on the subject (the *nous*, the "seer"), the latter on the objects of knowledge.

5.28. The intelligible "sword" is the spiritual word/Logos that cuts away the body from the soul, or evilness and ignorance.

This is one of the many short *kephalaia* in which Evagrius interprets elements, figures, and cultic prescriptions of the Bible in a spiritual way, on what he expressly indicates as the "intelligible" or "noetic" plane. Here the reference might be to Eph 6:17, "the sword of the Spirit, which is the word of God," and to Heb 4:12, "the word of God is living and active, sharper than any two-edged sword, piercing to the division of soul and spirit" (RSV), but also maybe to Matt 10:34, in which Jesus says: "I came not to send peace, but a sword" (KJV), and above all to several references in Revelation to a two-edged sword that is attributed to Christ and is described as "sharp" (1:16; 2:12, 16; 19:15). Very interestingly, these are passages that were commented on by Origen, whose exegesis I deem known to Evagrius, who was probably also influenced by it. In the *Scholia on Revelation*—whose authorship is uncertain but whose content seem to go back to Origen in large part, more or less directly—in scholium 6 Origen offers a positive exegesis of violence in this biblical book, thanks to the allegorical interpretation of destruction therein as a reference to the eventual annihilation, not of sinners, but of sin and evil, so that this violence can be interpreted by him as salvific. For liberation from evil produces the salvation of the evildoer. Thus, Origen can state that the sword that comes out of Christ's mouth (Rev 1:16–17) is a source of good violence against evil and sin (τὸ πονηρόν, ἡ ἁμαρτία); it is "a tongue that becomes a sharp sword *for the sake of salvation*," γλῶσσαν ἐπὶ σωτηρίᾳ μάχαιραν ὀξεῖαν γεγενημένην. Origen renders the concept of violence even more positive by applying it to *agapē*. The wicked—he adds—wound by a sword, but the good by charity-love (τιτρώσκουσιν ἀγάπῃ), and "the Lord wounded us by means of charity-love" (τῇ ἀγάπῃ οὖν ἔτρωσεν ἡμᾶς ὁ Κύριος).

Similarly, in scholium 12 Origen insists on the positive and salvific value of the violence represented in Revelation. He stresses that the sword that comes out of Christ's mouth cuts away all evil, "the buds and offshoots of evil," τὰ τῆς κακίας βλαστήματα, and "false convictions in thoughts," τὰς τῶν φρονημάτων ψευδοδοξίας. Likewise, Christ's eyes are fiery (Rev 2:18–20) because their sights dry up evil and eliminate it. Once again, violence in the Apocalypse is interpreted by Origen as directed against evil, and as good precisely for this reason, in that it cooperates to the salvific end. As is evident, Evagrius's interpretation of the "intelligible 'sword'" is the same as Origen's interpretation of Christ's two-edged sword in Revelation: it is the agent of the destruction of evil and therefore of ignorance. The Logos cuts away evilness and ignorance. As for the mention of the separation of the mortal body from the soul, this is clearly a reference to ordinary death, of which I have already pointed out the very positive conception in Evagrius's thought, just as in that of Origen, Methodius, and Nyssen. This definitely cooperates to the eventual elimination of evil.

A possible Greek parallel to this *kephalaion* is found in *Selected Passages on Psalms* 149:6 (PG 12:1681B).

5.29. Just as those who visit cities to see their beauties are filled with wonder when they observe each of the artworks, so will also the intellect, when it comes close to the intellections of beings, be filled with desire of the spirit and not abandon admiration.

Evagrius drawns here a simile between the awe inspired by sense-perceptible beauty and the unquenchable awe and spiritual desire inspired by the intellections of beings. It is probable that Evagrius in the last sentence is relying on a concept of infinite contemplation and desire that was developed especially by Origen and Gregory of Nyssa. The latter famously developed the concept of *epektasis* and of the infinite desire of each intellectual soul for God on which this is based. I have demonstrated that Gregory's doctrine of *epektasis* was inspired by Origen (in "*Apokatastasis* and *Epektasis* in *Hom. in Cant.*: The Relation between Two Core Doctrines in Gregory and Roots in Origen," in *Proceedings of the XIII International Colloquium on Gregory of Nyssa, Rome, 17–20 September 2014* [ed. Giulio Maspero; Leiden: Brill, 2016], a systematic investigation into Origen's influence upon Gregory with respect to this and many other doctrines is in program). Evagrius was well acquainted with both Gregory's and Origen's writings and is likely to have been inspired by both for this *kephalaion*, just as in many other cases. Moreover, Evagrius seems to have been a personal disciple of Gregory Nyssen, as many convergent clues suggest. See Ramelli, "Evagrius and Gregory." The more the intellect contemplates the existing beings and receives their intellections, the more it fills with awe and desire for more knowledge.

5.30. If it is true that the kingdom of heavens is the contemplation of beings, and that, according to our Lord's saying, it is "inside us," but if our inside is occupied by demons, then it is right to say that the Philistines occupy the Land of the Promise.

Strong is the continuity between this *kephalaion* and *KG* 5.29; Evagrius goes on reflecting on the contemplation of beings. In *KG* 5.29 he used a simile; here he uses allegoresis applied to scriptural details: the kingdom of heavens, the Philistines, and the promised land. He has already spoken of the kingdom of heavens in *KG* 1.44; 4.30, and 40. In *KG* 4.30 he has described it as "the spiritual contemplation of the worlds/aeons that will come into existence," and in *KG* 4.40 he has identified it with the revelation of "the intellections of the *praktikē* and of nature, and of the *logoi* concerning God" (see above, the relevant commentaries). Here, more simply but consistently, Evagrius identifies the kingdom of heavens with the contemplation of beings. Now, this contemplation is inside us, in our (intellectual) souls. The interiority of the human being—Evagrius argues—should harbor the kingdom of heavens, that is, the contemplation of beings. But one's intellect, on the contrary, could also harbor demons, and in this case it is driven away from contemplation.

The scriptural passage on which Evagrius relies is Luke 17:12, which in modern versions is usually translated, "The kingdom of God is among you," or "in the midst of you," but which should better be rendered, "The kingdom of God is inside you." I have thoroughly demonstrated elsewhere that the ancient Syriac versions support the correct interpretation of the Greek (see Ilaria L. E. Ramelli, "Luke 17:12: 'God's Kingdom Is inside You'; The Ancient Syriac Versions in Support of the Correct Translation," *Hugoye* 12.2 [2009]: 259–86). This *kephalaion* strongly confirms my interpretation, not only in its Syriac translation—which of course relies on the ancient Syriac versions of the New Testament—but evidently also in the underlying Greek, since the sense of the whole *kephalaion* conveys the idea that the kingdom of heavens is, or should be, in the interiority of each human being, just as contemplation is.

As for the Philistines, here allegorized as demons who occupy one's soul, see below, *KG* 5.36 and the relevant commentary.

5.31. The intelligible "shield" is practical knowledge, which preserves the part of the soul subject to passion without harm.

This is one of the many *kephalaia* in which Evagrius offers allegorical, spiritual interpretations of details in the Old Testament and the New, in the footsteps of Origen. In this type of *kephalaia* he regularly indicates the "intelligible" counterpart of objects that appear in the Bible. For instance, in *KG* 3.41 he explains what is the intelligible sun, in *KG* 3.52 what is the intelligible moon, in *KG* 4.12 what is the intelligible circumcision, in *KG* 4.18 the intelligible anointing, in *KG* 4.28 the intelligible unleavened breads, in *KG* 4.36 the intelligible fat presumably of sacrifices, in *KG* 4.48 the intelligible turban, in *KG* 4.52 the intelligible plate, in *KG* 4.63 the intelligible mercy seat, in *KG* 4.66 the intelligible pectoral of the high priest, in *KG* 4.69 the intelligible mantle, in *KG* 4.72 the intelligible breeches, in *KG* 4.75 the intelligible ephod of the high priest, in *KG* 4.79 the intelligible belt of the high priest, in *KG* 4.82 the intelligible refuge, in *KG* 5.2 the intelligible church, in *KG* 5.13 the intelligible cloud, in *KG* 5.16 the intelligible darkness, and in *KG* 5.28 the intelligible sword. See all the relevant commentaries above. The present *kephalaion* is related to *KG* 5.28 and continues its exegetical discourse in that it interprets another piece of armory mentioned in Scripture: the shield.

Here the scriptural reference, according to Guillaumont (p. 189), seems to be Eph 6:16, where Paul, or the Pauline author, mentions the "shield of faith," but of course in the Old Testament references to shields are legion. Some among these may be singled out, in which the Lord is identified with the shield of the believer, such as Deut 33:29; 2 Sam 22:3; Pss 115:9–11; 119:114; 144:2; Prov 30:5. In 2 Sam 22:36 and Ps 3:3 God is said to have granted to David, and the psalmist, respectively, "the shield of his salvation." Evagrius may be referring to the last two passages as well, for instance. In any case, the defensive function of the shield was naturally liable to a noetic interpretation as the defense of the *praktikē* soul. soul. But I think that a probable, specific reference to Exod 28:13–14 and 25 (LXX) read through Gregory of Nyssa can be detected here. What these Septuagint verses call "little shields" (ἀσπιδίσκαι) in the garments of the high priest, Gregory in his comments on this passage in *Life of Moses* 2.197–199 called "shields" (ἀσπίδες). These, hanging from the shoulders of the high priest, were interpreted by Gregory as symbols of "the double nature of the armory against the adversary," the weapons of righteousness that protect the soul from the darts of the devil.

5.32. Whatever is contained in the first cup is like the wine that is the knowledge of incorporeal beings, whereas what is in the second (cup) bears the symbol of water, I mean, the contemplation of bodies. And this is the cup that, from these two (cups), by Wisdom has been mixed for us.

Like the previous *kephalaion*, the present too is concerned with the spiritual interpretation of objects mentioned in the Old Testament; the reference here is to Prov 9:2, where Wisdom is said to have mixed her wine. Wine and water represent the knowledge of incorporeal and corporeal beings respectively. In turn, Wisdom is Christ, and wine and water are the sacramental representation of the blood and water that were effused on the cross (John 19:34). It is probable that Evagrius had this connotation in mind as well, given that Christ, Wisdom and Logos, is the source of all knowledge for the *logika.*

5.33. The dishonest steward is unable to work the earth. For he has abandoned the virtues of his soul. As for begging, this miserable chap is ashamed, he who is the teacher of the others. And those who are are still further below (him), he teaches (them) in an irate manner, he who has withdrawn just to remain among contentious men.

The biblical passage that Evagrius is interpreting here in the moral sense is Luke 16:3, where the steward ruminates on what he can do and realizes that he cannot either work the earth or beg (interestingly, it is slightly different from that of the Syriac version S_1, which rather bears on Luke 16:5–6). "Begging" is based on a marginal emendation in the Syriac manuscript, ܘܕܚܘܪ, instead of the reading ܘܪܚܘܪ in the body of the text. Evagrius seems to target here people who teach others but are not virtuous.

The spiritual meaning of working the earth as doing God's work has a long history that goes back to Philo's *On Agriculture*, as well as Origen and Gregory of Nyssa, who represent God himself as a farmer and his work on human souls as agricultural work. Gregory of Nyssa at the end of his dialogue *On the Soul and the Resurrection* has a long development of God as a farmer and his work of purification and growth on the souls. This farming metaphor was very dear to Evagrius, who uses it in reference to God also toward the end of his *Letter to Melania*. The conclusive metaphor in this letter is that of God as a merciful farmer, and it is exactly the same as that of the final section of Gregory of Nyssa's *On the Soul and the Resurrection*, where God, the good farmer, is said to take care even of the most damaged seeds and to make sure that absolutely all of them become fruitful. As Gregory concludes, "the earth will be blessed, and the farmer, the soil, and those who have been fed will sing glory and praise to the First Farmer, to whom all the seeds of blessing belong, for eternity." This is not the only *kephalaion* in which Evagrius uses agricultural metaphors. See also *KG* 2.25 and 4.1 and the relevant commentaries above.

5.34. The intelligible "helmet" is the spiritual knowledge, that which preserves the intelligent faculty of the soul unharmed.

This *kephalaion* stands in obvious continuity with *KG* 5.31, where Evagrius was interpreting on the intelligible plane another piece of defensive armory, the shield. While the shield represents practical science, the helmet represents spiritual science. The former defends the *praktikē* soul, the latter the *nous*.

The scriptural reference is here, according to Guillaumont (p. 191), Eph 6:17, where Paul (or the Pauline author) invites readers to take on "the helmet of salvation." It must be noted that in 1 Thess 5:8 Paul identifies the helmet with "the hope for salvation." Also, references to helmets, as well as to other pieces of armory, abound in the Old Testament too. Shield and helmet are associated not only in Eph 6:17 but also, for instance, in Ezek 23:24, "they shall set themselves against you on every side with buckler, shield, and helmet, and I will commit the judgment to them, and they shall judge you according to their judgments"; 27:10, "Persia and Lud and Put were in your army as your men of war; they hung the shield and helmet in you; they gave you splendor"; and 38:4–5, "all of them clothed in full armor ... all of them with shield and helmet." What is more, Isa 59:17 is the direct inspirer of 1 Thess 5:8, and, probably through this, of Eph 6:17: the Lord "put on righteousness as a breastplate, and a helmet of salvation upon his head" (RSV).

5.35. If it is true that the bread of the rational nature is the contemplation of beings, and that this we have been ordered to eat by means of the sweat of our faces, it is evident that it is by means of the *praktikē* that we eat this (bread).

Evagrius is going on with the allegorical interpretation of Scripture, which is so prominent in the present group of *kephalaia*. This particular *kephalaion* is clearly linked with *KG* 5.30, where the contemplation of beings is said to coincide with the kingdom of heavens. Here it is said to coincide with the bread of rational creatures. In *KG* 1.23 the bread of the angels is said to be the Ideas of the beings that are on earth. Here the bread of the rational nature, which includes angels, is said to be the contemplation of beings in general. Here Evagrius argues that the contemplation of beings is attained through *praktikē*—given that asceticism is an effort, *praktikē* is here symbolized by the sweat mentioned in Gen 3:19 as a malediction to men. Indeed, one must purify one's soul from passions and bad movements before one can attain contemplation. This sequence, purification first and then contemplation, was typical of both "pagan" and Christian Platonism. See Blossom Stefaniw, "Exegetical Curricula in Origen, Didymus, and Evagrius: Pedagogical Agenda and the Case for Neoplatonist Influence," *StPatr* 44 (2010): 281–95. In *On Thoughts* 26 Evagrius is clear that it is impossible to acquire science without having renounced mundane things, evil, and, after these, ignorance. See also *KG* 1.78–80, with the relevant commentary above, and already in Clement the passage from the cathartic to the epoptic mode in *Stromateis* 5.70.7–71.2.

5.36. Those who have inherited the Land of the Promise with all their force will kill the Philistines who are in it, lest, when Joshua grows old in them, he desist from going out in their force, and they be enslaved again to the Philistines.

This is another *kephalaion* that interprets Old Testament facts allegorically. In *KG* 5.30 the Philistines are identified with demons, who, through evil thoughts and passions, drive human beings to sin. There we have already found allegorization of the Philistines as demons and their opposition to the promised land (see above, the relevant commentary). Faithful to his ideal of *apatheia*, Evagrius insists that passions must be completely eradicated once and for all, and not fought all the time by the rational faculty of the soul, represented by Joshua (which already Origen took as a figure of Christ-Logos). The biblical reference is Josh 13:1–2, where Joshua is said to have grown old and to be unable to sustain further battles, while a great part of the promised land must still be conquered. The Philistines are identified with tempting demons also in the prologue to Evagrius's *Talking Back*, 3: "We have carefully selected words from the Holy Scriptures, so that we may equip ourselves with them and drive out the Philistines forcefully, standing firm in the battle, as warriors and soldiers for our victorious King, Jesus Christ."

Origen referred frequently to allegorical "Philistines," who were his adversaries from within the church and criticized both his allegorical exegesis of Scripture and his theology. In *Homilies on Genesis* 13.4 Origen identifies the Philistines with those Christians who do not want him to speculate about the causes for Jacob's election and Esau's repudiation—which according to Origen lie in his grand doctrine of the *logika*, their fall, and their restoration: "I too wanted to ask him: 'Lord, who sinned, this man, Esau, or his parents, that he should be born all full of hair like this, and that he should be supplanted by his brother already in the womb?' But if I want to ask God's Logos about this and make an investigation, some Philistines will immediately attack me and level calumnies against me!" *Et ego uolebam interrogare eum et dicere: Domine, quis peccauit, hic Esau aut parentes eius, ut sic totus hirsutus et horridus nasceretur, ut in utero supplantaretur a fratre? Sed si uoluero de his interrogare Uerbum Dei et inquirere, statim mihi lites Philistini et calumnias mouent.* These were Christians who criticized Origen's allegorical exegesis of Scripture and the theological and anthropological doctrines that he drew from it. In the same passage Origen is clear that these people opposed his spiritual and allegorical interpretation of the Old Testament, here represented by the notion of digging deep to find living water, that is, the hidden and salvific meaning of Scripture: "For if I want to dig deep and open hidden veins of living water, immediately some Philistines will appear and attack me; they will altercate and level calumnies against me and will begin to fill my wells with their earth and mud," *Si enim uoluero in altum fodere et aquae uiuae latentes uenas aperire, continuo aderunt Philistini et litigabunt mecum, rixas mihi et calumnias commouebunt, et incipient replere terra sua et luto puteos meos.* The identity of these opponents of Origen as Christian literalists, present even in the congregation he was addressing, is confirmed in 13.2–3:

> Who are these Philistines, who fill wells with earth? No doubt they are those who limit the interpretation of the law [i.e., the Old Testament] to the earthly and fleshly level, while they preclude the spiritual and mystical interpretation.... If I attempt to find out the spiritual sense of Scripture, to remove the veil of the law and show that what is written is allegorical, indeed I dig wells, but immediately the friends of literal exegesis will level calumnies against me and will ambush me; they will instantly machinate, preparing hostilities and persecutions, claiming that truth cannot be found but on earth.
>
> *Qui sunt isti, qui terra puteos replent? Illi sine dubio, qui in legem terrenam et carnalem intelligentiam ponunt, et spiritalem ac mysticam claudunt.... Si sensum in iis quaerere spiritalem, si conatus fuero uelamen legis amouere et ostendere allegorica esse quae scripta sunt, fodio quidem puteos, sed statim mihi mouebunt calumnias amici litterae et insidiabuntur mihi, inimicitias continuo et persecutiones parabunt, ueritatem negantes stare posse nisi super terram.*

5.37. The intelligible hook is the spiritual teaching, that which raises up the rational soul from the depths of evilness toward virtue.

Here is yet another case of noetic exegesis of a scriptural detail in the *KG*. Guillaumont (p. 193) refers to Job 40:25 as the scriptural passage that Evagrius has here in mind, though this is not the only possible one. There are some, albeit not many, scriptural references to the hook that Evagrius could so allegorize. In Matt 17:27 a fish is ordered by Jesus to be fished by means of a hook; it will have a coin in its mouth, by which to pay the tribute. More references are in the Old Testament. In 2 Kgs 19:28 and in Isa 37:29 the Lord is speaking to Hezekiah by means of Isaiah: "Because you have raged against me and your arrogance has come into my ears, I will put my hook in your nose and my bit in your mouth, and I will turn you back on the way by which you came." In this case, as in the *kephalaion* under examination here, the hook is a means of moral improvement, albeit forced. In Job 41:1–2, the Lord asks Job: "Can you draw out Leviathan with a fishhook, or press down his tongue with a cord? Can you put a rope in his nose, or pierce his jaw with a hook?" This sea monster is identified with the devil on the basis of Isa 27:1, where Leviathan is described as a serpent or dragon that will be slain by the Lord. In Job 40:25, likewise, in reference to Behemoth, God asks Job whether it is possible to take him with hooks. Since Behemoth can be interpreted as the devil, it is all the more relevant that Gregory of Nyssa used the metaphor of the fishhook in order to illustrate the action of Christ on the devil. Indeed Gregory, well known to Evagrius and perhaps his spiritual father, used the metaphor of the fishhook in reference to the devil in his *Catechetical Oration* 24, which is deeply inspired by Origen. Gregory states that, when the divine fishhook was gulped by the devil, "life was introduced into the house of death, and light shone forth in darkness; thus, that which is diametrically opposed to light and life vanished, for it is not in the nature of darkness to remain when light is present, or of death to exist when life is active." Now, the same argument that life (i.e., Christ, eternal life), being diametrically opposed to death, will make it vanish was brought about by Origen in *Commentary on Romans* 5.7.78–88. Gregory added that the deception of the devil by means of the hook was for him salvific, since it enabled his healing by Christ. Evagrius, too, here allegorizes the fishhook as a drawing force that acts upon the soul, dragging it upward from evilness and vice to virtue. The act of drawing upward to the Good is ascribed to Christ thanks to his cross in John 12:32: "And I, when I am lifted up from earth, shall draw all human beings to myself."

5.38. The one who fights in view of the impassivity will arm him or herself with the precepts, while the one who does so in view of the truth, it

is with knowledge that he or she will destroy his or her enemies. Now, the defeat of the former is when he does something that is condemned by the law, while that of the second is when he becomes head of false teachings and ideas.

Following the precepts of the moral law, the commandments, which aim at *apatheia*, is the way of the *praktikē*; science is the way of contemplation, aiming at the knowledge of the truth, the goal of gnosis. Evagrius illustrates here the shortcomings in each of these two paths.

5.39. In pure thought there lie impressed a sky/heaven, luminous to see, and a vast region, in which it appears how the intellections of beings and the holy angels go toward those who are worthy of this. Now, this vision that is impressed, resentment lets it be seen in a blurred way, while rage, when it is enflamed, definitely annihilates it.

Evagrius, playing with the metaphor of light for contemplation and knowledge, a metaphor that is dear to him, is explaining here the more or less destructive effects of passions upon knowledge. He has already explained the negative, blinding effects of an excess of the irascible and the concupiscible faculties of the soul, that is, anger and desire, in *KG* 5.27 (see above, the relevant commentary). Here he meditates more specifically on the degrees of anger, so dangerous in his view that in *Letter* 56.4 Evagrius warns that anger can transform a human *nous* into a demon. Irritation is a milder form of rage and limits itself to obscuring the intellections of beings, while rage, at its culmination, blinds people, completely destroying their intellectual vision and their capacity for receiving any intellections. See also Evagrius, *Letter* 38.592.23–25.

5.40. The intelligible mountain is spiritual contemplation, that which lies on a high peak to which it is hard to come close. Once the intellect has arrived at it, it will be a seer of all the intellections of the objects that are beneath it.

The biblical reference may be the mountain on which Moses met the Lord in Sinai (Exod 19:3–25), after the liberation of the Hebrews from Egypt. This is also called Mount Sinai. Moses's ascent to the mountain was a mystical metaphor for Gregory of Nyssa in his *Life of Moses*, which Evagrius knew very well. For both Gregory and Evagrius the ascent to the mountain represents spiritual contemplation, although Gregory emphasized negative theology more. Evagrius highlights the difficulty of spiritual contemplation, but not any impossibility. The intellect can arrive at the summit of the mountain and attain spiritual contemplation. Note, however, that the intellections that the intellect will attain are said to be those of beings below, and not of the divinity. In this *kephalaion* Evagrius wants to present spiritual contemplation as subsuming all inferior contemplations. So far in these *kephalaia* Evagrius has spoken of a mountain at *KG* 5.6 and 5.21, but there it was detailed that it was Mount Zion (see the relevant commentaries for the allegorical interpretation of Zion). Here no specification is given. The very notion of a mountain, however, conveys the idea of elevation.

5.41. The person in whose soul the intelligible world is wholly impressed refrains from all corruptible desire. Indeed, (this person) is ashamed of the things in which she delighted beforehand, when her thought rebukes her for her past stupidity.

The idea of the intelligible world as "impressed" goes back to *KG* 5.39 above. There are people in whose rational soul the whole intelligible world (*κόσμος νοητός*) is impressed. This intellectual excellence, as is typical in Evagrius's thought, goes hand in hand with moral excellence. This is also why morally wrong choices are tantamount not only to immorality but also to foolishness and stupidity. Already Bardaisan of Edessa described sinners as "fools" at the end of the *Book of the Laws of Countries* (see Ramelli, "Origen, Bardaisan, and the Origin of Universal Salvation"; and the translation and commentary in Ramelli, ed., *Bardaisan on Free Will*). Of course the ultimate philosophical basis for this position was Socratic-Platonic and Stoic ethical intellectualism.

5.42. That world that is built up in mind is regarded as difficult to see during the day. For the intellect is distracted by the senses and by sense-perceptible light, which shines forth. However, during the night it is possible to see it, when during prayer time it is luminously impressed.

Evagrius continues here, from *KG* 5.41, his reflection on the intelligible world, or *κόσμος νοητός*—not primarily, however, that which is in Christ-Logos-Wisdom but that which is impressed in a human being's intellect. Here Evagrius takes up the Platonic tension between sense perceptible and intelligible, which was developed also by Origen and Gregory of Nyssa in his dialogue *On the Soul and the Resurrection*. Sense perception distracts the intellect and somehow blurs its vision. During the time of prayer, sense perception is driven out, so that attention can be entirely focused on the intelligible world. Indeed, in Evagrius's view the ascetic life that imitates the life of angels—as in Gregory Nyssen's view—consists especially in prayer; the ascetics' imitation of the angelic life passes primarily through prayer, the fruit of both practical virtue and knowledge (see Evagrius [under Nilus's name], *On Prayer* 72 and 111 [PG 79:1181D and 1192C]). Evagrius is clear that prayer is even more important in *praktikē* than other ascetic practices, such as vigil, fasting, and the like, because the latter need also the body and cannot be performed continuously, while prayer needs only the intellect and must be incessant according to 1 Thess 5:17 (*Praktikos* 49). Evagrius's own definition of prayer is found in *Skemmata* 26–27: "Prayer is a state of the intellect destructive of every earthly intellection and produced only by the light of the Holy Trinity." Evagrius devoted his *Propositions on Prayer* to this topic, as the earliest treatise on apophatic prayer. See Monica Tobon, "From Evagrian Prayer to Centering Prayer," in *Colloquium Origenianum Undecimum, Aarhus, 26–31 August 2013* (ed. Anders-Christian Jacobsen; Leuven: Peeters, 2016).

5.43. The intelligible "way" is the condition of the rational soul in which the intellect, when it makes progress in it, will meet the objects and understand their intellections.

This is another of the many *kephalaia* in which Evagrius offers a spiritual interpretation of an object that appears in the Old or in the New Testament. Here the most conspicuous biblical reference that comes to mind is John 14:6, where Jesus declares: "I am the Way, Truth, and Life," even though in the whole Bible references to ways and paths are numerous. Among all these occurrences, those referring to "the way of the Lord" (Gen 18:19; Judg 2:22; 2 Kgs 21:22; Isa 40:3; Jer 5:5; Ezek 18:25; Pss 18:30; 27:11; 37:34; 77:13; 86:11; etc.) are to be singled out, as well as the use of "way" in the sense of conduct of life in Ps 1 and other psalms and proverbs, but also in Isaiah, Jeremiah, Ezekiel. The "way" in this *kephalaion* is the way to intellectual knowledge. On this way the *nous* meets the object of knowledge and can understand the intellections of these objects.

5.44. If it is true that "wine is the rage of serpents" and that it is from wine that the Nazirites abstain, then the Nazirites are ordered to be without rage.

The scriptural reference, Deut 32:33, is here easy to track down, even if it has a slightly different meaning in the Hebrew: "their wine is the poison of serpents." But in the Septuagint, which Evagrius has in mind, the quotation is: "Their wine is the rage of serpents." As for the law of the Nazirites, who could not drink wine, the relevant reference is Num 6:3. The same biblical quotations, and the same interpretation of them, are found in Evagrius's *On Evil Thoughts* 5: "There should be no wrath in those who pray. 'Their wine is the rage of serpents'; this is why the Nazirites abstained from wine." And in *Praktikos* 38 Evagrius notes that charity-love bridles rage, and this is why Moses calls it "fighter of serpents" (Lev 11:22), to whom rage is ascribed. Through the spiritual exegesis of the Nazirite prescriptions, Evagrius condemns again the passion of rage (that of Plato's irascible soul), as in *KG* 5.39, and just as in 5.41 he has condemned the passion of desire (that of Plato's concupiscible soul). These two groups embrace and represent all passions. Rage or anger, as I have often remarked, is singled out by Evagrius as particularly destructive in *Letter* 56.4, since it can turn human intellects into demons, the latter in turn associated with serpents.

5.45. The intellect is called the head/guide of the soul. Virtues, then, are the symbolic meaning of the hair, once deprived of which, the Nazirite will be separate from knowledge and will be led away by his enemies in bonds.

The definition of the intellect (*νοῦς*) as guide or leader of the soul is a clear reference to the Greek philosophical designation of *ἡγεμονικόν*, which was used in both the Stoic and the Platonic traditions. Virtues, again, relate to the intellect; virtue and knowledge cannot be separated, so that, if one is without virtues, one must necessarily also be without science. The enemies—here the Philistines, the enemies of Samson, who symbolize demons in *KG* 5.30 and 5.36—are likely again demons, of whom a soul without virtue and knowledge easily falls prey. The scriptural passage of which Evagrius is reminiscent is the part of the story of Samson in Judg 16:19–21: "She [Delilah] made him sleep upon her knees; and she called a man, and had him shave off the seven locks of his head. Then she began to torment him, and his strength left him. And she said, 'The Philistines are upon you, Samson!' And he awoke from his sleep, and said, 'I will go out as at other times, and shake myself free.' And he did not know that the Lord had left him. And the Philistines seized him and gouged out his eyes, and brought him down to Gaza, and bound him with bronze fetters; and he ground at the mill in the prison" (RSV).

5.46. The high priest is the one who on behalf of the whole rational nature intercedes before God. And some of them he separates from evilness, and some others of them from ignorance.

This high priest is clearly Christ-Logos. Unlike the Hebrew high priest, who intercedes for Israel alone, Christ intercedes for all rational creatures. His work is, again, twofold, leading to both virtue and knowledge. Origen, in his exegesis of Hebrews, had much insisted on Christ's capacity as high priest precisely in respect to the universality of his priestly intercessory ministry (see Ilaria L. E. Ramelli, "The Universal and Eternal Validity of Jesus's High-Priestly Sacrifice: The Epistle to the Hebrews in Support of Origen's Theory of Apokatastasis," in *A Cloud of Witnesses: The Theology of Hebrews in Its Ancient Contexts* [ed. Richard J. Bauckham et al.; London: T&T Clark, 2008], 210–21). That Christ's sacrifice, performed both as a high priest and as a victim, has an effectiveness that extends to all rational creatures—exactly as Evagrius declares here—was stressed by Origen in *Commentary on Romans* 5.10.187–195, where Origen insists that the power and effectiveness of Christ's cross is so great as to be enough for all rational creatures (see below). And Evagrius here recalls Origen's exegesis of the Epistle to the Hebrews, where he stresses that Christ, as a high priest, has accomplished a sacrifice, that of himself, which has universal and eternal validity. In his *Commentary on Romans* indeed Origen quotes Heb 9:26 and explains the necessity of Jesus's work as a propitiatory victim: "At the end of the world, in the very last time, God manifested his justice and offered as redemption him, whom he made a propitiator.... For God is just, and the just could not justify unjust people. Therefore, he wanted that there might be the intervention of a propitiator, so that those who could not be justified by their own works might be justified by his faithfulness / by faith in him," *In consummatione etenim saeculi in nouissimo tempore manifestauit Deus iustitiam suam et redemptionem dedit eum quem propitiatorem fecit.... Deus enim iustus est, et iustus iustificare non poterat iniustos: ideo interuentum uoluit esse propitiatoris ut per eius fidem iustificarentur qui per opera propria iustificari non poterant* (3.5.19–26). And soon after Origen explains, on the basis of 1 John 2:2, that this work was done not only for the Christians but for the whole world:

> John said that Christ is the expiation or propitiation for our sins, and not only ours, but also those of the whole world. Now these words have seemed to us to introduce some deeper mystery: they show that Jesus is the propitiator not only of the believers and faithful but also of all the world, however, not of the world first and of us after, but of us first, and then, in the end, of the whole world. Indeed, even if each and every creature awaits the Redeemer's grace, nevertheless each one will come to salvation when it is his or her turn.… All these details, if understood mystically, indicate Christ's future propitiatory work not only for our sins but also for the whole world.
>
> *Quod dixit Iohannes, quia ipse est exoratio siue propitiatio pro peccatis nostris, et non solum pro nostris, sed et pro uniuerso mundo, quaedam nobis intulisse uidetur augmenta mysterii, ut ostendat Iesum propitiatorem esse non solum credentium et fidelium, uerum et totius mundi, non tamen prius mundi et tunc nostrum, sed prius nostrum et ita demum totius mundi. Quamuis enim uniuersa creatura gratiam redemptoris expectet, unusquisque tamen in suo ordine ueniet ad salutem … quae singula mystico intellectu futuram Christi propitiationem non solum pro peccatis nostris sed et pro uniuerso mundo.* (3.5.205–222)

In his *Commentary on John* 1.35.255, Origen, after presenting again Jesus as "propitiation," says, evidently grounding his argument in the Epistle to the Hebrews, that he is "the high priest" (Heb 4:14; cf. 10:19) who has offered himself in sacrifice once and for all, "not only for the sake of human beings, but also for all rational creatures." Origen affirms this on the basis of Heb 2:9, according to both its attested variant readings, χάριτι Θεοῦ ὑπὲρ παντὸς ἐγεύσατο θανάτου, which is the reading of P[46] (third century) and of the majority of manuscripts, and χωρὶς Θεοῦ ὑπὲρ παντὸς ἐγεύσατο θανάτου, which is the reading of MSS 1379, 424c, Eusebius, Ambrose, Jerome, and Oecumenius. Now, both of these readings support the absolute universality of the intention and effectiveness of Jesus's sacrifice, whether we read, "He tasted death for all for God's grace," or "He tasted death for all except God," since God obviously did not need to be saved. Thus, referring to the latter reading, Origen concludes: "If he experienced death for the sake of all apart from God, then he died not only for human beings, but also for all other rational creatures." This is famously one of the tenets of Origen's eschatological conception: salvation will eventually extend not only to the whole of humanity but also to all rational creatures, including fallen angels and the devil. This doctrine was already criticized during Origen's life but was taken up in all its radical implications not only by Evagrius but also by Didymus and by Gregory of Nyssa, especially in his *In illud: Tunc et ipse Filius* (commentary on 1 Cor 15:28), where he proclaims that finally "no being will remain outside the number of the saved," and in *On the Soul and the Resurrection*, and in his *Catechetical Oration*, where he clearly announces the eventual healing and salvation of the devil. On this point see Ramelli, *Christian Doctrine of Apokatastasis*, the chapters on Didymus, Gregory, and Evagrius.

An important argument, well known to Evagrius and connected to the Epistle to the Hebrews and to the universal and eternal validity of Christ's sacrifice as a high priest, is developed by Origen, as I briefly mentioned, in his *Commentary on Romans* 5.10.158–240. Origen begins with a refutation of those who think that Christ's sacrifice would have to be repeated over and over again (an accusation that was curiously leveled against him during the "Origenistic controversy," whereas it is clear that Origen himself disproved it): "This is why I wonder how some people can contradict this statement of Paul [Rom 6:9: "Christ, being raised from the dead, will never die again"], even if it is absolutely clear, and want to claim that Christ will necessarily have to suffer the same or something similar again in the future aeons, to liberate also those whom his salvific medication could not heal in the present life," *Unde miror quosdam contra hanc euidentissimam Pauli sententiam uelle asserere quod in futuris iterum saeculis uel eadem uel similia pati necesse sit Christum ut liberari possint etiam hi quos in praesenti uita dispensationis eius medicina sanare non potuit.* The point of at least some of Origen's opponents was based on the possibility of ever new falls on the part of rational creatures. Origen is adamant that this is not at all what he personally teaches and in fact cannot be the case ("They think that Christ will have to repeat the same salvific deeds also in the future aeons. But to this we shall reply briefly, as we can," *Easdem etiam in futuris saeculis dispensationes a Christo repetenda esse arbitrantur. Sed ad haec nos breuiter prout possumus respondebimus*). Origen's reply is grounded in two main tenets:

(1) It is impossible and unnecessary that Christ's sacrifice be reiterated, because, even though it occurred once and for all, its effectiveness was such as to reach absolutely all rational creatures and all aeons:

> Christ died to sin once and for all and will not die again.... I do not deny in the least that rational creatures will always keep their free will, but I maintain that the power and effectiveness of Christ's cross and death is so great as to be enough to set right and heal not only the present and the future aeon but also the past ones, and not only this order of us humans but also the heavenly powers and orders. For, according to the declaration of the apostle Paul himself, Christ, by means of the blood of his cross, pacified not only the creatures that are on earth but also those in heaven.
>
> *Semel Christus mortuus est peccato, et ultra iam non moritur.... Manere quidem naturae rationabili semper liberum arbitrium non negamus, sed tantam esse uim crucis Christi et mortis huius ... asserimus, quae ad sanitatem et remedium non solum praesentis et futuri, sed etiam praeteritorum saeculorum, et non solum humano huic nostro ordini, sed etiam caelestibus uirtutibus ordinibusque sufficiat. Secundum sententiam namque ipsius Pauli apostoli Christus pacificauit per sanguinem crucis suae non solum quae in terra sunt, sed et quae in caelis.* (*Commentary on Romans* 5.10.235–236, 187–195)

Hence, it is also clear that for Origen the salvation of all rational creatures entirely depends, not on a metaphysical necessity, but on Christ's cross (both this tenet and the universal validity of Christ's sacrifice are stated also in 2.9.524–527: "The devil was keeping us prisoners; we were dragged to him, and far from God, by our sins; thus he asked for Christ's blood as the price of our ransom.... Jesus's blood would be given, which was so precious as to be enough for the redemption of all," *Tenebat autem nos diabolus, cui distracti fueramus peccatis nostris; poposcit ergo pretium nostrum sanguinem Christi.... Iesu sanguis daretur, qui tam pretiosus fuit ut solus pro omnium redemptione sufficeret*).

(2) It is not the case that the fall of all rational creatures, humans and angels, will take place over and over again, indefinitely, because there will come an end of all aeons, which will be the eventual *apokatastasis*, and in that condition no fall will occur any longer, because perfect charity-love will prevent this:

> But what is that which in the future aeons will prevent free will from falling again into sin? Well, the apostle Paul teaches us this quite pithily when he says, "Love never falls" [1 Cor 13:8]. Indeed, this is why charity-love is said to be greater than faith and hope, because it is the only factor thanks to which it will be impossible to sin again. For, if a soul has

> reached such a degree of perfection as to love God with its whole heart, its whole mind, and all of its forces, and to love its neighbor as much as it loves itself, where will be a place (an occasion) for sin? … Charity-love will prevent every creature from falling again, at that stage when God will be "all in all." Indeed, the apostle Paul reached such a degree of perfection and from there declared with confidence: "Who will be able to separate us from God's charity-love, which is in Christ Jesus?" … The power of charity-love is so great as to drag all beings to itself…, especially in that God has been the first to give us reasons for charity-love, since he did not spare his only Child but gave him for the sake of all of us.
>
> *Quod autem sit quod in futuris saeculis teneat arbitrii libertatem ne rursum corruat in peccatum breui nos sermone apostolus docet dicens: "Caritas numquam cadit." Idcirco enim et fide et spe maior caritas dicitur, quia sola erit per quam delinqui ultra non poterit. Si enim in id anima perfectionis ascenderit ut ex toto corde suo et ex tota mente sua et ex totis uiribus suis diligat Deum et proximum suum tamquam se ipsam, ubi erit peccati locum?… Caritas omnem creaturam continebit a lapsu, tunc cum erit Deus omnia in omnibus. Ad hunc namque perfectionis gradum ascenderat apostolus Paulus et in hoc stans confidens dicebat: "Quis enim nos separabit a caritate Dei quae est in Christo Iesu?" … Tanta caritatis uis est ut ad se omnia trahat…, maxime cum caritatis causas prior nobis dederit Deus qui unico filio suo non pepercit, sed pro nobis omnibus tradidit.* (*Commentary on Romans* 5.10.195–226)

To the implicit objection that charity-love (ἀγάπη) could not impede Satan's fall, or Adam's, Origen replies that this took place not in the final *apokatastasis* but before the manifestation of Christ's charity-love: "The one who was the morning star, Lucifer, and used to rise in the sky [i.e., Satan], or the one who was immaculate from his birth and was put together with the cherubim [i.e., Adam], could fall only before being tied by the bonds of charity-love to the good done by God's Child," *Uel ille qui Lucifer fuit et in caelo oriebatur, uel ille qui immaculatus erat a natiuitate sua et cum cherubin positus, labi potuit antequam erga beneficia Filii Dei caritatis uinculis stringeretur* (*Commentary on Romans* 5.10.227–230). This is also one of the reasons why Origen thought that the end would be not only similar to, but even better than, the beginning. The preeminence of charity-love is stressed by Origen over and over again, especially in *Commentary on Romans* 9.6, where love is said to have to be extended to all, after Christ's example: "Therefore, my brothers and sisters, we are ordered to love and not to judge. For if you think that a certain man is impious, and for this reason you think he is not to be loved, please listen: Christ died for the sake of the impious. Or if, because your brother is a sinner, for this reason you think he is not to be loved, please listen: Jesus Christ came into this world in order to save sinners," *Fratres ergo iubemur diligere, non iudicare. Si enim putas aliquem impium esse et ideo eum non iudicas diligendum, audi quia Christus pro impiis mortuus est. Aut si quia peccator est frater tuus, ideo eum non putas diligendum, audi quia Christus Iesus in hunc mundum uenit peccatores saluos facere.*

In this *kephalaion* it is also clear that Evagrius presents Christ as the chief intercessor, and this is another trait he shares with Origen. The latter, in fact, in *On First Principles* 2.7.3, offers an etymological analysis of the term παράκλητος and explains that, if it refers to the Holy Spirit, it means "consoler"; if it refers to Christ, it means "intercessor." So too, in *On Prayer* 10.15.4, Christ is the intercessor who beseeches the Father, and in *Against Celsus* 3.49 and 4.28, on the basis of Paul, Christ is presented as universal intercessor, whose sacrifice has universal efficacy, for all creatures: "Christ is the Savior of all human beings, and especially of those who believe, be these intelligent or simpler, and is a propitiator before the Father for our sins, and not only ours, but those of the whole world" (3.49); "Indeed, God is called the Savior of all human beings, and especially of those who believe, and God's Christ is said to be the propitiator for our sins, and not only ours, but those of the whole world" (4.28). See Ilaria L. E. Ramelli, "Alle origini della figura dell'intercessore in età paleocristiana," in *Mediadores con lo divino en el Mediterráneo antiguo, Actas del Congreso Internacional de Historia de las Religiones, Palma de Mallorca 13–15.X.2005* (Palma de Mallorca: Universitat de les Illes Balears, 2011), 2:1003–49.

5.47. We honor angels, not because of their nature, but because of their virtue. And we despise demons because of the evilness that is in them.

In the case of demons, just as in that of angels and all rational creatures, their nature is good, because it was created by God; it is their moral choices that can be evil. Reproaches and merits therefore regard the latter, that is, their moral choices, and not the former, their nature. This was already a stronghold of Origen's polemic against the (especially "Valentinian") determinism of natures. There are not good or evil natures among rational creatures; all natures are good, but the movements of their free will can go toward evil. See Ramelli, *Christian Doctrine of Apokatastasis*, the chapter on Origen. This was also the position of Bardaisan of Edessa, who, far from being a "Gnostic," as he was accused of being, was an anti-Gnostic. See full argument in Ramelli, *Bardaisan of Edessa*, with whom agree Crone, "Daysanis"; Heidi Marx-Wolf, "Bardesanes," in *The Encyclopedia of Ancient History* (ed. Roger S. Bagnall et al.; London: Wiley-Blackwell, 2013), doi:10.1002/9781444338386.wbeah05032; and Michael Speidel, "Making Use of History beyond the Euphrates," in *Mara bar Serapion in Context* (ed. Annette Merz and Teun Tieleman; Leiden: Brill, 2012), 11–41, esp. 36 nn. 94, 96, 99; 37 nn. 104, 106, 108; 38 nn. 110–12; 39 n. 114; 40 n. 118; 41 n. 119. Evagrius, who certainly knew Origen and probably also Bardaisan, followed in their footsteps in this respect.

5.48. Unique among all bodily beings, Christ is for us worthy of worship/adored, because this is the only one that has in himself God the Logos.

The Syriac word for "bodies" here encompasses not only mortal bodies but also spiritual bodies, such as that which Jesus put on after his resurrection (I have translated "bodily beings" because Christ is not simply a body, whether mortal or glorious). As for Origen, so for Evagrius too the rational creature Jesus Christ contains the divine Logos. In Origen's view Christ, thanks to an extremely strong and immutable love for God, was the only rational creature who escaped the fall (*On First Principles* 2.6.3–5) and has become united to God "in an inseparable and indissoluble union," thus acquiring divine characteristics and becoming God. What first depended on this rational soul's free will—to love God, the supreme Good—due to the intensity and the steadfastness of this love has become nature for it, so that the union of this soul with God/Good is a natural union and Christ has become entirely good, that is, divine and thus incapable of sinning (*On First Principles* 2.6.5). This rational creature is divine on account of its union with God and in particular with the divine Logos, the second person of the Trinity, who is God's Logos and Wisdom. Thanks to this union, God the Logos is in Jesus's soul, and Jesus's soul is in the Logos. Origen indeed describes Christ's soul as "a medium between God and the flesh," so that "the Logos could become the human being Jesus" (*Against Celsus* 2.42). This soul was sent by God the Father to receive a human body from Mary (*Commentary on John* 20.162); thus, the incarnate Christ turns out to be a σύνθετόν τι χρῆμα (*Against Celsus* 1.66), and this is possible precisely thanks to the mediation of his soul (*On First Principles* 2.6.3), which provides a link between Christ's divinity and his human body. See my "Atticus and Origen on the Soul of God the Creator:

From the 'Pagan' to the Christian Side of Middle Platonism," *Jahrbuch für Religionsphilosophie* 10 (2011): 13–35. This rational creature's participation in the Logos is perfect (whereas the participation of human souls, and even angelic souls, therein is not). Indeed, since this *logikon* (soul and body, a spiritual and then a mortal body, then again spiritual after the resurrection) has been united to the Logos in such a perfect way, in a supreme participation with God the Son, they have become one and the same thing, ἕν (*Against Celsus* 6.47).

5.49. The strange God is the one that cannot create anything, or the one that is joined to evil(ness).

The scriptural reference here is Ps 80:10, and indeed the corresponding Greek is found in *Selected Passages on Psalms* 80:10 (PG 12:1544D). That which Evagrius gives here is the definition of a "pagan" deity, or a deity that is no God, first because, unlike God the Creator, it cannot create anything from nothing, and second because, unlike God, it is not Goodness itself, pure Good unmixed with evil. The devil, like all demons—with whom "pagan" deities were assimilated from Justin onward—is a creature who is good qua creature but has evil(ness) as a result of his bad choices (see also *KG* 5.47, above, and the relevant commentary).

5.50. The Holy Trinity is uniquely worthy of worship because of itself, since from it at a certain point the incorporeal nature and the corporeal one, from the beginning, from nothing became something.

God the Trinity, as opposed to the false deities just mentioned in *KG* 5.49, is the only Creator and is Creator *ex nihilo* of all existing beings, here classified according to the main partition into incorporeal and corporeal creatures (here, the adjective for "corporeal" means "having a body," not necessarily mortal, but also spiritual and immortal). This is why God—including the divine side of Christ—is the only being worthy of worship. Origen had supported the doctrine of *creatio ex nihilo* for the first time with philosophical arguments (it had been supported even earlier, but not by means of philosophical arguments), and Evagrius is on the same line (see here above, the wide-ranging commentary on *KG* 2.2). Gregory of Nyssa, also well known to Evagrius, elaborated a doctrine of creation on the part of God, who is immaterial, as the creation of the intelligible qualities that make up matter. Thus, God created only immaterial, intelligible things, and matter was constituted by their very concourse. In this way, Gregory could uphold the doctrine of *creatio ex nihilo*, including the creation of matter from nothing—as opposed to the "pagan" notion of preexistent matter—without positing that the immaterial God directly created matter. See Arruzza, "La matière immatérielle"; idem, *Les mésaventures de la théodicée: Plotin, Origène, Grégoire de Nysse* (Turnhout: Brepols, 2011), part 3, with my review in *Bryn Mawr Classical Review*, December 2012, http://bmcr.brynmawr.edu/2012/2012-12-31.html, and the works by Marmodoro and Karamanolis cited above, in the commentary on *KG* 2.1.

5.51. The person who, on the basis of the harmony of beings, sees the Creator, it is not God's nature that she knows, but it is God's Wisdom that she knows, that in which God created everything. Now, with Wisdom I mean, not the essential one, but that which is manifested in the existent beings, that which those who are experts in these matters usually call "natural contemplation." And if this is so, what is the foolishness of those who claim that they know the nature of God?

That God's own nature cannot be known, but only God's activities can, was already a clear tenet of Origen's and Gregory Nyssen's theology (see full documentation in Ramelli, "Divine as an Inaccessible Epistemological Object"). As already Philo did, Origen too supported the thesis of the incomprehensibility of God's nature or essence on the gnoseological plane, and the possibility for humans to know only God's works and activities (ἔργα and ἐνέργειαι). Origen states: "In the limits of our scarce forces, we have known the divine nature by considering it more from its works than through our cognitive capacity; we have observed its visible creatures and have known by faith those invisible, because human frailty cannot see everything with its eyes and know everything with its reason, since the human being is the weakest and most imperfect among all rational beings" (*On First Principles* 2.6.1). In his *Commentary on John* 19.6.37–38, a passage that will exert a strong influence on Gregory of Nyssa, Origen claims that God's nature and power (φύσις and δύναμις) are even beyond being (οὐσία) and that humans cannot reach them with their cognitive capacities: they cannot be "grasped and observed" but barely "peered at." This is the verb for a forbidden object of sight, be it physical or intellectual sight (i.e., cognitive faculty). According to Origen, the Godhead cannot be known by human reason (*Against Celsus* 6.65), and yet it is mysteriously intelligible,

"intelligible thanks to an ineffable power or faculty" (ἀῤῥήτῳ τινι δυνάμει νοητός), even though it transcends everything (πάντων ἐπέκεινα; *Against Celsus* 7.45). In particular, God transcends being and intellect (*Against Celsus* 6.64; 7.38) but at the same time is also the supreme Being (οὐσία; *Against Celsus* 6.64; *On First Principles* 1.3.5). Indeed, only the "invisible and incorporeal nature" of God is Being (οὐσία) in the fullest and most proper sense (*Commentary on John* 20.18.159; cf. "invisible and incorporeal οὐσία" said of God in *Against Celsus* 6.71). Every other being is a being, an οὐσία, by virtue of participation in the Being that is God (*Against Celsus* 6.64).

Origen felt the need to maintain the identity between God and the absolute Being because of Exod 3:14 (in the Septuagint: ἐγώ εἰμι ὁ ὤν, "I am the One who Is"), from the biblical side, but also in order to identify, with Plato, the Being and the Good. The divinity is the Good and the Being, while evil, its opposite, is nonbeing (an idea that will return in Gregory of Nyssa and other Christian Platonists, such as Evagrius himself). The divinity is the Good, not only by virtue of possessing the good—as is the case with creatures, which are good insofar as they participate in the Good—but because it is the Good itself, αὐτοαγαθόν (a Numenian term) by essence (κατ' οὐσίαν; Origen, *Selected Passages on Numbers* [PG 12:577D]). God is the absolute Good, the Good per se. If God is the absolute Good, Origen deduces that God's power (δύναμις) must also be good, and God's operation or activity (ἐνέργεια) manifests itself in the goodness of the divine creation and of divine providence (*On First Principles* 2.9.1; 3.5.2; 4.4.8). After speaking of the gnoseological process of deducing God's essence on the basis of God's activity and works in creation, Origen describes God as a Monad and Henad in *On First Principles* 1.1.6, a definition that Evagrius will keep in mind: since the Divinity is "of an intelligible nature," and not of a material or corporeal nature, the Godhead is "simple; absolutely nothing can be added to it … but it is a Monad [μονάς] in an absolute sense, and, so to say, a Henad [ἑνάς]: intelligence and spring from which every intelligence gushes out.… The Godhead is the principle of everything, and therefore we must not deem it composite." This absolute simplicity takes God away from the grasp of human knowledge. Thus, in *On First Principles* 1.1.5 Origen illustrates the excellence and cognitive incomprehensibility of God, who is incomprehensible and impenetrable in its reality. Every human thought is inevitably inferior to, and cannot grasp, the Godhead itself, just as a spark is infinitely inferior to the splendor of the sun. So is human intelligence inferior to the intellectual and spiritual realities, and these in turn are inferior to God. God is superior to all of these, ineffably and inestimably excellent. This is a development of the Platonic metaphysical model of transcendence.

Gregory of Nyssa, the most philosophically minded of the Cappadocians, is the most insightful follower of Origen and the greatest patristic Platonist along with Origen himself and Augustine. His reflections on the human gnoseological limit before God are marked by a profound influence of Philo and, above all, Origen and Plotinus. He was very well acquainted with the works and thought of all of these Platonists. In *Homilies on Ecclesiastes* (GNO 5:414) Gregory interprets Eccl 3:7 (a verse concerning "a time to speak and a time to be silent") as follows: "the time to be silent is when one wants to investigate the nature of God, whereas the time to speak is when one wants to announce the wonders of his works." Like Plotinus, Gregory thinks that the very essence or nature of God is impossible to express and must lie in silence. In *Against Eunomius* 2.1.105, Gregory declares that the divine realities must be "honored with silence." What can be grasped cognitively and can therefore be expressed is God's activity in the world, first of all the creation. Gregory's apophatic theology—the awareness that the divinity in itself can be known and spoken of only in negative terms—refers to the specific area of God's transcendence: God's nature or essence (φύσις or οὐσία) cannot be known, whereas God's activities or operations (ἐνέργειαι) can be known and spoken of. This is the same line as Philo's and Origen's. In his treatise *To Ablabius* Gregory states that names describe not God's nature but something of what pertains to it (literally, what is "about/around it" [περὶ αὐτήν]: an idea that was already present in Plotinus and that was very well known to Gregory). Now, this something "does not at all indicate *what divine nature is in its essence* [κατ' οὐσίαν]" (GNO 3.1:42–43). This is exactly what Evagrius too maintains in the *kephalaion* under examination.

According to Gregory, the divinity, unknowable in its nature, becomes knowable in its works and can thus be understood by the human intellect in some respects concerning its nature (literally, again, "about/around it" [περὶ αὐτήν]). Here too, Gregory relies not only on Plotinus but also on Origen, who used in a similar sense the expression "what is around/about," τὰ περί (*Against Celsus* 6.65), which was already employed by Clement of Alexandria in a passage that precisely deals with the abstractive process in the human cognitive grasp of God (*Stromateis* 5.11.71.3). Origen elaborated on the same concept and expression in *Commentary on John*

13.21.124: it is possible to find in Scripture—in divine revelation, an extension of human limited cognitive capacities when it comes to God—clues to say "something" (τι) "regarding God's nature or essence," περὶ οὐσίας θεοῦ. The same concept and expression is also found in Plotinus, *Enneads* 5.3.14 (the One is ineffable, ἄῤῥητον, because to say "something about it" is, after all, "to say something," τι, but the One is not merely "some thing," that is, a thing among the others), and will be found again in another Origenian and milestone in Christian apophaticism, the Neoplatonist called Pseudo-Dionysius the Areopagite (*The Heavenly Hierarchy* 2.3), who was deeply influenced by Proclus.

In the second of Gregory's *Homilies on the Song of Songs*, the soul, personified as a character in a dialogue, addresses God as follows: "Your Name is beyond any other name and is inexpressible and incomprehensible to any rational being." Indeed, "the divine, *from the point of view of its nature, is ungraspable/untouchable* [ἀνέπαφον] and incomprehensible [ἀκατανόητον] … ineffable [ἄῤῥητον] and inaccessible [ἀνεπίβατον] to reasoning" (*Against Eunomius* 2 [GNO 1:265–66]). This is why we know only its existence and not its essence or nature (GNO 1:247–48). This is what Philo also maintained. In *Homilies on the Beatitudes* 6, Gregory insists that "*the divine nature, in what it is per se, is beyond any thought* that can comprehend it, inaccessible and unapproachable to every conjectural intuition." Again, this is the same position as expressed by Evagrius in the present *kephalaion*. And in *Homilies on the Song of Songs* 12, Gregory hammers home and further develops his thesis:

> As for what always turns out to be beyond any impression that can reveal it, how could it ever be understood by means of an indication included in this or that name? This is why the soul excogitates every meaning of names, in order to indicate that inexpressible Good, but every discursive capacity of reasoning is always defeated and declared inferior to the object that it is looking for. This is why the soul says: "I have called him as I could, excogitating words that indicate its inexpressible beatitude, but he was always superior to the indication suggested by their meanings." The same experience often happens to the great David as well, who invokes God with an infinity of names and yet recognizes that he has remained inferior to the truth.

For Gregory, as already for Philo, by means of names we can only say "how God is" (πῶς ἐστι) and not "what God is" (τί ἐστι; *To Ablabius* [GNO 3.1:56]), since divine names are established by humans "on the basis of each of the divine activities [ἐνέργειαι] we know" (GNO 3.1:44); "the divine is denominated with different appellatives that refer to its manifold activities" (*Against Eunomius* [GNO 1:315]). For, the divinity, "who is invisible in its nature, becomes visible in its activities" (*On the Beatitudes* [GNO 7.2:141]). Per se, God's nature "transcends every movement of our mind" or διάνοια, the discursive mind. This is what Evagrius in turn hammers home here in *KG* 5.51.

5.52. The intellections of corporeal beings need a pure intellect; the intellections of incorporeal beings need a purer intellect; the Holy Trinity needs an intellect that is still purer than these.

I have again translated with "corporeal beings" the Syriac word that means "bodies," not necessarily mortal, but also spiritual. This term embraces every kind of bodies. This *kephalaion* at first sight may seem to stand in contrast with *KG* 5.51, since in 5.51 Evagrius explains that God's nature cannot be known, but only God's activity and its results can (see above, the relevant commentary). Now in *KG* 5.52, as elsewhere, Evagrius speaks of the intellections of the Trinity, which are superior to those of bodily creatures and to those of intellectual beings. An extraordinarily pure intellect is required for these intellections of the Trinity, but they are not said to be precluded to the intellect. In fact there is no contradiction, since these intellections of the Trinity do not seem to give access to the essential nature of God.

Indeed, so far in the *KG* Evagrius has often spoken of contemplation and knowledge of the Trinity, making it clear that it is possible to know God the Trinity. However, he never states that this knowledge of the Trinity is a knowledge of the essence or nature of the Trinity. In *KG* 1.27 he lists the main contemplations, in number of five, the first of which is the contemplation of the Trinity, the second and third being the contemplation of incorporeal and corporeal beings, and the fourth and fifth the contemplation of the Judgment and of Providence. In *KG* 1.52 the knowledge of the Trinity is presented as the culmination of all knowledge (see above, the relevant commentary). In *KG* 1.70 Evagrius constructs an axiological gradation, at the top of which is the knowledge of the Holy Trinity; then come the contemplation of the intellections of the intelligible beings, then that of incorporeal realities, then the contemplation of the worlds/aeons, and last the impassivity of the soul, with which we exit the realm of gnosis and enter that of *praktikē*. In *KG* 1.74 Evagrius explains the tripartition of "the light of the intellect": again the knowledge of the Trinity, that of the incorporeal nature, and the contemplation of the beings (see the commentary above). In *KG* 2.4 he delineates a progression: the passage from evilness to virtue, that from impassivity—the goal of *praktikē*—to the secondary natural contemplation, then from the latter to the knowledge concerning rational creatures, and finally the passage of all to the knowledge of the Holy Trinity. In the commentary on 2.4 I have already highlighted the influence of Origen.

In *KG* 2.11 Evagrius comes close to the problem at stake, concerning the limits of human knowledge. What humans cannot know is only their own intellect, the knower and seer, and God, its author. For we can grasp neither what is a nature susceptible of the Trinity, such as the intellect itself, nor the Unity, substantial/essential knowledge, which is God. This *kephalaion* confirms *KG* 5.51 (we cannot know the nature of the Trinity) and 5.52, the present *kephalaion*. In *KG* 2.29 Evagrius is not asserting the possibility of knowing the nature of the Trinity but is rather adumbrating the eschatological state in which the intellect will pervade the soul, when it comes to be mingled with the light of the Trinity. The substantial gap between the Trinity and creatures, be these sense perceptible or intelligible, underlies *KG* 2.47: the Trinity is not placed together with the contemplation of either sense-perceptible or intelligible realities, nor is it counted with any object, since these are creatures, whereas the Holy Trinity is the Creator and is only essential knowledge. This is also why the Trinity in its essence cannot be an object of knowledge. When Evagrius speaks of the knowledge of the Trinity on the part of a pure or bare intellect, such as in *KG* 3.6, he never states that this knowledge involves a knowledge of the nature of God. He rather indicates that the intellect joins the knowledge of the Trinity, thus knowing what the Trinity knows about beings. The Trinity, being essential knowledge, knows their natures or essences, clearly because the Trinity is their very creator. But nothing is said about human intellect being able to know the nature of the Trinity. This is also in line with what Evagrius explains in *KG* 3.13: we have known the Wisdom of the Unity, while joined to the nature that is below it; Unity itself, however, cannot be seen, while joined to some of the beings, and for this reason the incorporeal *nous* sees the Holy Trinity in incorporeal beings, but not in itself. Even in the ultimate end, when "the intellect, finally bare, will become a seer of the Trinity" (*KG* 3.15; cf. 3.30, 33, 41, 71; see the relevant commentaries above), it is uncertain, and at any rate it is not stated, that the intellect can see the *nature* of the Trinity. Actually, in *KG* 4.40, after the intellections of the *praktikē* and of nature, Evagrius posits the *logoi* concerning God, which does not indicate a knowledge of God's very nature (see above, the relevant commentary).

In *KG* 4.10 Evagrius draws a distinction between three contemplations: the primary contemplation of nature (i.e., intelligible objects), the secondary one (i.e., sense-perceptible objects), and that of the Trinity. Likewise, in *KG* 4.42 the contemplation of the existent beings is ranked one step below the knowledge of the Trinity, which is evoked again in *KG* 4.52, where it is identified with the intelligible meaning of the high-priestly plate on which the holy tetragram was inscribed. In *KG* 4.77 Evagrius opposes the dualism between objects, which are outside the intellect, and the contemplation concerning them, which is inside the intellect, and the Trinity, which rules out any dualism, being only essential knowledge. This seems to primarily refer to the kind of knowledge that the Trinity has, without any dualism between intellect (knower) and object (known). Finally, in *KG* 5.3 Evagrius presents an eschatological perspective: rational creatures in this aeon have only a small sight over the aeon to come, and those in the last aeon—after which there will be no more aeons but a leap into the Trinity, as Origen already maintained—see some of the Trinity's light, which enhances rational creatures' knowledge. This, again, is not explicitly declared to be tantamount to seeing the nature of the Trinity.

5.53. The spiritual sacrifice is a pure conscience, that which is laid (offered) on the state of the intellect as on an altar.

Persius Flaccus, the Roman Stoic who wrote philosophical satires, also identified the pureness of one's thoughts and the honesty of one's heart as the true and best sacrifice, besides which no further sacrifice is needed (*Satire* 2.71–75). See Ramelli, *Stoici romani minori*, 1361–515, also with the review by Gretchen Reydams-Schils in *Bryn Mawr Classical Review*, October 2009, http://bmcr.brynmawr.edu/2009/2009-10-10.html. A parallel concept is found in Paul's "rational cult," or λογικὴ λατρεία; moreover, in Paul the notion of "conscience," or συνείδησις, is paramount (see Philip Bosman, *Conscience in Philo and Paul* [Tübingen: Mohr Siebeck, 2003]), and from him it was picked up by Christian authors. See Ilaria L. E. Ramelli, "Conscience. IV. Christianity," in *Encyclopedia of the Bible and Its Reception* (ed. Hans-Joseph Klauck et al.; Berlin: de Gruyter, 2011), 3:650–52. It is a Christian, Theophilus, who attests (*To Autolycus* 2.4) that in Stoicism each one's conscience is so important as to be divine; indeed, especially the Roman Stoics and authors who were strongly influenced by them, such as Seneca and Juvenal, emphasized the role of conscience (see Ramelli, *Stoici romani minori*, 2599–626, s.v. "coscienza," and passim in the essays and commentaries therein). Juvenal, *Satire* 13, observes that conscience produces remorse for one's sins and works as the divinity's principal instrument to punish human sins. Paul was probably acquainted with the Stoic conception of conscience, and Evagrius was surely acquainted with Paul's notion.

5.54. Just as it is more difficult for us to see the intellections of incorporeal beings than to approach objects by means of the senses, in the same way it is for us more difficult to know the intellections of corporeal beings than to see the corporeal beings themselves.

Another gnoseological *kephalaion.* By means of a comparison, sense-perceptible knowledge is declared to be easier than intellectual knowledge.

5.55. The Holy Trinity is not a thing that is mixed in contemplation. For this pertains exclusively to creatures. Therefore, one will call it "essential knowledge" in a pious way.

See *KG* 5.51 and the relevant commentary about the knowledge of the Trinity that creatures can have. The knowledge of the very nature of the Trinity is there declared to be precluded. In the present *kephalaion*, as in *KG* 4.77, Evagrius concentrates on the dualism that is entailed by human knowledge and contemplation (contemplation being inside the intellect, but the objects being outside) and the lack of dualism in the Trinity, which is essential knowledge and knows all things in their essence or substance—being their creator—and not as representations inside the intellect.

Evagrius speaks of "essential knowledge" several times in the *KG*. He has mentioned it in *KG* 1.89, in which "essential knowledge" is identified with God; *KG* 2.47, in which it is identified with the Trinity; *KG* 3.12, in which Evagrius states that only the perfect intellect can receive it. In *KG* 3.49 essential knowledge is presented as a prize for the intellect that has rejected ignorance. In *KG* 4.77 objects are said to be outside the intellect, whereas the contemplation concerning them is constituted inside it. This is not the case, however, with the Holy Trinity, who is only essential knowledge. Evagrius will speak of essential knowledge again in *KG* 6.34, in which the "essential knowledge" of God the Father is identified with the Son's image (see the commentary there, below).

5.56. The one who has been separated from objects, it is not the case that he has fallen also from the contemplation that is directed toward them, nor is it the case with the one who has lost the contemplation that this person is outside of objects. But this is not so with respect to the Holy Trinity: for we believe that it is exclusively essential knowledge.

The notion of the Trinity as "essential knowledge" is taken over from the preceding *kephalaion* (see the relevant commentary there). The same differentiation between the Trinity as essential knowledge and the objects of knowledge, which are outside the intellect, and their intellections, which are inside it like their contemplation, was drawn in *KG* 4.77 (see the commentary above). The Trinity does not know from outside, forming intellections inside the intellect, but knows every being in its very essence, since the Trinity created every being.

5.57. Just as now by means of the senses we approach sense-perceptible objects, but in the end, after being purified, we shall know their intellections too, in the same way first we see the objects themselves, and after being purified more, we shall also know the contemplation about them, after which it is possible to know, from that point on, also the Holy Trinity.

This is another gnoseological *kephalaion*, which hammers home the progression between knowledge of corporeal realities by means of sense perception, knowledge of incorporeal realities such as the intellections of sense-perceptible objects, the *theōria* of the object, and knowledge of the Trinity. For this progression, see also above, the commentaries on *KG* 5.52, 55, and 56. Here a distinction is drawn between the present imperfect condition and the state of perfection, after purification, which will enable the knowledge not only of objects themselves but also of their intellections, and, at the highest stage, the knowledge of the Trinity.

5.58. The intellect apprehends sense perception not qua sense perceptible but qua sense perception. On the other hand, sense perception apprehends sense-perceptible objects not qua objects but qua sense-perceptible objects.

The intellect as faculty knows in an intellectual modality, and not in a sense-perceptible modality, whereas sense perception knows in a sense-perceptible modality. This is also a rather common conviction in the Platonic tradition; see, for instance, Porphyry, *Sentences Leading to the Intelligible* 16 and 22.

5.59. Sense perception does not apprehend sense perception; rather, it exclusively apprehends the organs of sense perception, not qua organs of sense perception, but qua sense perceptible. The intellect, instead, apprehends sense perception qua sense perception, and the organs of sense perception qua organs of sense perception.

The same distinction between the modality of knowledge of the intellect and of sense perception as drawn in *KG* 5.58 is explicated here.

5.60. One is the power of the intellect, to see spiritual natures, and another is (the power) to know the contemplation concerning them. But one and the same is the following power: that to see and know the Holy Trinity.

In the case of creatures, in this case spiritual creatures, Evagrius posits a dualism between seeing them by means of the intellect and knowing the contemplation (θεωρία) concerning them. Again, he contrasts this creatural dualism with the case of the Trinity: seeing it by means of the intellect and knowing it is one and the same thing. Nothing is specified, however, about knowing the very nature or essence of the Trinity. On this point, see also above, the commentary on 5.52.

5.61. All the times when we consider material things [ὕλη, pl.], we come to the memory of the contemplation of these (things). And once we have received the contemplation, in turn we get far from material things. But this does not happen to us with regard to the Holy Trinity; for this is exclusively essential contemplation.

This is another gnoseological *kephalaion* in which, as in *KG* 5.60 and 5.56, and other *kephalaia*, the Trinity is contrasted with creatures and their knowledge (see above, the relevant commentaries). In *KG* 5.56 the contrast was between the objects of knowledge outside the intellect; their contemplation or *theōria* inside the intellect; and the Trinity, who is essential knowledge and knows all beings from inside, in their essence, since the Trinity created everything. In *KG* 5.60 the contrast was between the knowledge of the Trinity and the knowledge of spiritual creatures; the intellect's seeing spiritual creatures is said to be different from contemplating them, but seeing and knowing the Trinity is said to be performed by one and the same power. In the present *kephalaion* the contrast is between the contemplation of the Trinity and that of material creatures. The contemplation of material beings is different from their apprehension by sense perception and is formed inside the intellect; thus, their contemplation brings the intellect far from those material creatures themselves. This is not the case with the Trinity, which has no matter whatsoever in it, as Origen also stressed; its contemplation is essential or substantial. When the Trinity is contemplated by us (this is why Evagrius says, "This does not happen to us with regard to the Holy Trinity") there is no opposition between an object outside and contemplation inside. Memory too is associated with the contemplation of material beings. After the contemplation itself, there comes the memory of this contemplation. The central role of memory in Evagrius's writings, as well as in those of his admirer Palladius, is highlighted by Rebecca Krawiec, "Literacy and Memory in Evagrius's Monasticism," *JECS* 21 (2013): 363–90. The very memorization of Scripture is an indisputable monastic ideal. Though, Evagrius here points to the perfection of the contemplation of the Trinity and the eschatological state, in which presence will supersede memory and immateriality will supplant material objects.

5.62. The nature of the Trinity is not known in ascents and descents; for there are not, in this case, objects that underlie, and its nature does not admit of division. The one who divides the nature of bodies has it consist, in all, of matter and form. On the other hand, the incorporeal nature, when one divides it, one resolves it in common contemplation and substance that can receive opposition. Not in this way, instead, is it possible to know the nature of the Holy Trinity.

In the previous *kephalaion* Evagrius has already pointed out one consequence of the immateriality of the Trinity on its contemplation by a created intellect. Here, as already several times, Evagrius stresses the impossibility of knowing the Trinity by means of discursive reason ("in ascents and descents") because of the nondualism that characterizes the Trinity, supreme Unity, and its knowledge. Here the Syriac word for "bodies" includes spiritual bodies, and thus refers to bodies in general, and not only mortal bodies. Both corporeal and incorporeal creatures are divisible, bodies into matter (ὕλη) and form (εἶδος)—the basic Aristotelian division—and incorporeal creatures into common contemplation and substance liable to opposition, as Evagrius explains in this *kephalaion*, but the Trinity is absolutely simple and is neither divisible nor susceptible of any opposition. The simplicity of God was already a tenet of Origen's theology, as well as that of Rufinus and of the Cappadocians. Especially for Basil and Gregory Nyssen—who both exerted a remarkable influence on Evagrius—see Andrew Radde-Gallwitz, *Basil of Caesarea, Gregory of Nyssa, and the Transformation of Divine Simplicity* (Oxford: Oxford University Press, 2009). As for God as not susceptible of opposition, this is the tenet with which Evagrius has opened the *KG* themselves (see *KG* 1.1 and the relevant commentary). The nature of the Trinity cannot be known the way corporeal and incorporeal creatures are known; it should be known all together, suddenly, without division. Though Evagrius does not say whether human intellects are equipped with the capacity for such a knowledge, in the same way as they are equipped with the capacity for knowing corporeal and incorporeal creatures. In *KG* 5.51 indeed Evagrius—in line with Philo, Origen, Gregory of Nyssa, and Plotinus—seems to deny that humans can know the very nature of God: "what is the foolishness of those who claim that they know the nature of God?" (see above, the relevant commentary). This may be reserved for a mystical, that is, noncognitive, experience and/or the final "deification."

5.63. Partition allows us to go back to the genesis of the existing objects. The knowledge that is according to measure manifests the Wisdom of the Creator. But it is not in these signs that we see the Holy Trinity. For there is no beginning to it. As for the wisdom that is in these objects, we do not say that it is God either, if these principles harmonize, in the study of nature, with those things of which they are the principles. For a wisdom such as this is a knowledge without substance, which manifests itself exclusively in the objects.

Evagrius in the first sentence is speaking of the part of the Platonic dialectic method that is based on division, partition, and analysis (diairetic). This brings the philosopher back to the genesis or very beginning of the objects we can know. The Syriac expression that I have translated with "genesis" is *bršyt*, which corresponds to the Hebrew title of the book of

Genesis. In the second sentence, the relation of Wisdom to measure is probably based on Wis 11:20–21 ("You have arranged all things by measure and number and weight"; LXX: πάντα μέτρῳ καὶ ἀριθμῷ καὶ σταθμῷ διέταξας; Vulgate: *omnia in mensura, et numero et pondere disposuisti*).

In the subsequent part of this *kephalaion* Evagrius highlights again the exception that is represented by the Trinity. While of the objects of our knowledge we can trace the genesis through a dialectic process, of God the Creator we cannot, since God is beginningless. God the Trinity has neither beginning nor principle (ἀρχή), being totally uncreated, but is rather the ἀρχή of all, since the Trinity has created all. In Origen's *On First Principles*, likewise, the principles (ἀρχαί) at stake are the three hypostases of the Trinity. See my "Origen, Greek Philosophy" and "Ethos and Logos: A Second-Century Apologetical Debate between 'Pagan' and Christian Philosophers," *VC* 69 (2015): 123–56. In the objects of our knowledge we can see God's Wisdom, in that they were created according to measure and order, but we cannot see God's very nature. In *KG* 5.51 Evagrius drew a distinction between the Wisdom manifested in creatures and essential Wisdom, and remarked that knowing the former does not imply knowledge of the latter.

5.64. Just as a mirror, which is not stained by the images that are seen in it, so is the impassible soul (unsullied) by things on earth.

A simile illustrates the detachment from earthly things in the soul that has attained *apatheia* (this is the soul of the *praktikos*, mentioned in the following *kephalaion*). The soul sees in itself the intellections of things on earth but is not stained by them.

5.65. The *praktikos* is the minister of separation. The *gnōstikos* is the assistant of wisdom.

Praktikos and *Gnōstikos* are the titles of the two homonymous treatises by Evagrius. The *praktikos* is the person who engages in *praktikē*, that is, ascesis, purification of the soul, and the pursuit of *apatheia*. Without this basis, as I have pointed out more than once, according to Evagrius—and to most "pagan" and Christian Neoplatonists—it is impossible to attain knowledge. One cannot be a *gnōstikos* without having been a *praktikos*. Here the latter type is associated with separation, probably because of his or her separation from passions and worldly values, otherwise said, the separation of the soul from the body, and because of his or her purification and ascesis. The same is explained in *Praktikos* 52: "To separate the body from the soul belongs exclusively to the One who united them; but to separate the soul from the body belongs to anyone who desires virtue. The life of withdrawal has been called by the fathers a rehearsal for death and flight from the body" (trans. Dysinger, slightly modified). Kevin Corrigan glosses this as "separation of the soul from its uncritical slumber in the body" (*Evagrius and Gregory*, 50). According to Monica Tobon, this encompasses *xeniteia*, or voluntary exile, from "homeland, family, and possessions," as Evagrius has it in *Eulogius* 2 (see Monica Tobon, "Evagrius as Writer: The Example of *Eulogios* 2's Discussion of *Xeniteia*" in *Origeniana Decima* [ed. H. Pietras and S. Kaczmarek; BETL 244; Leuven: Peeters, 2011], 765–68). The *gnōstikos* is associated with Wisdom because of his or her pursuit of knowledge.

5.66. The intellect is not joined to knowledge, before joining to its own virtues the part of its soul that is subject to passions.

This *kephalaion* is again about *praktikē* coming before gnosis or knowledge. If one has not purified the part of one's soul that is subject to passions—that is, the inferior faculties: irascible and concupiscible—one cannot attain knowledge through the rational or intellectual faculty.

5.67. If it is true that rational natures bear the symbol of trees, and that these grow in water, knowledge is rightly called "water of the spirit" [or "spiritual water"], which gushes forth from the fountain of life.

This is one of the many *kephalaia* in which Evagrius interprets spiritually a point in the Old Testament. The *logika*, like trees, grow in a (spiritual) water that is knowledge. A rational creature needs gnosis as a nourishment to grow. For knowledge is life for a rational creature. And knowledge comes from the fountain of life, which is undoubtedly God or God's Logos or Wisdom, as is clear from the scriptural allusion to Ps 35:10 (36:9): "For with thee is the fountain of life; in thy light do we see light" (RSV). In this verse God is the source of both life and knowledge (in the mention of light) at the same time, which Evagrius interprets as an identification of life with knowledge for rational creatures.

5.68. The intelligible Philistine is the one who stands against those who enter to inherit the Land of the Promise.

Evagrius has already interpreted the Philistines spiritually in *KG* 5.36, where the Philistines are likewise opposed to those who inherit the promised land. See commentary there, with consideration of Origen's interpretation of the Philistines. Evagrius consistently associates the Philistines with demons as opposing powers. This is one of the many *kephalaia* in which Evagrius offers a spiritual exegesis of Scripture.

5.69. The holy water is the symbol of the Holy Trinity, and the tree of life is Christ, who drinks from it.

The tree of life appears in Scripture both in Gen 2:9 and in Revelation, where it is a reminiscence of Gen 2:9. Here Evagrius, I think, has in mind not so much the inferiority of Christ to the Trinity (as suggested by Konstantinovsky, *Evagrius*, 144), all the more so in that Christ in his divine nature is a person of the Trinity, but Rev 22:1–2, where in the heavenly Jerusalem both the holy vivifying water and the tree of life are located: "Then he showed me the *river of the water of life*, bright as crystal, flowing *from the throne of God and of the Lamb* through the middle of the street of the city; also, on either side of the river, *the tree of life* with its twelve kinds of fruit, yielding its fruit each month; and the leaves of the tree for the therapy of the nations." The association of the holy water and the tree of life makes it very probable that Evagrius is referring precisely to this scriptural passage. The tree, whose leaves are "the therapy of the nations," is Christ, due to his cross (see Ramelli, *Christian Doctrine of Apokatastasis*, 54–59). Oecumenius, *Commentary on the Apocalypse* 248 and 252–253, interprets the tree of life as Christ, and the leaves as the patriarchs, prophets, apostles, evangelists, martyrs, confessors, ecclesiastical shepherds, "and every righteous soul," who all cure the people's souls (ibid., 249). The tree of life, Evagrius explains, is Christ, who is nourished by the water of the Trinity and dwells in the Trinity itself, being one of the Trinity in his divine nature. The idea of trees who are nourished by God-water is the same as appears in *KG* 5.67 (see above, the relevant commentary). However, since the trees in *KG* 5.67 symbolize rational creatures, they are not said to presently *dwell* in God-water, something that only Christ does, who is a rational creature in his human nature but one of the Trinity in his divine nature. The tree of life is identified by Evagrius with the Lord also in *Letter to Anatolius* 7: "The staff is a tree of life to all who hold it, reliable for those who lean on it as on the Lord" (Prov 3:18).

5.70. Just as our mortal body is said to be in a place, so also is the intellect in this or that knowledge. For this reason science is appropriately said to be its place.

The intellect, like all intelligible realities, is adiastematic, meaning that it is not located in temporal or spatial dimension. This is an aspect that Gregory of Nyssa had especially emphasized (see Ramelli, *Gregorio di Nissa: Sull'anima*; and Boersma, *Embodiment and Virtue*). Evagrius here describes only the mortal body as diastematic, thus leaving the possibility open that spiritual bodies may be adiastematic. He does not specify this. The intellect itself is surely adiastematic: it is not in a physical place but is rather in a science or type of knowledge.

5.71. The intelligible hero is that one who endeavors to drive those who have entered the Land of the Promise out of it.

This *kephalaion* is connected with *KG* 5.36 and 5.68, which concern the Philistines as invaders of the promised land, identified with demons who attack one's soul. Evagrius offers an interpretation, as often so, of facts and figures of the Old Testament on the spiritual plane.

5.72. If it is true that four ramifications from one single river have parted, let someone indicate (literally, "say") the world in which there was only one river, that the body may understand also the paradise from which it will drink.

The scriptural reference is Gen 2:10. Just after the mention of the tree of life in Gen 2:9, to which Evagrius referred in *KG* 5.69, in verse 10 the river of which Evagrius speaks here is mentioned: "A river flowed out of Eden to water the garden, and there it divided and became four rivers." Within Eden the river is one; only when it exits Eden it becomes four. Evagrius very probably sees in this a symbol of the initial situation in which there was a harmonic henad, whereas division and disagreement came afterward. See Ramelli, "Harmony between *Arkhē* and *Telos*." The body mentioned in this *kephalaion* is not the mortal body but the body tout court or the spiritual body. Indeed, the body that will enter paradise is the resurrected spiritual body. Note that, in fact, just as the tree of life mentioned in Genesis will return again in the Apocalypse (Revelation), so will also the single river of Eden appear again in the heavenly Jerusalem in the Apocalypse. Both the tree of life and the water of the river are cited together in *KG* 5.69, where I have suggested a reference to Rev 22:1–2. The present *kephalaion*, with its protological and eschatological thrust, confirms that in *KG* 5.69 too Evagrius had in mind both the tree and river of Genesis and those of Revelation, and not only those of Genesis.

5.73. The intellect is in awe when it sees the objects, and in the contemplation of these it is not troubled, but as toward relatives and toward friends it runs.

Evagrius stresses how contemplation is connatural with the intellect. The simile with relatives and friends may point to Evagrius's use of the notion of *oikeiōsis* in this respect. Interestingly, Origen and Gregory of Nyssa were the Christian philosophers who made the most of the doctrine of *oikeiōsis*. See my "The Stoic Doctrine of Oikeiosis and Its Transformation in Christian Platonism," *Apeiron* 47 (2014): 116–40.

5.74. The intelligible city is the spiritual contemplation that embraces spiritual natures.

The reference to the "city" is difficult to trace to one single biblical passage. Guillaumont (p. 209) indicated Matt 5:14, "a city set on a hill cannot be hidden," but it is also possible that Evagrius had in mind the holy city of the Apocalypse (Rev 21–22). Actually, I deem this probable, given that in other close *kephalaia* he has interpreted spiritually the river and the tree of life in Rev 22 (*KG* 5.69 and 5.72; see above, the relevant commentary). It is therefore likely that the city that here is interpreted noetically is that mentioned in Rev 22, the heavenly Jerusalem. Evagrius allegorizes it as spiritual contemplation, or *theōria*. As in many other *kephalaia*, Evagrius is offering a spiritual interpretation of objects mentioned in the Bible.

5.75. The intellect, the more it is stripped from passions, the closer it gets to the objects and, according to the degree of its order [τάξις], also receives knowledge. And every order in which it will stay, it will know the contemplation of that order like its own.

In the first part of this *kephalaion* Evagrius hammers home again that knowledge is impossible without previous purification and that *praktikē* and gnosis are mutually interdependent. Here in particular Evagrius states that purification enables a better knowledge. Then he highlights the notion of order (the Syriac word is a transliteration of Greek τάξις), which was dear to Origen and the Neoplatonists as well. The knowledge that the intellect receives depends on the place it occupies in the order; from the last sentence it is clear that the *nous* can stay in different orders.

5.76. The knowing natures investigate the (existing) objects, and the knowledge of the objects purifies the knowers.

I have already pointed out several times that Evagrius posits purification as a necessary step before knowledge, and this was made clear once again by the immediately preceding *kephalaion* (*KG* 5.75; see the commentary above). From this *kephalaion* it is clear that the relation is double oriented: knowledge not only requires purification but in turn also provides it.

5.77. The intelligible doors/gates are the virtues of the rational soul and the *praktikē*, which have been established by God's power.

Here is yet another *kephalaion* in which Evagrius interprets spiritually a biblical detail. References to doors or gates in Scripture are copious, the most conspicuous being Jesus's self-definition as Door or Gate in John 10:7–9. One can also think of the many references to the gates of the Jerusalem temple. Another possible reference is to the gates of the heavenly Jerusalem in Rev 21–22: this is probable because it comes after a series of *kephalaia* that interpret allegorically several details in Rev 21–22, such as the heavenly city itself and the tree of life and the river in it. In Rev 21:25 and 22:14 the gates of the heavenly city are said to be permanently open, for those who want to wash their robes, that is, to purify themselves, and enter the city of the saints: "By its light shall the nations walk; and the kings of the earth shall bring their glory into it, and its gates shall never be shut by day—and there shall be no night there; they shall bring into it the glory and the honor of the nations. Blessed are those who wash their robes, that they may have the right to the tree of life and that they may enter the city by the gates" (RSV). In all cases these gates, or doors, are conceived as passages that bring people to God. Thus, virtues and ascesis—the noetic meaning of the gates or doors, according to Evagrius—bring people to God, having been established by the Godhead itself for this purpose.

5.78. Demons' bodies neither grow nor diminish. A terrible stench surrounds them, by means of which they stir up our passions. They are easily recognized by those who from the Lord have received the capacity for perceiving that smell.

Just as the bodies of demons are neither sense perceptible nor mortal (and indeed the Syriac word for "bodies," *gwšm'*, here indicates spiritual bodies and not mortal bodies), so also their "fetor" is not sense perceptible. This is why not everybody can perceive it but only those who have received this faculty from God. Demons are represented as responsible for the tempting action of arousing passions. Origen too conceived them this way but was quick to assert that they do not undermine human free will (see Lekkas, *Liberté et progrès*; Ramelli, "La coerenza della soteriologia origeniana"; and *KG* 3.41, with the relevant commentary above). Evagrius thinks the same. He also insists that demons cannot enter our mind, but only God can do so (*Praktikos* 47). He devotes a good part of his *Praktikos* to demons and their tempting actions.

5.79. Everything that falls under that faculty of the intellect that sees the incorporeal beings, this is entirely also of its nature, whereas whatever is seen by the other (faculty), this cannot be of its own nature, if this is the same faculty that knows the intellections of incorporeal beings and also the Holy Trinity.

The capacity for seeing incorporeal beings (that is, everything that has no body, be this mortal or immortal and spiritual, as the Syriac word makes clear) is a natural faculty of the intellect, but that for knowing the Trinity and the intellections of incorporeal beings—situated inside the intellect—is no natural faculty. This seems to be meant as a gift of divine grace. This is why this faculty is said to be different from all that it sees.

5.80. The intelligible lock is free will, sovereign upon itself, which is not swayed because of beauty.

What in Syriac is "beauty" is likely to be the translation of Greek *καλόν*, which means both "beauty" and "goodness." Free will is a key feature in Origen's, Bardaisan's, and Gregory of Nyssa's thought. Especially Origen and Bardaisan emphasized it in their polemic against "Gnostic" determinism. Evagrius embraces their line that true freedom is the freedom to do the good, and not to do evil. From the typological point of view, this is one of the many *kephalaia* in which Evagrius interprets allegorically, on the spiritual plane, a detail mentioned in Scripture. Mentions of a lock or a bolt or a bar in Scripture are several, making it very difficult to individuate which of them Evagrius had in mind. Since the bolt pertains to a door or gate, this seems to link the present *kephalaion* with *KG* 5.77, which contains the noetic interpretation of the doors or gates, possibly of the heavenly Jerusalem. Now the lock of the gates that lead to God—such as those of the heavenly Jerusalem—is free will, meaning that it depends on one's free choice whether to direct oneself toward God. If free will adheres to the Good, it is never swayed. The importance of free will in Origen (who emphasized it against the "Gnostics"), Gregory of Nyssa, and Evagrius can hardly be overestimated. At the same time, all of these theologians deemed human free will perfectly compatible with God's grace and universal salvation.

5.81. When the intellect receives essential knowledge, then it will also be called God, due to its capacity for establishing variegated worlds/aeons as well.

Evagrius has repeatedly characterized God the Trinity as "essential knowledge," in that the Trinity knows all beings in their very essence, since the Trinity created them. The Trinity's essential knowledge can therefore be considered as creative, all the more so in that the creation was performed on the basis of the Ideas or paradigmatic Forms of all things that are in the mind of God as God's thoughts (which is also Origen's view; see *On First Principles* 1.4.5, and the commentary on *KG* 1.14 above). This *kephalaion* seems to propose an interpretation of θέωσις. In this case, it is the creative capacity of the intellect possessing essential knowledge that is considered to be a divine prerogative. This is why the intellect is called "God," since, like God, it has essential knowledge (in the case of the created intellect, it has "received" essential knowledge, while the Trinity possesses it substantially).

5.82. The intelligible wall is the impassivity (*apatheia*) of the soul, that which demons cannot reach.

This *kephalaion* continues along the lines of *KG* 5.80 and 5.77, with the spiritual interpretation of details related to a building; there the door, or gates, and the lock, here the wall, of a building or of a whole city. These *kephalaia* are indeed connected with *KG* 5.74, which offers the spiritual interpretation of a city—possibly the holy city of the Apocalypse (see the relevant commentary above). In this case the biblical reference is to Rev 21:12–14, where a long description of the wall of the heavenly Jerusalem is offered. *Apatheia*—the goal of *praktikē*, according to Evagrius—is described in the present *kephalaion* as the protection of the soul against the attacks of demons, since demons try to elicit passions in a soul.

5.83. All circumcisions, we have found, are seven. Four of them belong to the sixth day, one of them to the seventh day, and the others to the eighth day.

Evagrius goes on with remarks on objects and rituals mentioned in the Bible. Here he expounds the results of a research of his into circumcision, which he divides according to the time in which each circumcision takes place. Evagrius has already remarked on circumcision in *KG* 4.12, where he interpreted it on the intelligible plane as the avoidance of passions (in line with Philo's and Origen' exegesis; see the relevant commentary above). Here it turns out that the intelligible circumcisions—probably to be understood as purifications—are seven, and they are distributed onto three days—again to be understood as different stages in the history of salvation. The sixth day is the last day of history proper; the seventh day is the rest after history, the Sabbath, like the Holy Saturday between the crucifixion and the resurrection; and the eighth day is the ultimate *telos*, the resurrection-restoration of all (see *KG* 6.7 and the relevant commentary). Evagrius seems to suggest that there are several opportunities for purification both in history and in the eschatological scenario, though more in history, and especially toward the end of history. In this case, this *kephalaion* would be very much in line with Origen's and Gregory Nyssen's thinking.

5.84. The intelligible temple is the pure intellect, that in which now there is the Wisdom of God, "full of varieties/modalities." Indeed, God's temple is the one who is a seer of the holy Unity, and God's altar is the contemplation of the Holy Trinity.

Evagrius continues his series of interpretations of elements related to buildings and the city (5.74, 77, 80, 82). If, as I suggested, the city he has in mind is the holy city of the Apocalypse (Rev 21–22), this would perfectly fit his present interpretation of the temple as the bare/pure intellect, since the temple of the Apocalypse is explicitly identified, not with a temple of stones, but with God and Christ (Rev 21:22). Likewise the stones that make up the holy city are identified by Origen with rational creatures (*On First Principles* 2.11.2–3; see above, the commentary on *KG* 4.30), and John himself in the Apocalypse says that the victor in the battle against evil will be a pillar in the temple of God, which will never go out (Rev 3:12, a passage that was dear to Origen). Moreover, mentions of the temple and temple imagery are scattered throughout the Apocalypse. See Ilaria L. E. Ramelli, "Jesus, James the Just, a Gate, and an Epigraph," in *Kein Jota und kein Häkchen des Gesetzes werden vergehen (vgl. Q 16,17): Das Gesetzesverständnis der Logienquelle auf dem Hintergrund frühjüdischer Theologie* (ed. Markus Tiwald; BWANT 200; Stuttgart: Kohlhammer, 2013), 203–29.

The definition of God's Wisdom, who is Christ, as "full of varieties/modalities" comes from Eph 3:10. This biblical quotation is a favorite of Evagrius's, who uses it also in *KG* 1.43; 2.2, 21; 3.11; and 4.7 (see above, the relevant commentaries). Origen elaborated on it for his image of Christ-Logos-Wisdom bearing the paradigmatic Ideas or *logoi* of all beings on his surface, notably the same image that was used by Bardaisan of Edessa. See Ramelli, *Bardaisan of Edessa*, 107–24, and new remarks in Ramelli, "Preexistence of Souls," the section on Bardaisan. See also above, the commentary on *KG* 2.2.

The altar too is often mentioned in the Apocalypse (Rev 6:9; 8:3, 5; 9:13; 11:1; 14:18; 16:7). In this *kephalaion* the temple and the altar as symbols of the contemplation (θεωρία) of the divine Unity and Trinity remind readers of the mystery of God as one nature in three hypostases. Evagrius in this respect was in perfect continuity with the Cappadocians, who had inherited this theological point from Origen. See Ilaria Ramelli, "Origen's Anti-Subordinationism and Its Heritage in the Nicene and Cappadocian Line," *VC* 65 (2011): 21–49; idem, "Origen, Greek Philosophy."

5.85. The primary nature is because of the One, and the secondary (nature) toward the One, and this same in the One.

The "primary nature" is probably to be identified, as elsewhere, with the intelligible nature. Its relation to the One, God, is expressed by the preposition "because of," which may mean both a causal relationship and a final one. In the former sense, Evagrius would mean that the Godhead created the intelligible nature as its primary creation, which indeed is a tenet of Evagrius's thought; in the latter sense, he would mean that intellectual creatures are oriented to God as their final cause, to which they all tend. Both meanings fit well with Evagrius's frame of thought. The secondary nature is probably to be understood as the material one, created in the service of the primary nature and oriented toward God. The One encompasses all; this is why, notwithstanding its transcendence, creatures can be said to be "in the One." The identification of the One with God, or at least the supreme God, is already found in Plotinus, Origen, and Porphyry (for Porphyry, see now Aaron Johnson, *Religion and Identity in Porphyry of Tyre: The Limits of Hellenism in Late Antiquity* [Cambridge: Cambridge University Press, 2013], 60–62) and was already hinted at in Plato's protology.

5.86. The monk who loves vainglory is the one who, rather than (aiming at) impassivity, endeavors to be praised by human beings, in those things that are not done for the sake of impassivity and for the sake of the knowledge of God.

This *kephalaion* resembles in its tenor other works of Evagrius that aim at the spiritual direction of monks. This is the first of the *KG* in which monks are named, and actually the only one. Monks, Evagrius warns, should not pay attention to human glory. Worldly honors, power, and money have nothing to do with the goals of monastic life, namely, impassivity (*apatheia*, attained by means of the *praktikē*) and knowledge of God (the domain of gnosis). I have translated as "monk" the Syriac word that means "solitary" (*yḥydy*'), corresponding to Greek μοναχός.

5.87. The knowledge of the secondary is in the primary, and that of the primary is in itself, whereas the secondary is not knowing.

The intellectual nature, or primary nature, can know the secondary nature, or corporeal nature, as well as itself. The corporeal nature, on the contrary, has no capacity for knowledge. All knowledge belongs to the intellect. This is a tenet of Platonism—and not only of this philosophical school—that on the Christian side was especially developed by Gregory of Nyssa. In his dialogue *On the Soul and the Resurrection* Macrina argues at length that what knows is the intellect. Sense perception apprehends only sense-perceptible objects—that is, corporeal beings—but does not know them. What knows both sensible and intellectual objects is the intellect. See my commentary in Ramelli, *Gregorio di Nissa: Sull'anima*, also with references to the philosophical tradition behind it.

5.88. Zion is the symbol of the primary knowledge, whereas the emblem of every evilness is Egypt. The token, then, of natural contemplation is Jerusalem, that in which is Mount Zion, the head of the city (the citadel).

The allegorization of Egypt as evilness and vice goes back especially to Philo and Origen, and Evagrius himself has already presented this symbolic interpretation in *KG* 5.6 and 5.21, where Egypt is contrasted with Jerusalem and Mount Zion, exactly like here. What Evagrius suggests in the present *kephalaion* is that the highest peak of natural contemplation—just as Mount Zion is the highest peak of Jerusalem—is primary knowledge, the knowledge of primary beings (that is, intelligible realities). Note the opposition between knowledge and evilness. One would expect an opposition between knowledge and ignorance, but—as I have already remarked more than once—ignorance and evilness are almost interchangeable in Evagrius's thought, just as virtue and knowledge are.

5.89. Just as the destruction of the last aeon will not be followed by a new creation, so also the creation of the first aeon was not preceded by a destruction.

Against most "pagan" philosophers who upheld the eternity of the world, in infinite cycles of genesis and destruction, Evagrius closely adheres to Origen in claiming that the succession of aeons, and therefore the duration of the world, is not infinite but had a beginning and will thus have an end. Aeons are necessary to rational creatures' spiritual and intellectual development precisely for these reasons; they cannot succeed to one another in infinite series of repetitions without an orientation to a *telos*. According to Evagrius, as well as to Origen and Gregory of Nyssa, the *telos* is the removal of evil and ignorance, the restoration of intellectual creatures, and deification. For Origen's doctrine of the aeons, see Ramelli, *Christian Doctrine of Apokatastasis*, introductory chapter, and the section on Origen. See also Ramelli and Konstan, *Terms for Eternity*, with the reviews by O'Brien; by Ghira; and by Shawn Keough in *ETL* 84.4 (2008): 601; and now my *Tempo ed eternità in età antica e patristica* (Assisi: Cittadella, 2015). Evagrius has has already introduced the motif of the succession of the aeons in *KG* 2.17, in which the end of all aeons is expressly mentioned; *KG* 2.25, in which Evagrius remarks that each aeon's arrangement depends on the previous aeon, that is, on the moral choices of rational creatures in the previous aeon; *KG* 2.75, where Evagrius makes it clear that each aeon follows a divine judgment of rational creatures; *KG* 3.9, where the purificatory function of the aeons is stated; *KG* 3.26, where the aeons are said to be created by Christ; *KG* 3.36, with the very definition of aeon as a natural system that includes the various and different bodies of rational creatures, because of the knowledge of God; *KG* 3.38, where the sequence of one judgment–one aeon is affirmed again; *KG* 4.49, in which the passing away of the aeons is mentioned again; *KG* 4.58, in which the aeons are said to be created by God in Christ; *KG* 4.89, where the aeons are declared to be aimed at leading rational creatures to unity in God; *KG* 5.3, where again the aeons are described as aimed at the spiritual progress of rational creatures on their path toward God; *KG* 5.5, where the aeons are connected with the purification of the *logika*; *KG* 5.21, where the last of the future aeons are said to be free from evil; as well as in *KG* 1.7, 8, 9, 11, 17, 26, 65, 70, 75; 2.2, 14, 58, 59, 65, 74, 85; 3.23, 51; 4.15, 30, 34, 38, 39, 43; 5.7, 10, 81 (see above, the relevant commentaries). From the sheer bulk of these *kephalaia* it is clear how profoundly Evagrius was influenced by Origen's doctrine of the aeons and their meaning for rational creatures.

5.90. The (existing) objects, the way they are in their nature, either the bare intellect sees them, or the discourse of wise people reveals them. The one who, on the contrary, is deprived of both of them comes to the discredit of the writer.

Common human knowledge cannot reach the very nature of things. This requires the "bare intellect," which, as already pointed out, is the most purified intellect, and thus the purest intellect, which is also the seer of the Trinity. See above, *KG* 3.6 and 3.17, with the relevant commentaries, and 3.70: "It is proper to the bare intellect to say what its nature is," where Evagrius stresses the bare intellect's capacity for knowing the nature of the objects of knowledge, including itself. In *KG* 5.84 too the bare intellect is described as a seer of the holy Unity, as a pendant to the contemplation of the Holy Trinity. If one is not endowed with a bare intellect and does not pay attention to the wise either, one cannot have knowledge of the nature of the objects, and (Evagrius seems to imply) cannot write about them, otherwise he will gather only discredit.

***

After the end of this *kephalaion* the manuscript has: "The fifth discourse/book is concluded."

Sixth Discourse

6.1. What the contemplation of beings is, the Divine Book (Holy Scripture) has not clarified. However, how one can get close to it by means of the practice of the commandments and by means of (the) true teachings, it has clearly taught.

The Bible does not explain the contemplation (θεωρία) of existing beings. This may be one of the points that, as Origen remarked in the preface to his *On First Principles*, have been left unclarified by Scripture and therefore need to be researched by means of rational investigation. In the case under examination in the present *kephalaion*, Evagrius observes that in Scripture there are at least indications of how to come close to the contemplation of beings. These ways are mainly two: one is to obey the commandments, which pertains to *praktikē*, and the other is to pay attention to the true teachings revealed in Scripture.

6.2. Twofold is the contemplation of this aeon. One sense perceptible and thick, and the other intelligible and spiritual. And to the former contemplation impious men and demons come close, while to the latter the righteous and the angels of God (come close). And just as more than righteous human beings the angels know the spiritual contemplation, so also more than impious men do the demons know the thick contemplation, that which they are also considered to give to some of those who belong to them. In turn, we have learned from the Divine Book (Holy Scripture) that the holy angels too do so.

Evagrius draws here a dichotomy between two kinds of contemplation (θεωρία) of the present aeon: one is sensible and the other intellectual. He has spoken already elsewhere in the *KG* of different kinds of contemplation. In *KG* 1.27 he has explained that the main contemplations are five: that of the Trinity, those of incorporeal and corporeal realities, and those of the Judgment and of Providence. In *KG* 3.19 he has concentrated on the primary and the secondary contemplation, the former immaterial, and the other in matter. Here he adds that the righteous are helped by angels in their intellectual—and thereby immaterial—contemplation, while the impious are helped by demons in their sensible—and therefore material—contemplation. Clearly a distinctive axiological overtone is here attached to the two kinds of contemplation, positive in the case of the former and negative in the case of the latter.

6.3. Sense-perceptible peoples are distinct from one another in places, and in laws/customs, and in languages, and in dresses—sometimes also in qualities [lit. "mixtures"]. On the other hand, the intelligible and holy ones (are distinct from one another) in aeons and in spiritual bodies and in kinds of knowledge—also, they say, in languages. And the father of the former is Adam, while that of the latter is Christ, the one whose typological figure is Adam.

Origen had centered much of his reflection on the Adam-Christ typology (here the Syriac word I have translated with "typological figure" is a transliteration of the Greek technical term τύπος). Of course he based himself mainly on Paul (see Ramelli, "Typology"; idem, "Allegory. II. Judaism," in *Encyclopedia of the Bible and Its Reception* [ed. Hans-Joseph Klauck et al.; Berlin: de Gruyter, 2009], 1:785–93). Aeons are not worlds but stretches of time characterized by a given arrangement of creatures and their states—exactly as in Origen—and the bodies mentioned in connection with the intelligible peoples, that is, angels, are not the mortal ones, as is clear from the Syriac word (*gwšm'* and not *pgr'*), but the immortal and spiritual ones. Sense-perceptible peoples are human populations, while intelligible peoples are orders of angels. Christ, presumably qua *logikon*, is the originator of the latter, just as Adam of the former. The typological connection between Adam and Christ seems to prelude the elevation of humans to the rank of angels.

6.4. The Father is deemed anterior to the Son qua Father, and on the other hand anterior to the Holy Spirit qua Principle. But he is prior to both corporeal and incorporeal creatures qua Creator.

There is no question here of temporal anteriority of the Father with respect to the Son and the Spirit, but rather it is a question of an anteriority of the principle. The first person of the Trinity is the Father, who eternally generates the Son and is the Principle from which the Spirit proceeds. Evagrius agrees with Origen, who had insisted on the coeternity of the Son with the Father (see Ramelli, "Origen's Anti-Subordinationism") and on the Father as ἀρχή, or metaphysical principle (see Ramelli, "Origen, Greek Philosophy"). These two intra-Trinitarian aspects of God are kept distinct from the extra-Trinitarian aspect of God as Creator of all creatures, intellectual and corporeal alike. In this case, the Father is prior to creatures, both from the temporal point of view and from the ontological and protological point of view.

6.5. The noncreated is that anterior to which, since it IS in its own essence, there is nothing.

The present *kephalaion* is the continuation of the preceding one, where an ontological divide has been introduced between the Trinity and creation. Here Evagrius explains that God is the Creator and is the only noncreated being. Therefore, there is no being anterior to it. The Godhead is Being in its very essence: it is Being itself, just as it is also Good itself, that is, Goodness in its very essence (*KG* 1.1; see the relevant commentary there). According to Evagrius, just as to Origen, the Godhead has no principle, or ἀρχή, before itself and is the only being that is Being in itself; all other beings, that is, creatures, possess Being only by participation in God, the supreme Being. In the same way, all other beings possess Goodness only by participation in God, the supreme Good. Origen expanded a great deal on this point. See Ramelli, *Christian Doctrine of Apokatastasis*, the chapter on Origen.

6.6. Just as the knife circumcises the sense-perceptible Jew, so does also the *praktikē* circumcise the intelligible Jew. Christ called it allegorically the sword that he has cast into the world.

Evagrius offers a spiritual interpretation of the Jewish circumcision as *praktikē*, ascesis and moral striving toward *apatheia*. In *KG* 4.12 too he interpreted circumcision on the intelligible plane as the avoidance of passions, which is precisely the main aspect of *praktikē*. The knife of circumcision is assimilated to the sword mentioned in Matt 10:34; both allude to the action of cutting away passions proper to asceticism and moral training.

6.7. If it is the case that the eighth day is the symbol of the resurrection, and on the other hand the resurrection is Christ, then those who are circumcised on the eighth day, it is in Christ that they are circumcised.

Evagrius continues his reflection on circumcision, here linking it with the theme of the eighth day and of the resurrection. The connection between the eighth day and the resurrection is strong in patristic thinkers and is developed especially by Maximus the Confessor (see Ramelli, *Christian Doctrine of Apokatastasis*, the chapter devoted to him). Here Evagrius is referring to Gen 17:12, where the prescription is given to circumcise babies on the eighth day, and John 11:25, where Jesus identifies himself with the resurrection and life. In this way Evagrius, as Origen often did, puts together the Old and the New Testament: the Hebrew circumcision was in fact already made in Christ, as a token of the resurrection. The circumcision on the eighth day is one of the circumcisions listed by Evagrius in *KG* 5.83.

6.8. Just as paradise is the place of instruction of the righteous, so also is hell the torment of the impious.

The concept of paradise as a place of instruction for the just was widely elaborated by Origen, who thought of an instruction first imparted by angels and then by Christ himself (see Ramelli, *Christian Doctrine of Apokatastasis*, the chapter on Origen). The word I translated as "hell" is properly Sheol, a more neutral term that can also mean "place of the dead." But I have opted for the translation "hell" because of its specific description as a place of torment and because of its opposition to paradise. In this case, therefore, the death that reigns in Sheol is to be understood as spiritual death; this is why Evagrius characterizes Sheol as the place of the damned. As a place of torment opposed to the instruction administered in Paradise, hell is thus by implication characterized by ignorance. It is to be noted that Evagrius does not specify in any way that hell will be eternal. On the contrary, in *KG* 3.60 he indicates very clearly that the opposition between the damned and the righteous will come to an end at the eventual *apokatastasis* (see the relevant commentary above).

6.9. If it is together with genesis and destruction that time is contemplated, it is without time that the genesis of incorporeal beings is, because genesis for them was not preceded by a destruction.

The θεωρία of time cannot be separated from that of genesis and destruction (γένεσις and φθορά). Where these factors of mutability are lacking, time as a dimension is not existing, but there is rather adiastematic eternity (without space or time). This reflection owes much to both Origen and Gregory of Nyssa. See Ramelli, *Gregorio di Nissa: Sull'anima*; idem, "Αἰώνιος and Αἰών"; Boersma, *Embodiment and Virtue*. Gregory regarded intelligible beings as adiastematic realities, as Evagrius does here. Even though they are creatures and began to exist at a certain point out of nothing, nevertheless they are adiastematic and were not created in time (otherwise they would also have to perish in time—this is a tenet of all Platonism, the so-called perishability axiom, well known also to Christian Platonists such as Origen, Basil, and Gregory of Nyssa; see Ramelli, "Preexistence of Souls." This is also clear from *KG* 2.87 (see above, the relevant commentary) and the *Chapters of the Disciples of Evagrius* 25, which states that the intellect "preexists [προϋπάρχει] the body, but not chronologically [χρόνῳ], since time pertains to the corporeal [σωματική] nature."

The coming into being of the *logika* as independent substances was not preceded by any destruction, because there were no corruptible bodies before them. Corruptible bodies arose only as a result of the fall of the *logika*, but before corruptible bodies there was no destruction. This does not rule out that the *logika* at their creation as independent substances were equipped with incorruptible bodies, which do not entail any destruction. This supposition is indeed confirmed by the above-quoted *Chapters of the Disciples of Evagrius* 25, in which intellects are said to preexist bodies, but not chronologically. Bodies alone are created in time, but, as Origen also seems to have maintained, there was no time in which intellects existed without bodies.

6.10. The Holy Trinity is not like a tetrad, or a pentad, or a hexad. For these, being arithmetical, are forms without substance, whereas the Holy Trinity is essential/substantial knowledge.

Evagrius is concerned about the possible confusion of the Trinity with a (Platonic-Pythagorean) mathematical entity. The divide between these and the Trinity is given by their lack of substance. The definition of the Trinity as essential or substantial knowledge occurs frequently in the *KG*. Plotinus too had insisted that the One, the first, transcendent principle, must not be confused with a numerical entity. Svetla Slaveva-Griffin, *Plotinus on Number* (Oxford: Oxford University Press, 2009), has demonstrated that Plotinus discussed number in depth, in relation to each principle, the One, the Intellect, and the Soul, and even that "Plotinus' conception of number is the fundamental framework on which his entire philosophical system is built" (11). She also offers an account of Plato's and the Neopythagoreans' theory of number and its influence on Porphyry's organization of the *Enneads* (ch. 6). Drawing on Plato—whose doctrine of ideal numbers he defended against Aristotle—and the Neopythagoreans, Plotinus placed number in the foundation of the intelligible realm and in the construction of the universe. After Plato, and unlike Aristotle, Plotinus drew a distinction between intelligible numbers and mathematical/arithmetical numbers and is "the first post-Platonic philosopher who develops a theory of numbers" (Slaveva-Griffin, *Plotinus on Number*, 12). Plotinus constructs the hierarchy One (not participating in quantity) > substantial number (not participating in quantity and expression of the Intellect) > monadic number (to which quantity pertains). He views multiplicity as number, a notion that Evagrius shared with him, and as a derivation from the One in a mathematical procession. Indeed, Plotinus's idea of the universe as a multiplicity that results from a separation from the One is remarkably similar to Origen's and Evagrius's idea. Slaveva-Griffin (*Plotinus on Number*, ch. 1) rightly observes the inversion of direction between Plato's cosmogonical scheme in his *Timaeus* and Plotinus's especially in *Enneads* 6.6: while Plato considers the universe to result from a composition operated by the Demiurge, with a bottom-to-top scheme, Plotinus uses a top-to-bottom scheme, from the One to the multiplicity of the universe. This, I note, is also Origen's and Evagrius's scheme. Evagrius knew Plotinus's theory of numbers and their distinction from the One as a supreme principle and is no less keen to emphasize this distinction.

6.11. The arithmetic triad is followed by a tetrad. The Holy Trinity, on the contrary, is not followed by a tetrad. Therefore, it is not an arithmetic triad.

Evagrius continues here, in this syllogistic reasoning, the argument he has put forward in the preceding *kephalaion* (see above, the relevant commentary). God the Trinity is not an arithmetical or numerical or mathematical entity. The next two *kephalaia*, too, will continue this argument.

6.12. The arithmetic triad is preceded by a dyad. The Holy Trinity, on the contrary, is not preceded by a dyad. For it is not an arithmetic triad.

The argument in this *kephalaion* evidently parallels almost exactly that which is used in *KG* 6.11. The only difference is the key verb, here "preceding," there "following," as well as the particle of the last sentence, here "for," "indeed" (corresponding to Greek γάρ), there "therefore," "as a consequence." This is why *KG* 6.11 corresponds more closely to the formal structure of a syllogism. Note Evagrius's ongoing concern to distinguish the Trinity from a mathematical entity or a number.

6.13. The arithmetic triad is formed by addition of unity to unity without substance. The blessed Trinity, on the contrary, is not formed by addition of unities like those. Therefore, it is not a triad that is in numbers.

The structure of the argument is similar to that of the two preceding *kephalaia*. As in this whole series of *kephalaia* (*KG* 6.10–13), Evagrius is concerned about the distinction between the Trinity and the arithmetic triad. The units of the arithmetic triad have no substance, unlike the hypostases of the Trinity.

6.14. "Christ is NOT *homoousios* with the Trinity; indeed, he is not substantial knowledge as well." But Christ is the only one who always and inseparably possesses substantial knowledge in himself. What I claim is that Christ is the one who went together with God the Logos; in spirit, Christ IS the Lord [i.e., God]. He is inseparable from his body and in unity IS *homoousios* with the Father.

After speaking of the Trinity in the preceding *kephalaia*, and carefully distinguishing it from a mathematical entity, Evagrius focuses on Christ—God and *logikon* and human being together—as a person of the Trinity. The adversative particle ("but, though") indicates that what comes before it is the expression of the opinion of an interlocutor, which Evagrius overturns (as is also clear from the marker: "What I claim is…"). This is why I put the first sentence within quotation marks in my edition. Indeed, the last sentence of Evagrius's own refutation is the contradictory opposite of the first: "Christ is NOT *homoousios* with the Trinity" versus "[Christ] IS *homoousios* with the Father," and "IS the Lord" God. On this interpretation, this *kephalaion* is far from demonstrating that—as is often assumed (see, e.g., Konstantinovsky, *Evagrius*, 144–45)—Evagrius regarded Christ as extraneous to God and not consubstantial with the other persons of the

Trinity. Moreover, on my interpretation this *kephalaion* is perfectly consistent with Evagrius's declaration in his *Letter on Faith* 3 that the Father and the Son have the same essence. For Christ is the Son, who at the same time has also assumed humanity. This is why Evagrius states that Christ has God the Logos in himself (ibid. 4).

The adverb "inseparably" here in Syriac is the same as either of those that at Chalcedon will describe the inseparability of the two natures of Christ, human and divine (ἀχωρίστως, ἀδιαιρέτως). Not accidentally, the adjective "inseparable" is used here explicitly to describe the union of the divine and human nature in Christ. Christ is both fully God and fully human; the fact that he is a *logikon* and a human being does not mean that he is God to a lesser degree or not at all.

6.15. Christ's feet are practical virtue and contemplation. Now, if he "puts all his enemies under his feet," all of them will know practical virtue and contemplation.

In his reflection on Christ, which he has carried forward also in the immediately preceding *kephalaion*, Evagrius comes to the eschatological point of the submission of all to Christ, "under his feet," announced by Paul in 1 Cor 15:25. This verse, remarkably, is part of the eschatological revelation of 1 Cor 15:24–28 that Origen and Gregory of Nyssa used as a major biblical pillar for their *apokatastasis* doctrine, in that it announces that in the end God will be "all in all" (see Ramelli, "Christian Soteriology and Christian Platonism"). Evagrius here focuses on verse 25 and takes over Origen's identification of the eventual submission of all to Christ as universal salvation. He interprets the submission of all under Christ's feet as their acquisition of practical virtue (the goal of *praktikē*) and contemplation, or *theōria*. This will clearly lead to their perfection. See also below, *KG* 6.27 and the relevant commentary.

The Syriac word for "contemplation" is ܬܐܘܪܝܐ, the transliteration of θεωρία. Thus, Christ's feet are allegorized as active and contemplative virtue, action and contemplation, and the submission of all enemies to Christ, who will have them all "under his feet" according to 1 Cor 15:25 (which in turn quotes Ps 109:1 [LXX]), is interpreted as their salvation—just as in Origen—through the attainment of practical and contemplative virtue. Origen's interpretation of the universal subjection announced in 1 Cor 15:25–28 and in Ps 109:1 as universal salvation is evident, for example, in his *Commentary on John* 6.295–296: "The Father says to him who is the

Lord of each of us, 'Take your seat to my right, until I place your enemies as a stool for your feet,' which will occur when the last enemy, Death, will be annihilated by him [1 Cor 15:26]. So, if we grasp what it means to be subjected to Christ, especially in the light of this passage: 'And when all will be subjected to him, he himself, the Son, will be subjected to him who has subjected everything to himself' [1 Cor 15:28], then we shall understand God's lamb, who takes up the sin of the world, in a way worthy of the goodness of the God of the universe." Universal subjection in 1 Cor 15:25–28 is even more clearly understood as universal salvation in *On First Principles* 1.6.1: "Now, what kind of subjection is this in which all beings must be subject to Christ? I believe this is the kind of subjection in which we also wish to be subject to him, the one in which the apostles and all saints, who have followed Christ, are also subject to him. For the word 'subjection,' in the case of the subjection in which we are subject to Christ, means the salvation of those who are subject, a salvation that comes from Christ," *Quae ergo est subiectio, qua Christo omnia debent esse subiecta? Ego arbitror quia haec ipsa qua nos quoque optamus ei esse subiecti, qua subiecti ei sunt et apostoli et omnes sancti qui secuti sunt Christum. Subiectionis enim nomen, qua Christo subicimur, salutem quae a Christo est indicat subiectorum.* This equation was developed also by Gregory of Nyssa in his commentary on 1 Cor 15:28 (*In illud: Tunc et ipse Filius*), in strict accord with Origen, by means of the same quotations and the selfsame interpretation.

In another passage, as in the present *kephalaion*, Evagrius relates Christ allegorically to the *praktikē* and contemplation: scholium 2 on Ps 126:1. However, while in the *kephalaion* under examination the structure is binary, in the scholium it is threefold: "by means of practical life/asceticism [πρακτική] the soul has Christ as master of the house; by means of natural contemplation [φυσική] it has him as king; and by means of theology [θεολογία], as God. The first two states are necessarily implied by the third, just as the first is by the second; but the second and third states, for now, are not necessarily implied by the first."

6.16. Christ is the one who, from the essential knowledge and from the incorporeal nature and the corporeal one, has manifested himself to us. Now, the man who says, "two Christs" or "two Sons," is like one who calls the wise and his or her wisdom "two wise" or "two wisdoms."

This *kephalaion* is directly connected to *KG* 6.14 and confirms my interpretation of 6.14 (see above, the relevant commentary) by denying the duplicity of Christ and the Son. Christ is the Son of God, consubstantial with the Father, and person of the Trinity. With the three components—essential knowledge, incorporeal nature, and corporeal natures—Evagrius indicates the three components of Christ: (1) God the Logos, the Son (God being essential knowledge), (2) rational soul or intellect, that of a *logikon*, and (3) human body, that of a human being. These are the same components of Christ as Origen indicated and were taken over by Gregory Nyssen and Nazianzen as well.

6.17. The holy power is that which, from the contemplation of beings and from the incorporeal and the corporeal nature, has been constituted.

The present *kephalaion* has the same structure as the first half of the preceding *kephalaion*. The Syriac noun for "power" probably renders a Greek δύναμις here. The definition of power given here can correspond to an angel (angels being often called holy powers). Angels have an incorporeal intellect or rational soul and a corporeal, albeit not mortal, body and are capable of the contemplation of beings.

6.18. There was a time when Christ did not possess a body. But there was no time when in him there was not God the Logos. For together with his (coming into) being, also God the Logos has dwelled in him.

The train of thought of this *kephalaion* goes back to *KG* 6.16 and 6.14 about the identity and components of Christ (see the relevant commentaries above). Evagrius uses the key formulas "there was a time when it did not…" and "there was no time when it did not…" that he also uses in *KG* 1.40, about evil and virtue, and 2.84. Origen had imported this formula from the philosophical cosmological debate about the eternity of the world into the Christian theological debate about the coeternity of the Son with the Father and his divinity, where it became the focus of the "Arian" controversy (see above, the commentary on *KG* 1.40; and Ramelli, "Alexander of Aphrodisias").

God the Logos, who is absolutely eternal, has been in Christ from the very beginning; there was no time when God the Logos was not in Christ. This pertains to the divinity of Christ, and in reference to this Evagrius uses the eternity formula, "there was no time when it did not…" What pertains to the creaturely aspect of Christ, instead, is the body (not only his mortal body but also that of his resurrection and possibly the immortal body of a nonfallen *logikon*; this is why the Syriac word for "body" in this *kephalaion* embraces all kinds of bodies and not only mortal bodies). Consistently with this, for the creaturely nature of Christ Evagrius uses the formula, "there was a time when it did not…," which is the formula of noneternity but temporality. It applies to created, diastematic realities. But for the divine nature of Christ he uses the eternity formula: "there was no time when it did not…." From the coming into being of Christ as *logikon*, God the Logos has dwelled in him.

6.19. Conversion is the ascent from movement and from evilness and from ignorance toward the knowledge of the Holy Trinity.

The underlying Greek word for "conversion" is probably μετάνοια. For the New Testament basis of this notion, see Richard V. Peace, *Conversion in the New Testament: Paul and the Twelve* (Grand Rapids: Eerdmans, 1999); Guy D. Nave, *The Role and Function of Repentance in Luke-Acts* (Atlanta: Society of Biblical Literature, 2002); and David Konstan, "Regret, Repentance, and Change of Heart in Paul: *Metanoia* in its Greek Context," in *Paul's Greco-Roman Context* (ed. Cilliers Breytenbach; BETL; Leuven: Peeters, forthcoming). For the patristic panorama, although very selectively, see also Alexis Torrance, *Repentance in Late Antiquity: Eastern Asceticism and the Framing of the Christian Life c. 400–650 CE* (Oxford: Oxford University Press, 2013). Another probable candidate is Greek ἐπιστροφή, which was also used by Origen with reference to *apokatastasis* and denoted the third Neoplatonic movement, that of reversal or return or restoration, after μονή and πρόοδος. Evagrius underlines the aspect of ascent that is inherent in conversion. Note that "movement," according to Evagrius's and Origen's terminology, is a movement of will, here denoting a diversification of wills toward minor goods that must be left behind in the ascent (see Ramelli, "Harmony between *Arkhē* and *Telos*"). The same terminology of movement is used again by Evagrius in the next *kephalaion*. It is also to be remarked that Evagrius, once again, associates here evilness and ignorance: both, and not only ignorance, must be left aside in the ascent to the knowledge of the Trinity. If one does not renounce vice, one cannot acquire true knowledge.

6.20. Before the movement God was good and powerful and wise, and creator of incorporeal beings, and father of rational creatures, and omnipotent. But after the movement God has become creator of bodies, and judge and ruler and physician and shepherd and teacher, and merci-

ful and patient, and also door/gate, way, lamb, high priest, together with the other epithets that are said in modes. But Father and Principle he is also before the creation of the incorporeal beings: Father of Christ, Principle of the Holy Spirit.

As in the immediately preceding *kephalaion*, here too "movement" (reflecting Greek κίνησις) refers to the movements of free will of rational creatures. This movement allowed for the fall. In this *kephalaion* this is taken as a turning point in the history of rational creatures and in God's relation to them, as it was also in Origen. The term for "bodies" here is generic and can include both mortal and immortal bodies. Rational creatures equipped with individuality and free will have bodies for their individuation. The *epinoiai* of God came only after the differentiation of wills of rational creatures. Origen had devoted a great deal of attention to the *epinoiai* of Christ.

The last sentence links this *kephalaion* with *KG* 6.4, where God the Father is said to be Father of the Son and Principle of the Spirit. The intra-Trinitarian relation, which is eternal *a parte ante* and *a parte post*, is kept distinct from the creation of incorporeal and corporeal beings. Note that by saying "Father of Christ," and by saying that God is such also before the creation of rational creatures, Evagrius here further confirms my interpretation of *KG* 6.14 about Christ's consubstantiality with the Father (see above, the relevant commentary), since he asserts the coeternity of Christ with the Father and sets him apart from all creatures, including rational creatures. Evagrius here clearly places Christ within the intra-Trinitarian sphere and not outside with the creaturely world, as is also clear from his attributing to God the *epinoiai* of Christ, as Gregory of Nyssa also had done. This obviously means that Christ is God.

6.21. Virtue is the rational soul's condition in which (the soul) hardly moves toward evil.

This is the third *kephalaion* in a row in which Evagrius reflects on the movements of rational creatures' free will. Of course Evagrius cannot state that virtue is the state in which a rational soul cannot sin at all and cannot utterly move toward evil by means of an evil choice of free will, since free will, and the possibility of choosing evil, is constitutive of all rational creatures, apart from the *logikon* of Christ, who is inseparable from God. This is perfectly in line with Origen's thought. See also Lekkas,

Liberté et progrès. Virtue is the state in which it is very difficult or unlikely, albeit not impossible, that the soul chooses evil and sins. It will become utterly impossible only in the ultimate *telos*, when there will be no further fall from *apokatastasis*. This will bee guaranteed by perfect charity-love (see above, the commentary on *KG* 1.86 and 5.46).

6.22. If it is true that sense-perceptible words also in the aeon to come indicate objects, it is clear that the wise of this aeon too will inherit the kingdom of heavens. If, on the other hand, it is the pureness of the intellect that sees, and the word fitting it that reveals, the wise of this aeon will be kept far from the knowledge of God.

In the present *kephalaion*, just as in the following one, Evagrius distinguishes two kinds of words, which provide two kinds of knowledge. A distinction is also drawn between the kingdom of heavens and the knowledge of God, two states of which the latter is higher than the former. Indeed, in *KG* 5.30 the kingdom of heavens is the contemplation of beings, but the knowledge of God, by virtue of its object, is superior. However, the opposition on which Evagrius focuses here is between the wise of this world and the real wise, that is, those who possess a pure intellect.

6.23. Just as this word indicates objects in this aeon, so will the word of the spiritual body indicate the objects of the aeon(s) to come.

Again two kinds of words are kept distinct and associated with the respective objects in the present and the future aeon (or aeons: in Syriac the distinction between "aeon" and "aeons" is only clear from the vocalization). The word for "body" here is not that which in Syriac indicates a mortal body, but it is *gwšm'*, which can indicate all types of bodies; here the qualifier "spiritual" (*rwḥn'*) makes it clear what kind of body this is. This is also why it is associated with the future aeon or aeons.

6.24. If it is true that those who in the aeon to come will be angels will also be in charge of five or six cities, it is obvious that they will receive knowledge too, that which can urge rational souls from evilness to virtue and from ignorance to the knowledge of God.

As in the two preceding *kephalaia*, here too Evagrius reflects on the aeon to come. This can entail the passage of some rational creatures—who now are humans, presumably—to the rank of angels. Note once again the association of virtue and knowledge, which occurs so often in Evagrius. The passage from evilness to virtue and from ignorance to knowledge is indispensable on the path of the final restoration. Luke 19:17–19, where the good servants are rewarded with rule over five or ten cities, is here interpreted as a reference to the reward of those who will be angels in the aeon to come.

6.25. When demons have been unable to move evil thoughts in the gnostic, then they close his eyes with much cold and drive them [i.e., the eyes] into a deep sleep. Very cold, indeed, are demons' bodies, in the likeness of ice.

The very same idea, that demons cause monks to fall asleep during the reading of the Bible, by sitting on their head and cooling it down with their cold bodies, is expressed by Evagrius with much concern also in *On Evil Thoughts* (Περὶ λογισμῶν) 33. Indeed, both in this treatise and in the present *kephalaion* the point is the same: evil thoughts inspired by demons and other cases of demons' pernicious influence on humans. Here the word denoting the bodies of demons is the Syriac word that includes imperishable bodies (*gwšm'*), and not that which denotes earthly, mortal bodies. Demons cause ascetics to sleep, while the latter would better wake; deprivation of sleep was practiced by Evagrius and his fellow monks within the framework of the *praktikē*. Thus, in *Sentences to the Monks* (*Sententiae ad monachos*) 97 he warns: "Do not give yourself to feasting your stomach, nor do you fill yourself with nighttime sleep, since in this way you will become pure, and the Spirit of the Lord will come upon you." On asceticism with respect to sleep in Evagrius's day, see now Leslie Dossey, "Watchful Greeks and Lazy Romans: Disciplining Sleep in Late Antiquity," *JECS* 21 (2013): 209–39, esp. 224 on Evagrius and Basil. The coldness of demonic bodies was consistently maintained by Evagrius and was already postulated by Origen, in whose system it made a lot of sense, because the ardor of love is the factor that, in his view, keeps rational creatures close to God. The farther removed one is from God, the colder one is. Indeed, the very fall of rational creatures from God was described by Origen as a ψῦξις, a "cooling down."

6.26. Just as it is not fire itself that is in our bodies, but rather its quality [lit. "a mixture of it"] has been constituted in them, so in the bodies of

demons it is not earth itself, or water itself, but their qualities [lit. "mixtures of them"] that the Creator has inserted in them.

After declaring in the preceding *kephalaion* that demons' bodies are cold, Evagrius goes on to reflect on the qualities of their bodies and of human beings' bodies. The latter are designated in Syriac with the word (*gwšm'*) that also includes spiritual and immortal bodies—such as the prelapsarian body and the body of the resurrection—and not only mortal bodies. Evagrius insists that God has not created the elements themselves as constitutive of the bodies of humans and demons, but rather that God has created their qualities, or mixtures of them. Especially if one sticks to the translation "qualities," this seems to reflect closely Gregory of Nyssa's solution that God created immaterial, intelligible qualities, and these constituted matter. See my commentary on *KG* 5.50 above. This would point to one more element of Evagrius's dependence on Gregory of Nyssa, which needs to be investigated further. See Ramelli, "Evagrius and Gregory." Evagrius has already spoken of the elemental composition of demonic bodies in *KG* 2.51, where he opposed the "chariot of knowledge"—probably the angelic body, with a prevalence of fire and air—to "the chariot of ignorance," with a prevalence of air and water (see the relevant commentary above). In the present *kephalaion*, Evagrius mentions water and air as constituents of demonic bodies.

6.27. If it is the case that "all peoples will come and will worship before the Lord," it is evident that the peoples who want war will also come. Now, if this is true, the whole nature of rational creatures will adore the Name of the Lord, the one who reveals the Father who is in him. For this is the Name that is "above all names."

This *kephalaion* clearly interprets the eschatological universal submission to Christ and God (announced by Paul also in 1 Cor 15:24–28) as universal salvation, in that this submission will be voluntary. Origen and Gregory of Nyssa reasoned along the same lines (see Ramelli, "Christian Soteriology and Christian Platonism"). In Phil 2:9–11 Paul states that "God has highly exalted him and bestowed on him the name which is above every name, that at the name of Jesus every knee should bow, in heaven and on earth and under the earth, and every tongue confess that Jesus Christ is Lord, to the glory of God the Father" (RSV). Evagrius directly identifies Christ the Son with the name of God, which reveals the Father. In Heb

1:4 Christ is declared to be "as much superior to angels as the name he has obtained is more excellent than theirs" (RSV). In Rev 15:4, which is the main biblical reference for this *kephalaion*, the prophecy is uttered that Evagrius uses here: "All nations shall come and worship thee, for thy judgments have been revealed" (RSV).

Here the universal adoration before the Lord is described by Evagrius in the words of Ps 85:9, and it is understood as universal salvation, including the enemies who are said to be subjected in the end (cf. 1 Cor 15:24–26), given that it will be the adoration of the Name that reveals the Father, which for this reason is said to be superior to all names in Phil 2:9. Consequently, even the enemies will know the Father—and this knowledge, according to Evagrius's ethical intellectualism, must entail voluntary adhesion. Should one understand the Name to be Jesus's name, its meaning would be "God saves" or "God is salvation," which perfectly fits Evagrius's (and Origen's and Gregory Nyssen's) conviction that universal subjection will coincide with universal salvation.

6.28. The Father is the begetter of essential knowledge.

This *kephalaion* begins a group of four where Evagrius reflects on the Father, the first person of the Trinity. Essential knowledge is often identified by Evagrius with the whole Trinity, as a kind of definition of God the Trinity. Here he claims that essential knowledge is begotten by the Father, which points to a more special identification with the Son, the Logos of God, who is also the divine component of Christ-Logos.

6.29. The Father is the one who possesses a rational nature that is united with the knowledge of the Trinity.

Evagrius may here refer to Christ, whose *logikon*—that is, his creaturely component, which exists together with his divine component—is possessed by God the Father and is permanently united with the knowledge of the Trinity. In this sense, the Son is essential knowledge, begotten by the Father, and Christ—who in his divine component is the Son and the Logos of God, but also has a creatural component as a *logikon* and a human being—is permanently joined to that knowledge. Christ is said to be possessed by the Father, being the Logos of God the Father in his divine component, and a *logikon* who loves God.

6.30. The Father is the one who possesses a rational nature that is joined to the contemplation of beings.

Christ, who is God and a *logikon*, is oriented both to the Trinity and to creatures. So he is joined not only to the knowledge of the Trinity but also to the contemplation of created beings. The Father possesses Christ both as his own Logos and as a *logikon.*

6.31. Begotten is the one who has been begotten by some factor as by a father.

The object of this *kephalaion* is the Son as a Person of the Trinity, and his relation to the Father. Here Christ is considered in his divine component, and not in his creatural component as a *logikon.*

6.32. Brought to being is that which has been brought to being by some factor as by a creator.

I have already highlighted the distinction drawn by Evagrius in *KG* 6.4 and 6.20 between God as the Father of Christ (and Principle of the Holy Spirit) and as the Creator of creatures (see above, the relevant commentaries). The same distinction underlies *KG* 6.31 and 6.32. This is why I have translated the same Syriac word *ylyd'* with "begotten" in *KG* 6.31 and with "brought to being" in *KG* 6.32. It is probable that the Greek *Vorlage* had γεννητός in the former case and γενητός in the latter, but in manuscripts the two are often confused, and this probably happened also in the manuscript available to the Syriac translator.

6.33. When Christ will no longer be imprinted on the various aeons and in names of every sort, then he too "will submit to God the Father," and he alone will rejoice in the knowledge of God, a knowledge that is not distributed over the aeons and the progresses of rational creatures.

Note the claim that Christ alone will rejoice in the knowledge of God, which separates Evagrius from the ideas of the Isochristoi, to whom he is often associated. The submission of all to Christ, who will in turn submit to God, according to 1 Cor 15:28, will take place at the end of all aeons, in the very *telos*, when all will be brought to unity. Indeed, Evagrius's conception of aeons is close to Origen's: there are several aeons (αἰῶνες, not worlds, or κόσμοι) before the final *apokatastasis*. During the aeons, rational creatures increase their virtue and knowledge and get purified; after all this has been accomplished, the series of aeons will cease, and the fullness of divine ἀϊδιότης, or absolute eternity, will remain. Evagrius closely adheres to Origen in claiming that the succession of aeons is not infinite—as Origen's notion of aeons was misrepresented by Augustine and others during the Origenistic controversy—but it had a beginning and will thus have an end: "Just as the destruction of the last aeon will not be followed by a new creation, so also the creation of the first aeon was not preceded by a destruction" (*KG* 5.89; see above, the relevant commentary). Aeons are necessary to rational creatures' spiritual and intellectual development. In this *kephalaion* Evagrius is interpreting 1 Cor 15:28 in the same way as Gregory of Nyssa, his inspirer, did in his *In illud: Tunc et ipse Filius*. See Ramelli, "Gregory of Nyssa's Trinitarian Theology."

The eventual subjection of the Son to the Father, which is mentioned and interpreted by Evagrius in the present *kephalaion*, is announced by Paul in 1 Cor 15:28, the same passage that Gregory comments on in his *In illud: Tunc et ipse Filius* in order to support the doctrine of *apokatastasis* and that is repeatedly used by Origen as the main biblical support for this doctrine. Both Origen and Gregory interpret the final subjection of the Son to the Father not as a sign of inferiority but as the subjection of humanity or even all *logika*, that is, the creaturely component of Christ-*logikon* (not the divine one); this is implicitly the whole of humanity, which Christ has taken up. We have already seen that this subjection of all humanity to Christ, and then, through Christ, to God, will be not forced but voluntary and will mean the salvation of all of humanity, as Origen, Gregory, and Evagrius understood to be confirmed by the last words of 1 Cor 15:28: "God will be all in all."

This is the most crucial passage, and the one most often quoted by Origen, in defense of his theory of universal salvation. One of the best examples is to be found in his *On First Principles* 3.5.6–8:

The only begotten son of God, Logos and Wisdom of the Father, must reign until he has put his enemies under his feet and destroyed the last enemy, Death, embracing in himself, at the end of the world, all those whom he subjects to the Father and who come to salvation thanks to him.… This is the meaning of what the apostle says about him: "When all is subjected to him, then the Son himself will be subjected to him who has subjected everything to him, so that God may be all in all" [1 Cor 15:28].… As the Son's subjection to the Father means the perfect reintegration of all creation [i.e., universal *apokatastasis*], so the subjection of his enemies to the

Son means the salvation of his subjects and the reintegration of the lost.... This subjection will take place in certain ways and times and according to precise rules: the entire world will be subjected to the Father, not as a result of violence, nor by necessity that compels subjection, but thanks to words, reason, teaching, emulation of the best, good norms, and also threats, when deserved and apt.... Providence operates in favor of each one, safeguarding the rational creatures' free will.

Evagrius takes over this conception of Origen and refers 1 Cor 15:28 to the eventual *apokatastasis*, at the end of all aeons.

6.34. During the aeons God "will change the body of our humiliation into the likeness of the glorious body" of the Lord. Then, after all aeons, he will also make us "in the likeness of his Son's image," if it is the case that the Son's image is the essential knowledge of God the Father.

Here, once again, it is clear that Evagrius adopts the same scheme as Origen had done: a succession of aeons for the moral improvement of rational creatures and the resurrection of mortal bodies, followed by the eternity of *apokatastasis*, when all rational creatures will attain the knowledge of God. The biblical references are to Phil 3:21, about the transformation of the body of our humiliation into the likeness of Christ's risen body, and Rom 8:29, about the conformation of human beings to the image of God's Son. Clearly, when he speaks of Christ's risen body, he refers to the humanity of Christ; when he speaks of God's Son, he refers to the divinity of Christ.

Evagrius states here that the resurrection—with the transformation of the mortal body into a glorious and immortal body, like that of the risen Christ—will take place during the aeons, in the other aeon but not after the end of all aeons, which will coincide with the *apokatastasis*, in Evagrius's just as in Origen's view. Resurrection—or more precisely, the resurrection of the body, since we have seen that Evagrius conceives of resurrection in three different ways—will come first, and it is described by Evagrius in the words of Phil 3:21.

The resurrection of the intellect, instead, will be the perfection of *apokatastasis*, after the end of all aeons—and it will coincide with our acquisition of "the likeness of his Son's image." Here Evagrius is working with the interpretation of Rom 8:29. He is certainly recalling Origen's distinction between image and likeness: human beings were made in the image of God, as is stated in Genesis, but God's likeness, which was part of God's original plan for humans, must be voluntarily pursued by each one, and its complete realization will be in the *telos* (see, e.g., Origen's *Commentary on Romans* 4.5.161–165: "In the beginning God's intention was that the human being be in the image and likeness of God. Then the human being was created indeed in the image of God, but the likeness was postponed, that first the human being might trust in God, and in this way might become like God," *In initiis homo, cum propositum fuisset ut ad imaginem et similitudinem Dei fieret, ad imaginem quidem factus est, similitudo autem dilata est, ut prius confideret in Deum et ita similis fieret ei*). Evagrius also places the acquisition of this likeness in the *telos*, after the end of all aeons, and makes it consist in the essential knowledge of the Father. This, of course, passes through the Son, who is the image of the Father and reveals the Father. That the ultimate end for all human beings in the plan of God is their acquisition of the knowledge of the truth, which is God, is clear from 1 Tim 2:4. In John 17:3 Jesus defines eternal life as the knowledge of the Father, the only true God, and of Jesus Christ, sent by the Father.

6.35. With intellections of exhortation the holy angels purify us from evilness and render us impassive. With (the intellections) of nature, on the other hand, and with the divine words they free us from ignorance and make us wise and gnostic.

Note again knowledge's close relationship to virtue, which Evagrius often emphasizes. Purification from passions and evilness and purification from ignorance are inseparable from one another. The role of angels in the process of purification and instruction of human beings was already stressed by Origen and Gregory Nyssen (see Ramelli, *Christian Doctrine of Apokatastasis*, the chapters devoted to them). Origen in particular conceived of an instruction by angels followed by instruction by Christ. See above, *KG* 3.65 and the relevant commentary.

6.36. The one who "was made to be the object of derision of the angels of God," is it not he who initiated movement and in the beginning broke the boundaries of evilness? And because of this he was called "the principle [or "the first"] of the works of God."

Evagrius is manifestly inspired by Origen, who in *Commentary on John* 20.22.182 comments on the same quotations in reference to the devil (Job 40:19 according to the Septuagint: an unspecified beast is "the first of the molding of the Lord, made to be the object of derision of the angels of God," τοῦτ' ἔστιν ἀρχὴ πλάσματος κυρίου, πεποιημένον ἐγκαταπαίζεσθαι ὑπὸ τῶν ἀγγέλων αὐτοῦ). Origen insists that the devil was not the principle of God's creation but only of God's molding from the earth, ἀρχὴ πλάσματος Κυρίου, which came only after the fall. See Pietras, "L'apocrifo giudaico *Preghiera di Giuseppe*"; idem, "L'inizio del mondo materiale"; Ramelli, *Christian Doctrine of Apokatastasis*, the chapter devoted to Origen. Evagrius states that Satan's sin initiated movement, that is, volition, and specifically bad volition; the devil was the first who moved his free will away from God.

6.37. Just as cranes fly in the type (shape) of letters, while they do not know letters, so do also demons recite the words of the fear of God, while they do not know the fear of God.

After speaking of the devil, Evagrius goes on reflecting on demons. Since the fear of God is the beginning of all wisdom, demons cannot possess it (since they are characterized by ignorance), but they pretend to have it, which becomes their falsity. Indeed, in Jas 2:19—which I think Evagrius had in mind here—it is stated that "demons too believe and tremble," but Evagrius seems to suggest that their faith, as well as their fear of God, is only nominal.

6.38. The intelligible cross is the mortification of one's mortal body out of one's own will, which completes Christ's chastity.

In this and in the following *kephalaia* Evagrius interprets details of the life of Christ and reflects on their spiritual meaning, offering, as he often does in the *KG*, a noetic exegesis. Here the word for body is *pgr'*, which indicates the mortal body, the result of sin, prone to passions and corruption. This is the body that one has to mortify (spiritually reproducing the death of Christ on the cross), but not so the immortal body of the resurrection. When Christ mortified his mortal body on the cross, he completed its mortification by chastity on earth. This is what his followers too should do. Note the broad meaning of chastity as the mortification of passions, which Evagrius maintains in Origen's, Methodius's, and Gregory Nyssen's line (see Ilaria L. E. Ramelli, "L'Inno a Cristo-Logos nel *Simposio* di Metodio," in *Motivi e forme della poesia cristiana antica tra scrittura e tradizione classica* [SEAug 108; Rome: Institutum patristicum Augustinianum, 2008], 257–80). Of course, here Christ is considered in his creaturely nature, and not in his divine nature.

6.39. The birth of Christ is the birth of our inner human being, which is from the beginning, that which Christ, like a good builder, has founded and built upon the head stone of the building of his body.

After speaking of the spiritual-noetic meaning of the death of Christ, Evagrius tackles that of the birth of Christ. Here the word for body, in reference to the body of Christ, is *gwšm'*, which indicates not only Jesus's mortal body but also the body of his resurrection and the mystical body of Christ. The motif of the birth of Christ in one's heart is typical of Origen (e.g., *Homilies on Jeremiah* 9.4; *Homilies on Luke* 22.3; *Homilies on Numbers* 23, etc.) and is taken up not only here by Evagrius but also, much later, by Meister Eckhart.

Evagrius, just like Origen (and earlier Philo), speaks of an inner and an outer human being, the former made after the image of God, the latter corruptible and liable to passions. One of the many passages in which this conception is to be found in Origen is *Commentary on Romans* 2.9.569–575: "The apostle Paul often deals with anthropology in such a way as to declare that for every single person there are two human beings, one of which he usually calls exterior, and the other interior. He says that the former is according to the flesh, and the latter according to the spirit. I suppose he was inspired by the passage in Genesis where one human being is declared to have been created in the image of God and another to have been molded from the earth," *Frequens est apostolo iste tractatus quo per singulos quosque binos homines esse designat, quorum alterum exteriorem nominare alterum interiorem solet, eorumque alterum secundum carnem esse alterum secundum spiritum dicit, opinor ex illis institutus quae in Genesi scripta sunt ubi alius ad imaginem Dei factus alius de limo terrae fictus refertur.* In the same commentary, 7.2.108–111, Origen remarks again that this threefold anthropology was taught by St. Paul: "That interior human being who was created after the model of God and made in the image of God is incorruptible, invisible, and, in relation to itself, can also be called incorporeal. The exterior human being, on the contrary, is said to be both corporeal and corruptible," *Ille interior homo qui secundum Deum creatus est et ad imaginem Dei factus incorruptibilis est et inuisibilis et secundum propriam sui rationem etiam incorporeus dici potest. Exterior uero homo et corporeus et corruptibilis dicitur.* This division Origen inherited not only from Paul but also from Philo and is connected with the theory of the so-called double creation, which is shared by Philo, Origen, and Gregory of Nyssa. For Philo, the creation of the human being was double, not in time but in principle (*On the Creation of the World* 69–71; *Allegorical Interpretation* 1.31, 53, 88–90): intelligible, according to Gen 1:26–27, and corporeal, according to Gen 2:7. The human being (ἄνθρωπος) who is in the image and likeness of God is the noetic human being, since the human being is image of God not in the body but in the intellect (*On the Creation of the World* 69). The ἄνθρωπος / image of God is an Idea, a *typos*, intelligible, incorporeal, neither male nor female, immortal; the man of Gen 2:7, derived from mold, is corporeal, mortal, and divided into genders (*On the Creation of the World* 134; *Allegorical Interpretation* 1.31). The body derives from the earth, the soul from God, "the Father and leader of all" (*On the Creation of the World* 135; *On the Migration of Abraham* 3; see *Allegorical Interpretation* 1.53, 88–90; 2.4). Such "double creation" is clearly present in Origen (*Homilies on Genesis* 1.13; *On First Principles* 1.2.6; *Dialogue with Heraclides* 15.28; *Homilies on Jeremiah* 1.10; *Commentary on Mathew* 14.16) and Gregory Nyssen (*On the Creation of the Human Being* 181AD) too, and so is Philo's threefold division of the human being. See my philosophical essay in Ramelli, *Gregorio di Nissa: Sull'anima*, with documentation; idem, "Tricotomia."

6.40. The crucifying of Christ is the mortification/killing of our old human being, and the cancellation of the condemnation pronounced against us, and forgiveness that brings us back to life.

This *kephalaion* is closely related to *KG* 6.38, where Evagrius offered the spiritual interpretation of the death of Christ on the cross, identifying it with the mortification of passions and the fleshly body (see the relevant commentary above). Here, again, the killing of Christ is seen as the killing of our old, sinful human being. Evagrius here also confirms the centrality of Christ in the history of salvation, and in *apokatastasis* itself—just as for Origen. See Ramelli, "Origen's Doctrine of the Apokatastasis." Christ with his death, which is the killing of the sinful human being, has cancelled the condemnation pronounced by God against us humans, thus enabling God's forgiveness of our sins, which vivifies us. At the same time this *kephalaion* means that Christ's death must be actualized by each human being by the mortification of his or her old and sinful self.

The expression "our old human being," meaning the postlapsarian human being before and without the regeneration in Christ and the Holy Spirit, the human being that must be destroyed, is Pauline. See Rom 6:6: "Our old self was crucified with him so that the sinful body might be destroyed, and we might no longer be enslaved to sin"; 2 Cor 5:17: "If any one is in Christ, he is a new creation; the old has passed away, behold, the new has come"; Eph 4:22–24: "Put off your old nature which belongs to your former manner of life and is corrupt through deceitful lusts, and be renewed in the spirit of your minds, and put on the new nature, created after the likeness of God in true righteousness and holiness"; Col 3:9–10: "You have put off the old nature with its practices and have put on the new nature, which is being renewed in knowledge after the image of its creator" (RSV).

6.41. Complete distancing softens the concupiscible/appetitive faculty of the soul, while it hardens its irascible faculty.

Evagrius clearly follows Plato's tripartition of the soul into rational, irascible, and concupiscible or appetitive (see, e.g., *KG* 4.79; 5.27; and the relevant commentaries). The distancing he is referring to here may be the detachment from passions and the world. Evagrius probably means the solitary life of monks, their ascesis (*praktikē*).

6.42. The death of Christ is the realization of the mystery that brings back to the life of the aeon to come those who have hoped in him in this life.

This *kephalaion* is connected with *KG* 6.38 and 6.40, which both interpret the death of Christ (see above, the relevant commentaries). Like *KG* 6.40, this *kephalaion* underscores the salvific value of the death of Christ and confirms the centrality of Christ and his sacrifice to Evagrius's soteriology, just as to Origen's. Origen definitely rejected all docetic Christology; this is clear in the argument he uses against this doctrine in *Commentary on Romans* 5.9.45–60, where he refutes docetism through a *reductio ad absurdum*:

> Some heretics have tried to claim that Christ did not truly die but underwent an apparent death; it *seemed* that he had died, rather than he actually died. Now it is extremely easy to respond to these people.... If an apparent death was in Christ, and not a true death, then also his resurrection was apparent and not true; therefore, we too will seem to rise but will not really rise; we will seem to die to sin but will not really die. In sum, all that has been done has not been really done. As a consequence, as for our salvation, it results that we *seem* to have been saved, but in fact we have not been saved.... Now this conclusion is so absurd that there is no need for proofs.

> *Quidam haereticorum conati sunt ... asserere quod Christus non uere mortuus sit, sed similitudinem mortis habuerit et uisus sit mori magis quam uere mortuus sit. Quibus respondere perfacile est ... si similitudo fuit mortis in eo et non uera mors, ergo et resurrectionis similitudo fuit et non uera resurrectio, et nos ergo uidebimur resurgere et non uere resurgemus, et uidebimur mori peccato et non uere moriemur, et omne ergo quod gestum est ... non est gestum. Superest igitur ut et quod saluati sumus uisi simus saluari sed non uere saluati simus.... Haec tam absurda sunt ut non indigeant probationibus.*

See also Origen, *Against Celsus* 2.16; *Commentary on John* 10.6.

6.43. God's providence accompanies the freedom of will, whereas God's judgment takes into account the order of rational creatures.

This *kephalaion*, with the synergy of divine providence and rational creatures' free will and merits that it indicates, is in perfect agreement with Origen's theory. God's providence never forces rational creatures' free will, but it brings them to salvation, always respecting their free will. God's judgment is entirely based on rational creatures' merits and demerits, which determine their "order," but it does not contradict God's providence. See Lekkas, *Liberté et progrès*; and Ramelli, *Christian Doctrine of Apokatastasis*, the chapter on Origen. The compatibility between divine providence, creaturely free will, and justice is one of the main pillars of Origen's and Evagrius's doctrine of *apokatastasis*. In *KG* 1.27 Evagrius has pointed out that the contemplation of the Judgment, based on each *logikon*'s deserts, is not the last one but is followed by the contemplation of divine providence. The notion of "order" was central to Origen's soteriology as well: in his view, all rational creatures will attain the blessed *telos* and salvation, but each of them according to its order—that is, the more virtuous first, and the less last.

6.44. The spiritual showing/manifestation is the fulfillment of those things that have been divinely said in advance by the Holy Spirit.

Evagrius is reflecting on prophecies inspired by the Holy Spirit, such as those that appear in the Bible, and their coming true.

6.45. Not one of the worlds/aeons was more excellent than the first world/aeon. This, indeed, they say was made out of the principal [or

"original"] mixture [or "quality"]. And that in it all the aeons will be perfected, a minister and gnostic taught us.

The excellence of the first aeon might be considered to be due to its initially prelapsarian condition; however, Evagrius is clear elsewhere that the first aeon results from the first judgment, which occurred after the fall (see also below, the commentary on *KG* 6.47). The first aeon, at any rate, is declared excellent vis-à-vis the subsequent aeons, not vis-à-vis the prelapsarian state. The perfection of all aeons will be in the restoration of the original condition; this is why it is declared to be accomplished in the first aeon, as a kind of Irenaean recapitulation (ἀνακεφαλαίωσις). The notion of the correspondence between ἀρχή and τέλος is clearly at work here. The Origenian overtones of this conception are evident. The principal or royal or dominant (ἀρχική, also meaning "original") mixture or quality (Guillaumont translates "qualité," followed by Dysinger and Fr. Theophanes: "quality") of the first aeon/world/arrangement is here emphasized. Evagrius probably had in mind also Plato's account of the creation of souls in the *Timaeus* from precise mixtures.

The "gnostic" to whom Evagrius refers as an authority might be Origen himself, or Gregory of Nyssa, who was Evagrius's inspirer and had a closer relation to him than commonly assumed (see Ramelli, "Evagrius and Gregory"), or some other Origenian. Both Origen and Gregory were ministers in the church, respectively a presbyter and a bishop. The Syriac word *gzry'*, which Guillaumont tentatively translated "athlète" (p. 235), is rendered by Sokoloff (*Syriac Lexicon*, 224) as "magistrate" in reference to officers who carry out judgment. If this meaning is to be taken in a spiritual sense, as often in Evagrius, it may well refer to a minister of the church, or more generally to a spiritually advanced person endowed with judgment.

6.46. The lyre is the ascetic soul that is moved by the commandments of Christ.

Evagrius in this *kephalaion*, as in many others before this, offers a spiritual interpretation of a scriptural detail. Here it is the harp or lyre (a small harp), which is mentioned a number of times in Scripture, but especially in connection with the Psalms and King David. Here the lyre is interpreted as the soul that engages in practical virtues and moves according to the moral law of Christ. It is the soul that engages in *praktikē*. The Greek text of this passage is found in *Selected Passages on Psalms* 32:2; 91:4; 150:3–5.

Given the exegesis of the lyre offered in this *kephalaion*, it is not accidental that the Greek was excerpted in a collection of passages that comment on the Psalms.

6.47. God's judgment will have every person who has followed Joshua enter the Land of the Promise, when it gives her a spiritual body and a world/aeon appropriate to her. On the contrary, those who, because of the abundance of their possessions, have been unable to attain it, these people (God's judgment) will settle on the banks of the Jordan, according to their rank.

According to Evagrius, every aeon is followed by a judgment, performed by Christ-Logos, which determines the state of a rational creature in the subsequent aeon. In *KG* 1.65 and 3.2 the judgment is said to be performed by Christ, in *KG* 1.82 by God more generically (see commentaries above). Evagrius has often spoken of the judgment that follows each aeon in his *KG*, for instance in *KG* 6.43, where the judgment is related to rational creatures' free will; *KG* 1.27, where the *logoi* concerning the judgment are said to be followed by the *logoi* concerning divine providence (cf. *KG* 5.27 and 5.16); *KG* 4.4 (see the relevant commentaries above). In *KG* 2.59, 75; 3.38; 5.4, 7, judgments are related by Evagrius precisely to the aeons; in *KG* 3.47 and 2.59 judgments are said to establish the kind of body and the rank of rational creatures (which depends on their development in virtue and knowledge), exactly as in the *kephalaion* under examination here, which must be read against this backdrop. The principle that every person will receive a position that fits the degree of his or her spiritual advancement is a stronghold of both Origen's and Evagrius's thought. The last Judgment will be at the end of all aeons (*KG* 2.77).

The scriptural reference is Josh 1:14–15. The spiritual interpretation of Joshua, the leader who enabled the Hebrews to enter the promised land, is also offered by Evagrius in *KG* 5.36 (see above, the relevant commentary). Those who cannot enter the Holy Land—which in *KG* 5.30 is interpreted as the kingdom of heavens—are identified with those who possess too many material goods. This perspective is in line with Evagrius's asceticism. Evagrius, in turn, shared Origen's and Gregory Nyssen's viewpoint that possessions exceeding one's needs are tantamount to iniquity and theft. See my *Social Justice and the Legitimacy of Slavery: The Role of Philosophical Asceticism from Ancient Judaism to Late Antiquity* (Oxford University Press, forthcoming).

6.48. The harp is the pure intellect, which is moved by spiritual knowledge.

This *kephalaion* is the continuation of *KG* 6.46. There Evagrius interpreted spiritually the lyre or small harp (see the commentary above); here he focuses on the harp. The small harp is related to the level of *praktikē*, the big harp to that of knowledge or gnosis. The Greek of this passage too, like that of *KG* 6.46, is preserved in the *Selected Passages on Psalms* (32:2; 91:3–5). On the bare or pure intellect, see above, *KG* 5.90 with the relevant commentary and the other references there.

6.49. Egypt indicates evil; the desert, practical virtue; the land of Judah, the contemplation of corporeal beings; Jerusalem, that of incorporeal beings; Zion is the symbol of the Trinity.

Evagrius inherited from Origen the allegorical exegesis of the Bible. This is clear from several passages of the *KG* that I have commented on so far. In particular, in this passage allegory finds an ascending route to perfection, from evil and vice to *praktikē*, which pursues virtue, up to the contemplation of corporeal and then incorporeal realities, and finally God the Trinity, who is essential knowledge. The negative symbolism of Egypt is already found in *KG* 4.64; 5.6, 21, and in *KG* 5.88, where Egypt is labeled "the emblem of every evilness." Here Evagrius takes up this negative connotation once again. The allegorization of Egypt as a symbol of evil or evilness and vice (κακία) has a long history going back to Philo. Israel's captivity in Egypt was equated by Philo with a life according to bodily passions, and Pharaoh with a lover of the body, of matter, and of pleasures (*Allegorical Interpretation* 3.13, 38, 212, 243; *On Drunkenness* 209; *On Abraham* 103), a godless man and opposer of God (e.g., *Allegorical Interpretation* 3.12, 212; *On Drunkenness* 19; *On the Confusion of Tongues* 88), and a symbol of those who do not know God and thus forget their humanity because of their enjoyment of bodily things (*On the Posterity of Cain* 115). He is a lover of passions who dwells in the darkness (*On Drunkenness* 209). The making of bricks in Egypt in *On the Confusion of Tongues* 83–100 is assimilated to those employed in the tower of Babel and is interpreted as involvement in material and earthly activities characterized by passions and vices.

Origen was inspired by Philo, although he of course had his differences (for instance, while Philo thought that evil souls will vanish, Origen did not admit of the ontological annihilation of any soul); Gregory of Nyssa—whose ideas Evagrius knew well—relies on both Philo and Origen for his own allegorization of Egypt. Gregory follows Origen more than Philo, though, in that he avoids an exegesis in which the body per se is judged negatively, as in Philo's equation of Egypt with corporeality; thus, he transfers all negativity to vices and the passions rather than corporeality as such. See Ramelli, "Philosophical Allegoresis of Scripture." Philo's interpretation of Egypt as the body and its passions and sense perception—perfectly in line with his statement that the principle of all salvation consists in abandoning the body, with its sense perception, its pleasures, and its desires, as Abraham abandoned his land and family (*On the Migration of Abraham* 2, 9)—is transformed by Origen into a reference to the passions of this world and to sin, with a stress on sin rather than on the body. This will be retained by Gregory: in both Fathers the emphasis lies, not on the body, which is absent in their exegesis, but on passions and sins. In fact, in his *Homilies on Exodus* 3.3, Origen interprets Egypt as a symbol of this world and its passions and darkness, and in 7.2 he considers it to be a figure for the passions: luxury, voluptuousness, and sensuality. Pharaoh is understood by him as a symbol of the devil—Philo's opposer of God—the ruler of this world's darkness (*Homilies on Exodus* 1.5; 2.1; 3.3; 6.1; *Homilies on Psalm 36* 3.1), an interpretation that was adopted also by the Origenian Methodius in *Symposium* 4.2. The making of bricks in Egypt is allegorized by Origen in *Homilies on Exodus* 1.5 as earthly works.

In *The Life of Moses* 2.26–27 Gregory Nyssen interprets Pharaoh's tyranny over the Hebrews in Egypt as a symbol of the tyranny of passions and sin over the human being, who is an image of God and thus has freedom as an essential feature. This image was blurred by the fall, and human freedom was partially lost, but both can be recovered through *apatheia*. Thus, the exodus from Egypt is read as the liberation of the soul from the tyranny of passions. Accordingly, in 2.54–62 Gregory interprets the making of bricks in the land of Egypt as material enjoyment and the pursuit of pleasures, and Pharaoh as a lover of the material life (2.35). Gregory seems to follow Origen in dropping the negative characterization of the body, implicit in Philo's exegesis of Egypt as body and Pharaoh as lover of the body, and in retaining the reference to passions and sin derived from bad will and from the lessened status of humanity after the fall. Like Gregory, Evagrius also follows Origen's line in that he sees in Egypt a symbol of evil and wickedness rather than a symbol of matter and corporeality, which Philo tended to associate with evil.

Mount Zion, as the citadel of Jerusalem, is the knowledge of the Trinity, as the culmination of the contemplation of the incorporeal beings.

Origen in *Commentary on the Song of Songs* 3.13.42 had likewise allegorized the highest mountains with the knowledge of the Trinity. In reference to Ps 103:18, indeed, "the highest mountains are for deer," *montes excelsi cervis*, he interprets *cervi* as a symbol of the saints and *montes excelsi* as an allegory of the knowledge of the Trinity: Scripture "called 'highest mountains' the science of the Trinity," *scientiam Trinitatis montes excelsos appellaverit.*

6.50. All that which is a part of this world/aeon is from the (mortal) corporeal nature, and all that which is from the (mortal) corporeal nature is a part of this world/aeon.

Evagrius squarely identifies this world with the realm of mortal bodies (he uses a double logical correspondence or bijective correspondence for this, <=>). The adjective that means "made of mortal corporeal nature" or "pertaining to mortal corporeal nature" is *pgrn'*, which derives from the noun *pgr'*, meaning, as I have repeatedly mentioned, a mortal body or even a corpse.

6.51. If it is true that the intelligent part is the most excellent among all the faculties of the soul, because this alone is joined to wisdom, then the first of all virtues is knowledge. Our wise teacher, indeed, called this too "spirit of filial adoption."

The words "spirit of adoption" come from Rom 8:15; the identification of the spirit of adoption with knowledge is here attributed to Evagrius's "wise teacher." The latter is unnamed, but Gregory of Nyssa might be identified with this teacher. He commented on that biblical verse thrice, in *Homilies on the Song of Songs* 4 (115.14); *Against Eunomius* 1.572, and 3.8.53. Now, in the first passage Gregory links the acquisition of the spirit of filial adoption with the third ascent of the soul, in which the soul looks at the Father and the Son and becomes daughter of the Father and sister of the Son. This ascent is performed through knowledge and coincides with the acquisition of the spirit of adoption. If Gregory, as is probable, inspired Evagrius here and is to be identified with his "wise teacher," this would point again to a greater importance of Gregory Nyssen in Evagrius's thought, which is suggested by both biographical and philosophico-theological elements. See Ramelli, "Evagrius and Gregory." Being adopted by God as children means, according to Evagrius and his teacher, reaching knowledge. This is clear if one keeps in mind Evagrius's definition of God as "essential knowledge."

6.52. Many passions hide in our souls, those that, when they escape us, strong temptations reveal to us. And it is necessary that "with all solicitude we keep our heart," lest, when the object of our passion presents itself, we immediately be drawn by demons and make any of those things that are odious to God.

The scriptural reference here is Prov 4:23, "Keep your heart with all vigilance." The πάθη, or passions—meaning bad emotions—that inhabit one's soul are revealed by the temptations they give rise to. (As for the clause I have translated, "when the object of our passion presents itself," I follow Guillaumont's conjecture against a manuscript reading that makes no sense). The mechanism delineated by Evagrius is the following: temptations reveal that passions are hiding in one's soul; when the objects of these passions appear, demons instantly take advantage of this to push the soul toward sin. Evagrius has already spoken of the tempting role performed by demons in several *kephalaia*: *KG* 1.25; 3.41; 4.35, 73, 85; 5.78; see above, the relevant commentaries.

6.53. The intelligible arrow is an evil thought, which is formed by the passible part of the soul.

This is one of the many *kephalaia* that interpret biblical details spiritually, on the noetic plane. The detail of the arrow is difficult to locate in the Bible, since this element appears many a time, for example, in 1 Sam 20:36; 2 Kgs 9:24; Job 41:28; Pss 11:12; 64:7; 91:5; Prov 25:18; Isa 37:33; Jer 9:8; and Zech 9:14.

This *kephalaion* is in full continuity with *KG* 6.52, where demons and their temptations were treated, all the more so in that Evagrius explicitly associated evil thoughts with demons. He devoted a specific work (*On Thoughts*) to evil thoughts, that is, tempting reasonings, or *logismoi* (λογισμοί). Their association with demons is so tight that the very first section of this work on tempting thoughts is devoted to demons, who oppose *praktikē*, or ascetic life, and how these tempt humans and are related to one another. Moreover, in *On Thoughts* 2 Evagrius expressly identifies the evil thoughts with demons and describes the *logismoi* as "demonic" or "inspired by demons." Likewise in the same section Evagrius warns that "all thoughts producing anger or desire in a way that is contrary to nature are caused by demons." In section 8 thus Evagrius classifies different kinds of thoughts: "angelic thoughts, human thoughts, and thoughts that come from demons." The first are good and lead to knowledge, the last are bad and lead to evilness. Evagrius meditates on demonic thoughts also in *Skemmata* 13: "A demonic thought is an image of the sense-perceptible human being, an image constituted according to discursive thinking. The intellect that is moved with it says something passionately, or acts against the law in secret," Λογισμὸς δαιμονιώδης ἐστὶν εἰκὼν τοῦ αἰσθητοῦ ἀνθρώπου, συνισταμένη κατὰ διάνοιαν, μεθ' ἧς ὁ νοῦς κινούμενος ἐμπαθῶς λέγει τί ἢ πράττει ἀνόμως ἐν τῷ κρυπτῷ. Reflections on evil thoughts are scattered throughout Evagrius's works and frequently appear; for instance, *Praktikos* 6–33 is all devoted to tempting *logismoi* and the way to contrast them. In *Praktikos* 6, after listing the eight main tempting thoughts, Evagrius observes that "whether these *logismoi* are able to disturb the soul or not is not up to us; but whether they linger or not, and whether they arouse passions or not, that is up to us." So, even the person who has attained *apatheia* is still tempted by *logismoi*, but these cannot arouse passions in her and cannot cause her to sin, thanks to her purity of heart (in scholium 199 on Prov 19:17 Evagrius identifies purity of heart with *apatheia*). *Praktikos* 34–39 is thus all devoted to passions. *Logismoi* are called "fleshly" and are related to desires and greed (ἐπιθυμίαι) in *Foundation of the Monastic Life* 1.

6.54. If it is true that the intellect discerns the *logoi*, and that in turn names and *logoi* indicate the objects, then the intellect discerns the objects.

The intellect knows and discerns the objects through their *logoi*, their metaphysical forms and very principles of being. Origen already used both λόγοι and εἴδη to indicate the metaphysical principles and forms of all creatures, and very Middle Platonically he located them inside the divine Logos, as though these were God's thoughts. Indeed, Origen claims in *On First Principles* 1.2.2 that the Son-Logos-Wisdom contained in itself *ab aeterno* the "principles," "reasons," and "forms" of the whole creation (*initia*, *rationes*, and *species* in Rufinus's version, corresponding to ἀρχαί, λόγοι, and εἴδη). These are, at the same time, the Ideas in which, according to the Platonic category of "participation" (μέθεξις), every existing being participates. Take, for example, the Idea of Justice: Christ-Logos can be said to be Justice itself, and every being that is just is such insofar as it participates in the Idea of Justice, that is, in Christ: "Our Savior does not participate in Justice but rather, being Justice itself, is participated in by the just" (Origen, *Against Celsus* 6.64).

6.55. It is then that the intellect approaches the intelligible things: when it is no longer joined to the evil thoughts that arise from the passible part of the soul.

The purification of the intellect requires the detachment from evil thoughts, which come from the part of the soul that is liable to passions. This *kephalaion* clearly rejoins *KG* 6.53, on evil thoughts, and 6.54, on the intellect's proper activity of knowing the intelligible things (the *logoi* of all things, including sense-perceptible objects, of which the intellect knows the intelligible *logoi*). See above, the relevant commentaries.

6.56. If it is true that vision is said to be in sense perception and in thought—now it is in this way that Christ will come, just as when the disciples saw him ascend to heaven—someone might say, "How did they see him?" However, one should realize that in every time in the saints Christ is actually ascending, even if to others he seems to be descending.

It was typical of Origen to interiorize, spiritualize, and actualize key events in Jesus's life (such as his birth and his resurrection) in each Christian. He used to say, for instance, that it is useless that Christ was born, if he is not also born and nurtured in the heart of each Christian (see also above, the commentary on *KG* 6.38, where Evagrius takes over this notion). In the same way, Christ must rise from the dead also in the heart of each Christian. Likewise, Evagrius here asserts that Christ's ascension is not only that which occurred in 30 C.E. and is described in Acts 1:11 but also that which occurs in every saint. Toward those who are not saints Christ descends, because these are placed low in the rank of purification and holiness, but since the saints ascend toward perfection, Christ is considered to ascend in them.

Origen explains that what Scriptures call "heart" is often meant to indicate our intellectual faculty: the Bible "usually calls 'heart' the rational faculty of the soul," *rationabilem animae uirtutem cor solere nominari* (*Commentary on Romans* 2.7.36–37). He, like some other Fathers, drawing inspiration from Gal 4:19, speaks of the formation and birth of Christ, as Logos and all virtues, in the heart of human beings (*Commentary on Romans* 7.5.41–51):

> "My small children, whom I bear again with pains, until Christ is formed in you" [Gal 4:19]. Paul says that Christ is formed in those who tend to perfection in that Christ is the Logos, that in these people the Logos of God may be formed in all purity, and in that Christ is the Truth … and in that Christ is Wisdom … and in the same way according to all that which Christ is, such as justice, sanctification, and all other virtues: if each of these is formed in them in the purest way, these people will clearly be conformed to that form that is in the form of God, because they have been made images of that form.
>
> *Filioli mei quos iterum parturio donec formetur Christus in uobis: formari in his qui ad perfectionem tendunt Christum dicat secundum hoc quod Uerbum est, ut in eis Uerbum Dei ad purum sinceritatis informetur, et secundum hoc quod ueritas est … et secundum hoc quod sapientia est … sic et secundum omnia quae Christus est, uel iustitia uel sanctificatio uel ceterae quaequae uirtutes, si in eis formentur ad liquidum isti uidebuntur ad illam formam quae in forma Dei est conformes imagines eius effecti.*

Evagrius too, like Origen, notes that Scripture often calls "heart" the intellect (scholium 1 on Ps 15:9) and the soul and its intellection or *νοήματα* (scholium 371 on Prov 25:26).

6.57. What the rational nature will receive in reward before the tribunal of Christ, these are spiritual bodies or dark (bodies), and contemplation or ignorance, which become these. And because of this, Christ, the one we wait for, for some of them will come in this way, and for some others in that other way.

This *kephalaion* rejoins the reflection on the Judgment in *KG* 6.47 and in preceding *kephalaia* (see above, the relevant commentaries). The different bodies that rational creatures will receive upon the Judgment will depend on their deserts. Likewise, contemplation or ignorance will be in line with their deserts. Those who have progressed spiritually will receive spiritual bodies and contemplation; those who have regressed will receive dark bodies, like those of demons, and ignorance. Christ therefore will be contemplation for those who deserve contemplation, and ignorance for those who deserve ignorance.

6.58. Among bodies, those that will have been reestablished by the transformation are said to result in spiritual bodies. However, whether it is from the matter or from the organs that were at the end that this will take place, you too, please, investigate this in truth.

Evagrius has just spoken of spiritual bodies—as opposed to dark, demonic bodies—as a reward for spiritual advancement to be received at the Judgment by some rational creatures (*KG* 6.57; see the commentary above). Here he speaks of spiritual bodies that are the result of the resurrection of human mortal bodies. For the transformation that reestablishes (dead) bodies, turning them into spiritual bodies, seems to be identifiable with the resurrection. Gregory of Nyssa, too, in *On the Soul and the Resurrection*, described the resurrection as a reestablishment of a dead body as a spiritual body, within the allegoresis of the Feast of the Tabernacles (see my *Gregorio di Nissa sull'Anima*).

Just as Origen often did, with much humility and in accord with his zetetic spirit, Evagrius too here invites his readers to examine the question at stake themselves (something he also does elsewhere, e.g., in *Logismoi* [*On Thoughts*] 41: "you will investigate [ζητήσεις] whether…"). After the resurrection (which Evagrius here calls "transformation"), mortal bodies will become spiritual. The question is whether spiritual bodies will come out of the matter of mortal bodies or the organic, instrumental body. Origen was clear that it was not the material substratum, or *hypokeimenon*, that will be taken over at the resurrection but its metaphysical form. In his *On the Resurrection* Origen—like Gregory Nyssen in his footsteps in his own *On the Soul and the Resurrection*—endeavored to present the Christian doctrine of the resurrection in a philosophically sustainable manner. He read the resurrection on a twofold plane, physical and spiritual, as a resurrection of both the body and the soul, which is liberated from its own death. For the death of the soul was due to sin (Origen in *Dialogue with Heraclides* 26, preserved in Greek, maintains that "the soul is mortal of the real death": not an ontological destruction—or a disaggregation, since the soul is simple—but the death of sin). Origen's treatise is unfortunately lost; his ideas on the resurrection must be gleaned from later sources, which, however, must be read critically, since they also misunderstood Origen's thought. One of these sources is Methodius.

Methodius, in *On the Resurrection* 1.20–24, reports a long passage from Origen. The latter argues here that the material substratum, or ὑποκείμενον, which is always in flux, will not be resurrected, but the εἶδος will, which is the metaphysical form of the body and will guarantee the permanence of its identity from the earthly to the risen body. Methodius misunderstood the metaphysical meaning of εἶδος, mistaking εἶδος—the metaphysical form meant by Origen—for μορφή or σχῆμα, a sense-perceptible shape or figure. This misunderstanding is especially clear in the excerpts from Methodius's *On the Resurrection* preserved by Photius in *Library* codex 234, pp. 299a–300a, where Methodius reads εἶδος as a synonym of μορφή or σχῆμα, for example, when he refutes Origen by asking: "Is it the *shape* that will be resurrected? But the changes of *shapes* are very many. The *change of shape* into impassibility and glory is *apokatastasis*," Σχῆμα τὸ ἀνιστάμενον; πλεῖσται γὰρ τῶν σχημάτων αἱ παραλλαγαί. ὁ μετασχηματισμὸς ἡ εἰς τὸ ἀπαθὲς καὶ ἔνδοξόν ἐστιν ἀποκατάστασις). Methodius's misunderstanding is manifest in his mistaken paraphrase of Origen's thought in the same report by Photius:

> Origen wants that what is restored [ἀποκαθίστασθαι] to the soul is not the same flesh but a *certain shape* [ποιὰν μορφήν] of each one, *according to the appearance* that now too characterizes the flesh … that each one may *look* [φανῇ] *the same* again in his or her *shape* [μορφήν].… The material body is in flux and never remains the same, but it increases and decreases around *the appearance* that *characterizes the shape* [μορφήν] and by which the *figure* [σχῆμα] is also controlled; therefore, the resurrection (according to Origen) will necessarily be of *the appearance alone*.… Dear Origen, you affirm with confidence that we should expect a resurrection *of the sole appearance* that will be transposed into a pneumatic body.… It is absolutely absurd to limit the resurrection to *the sole appearance*, since souls, even after exiting the flesh, never seem to abandon *the appearance, which Origen says to be resurrected*.… Origen says that *the appearance* is dissociated from the body and given to the soul.… It is inconsistent to claim that *the appearance rises again* without undergoing any damage, while the body, in which *this appearance was stamped*, is destroyed.… In Origen's view, perhaps *the figure of the soul at death has an appearance that is similar to the dense and earthly body.*

Origen himself was aware that his technical philosophical terminology could be misunderstood, and therefore he renounced using it when speaking to people who had no philosophical formation. The same was done by his fourth-century follower Didymus the Blind, who took over Origen's terminology—and was himself well steeped in philosophy, including Aristotelianism—but only in the works that addressed a philosophically learned public. In his *Commentary on Zechariah*, for instance, whose public was not restricted to his own disciples, Didymus simplified Origen's theory, explicitly preferring a "more introductory" treatment (εἰσαγωγικώτερον). Thus, in this work Origen's technical terms εἶδος and ὑποκείμενον—which were crucial to the description of the resurrection in Origen's *On the Resurrection*—are *not* employed. Didymus clearly aimed at avoiding the misunderstanding that these Aristotelian notions had given rise to.

According to Origen, what will remain the same in the present and in the risen body is the εἶδος of the body, of which he speaks also in *On First Principles* 2.10.2: "every body is endowed with its individual form." In fact, every individual has his or her own εἶδος, which endures throughout his or her life and will endure also in the next world, at the resurrection: "The same metaphysical form [εἶδος] endures in us, from babyhood until old age.... The metaphysical form will remain the same also in the future body, but with a startling transformation into the better and the more glorious.... For this metaphysical form [εἶδος] will not be destroyed, even if it will be changed and will become more glorious," *Eadem in nobis* speciem [εἶδος] *permanet ab infantia usque ad senectutem ... ipsam permansuram etiam in futuro, plurima tamen immutatione in melius et gloriosius facta ... nec haec* species [εἶδος] *exterminabitur licet gloriosior eius effecta sit permutatio* (*Commentary on Psalm* 1, *apud* Pamphilus, *Apology for Origen* 141). With εἶδος Origen meant the form as the *metaphysical* principle, in an Aristotelian sense, and more specifically in a sense that was typical of Alexander of Aphrodisias, who was very probably known to him (see Ramelli, "Alexander of Aphrodisias").

6.59. God's providence is twofold: and they say that a part of it preserves the substance of corporeal and incorporeal beings, and the other part urges on rational creatures from evil and ignorance to virtue and knowledge.

Evagrius has already spoken many times of God's providence in his *KG*: in *KG* 1.27 he has claimed that the main contemplations are five, the fourth and fifth of which are the contemplation of the Judgment and of Providence. One consequence of this declaration is that the contemplation of the Judgment is not the last and definitive but is followed by that of God's providence. This is fully confirmed by what Evagrius states in *KG* 5.24: the *logoi* concerning the Judgment are secondary vis-à-vis those concerning rational creatures' free will and God's providence. Judgment and

Providence are again associated in *KG* 2.59: Christ judges rational creatures in a righteous way at the end of every aeon but also shows mercy, in that he guides by means of his Providence *logika* who are unworthy of it. In *KG* 5.4 and 5.7 both angels and archangels are said to have been entrusted with the *logoi* of Providence. Both *KG* 5.16 and 5.23 also concern divine providence, and in *KG* 6.43 God's providence is said by Evagrius—as by Origen—to respect rational creatures' free will, whereas God's judgment takes into account their deserts. In *KG* 4.89 the grace of God is associated to divine providence, whose action is described as Christ's leading the rational nature through various aeons, toward union in the holy Unity. This *kephalaion* comes particularly close to the one at stake here, in that it describes the second of the tasks of divine providence: leading rational creatures toward virtue and knowledge, which in turn enables them to reach union with the Holy Trinity.

Here in *KG* 6.59, in fact, Evagrius details the two main actions of divine providence: keeping all creatures in existence and leading rational creatures toward the best and their own *telos*. Clearly, indeed, this continual and universal action of Providence will fully accomplish its purpose in the end, when not only will all corporeal substance be restored after the universal resurrection, but all rational creatures will be restored to goodness and knowledge, after the due purification and illumination. That knowledge is part of God's plan for all human beings is also declared in 1 Tim 2:4, a passage that Origen used to support his doctrine of *apokatastasis*, and which Evagrius had very well present to his mind: "God wants *all human beings* to be saved and to attain the knowledge of truth." This can be related to John 17:1–2: "Father … glorify your Son, that the Son may glorify you, as you have entrusted him with *every human being*, that he may give life to every being you have given him. Now, eternal life is that they know you."

Note, once again, the association of virtue and knowledge that is especially dear to Evagrius.

6.60. Barren is the intellect that is deprived of spiritual doctrine or that lacks the seeds the Holy Spirit has sown.

To attain true knowledge the intellect must be "fertilized" by the divine Spirit. Evagrius, like patristic thinkers in general, has no confidence in knowledge without faith, just as he has none in knowledge without virtue.

6.61. If God is the God of the living and is not of the dead, and on the other hand, according to the word of the holy Moses, necromancers ask the dead questions, the female necromancer did not evoke Samuel from among the dead, if it is true that he is not dead but living.

Evagrius's major premise here, that "God is the God of the living and is not of the dead," is grounded in Matt 22:32 and its parallels, where Jesus declares this.

The biblical episode Evagrius refers to in the minor premise and in the conclusion is that of the witch of Endor in 1 Sam 28:7–20. This passage was hotly debated among the Fathers, not least because of the controversy over Origen's interpretation of it and the criticisms of Eustathius of Antioch (see Rowan Greer and Margaret Mitchell, eds. and trans., *The "Belly-Myther" of Endor* [WGRW 16; Atlanta: Society of Biblical Literature, 2007]). Evagrius sides with Gregory of Nyssa, who probably exerted much more influence on him than is usually assumed (see Ramelli, "Evagrius and Gregory"). In his *Letter to Theodosius*, Gregory observes: "Since Samuel is great among the saints but sorcery is an evil attainment, I am not persuaded that Samuel, established as he was in so great a place of his own rest, would have passed over that trackless chasm [Luke 16:26] and remove the saint who was in the chorus of the holy ones" (GNO 3:103; trans. Greer and Mitchell). According to Gregory, it was rather a demon who appeared to the sorceress, because necromancy was invented by demons. Indeed, Deut 18:11 prohibited necromancy among the Hebrews.

6.62. Barren is the rational soul that continually learns and yet never can arrive at true knowledge.

This *kephalaion* takes over *KG* 6.60 about the sterility of the intellect, which was described as the absence of fertilization by the Holy Spirit. Here the question is of the sterility of the soul, when it continually receives seeds of knowledge but never produces true knowledge, which is always joined with virtue.

6.63. Just as those whose sight is ill and gaze at the sun are impeded by their own tears, and in the air see ghosts, so also cannot the pure intellect, when it is disturbed by anger, receive contemplation of spirit, but it sees a kind of fog lying on the objects.

Passions interfere with knowledge, disturbing the intellect's apprehension of its objects. Hence, once again, the necessity of purification from passions with a view to knowledge and further spiritual contemplation. *Apatheia* and knowledge, as I have frequently remarked, go hand in hand in Evagrius's view. Passions, such as anger, are considered to be a kind of illness of the intellect here, by virtue of the parallel with the illness of one's sight, just as in *KG* 1.41 evilness was defined as the illness of the soul. In particular, anger's blinding effect on the soul was already pointed out by Evagrius in *KG* 5.39 (see above, the commentary). Anger forestalls intellectual sight, and therefore knowledge, and this is why Evagrius associates it with demons, who are characterized by ignorance.

6.64. Just as by means of the physical healing of the paralytic our Savior has illuminated us about the intelligible healing, and by means of the evident has affirmed the hidden, in the same way by means of the physical exodus of the children of Israel he has indicated to us the exodus that (occurs) from evilness and ignorance.

The interpretation of Jesus's miracles in the New Testament on the intelligible plane (here the specific reference is to Matt 9:2–7) parallels that of the Hebrews' exodus in the Old Testament on the intelligible plane. Likewise, Origen offered a spiritual interpretation of both the Old and the New Testament. Note again, in the last sentence, the association between evilness and ignorance, as the negative counterpart of that between virtue and knowledge, which surfaces very often in the *KG*. The abandonment of evilness and ignorance, symbolized by the Israelites' exodus from Egypt (which indeed represents evil in *KG* 6.49), is what leads to the *telos* of all. This *telos*, according to both Origen and Gregory Nyssen, on whose ideas Evagrius draws, is "the complete eradication of evil(ness)," τὸ τέλος τῶν πραγμάτων ἀναιρεθῆναί ἐστι τὴν κακίαν (Origen, *Against Celsus* 8.72). For "evil(ness) must necessarily be eliminated, absolutely and in every respect, once and for all, from all that exists" (Gregory of Nyssa, *On the Soul and the Resurrection* 101). Evagrius is on the same line, as is also clear from *KG* 1.40–41 (see above, the relevant commentary).

6.65. Mystery is spiritual contemplation, that which not to everybody is accessible.

Evagrius interprets as spiritual contemplation what the Bible calls μυστήριον and was translated into Latin by both *sacramentum* and *mysterium* (see Ilaria L. E. Ramelli, "Μυστήριον negli *Stromateis* di Clemente Alessandrino: Aspetti di continuità con la tradizione allegorica greca," in *Il volto del mistero: Mistero e religione nella cultura religiosa tardoantica* [ed. Angela Maria Mazzanti; Castel Bolognese: Itaca Libri, 2006], 83–120; and idem, "*Mysterium* and *Sacramentum* in the Vetus Afra: What Differing Interpretations by African Patristic Authors Reveal about Paganism and Donatism," in *The Uniquely African Controversy: Studies on Donatist Christianity* [ed. Anthony Dupont, Matthew Gaumer, and Mathijs Lamberigts; Leuven: Peeters, 2014], 349–75). Indeed, μυστήριον, the symbolic and mystical meaning of points in Scripture, is not for everybody; most people limit themselves to the literal meaning—Clement and Origen had already insisted a lot on this—and likewise spiritual contemplation is not attained by everybody.

6.66. The knife of stone is the teaching of Christ our Savior, the one who circumcises the intellect, which is covered with passions, through knowledge.

The biblical reference is to Josh 5:2–3: "At that time the Lord said to Joshua, 'Make flint knives and circumcise the people of Israel again the second time.' So Joshua made flint knives, and circumcised the people of Israel at Gibeath-haaraloth" (RSV). This *kephalaion* is clearly connected with other *kephalaia* concerning the spiritual interpretation of circumcision: *KG* 4.12, where circumcision is identified with purification from passions, which can take place thanks to the knowledge of God (with the connection between virtue and knowledge that Evagrius constantly makes); 5.83; and 6.6–7. In the present *kephalaion* too, knowledge and purification from passions, and therefore the pursuit of virtue, are closely interrelated.

6.67. The more the aeons will increase, the more also the names and the intellections that are proper to them will indicate to us the Holy Trinity.

Evagrius is clearly following once again Origen's scheme of a succession of aeons that are functional to the spiritual development of rational creatures and an increment of their knowledge. The culmination of knowledge is the knowledge of the Trinity—identified by Evagrius with "essential knowledge." At the end of the aeons there will come the *telos*, with the revelation of the Trinity. This revelation, according to both Evagrius and Origen, will coincide with θέωσις ("deification"). On deification in Origen, see my *The Christian Doctrine of Apokatastasis*, the chapter on Origen.

6.68. Submission is the assent of the rational nature's will toward the knowledge of God.

The equation between submission to Christ and God and salvation was posited by Origen, who was closely followed in this respect by Gregory of Nyssa (see Ramelli, "Christian Soteriology and Christian Platonism"; and idem, "*In illud: Tunc et ipse Filius*...: Gregory of Nyssa's Exegesis, Its Derivations from Origen, and Early Patristic Interpretations Related to Origen's," *StPatr* 44 [2010]: 259–74). Now, for this equation to stand, one must posit that submission to God will be voluntary. This is what Origen and Gregory postulated and what Evagrius too makes clear in this *kephalaion*, speaking of the assent of rational creatures' will. That salvation coincides with the knowledge of God not only was upheld by Origen and Gregory of Nyssa but is strongly suggested by Scripture (1 Tim 2:4–6: "God our Savior wants all human beings to be *saved* and to *reach the knowledge of the truth*. For God is one, and one is the mediator between God and humans: the human being Christ Jesus, who has given himself in ransom for all").

The Greek of this *kephalaion* is preserved in *Selected Passages on Psalms* 36:7 (PG 12:1316CD).

6.69. Angels see human beings and demons; human beings, on the contrary, are deprived of the sight of angels and demons, while demons see only human beings.

Humans cannot see either angels or demons, because they live in a sense-perceptible and mortal body, while angels and demons live in bodies that are immortal and not sense perceptible (even though the spiritual bodies of angels are very different from the "ridiculous" and "dark" bodies of demons). This is also why angels, conversely, are said to be able to see both humans and demons, and why demons—who obviously rank lower than angels—can see humans. Indeed, in *KG* 1.22 Evagrius has declared that the bodies of demons have a color and a shape—so they are less spiritual than the bodies of angels—but they escape our sense perception, in that their quality is not similar to the quality of the bodies that fall under our senses. So, whenever they want to appear to humans, they turn themselves into a resemblance of a human body, without showing us their own bodies. Demons, however, as Evagrius declares in the present *kephalaion*, cannot see angels, arguably because the bodies of angels are subtler than their own. The bodies of demons are not fleshly, but they are different from the spiritual and luminous bodies of angels: as Origen maintains, they are such as to arouse the angels' laughter. Evagrius, in fact, deemed the bodies of angels fiery (ethereal), those of humans earthy, and those of demons pneumatic. See Stewart, "Imageless Prayer," 176. See *KG* 1.22 and the relevant commentary.

6.70. Submission is the weakness of the rational nature, which cannot cross the boundaries of its rank. In this way, indeed, he "has put everything under his feet," according to Paul's saying.

This *kephalaion* is clearly connected with *KG* 6.68, which also deals with the salvific submission of rational creatures (see commentary there). Both of these *kephalaia* investigate the meaning of submission, and particularly of the eschatological submission of rational creatures to Christ and, through Christ, to God (cf. 1 Cor 15:24–28). In *KG* 6.68 the stress lay on the voluntary nature of this submission; here this submission is said to reveal the inferiority of rational creatures—qua creatures—to Christ and God, the Creator. The specific verse quoted by Evagrius here is 1 Cor 15:27. This is why Christ, after submitting all rational creatures, will hand them to God, who will be "all in all." In this way Christ will enable all rational creatures to transcend their rank and enjoy "deification" (θέωσις).

6.71. Just as to the sense-perceptible Israel sense-perceptible nations are opposed, likewise to the intelligible Israel intelligible nations are opposed.

Evagrius refers to what the Septuagint and the New Testament, up to the Apocalypse of John, or Revelation, call ἔθνη, or "nations," typically Gentiles, unbelievers. In Revelation they are repeatedly said to be destroyed, but then they appear again, and the leaves of the tree of life (Christ) in the eschatological Jerusalem are said to heal them (see Ramelli, *Christian Doctrine of Apokatastasis*, ch. 1). Here the attention focuses on the double meaning that "Israel" and "the nations" can bear, as everything in Scripture: both historical/sensible and spiritual/intelligible. As for the exact meaning of the "intelligible Israel," Evagrius may have had in mind the etymology of Israel as "the one who sees God." In this case, the "intelligible

Israel" would be composed of those who have achieved the contemplation of the Trinity. Those who oppose these people may easily be demons and the evil thoughts they inspire, which distract from contemplation and impede knowledge (and not only virtue).

6.72. One thing is the intellection of matter, and another is that of the mixtures that reveal it. And one is that of their inside, which is close to the elements, and another is that of sense-perceptible elements. And one is the contemplation of the spiritual body, and another is that of the human instrumental body.

Evagrius is not differentiating here six single elements (as it may appear from Guillaumont's translation, followed by Dysinger and Fr. Theophanes) but is rather distinguishing two elements within three couples. The intellection of matter is thus distinguished from the intellection of the mixtures that compose matter and give rise to its qualities (Gregory of Nyssa famously reduced matter to its qualities, and Evagrius knew his ideas well). I correct the singular "mixture" in the manuscript, preserved by Guillaumont (who translates "qualité," followed by Dysinger and Fr. Theophanes: "quality"), into the plural "mixtures" (which merely entails the addition of a diacritical mark; the term itself is identical in the singular and the plural) because "their inside" or "their inner part" seems to refer to "mixtures." If "mixture" were singular, there would be no plural to which refers "their." Matter is made up of mixtures of the various sense-perceptible elements that compose it and that indeed are mentioned in the following sentences. Different mixtures constitute different mortal bodies (see also below, *KG* 6.78 and the relevant commentary). Finally, the spiritual body, or the body tout court (the Syriac term here designates not only a mortal body but also a spiritual body and any kind of bodies), is contrasted with the human mortal body, the "instrumental body" (*σῶμα ὀργανικόν* in Aristotle's definition), which is an instrument (*ὄργανον*) of the soul and is equipped with organs (*ὄργανα*) of sense perception. The expression "instrumental body" (*σῶμα ὀργανικόν*) is frequently found in Neoplatonism too and is used by Gregory of Nyssa in his very definition of the human soul in *On the Soul and the Resurrection* 29B = GNO 3/3.15.6–9: "The soul is a created substance, a living, intellectual substance, which into a body equipped with organs of sense perception infuses, by virtue of itself, vital force and the faculty of apprehending sense-perceptible objects, as long as the nature susceptible of these faculties [i.e., the mortal body] subsists," Ψυχή ἐστιν οὐσία γεννητή, οὐσία ζῶσα, νοερά, σώματι ὀργανικῷ καὶ αἰσθητικῷ δύναμιν ζωτικὴν καὶ τῶν αἰσθητῶν ἀντιληπτικὴν δι' ἑαυτῆς ἐνιεῖσα, ἕως ἂν ἡ δεκτικὴ τούτων συνέστηκε φύσις (I use the text established in my edition [Ramelli, *Gregorio di Nissa: Sull'anima*], which differs here from Migne's text, which has ἐνιοῦσα instead of ἐνιεῖσα; this is my Italian translation: "L'anima è una sostanza generata, una sostanza vivente, intellettuale, che in un corpo dotato di organi di senso immette, in virtù di se stessa, la forza vitale e la facoltà di percepire gli oggetti sensibili, finché sussiste la natura suscettibile di queste"). Here ὀργανικῷ καὶ αἰσθητικῷ is endyadic. George Karamanolis, *The Philosophy of Early Christianity* (Durham: Acumen, 2013), 279, expressly follows my reading ἐνιεῖσα, which is now also kept in Ekkehard Mühlenberg's GNO edition, p. 15.8.

6.73. It is not in that the intellect is incorporeal that it is in the likeness of God, but rather in that it was (created) susceptible of Him. On the other hand, if it is in that it is incorporeal that it is in the likeness of God, then it is essential knowledge, and it is not as a result of its susceptibility (of God) that it was (created) as an image of God. Yet, consider whether it is the same statement that it is incorporeal and that it is susceptible of knowledge, or differently put, as with respect to a statue and its bronze.

Evagrius is referring to Gen 1:26, where the divinity declares that it will make the human being in its own image (εἰκών) and after its likeness (ὁμοίωσις), a passage that was fundamental for many Fathers' "theology of the image" and especially for Origen and Gregory of Nyssa. Origen stressed more the distinction between image, as an initial datum for all human beings, and likeness, as something to be acquired by means of personal endeavor in virtue (since in Gen 1:27 likeness is not mentioned as a datum, from which Origen deduced that it is rather posited as a target). Evagrius takes it for granted—with Philo, Origen, and Gregory Nyssen—that this likeness of God in the human being cannot be situated in the body, since God is incorporeal, but must be located in the intellect. However, the reason why the intellect can be the likeness of God is not simply because it is incorporeal—which would be a mere datum—but because it can become a recipient of God, and this is not a datum but depends one one's own engagement in virtue and knowledge. But in turn, the very fact that it can receive knowledge depends on its being incorporeal. Evagrius here, like Origen, is reasoning by considering different possibilities, in this case a thesis (the intellect is in the likeness of God not because it is incorporeal but because it is susceptible of God), an antithesis (the intellect is in the likeness of God because it is incorporeal and is essential knowledge), and finally a synthesis (being incorporeal and being susceptible of essential knowledge are the very same thing). In the antithesis the use of "image" and no longer of "likeness" makes one wonder whether here Evagrius uses the two terms rather indifferently, as Gregory Nyssen did more often than Origen. The final exhortation to the reader to consider and decide the question personally resembles what one often finds also in Origen. Evagrius suggests that being incorporeal and being susceptible of knowledge, and primarily of the knowledge of God (i.e., essential knowledge), are the same thing, like an inanimate object and the matter that composes it (since there is nothing more than matter to it, which has no soul).

6.74. Christ will in fact come before the Judgment, to judge those alive and the dead. But he will be known after the Judgment, if it is true that "the Lord is known by means of the Judgment he makes."

The scriptural quotation is from Ps 9:16. Christ's judgment will reveal the character of the Judge. Evagrius too, like Origen (and Clement and Gregory of Nyssa), thinks that in case of condemnation Christ will establish a period, however long, of purifying suffering and not an eternity of retributive suffering. And this because only this kind of judgment will be worthy of God—not only of God's goodness but also of God's justice. This is a theological argument; the Judgment reveals the character of God and therefore must be worthy of God (see Ramelli, *Christian Doctrine of Apokatastasis*, the sections on Origen and Gregory Nyssen). In the very next *kephalaion*, indeed, Evagrius is quite clear that divine providence is always there to correct the negative effects of rational creatures' free will, at every judgment after every single aeon.

6.75. The primary knowledge that was found in rational creatures is that of the Holy Trinity; then, there occurred the movement of free will, and Providence, which rescues and never abandons anyone, and then the Judgment, and again the movement of free will, and Providence, and the Judgment, and so on up to the Holy Trinity. Thus, every judgment comes between the movement of free will and God's providence.

According to Evagrius, just as to Origen, each aeon begins with the end of the preceding one and the judgment that follows the latter. Aeons, which are the result of each judgment, come after the first movement of rational creatures' free will and their fall but come before the final and most perfect manifestation of God's providence, which will be *apokatastasis*, after the end of all aeons. Then, not only for Origen, but for Evagrius as well, no one will be in any aeon anymore, but God will be "all in all." Indeed, Evagrius thinks of *apokatastasis* in terms of θέωσις to the point of calling it "the Holy Trinity" outright in this *kephalaion*: aeons, judgments, and Providence's action will succeed to one another "up to the Holy Trinity" or "until the Holy Trinity" (Origen also thought of the *telos* as a "leap into the Holy Trinity," *Commentary on John* 13.3). Once all have reached God the Trinity, there will be no more movements of free will and no more aeons.

In each judgment, God establishes the role and the kind of body that each rational creature will have in the new aeon, on the basis of the moral and spiritual development of each one: "A judgment of God is the coming into being of a world/aeon, to which he gives a mortal body, in accord with the degree (of development) of each one of the rational creatures" (*KG* 3.38; see above, the relevant commentary). Likewise in scholium 275 on Prov 24:22: "A judgment is the creation of an aeon that allots bodies to every intellectual creature according to" its spiritual development; scholium 16 on Prov 1:32: "Just as babies are between the just and the impious, so all human beings are between angels and demons, since they neither are demons, nor are called angels until the completion of the aeon [μέχρι τῆς συντελείας τοῦ αἰῶνος]"; scholium 2 on Ps 134:6: the division of rational creatures into angels, humans, and demons, and their allotment to different realms, places, or states is the result of every judgment. This is why Evagrius claims that "the exact knowledge of these realms/states and the different bodies [i.e., allotted to angels, humans, and demons] consists in the *logoi* regarding the Judgment" (ibid.).

Christ's justice is therefore evident in the partial judgments that take place after each aeon, and in which each rational creature is assigned a given body and place in the world according to its spiritual progress, but Christ's mercy is evident from the fact that he extends divine providence to all, including those who would not deserve it (see above, *KG* 2.59). Christ himself was the agent of the second creation (that which followed rational creatures' fall) and of all aeons, each of which—again as in Origen's view as well—is the result of a judgment (see *KG* 2.75 and the commentary on it). In *Gnostikos* 36 Evagrius remarks that "the loftier doctrine concerning the

Judgment should be kept undisclosed to secular people and young people." Evagrius, like Origen, shows a pastoral concern in respect to the divulgation of the doctrine of *apokatastasis*, especially among spiritually immature people, who do good out of fear and not for love. It is better for such persons to believe in threats of eternal punishments, in order for them to keep their fear, which prevents them from sinning. Indeed, for Evagrius, just as for Origen, fear of punishments as a deterrent from doing evil is typical of scarcely mature people: "A person who has established the virtues in herself and is entirely permeated with them no longer remembers the law, the commandments, or punishment [κολάσεως]. Rather, she says and does what her excellent condition inspires her" (*Praktikos* 70).

In *Gnostikos* 48 Evagrius cites with great veneration an exhortation of Didymus the Blind, the close follower of Origen and director of the Alexandrian Didaskaleion, on the necessity of meditating God's judgment and God's providence together: "Always exercise yourself in the meditation of the *logoi* concerning Providence and Judgment—said Didymus, the great 'gnostic' teacher—and endeavor to remember their materials, since almost all people err in these topics. As for the *logos* of Judgment, you will find that this lies in the variety of bodies and worlds; that concerning Providence, instead, lies in the turns that from evilness and ignorance bring us back to virtue or knowledge." Clearly the *logos* of Providence, for Didymus just as for Origen and Evagrius, is that which leads to the restoration of rational creatures.

Evagrius never separates the idea of the Judgment, with the retribution of rational creatures' deeds and passions or virtues, from that of God's providence, which is prior to that of the Judgment, because it was anterior to the fall, which brought about the necessity of the Judgment: "The *logoi* concerning the Judgment are secondary, as has been said, vis-à-vis the *logoi* concerning movement and concerning Providence" (see above, *KG* 5.24 and the relevant commentary). That God's judgment is inseparable from God's providence is also clear from scholium 8 on Ps 138:16, where also the *logoi* of Providence and Judgment are joined. Providence cares for the spiritual therapy of rational creatures and operates on their intellects, which take care of their own souls (*Praktikos* 82). Such a therapy is salvific because it performs the destruction of sin (*KG* 1.28; see above, the commentary). Evagrius, indeed, is exactly on Origen's line in thinking that divine providence, which is universally salvific, is not at odds with individual free will, but divine justice rewards each one according to his or her deserts (which determine the order or rank of rational creatures), and divine providence operates at the same time, always allowing each one's will to be free: "God's *providence accompanies the freedom of will*, whereas God's judgment takes into account the order of rational creatures" (*KG* 6.43; see above, the commentary).

6.76. If it is true that "the One who has ascended beyond all heavens" has "fulfilled everything," it is manifest that each of the hosts/orders of the heavenly powers has truly learned the intellections that concern Providence, by means of which (intellections) they urge on those who are inferior to them quickly toward virtue and toward the knowledge of God.

The cooperation of angels to the salvation of rational creatures is repeatedly highlighted by Evagrius; see also below, *KG* 6.86, and the relevant commentary. Both Origen and Gregory of Nyssa highlighted this role played by angels (for Origen, their work of instruction will be followed by the work of Christ-Logos). According to Evagrius, not only angels cooperate with Providence, but even celestial bodies do—which Evagrius, like other ancient authors, regarded as animated—and whatever creature endowed with spiritual knowledge. This is clear from other *kephalaia*, especially *KG* 6.88 and 6.90 (see the relevant commentaries below). The scriptural reference here is Eph 4:10, in reference to Jesus Christ: "He who descended is he who also ascended far above all the heavens, that he might fill all things" (RSV). The Syriac word for "host/order" is the transliteration of Greek τάγμα, "order, status," but also "body of soldiers, legion." This refers to the various orders of angels. Note again at the end of the *kephalaion* the association of virtue and knowledge, which Evagrius stresses everywhere.

6.77. Is it the exit of Christ from the Father that Gabriel announced to Mary, or his coming from the world of angels to that of human beings? Now please investigate again also regarding the disciples who lived with him during his bodily existence, whether it is from the world that is seen by us that they came with him, or from another, or from others (worlds/aeons), and whether some of these, or all. And moreover investigate further whether on the basis of the psychic state they had, they happened to become disciples of Christ.

Like Origen, Evagrius once again invites his readers—primarily, his disciples and monks—to examine questions by themselves. The very first question implies, of course, a radical distinction between the eternal generation of Christ and his incarnation. Christ as God is the Son, while Christ as a *logikon* is a creature, and as such has taken up a mortal human body. Note again Evagrius's identification between Christ and the Son in the first sentence. Christ-Logos, moreover, as a *logikon* passed on from the angels, who are all *logika*, to human beings through the incarnation, or better, inhumanation. The disciples of Christ have lived, and will live, during several aeons, or better, all the aeons, as all rational creatures. But Christ, as Origen too maintained, became incarnate in one single aeon and sacrificed himself in one single aeon, although the effectiveness of his sacrifice is eternal (see Ramelli, "Universal and Eternal Validity"). The disciples were chosen to become disciples of Christ in that specific aeon because of the state of their soul.

6.78. The equivalent of a mortal body is that which is like it in mixture.

The Syriac noun for "body" here, *pgr'*, designates, not any body, but a mortal body. Indeed, mortal, heavy bodies result from a mixture of elements; these in turn determine given qualities. The Syriac word I have translated "mixture" is *mwzg'*, from the verb *mzg*, "to mix." Guillaumont renders "qualité" (p. 251), followed by Dysinger and Fr. Theophanes ("quality"). Here in fact *mwzg'* renders an original Greek κρᾶσις. Compare *Chapters of the Disciples of Evagrius* 113.1–5: "A soul has the same substance as a soul, and a body as a body, but the mixture [κρᾶσις] is different: for the latter has come from the Creator, depending on our free choices. For mixture [κρᾶσις] varies according to the abundance or lack of elements, of this or that virtue." Once again Evagrius is explaining that the mixture that determines the quality of a body, light or heavy, mortal or immortal, depends on the choices that rational creatures have made through their free will. God decrees whether a rational creature must have an angelic, mortal, or demonic body based on the moral progress of that creature. In this Evagrius is following Origen quite closely.

6.79. The mortal body of Christ is of the same nature as our own mortal body, and his soul is of the nature of our souls. But the Logos that is in him in an essential way is *homoousios* (coessential, consubstantial) with the Father.

This is the very same doctrine as Origen's and the Cappadocians' concerning Christ. His mortal body is a human body, like that of all other human beings; his rational soul is a *logikon*, like that of all other rational creatures; but the Logos in Christ is divine, and indeed consubstantial with the rest of the Trinity: it is the Logos of God, the Son. Evagrius even takes over the Nicene ὁμοούσιος formula, which was anticipated by Origen and was then developed by the Cappadocians into the Trinitarian doctrine of *μία οὐσία, τρεῖς ὑποστάσεις* (see Ramelli, "Origen's Anti-Subordinationism"; and idem, "Origen, Greek Philosophy"). Note also that the union of God the Logos with a mortal body and a rational soul is not loose but is rather essential, a union of essence. See also above, *KG* 4.9; 5.69; and 6.14, with the relevant commentaries. These *kephalaia* indicate, against current interpretations (e.g., François Refoulé, "La christologie d'Évagre et l'origénisme," *OCP* 27 [1961]: 221–66, esp. 255), that a subordinationistic Christology should not be attached to Evagrius. In his view, Christ is not only a rational creature (as Antione Guillaumont states in *Les "Képhalaia gnostica" d'Évagre le Pontique et l'histoire de l'origénisme chez les grecs et chez les syriens* [Paris: Éditions du Seuil, 1962], 119: "le Christ, nature raisonnable") but the union of God and human being, of the divine Logos and a rational nature.

6.80. The equivalent of a rational substance is that which is like it in knowledge.

This *kephalaion* parallels *KG* 6.78. There the question was of the equivalent of a mortal body, which was identified with another body with the same mixture; here the question is of the equivalent of a rational substance, probably a *nous* or a *logikon*. While bodies are defined by various mixtures of elements, the *logika* are defined by various degrees of knowledge.

6.81. Just as it is impossible that a rational nature with the mortal body exist apart from the world [or "this aeon"], likewise it is impossible that apart from the mortal body it be in the world [or "in this aeon"].

Rational creatures are in this world, or in the present aeon, only with their mortal body—indeed, human beings are the only rational creatures who inhabit this sense-perceptible world—but if their rational soul is detached from the body, their rational soul is out of this world. After death, humans migrate to "the other world." That of the separation of the soul from the mortal body and the world already during this life was a topic dear to Plato and the Neoplatonists. Origen maintained that as long as there will be mortal bodies there will be aeons; at the end all mortal bodies will be transformed into spiritual bodies at the resurrection. The eventual *apokatastasis* will be the final state in which no one will be in an aeon anymore, but rather God will be "all in all." At that stage, there will be no longer mortal bodies. Origen, like Evagrius in this *kephalaion*, claimed that the soul always needs a body that is suited to the place/state in which it happens to be, according to its spiritual progress (ψυχὴ ἐν παντὶ σωματικῷ τόπῳ τυγχάνουσα δέεται σώματος οἰκείου τῇ φύσει τῷ τόπῳ ἐκείνῳ, *Against Celsus* 7.32); "A soul that inhabits corporeal places must necessarily make use of such bodies that are suited to the places in which she dwells" (*Necesse est animam in locis corporeis habitantem uti corporibus talibus quae apta sint his locis in quibus degit*, commentary on Ps 1 quoted by Pamphilus, *Apology* 141).

6.82. God is said to be in the mortal bodily nature just like the architect in those things that were (made) by him. And likewise he is said to be as in a statue, if he happens to make for himself a statue of wood.

God is in mortal bodies qua their Cause, their Creator. This is a causal presence, which keeps God's transcendence intact. Evagrius is elsewhere clear that Christ is the creator of the corporeal nature and of the aeons (see *KG* 2.2, 21–22, with the relevant commentaries). The metaphor of the architect was used especially by Philo and Origen to express the way God the Logos created the world on the basis of a project devised by him (and assimilated to the noetic world of the divine Logos itself). See Ramelli, "Cristo-Logos in Origene." A statue that represents Christ-Logos, both as the Creator and as the created world, was a prominent feature in Bardaisan's work *On India*, two authentic fragments of which survive thanks to Porphyry's *De Styge*. For a detailed analysis of the statue passage in Bardaisan and its philosophical significance, see Ramelli, *Bardaisan of Edessa*, 107–24; and new remarks in idem, "Preexistence of Souls," the section on Bardaisan. Since this passage was known to, and reported by, Porphyry, it is quite probable that Gregory Nyssen too knew it.

6.83. The intellect is said to know those things that it sees, and not to see those things that it does not know. And for this reason not all thoughts hinder it from knowing God, but those that attack it from the irascible and the concupiscible/appetitive (parts of the soul), which assail it (going) against what properly belongs to (human) nature.

There is a complete coincidence between seeing and knowing in the case of the intellect. This is what the first sentence of this *kephalaion* points out. The idea that evil thoughts (λογισμοί) and passions, coming from the *thymikon* and the *epithymētikon*, are against nature, that is, against human rational nature, was especially developed in the dialogue *On the Soul and the Resurrection* by Gregory of Nyssa, who even represented them as a kind of subsequent accretion over one's soul (see my commentary in Ramelli, *Gregorio di Nissa: Sull'anima*). Here as elsewhere in the *KG*, Evagrius follows Plato's terminology for the tripartition of the soul into rational, irascible, and concupiscible or appetitive; see also, for instance, *KG* 1.53, 68, 84; 3.35, 59; 4.73, 79; 5.27, 39, 66; 6.41, 84, 85, with all the relevant commentaries. As is typical of Evagrius's close correspondence between virtue and knowledge, what is strongly implied here is that passions hinder not only virtue but also knowledge.

6.84. The irascible part of the soul is joined with the heart, where its intelligence too is; its concupiscible/appetitive part, instead, is joined with the flesh and the blood, if it is true that we ought to remove rage in the heart and evilness in the flesh.

This *kephalaion* is a continuation and a development of the preceding one, where the irascible and concupiscible faculties of the soul have been declared to be opposite to nature—that is, for a human being, its rational nature. The present *kephalaion* analyzes the two inferior faculties and parts of the soul, *thymikon* and *epithymētikon*, and their location. The scriptural reference is Eccl 11:10: "Therefore remove sorrow from thy heart, and put away evil from thy flesh" (KJV). From this Evagrius deduces the locations of the two inferior faculties of the soul: Rage, which is associated with the irascible faculty, is located in the heart, where the intellect too dwells (Origen had often treated biblical mentions of the "heart" as references to the intellect, though without speaking of a physical location of the intellect). Evilness/vice, which is associated with the concupiscible faculty, is located in the "flesh and blood" (here there may also be an echo of Paul's claim in 1 Cor 15:50 that "flesh and blood cannot inherit the kingdom of God," as evilness certainly cannot). The location of the soul as a whole, or the rational soul, was a matter of discussion in ancient philosophy. The head and the heart were the two most popular identifications. See Teun Tieleman, *Galen and Chrysippus on the Soul: Argument and Refutation in the De Placitis II–III* (Leiden: Brill, 1996).

The biblical book of Ecclesiastes, or Qohelet, is often referred to, and commented on, by Evagrius; we also have an entire work, the scholia, devoted to this book by Evagrius. It is remarkable that in this connection one more convergence is to be found between Evagrius and Gregory of Nyssa: both of them identified the Ecclesiastes, or Preacher, with Christ himself, as is clear from Evagrius's first scholium on Ecclesiastes.

6.85. If it is true that all those faculties that we have in common with animals belong to the mortal corporeal nature, it is evident that the irascible and the appetitive faculties do not seem to have been created together with the rational nature before the movement.

This *kephalaion* continues the discourse on the irrational parts of the soul that Evagrius has been conducting in the two preceding *kephalaia* (see the relevant commentaries there). Here it is particularly clear that Evagrius is following Gregory Nyssen's line—once again—concerning the secondary, later, and adventitious nature of the inferior faculties of the soul liable to passions (Gregory uses terms such as ἐπιγεννήματα in this regard). They are parts of those animal aspects that entered human life after the fall, when it became mortal and shared in animal life. Indeed, the movement of which Evagrius speaks here is the movement of will that determined the fall. Gregory has a long treatment of this point in his dialogue *On the Soul and the Resurrection* (see my commentary in Ramelli, *Gregorio di Nissa: Sull'anima*). The inferior faculties of the soul, just as mortality itself, did not exist before the movement of free will toward evil, and will not exist any longer in the *telos*.

6.86. The holy angels instruct some of the human beings through words, recover others by means of dreams, and make others chaste thanks to nocturnal scares—and bring yet others back to virtue by means of blows.

The help given by angels to the spiritual progress of rational creatures has already been highlighted by Evagrius in *KG* 6.76 (see the relevant commentary above). Angels do not refrain from the most radical therapies to bring people back to virtue. It is the same pedagogical strategy used by the Godhead itself, according to Clement and Origen. See Ramelli, *Christian Doctrine of Apokatastasis*, the chapters on Clement and Origen.

6.87. The intellect, according to the sentence of Solomon, is joined with the heart, while the light that appears to it is considered to come from the sense-perceptible head.

After situating the inferior faculties of the soul in given parts of the body in *KG* 6.84 (see above, the relevant commentary), Evagrius in the present *kephalaion* associates the highest faculty, the intellect, with the heart. The reference to Solomon seems to point to the books of Proverbs and Ecclesiastes, where the heart is treated many times as the seat of human intellect. Especially relevant are, for instance, Prov 2:2 ("Apply your heart to understanding"); 8:5 ("Be you of an understanding heart!"); 15:14 ("the heart of the person who has understanding"); 20:5 ("counsel in the heart of a human being"); 22:17 ("Apply your heart to my knowledge"), 23:7 ("He thinks in his heart"), 12 ("Apply your heart to instruction"), 15 ("my son, if your heart be wise"); Eccl 1:17 ("I gave my heart to know wisdom"); 2:3 ("acquainting my heart with wisdom"); 3:17 ("I said in my heart, God shall judge"); 7:25 and 8:16 ("I applied my heart to know"); and 9:1 ("I considered in my heart"). The location of intellect in the heart is therefore established on the basis of Scripture (as I have mentioned earlier, Origen explained that what Scriptures call "heart" is often meant to indicate our intellectual or rational faculty: "Scripture usually calls 'heart' the rational faculty of the soul," *Rationabilem animae uirtutem cor solere nominari*; *Commentary on Romans* 2.7.36–37). The head is rather the apparent source of the light that enlightens the intellect. In the second half of the *kephalaion* there is probably a reference to Eccl 2:14: "The wise have eyes in their heads, while the fool walks in the darkness; but I came to realize that the same fate overtakes them both."

6.88. It is not only the holy angels who collaborate with us for the sake of our salvation but stars as well, if it is true that in the days of Barak from heaven they waged war against [lit. "with"] Sisara.

In *KG* 6.76 and 6.86 Evagrius has already emphasized that angels are the instruments of divine providence, working for the salvation of human beings (see the commentaries above). Here he adds that heavenly bodies do the same, with a scriptural reference to Judg 5:20: "From heaven fought the stars, from their courses they fought against Sisera." The notion that heavenly bodies were intelligent beings was widespread in antiquity. It is found also in Origen (see Ramelli, *Bardaisan of Edessa*). Evagrius here focuses on the providential role played by the stars, as well as by angels, in the salvific economy. Angels and stars work for the salvation of human beings. In *KG* 3.37 Evagrius has reflected on the stars' orders and the government they have been entrusted with by God (see the relevant commentary above, and *KG* 3.62, 3.84, 4.29 and commentaries).

6.89. Just as in this aeon our Lord was the firstborn from among the dead, so will he be in the aeon to come the firstborn of many siblings.

The resurrection is in the focus of this *kephalaion.* That of Christ himself has already occurred in the present aeon, but in the future aeon that of the other human beings will also occur. Evagrius here quotes Col 1:18 ("He is the beginning, the first-born from the dead," RSV) and Rom 8:29 ("Those whom he foreknew he also predestined to be conformed to the image of his Son, in order that he might be the first-born among many brethren," RSV). It must be taken into consideration that Evagrius thinks of the future resurrection as holistic—as did Origen—as a resurrection-restoration not only of bodies but also of souls and intellects. This is indeed confirmed by *KG* 5.22 and 5.25 (see above, the relevant commentary). On Origen's idea of the eschatological resurrection-restoration as the glorious resurrection of the "body of Christ" (that is, all humanity and all rational creatures), see above, the commentary on *KG* 2.6, where I also report the main passages from his *Commentary on John.*

6.90. Whoever has been held worthy of spiritual knowledge will help the holy angels and bring back rational souls from evilness to virtue and from ignorance to knowledge.

This *kephalaion* is closely connected with *KG* 6.88. Not only angels and heavenly bodies, but also those human beings who have attained spiritual knowledge, help drag other rational souls to salvation. The latter, once again, is represented by Evagrius as a passage from vice and ignorance to virtue and knowledge, with the usual association of the ethical and the cognitive planes. Only purification from evil allows rational creatures to attain knowledge. The link between purification and knowledge was already stressed by Gregory Nyssen—one of Evagrius's main inspirers—in *Homilies on the Beatitudes* 6, on Matt 5:8: "Blessed are the pure of heart, because they will see God" (purification enables the highest knowledge):

> I think that in this short saying the Word expresses some such counsel as this: there is in you, human beings, a desire to contemplate the true Good. But when you hear that the divine majesty is exalted above the heavens, that its glory is inexpressible, its beauty ineffable, and its nature inaccessible, do not despair of beholding what you desire. It is indeed within your reach; you have within yourselves the standard by which to apprehend the divine. For he who made you did at the same time endow your nature with this wonderful quality. For God imprinted on it the likeness of the glories of his own nature, as if molding the form of carving into wax. But the evil that has been poured all around the nature bearing the divine image has rendered useless to you this wonderful thing that lies hidden under vile coverings. If, therefore, you wash off by a good life the filth that has been stuck on your heart like plaster, that beauty that is in the image of God will again shine forth in you.... Hence, if a person who is pure of heart sees herself, she sees in herself what she desires; and thus she becomes blessed, because when she looks at her own purity, she sees the archetype in the image.

Investigate our words, our brothers, and interpret with diligence the riddles of these discourses/centuries, which are in the number of the six days of creation.

Here end the six discourses/centuries of the blessed Evagrius.

The final exhortation to investigation (ἐρευνᾶν) is in the spirit of Origen the "zetetic." I deem it probable that the underlying Greek verb was ἐρευνάω (more than ἐξιχνεύω, proposed by Dysinger), because in the extant Greek works of Evagrius ἐρευνάω/διερευνάω/ἔρευνα occurs seven times (*Sentences to the Monks* 108: Ἀνὴρ σοφὸς ἐρευνήσει λόγους θεοῦ; *Eulogius* [PG 79:1116,8], twice: Ὁ τὰς ἑτέρων σκέψεις πειρώμενος ἐρευνᾷν, τὰς ἑαυτοῦ πράξεις ἔργῳ οὐκ ἐρευνᾷ; ibid. 1132,19: ὅσον γὰρ ἐπὶ πλεῖον σκληραγωγεῖς σου τὸ σῶμα, τοσοῦτον διερευνᾷς σου τὸ συνειδός; *Scholia on Proverbs* 221: φῶς κυρίου πνοὴ ἀνθρώπων, ἢ λύχνος ὃς ἐρευνᾷ ταμίεια κοιλίας; *Scholia on Ecclesiastes* 68,2: Ὁ μὲν ἄνθρωπος προσάγει τῇ καρδίᾳ τὰ πράγματα πρὸς τὴν ἔρευναν αὐτῶν ἀποκλίνων; *On Evil Thoughts* 19.20: ταῦτά σου διερευνωμένου, φθαρήσεται μὲν ὁ λογισμὸς εἰς τὴν ἰδίαν ἀναλυόμενος θεωρίαν, φεύξεται δὲ ἀπὸ σοῦ τὸ δαιμόνιον, τῆς διανοίας σου ὑπὸ ταύτης τῆς γνώσεως εἰς ὕψος ἀρθείσης), while there is not one single occurrence of ἐξιχνεύω. Moreover, ἐρευνάω belongs to the terminology of Origen, Evagrius's great inspirer. Origen applied investigation to Scripture or some philosophical problems, and he exhorted his public to do so, while here readers, that is, monks, are encouraged to investigate and interpret Evagrius's own enigmatic words. The rationale for the number of discourses, six, under which all the *kephalaia*, or propositions, are grouped, is explained here at the end: it coincides with the Hexaemeron. In this light, Evagrius's reflections have a wideness that encompasses that of creation; they suggest the intention of producing a foundational work on the principles of reality. In this sense the closest work one can think of—albeit the propositional structure of Evagrius's work is different—is Origen's *On First Principles.*

Bibliography

Primary Sources

Chapters of the Disciples of Evagrius. Paul Géhin, ed. *Chapitres des disciples d'Evagre*. SC 514. Paris: Cerf, 2007.

Ephrem. *Prose Refutations*. C. W. Mitchell, A. A. Bevan, and F. Crawford Burkitt, eds. *S. Ephraim's Prose Refutations of Mani, Marcion, and Bardaisan*. 2 vols. London: Williams & Norgate, 1912–1921.

Eustathius of Antioch. *On the Belly-Myther, Against Origen*. Rowan Greer and Margaret Mitchell, eds. and trans. *The "Belly-Myther" of Endor: Interpretations of 1 Kingdoms 28 in the Early Church*. WGRW 16. Atlanta: Society of Biblical Literature, 2007.

Evagrius Ponticus. *Antirrheticus* (*On Talking Back*). David Brakke, trans. *Evagrius of Pontus: Talking Back (Antirrhetikos); A Monastic Handbook for Combating Demons*. Collegeville, Minn.: Liturgical Press, 2009.

———. *Gnostikos* (*The Gnostic*). Luke Dysinger, trans. "Evagrius: Gnostikos (CPG 2431) and Kephalaia Gnostika." http://www.ldysinger.com/Evagrius/02_Gno-Keph/00a_start.htm.

———. *Gnostikos* (*The Gnostic*). Antoine Guillaumont and Claire Guillaumont, eds. and trans. *Évagre le Pontique: Le gnostique, ou À celui qui est devenu digne de la science*. SC 356. Paris: Cerf, 1989.

———. *Kephalaia Gnostika* (*Propositions on Knowledge*). Luke Dysinger, trans. "Evagrius: Gnostikos (CPG 2431) and Kephalaia Gnostika." http://www.ldysinger.com/Evagrius/02_Gno-Keph/00a_start.htm.

———. *Kephalaia Gnostika* (*Propositions on Knowledge*). W. Frankenberg, ed. *Evagrius Ponticus*. Abhandlungen der Königlichen Gesellschaft der Wissenschaften zu Göttingen, Philologisch-Historische Klasse n.s. 13.2. Berlin: Weidmann, 1912.

———. *Kephalaia Gnostika* (*Propositions on Knowledge*). Antoine Guillaumont, ed. and trans. *Les six centuries des "Kephalaia gnostica."* PO 28.1. Paris: Firmin-Didot, 1958.

——. *Kephalaia Gnostika (Propositions on Knowledge)*. Fr. Theophanes (Constantine), trans. *The Evagrian Ascetical System*. Vol. 2 of *The Psychological Basis of Mental Prayer in the Heart*. Mount Athos: Timios Prodromos, 2006.

——. *Letters*. W. Frankenberg, ed. *Evagrius Ponticus*. Abhandlungen der Königlichen Gesellschaft der Wissenschaften zu Göttingen, Philologisch-Historische Klasse n.s. 13.2. Berlin: Weidmann, 1912.

——. *Letter to Melania*. W. Frankenberg, ed. *Evagrius Ponticus*. Abhandlungen der Königlichen Gesellschaft der Wissenschaften zu Göttingen, Philologisch-Historische Klasse n.s. 13.2. Berlin: Weidmann, 1912.

——. *Letter to Melania*. Gösta Vitestam, ed. *Seconde partie du traité, qui passe sous le nom de La grande lettre d'Évagre le Pontique à Mélanie l'ancienne, d'après le manuscrit du British Museum Add. 17192*. Lund: Gleerup, 1964.

——. *On Thoughts*. Paul Géhin, Antoine Guillaumont, and Claire Guillaumont, eds. and trans. *Évagre le Pontique: Sur le pensées*. SC 438. Paris: Cerf, 1998.

——. *Praktikos (The Ascetic)*. Antoine Guillaumont and Claire Guillaumont, eds. and trans. *Évagre le Pontique: Traité pratique, ou Le moine*. 2 vols. SC 170–171. Paris: Cerf, 1971.

——. *Praktikos (The Ascetic)*. Luke Dysinger, trans. "Evagrius: Praktikos." http://www.ldysinger.com/Evagrius/01_Prak/00a_start.htm.

——. *Praktikos (The Ascetic)*. Robert E. Sinkewicz, trans. *Evagrius of Pontus: The Greek Ascetic Corpus*. Oxford: Oxford University Press, 2003.

——. *Scholia on Proverbs*. Paul Géhin, ed. *Scholies aux Proverbes*. SC 340. Paris: Cerf, 1987.

Galen. *The Formation of a Fetus*. Karl Gottlob Kühn, ed. *Claudii Galeni opera omnia*. 20 vols. Leipzig: Knobloch, 1821–33.

Géhin, Paul. "Nouveaux fragments grecs des Lettres d'Évagre." *Revue d'histoire des textes* 24 (1994): 117–47.

Gregory of Nyssa. *Letter to Theodosius*. Rowan Greer and Margaret Mitchell, eds. and trans. *The "Belly-Myther" of Endor: Interpretations of 1 Kingdoms 28 in the Early Church*. WGRW 16. Atlanta: Society of Biblical Literature, 2007.

——. *On the Soul and the Resurrection*. Ilaria L. E. Ramelli, ed. and trans. *Gregorio di Nissa: Sull'anima e la resurrezione*. Milan: Bompiani–Catholic University, 2007.

———. Andreas Spira and Ekkehardus Mühlenberg, eds. *Gregorii Nysseni, De anima et resurrectione.* GNO 3.3. Leiden: Brill, 2014.

Iamblichus. *On the Soul.* J. F. Finamore and J. M. Dillon, eds. and trans. *Iamblichus, De anima: Text, Translation, and Commentary.* Philosophia Antiqua 92. Leiden: Brill, 2002.

Palladius. *Lausiac History.* Gabriel Bunge and Adalbert de Vogüé, eds. and trans. *Quatre ermites égyptiens, d'après les fragments coptes de l'Histoire Lausiaque.* Bégrolles-en-Mauges: Bellefontaine, 1994.

Porphyry. *Fragments.* Andrew Smith, ed. *Porphyrii Philosophi fragmenta.* Stuttgart: Teubner, 1993.

Secondary Sources

Aptsiauri, Tamara. "Die Allegorese in der Schrift *Leben des Mose* Gregors von Nyssa im Kontext seiner Epinoia-Theorie." Pages in 495–504 in vol. 2 of *Gregory of Nyssa Contra Eunomium.* Edited by Lenka Karfíková. Leiden: Brill, 2007.

Arruzza, Cinzia. "La matière immatérielle chez Grégoire de Nysse." *FZPhTh* 54 (2007): 215–23.

———. *Les mésaventures de la théodicée: Plotin, Origène, Grégoire de Nysse.* Turnhout: Brepols, 2011.

Augst, Rüdiger. *Lebensverwirklichung und christlicher Glaube, Acedia, religiöse Gleichgültigkeit als Problem der Spiritualität bei Evagrius Ponticus.* Frankfurt: Lang,1990.

Balthasar, Hans Urs von. "Metaphysik und Mystik des Evagrius Pontikus." *Zeitschrift für Askese und Mystik* (1939): 31–47.

Barnes, Jonathan. "Justice Writ Large." Pages 31–49 in *Virtue and Happiness: Essays in Honour of Julia Annas.* Edited by Rachana Kamtekar. Oxford Studies in Ancient Philosophy Supplements. New York: Oxford University Press, 2012.

Beeley, Christopher. *The Unity of Christ: Continuity and Conflict in Patristic Tradition.* New Haven: Yale University Press, 2012.

Bergjan, Silke-Petra. "Clement of Alexandria on God's Providence and the Gnostic's Life Choice: The Concept of *Pronoia* in the *Stromateis*, Book VII." Pages 63–92 in *The Seventh Book of the Stromateis.* Edited by Matyas Havrda, Vit Husek, and Jana Platova. Leiden: Brill, 2012.

Bettiolo, Paolo, ed. *L'*Epistula fidei *di Evagrio Pontico: Temi, contesti, sviluppi.* Rome: Augustinianum, 2000.

———. *Evagrio Pontico: Lo scrigno della sapienza; Lettera a Melania*. Magnano, Biella: Edizioni Qiqajon, 1997.

Blowers, Paul. *Drama of the Divine Economy*. Oxford: Oxford University Press, 2012.

———. "Maximus the Confessor, Gregory of Nyssa, and the Concept of Perpetual Progress." *VC* 46 (1992): 151–71.

Boersma, Hans. *Embodiment and Virtue in Gregory of Nyssa*. Oxford: Oxford University Press, 2013.

Bos, Abraham. *The Soul and Its Instrumental Body*. Leiden: Brill, 2003.

Bos, Abraham, and Rein Ferwerda. *Aristotle, On the Life-Bearing Spirit*. Leiden: Brill, 2008.

Bosman, Philip. *Conscience in Philo and Paul*. Tübingen: Mohr Siebeck, 2003.

Bousset, Wilhelm. *Apophthegmata: Studien zur Geschichte des ältesten Mönchtums*. Tübingen: Mohr, 1923.

Bouyer, Louis. *The Spirituality of the New Testament and the Fathers*. Translated by M. P. Ryan. London: Burns & Oates, 1963.

Bradford, David. "Evagrius Ponticus and the Psychology of Natural Contemplation." *Studies in Spirituality* 22 (2012): 109–25.

Brock, Sebastian. *The Bible in the Syriac Tradition*. Piscataway, N.J.: Gorgias, 2006.

Bucur, Bogdan. *Angelomorphic Pneumatology: Clement of Alexandria and Other Early Christian Witnesses*. Leiden: Brill, 2009.

———. "The Early Christian Reception of Gen 18." *JECS* 23 (2015): 245–72.

Bundy, David. "The Kephalaia Gnostika." Pages 175–86 in *Ascetic Behavior in Greco-Roman Antiquity: A Sourcebook*. Edited by Vincent L. Wimbush. Minneapolis: Fortress, 1990.

———. "The Philosophical Structures of Origenism: The Case of the Expurgated Syriac Version S1 of the *Kephalaia Gnostika* of Evagrius." Pages 577–84 in *Origeniana Quinta*. Edited by Robert J. Daly. Leuven: Peeters, 1992.

Bunge, Gabriel. "Aktive und kontemplative Weise des Betens im Traktat *De oratione* des Evagrios Pontikos." *StudMon* 41 (1999): 211–27.

———. "Créé pour être." *BLE* 98 (1997): 21–29.

———. *Despondency: The Spiritual Teaching of Evagrius Ponticus*. Translated by Anthony P. Gythiel. Crestwood, N.Y.: St. Vladimir's Seminary Press, 2012. Translation of *Akedia: Die geistliche Lehre des Evagrios Pontikos vom Überdruss*. Köln: Luthe, 1983.

———. "Encore une fois: Hénade ou Monade?" *Adamantius* 15 (2009): 9–42.

———. *Evagrios Pontikos, Briefe aus der Wüste.* Trier: Paulinus, 1986.

———. *Das Geistgebet: Studien zum Traktat* De oratione *des Evagrios Pontikos.* Köln: Luthe, 1987.

———. "Hénade ou Monade? Au sujet de deux notions centrales de la terminologie évagrienne." *Mus* 102 (1989): 69–91.

———. "*Mysterium Unitatis*: Der Gedanke der Einheit von Schöpfer und Geschöpf in der evagrianischen Mystik." *FZPhTh* 36 (1989): 449–69.

———. "Priez sans cesse: Aux origines de la prière hésychaste." *StudMon* 30 (1988): 7–16.

———. "'Nach dem Intellekt Leben': Zum sog. 'Intellektualismus' der evagrianischen Spiritualität." Pages 95–109 in *Simandron, der Wachklopfer: Gedenkenschrift Gamber.* Edited by Wilhelm Nyssen. Köln: Luthe, 1989.

———. "Origenismus-Gnostizismus: Zum geistesgeschichtlichen Standort des Evagrios Pontikos." *VC* 40 (1986): 24–54.

Burns, Dylan. "Care or Prayer? Justin Martyr's *Dialogue with Trypho* 1.4 Revisited." *VC* 68 (2014): 178–91.

Casiday, Augustine. "Deification in Origen, Evagrius, and Cassian." Pages 995–1001 in vol. 2 of *Origeniana Octava.* Edited by Lorenzo Perrone. Leuven: Peeters, 2003.

———. *Reconstructing the Theology of Evagrius Ponticus.* Cambridge: Cambridge University Press, 2013.

———. "Universal Restoration in Evagrius Ponticus' 'Great Letter.'" *StPatr* 47 (2010): 223–28.

Conway-Jones, Ann. *Gregory of Nyssa's Tabernacle Imagery in Its Jewish and Christian Contexts.* Oxford: Oxford University Press, 2014.

Corrigan, Kevin. *Evagrius and Gregory: Mind, Soul and Body in the 4th Century.* Burlington, Vt.: Ashgate, 2009.

Corrigan, Kevin, and Gregory Yuri Glazov. "Compunction and Compassion: Two Overlooked Virtues in Evagrius of Pontus." *JECS* 22 (2014): 61–77.

Corsaro, Francesco. Review of Ilaria Ramelli, *Gregorio di Nissa: Sull'anima e la resurrezione. Aug* 51 (2011): 556–59.

Crone, Patricia. "Daysanis." Pages 116–18 in the *Encyclopedia of Islam.* Edited by Kate Fleet et al. 3d ed. Leiden: Brill, 2012.

Crouzel, Henri. "Recherches sur Origène et son influence." *BLE* 62 (1961): 3–15, 105–13.

Daley, Brian. *The Hope of the Early Church*. Cambridge: Cambridge University Press, 1991.

Dossey, Leslie. "Watchful Greeks and Lazy Romans: Disciplining Sleep in Late Antiquity." *JECS* 21 (2013): 209–39.

Draguet, René. "L'*Histoire Lausiaque*: Une oeuvre écrite dans l'esprit d'Évagre." *RHE* 41 (1946): 321–64; 42 (1947): 5–49.

Driscoll, Jeremy. *The* Ad monachos *of Evagrius Ponticus*. Rome: Augustinianum, 1991.

———. "*Apatheia* and Purity of Heart in Evagrius." Pages 141–59 in *Purity of Heart in Early Ascetic and Monastic Literature*. Edited by Harriet A. Luckman and Linda Kulzer. Collegeville, Minn.: Liturgical Press, 1999.

———. "Gentleness in the *Ad monachos* of Evagrius." *StudMon* 22 (1990): 295–321.

———. "A Key for Reading the *Ad monachos* of Evagrius." *Aug* 30 (1990): 361–92.

Dysinger, Luke. *Psalmody and Prayer in the Writings of Evagrius Ponticus*. Oxford: Oxford University Press, 2005.

Edwards, Mark J. Review of Ilaria Ramelli, *Gregorio di Nissa: Sull'anima e la resurrezione*. *JEH* 60 (2009): 764–65.

Elm, Susanna. "The *Sententiae ad virginem* by Evagrius Ponticus and the Problem of Early Monastic Rules." *Aug* 30 (1990): 393–404.

Fernández, Samuel. *Cristo médico, según Orígenes: La actividad médica como metáfora de la acción divina*. Rome: Augustinianum, 1999.

Finamore, John. *Iamblichus and the Theory of the Vehicle of the Soul*. Chico, Cal.: Scholars Press, 1985.

Géhin, Paul. "La place de la *Lettre sue la foi* dans l'oeuvre d'Evagre." Pages 25–58 in *L'*Epistula fidei *di Evagrio Pontico: Temi, contesti, sviluppi*. Edited by Paolo Bettiolo. Rome: Augustinianum, 2000.

Geljon, Albert. "Divine Infinity in Gregory of Nyssa and Philo of Alexandria." *VC* 59 (2005): 152–77.

Ghira, Danilo. Review of Ilaria Ramelli and David Konstan, *Terms for Eternity*. *Maia* 61 (2009): 732–34.

Graver, Margaret. *Stoicism and Emotion*. Chicago: University of Chicago Press, 2007.

Guillaumont, Antoine. *Études sur la spiritualité de l'Orient chrétien*. Bégrolles en Mauges: Bellefontaine, 1996.

———. "Évagre et les anathématismes anti-origénistes de 553." *StPatr* 3 (1961): 219–26.

———. "Le gnostique chez Clément d'Alexandrie et chez Évagre." Pages 195–201 in *Alexandria: Hellénisme, judaïsme et christianisme à Alexandrie; Mélanges Claude Mondésert*. Paris: Cerf, 1987. Repr. pages 151–60 in *Études sur la spiritualité de l'Orient chrétien*. Begrolles-en-Mauges: Bellefontaine, 1996.

———. *Les "Képhalaia gnostica" d'Évagre le Pontique et l'histoire de l'origénisme chez les grecs et chez les syriens*. Paris: Éditions du Seuil, 1962.

———. "Un philosophe au désert: Évagre le Pontique." *RHR* 181 (1972): 29–56. Repr. pages 185–212 in *Aux origines du monachisme chrétien*. Begrolles-en-Mauges: Bellefontaine, 1979.

———. *Un philosophe au désert: Évagre le Pontique*. Paris: Vrin, 2004.

———. "Le problème de la prière continuelle dans le monachisme ancien." Pages 285–94 in *L'experience de la prière dans les grandes religions*. Louvain-la-Neuve: Presses universitaires, 1980.

———. "Le rôle des versions orientales dans la récupération de l'oeuvre d'Évagre." Pages 64–74 in *Comptes rendus des séances de l'Académie des inscriptions*. Paris: Académie des inscriptions, 1985.

———. "Le texte véritable des *Gnostica* d'Évagre le Pontique." *RHR* 142 (1952): 156–205.

———. "Les versions syriaques de l'oeuvre d'Évagre." *OrChrAn* 221 (1983): 35–41.

———. "La vie gnostique selon Évagre le Pontique." *Annuaire du Collège de France* 80 (1979–80): 467–70.

Hägg, Henny F. "Prayer and Knowledge in Clement of Alexandria." Pages 131–42 in *The Seventh Book of the Stromateis*. Edited by Matyas Havrda, Vit Husek, and Jana Platova. Leiden: Brill, 2012.

Hausherr, Irenée. *Les leçons d'un contemplatif: Le Traité de l'oraison d'Evagre le Pontique*. Paris: Beauchesne, 1960.

———. "L'origine de la théorie orientale des huit péchés capitaux." *Orientalia Christiana* 30 (1933): 164–75.

———. "Le traité de l'oraison d'Évagre le Pontique (ps. Nil)." *Revue d'Ascétique et de Mystique* 15 (1934): 34–118.

Herrero de Jáuregui, M. Review of Ilaria Ramelli, *Gregorio di Nissa: Sull'anima e la resurrezione*. *'Ilu* 13 (2008): 334–36.

"Ilaria Ramelli and David Konstan, Terms for Eternity: *aiônios* and *aïdios* in Classical and Christian Texts." *IZBG* 54 (2009): 444, §1901.

Ivánka, Endre von. "ΚΕΦΑΛΑΙΑ: Eine byzantinische Literaturform und ihre antiken Wurzeln." *ByzZ* 47 (1954): 285–91.

Joest, Christoph. "Die Bedeutung von *Akedia* und *Apatheia* bei Evagrios Pontikos." *StudMon* 35 (1993): 7–53. English translation, "The Significance of *Acedia* and *Apatheia* in Evagrius Ponticus." *American Benedictine Review* 55 (2004): 121–50, 273–307.

Johnson, Aaron. *Religion and Identity in Porphyry of Tyre: The Limits of Hellenism in Late Antiquity.* Cambridge: Cambridge University Press, 2013.

Kalvesmaki, Joel. "The *Epistula fidei* of Evagrius of Pontus: An Answer to Constantinople." *JECS* 20 (2012): 113–39.

Kannengiesser, Charles. "Antony, Athanasius, Evagrius: The Egyptian Fate of Origenism." *Coptic Church Review* 16 (1995): 3–8.

Karamanolis, George. "Clement on Superstition and Religious Belief." Pages 113–30 in *The Seventh Book of the Stromateis.* Edited by Matyas Havrda, Vit Husek, and Jana Platova. Leiden: Brill, 2012.

———. *The Philosophy of Early Christianity.* Durham: Acumen, 2013.

———. *Plato and Aristotle in Agreement: Platonists on Aristotle from Antiochus to Porphyry.* Oxford: Oxford University Press, 2006.

Kavvadas, Nestor. *Isaak von Ninive und seine Kephalaia Gnostika: Die Pneumatologie und ihr Kontext.* Leiden: Brill, 2015.

Keough, Shawn. Review of Ilaria Ramelli and David Konstan, *Terms for Eternity. ETL* 84.4 (2008): 601.

Kline, Francis. "The Christology of Evagrius and the Parent System of Origen." *Cistercian Studies* 20 (1985): 155–83.

Konstan, David. "Regret, Repentance, and Change of Heart in Paul: *Metanoia* in its Greek Context." In *Paul's Greco-Roman Context.* Edited by Cilliers Breytenbach. BETL. Leuven: Peeters, forthcoming 2015.

Konstantinovsky, Julia. *Evagrius Ponticus: The Making of a Gnostic.* Burlington, Vt.: Ashgate, 2009.

———. "Soul and Body in Early Christian Thought: A Unified Duality?" *StPatr* 44 (2010): 349–55.

Kovacs, Judith. "Saint Paul as Apostle of *Apatheia.*" Pages 199–216 in *The Seventh Book of the Stromateis.* Edited by Matyas Havrda, Vit Husek, and Jana Platova. Leiden: Brill, 2012.

Krawiec, Rebecca. "Literacy and Memory in Evagrius's Monasticism." *JECS* 21 (2013): 363–90.

Le Boulluec, Alain. *Clément d'Alexandrie: Les Stromates; Stromate V, Tome II; Commentaire, bibliographie et index.* SC 279. Paris: Cerf, 1981.

Lekkas, Georgios. *Liberté et progrès chez Origène.* Turnhout: Brepols, 2001.

Lollar, Joshua. *To See into the Life of Things: The Contemplation of Nature in Maximus the Confessor and His Predecessors.* Turnhout: Brepols, 2013.

Ludlow, Morwenna. "Demons, Evil and Liminality in Cappadocian Theology." *JECS* 20 (2012): 179–211.

Luzárraga, Jesús. *El evangelio de Juán en las versiones siríacas.* SubBi 33. Rome: Pontifical Biblical Institute, 2008.

Maier, Barbara. "*Apatheia* bei den Stoikern und *Akedia* bei Evagrios Pontikos: Ein Ideal und die Kehrseite seiner Realität." *OrChr* 78 (1994): 230–49.

Marmodoro, Anna. "Gregory of Nyssa on the Creation of the World." Pages 94–110 in *Causation and Creation in Late Antiquity.* Edited by Anna Marmodoro and Brian Prince. Cambridge: Cambridge University Press, 2015.

Marsili, Salvatore. "Giovanni Cassiano ed Evagrio Pontico, Dottrina sulla Carità e Contemplazione." *Scriptorium* 5 (1951): 195–213.

Martens, Peter. "Revisiting the Allegory/Typology Distinction: The Case of Origen." *JECS* 16 (2008): 283–317.

Marx-Wolf, Heidi. "Bardesanes." In *The Encyclopedia of Ancient History.* Edited by Roger S. Bagnall et al. London: Wiley-Blackwell, 2013. doi:10.1002/9781444338386.wbeah05032.

Maspero, Giulio. Review of Ilaria Ramelli, *Gregorio di Nissa: Sull'anima e la resurrezione. ZAC* 15 (2011): 592–94.

McConnell, Timothy. *Illumination in Basil of Caesarea's Doctrine of the Holy Spirit.* Minneapolis: Fortress, 2014.

Melcher, Robert. *Der 8. Brief des hl. Basilius, ein Werk des Evagrius Pontikus.* Münsterische Beiträge zur Theologie 1. Münster: Aschendorff, 1923.

Meloni, Pietro. *Il profumo dell'immortalità: L'interpretazione patristica di Cantico, 1, 3.* Rome: Edizioni Studium, 1975.

Moreschini, Claudio. *I Padri Cappadoci: Storia, letteratura, teologia.* Rome: Città Nuova, 2008.

Muehlberger, Ellen. *Angels in Late Ancient Christianity.* Oxford: Oxford University Press, 2013.

Mühlenberg, Ekkehardt. *Die Unendlichkeit Gottes bei Gregor von Nyssa.* Göttingen: Vandenhoeck & Ruprecht, 1966.

Murphy, Francis X. "Evagrius Ponticus and Origenism." Pages 253–69 in *Origeniana Tertia.* Edited by Robert Hanson and Henri Crouzel. Rome: Augustinianum, 1985.

Nave, Guy D. *The Role and Function of Repentance in Luke-Acts.* Atlanta: Society of Biblical Literature, 2002.

O'Brien, Carl. Review of Ilaria Ramelli and David Konstan, *Terms for Eternity. The Classical Review* 60.2 (2010): 390–91.

O'Laughlin, Michael. "Elements of Fourth-Century Origenism." Pages 357–73 in *Origen of Alexandria*. Edited by Charles Kannengiesser. Notre Dame, Ind.: University of Notre Dame Press, 1988.

———. "New Questions concerning the Origenism of Evagrius." Pages 528–35 in *Origeniana Quinta*. Edited by Robert J. Daly. Leuven: Peeters, 1992.

———. "Origenism in the Desert: Anthropology and Integration in Evagrius Ponticus." Ph.D. diss., Harvard Divinity School, 1987.

Parmentier, Michel. "Evagrius of Pontus' Letter to Melania." *Bijdr* 46 (1985): 2–38. Repr. pages 272–309 in *Forms of Devotion, Conversion, Worship, Spirituality, and Asceticism*. Edited by Everett Ferguson. New York: Garland, 1999.

Payne Smith, J., ed. *A Compendious Syriac Dictionary*. 1903. Repr., Winona Lake, Ind.: Eisenbrauns, 1998.

Peace, Richard V. *Conversion in the New Testament: Paul and the Twelve*. Grand Rapids: Eerdmans, 1999.

Pearce, Sarah J. K. *The Land of the Body: Studies in Philo's Representation of Egypt*. WUNT 208. Tübingen: Mohr Siebeck, 2007.

Perczel, István. "Note sur la pensée systematique d'Évagre le Pontique." Pages 277–97 in *Origene e l'Alessandrinismo cappadoce*. Edited by Mario Girardi and Marcello Marin. Bari: Edipuglia, 2002.

Pesthy, Monika. "*Logismoi* origéniens—*logismoi* évagriens." Pages 1017–22 in vol. 2 of *Origeniana Octava*. Edited by Lorenzo Perrone. Leuven: Peeters, 2003.

Pietras, Henryk. "L'apocrifo giudaico *Preghiera di Giuseppe* nell'interpretazione origeniana." Pages 545–60 in *Origeniana Decima*. Edited by H. Pietras and S. Kaczmarek. BETL 244. Leuven: Peeters, 2011.

———. "L'inizio del mondo materiale e l'elezione divina in Origene." Pages 653–68 in *Origeniana Nona*. Edited by G. Heidl and R. Somos. Leuven: Peeters, 2009.

Possekel, Ute. "Bardaisan and Origen on Fate and the Power of the Stars." *JECS* 20 (2012): 515–42.

Proctor, Travis. "Daemonic Trickery, Platonic Mimicry." *VC* 68 (2014): 416–49.

Radde-Gallwitz, Andrew. *Basil of Caesarea, Gregory of Nyssa, and the Transformation of Divine Simplicity*. Oxford: Oxford University Press, 2009.

Ramelli, Ilaria L. E. "Αἰώνιος and Αἰών in Origen and Gregory of Nyssa." *StPatr* 47 (2010): 57–62.

———. "Alexander of Aphrodisias: A Source of Origen's Philosophy?" *Philosophie Antique* 14 (2014): 237–90.

———. *Allegoria, 1: L'età classica.* Milan: Vita e Pensiero, 2004.

———. "Allegory. II. Judaism." Pages 785–93 in vol. 1 of *Encyclopedia of the Bible and Its Reception.* Edited by Hans-Joseph Klauck et al. Berlin: de Gruyter, 2009.

———. "Alle origini della figura dell'intercessore in età paleocristiana." Pages 1003–49 in vol. 2 of *Mediadores con lo divino en el Mediterráneo antiguo, Actas del Congreso Internacional de Historia de las Religiones, Palma de Mallorca 13–15.X.2005.* Palma de Mallorca: Universitat de les Illes Balears, 2011.

———. "Apofatismo cristiano e relativismo pagano: Un confronto tra filosofi platonici." Pages 101–69 in *Verità e mistero nel pluralismo culturale della tarda antichità.* Edited by Angela M. Mazzanti. Bologna: Edizioni Studio Domenicano, 2009.

———. "Apokatastasis and Epektasis in *Hom. in Cant.*: The Relation between Two Core Doctrines in Gregory and Roots in Origen." In *Proceedings of the XIII International Colloquium on Gregory of Nyssa, Rome, 17–20 September 2014.* Edited by Giulio Maspero and Miguel Brugarolas. Leiden: Brill, 2016.

———. "Atticus and Origen on the Soul of God the Creator: From the 'Pagan' to the Christian Side of Middle Platonism." *Jahrbuch für Religionsphilosophie* 10 (2011): 13–35.

———. "Bardaisan as a Christian Philosopher: A Reassessment of His Christology." Pages 873–88 in *Religion in the History of European Culture: Proceedings of the 9th EASR Conference and IAHR Special Conference, 14–17 September 2009, Messina.* Edited by Giulia Sfameni Gasparro, Augusto Cosentino, and Mariangela Monaca. Palermo: Officina di Studi Medievali, 2013.

———. *Bardaisan of Edessa: A Reassessment of the Evidence and a New Interpretation.* Eastern Christian Studies 22. Piscataway, N.J.: Gorgias, 2009.

———, ed. *Bardaisan on Free Will, Fate, and Human Nature: The Book of the Laws of Countries.* Tübingen: Mohr Siebeck, 2016.

———. "Basil and Apokatastasis: New Findings." *Journal of Early Christian History* 4 (2014): 116–36.

———. "The Birth of the Rome–Alexandria Connection: The Early Sources on Mark and Philo, and the Petrine Tradition." *SPhilo* 23 (2011): 69–95.

———. *The Christian Doctrine of Apokatastasis: A Critical Assessment from the New Testament to Eriugena.* Supplements to Vigiliae Christianae 120. Leiden: Brill, 2013.

———. "Christian Soteriology and Christian Platonism: Origen, Gregory of Nyssa, and the Biblical and Philosophical Basis of the Doctrine of Apokatastasis." *VC* 61 (2007): 313–56.

———. "Clement's Notion of the Logos 'All Things as One': Its Alexandrian Background in Philo and Its Developments in Origen and Nyssen." In *Alexandrian Personae: Scholarly Culture and Religious Traditions in Ancient Alexandria (1st ct. BCE–4 ct. CE)*. Edited by Zlatko Plese. Tübingen: Mohr Siebeck, 2016.

———. "La coerenza della soteriologia origeniana: Dalla polemica contro il determinismo gnostico all'universale restaurazione escatologica." Pages 661–88 in *Pagani e cristiani alla ricerca della salvezza: Atti del XXXIV Incontro di Studiosi dell'Antichità Cristiana, Roma, Istituto Patristico Augustinianum, 5–7 maggio 2005.* SEAug 96. Rome: Augustinianum, 2006.

———. "La colpa antecedente come ermeneutica del male in sede storico-religiosa e nei testi biblici." Pages 11–64 in *Atti del XIV Convegno di Studî vetero-testamentarî dell'Associazione Biblica Italiana: Origine e fenomenologia del male; Le vie della catarsi vetero-testamentaria, Roma-Ciampino, Istituto Il Carmelo, 5–7 settembre 2005.* Edited by Ignazio Cardellini. Bologna: Dehoniane, 2007 = *Ricerche Storico-Bibliche* 19 (2007).

———. "Conscience. IV. Christianity." Pages 650–52 in vol. 3 of *Encyclopedia of the Bible and Its Reception.* Edited by Hans-Joseph Klauck et al. Berlin: de Gruyter, 2011.

———. "Cristo-Logos in Origene: Ascendenze filoniane, passaggi in Bardesane e Clemente, e negazione del subordinazionismo." Pages 295–317 in *Dal Logos dei Greci e dei Romani al Logos di Dio: Ricordando Marta Sordi.* Edited by Alfredo Valvo and Roberto Radice. Milan: Vita e Pensiero, 2011.

———. "Death." Pages 673–81 in vol. 1 of *Nuovo Dizionario Patristico e di Antichità Cristiane.* Edited by Angelo Di Berardino. 4 vols. Genova: Marietti, 2006–10.

———. "Deification (*Theosis*)." Pages 468–70 in vol. 6 of the *Encyclopedia of the Bible and Its Reception*. Edited by Hans-Joseph Klauck et al. Berlin: de Gruyter, 2013.

———. "The *Dialogue of Adamantius*: A Document of Origen's Thought? (Part One)." *StPatr* 52 (2012): 71–98.

———. "The *Dialogue of Adamantius*: A Document of Origen's Thought? (Part Two)." *StPatr* 56 (2013): 227–73.

———. "Disability in Bardaisan and Origen: Between the Stoic *Adiaphora* and the Lord's Grace." Pages 141–59 in *Gestörte Lektüre: Disability als hermeneutische Leitkategorie biblischer Exegese*. Edited by Wolfgang Grünstäudl and Markus Schiefer Ferrari. Stuttgart: Kohlhammer, 2012.

———. "The Divine as an Inaccessible Epistemological Object in Ancient Jewish, 'Pagan,' and Christian Platonists: A Common Cognitive Pattern across Different Religion Traditions." *JHI* 75 (2014): 167–88.

———. "Eriugena's Commentary on Martianus in the Framework of His Thought and the Philosophical Debate of His Time." Pages 245–72 in *Carolingian Scholarship and Martianus Capella*. Edited by Sinead O'Sullivan and Mariken Teeuwen. Cultural Encounters in Late Antiquity and the Middle Ages 12. Turnhout: Brepols, 2012.

———. "Ethos and Logos: A Second-Century Apologetical Debate between 'Pagan' and Christian Philosophers." *VC* 69 (2015): 123–56.

———. "Evagrius and Gregory: Nazianzen or Nyssen? A Remarkable Issue That Bears on the Cappadocian (and Origenian) Influence on Evagrius." *GRBS* 53 (2013): 117–37.

———. "1 Cor 15:24–26: Submission of Enemies and Annihilation of Evil and Death; A Case for a New Translation and a History of Interpretation." *SMSR* 74.2 (2008): 241–58.

———. "1 Tim 5:6 and the Notion and Terminology of Spiritual Death: Hellenistic Moral Philosophy in the Pastoral Epistles." *Aev* 84 (2010): 3–16.

———. *Gospel according to John III*. Novum Testamentum Patristicum. Göttingen: Vandenhoeck & Ruprecht, forthcoming.

———. *Gregorio di Nissa: Sull'anima e la resurrezione*. Milan: Bompiani–Catholic University, 2007.

———. "Gregory of Nyssa's Trinitarian Theology in *In illud: Tunc et ipse Filius*: His Polemic against 'Arian' Subordinationism and Apokatastasis." Pages 445–78 in *Gregory of Nyssa: The Minor Treatises on Trinitarian Theology and Apollinarism; Proceedings of the 11th International Colloquium on Gregory of Nyssa (Tübingen, 17–20 September 2008)*.

Edited by Volker Henning Drecoll and Margitta Berghaus. Leiden: Brill, 2011.

———. "Harmony between *Arkhē* and *Telos* in Patristic Platonism and the Imagery of Astronomical Harmony Applied to the Apokatastasis Theory." *International Journal of the Platonic Tradition* 7 (2013): 1–49.

———. *Hierocles the Stoic.* Translated by David Konstan. Leiden: Brill, 2009.

———. "Iamblichus, *De anima* 38 (66,12–15 Finamore/Dillon): A Resolving Conjecture?" *Rheinisches Museum für Philologie* 157 (2014): 106–11.

———. "*In illud: Tunc et ipse Filius*...: Gregory of Nyssa's Exegesis, Its Derivations from Origen, and Early Patristic Interpretations Related to Origen's." *StPatr* 44 (2010): 259–74.

———. "L'Inno a Cristo-Logos nel *Simposio* di Metodio." Pages 257–80 in *Motivi e forme della poesia cristiana antica tra scrittura e tradizione classica.* SEAug 108. Rome: Institutum patristicum Augustinianum, 2008.

———.Jesus, James the Just, a Gate, and an Epigraph." Pages 203–29 in *Kein Jota und kein Häkchen des Gesetzes werden vergehen (vgl. Q 16,17): Das Gesetzesverständnis der Logienquelle auf dem Hintergrund frühjüdischer Theologie.* Edited by Markus Tiwald. BWANT 200. Stuttgart: Kohlhammer, 2013.

———. "ΚΟΙΜΩΜΕΝΟΥΣ ΑΠΟ ΤΗΣ ΛΥΠΗΣ (Luke 22,45): A Deliberate Change." *ZNW* 102 (2011): 59–76.

———. "Love." Pages 611–26 of vol. 2 in *Encyclopedia of Ancient Christianity.* Edited by Angelo Di Berardino. Downers Grove, Ill.: InterVarsity, 2014.

———. "Luke 17:12: 'God's Kingdom Is inside You'; The Ancient Syriac Versions in Support of the Correct Translation." *Hugoye* 12.2 (2009): 259–86.

———. "Mansuetudine, grazia e salvezza negli *Acta Philippi.*" *Invigilata Lucernis* 29 (2007): 215–28.

———. "The Mysteries of Scripture: Allegorical Exegesis and the Heritage of Stoicism, Philo, and Pantaenus in Clement." Second *Internationale Colloquium Clementinum*, Prague-Olomouc 29–31 May 2014. Edited by Veronica Cernuskova, Vit Husek, and Jana Platova. Leiden: Brill, 2016.

———. "Μυστήριον negli *Stromateis* di Clemente Alessandrino: Aspetti di continuità con la tradizione allegorica greca." Pages 83–120 in *Il volto del mistero: Mistero e religione nella cultura religiosa tardoantica.* Edited by Angela Maria Mazzanti. Castel Bolognese: Itaca Libri, 2006.

———. "*Mysterium* and *Sacramentum* in the Vetus Afra: What Differing Interpretations by African Patristic Authors Reveal about Paganism and Donatism." Pages 349–75 in *The Uniquely African Controversy: Studies on Donatist Christianity.* Edited by Anthony Dupont, Matthew Gaumer, and Mathijs Lamberigts. Leuven: Peeters, 2014.

———. "Mysticism and Mystic Apophaticism in Middle and Neoplatonism across Judaism, 'Paganism' and Christianity." In *Constructions of Mysticism: Inventions and Interactions across the Borders.* Edited by Annette Wilke. Wiesbaden: Harassowitz, 2015.

———. "L'*omen* per Acilio Glabrione e per Traiano: Una corona?" *Rivista di Storia della Chiesa in Italia* 55.2 (2001): 389–94.

———. "Origen and the Stoic Allegorical Tradition: Continuity and Innovation." *Invigilata Lucernis* 28 (2006): 195–226.

———. "Origen, Bardaisan, and the Origin of Universal Salvation." *HTR* 102 (2009): 135–68.

———. "Origen, Eusebius, and the Doctrine of Apokatastasis." Pages 307–23 in *Eusebius of Caesarea: Traditions and Innovations.* Edited by Aaron Johnson and Jeremy Schott. Hellenic Studies 60. Cambridge: Harvard University Press, 2013.

———. "Origen, Greek Philosophy, and the Birth of the Trinitarian Meaning of Hypostasis." *HTR* 105 (2012): 302–50.

———. "Origen in Augustine: A Paradoxical Reception." *Numen* 60 (2013): 280–307.

———. "Origen, Patristic Philosophy, and Christian Platonism: Re-Thinking the Christianisation of Hellenism." *VC* 63 (2009): 217–63.

———. "Origen's Anti-Subordinationism and Its Heritage in the Nicene and Cappadocian Line." *VC* 65 (2011): 21–49.

———. "Origen's Doctrine of the Apokatastasis: A Reassessment." Pages 649–70 in *Origeniana Decima.* Edited by H. Pietras and S. Kaczmarek. BETL 244. Leuven: Peeters, 2011.

———. "Origen's Exegesis of Jeremiah: Resurrection Announced throughout the Bible and Its Twofold Conception." *Aug* 48 (2008): 59–78.

———. "Philosophical Allegoresis of Scripture in Philo and Its Legacy in Gregory of Nyssa." *SPhilo* 20 (2008): 55–99.

———. "The Philosophical Stance of Allegory in Stoicism and Its Reception in Platonism, 'Pagan' and Christian: Origen in Dialogue with the Stoics

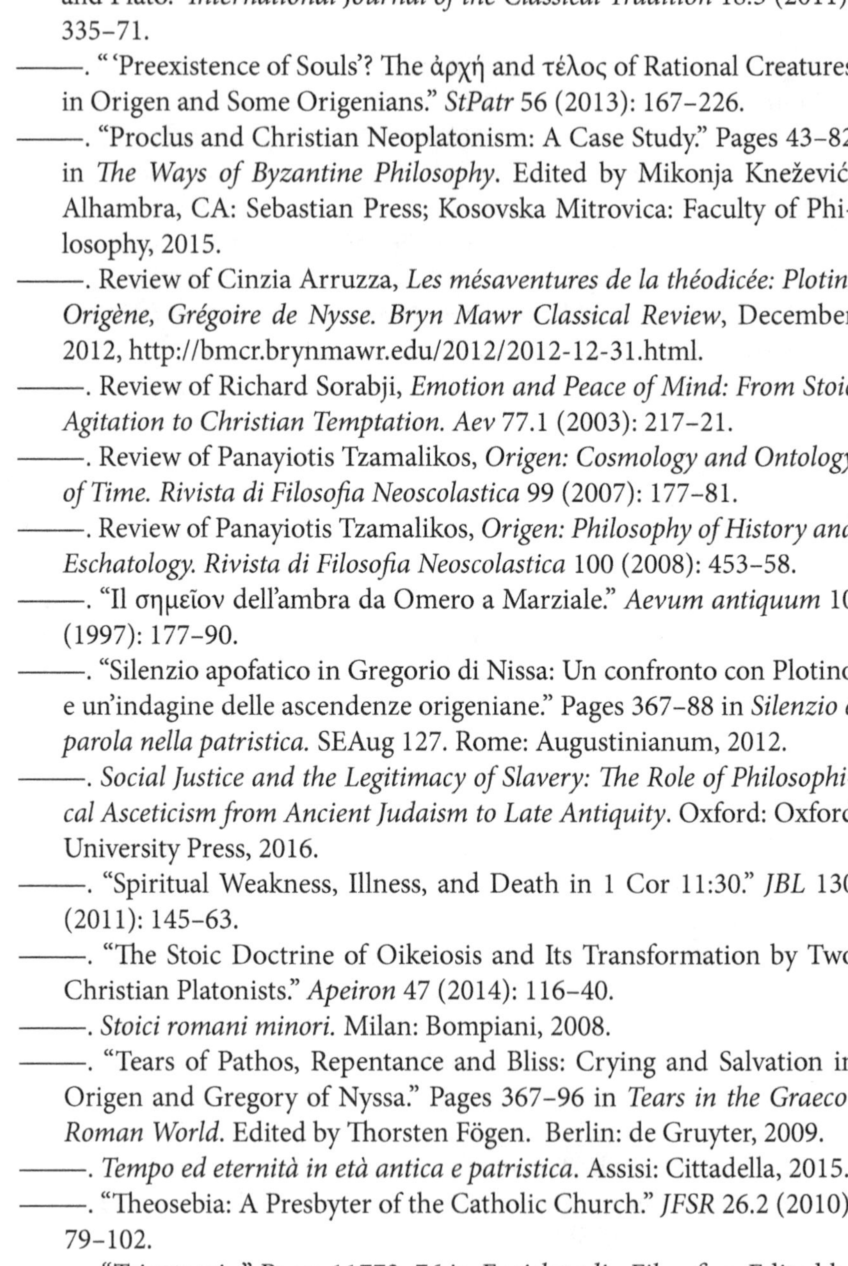

and Plato." *International Journal of the Classical Tradition* 18.3 (2011): 335–71.

——. "'Preexistence of Souls'? The ἀρχή and τέλος of Rational Creatures in Origen and Some Origenians." *StPatr* 56 (2013): 167–226.

——. "Proclus and Christian Neoplatonism: A Case Study." Pages 43–82 in *The Ways of Byzantine Philosophy*. Edited by Mikonja Knežević; Alhambra, CA: Sebastian Press; Kosovska Mitrovica: Faculty of Philosophy, 2015.

——. Review of Cinzia Arruzza, *Les mésaventures de la théodicée: Plotin, Origène, Grégoire de Nysse*. *Bryn Mawr Classical Review*, December 2012, http://bmcr.brynmawr.edu/2012/2012-12-31.html.

——. Review of Richard Sorabji, *Emotion and Peace of Mind: From Stoic Agitation to Christian Temptation*. *Aev* 77.1 (2003): 217–21.

——. Review of Panayiotis Tzamalikos, *Origen: Cosmology and Ontology of Time*. *Rivista di Filosofia Neoscolastica* 99 (2007): 177–81.

——. Review of Panayiotis Tzamalikos, *Origen: Philosophy of History and Eschatology*. *Rivista di Filosofia Neoscolastica* 100 (2008): 453–58.

——. "Il σημεῖον dell'ambra da Omero a Marziale." *Aevum antiquum* 10 (1997): 177–90.

——. "Silenzio apofatico in Gregorio di Nissa: Un confronto con Plotino e un'indagine delle ascendenze origeniane." Pages 367–88 in *Silenzio e parola nella patristica*. SEAug 127. Rome: Augustinianum, 2012.

——. *Social Justice and the Legitimacy of Slavery: The Role of Philosophical Asceticism from Ancient Judaism to Late Antiquity*. Oxford: Oxford University Press, 2016.

——. "Spiritual Weakness, Illness, and Death in 1 Cor 11:30." *JBL* 130 (2011): 145–63.

——. "The Stoic Doctrine of Oikeiosis and Its Transformation by Two Christian Platonists." *Apeiron* 47 (2014): 116–40.

——. *Stoici romani minori*. Milan: Bompiani, 2008.

——. "Tears of Pathos, Repentance and Bliss: Crying and Salvation in Origen and Gregory of Nyssa." Pages 367–96 in *Tears in the Graeco-Roman World*. Edited by Thorsten Fögen. Berlin: de Gruyter, 2009.

——. *Tempo ed eternità in età antica e patristica*. Assisi: Cittadella, 2015.

——. "Theosebia: A Presbyter of the Catholic Church." *JFSR* 26.2 (2010): 79–102.

——. "Tricotomia." Pages 11772–76 in *Enciclopedia Filosofica*. Edited by V. Melchiorre. Milan: Bompiani, 2006.

———. "Typology." In *The Encyclopedia of Ancient History*. Edited by Roger S. Bagnall et al. London: Wiley-Blackwell, 2013. doi:10.1002/9781444338386.wbeah05187.

———. "The Universal and Eternal Validity of Jesus's High-Priestly Sacrifice: The Epistle to the Hebrews in Support of Origen's Theory of Apokatastasis." Pages 210–21 in *A Cloud of Witnesses: The Theology of Hebrews in Its Ancient Contexts*. Edited by Richard J. Bauckham et al. London: T&T Clark, 2008.

Ramelli, Ilaria, and David Konstan. *Terms for Eternity: Aiônios and Aïdios in Classical and Christian Authors*. 2d ed. Piscataway, N.J.: Gorgias, 2011.

Rapp, Claudia. *Holy Bishops in Late Antiquity: The Nature of Christian Leadership in an Age of Transition*. Berkeley: University of California Press, 2005.

Refoulé, François. "La christologie d'Évagre et l'origénisme." *OCP* 27 (1961): 221–66.

———. "Évagre fut-il origéniste?" *RSPT* 47 (1963): 398–402.

———. "La mystique d'Évagre et l'origénisme." *VSpir* suppl. 66 (1963): 453–63.

Reydams-Schils, Gretchen. Review of Ilaria Ramelli, *Stoici romani minori*. *Bryn Mawr Classical Review*, October 2009, http://bmcr.brynmawr.edu/2009/2009-10-10.html.

Rivas, R. Pereto. "Evagrio Póntico y la exclaustración de la acedia." *Car* 28 (2012): 23–35.

Runia, David, and Albert Geljon. *Philo of Alexandria, De Agricultura: Introduction, Translation and Commentary*. Philo of Alexandria Commentary Series 4. Leiden: Brill, 2012.

Russell, Norman. *The Doctrine of Deification in the Greek Patristic Tradition*. Oxford: Oxford University Press, 2004.

Samir, Khalil. "Évagre le Pontique dans la tradition arabo-copte." Pages 123–53 in vol. 2 of *Actes du IVe Congrès Copte*. Edited by M. Rassart-Debergh and J. Ries. Louvain-la-Neuve: Université catholique de Louvain, Institut orientaliste, 1992.

Scott, Mark S. M. "Guarding the Mysteries of Salvation: The Pastoral Pedagogy of Origen's Universalism." *JECS* 18 (2010): 347–68.

Scully, Jason. "Angelic Pneumatology in the Egyptian Desert." *JECS* 19 (2011): 287–305.

Simian-Yofre, Horacio. "La luce, metafora sapienziale nell'AT." Pages 49–66 in *Greeks, Jews, and Christians: Historical, Religious, and Philologi-*

cal Studies in Honor of Jesús Peláez del Rosal. Edited by Lautaro Roig Lanzillotta and Israel Muñoz Gallarte. EFN 10. Córdova: Ediciones El Almendro, 2013.

Sinkewicz, Robert E. *Evagrius of Pontus: The Greek Ascetic Corpus.* Oxford: Oxford University Press, 2003.

Slaveva-Griffin, Svetla. *Plotinus on Number.* Oxford: Oxford University Press, 2009.

Smith, Gregory. "How Thin Is a Demon?" *JECS* 16 (2008): 479–512.

Sokoloff, Michael, ed. *A Syriac Lexicon: A Translation from the Latin, Correction, Expansion, and Update of C. Brockelmann's* Lexicon Syriacum. Winona Lake, Ind.: Eisenbrauns, 2009.

Somos, Robert. "Origen, Evagrius Ponticus and the Ideal of Impassibility." Pages 365–73 in *Origeniana Septima: Origenes in den Auseinandersetzungen des 4. Jahrhunderts.* Edited by Wolfgang Bienert and Uwe Kühneweg. Leuven: Peeters, 1999.

Sorabji, Richard. *Emotion and Peace of Mind: From Stoic Agitation to Christian Temptation.* Oxford: Oxford University Press, 2000.

Speidel, Michael. "Making Use of History beyond the Euphrates." Pages 11–41 in *Mara bar Serapion in Context.* Edited by Annette Merz and Teun Tieleman. Leiden: Brill, 2012.

Stefaniw, Blossom. "Exegetical Curricula in Origen, Didymus, and Evagrius: Pedagogical Agenda and the Case for Neoplatonist Influence." *StPatr* 44 (2010): 281–95.

———. *Mind, Text, and Commentary: Noetic Exegesis in Origen of Alexandria, Didymus the Blind, and Evagrius Ponticus.* Frankfurt: Lang, 2010.

Stewart, Columba. *Cassian the Monk.* Oxford: Oxford University Press, 1998.

———. "Imageless Prayer and the Theological Vision of Evagrius Ponticus." *JECS* 9 (2001): 173–204.

———. "Monastic Attitudes toward Philosophy and Philosophers." *StPatr* 44 (2010): 321–27.

Suzuki, J. "The Evagrian Concept of *Apatheia* and Its Origenism." Pages 605–11 in *Origeniana Nona*. Edited by G. Heidl and R. Somos. Leuven: Peeters, 2009.

Taylor, David. "L'importance des Pères de l'Église dans l'oeuvre spéculative de Barhebraeus." *ParOr* 33 (2008): 63–85.

Thunberg, Lars, and A. M. Allchin. *Microcosm and Mediator: The Theological Anthropology of Maximus the Confessor.* 2d ed. Chicago: University of Chicago Press, 1995.

Tieleman, Teun. *Galen and Chrysippus on the Soul: Argument and Refutation in the De Placitis II-III.* Leiden: Brill, 1996.

Tischendorf, Constantine. *Notitia editionis codicis bibliorum Sinaitici.* Leipzig: Brockhaus, 1860.

Tobon, Monica. *Apatheia in the Teachings of Evagrius Ponticus: The Health of the Soul.* Burlington, Vt.: Ashgate, forthcoming.

———. "Evagrius as Writer: The Example of *Eulogios* 2's Discussion of *Xeniteia.*" Pages 765–68 in *Origeniana Decima.* Edited by H. Pietras and S. Kaczmarek. BETL 244. Leuven: Peeters, 2011.

———. "From Evagrian Prayer to Centering Prayer." In *Colloquium Origenianum Undecimum, Aarhus, 26–31 August 2013.* Edited by Anders-Christian Jacobsen. Leuven: Peeters, 2015.

———. "The Health of the Soul: ἀπάθεια in Evagrius Ponticus." *StPatr* 47 (2010): 187–202.

———. "Introduction." *StPatr* 57 (2013): 3–7.

———. "Raising Body and Soul to the Order of the Nous: Anthropology and Contemplation in Evagrius." *StPatr* 57 (2013): 51–74.

———. "Reply to Kevin Corrigan." *StPatr* 57 (2013): 27–29.

Torrance, Alexis. *Repentance in Late Antiquity: Eastern Asceticism and the Framing of the Christian Life c. 400–650 CE.* Oxford: Oxford University Press, 2013.

Trigg, Joseph W. "Christ and the Angelic Hierarchy in Origen's Theology." *JTS* 42 (1991): 35–51.

Tzamalikos, Panayiotis. *A Newly Discovered Greek Father: Cassian the Sabaite, Eclipsed by John Cassian of Marseilles.* Leiden: Brill, 2012.

———. *Origen: Cosmology and Ontology of Time.* Leiden: Brill, 2006.

———. *Origen: Philosophy of History and Eschatology.* Leiden: Brill, 2007.

———. *The Real Cassian Revisited: Monastic Life, Greek Paideia, and Origenism in the Sixth Century.* Leiden: Brill, 2012.

———. Review of Ilaria Ramelli, *Gregorio di Nissa: Sull'anima e la resurrezione. VC* 62 (2008): 515–23.

Tzvetkova-Glaser, Anna. *Pentateuchauslegung bei Origenes und den frühen Rabbinen.* Frankfurt: Lang, 2010.

Vannucci, Giovanni, ed. *Philokalia: Testi di ascetica e mistica della Chiesa orientale.* Florence: Libreria editrice fiorentina, 1978.

Ware, Kallistos. "Nous and Noesis in Plato, Aristotle and Evagrius of Pontus." *Diotima* 13 (1985): 158–63.

Watt, James W. "Philoxenus and the Old Syriac Version of Evagrius' Centuries." *OrChr* 64 (1980): 65–81.

———. "The Syriac Adapter of Evagrius' Centuries." *StPatr* 17.3 (1982): 1388–95.

Weedman, Mark. "The Polemical Context of Gregory of Nyssa's Doctrine of Divine Infinity." *JECS* 18 (2010): 81–104.

Wenzel, Siegfried. "Ακηδια: Additions to Lampe's Patristic Greek Lexicon." *VC* 17 (1963): 173–76.

———. *The Sin of Sloth: Acedia in Medieval Thought and Literature.* Chapel Hill: University of North Carolina Press, 2012.

Woodruff, Paul. "Justice as a Virtue of the Soul." Pages 89–101 in *Virtue and Happiness: Essays in Honour of Julia Annas.* Edited by Rachana Kamtekar. Oxford Studies in Ancient Philosophy Supplements. New York: Oxford University Press, 2012.

Young, Robin Darling. "The Armenian Adaptation of Evagrius' *Kephalaia Gnostika.*" Pages 535–41 in *Origeniana Quinta.* Edited by Robert J. Daly. Leuven: Peeters, 1992.

———. "Evagrius the Iconographer: Monastic Pedagogy in the *Gnostikos.*" *JECS* 9 (2001): 53–71.

Index of Primary Sources

Index of Subjects and People

Printed in the USA
CPSIA information can be obtained
at www.ICGtesting.com
JSHW022252031024
71051JS00001B/6

9 781628 370393